1
HIDDEN PLACES
of
ENGLAND

Edited by
Joanna Billing

Published by:
Travel Publishing Ltd
7a Apollo House, Calleva Park
Aldermaston, Berks, RG7 8TN

ISBN 1-902-00705-0
© Travel Publishing Ltd 1997

Published: 1997

National Titles in the Hidden Places Series:

England	Ireland
Scotland	Wales

Regional Titles in the Hidden Places Series:

Channel Islands	Devon & Cornwall
Dorset, Hants & Isle of Wight	East Anglia
Gloucestershire	Heart of England
Lancashire & Cheshire	Lake District & Cumbria
North Wales	Northumberland & Durham
Peak District	Potteries
Somerset	South East
South Wales	Thames & Chilterns
Welsh Borders	Wiltshire
Yorkshire & Humberside	

Printing by: Nuffield Press, Abingdon
Cartography by: Estates Publications, Tenterden, Kent
Line Drawings: Sarah Bird
Editor: Joanna Billing
Cover : Clare Hackney

Born in 1961, Clare was educated at West Surrey College of Art and Design
as well as studying at Kingston University. She runs her own private water-
colour school based in Surrey and has exhibited both in the UK and
internationally. The cover is taken from an original water-colour of Warwick
Castle.

Foreword

The Hidden Places series is a collection of easy-to-read travel guides covering the U.K. and Ireland. They are ideal companions for the tourist who wishes to explore and experience the diverse character of these ancient islands in a relaxed but informative way. The series is now in its 9th year of publication reflecting its popularity with a wide range of readers.

Each guide contains a wealth of interesting geographical and historical information and promotes the less well-known visitor attractions and places to stay, eat and visit, many "off-the beaten track", as well as the more established places of interest.

The descriptive narrative in the book is accompanied by attractive line drawings and coloured maps. The guides do not award merit marks or rankings but concentrate on describing the more interesting, unusual or unique features of each place with the aim of making the reader's stay in the local area an enjoyable and stimulating experience.

The Hidden Places of England aims to show the reader the varied urban and rural landscape of this country as well as providing an insight into its social, agricultural and industrial heritage. At the same time it includes many places of interest which we hope will be a source of great satisfaction. In order to make this book both interesting and enjoyable, as well as usable, the selection of places incorporated has had to be rigorous. We have not included all information that is readily available elsewhere. So, whilst some cities, towns and villages are not given significant coverage, many smaller, less well known places receive unaccustomed attention.

This title cannot of course cover all the places of interest in England and for this reason *the Hidden Places* publishes a series of county guides, details of which can be found at the rear of the book. We are always interested in what readers think of places covered (or not covered) in our guides so please do not hesitate to use the reader reaction forms provided to give us your considered comments. We also welcome any general comments which will help us improve the guides themselves.

Contents

FOREWORD   iii

CONTENTS   v

GEOGRAPHICAL AREAS:

Southeast England   1

Southern England   73

Devon   135

Cornwall   197

Central England   245

Eastern England   _Essex 325_   323

Yorkshire   367

Northwest England   429

North England   481

INDEXES AND LISTS:

Tourist Information Centres   527

Town & Village Index   529

Places of Interest Index   535

ADDITIONAL INFORMATION:

Order Form   549

Reader Reaction Form   551

MAPS:

Key to Maps   553

Maps   555

Leicester 292
Lincoln 362

CHAPTER ONE
Southeast England

Canterbury Cathedral

1
Southeast England

Kent

INTRODUCTION

Known as the Garden of England, the county's fertile fields and orchards were ideally located for supplying the growing population of London with food during the last few hundred years. Trade, of another sort, travelled the other way as the wealth from the capital took to building themselves country retreats in Kent. One of the most famous of these, Chartwell, was the country home of Winston Churchill and today many of his personal possessions remain as they were during his time there.

Kent is also the nearest part of mainland Britain to France and Europe and it has always been open to attack by invading forces. As a result numerous defences were built over the centuries, many of which can still be seen today. One 'invader', St Augustine, however, came in peace, in AD 597, and he and his party settled in Canterbury where the magnificent Cathedral, the mother church of Anglican Christianity, still draws visitors.

While the south coast is dominated by holiday traffic to France and beyond through Dover and the Tunnel at Folkestone, the north coast and, in particular, Margate, remains home to seaside resorts of a wholly British nature. By contrast, the inland town of Royal Tunbridge Wells is smart and genteel, a reminder of the times when it was very much an upper class spa town. The towns along the Medway, again are different, and, while few of the once many dockyards now remain, many visiting the area will be reminded of the novel of Charles Dickens who found inspiration in this charming river valley.

CANTERBURY   *Map 7 ref R21*

This delightful walled city is dominated by its **Cathedral** which includes such highlights as the central late 15th century Bell Harry Tower designed by William Westall; Henry Yevele's lofty nave with its magnificent columns; the Trinity

3

Chapel, which houses the splendid tomb of Edward the Black Prince and the canopied tomb and alabaster effigies of Henry IV and his queen; the great north window; and the spectacular Crypt, the largest of any ecclesiastical building in the world. The cathedral was founded just after AD 597 by St Augustine after his arrival in Britain from Rome. Before his death some seven years later, he had converted large numbers of the native Saxons to Christianity and Canterbury became the seat of the Mother Church of the Anglicans. Nothing now, however, remains of the original, pre-Conquest buildings; the present cathedral having been constructed between 1071 and 1500.

It was here that the treacherous murder of Archbishop Thomas Becket by Henry II's knights took place, on the cathedral steps. The simple stone marking the spot states that Becket "died here Tuesday 29th December 1170". Although the knights apparently 'misinterpreted' the King's wishes, the horror of this treacherous act has been passed down the centuries. A penitent Henry, full of remorse for the death of his former friend, came here later as a pilgrim to Becket's shrine. The Archbishop's magnificent tomb was destroyed during the Dissolution of the Monasteries in 1538 but visitors to the cathedral can still see the Altar of the Swordpoint, commemorating the spot where the sword of one of his assassins shattered on the stone floor.

Canterbury is a compact city and any short walk around the centre brings the visitor face to face with its long and colourful history. As for shopping, there cannot be many cities in England that offer a greater variety. Specialist shops of every kind stand side by side with all the familiar high street names (many of these can be found in the attractive covered Marlowe Arcade in St Margaret's Street) and, surprisingly, neither look out of place in their medieval surroundings. Canterbury's foremost architectural gems are well marked and easy to spot but there are many more beautiful and interesting buildings that will elude the sightseer if they keep their eyes cast downwards. In particular there is the glorious 'chequer-board' effect above the entrance to the **Beaney Institute** at the end of the High Street. This is a splendid Victorian building which not only houses the public library but also the **Royal Museum and Art Gallery** and the **Buffs Regimental Museum**.

From the bridge across the River Stour can be seen the ducking-stool once used to immerse all manner of miscreants—as the sign implicitly warns: "Unfaithful Wives beware; Butchers, Bakers, Brewers, Apothecaries and all who give short measure". The bridge is now a favourite haunt for a motley collection of buskers who go down well with passing tourists but are not quite so popular with the captive audience of local traders who have become intimately familiar with the repertoire! Opposite The Weavers' Inn a flight of stone steps lead down, below street level, to the vaults of the 12th century **Eastbridge Hospital**, founded in 1180 by Edward Fitzodbold as a hostel for poor pilgrims visiting St Thomas' tomb.

The Poor Priests' Hospital in Stour Street dates back to the 14th century and was used as an almshouse for elderly clergy. Today it houses the award winning **Canterbury Heritage Museum**, which tells the story of the city from Roman times to the present day, making effective use of the latest computer, hologram and audiovisual technology. Highlights include an exciting video on the story of Thomas Becket, an audiovisual presentation on Canterbury during the Blitz, and displays and memorabilia concerning Mary Tourtel, the creator of Rupert Bear, who was born at 52 Palace Street in 1874. Those who like their history to be liberally spiced with fun should also make a point of visiting **The Canterbury Tales**, which is housed in a medieval church in St Margaret's Street. Here visitors can enjoy superb recreations of scenes from life in the Middle Ages, all based on Chaucer's famous stories.

The city is also renowned as a centre for the arts, the main event being the annual Canterbury Festival in autumn, when a varied programme of music, drama, dance, film, exhibitions, walks, talks and community events takes place. Among the many places which play host to these events are the **Gulbenkian Theatre**, at the University of Kent, and Canterbury's major theatrical venue, the **Marlowe Theatre**, relocated in recent years to The Friars, off St Peter's Street. The theatre was named after the playwright Christopher Marlowe, who was born in Canterbury in 1564. A contemporary of Shakespeare (who he most probably knew), his works include *Dr Faustus* and *Tamurlane the Great*. As a boy, Marlowe attended the famous King's School, situated in the cathedral precincts (whose Norman staircase is, incidentally, one of the most famous examples of Norman architecture in England), before going up to Benet—now better known as Corpus Christi College, Cambridge. As a friend of Sir Francis Walsingham, Elizabeth I's Secretary of State, Marlowe supplemented his literary career by taking an active role as a spy. At only 29 years of age, he was stabbed to death in Deptford following what was officially referred to as a tavern brawl, but was more likely to have been a deliberately planned assassination. He is buried at the church of St Nicholas and records simply state: "Christopher Marlowe, slain by ffrancis Archer 1 June 1593".

To the east of the city centre, lie the picturesque remains of **St Augustine's Abbey**, the oldest Anglo-Saxon abbey in England. It was also this eastern part of the city which took most of the force of the enemy bombing raids during World War II. Roughly, one third of the old city of Canterbury was destroyed but in one way some good did come from this mass destruction as, when the rubble had been cleared away, the ancient foundations of Canterbury were revealed. From these excavations, archaeologists have been able to piece together the history of the citizens of Canterbury from the Stone Age through to the Roman occupation and Middle Ages.

Chiefly known for its ecclesiastical buildings, Canterbury also has a **Castle**, found to the south of the city centre. Though much overlooked by visitors, it would be easy to mistake it for an elaborate section of the ancient city walls, it has, however, stood for over 900 years. William the Conqueror had the original motte and bailey castle built not long after the Battle of Hastings, and the site of this was just to the east of the present castle in what is now the Dane John Gardens. The mound of this Norman donjon survives today within the Dane John mound.

The 'new' castle would have been built sometime between 1080 and 1100 and it is first referred to in the Domesday Book of 1086. It would have consisted originally of a three-storied, rectangular keep with 9 foot thick walls, surrounded by an outer wall with a tower at each angle and a defensive ditch—the whole enclosure covering an area of some four and a half acres in all. The castle became the county gaol in the 11th century and served in that capacity for the next 400 years or so. By the end of the 18th century it had fallen into complete ruin and at this time the outer wall was demolished and the ditch filled in. Attempts were made to pull down the keep itself in 1817 but this was only partially successful; the castle was built of sterner stuff than the demolition crew could handle and only the top storey yielded to the hammer. The keep was then purchased by the Gas, Light and Coke Company, who used it first to store water pumping machinery and, ultimately, as a glorified coal bin! Such degradations happily came to an end in 1928, when Canterbury Castle was declared an historic monument and a long overdue programme of preservation began.

Yorke Lodge Guest House

Yorke Lodge Guest House is a spacious, elegant Victorian town house situated close to the city that offers hotel standard rooms at bed and breakfast prices. Recently restored and decorated to its period splendour, this attractive house offers its guests beautiful bedrooms, all with full en-suite facilities, colour television and modern conveniences. Guests can sit and enjoy a traditional English breakfast in the themed dining room before perusing through the well stocked library or exploring a few of the local attractions. Whether for business or pleasure, a stay at Yorke Lodge will be a most memorable one.

Yorke Lodge Guest House, 50 London Road, Canterbury, Kent CT2 8LF
Tel: 01227 451243 Fax: 01227 462006

Cathedral Gate Hotel

In the centre of Canterbury, the cathedral can be reached through Christ Church Gate, off Burgate. A little to the right of the gate, is a small doorway and steep staircase that lead to **The Cathedral Gate Hotel**. The tiny entrance gives little indication of the delightful establishment that can be found here. The hotel offers 24 bedrooms in all, sprawling the length of Burgate and guests quite literally have to walk the rooftops to reach some of the rooms! The views are well worth the trouble with one side overlooking Canterbury Cathedral and the other looking down on to the narrow pedestrianised street. The rooms are characterful, with most also offering en-suite facilities, and the atmosphere is relaxed and unhurried. There are several dining areas and the traditional menu offers freshly prepared, home-cooked dishes. This is a convenient location for anyone visiting this historic city.

Cathedral Gate Hotel, Burgate, Canterbury, Kent CT1 2HA
Tel: 01227 464381

WHITSTABLE   *Map 7 ref R21*

Anyone wandering around the busy commercial harbour, which was originally the port for Canterbury, and down the old fashioned streets will soon begin to realise that this is no seaside resort but very much a working town by, and of, the sea. The best way to get the authentic flavour of Whitstable itself is to take a stroll along the beach. To the east lies the harbour and to the west Seasalter and, from here in both directions, can be found the tightly packed rows of traditional black tarred oyster sheds and weatherboarded cottages that give the town so much of its atmosphere. There is always plenty of activity in and around the beach; fishing boats go about their business whilst hardy types, clad in wet suits, take to the water pursuing the watersports for which Whitstable is famous.

Otherwise known as Tankerton Tower, **Whitstable Castle** was originally built as an octagonal folly by Charles Pearson in 1792 and added to extensively 28 years later by his son. More recently it housed the old district council offices and it is currently used as a Community Centre.

Barnfield at Windy Ridge Guest House

Just over a mile from the centre of Whitstable, off the A299, is **Barnfield at Windy Ridge Guest House**. This bed and breakfast establishment, personally run by Elizabeth Dyke, enjoys a fabulous setting with views over the valley towards Canterbury and to the River Thames. The approach from the car park is through the mature, well laid out gardens which are most attractive. There are 10 en-suite bedrooms, all comfortably furnished, and the facilities that have earned a tourist board 3 Crown highly commended status. This is a nonsmoking establishment and children are welcome. Evening meals available on request.
Barnfield at Windy Ridge Guest House, Wraik Hill, Whitstable, Kent CT5 3BY Tel: 01227 263506

HERNE BAY   *Map 7 ref R21*

Originally a fishing village which developed a notorious reputation for its smuggling activities, Herne Bay is one of the main resorts on the north Kent coast. It was a favourite holiday haven for the Victorian middle classes and still retains the quiet atmosphere of that particular era—most of the town having been laid out no more than 150 years ago. The town's main landmark is the **Clock Tower** on the promenade; solid, dependable and just a little preposterous, it stands 80 feet high and was erected in 1836 by a wealthy Londoner, Mrs Anne Thwaytes, to commemorate Queen Victoria's coronation.

MARGATE

Map 7 ref S20

This town fulfils most people's expectations of the typical English seaside resort: long sweeping stretches of golden sand, promenades, amusement arcades, candyfloss and fun fairs. For many years, the resort has been a Mecca for day-trippers from London (greatly assisted by excellent water-transport along the River Thames) and there are still those faithful patrons who come back time and time again. As befits such a seaside resort, the covered bathing machine was invented here in 1753 by a Quaker and glovemaker called Benjamin Beale.

Visitors who come here for the beach may be surprised to learn of Margate's history and one excellent place to visit is the **Tudor House** in King Street. Built in the early 16th century, during the reign of Henry VIII, the house now contains an exhibition on the human occupation of the Isle of Thanet from earliest times through to the end of the Tudor period. Just to the south of the town is the medieval **Salmestone Grange** which was originally a farm of St Augustine's Abbey at Canterbury. Probably the best preserved example of a monastic grange (or farm) in England, the chapel, crypt and kitchen are open to the public.

Margate also has two truly hidden treasures which can be found within a few hundred yards of each other at the eastern end of town. Firstly, there are the **Margate Caves**; enormous caverns which were cut from the chalk cliffs over 1000 years ago. Used variously as a refuge, a medieval dungeon and church, and a hiding place for smugglers and their contraband, the caves are open daily throughout the summer. Nearby, on Grotto Hill, is **Shell Grotto**. Thought to have pagan origins, these underground passages and chambers have been skilfully decorated with literally millions of seashells.

Heading up the High Street towards the church, visitors will find Charlotte Square on their left. Here, backing onto the churchyard and in a delightfully quiet spot, is the **Quart in a Pint Pot** public house. Run by Pearl Underdown and

Quart in a Pint Pot

David Saffen, this is a free house offering a good selection of beers and wines. Dating back to 1782 the pub was known, until 15 years ago, as the George and Dragon. However, whatever the name, the traditional atmosphere remains as warm and welcoming as ever for locals and visitors. There is an attractive walled garden, which is ideal for children, and the seafront is just a short walk away.
Quart in a Pint Pot, 28 Charlotte Square, Margate, Kent CT9 1LR
Tel: 01843 223672

In the centre of Margate can be found **4 Hawley Square** a stylish, high class bistro serving seasonal produce with French and English themes that attracts customers from far and wide. Open for lunch Tuesday to Saturday and in the evenings on Thursday, Friday and Saturday only, booking ahead is recommended.

4 Hawley Square

Run by Valerie and Raymond Biddulph, Raymond's expertise as a chef is demonstrated by the fact he writes a food column for the local newspaper group. The menu is varied and interesting and occasionally features unusual dishes such as kangaroo and wild boar.
4 Hawley Square, Margate, Kent CT9 1PF
Tel: 01843 224347

BROADSTAIRS   *Map 7 ref S21*

This town is probably best known for its associations with Charles Dickens and those coming in search of **Bleak House** will find it high up on the cliffs at the northern end of town, overlooking the popular family beach at Viking Bay. The sands of the little harbour here—described by Dickens as "rare good sands"—are partly protected by a small 16th century pier, a replacement for one built during the reign of Henry VIII.

As well as Charles Dickens, other famous people associated with Broadstairs include Sir Edward Heath, who was born here in 1916, and another famous sailor, Sir Alec Rose, who lived here for many years. Frank Richards, the creator of Billy Bunter, also lived in the town, as did John Buchan, whose popular spy thriller, *The Thirty-Nine Steps*, has become an even more popular film. He wrote the story at a house called St Cuby on Cliff Promenade and the staircase that gave him his inspiration still stands opposite the house, its 78 steps halved by Buchan to make a better title.

Another native of Broadstairs was the eminent Victorian railway engineer, Thomas Russell Crampton. Opposite the railway station is, appropriately enough, **Crampton Tower**, a railway museum dedicated to his life and work, with exhibits of his blueprints, drawings and photographs. The Broadstairs Stagecoach is also on display and there is a superb 00 gauge model railway.

SANDWICH   *Map 7 ref S21*

One of the ancient Cinque Ports, Sandwich is a town full of historical interest. Though not a big place, one of the best ways of seeing the delights is to follow the Sandwich Town Trail. The starting point is the **Guildhall**, built in 1579 and enlarged in 1912 and again in 1973, when the New Hall and offices were added. It is well worth taking the time to seek out some of the fascinating historical pieces in the Guildhall. One of these is the ancient, brass Moot Horn which has been used to summon the people of Sandwich to hear important announcements from as far back as the 12th century. Today, it is still used to announce the death of a sovereign and the accession of the new. There is also the Hog Mace, which, as the name implies, was used to round up straying animals after the Goose Bell had rung from St Peter's Church at 4 am. All such animals, if not repossessed by their owners on payment of a fine, passed to the brothers and sisters of St John's Hospital. The evening curfew at 8 pm is still rung every day, continuing a tradition going back some 800 years.

The entire town centre has been declared a conservation area and this is where most of the historically interesting buildings can be found. Guarding the northern entrance to Sandwich is the **Barbican Gate**, a turreted 16th century gatehouse on the quayside. Sandwich is now almost two miles from the sea and, although its days as a major port have long since passed, it continues to be used as an inland berth by a colourful array of yachts and cruisers.

Though dissolute and corrupt it was John Montagu, the 4th Earl of Sandwich who is responsible for immortalising the town's name. The rogue Earl's lasting claim to fame was to order a slice of beef between two pieces of bread as a substitute for a more conventional meal—a snack he could eat without having to leave the gambling table—and thus the Great British sandwich was born!

DEAL   *Map 7 ref 21*

This charming fishing town has altered very little in character since the 18th century. The fact that its beach is of shingle rather than sand meant that it escaped Victorian development into a full-blown seaside resort. The seafront is one of the most picturesque to be found anywhere on the southeast coast and with its quiet alleyways, traditional cottages and houses (many of them colour-washed), and shingle beach festooned with fishing boats, Deal is a delightful place to explore.

The quiet waters just off the coast are known as The Downs and they create a safe natural anchorage for shipping that may otherwise run aground on the treacherous **Goodwin Sands**. The sands have been the setting for hundreds of tragic shipwrecks throughout the centuries and the sad sight of drowned ships, with their masts poking above the water, is still in evidence at low tide, serving as a permanent reminder of the darker side of the sea. The sands are mentioned in Shakespeare's *Merchant of Venice* as a place where the eponymous merchant lost one of his ships. As many as 50,000 men may have perished on these sands and there are many tales of ghost ships having been sighted here.

In St George's Road, in stables once used to house army mules, is the **Maritime and Local History Museum**, where a large collection of models, pictures and other memorabilia relate the maritime history of the town. Also on display are a number of original boats constructed by local boat builders up until the turn of the century. The **Costume and Accessories Museum**, a personal collection of original costumes and accessories put together by Doris Salter, can be found in a private house at 18 Gladstone Road; while in the Town Hall is the **Victoriana Museum**, its displays of toys, dolls, china, ornaments and jewellery from the Victorian and Edwardian eras illustrating the growth of the 19th century souvenir trade.

Near the start of the pier is the distinctive **Timeball Tower**; built in 1795 to give time signals to ships in the Channel. The four storey tower had a curious device whereby a black copper ball was dropped down its central shaft to register 1 pm Greenwich Mean Time each day—so sailors would always know when it was lunchtime! The original timeball has since been replaced by a modern radio time signal but a replica ball now drops down the shaft on the hour. On the fourth floor of the building there is a museum devoted to time and telegraphy.

Close to the Timeball Tower is **Deal Castle** with its unusual if not unique lily-pad shape which was built by Henry VIII during the early 1540s. The castle was actually designed to resemble a Tudor Rose and was the largest in a chain of five coastal defences (the Cinque Ports) built along the southeast coast against possible French invasion. The ruins of another of these, **Sandown Castle**, can be seen at the northern end of town; its few remaining buttresses holding out valiantly against the encroaching sea. Deal Castle was built very specifically as a war bastion and, with 119 guns trained across the sea, it must have been a formidable sight. A permanent exhibition here describes Henry VIII's various castles and their defensive role throughout history. Just to the south of Deal Castle lies another of Henry VIII's defences, **Walmer Castle**.

DOVER   *Map 7 ref S22*

Known as the Gateway to England to those coming in, Dover is one of the major routes to Europe for those going out. For many then, this busy cross-Channel port is nothing more than brief stopping point but there is plenty to see here though its history is, of course, dominated by the sea.

Dating back to 1180, the massive **Dover Castle** sits on a high hill above the clifftops, dominating the town from almost every angle. It was here, on the site of an Iron Age fort, that the Normans built this impressive stronghold during the last years of Henry II's reign at the then colossal cost of nearly £7,000. Today, it ranks among the greatest fortresses in Western Europe. Apart from an impressive 19th century scale model of the Battle of Waterloo which is displayed in one of the first floor rooms, the chambers and passageways are relatively bare—yet the castle exerts a forceful presence and it is not hard to visualise it as a busy working garrison, teeming with life.

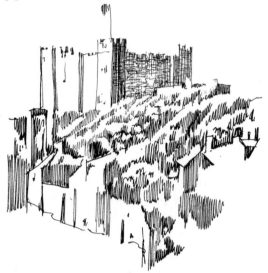

Dover Castle

There are also many popular attractions in the town centre and one of the most visited is the **Roman Painted House**. The main features of this Roman town house are a complex system of underfloor heating and the most beautifully preserved painted walls. First discovered in 1970, the house has won various awards for the way in which it has been preserved and excavation is currently still in progress. One of the team, Wendy Williams, has put together a very special display using the features of those who once lived here. Working on the skulls excavated at the site, she has painstakingly built up their features to produce an uncanny group of extremely lifelike faces.

At first sight, the Victorian Town Hall, in the High Street, may not look as though it warrants any special attention but inside it incorporates the magnificent **Maison Dieu**, a hostel for Canterbury pilgrims which was originally founded in 1203. Beneath the building lie the cells of Dover's **Old Town Gaol**, now open to the public throughout the year. However, one of the town's most exciting attractions is **The White Cliffs Experience**, housed in a modern glass and chrome building opposite the Market Square. Here visitors can chat to a centurion, encounter the warring Cantiacii tribe who greeted the Roman invaders, experience life as a galley slave, and wander through the rubble of a typical Dover street after it has endured the horrors of a World War II air raid attack. This area of the Experience is called the Historium but there is also a more conventional museum with displays of the history of Dover from its earliest days to the present.

FOLKESTONE   *Map 7 ref R22*

Though the town is the second busiest cross-Channel port on the south coast, Folkestone is a most unusual seaside resort as it does not have a recognizable seafront; instead, it has The Leas, a series of delightful clifftop lawns and flower gardens with a distinctly Mediterranean feel to them. A water-driven lift takes residents from the clifftop hotels to the beach below and the warm south-facing aspect makes this a very pleasant area to explore.

Much of Folkestone's history is conveniently condensed into an area known as **The Lanterns** on the Sandgate Road. The attractions centred in this part of town are many and varied. The Bayle was once the site of an ancient fort and the lovely 13th century church of St Mary and St Eanswythe (the oldest building in Folkestone) stands nearby. The bones of the latter patron saint are buried here.

Church Street, formerly called Mercery Lane, was home to the traders of silk and cloth and William Harvey, one of England's most famous physicians, was born here in 1578. Perhaps Harvey's greatest gift to medicine was his discovery of the circulation of the blood; his statue can be seen near the centre of The Leas, appropriately clutching a human heart in his hand. It would seem, however, that all of Harvey's skills in the world of medicine came to naught when it came to his own fate, for he is reputed to have committed suicide in 1657 after discovering that he was going blind.

One of Folkestone's most popular tourist attractions is the **Eurotunnel Exhibition Centre**, which can be found to the north of the town. A special viewing tower overlooks the Channel Tunnel terminal site here and the exhibition includes a superb model railway, an interactive map of Europe, a boring machine and many other items used during the construction of the tunnel. The exhibition also explains the various historical attempts that have been made to forge a channel link between England and France. Napoleon himself thought it would be an excellent idea, although Henry VIII was obviously not quite so keen!

HYTHE   *Map 7 ref R22*

The recorded history of Hythe goes back to AD 732, when Ethelred, King of the Saxons, first granted it a charter. Its name means 'landing place', and the town once played an important role as one of the five Cinque Ports. Its decline in this respect came with the silting up of its harbour, which left it completely high and dry—it is now over half a mile from the sea and no trace of the harbour remains.

A mile to the north of Hythe is **Saltwood Castle**, which although not open to the public can be seen from a nearby bridleway. It was once the residence of the Archbishop of Canterbury and it was here that Becket's murderers stayed the night before they performed their vile deed. More recently it was the home of the late Lord Clark, the famous art historian and presenter of the pioneering television series, *Civilisation*. His son, Alan Clark, also a renowned historian and TV presenter still lives here today

DYMCHURCH   *Map 7 ref R22*

The decidedly odd and not especially attractive building close to the beach here, which looks more like the truncated cooling tower of a power station, is a **Martello Tower**. The pride of Britain's defence against Napoleon, there were, at one time, 74 of these massive 'pepper pots' positioned along the coast. Their name derives from the similarity with a tower at Cape Mortella in Corsica; an ironic choice of model as Napoleon himself was born on that particular island!

At one time a quiet, secluded village, Dymchurch has now been transformed into a busy seaside resort. Amusement arcades, giftshops and cafés line the road, but those wanting to get onto the beach will have to clamber over the formidable Dymchurch Wall. This wall is the only thing that prevents the sea from flooding both town and marsh—Dymchurch lies about seven and a half feet below high tide level and a barrier of one sort or another has existed here since the Romans came to Kent.

TENTERDEN   *Map 7 ref Q22*

Firmly established as the Jewel of the Weald, this name is a far cry from its earliest days when it was known as Tenet-ware-den (pig pasture of the men of Thanet!). Despite the fact that pigs flourished here, sheep inevitably became the more profitable farm animal on these fertile lands and the wool trade quickly took off. In 1331, the far sighted Edward III prohibited the export of unwashed wool and encouraged weavers from Flanders to settle here and bring their dyeing and weaving techniques to the English. The town of Tenterden and some of its neighbouring villages were to become the most important centres for the manufacture of broadcloth.

Set off the main High Street, with its many quaint shops and stylish boutiques, is **Collina House Hotel**. The hotel has been owned and personally run by the Cotella family for over 18 years and offers its guests excellent hospitality. Each of the hotel's 14 bedrooms have private bathrooms, colour television and are individually decorated and furnished to a high standard. Enjoy professional home-cooking in the light and airy dining room, here guests can choose from a comprehensive à la carte or table d'hôte menus, all enhanced by the use of seasonal home-grown produce. A warm welcome awaits everyone for an aperitif in the bar, or guests can soak up the sun on the terrace during the warmer summer days, whilst the comfortable lounge is the perfect place to sit and relax on those colder days. The Collina House Hotel is conveniently placed for visiting many National Trust houses and gardens including Sissinghurst Castle, Smallhythe Place, Scotney Castle Gardens and Leeds Castle

Collina House Hotel

Collina House Hotel, East Hill, Tenterden, Kent TN30 6RL
Tel: 01580 764852 Fax: 01580 762224

BIDDENDEN   *Map 7 ref Q22*

Quite apart from the physical attractions of its architecture and picturesque High Street, there is something else here that has assured the village of a permanent place in the history books. Around the beginning of the 12th century, two of its most famous residents were born. Eliza and Mary Chulkhurst, Siamese twins, became known as the Biddenden Maids and they originated the Easter custom of distributing bread and cheese to pensioners at the Old Workhouse. To the north of the village green lies the **Old Cloth Hall**, a superb six-gabled building which was the centre of the local cloth trade in medieval and Tudor times and housed the workshops of the weavers.

Providing comfortable accommodation and nestled deep in the green valleys of the Weald of Kent, stands **Bishopsdale Oast**. This 18th century double kiln oast has been family run by owners Iain and Jane for many years and offers its guests a unique opportunity to relax and revive themselves in the peace and tranquillity of rural Kent. The accommodation comprises three large bedrooms, each offering full en-suite facilities, tea and coffee maker, colour television, super king sized bed and fantastic views across the valley and countryside.

Guests can enjoy breakfast or dinner in the dining room or on the sunny terrace and, as Iain and Jane are professional caterers, everyone is guaranteed a superb meal. As Bishopsdale Oast does not have its own liquor license, guests are encouraged to bring along their own alcohol to enjoy with their meal, before retiring to the sitting room in front of a roaring log fire or, in the warmer months, stroll around the four acres of wild and cultivated gardens or play a game of croquet. The Channel Tunnel is very close and a visit to Calais and a drive along the French coast is well advised whilst Jane and Iain can point guests to many good shopping areas and fine restaurants locally.

Bishopsdale Oast

Bishopsdale Oast, Biddenden, Kent TN27 8DR Tel: 01580 291027/292065 Fax: 01580 292321

SISSINGHURST   *Map 7 ref Q22*

This charming village with its main street of Wealden houses is often overlooked in favour of the famous castle and gardens. All that remains of the original Elizabethan manor house is the tall brick gatehouse and in 1930 the castle was bought, in a derelict condition, by Sir Harold Nicolson and his wife, Vita Sackville-West. Together they restored the buildings and planned and planted the now world famous **Sissinghurst Castle Gardens**, which include the White Garden—full of only white flowers and plants with silver leaves.

GOUDHURST   *Map 7 ref Q22*

This is a very pretty and typical Wealden village with tile-hung, weatherboarded cottages and its very own duckpond. Just to the west of Goudhurst is **Finchcocks**, a living museum of music. Housed in a beautiful Georgian building, the museum has a truly magnificent collection of musical instruments. The noted pianist Richard Burnett purchased the house in 1970 and this is his personal collection of restored keyboard instruments.

Just across the village duck pond is **Squirrels** restaurant, tearoom and flower shop, a light and airy building that is entered through a flower-banked arcade. The restaurant's name comes from the owner Ray Bailey's Royal Naval experiences when he found himself cast as a squirrel. A squirrel? Well, it's an intricate tale best told by Ray himself!

Ray looks after the flowers whilst his wife, Marian, does the cooking—creating a tasty range of home-make cakes, soups, traditional Sunday lunches and giant tea cakes the size of a tea plate. Marian is 'very fussy about quality'; a concern that is evident in all her cooking, especially in the cream teas, and the decor which consists of old photographs, beautiful dried flower arrangements and, of course,

The Squirrels

squirrels. The widely spaced tables and friendly atmosphere gives everyone a sense of visiting a village club that also happens to be an excellent tearoom and restaurant. Squirrels opens from 10 am until 5 pm (later from Easter— September) and is closed on Mondays, except for Bank Holidays.
The Squirrels, The Plain, Goudhurst, Kent TN17 1AP Tel: 01580 211807

LAMBERHURST   *Map 6 ref P22*

This charming village's former days of industrial glory hark back to the time when the iron furnaces blazed away and it was here that the ironwork for the balustrades at St Paul's Cathedral was cast. Teise, a wooded hillside, hides **Scotney Castle** from view. One footpath from the village churchyard crosses a footbridge over the River Teise and up a wooded hillside into the grounds of Scotney Castle.

A castle has stood on this site for well over 600 years and the current building's last private owner was Christopher Hussey, the former editor of *Country Life* magazine, who died in 1970. He lived in the newer Scotney Castle, the Tudor style house overlooking the old castle, which was built for his grandfather, Edward Hussey, in the late 1830s. Left to the National Trust, old Scotney is now open to the public from May to August, and its glorious gardens—created by Edward Hussey in the quarry from which the stone was cut to build his house— is now a perfect vision of fine trees surrounded by a blaze of rhododendrons, azaleas, waterlilies and wisteria. Open from April to November.

ROYAL TUNBRIDGE WELLS

Map 6 ref P22

In 1909, Edward VII decreed that Tunbridge Wells would, from that time on, be known as Royal Tunbridge Wells. As the name implies, the waters here were considered to be curative and members of the upper classes came to take advantage of their efficacious properties and to enjoy the pleasant social gatherings. Some 300 years before, Lord North had discovered a chalybeate spring rich in iron in the area where the Pantiles are now situated. After sampling the red-tinged waters his consumptive afflictions were apparently eased and he enthusiastically spread the word. The future of Tunbridge Wells as a popular spa was thus assured.

The Pantiles is a colonnaded tiled walk which gets its name from the square clay tiles originally laid in the 1700s on the instructions of Queen Anne. At one end of the original walk, a new area has been created with many excellent shops to browse in but the graceful older area is lovelier by far. Linking the High Street to the Pantiles is picturesque Chapel Place, a Victorian pedestrian precinct tucked behind the 17th century chapel of King Charles the Martyr.

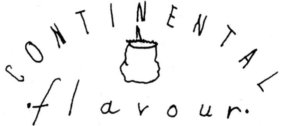

Opposite the Trinity Art Centre on Church Road is the **Continental Flavour Wholefood Restaurant and Shop** which promises traditional European dishes, freshly made on the premises with a strong emphasis on wholesome eating. Here visitors can enjoy vegetarian or nonvegetarian cuisine in the nonsmoking restaurant or sample the freshly made coffee, delicious cakes, interesting salads, sandwiches and savouries; there's also a take away service. Food can be prepared to order for special diets or any other particular requirements.

Outside catering is another service offered by Continental Flavour who will happily cater for any special function, be it a wedding, christening, corporate event or whatever, at other locations providing the same quality of service. Open Monday to Saturday 8 am to 6 pm.
Continental Flavour, 15 Ritz Buildings, Church Road, Royal Tunbridge Wells, Kent TN1 1HP Tel: 01892 512215

Half a mile from the town centre, just off Johns Road, is **The Downs Tavern**, a typical pub for the serious drinker! The pub has been run by new owners Roy and Denise since August 1996 and they stay open for business all day from 11.30 am until 11 pm. A very good range of beers are on offer at this free house and

The Downs Tavern

for those who feel the need for sustenance, bar snacks are available. Outside is a sunny garden with swings for the children and there's a massive car park at the back of the pub.

The Downs Tavern, 5 Culverden Down, Royal Tunbridge Wells, Kent
TN4 9SA Tel: 01892 524029

When travelling westwards out of Tunbridge Wells along the A264 towards Rusthall, the rather steep and winding road leads to the pretty village of **Toad Rock** and the attractive **Toad Rock Retreat**. This friendly pub dates back to the 16th century and can be found opposite the local landmark of Toad Rock, a large

Toad Rock Retreat

sandstone rock that proved inspiration for the naming of the inn back in the 18th century. Owned and very capably run by Chris and Celestine for the past decade, Toad Rock Retreat offers its visitors the best in home-cooked food with a good value for money menu and a large range of specialist O'Hagans sausage dishes. Visitors can sit in front of the open log fires and enjoy a pint of excellent beer from the large selection of guest ales whilst soaking in the welcoming ambiance that permeates through this traditional inn.

Toad Rock Retreat, 1 Harmony Street, Denny Bottom, Royal Tunbridge
Wells, Kent TN4 8NX Tel: 01892 520818

The Red Lion is found in the village of **Rushall** on the old London to Brighton Coach Road used by the Cavaliers during the English Civil War. Look upwards outside this historic inn and the old windows which were used to signal the warning and arrival of the Customs and Excise to the next pub across the valley can still be seen. Licensed since 1415, The Red Lion has an inglenook fireplace with logs roaring in the grate on colder days and many features from its past. John and Joan are the licensees and they offer some lovely speciality cooking, including that old favourite Spotted Dick pudding. There is also an enormous garden which is ideal for children and even dogs providing they are kept under control. Many traditional pub games are played here so take a chance and challenge the locals. Nearby is the 17th century walled garden and medieval moat of Groomridge Place and Royal Tunbridge Wells is only a mile away.

The Red Lion

The Red Lion, 82 Lower Green Road, Rusthall, near Royal Tunbridge Wells, Kent TN4 8TW Tel: 01892 520086

The Beacon is much more than a country pub, it's a comfortable and relaxing home-from-home in a beautiful setting with genuinely helpful people on hand make sure any event goes smoothly. For here, parties, celebrations and get-togethers of all kinds are the specialities of The Beacon. Whatever the season, proprietors John and Di Cullen are able to accommodate from 10 to 60 guests in a variety of settings. In the winter guests can enjoy the warm welcome of a log fire while, in the summer, they can spread out onto the terrace and into 16 acres of grounds, complete with lakes and woodland. Appropriately set in Happy Valley, the Beacon is a friendly and informal bar and restaurant with a reputation for good food and entertainment.

The house itself dates back to 1895 and was built as the country house of Sir Walter Harris, a former Lieutenant of the City of London and for those who are looking for really special surroundings for any sort of reception, anniversary or reunion, the Beacon should be at the top of the list. With a service tailored to individual needs, the management will do everything from decorating tables to ensuring that everyone's glass is filled. But if cost is a concern and a simple room is all that is necessary—then that's fine too. For every event help is on hand. Call at the Beacon and take a stroll around the gardens—any one who does will certainly agree that the setting is just perfect.

The Beacon

The Beacon, Tea Garden Lane, Rusthall, near Royal Tunbridge Wells, Kent TN3 9JH Tel: 01892 524252

TONBRIDGE   *Map 6 ref P21*

Tonbridge Castle preceded the town by many centuries: there is evidence of a castle on this site as far back as the Iron Age, while the Saxons and Normans added to the earlier building, and Edward I completed things by constructing the impressive gatehouse. The castle commands fine views standing on its mound overlooking the River Medway and a personal guided audio tour will teach visitors everything they need to know about its fascinating history.

HEVER   *Map 6 ref P21*

To the west of Tonbridge can be found **Hever Castle**, the home of Anne Boleyn, Henry VIII's second wife and mother of Elizabeth I. Hever is a picture, with an original moat and benefiting from extensive restoration at the turn of this century by the wealthy Astor family.

WESTERHAM   *Map 6 ref P21*

The westernmost village in the county, this charming village sits right up against the border with Surrey, with the North Downs above and the Greensand Ridge below. However, apart from its scenic location, the village is perhaps best remembered as the birthplace of General James Wolfe. The Elizabethan house, now called **Quebec House**, was his childhood home though he was actually born in the Vicarage in 1727. Quebec House now houses a museum dedicated to this famous soldier.

On the village green stands a statue of Wolfe brandishing a sword aloft, portraying him very much as the fighting man who defeated the French at the famous Battle of Quebec. Also worth a look is the statue of Churchill on the same green which depicts the distinguished statesman in his familiar hunched position, a rather weary ministerial figure in contrast to the more flamboyant hero nearby.

The other building here which has strong associations with Wolfe is **Squerryes Court**. In the grounds of the house, a memorial marks the spot where he first received his military orders at the tender age of 14. Built in 1681, the house has some fine paintings by Dutch Old Masters, together with mementos of Wolfe, who was a regular visitor to the house as a friend of the Warde family.

To the south of the village lies **Chartwell** a place which will always be associated with Winston Churchill. His home from 1922 until his death, the house contains many items from Churchill's life including some of his paintings. The gardens too are worthy of note and of particular interest is the brick wall which Churchill built himself.

ROCHESTER   *Map 6 ref P21*

Lying in the north of the county, this town, like many places in the Medway valley, has associations with Charles Dickens. It was here, in the grounds of the castle mound with its splendid views, that Dickens requested that his body be laid to rest. His wishes were not fulfilled, as he now lies in Westminster Abbey, but his spirit lingers on here in the streets of the town that he loved so much.

Rochester Cathedral is easily overlooked as it lies so close to Canterbury but it is a handsome building and should not be ignored. King Ethelbert encouraged his Saxon followers to take up the Christian teachings over 1300 years ago and he founded a church on this site. Bishop Gundulph established the cathedral some 400 years later and it is particularly beautiful, with a magnificent Norman nave and fine arches leading up and up to the oaken roof. A memorial plate to Charles Dickens can be found here, and the crypts are definitely worth a visit.

SITTINGBOURNE   *Map 7 ref Q21*

Many of the beautiful river barges, which once made their way along the Medway to the mouth of Thames, were built at the boat yards around the town. There were once as many as 11 boat yards here, but today only **Dolphin Yard** remains. Situated on the banks of Milton Creek near Crown Quay Lane, it is now a sailing boat museum. Although rather tucked away, this museum is really worth a visit to see the splendid barges with their ornate paintwork. Lovers of these romantic craft can trace their history and inspect several of them at close quarters.

LEEDS
Map 7 ref Q21

The beauty of **Leeds Castle** is renowned far and wide and it can be found between Leeds and the neighbouring village of **Broomfield**. The castle's setting is breathtaking as it stands on two islands in a man-made lake that was created by damming the River Len which flows through the surrounding 500 acres of parkland. Although it was first a Norman stronghold, Leeds Castle became the beautiful palace seen today under Henry VIII. The rooms are full of medieval furnishings, tapestries and fine English and French paintings. To add to the attractions of the beautiful place, a new maze has been planted and, once the middle has been reached there is an underground retreat to explore.

Sussex

INTRODUCTION

This county, once the kingdom of the South Saxons, is characterised by three distinct areas: the coast, the South Downs and the fertile Weald. In the northern part of the county, and closest to London, this rich farming country of the Weald was, at the time of the Roman invasion, a massive forest of which little remains today.

To the south lies the green slopes of the South Downs which meet the sea at the famous point of Beachy Head. Described by Rudyard Kipling as the "blunt, bow-headed, whale-backed Downs", they are a favourite place for ornithologists and walkers as well as a training ground for race horses.

However, Sussex is probably most famous for its coastline and, in particular, the famous and elegant resorts of Eastbourne and Brighton. Both offer the usual seaside facilities, but, particularly at Brighton, it is the wonderful Regency architecture that makes the town so popular. A must for antique hunters, the narrow Lanes, are full of shops and dealers and they cater for every taste and pocket. Eastbourne, the quieter of the two, is equally attractive.

BRIGHTON
Map 6 ref O23

Before Dr Richard Russell of Lewes published his famous dissertation on *The Use Of Sea Water In Diseases Of The Glands* in 1753, Brighton was a small and unassuming fishing village which went under the name of Brighthelmstone. At that time, the sea front was constantly under threat from the encroachment of the sea and those not directly involved in fishing, settled on higher ground in the area of densely packed streets and alleyways now known as **The Lanes**. Although most of the buildings here were renewed in the early 19th century, this highly picturesque quarter between West, North and East Streets retains its maze-like medieval street plan. The present day Lanes are inhabited by an interesting assortment of antique shops, street cafés and specialist retailers which together form a fascinating attraction.

During the 1750s, Dr Russell moved to Brighton and began to extol the virtues of both bathing in and drinking sea water (the original chalybeate spring where he treated his patients can still be seen in **St Anne's Well Gardens** in Hove). His ideas gradually gained favour amongst the rich and influential until, in 1783, the fashionable status of the town was affirmed when the Prince of Wales chose to sample the beneficial effects of the new resort for himself. The young prince, who was later to become the Prince Regent and then George IV, was so taken with the place that he decided to build a permanent **Royal Pavilion** in the resort. In 1787, architect Henry Holland designed a classical style building with a dome and rotunda; however, in 1815, John Nash, the architect responsible for London's Regent's Park and the Mall, was asked to remodel the building. Nash came up with a radical and exotic scheme based on an Indian maharajah's palace complete with minarets, onion-shaped domes and pinnacles. Inside, the flavour of the building moves from the Indian subcontinent to the Far East in what must be one of the finest examples of Regency chinoiserie in the world.

The nearby **Dome** was once an arena for exercising the royal horses and is now a major concert venue; likewise, the old stables in Church Street have been converted into Brighton's acclaimed **Museum and Art Gallery**. The town contains a number of other splendid Regency developments, most of which are dotted along the sea front on either side of the old medieval centre. Among the better known are Bedford Square, Regency Square, Russell Square, Kemp Town and, perhaps most famous of all, Royal Crescent; this elegant row of terraced houses is faced with dark 'mathematical' tiles, a characteristic feature of this part of eastern Sussex.

A hidden place which may be of interest to those keen on antique toys and model railways is situated in the arches underneath Brighton station. The **Sussex Toy and Model Museum** is well worth a visit or there is an interesting exhibition of steam engines, some of which can be seen in operation, at the **British Engineerium** in neighbouring **Hove**.

Modern Brighton is a vibrant seaside town which offers visitors an enormous range of recreational activities. Apart from its long shingle beach, there are two splendid Victorian piers (one of which is no longer open to the public), a combined aquarium and dolphinarium which was founded in 1872, a popular and scenic racecourse, an electric railway which was the first of its kind in the country, and an impressive marina which, at 126 acres, is the largest such development in Europe.

One of Brighton's lesser known attractions is, however, **Preston Manor**, a 13th century manor house which is set within beautiful landscaped grounds on the northern approaches to the town. The house was rebuilt in the 1730s and was left to the people of Brighton in 1932 on condition that it would remain an English country home. The interior contains a permanent display of 18th century furnishings, silverware and porcelain, and the grounds have been preserved in period style and contain some fine water-lily ponds and a famous scented rose garden.

Further to the west, a unique view of the Downs can be seen through a recently installed camera obscura at the **Foredown Tower Countryside Centre** on the outskirts of Hove.

Quietly situated at 17 Regency Square, Brighton, the **Topps Hotel and Restaurant** is ideally located only two minutes walk from the sea and the Metropole Conference Centre, with the Lanes and Royal Pavilion nearby. This charming hotel offers an attractive alternative to the more anonymous large establishments in the vicinity and is under the personal supervision of resident proprietors, Paul and Pauline Collins. With its friendly welcome and efficient service, the Topps Hotel is certainly deserving of its name.

Topps Hotel

The bedrooms are all elegantly appointed and every need of the discerning visitor has been anticipated, guests can even select a bedroom complete with four poster bed if they require a stay that is a little more special. Brighton has often been described as London-by-the-sea, with its urbane atmosphere and wide range of shops, clubs and theatres make it a popular town for visitors. Glyndebourne, Arundel, Chichester and Lewes are all within easy reach and London is only 52 minutes away by train, so the Topps Hotel is the ideal base for exploring the surrounding countryside and towns.

Topps Hotel, 17 Regency Square, Brighton, Sussex BN1 2FG Tel: 01273 729334 Fax: 01273 203679

LEWES   *Map 6 ref O23*

This historic settlement stands at the strategically important point where the River Ouse is crossed by an ancient east–west land route. Because of the area's close proximity to Normandy, William the Conqueror divided his newly acquired Sussex estates amongst some of his most trusted lieutenants. The lands around Lewes were granted to William de Warenne and his wife, Gundrada, who not only constructed a substantial double motte and bailey castle on a hillside above the river but also founded St Pancras Priory on the southern edge of the town. This once magnificent monastic house belonged to the abbey of Cluny in Burgundy and had a great church as large as Chichester Cathedral. The priory was the home of the renowned team of artists who painted the famous ecclesiastical murals at Hardham and Clayton during the 12th century. Following the Dissolution, the building was forcibly demolished and its stone used for constructing residential dwellings in the town.

One building thought to have benefited in this way is **Southover Grange**, a substantial gabled residence which was built in 1572 and was the childhood home of the famous 17th century diarist, John Evelyn. Today, the house is perhaps best known for its wonderful walled garden whose beautiful lawns, trees and flowering plants provide a secluded haven in the heart of the town. The garden is open daily, 7 am till dusk, all year round.

Although very little of the priory has survived, a substantial part of **Lewes Castle** still remains, including a section of the keep with two flanking towers dating from the 13th century and a fortified gateway, or Barbican, dating from the 14th century. Visitors climbing onto the battlements are rewarded with magnificent views over the surrounding town and countryside; the castle gardens also offer an attractive area for relaxing or picnicking. Nearby Barbican House contains both the **Museum of Sussex Archeology** and Lewes' **Living History Model**. The former charts human development from early hunting cultures, through the Roman, Saxon and Norman incursions, to the end of the medieval era; the latter is an audiovisual presentation which tells the story of Lewes since 1066 using a remarkable scale model of the town.

In 1264, Lewes was the site of a particularly bloody confrontation between the armies of Henry III and Simon de Montfort. The Battle of Lewes took place on Mount Harry, an exposed hillside on the western side of the town and resulted in the deaths of as many as 5000 troops. Henry's defeat led to his enforced signing of the Mise of Lewes, a document which strengthened the importance of the barons and laid the foundations of modern parliamentary democracy.

The town also has an **Anne of Cleves House**, an early 16th century Wealden hall-house which formed part of Henry VIII's divorce settlement with his fourth wife. The structure has been much altered over the centuries and has evolved into an attractive concoction of buildings set around a reconstructed Tudor garden. Now a museum run by the Sussex Archeological Society, its rooms and galleries have been arranged to create an impression of domestic and working life in Lewes in the 17th and 18th centuries.

Lewes developed strong Protestant roots following the Reformation and the burning of over a dozen Protestant martyrs in the town during the reign of Mary I established an anti-Catholic fanaticism which can still be detected in the town's modern bonfire night festivities. In what must be the most extravagant 5th November celebrations in the country, rival bonfire societies march through the streets carrying flaming torches and specially made guys. These are then carried to the edge of town and thrown onto huge bonfires—a spectacular, if somewhat sinister, annual custom.

In the 18th century, Lewes became something of a centre for radical political thought. During this period, a local excise officer, Tom Paine, became renowned as a human rights campaigner and leading supporter of the American and French Revolutions. Paine lived at Bull House in the High Street, now a restaurant, and married the daughter of his landlord before settling in America. On his return, he wrote the revolutionary work in support of the French Revolution, *The Rights of Man* in 1792 and was forced to flee across the Channel.

GLYNDE   *Map 6 ref P23*

Although this settlement is filled with well preserved traditional Sussex cottages, the 18th century village church is very atypical of the area in that it is built in Palladian style. The churchyard contains the grave of one of Glynde's most noted sons, John Ellman, who was a pioneer of selective breeding and was responsible for producing the black-faced Southdown sheep, the breed on which most of the flocks in New Zealand and Australia are based.

Glynde Place, the imposing brick and flint mansion near the church, was built in the mid-16th century for William Morley. Two centuries later, it was acquired by Richard Trevor, the Bishop of Durham, who added the stable block, remodelled the house and built the parish church. The house has an elegant wood-panelled long gallery and contains some exceptional works of art, and the grounds are beautifully laid out and incorporate an aviary and a pottery. Glynde Place is open to the public on a limited number of days each year.

The distinctive local landmark known as **Mount Caburn** lies to the west of Glynde and can be reached along a footpath from the village. Many thousands of years ago, this steep-sided chalk outcrop was separated from the rest of the Downs by the action of the River Glynde. This process created an artificial looking mound almost 500 feet in height whose natural defensive properties have long been exploited by man. The earthwork defences of an Iron Age hill fort can still be made out near the summit and evidence of an earlier Stone Age settlement has also been detected.

However, Glynde's international renown centres around the part-Tudor, part-Victorian country house lying one mile to the north of the village which is the home of the **Glyndebourne Opera House**. This unique institution was founded by John and Audrey Christie in 1934 and since then it has built up an international reputation for presenting the finest opera in the most idyllic of English surroundings. Each summer season, audiences wearing evening dress arrive by train from London and leave their champagne to cool in the lake while they listen to the first half of the evening's performance; they then picnic in the grounds during the long interval before returning to the auditorium to enjoy the second half. Fans preferring their opera in a less precious atmosphere often choose to attend the autumn performances by Glyndebourne's Touring Company. The beautiful grounds of Glyndebourne are regularly open to visitors throughout the year.

EASTBOURNE   *Map 6 ref P23*

This stylish and genteel seaside resort takes its name from the stream, or bourne, which has its source in the old reservoir in the area of open land now known as Motcombe Gardens. The town developed relatively recently as a seaside resort. Prior to 1780, when the children of George III spent the summer here, Eastbourne consisted of two separate villages, the larger of which lay over a mile inland. A period of gradual development then followed which gained momentum after the town was connected to the railway network in 1849.

The development of Eastbourne's sea front was relatively controlled, largely because most of the land belonged to only two individuals, the 7th Duke of Devonshire and, to a lesser extent, Carew Davis Gilbert. Between them they were able to plan the wide thoroughfares, graceful stuccoed buildings and spacious gardens which characterise the town's three mile long esplanade. Among the noteworthy buildings constructed around this time are the handsome Regency-style Burlington Hotel, St Saviour's Church, the town hall, and the unusually elegant railway station. Eastbourne's classic seaside pier was built in 1880s and is one of the finest examples of its type in the country.

Despite its distinctive Victorian flavour, a settlement has existed on the site for many centuries. The remains of a Roman ship were discovered here in the 1960s and the parish church of St Mary dates from around 1200. Other pre-Regency buildings include the flint and cobble built Old Rectory and the 13th century Lambe Inn in the High Street. A total of 14 Martello towers were built along the sea front in the early 19th century when a Napoleonic invasion seemed likely. One of these, the **Wish Tower**, has been restored and now houses the **Coastal Defence Museum**, an interesting place which chronicles Britain's attempts over the centuries to resist invasion from the sea.

The circular **Redoubt Tower** in Royal Parade is another, even larger, Martello tower which has been converted for modern use. As well as containing an aquarium and the popular Treasure Island children's play centre, it is also the home of the **Sussex Combined Services Museum**, an informative museum on the history of Sussex based military units. The **Royal National Lifeboat Museum** lies on the sea front within a few yards of the Wish Tower; when it first opened in 1937, it was the first of its kind in the country.

Eastbourne has a proud reputation for its floral gardens and, indeed, it would be hard to find a more typically British display of spring bulbs and summer bedding plants than here. The **Carpet Gardens** beside the pier have an international reputation and are one of the finest remaining examples of the art of carpet gardening, a style which first became popular in the 18th century. The acclaimed **Towner Art Gallery** and local history museum is housed in an 18th century manor house which also enjoys an attractive landscaped setting.

Some three miles to the west of the town centre is the summit of **Beachy Head**. This magnificent white chalk cliff marks the eastern end of the South Downs and from the pleasant grassy picnicking area at the top there is an almost sheer drop of well over 500 feet to the waves below. The views from here are superb: to the east it is possible to see as far as Dungeness, to the west as far as Selsey Bill and the Isle of Wight and to the south as far as the distant cargo ships which ply the busy shipping lanes of the English Channel. The colossal mass of Beachy Head dwarfs the red and white banded lighthouse which stands on the wave-cut platform at its base. Notwithstanding, this distinctive granite built structure throws out a beam of light which can be seen over 15 miles out to sea. This stretch of coastline was once known as the Devil's Cape because of its danger to shipping and to this day the lighthouse has to continue its vital task of deterring ships from straying too close to the cliffs.

The **Far End** guest house is situated at the eastern end of Eastbourne's sea front and is ideally located for the boating lake, pitch and putt, bowling green and numerous pleasant walks. Hosts Tony and Trish Callaghan make all their guests

Far End

feel at home from the moment that they walk through the door, they even provide them with a front door key so that everyone is free to come and go as they please. All of the double, twin and single bedrooms are centrally heated and come complete with colour television and complimentary tea and coffee tray, whilst some of the rooms also have full en-suite facilities. Trish believes in supplying her guests with only the best in traditional English cooking using only the freshest local ingredients and the friendly, personal service ensures that a stay at the Far End will be an enjoyable one. Guests will also find a fully licensed bar available for their convenience and a whole host of features that will make them feel like returning to Far End each time they return to Eastbourne.

Far End, 139 Royal Parade, Eastbourne, Sussex BN22 7LH
Tel: 01323 725666

Set just off of the seafront in a haven of peace and tranquillity, visitors can sit and enjoy some good, traditional English home-cooking at **The Black Cat Tea Rooms**. Everyone can always expect a warm and friendly greeting from Eve and Paul, who personally own and run this charming tea shop. They even bake all of the delicious cakes and fancies that are available throughout the day and are always on hand to recommend some tempting delicacies.

After a stroll along the promenade to Beachy Head, the Black Cat proves the perfect location of stop and enjoy a cup of tea and some freshly baked scones but don't expect acres of tables and chairs, this tea room is cosy and filled with a homely atmosphere. As well as cakes and scones, Eve and Paul also serve tempting hot snacks for those with a larger appetite

The Black Cat Tea Rooms

and provide a large selection of real English teas.

The Black Cat Tea Rooms, 50 Meads Street, Eastbourne, Sussex BN27 RH
Tel: 01323 646590

The Castle, a charming inn, is set well back off the road in its own grounds. Having recently been substantially refurbished by its owner Karen Kennedy, this attractive pub offers the very best in modern facilities including a nonsmoking family room and a spacious function hall which is used for live bands and some very American line dancing! Value for money has played a big part in Karen's plans and guests can sit back and enjoy a three course meal for under six pounds!! There are always plenty of specials, including specialist cooking nights, when delicious French or Italian dishes can be sampled. There is a good selection of

The Castle

real ales from local breweries, including a full range of the more well known brands, whilst a comprehensive array of wines are provided to complement the meals. It is also said that the ghost of Ma Morgan still oversees the cooking in the kitchens to make sure that the excellent cuisine reaches her high standards.
The Castle, 346 Seaside, Eastbourne, East Sussex BN22 7RJ
Tel: 01323 738411

HERSTMONCEUX   *Map 6 ref P23*

This attractive village has been a centre of the trug-making industry for over 160 years and, still made in the traditional way, these useful garden tools can be found here in many different sizes. Just outside the village is the famous **Herstmonceux Castle** and **Observatory**. The castle was built on the site of an earlier Norman manor house in 1440 and was one of the first large scale buildings in Britain to be constructed from redbrick; it was also one of the first fortifications to take into account both the defensive needs and the comfort of its residents.

Later, the castle passed into the hands of the Hare family who presided over a long period of decline which culminated in its virtual dismantling in 1777. The structure then remained in a state of dilapidation for some 150 years until a major programme of careful restoration began in the 1930s under the supervision of the Lewes architect, WH Godfrey. In 1948, the Royal Greenwich Observatory moved here from its original home in Greenwich Park, London to get away from the residual glare of the city. Over the following 20 years, the mighty Isaac Newton telescope was planned and built in the grounds which, when it was officially opened in 1967, was one of the five largest telescopes in the world. Recent advances in the field of astronomy necessitated a further move and the Royal Greenwich Observatory is now located in Cambridge. The observatory and grounds are open daily, Easter to end-September; the castle is open on a limited number of days each year (opening times displayed on site).

HASTINGS

Map 7 ref Q23

Long before William the Conqueror made his well publicised landing on the beaches of nearby Pevensey Bay, Hastings was the principal town of a small semi-independent Saxon province which straddled the Kent–Sussex border. By the mid-10th century, it had become an important port and Hastings even had its own mint. Following the Battle of Hastings, which in fact took place six miles inland at the place now called Battle, the Normans chose a promontory to the west of the old town to build their first stone **Castle** in England. Sections of the north and east walls, a gatehouse, tower and dungeons still remain, and the stiff walk up to the castle site is rewarded with some magnificent views of the town and surrounding coastline. Hastings Castle is forever linked with that most famous date in English history—1066. The ruins of William the Conqueror's 900 year old castle are also the home of the **1066 Story**. From within a medieval siege tent visitors are transported back in time with the help of high tech multi-track sound, lighting effects and projected images covering thousands of years of history.

From the castle, it is only a short walk across the West Hill to another great experience—**Smugglers Adventure**. Housed in the winding tunnels and caverns of St Clement's Caves, this themed experience includes a museum of smuggling, a video theatre and subterranean adventure walk.

Over the centuries, Hastings has been subjected to periodic attack from the sea, both from cross-Channel raids, which on at least one occasion left the town a smouldering ruin, and from the waves themselves, which would regularly flood the streets during stormy conditions. The town's busy fishing harbour started to silt up during the Elizabethan era and now lies buried beneath a 20th century shopping development. Nevertheless, the industry managed to survive and today, fishing vessels continue to be hoisted onto the shingle beach by motor winch. One of Hastings' most characteristic features are the tall, narrow wooded huts which are used for dying nets and storing fishing tackle; these date from the 17th century and are known as net shops or deezes. The old fishermen's church of St Nicholas now houses the **Fishermen's Museum**, an interesting exhibition which includes the full sized sailing lugger, *Enterprise*. This was the last vessel to be built in Hastings before the shipyard closed in 1909 and was actively involved in the Dunkirk evacuation of 1940.

The old part of Hastings consists of a network of narrow streets and alleyways, or twittens, which lie between Castle Hill and East Hill. The best way discover the many interesting old residential buildings, inns and churches is to take a walking tour along the High Street and All Saints Street. **St Clement's Church**, in the High Street, has two cannonballs embedded in its tower, one of which was fired from a French warship, and the **Stag Inn**, in All Saints Street, has a concealed entrance to a smugglers' secret passage and a pair of macabre 400 year old mummified cats.

Hastings also contains a variety of attractions for the traditional seaside holiday-maker. The 600 foot long **Pier** was completed in 1872 and had to be repaired after World War II when it was deliberately holed in two places to prevent it being used as a landing stage by Hitler's forces. According to local legend, the **Conqueror's Stone** at the head of the pier was used by William the Conqueror as a dining table for his first meal on English soil in 1066. A total of 81 events spanning 900 years of the town's history are remembered in the impressive **Hastings Embroidery**, on display in the town hall. Inspired by the Bayeux Tapestry, this remarkable 240 foot long embroidery was made by the Royal School of Needlework in 1966 to commemorate the ninth centenary of the Norman Invasion. Among the characters to be depicted is John Logie Baird, the pioneer of television who carried out his early experiments here in the 1920s.

At **Guestling**, located only a few miles east of Hastings on the A259, stands **The Three Oaks**, an attractive and traditional free house inn. Owned and run by Craig and Chrissie, the Three Oaks has been reputedly haunted by a mischievous ghost for many years and customers are encouraged to partake in a little ghost busting whilst enjoying a pint of real ale from Craig's excellent casked beers. Mentioned in the *Good Beer Guide*, Three Oaks is locally known for its good

The Three Oaks

quality restaurant and bar menus, each offering its guests the opportunity to sample delicious home-cooked dishes, freshly prepared using only the finest local ingredients. Those visiting this delightful pub in winter time will be greeted by roaring log fires crackling in the grate and a cosy atmosphere pervades throughout the inn but, if visited in the long summer months, the flower filled beer garden is the perfect place to enjoy a cool drink and soak up the sun. Whatever the time of year, Three Oaks offers a friendly welcome and excellent hospitality that has people returning again and again.

The Three Oaks, Butchers Lane, Three Oaks, Guestling, near Hastings, Sussex TN35 4NH Tel: 01424 813303

RYE

Along with its neighbour, Winchelsea, Rye was added to the five existing Cinque Ports of Hastings, Romney, Hythe, Dover and Sandwich in the 12th century. The town was also subjected to ferocious cross-Channel raids and almost every non-stone built structure in the town was burnt to the ground in the notorious French raid of 1377. Later, the harbour suffered from the problems of a receding coastline, a dilemma which eventually required the building of a new port, Rye Harbour, closer to the repositioned mouth of the River Rother.

Rye's prominent hilltop site is partially ringed by the rivers Rother, Brede and Tillingham, a factor which has made it an easily defendable hill fort since early times. A substantial perimeter wall was built to defend the open northern approaches and one of its four great gateways, the **Land Gate**, still survives in the northeastern corner of the old town. This imposing 14th century structure once had oak gates, a drawbridge and a portcullis. The clock was added in 1863 in memory of Prince Albert and was restored at the time of the Royal Wedding in 1981.

Rye grew prosperous in the late medieval period due to the activities of its fishing and merchant fleets who brought in fish and cloth and sent out wool and processed iron to Europe. However, the silting up of the harbour gradually denied the town a means of earning a living and heralded a lengthy period of decline. This economic downturn halted the process of organic change in Rye and many of the buildings which would have been updated in more prosperous circumstances remained unchanged. As a result, present day Rye has inherited a superb legacy of late medieval buildings, most of which have been restored in the years since the town was rediscovered in the 19th century.

Of interest is the National Trust owned **Lamb House**, a handsome redbrick Georgian residence which was built by a local wine merchant, James Lamb, in 1723. The new building incorporated a number of earlier structures, including a deese for drying herrings and a brewery which occupied the site of what is now the walled garden. In 1726, George I paid an impromptu visit to Lamb House after his ship was driven onto nearby Camber Sands during a storm. He ended up being snowed in for four nights during which time Lamb's wife, Martha, gave birth to a son; the King agreed to be child's godfather and two days later the baby was baptised George. An inscribed silver bowl given by the King as a christening present was later revealed to be silver plate.

In 1742, an attempt was made on James Lamb's life by a local butcher, John Breads. As mayor, Lamb had fined Breads for selling short measures and, in revenge, Breads attacked a man wearing the red mayoral cloak as he was walking through the churchyard late one night. The man turned out to be Lamb's brother-in-law, Allen Grebell, who had agreed to represent him at a dinner on board a visiting ship. Grebell later died from his injuries and Breads was tried and hanged. His body was then chained to a public gibbet as a deterrent to others. Later, the murderer's bones were taken down and boiled into an infusion which was thought to cure rheumatism and the remainder of the his skull, still in its gibbet cage, was put on display in Rye's 18th century town hall where it can still be seen to this day. The ghost of Allen Grebell has been known to appear both in Lamb House and in the churchyard.

Lamb House became the home of the American writer Henry James from 1898 until his death in 1916 and many of his finest later novels were dictated to his secretary either in the Green Room or, during warmer weather, in the Garden Room. James laid out the delightful walled garden and invited many of his literary friends to the house, including HG Wells, Rudyard Kipling, GK Chesterton and Joseph Conrad. During the 1920s, Lamb House was leased to another writer, EF Benson, the author of the *Mapp and Lucia* books, who thinly disguised the house as Mallards and the town as Tilling. Today, Lamb House contains a number of Henry James' personal effects and is open to the public.

Rye's wonderful centrepiece, Church Square, contains some of the town's finest late medieval buildings. The parish **Church of St Mary the Virgin** was severely damaged during the French raid of 1377, although not before its church bells were taken down and carried off to Normandy. However, a retaliatory raid the following year not only inflicted a similar fate on two French towns but succeeded in recapturing the bells of St Mary. Built of red brick in 1735, the town cistern, or **Water House**, stands on top of an underground tank which once held the town's water supply. The tank was filled by raising water through wooden pipes from the bottom of Conduit Hill using horse drawn machinery. Southwest of here is the **Ypres Tower**; one of the oldest surviving buildings in Rye, it was constructed around 1250 as a defensive fort. Two centuries later, it was acquired by John de Ypres as a private residence then, subsequently, it became the town's courthouse, gaol and mortuary. Today, it houses the award-winning **Rye Museum** and offers some magnificent views over the surrounding coastal plain.

The nearby **Dormy House Club** stands on the site of the old Tower House, the former home of a beautiful young woman who is said to have fallen in love with a friar with a particularly fine singing voice. The pair ran away together, but were caught, brought back and punished by being buried alive. Years later, the skeletons of the lovers, still wrapped in each other's arms, were discovered during excavations for the railway. Their ghosts, who regularly haunted nearby Turkey Cock Lane, have not been seen since their remains were given a formal reburial.

South of Rye lie the ruins of **Camber Castle**, a fortification built in 1539 by Henry VIII as part of the Tudor coastal defences. Although originally constructed near the shoreline, the shifting sands have marooned the structure over a mile inland.

BATTLE

Map 7 ref Q23

This historic settlement is renowned as the location of the momentous battle on 14th October 1066 between the forces of Harold, the Saxon King of England and William, Duke of Normandy. The Battle of Hastings actually took place on a hill which the Normans named Senlac, meaning lake of blood and, even today, some believe in the myth that blood seeps from the battlefield after heavy rain (any discolouring of the water is, in fact, due to iron oxide in the subsoil).

Any visit to Battle must take in **The Almonry**, on the High Street, where visitors can follow a tour of the town through a model, with synchronised commentary and lighting. The Almonry building itself is a 14th century, five bay medieval hall house and is one of only four oak-framed buildings remaining in east Sussex. The 17th century panelled staircase features a 300 year old Guy Fawkes and, beneath the house, a secret passage links the building directly with the Abbey.

Prior to 1066, the site of Battle was virtually uninhabited; however, one of William the Conqueror's first tasks on becoming King of England was to found a substantial Benedictine abbey on this exposed hillside in order to make amends for the loss of life in battle and so secure his future salvation. **St Martin's Abbey** was finally consecrated in 1094, the high altar in the great church being placed on the very spot where Harold was struck in the eye by an arrow from a Norman bow. Throughout the late Middle Ages, the abbey grew wealthy and powerful as it extended its influence over a wide area of east Sussex. This period of prosperity came to an abrupt end, however, following the Dissolution. The abbey site is now under the ownership of English Heritage and several of the old monastic buildings are open to visitors. The imposing 14th century gatehouse contains a recently opened exhibition which brings the history of the abbey to life and the mile long Battlefield Walk guides visitors around the edge of Senlac Hill and describes the course of the battle with the help of models and information boards.

Battle offers a number of other noteworthy attractions, apart from the battle site and abbey. In particular, the **Battle Museum of Local History** in Langton House contains a half-size reproduction of the Bayeux Tapestry, a facsimile of the Sussex volume of the Domesday Book and an interesting collection of old maps, coins, toys and games.

FRANT

Map 6 ref P22

A former iron founding community, the early 19th century village church contains some unusual interior features and the country house, Shernfold Park, was once the home of the founder of Ottawa in Canada.

Bassetts Restaurant occupies a charming cottage style building which exudes charm and character and creates the perfect impression for what is to come. Bassetts has been trading as a restaurant for the past 15 years and is renowned for its fine cuisine. It recently gained it's first entry in the *AA Best Restaurants Guide* for 1997.

Nicholas Mott has been a co-owner and maitre d' at Bassetts since 1985. Prior to that, he spent several years pursuing his great love of sailing. Following the racing circuit, he competed in many events including the Whitbread Round the World Race—on board the British yacht *United Friendly* which was skippered by Chay Blyth. Still sailing whenever possible, he now lives in Frant and is responsible for the smooth running of Bassetts front of house. Duncan Morley, on the other hand, joined Bassetts as chef de cuisine in May 1996 having previously worked in the kitchens of a number of award winning restaurants, including Gidleigh Park (Devon), Amberley Castle and Gravetye Manor (West Sussex) and Horsed Place (East Sussex). His great enthusiasm for his work is admirably demonstrated by his demand for high quality local produce, his varied and frequently changing menu and the importance he places on customer satisfaction.

Bassetts Restaurant

Bassetts present Gourmet Evenings, Theme Evenings, Wine Tastings and other special events which have now become a popular feature of the restaurant and they are much in demand. They cater for up to 36 guests and will be pleased to keep anyone interested informed by adding their name to the mailing list. Bassetts also provide outside catering to the same high standards as their restaurant and will cater for dinner parties at home, barbecues, buffets, parties, formal dinners or wedding breakfasts. They offer a full service for any occasion.
Bassetts Restaurant, 37 High Street, Frant, Sussex TN3 9DT
Tel: 01892 750635 Fax: 01892 750913

Situated on the edge of this pretty Wealden village, **Cornhill** is a timber framed former gamekeepers' cottage with many period features. Originally built by the monks of Bayham Abbey, its origins date back to the 13th century. It is set in six acres of grounds with an abundance of wildlife including a herd of fallow deer and surrounded by some of the most attractive and unspoilt countryside in

Cornhill

Sussex. The area is perfect for a long weekend holiday with many places of interest nearby. The accommodation consists of a family sitting room complete with large inglenook fireplace and open fires all year round and two charming double bedrooms with en-suite facilities. Both rooms have brass and iron beds, hot drinks facilities, colour TV and lovely views. A full English breakfast is served.

Cornhill, Manor Farm, Frant, Sussex TN3 9BN Tel & Fax: 01892 750604

PILTDOWN
Map 6 ref P22

This village is notorious in academic circles for being the site of one the greatest archeological hoaxes of all time. In 1912, an ancient skull was discovered by the amateur archeologist, Charles Dawson, which was believed to form the missing link between man and the apes. The Piltdown Skull was believed to be about 150,000 years old; however, the improved methods of dating which came into use during the 1950s revealed that the jaw bone in fact belonged to a modern ape, whilst the rest was a human skull dating from around 50,000 BC. The perpetrator of the hoax was never discovered although various theories point the finger at Sir Arthur Conan Doyle, at an evangelical Christian fundamentalist and, perhaps most likely, at Charles Dawson himself.

CLAYTON
Map 6 ref O24

This is an unusual village whose parish church contains a series of 12th century wall paintings which are thought to be by the same group of artists from the St Pancras Priory in Lewes who were responsible for those at Hardham and Coombes. Rediscovered in the 1890s, the murals depict some salutary scenes of eternal damnation from the *Last Judgment*.

The village stands at the northern end of the one-and-a-quarter-mile long **Clayton Tunnel**, an engineering wonder of its day which opened in 1846 and still carries the busy London to Brighton trains. A towering Victorian folly known as **Tunnel House** stands at the tunnel's northern portal. Built to house the resident tunnel keeper, this castellated mock-Tudor fortress is still occupied.

A unique pair of windmills known as **Jack and Jill** stands above the village on Clayton Hill. Jack is a black painted tower mill which fell into disuse in the 1920s and has since been converted into an unusual private home; Jill is a smaller timber built post mill dating from 1821 that was removed from its original site in Dyke Road, Brighton by a team of oxen around 1850. Now restored, it is still capable of grinding corn and is occasionally open to visitors.

WORTHING   *Map 6 ref N23*

Despite having been inhabited since the Stone Age, Worthing remained a small and isolated fishing community until the end of the 18th century when the combined effects of a new northern road link through the Findon Gap and the sudden popularity of sea-bathing amongst the rich and fashionable set led to a period of rapid development. This reached its peak after 1798 when George III sent his 16 year old daughter, Princess Amelia, to Worthing to recuperate from an ill chosen affair with one of his royal equerries. During this period, several fine Regency thoroughfares were constructed, most notably Warwick Road, Montague Place, Liverpool Terrace and Park Terrace, all of which survive today.

By 1830, however, Worthing's Golden Age had come to an end. Further expansion was interrupted by the cholera and typhoid outbreaks of the 1850s and 1890s and it was not until the inter-war years of the 20th century that the town once again saw a period of development, albeit of a less grandiose kind. Today, Worthing is a bustling seaside town with a pier, theatre and cinemas which offers some excellent shopping and entertainment facilities in an atmosphere of dignified Regency charm.

Visitors interested in finding out more about the town's history from Neolithic times to the present day should make a point of finding the award winning **Worthing Museum and Art Gallery** in Chapel Road. Exhibits here include a model of a Neolithic flint mine, Anglo-Saxon glass and jewellery, a fascinating collection of antique toys and dolls and a display of English paintings, glassware and china from the Regency period onwards.

ARUNDEL   *Map 6 ref N23*

A settlement since pre-Roman times, Arundel stands at the strategically impor-tant point where the major east–west land route through Sussex crosses the River Arun. One of William the Conqueror's most favoured knights, Roger de Montgomery, first built a castle on the high ground above the river. This was similar to the castle at Windsor in that it consisted of a motte and double bailey, a plan which, despite several alterations to the fabric of the building, remains largely unaltered to this day.

The period of stability the castle brought to the town in the late medieval period made Arundel into an important port and market town. It was during this era that the 14th century Parish **Church of St Nicholas** was built, a unique building in that it is now divided into separate Catholic and Anglican areas by a Sussex iron screen. The Fitzalan Chapel in the choir houses the tombs of the Catholic Earls of Arundel and Dukes of Norfolk, in whose family the castle has remained for the past 500 years.

During the English Civil War, Parliamentarian forces bombarded the castle using cannons fired from the church tower. This bombardment led to the destruction of most of the Norman fortifications, the only parts to survive being the 12th century shell keep on the central mound and parts of the 13th century barbican and curtain wall. The rest of the structure remained in ruins until a programme of restoration during the 1790s made the castle habitable once again. (One of the finest rooms in Arundel Castle, the mahogany lined library, dates from this period.) A second restoration, amounting to a virtual rebuilding, was carried out about 100 years later by the 15th Duke, funded by profits from the family's ownership of the newly prosperous steel town of Sheffield.

Most of the colossal **Arundel Castle** structure which can be seen today is, therefore, a 19th century Gothic reproduction. However, the state apartments and main rooms contain some fine period furniture dating from the 16th century and paintings by such artists as Reynolds, Van Dyck, Gainsborough, Holbein and Constable. Members of the public also have unrestricted access to the nearby 1000 acre Arundel Castle grounds; dogs, however, are not allowed.

Despite religious persecution, particularly during the 16th century, the Fitzalan family and the successive Dukes of Norfolk remained staunchly Roman Catholic. The 15th Duke who was responsible for the 19th century rebuilding of the castle also commissioned the substantial Catholic Church of St Philip Neri which was designed in French Gothic style by Joseph Hansom, the inventor of the Hansom cab. In 1965, this impressive building became the seat of the Catholic bishopric of Brighton and Arundel and was renamed the **Cathedral of Our Lady and St Philip Howard**. (St Philip Howard was the 13th Earl of Arundel who died in prison after being sentenced to death by Elizabeth I for his Catholic beliefs; his remains are now in the cathedral, along with an impressive memorial shrine.) Each June, the cathedral hosts the two day Corpus Christ Festival during which the entire length of the aisle is laid out with a carpet of fresh flowers.

Other historic sites in Arundel include the **Maison Dieu**, a medieval hospital which can be found outside the Mill Road lodge of Arundel Castle. Founded around 1380 and dissolved in 1546, this semi-monastic institution combined the roles of clinic, hotel and almshouse.

Arundel also contains a couple of interesting museums; the privately owned **Arundel Toy and Military Museum** is located in a charming Georgian cottage in the High Street known as the Doll's House. Inside, visitors can see a unique collection of antique dolls, teddy bears, puppets, games, boats, tin toys and around 3000 toy soldiers. Further along the High Street, the **Arundel Museum and Heritage Centre** gives an fascinating insight into the people and activities of the town through imaginative use of models, old photographs and historic artefacts.

Just to the north of the town is the 60 acre woodland site run by the **Wildfowl and Wetlands Trust** which contains a wide variety of ducks, geese, swans and other wildfowl from all over the world. Many of the birds can be viewed at close quarters, with Arundel Castle providing a dramatic backdrop.

A little to the south of Arundel, between Littlehampton and Bognor Regis, can be found the village of **Climping** and the delightful **Amberley Court**— converted Sussex barns around a quiet courtyard setting. But these are no ordinary barns, this is a quality conversion, beautifully restored, creating a luxury home. A huge display of colour around the courtyard comes from the

Amberley Court

many varieties of flowers and shrubs planted there. A log burning stove produces a warm glow in the beamed guest lounge whilst the accommodation provides for single, twin and double bedrooms, mostly en-suite. Situated off the A259 between Bognor and Littlehampton with Climping Beach nearby. Modestly priced. ETB 2 Crowns Highly Commended.
Amberley Court, Crookthorn Lane, Climping, near Littlehampton, Sussex BN17 5QU Tel: 01903 725131 Fax: 01903 734555

CHICHESTER   *Map 6 ref M23*

Founded by the Romans in the 1st century, Chichester still retains its original street plan; its four major thoroughfares—North, East, South and West Streets—intersecting at the point where the **Market Cross** now stands. This ornate 50 foot octagonal structure was built around 1500 by Bishop Edward Story to provide shelter for traders who came to ply their wares at the city's busy market.

Chichester was used as a base camp by the invading Roman legions who named it Noviomagus, the new city of the plain. The Romans were also responsible for constructing Chichester's city walls around AD 200. These originally consisted of raised earthwork embankments which were built in an irregular 11 sided polygon. The following centuries, however, saw a series of alterations and improvements and, today, large sections of the mainly medieval stone walls can be seen on the boundary of the old city. The city's modern name is derived from Cissa's ceaster (or castle) after the Saxon King Cissa who ruled this part of Sussex around AD 500.

In the post Roman era, Chichester remained an important administrative centre and market town. Between the 14th and 18th centuries, it was a major trading and exporting centre for the Sussex wool industry and many handsome merchants' houses remain, especially around St Martin's Square and the elegant Georgian enclave known as **The Pallants**. Pallant House is a fine example of a redbrick town house built in 1713 by the local wine merchant Henry 'Lisbon' Peckham.

The city has had a long military history and is home to the **Royal Military Police**, or Redcaps, whose museum is open to the public. Chichester also has a long and colourful ecclesiastical history. Although St Wilfrid chose nearby Selsey as the site for the area's first cathedral in the 8th century, the conquering Normans decided to build a new cathedral in its present location at the end of the 11th century. (This turned out to be a wise decision as the site of the original building has been washed away and now lies in the sea somewhere off Selsey Bill.) Construction work began in 1091 and the new cathedral was finally consecrated in 1184. Three years later, however, it was reduced to a shell by fire, requiring a rebuilding programme which was carried out in the 13th century by Richard of Chichester, a venerated bishop who was canonised in 1262 and subsequently adopted as the city's saint.

Chichester Cathedral is unique on two counts: it is the only medieval English cathedral which can be seen from the sea and it has a detached bell tower. This was so built because it was feared the existing tower was insufficiently sturdy to hold the cathedral bells; a justifiable concern as it turned out for, in 1861, the spire blew down in storm, demolishing a large section of the nave. The present 277 foot spire was designed by Sir Gilbert Scott in sympathy with the original style and can been seen for miles around in every direction. The **Prebendal School**, the cathedral choir school and the oldest school in Sussex, stands alongside the main building. A little further south, the **Bishop's Palace** has a delightful garden and a 12th century chapel containing a unique wall painting.

One of Chichester's most distinctive modern buildings can be found at Oaklands Park, just north of the city walls. Since the hexagonally shaped **Festival Theatre** was opened in 1962, it has built up an international reputation for staging the finest classical and contemporary drama, opera and ballet. The theatre is one of the focal points of the annual Chichester Festival, a two week programme of cultural events which takes place each July. Festivities include classical concerts in the cathedral and fireworks displays at Goodwood Racecourse. Along with Salisbury and Winchester, Chichester also plays its part in the summer Southern Cathedrals Festival.

The acclaimed **Chichester District Museum** is located in the area of the city known as Little London. This interesting and well laid out museum creates a vivid picture of life in this part of west Sussex from the Stone Age to the present day. There is a particularly good collection of artefacts from the Roman period, along with a recently opened exhibition illustrating the many changes which have affected Chichester during the last 100 years. The museum also contains a special section dedicated to the history of the Royal Sussex Regiment from its foundation in 1701 to the present day.

Reviewed and acclaimed by the Sunday Telegraph for its unusual and exotic cuisine, **The Brasserie** is truly a dining experience with a difference. It's a bustling 18th century style restaurant by day and in the evening an incredibly discreet and intimate venue with the glow of candlelight. Resident chef and

proprietor Achim Klein knows only too well how to present his inventive dishes maintaining a most agreeable ambience and high level of service.

Between the very large menu and an even larger blackboard, selection of food is a painstaking process, so allow time to choose. An ever changing selection of at least 15 seasonal starters are listed; emu, kangaroo and bison are some of the main meat dishes guests can expect to find on the menu, whilst mahi-mahi, Oman hornbilled bream, flying fish and tipsy prawns are just some of the sea and fresh-water creature creations normally avail-able. Exotic fish from the Pacific and Indian Ocean and from local suppliers all

The Brasserie

create a magnificent selection of culinary creations to be savoured here. Calorie conscious and healthy eating diners will appreciate the benefits of the many high and low calories dishes, as will the dieting and discerning patrons. The puddings are equally imaginative and delicious. Achim is always happy to entertain families and corporate users will find The Brasserie a perfect venue. Naturally, bookings are preferred and advisable.

The Brasserie, 14 St Pancras, Chichester, Sussex PO19 1SJ
Tel: 01243 538282 Fax: 01243 782210

Set back from the road, is **The Bulls Head** where hosts Roger and Jools Jackson have created a popular venue in this old 17th century farmhouse. It has a south facing courtyard and Sussex barn in which there is a skittle alley. A slightly French influence has crept in with the introduction of the game of boules, now gaining popularity in this country. The restaurant offers home-cooked English meat and fish dishes with game on the menu in season. Six real ales are available and, of course, there's a good selection of other beers, lagers, wines and spirits. The seashore can be reached at the end of the road past the pond and Fishbourne Roman Palace is just a few hundred yards away.

The Bulls Head, 99 Fishbourne Road, Chichester, Sussex Tel: 01243 785707

Jackson's Cellar

Jackson's Cellar, also hosted by Roger and Jools Jackson, was converted from three 18th century vaulted tunnels and it has a unique below ground atmosphere with interesting arrangements for meals and candlelight evenings. Jacksons Cellar has great possibilities for partying and special functions. The cuisine has a strong Belgian influence which can be enjoyed between 11 am and 11 pm Monday to Friday. A well stocked bar can provide drinks for all preferences including an incredibly wide selection of quality beers. Well worth coming to for dining with a difference.

Jackson's Cellar, 3 Little London, Chichester, Sussex Tel: 01243 771771

Crouchers Bottom Country Hotel offers an interesting blend of country house with hotel standards thus ensuring all the creature comforts in a relaxed and informal atmosphere. Situated close to Chichester Harbour, just half a mile from the Yacht Basin and only two miles from the centre of the city. The house is surrounded by fields, with picturesque views of Chichester Cathedral, Goodwood and the South Downs.

The nine en-suite guest rooms are located in the separate coach house, seven of which are on the ground floor. One of the rooms is particularly suitable for wheel-chair users. All the bedrooms have direct dial telephones, colour television, clock radio, hair dryer and tea and coffee making facilities. The south-facing ground floor rooms open onto the large patio which overlooks the garden and pond with its resident waterfowl. There is a large guests' lounge (with log fire in the winter) adjacent to the dining room. Dinner is available to

Crouchers Bottom Country Hotel

residents and their guests with an interesting choice of freshly prepared dishes, which changes daily. A nice selection of wines are offered to complement the meal. With afternoon teas and high teas on offer for younger children, the proprietors Mr and Mrs Wilson clearly provide a very high standard of service for their guests. Awarded 3 Crown Highly Commended by the ETB.
Crouchers Bottom Country Hotel, Birdham Road, Apuldram, Chichester, Sussex PO20 7EH Tel: 01243 784995 Fax: 01243 539797

MIDHURST   *Map 6 ref N22*

This quiet and prosperous country town possesses a number of noteworthy buildings, including the tall timber-framed Elizabeth House, the 15th century Spread Eagle coaching inn and the 19th century cottage library in **Knockhundred Row**. This delightfully named thoroughfare is believed to have been the focal point for the ancient custom of knocking for 100 militia men when there was a call to defend the town. Midhurst's renowned **Grammar School** was founded in the 1670s in the Old Market Hall. Over two centuries later, it was attended by the young HG Wells when his mother was a housekeeper at nearby Uppark House.

The town though is perhaps better known for the ruins of **Cowdray House**, which lie just to the northeast. This once magnificent courtyard mansion was built of local sandstone around 1530 by the Earl of Southampton on the site of an earlier 13th century manor house. Elizabeth I was a regular visitor and, on one occasion, the Queen and her entourage were said to have consumed three oxen and 140 geese during a week long stay, no doubt making her departure something of a relief for her overstretched host, Viscount Montague.

In 1793, Cowdray House was gutted by fire and a week later, its owner, the last Lord Montague, was drowned whilst on a visit to Germany. This fulfilled a legendary curse placed on the owners of Cowdray House by a monk evicted from Battle Abbey by the first owner during the Dissolution. Today, visitors can view the roofless remains of the east side of the quadrangle court, along with parts of the west side where the turreted three storey gatehouse remains largely intact. The 17,000 acre **Cowdray Park** is one of the largest private estates in Sussex and is a well established for venue for summer polo tournaments.

PETWORTH   *Map 6 ref N22*

Between the 14th and 16th centuries, Petworth was an important cloth-weaving centre and a number of fine merchants' and landowners' residences, including Daintrey House, North House and Tudor House, were built during those prosperous days. The cramped Market Place contains a fine late 18th century arcaded town hall and a striking bank building, the National Westminster, built in baroque style in 1901.

However, the most dominant feature of Petworth is the grand house and park which together make up the National Trust owned Petworth Estate. Surrounded by a wall over 13 miles long, the 700 acre **Petworth Park** was landscaped by Lancelot 'Capability' Brown in the 1750s. The sweeping grounds contain a lake and a deer park and are a fine example of 18th century emparking. **Petworth House** was built between 1688 and 1696 on the site of a 13th century manor house and the present building incorporates the original medieval chapel and hall undercroft. The house, with its magnificent 320 foot west front, was built in French style on the instructions of Charles, 6th Duke of Somerset. The galleries and state rooms house one of the finest art collections in the country and paintings on show include work by Turner, who was a regular visitor, Rembrandt, Van Dyck, Holbein and Gainsborough.

At **Balls Cross**, to the north of Petworth, can be found **The Stag**, run by licensees Hamish and Sue Hiddleston and their friendly dogs. The perfect place to make for while explore this area of Sussex, locals come to this watering hole not just

The Stag

for the fine ales but also for the seasonal game on the menu. Surrounded on all sides by marvellous woodland, this is an ideal place to enjoy a walk or leisurely stroll to work up an appetite and get full value from the ale on tap. The Stag also offers bed and breakfast, the bedrooms (mind the low beams) are comfortable and there is a sitting room for guests' use. Back in the bar guests can join in with a game of dominoes, bar skittles or darts. In particular the Steak and Kidney Pie is to be recommended.

The Stag, Balls Cross, Petworth, West Sussex GU28 JP Tel: 01403 820241

LURGASHALL   *Map 6 ref N22*

A little to the north of Petworth and nestling beneath Blackdown, the highest point in West Sussex, where Alfred Lord Tennyson once had his home, Aldworth, stands the **Lurgashall Winery**, housed in a complex of converted 17th and 19th century farm buildings. Visitors are encouraged to 'try before they buy' at the well stocked winery shop and time should be made to browse around the range of English products, including a selection of "A Taste of Sussex" food and beverage items. English wine, cider, glasses, honey, mead mustard, fudge, chocolates and beeswax candles are just some of the items to be found on sale here, together with a good selection of tourist information leaflets. Tea and coffee are always available and self-guided Winery tours can be taken at weekends only during Shop opening hours by purchasing a leaflet at the Shop for a small charge. Guided Winery Tours, with English cheese and tutored wine tastings can be booked for groups of between 15 and 50 people for weekday evenings and weekends.

Lurgashall Winery

There is also a Medieval herb garden to be visited and an orienteering course is available for pre-booked groups. For those who cannot make a visit here a full mail order service is available from the Winery shop which is open every day except Christmas Day, Boxing Day and New Year's Day from Monday to Saturday 9 am to 5 pm and on Sunday from 11 am to 5 pm.

Lurgashall Winery, Windfallwood, Lurgashall, West Sussex GU28 9HA
Tel: 01428 707292 Fax: 01428 707654

Surrey

INTRODUCTION

The county of Surrey is conveniently placed close to London and is an ideal area for those people who have perhaps seen and experienced the more obvious tourist attractions of the capital, to begin to broaden their horizons. Although many of the towns and villages in the northern and eastern areas of the county are very much the homes of commuters to the City, many have retained their ancient centres and a little exploration will reveal the older buildings amidst the modern amenities.

Further south and west the county becomes more rural and, in its southwest corner, can be found Chiddingfold, the quintessential English village. Surrounding the large village green, on which cricket is still played, there are charming 16th and 17th century houses as well as an ancient village pub. Also hidden away are many interesting manor houses that have stood the test of time.

The county is also home to some interesting and unforgettably named natural features. The North Downs run across northern Surrey and Box Hill, a noted beauty spot, overlooks the valley of the River Mole to the north of Dorking. To the west of Guildford is the narrow ridge of the Hog's Back while, at Hindhead and close to the Hampshire border, there is the deep chasm of the Devil's Punchbowl.

GUILDFORD   *Map 6 ref N21*

Guildford Cathedral, which dominates the northwest approaches to the city, is one of only two new Anglican cathedrals to have been built in this country since the Reformation (the other is Liverpool). This impressive redbrick building stands on top of Stag Hill, a prominent local landmark which enjoys panoramic views over the surrounding landscape. The building was designed by Sir Edward Maufe with a superb high-arched interior and was begun in 1936. However, work was halted during World War II and members of the local diocese had to wait until 1961 for the new cathedral to be finally consecrated. In 1968, the **University of Surrey** relocated from London to a site on a hillside to the northwest of the cathedral. Pleasant and leafy, the campus contains a number of striking buildings including the university library and art gallery.

From the university, it is only a mile to the heart of the city, the ancient county town of Surrey. Guildford has been the capital of the region since pre-Norman times and, in the 10th century, it even had its own mint. Henry II built a **Castle** here on high ground in the 12th century which later became the county gaol; today, the remains of the castle house a renowned brass-rubbing centre and the ruined keep provides a fascinating place from which to view the surrounding area.

Those visiting the town for the first time should make straight for the old **High Street**, a wonderful cobbled thoroughfare of Georgian and older buildings which rises steeply from the River Wey. Perhaps the most noteworthy of these is the **Guildhall**, a Tudor structure with an elaborately decorated 17th century frontage which incorporates a bell-tower, balcony and distinctive gilded clock. The timber-framed Guildford House is also 17th century and is known for its carved staircase and ornate painted plasterwork ceilings. Abbot's Hospital, a little further along, is an imposing turreted almshouse which was built in 1619 by the Guildford born Archbishop of Canterbury, George Abbot. At the top of the High Street lies the Royal Grammar School; dating from the early 1500s and was subsequently endowed by Edward VI.

A number of interesting streets and alleyways run off Guildford High Street, including Quarry Street with its medieval St Mary's Church and old Castle Arch. The latter houses the **Guildford Museum**, an informative museum of local history and archeology which also contains an exhibition devoted to Lewis Carroll, the creator of *Alice In Wonderland* who died in the town in 1898. A charming bronze memorial to Lewis Carroll, which is composed of a life sized Alice chasing the White Rabbit into his hole, can be found on the far bank of the River Wey, midway between the two footbridges.

To the east of Guildford on the A25 is the splendid country mansion, **Clandon Park**, which was designed in the 1730s by Giacomo Leoni, a Venetian architect who combined Palladian, Baroque and European styles to create one of the grandest 18th century houses in England. The interior is renowned for its magnificent two storey marble hall, sumptuous decoration and fine Italian plasterwork depicting scenes from mythology. The Gubbay collection of furniture and porcelain is also housed here, along with the Ivo Forde collection of humorous Meissen figures. The surrounding parkland was landscaped by Capability Brown in characteristic style and includes a parterre, grotto and brightly painted New Zealand Maori house.

RIPLEY   *Map 6 ref N21*

This attractive village is a former staging post on the old coaching route between London and Portsmouth and its main street contains a number of exceptional brick and half-timbered buildings, including the charming Vintage Cottage with its unusual crownpost roof.

A lovely welcome is given to everyone who visits **The Seven Stars**, a family pub run by Sheila, Paul and their son David—the hard working Chef responsible for extensive catering in this popular hostelry. Ripley is a picturesque village in beautiful countryside surroundings and The Seven Stars is an ideal spot for lunchtime meetings and evening dining. Food is available at all opening times and may be enjoyed in the restaurant, whilst bar meals are also available with a wide selection of dishes are displayed on the specials' board. All meals are

The Seven Stars

prepared and cooked to order. The award winning pizzas are well worth trying and Sunday roast lunches are highly rated by all in the know! The Seven Stars also offers good food, real ales and fine wines all at reasonable prices.
The Seven Stars, Newark Lane, Ripley, Surrey Tel: 01483 225128

WEYBRIDGE   *Map 6 ref N21*

The town once possessed a palace, Oatlands Park, in which Henry VIII married his fifth wife, Catherine Howard, in 1540. Just over a century later, the building was demolished and the stone used in the construction of the **Wey Navigation**. Weybridge stands at the northern end of this historic inland waterway which was one of the first examples of its kind when it was completed in 1670. It extends for almost 20 miles southwards to Godalming and incorporates large sections of the main river.

In 1907, the world's first purpose built motor racing track was constructed on the **Brooklands** estate, near Weybridge, and in the years which followed, this legendary banked circuit hosted competitions between some of the most formidable racing cars ever made. With the outbreak of World War I, however, racing came to an end: the track fell into disrepair and Brooklands was never again able to regain its once pre-eminent position in British motor racing.

For years, the only thing to interrupt the tranquillity of the empty track was the occasional eerie sound of screeching tyres and roaring engines or the appearance of the goggled ghost of Percy Lambert, who tragically died after his car smashed into the end of the Railway Straight in 1913. Recently, the circuit has undergone something of a revival with the opening of the **Brooklands Museum**, a fascinating establishment centred around the old Edwardian clubhouse which features a unique collection of historic racing cars, motorcycles and aircraft.

ESHER   *Map 6 ref N21*

Thought of as a residential suburb within easy commuting distance from London, there is more of interest here than the excellent racecourse, Sandown

Park. The part 16th century **Church of St George** has an unusual three tier pulpit and a marble monument to Princess Charlotte of Wales who died at nearby Claremont House in 1817.

The beautiful National Trust owned **Claremont Landscape Garden** was laid out in the 1710s and it is believed to be one of the earliest surviving examples of an English landscape garden. Later in the 18th century, it was remodelled by William Kent whose work was continued by Capability Brown. The grounds have been designed to include a number of striking vistas and contain a grassed amphitheatre, grotto, lake, and an island with a pavilion. Nearby **Claremont House** operates as a school and is only occasionally open to visitors. Designed in the 1700s by Vanbrugh, it was substantially remodelled in 1772 for Clive of India.

EPSOM   *Map 6 ref O21*

In the early 17th century, it was observed that cattle were refusing to drink from a spring on the common above the town and subsequent tests revealed the water to be high in magnesium sulphate, a mineral believed to have highly beneficial medicinal properties. As the fashion for 'taking the waters' grew towards the end of the century, wealthy people from London came in increasing numbers to sample the benefits of Epsom salts and the settlement grew from a small village to a town with its own street market, a charter for which was granted in 1685.

By the end of the 18th century, the popularity of Epsom's spa was on the decline but, by this time, the town's pleasant rural location within easy reach of the City of London was already starting to attract well-to-do business people; a number of substantial residential homes were built in and around the town during this period, several of which survive to this day.

Epsom's other main claim to fame is its **Racecourse**. Each year in early June, the Downs to the southeast of the town take on a carnival atmosphere as tens of thousands of racing enthusiasts come to experience the annual Classic race meeting and the colourful funfair which accompanies it. Informal horse racing took place on Epsom Downs as long ago as 1683 when Charles II is said to have been in attendance. Racing was formalised in 1779 when a party of aristocratic sportsmen led by Lord Derby established a race for three year old fillies which was named after the Derbys' family home at Banstead, The Oaks; this was followed a year later by a race for all three year olds, The Derby, which was named after the founder himself, although only after he won a toss of a coin with the race's co-founder, Sir Charles Bunbury. (Had Lord Derby lost, the race would have become known as The Bunbury.) The Oaks and The Derby were a great success and soon achieved Classic status along with the St Leger at Doncaster, the earliest to be established in 1776, and the 1000 Guineas and 2000 Guineas at Newmarket, established in 1814 and 1809 respectively.

REIGATE   *Map 6 ref O21*

A prosperous residential town expansion at the hands of postwar developers has done much to conceal its long and distinguished history. The settlement was once an important outpost of the de Warenne family, the assertive Norman rulers whose sphere of influence stretched from the Channel coast to the North Downs. As at Lewes, they built a castle on a rise above the village streets of which nothing remains today except for an arch which was reconstructed in the 1770s from material recovered from the original castle walls. Today, this striking neo-Gothic reproduction stands at the heart of a pleasant public park.

A steep path leads down from the castle mound to the attractive mixture of Victorian, Georgian and older buildings which line Reigate's High Street. The old Town Hall, a handsome redbrick building constructed in 1729, stands at its eastern end and, a short distance away to the north, the entrance to a disused road tunnel can be seen which was built beneath the castle mound in 1824 to ease the through-flow of traffic on the busy London to Brighton coaching route.

To the west of this town lies Reigate Heath; a narrow area of open heathland that is the home of the unique **Windmill Church**, the only church in the world to be situated in a windmill.

HORLEY   *Map 6 ref O22*

The original medieval village has been lost amid the houses and villas which sprang up in the late 19th century. Ideally located close to Gatwick Airport and Horley town centre, **Springwood Guest House** is an elegant Victorian detached house set in a quiet, residential road. Owned and very personally run by Ernest and Marcia, this attractive guest house has a distinctly Chinese feel about it. The professionally landscaped gardens are delicately illuminated by night and some traditional wind chimes can be heard, melodious in the soft breeze that passes through the Oriental pergola. All of the seven guest bedrooms are furnished and decorated to a very high standard, all having full en-suite facilities, central

Springwood Guest House

heating, colour television and a complimentary tea and coffee tray. There is also a light and airy family room available, with plenty of facilities for children in the large, tree lined gardens. Springwood Guest House is the perfect location for those wanting an out of season break and, during the long summer months the barbecues, that are held in the garden prove very popular amongst the guests that return again and again to sample Ernest and Marcia's unique hospitality.
Springwood Guest House, 58 Massetts Road, Horley, Surrey RH6 7DS
Tel: 01293 775998

Gainsborough Lodge

Conveniently situated only 35 minutes train journey from central London, **Gainsborough Lodge** is an attractive, family run bed and breakfast establishment that offers its guests the very best in home comforts. Owned and very personally run by Graham and Rosina for the past four years, Gainsborough Lodge is a credit to the couple's commitment to good old British hospitality. All of the 18 guest bedrooms are individually decorated and furnished to a very high standard. For those who are flying in to Gatwick Airport, there is a courtesy pickup that is available from 9 am right through until 11 pm, following a free phone call. Gainsborough Lodge is certainly the ideal base from which to explore all of the sights and sounds of London and its surrounding scenery and guests are safe in the knowledge that they will be returning to a warm and welcoming environment at the end of their busy day.
Gainsborough Lodge, 39 Massetts Road, Horley, Surrey RH6 7DT
Tel: 01293 783982

DORKING   *Map 6 ref O21*

This long established settlement stands at the intersection of Stane Street, the Roman road which once connected London with Chichester, and the ancient Pilgrims' Way, the east–west ridgeway route which is roughly followed by the modern North Downs Way. Despite evidence of Saxon and Viking occupation, present day Dorking is a congested commuter town which owes most of character to the Victorians. There are a small number of older buildings, most notably the part 15th century former coaching inn, the **White Horse**, and the shops and houses in North Street, West Street and at the western end of the High Street; however, the town's two most distinctive architectural features are characteristically 19th century: the unexpectedly grand **Parish Church**, with its soaring spire, and the **Rose Hill** housing development, an assortment of Victorian villas arranged around a green and entered from South Street through an unusual neo-Gothic arch.

The 563 foot **Box Hill**, to the north of the town and overlooking the River Mole, is a popular local landmark. The hill takes its name from the mature box trees which once grew here in profusion but which were seriously depleted in the 18th century to supply the needs of London wood-engravers. By then, the site had already been known for over a century as a beauty spot and had been visited by, among others, the diarist John Evelyn.

Today, the National Trust owns over 800 acres of land around Box Hill which has now been designated a country park. The area around the summit incorporates an exhibition centre, a late 19th century fort and a take-away café and can be reached either by footpath or by a narrow winding road which leads up from Burford Bridge. The hillside is traversed by a series of nature walks, and there are also several picnic sites which enjoy breathtaking views across the Weald to the South Downs.

GREAT BOOKHAM   *Map 6 ref N21*

Although heavily built up since World War II, this residential area has managed to retain something of its historic past. The earliest mention of a settlement here dates back to the 660s when a manor at Bocheham is recorded as belonging to Chertsey Abbey. Present day Great Bookham contains an exceptional parish church, **St Nicholas'**, which has an unusual flint tower with a shingled spire dating back to the Norman era in the 12th century. A substantial part of the building, including the chancel, is known to have been rebuilt in the 1340s by the Abbot of Chertsey and the church was again remodelled by the Victorians. Inside, there is some fine 15th century stained glass and a number of noteworthy monumental brasses and memorials to the local lords of the manor. An early 18th century owner of the Bookham estate, Dr Hugh Shortrudge, left an endowment in his will to four local churches on condition that an annual sermon was preached on the subject of the martyrdom of Charles I. St Nicholas' continues to uphold the tradition of the Shortrudge sermon which is preached each year on the final Sunday in January.

Nearby **Little Bookham** has a small single roomed church with a wooden belfry which is believed to date from the 12th century. The adjacent 18th century manor house now operates as a school. **Bookham** and **Banks Commons** to the northwest of Little Bookham provide some welcome relief from the commuter estates and offer some pleasant walking through relatively unspoilt open heathland. The commons are recorded in the Domesday Book as providing pannage, the right to graze pigs on acorns, for Chertsey Abbey. Now under the ownership of the National Trust, they are particularly known for their rich and varied birdlife.

Another National Trust owned property, **Polesden Lacey**, stands on high ground two miles to the south of Great Bookham. The estate was once owned by the writer RB Sheridan who purchased it in 1797 with the intention of restoring its decaying 17th century manor house. However, a lack of funds prevented him from realising his ambitions and, following his death in 1816, the building was demolished and the estate sold. Then, during the 1820s, the architect Thomas Cubitt built a substantial Regency villa in its place which was subsequently remodelled and enlarged by successive owners throughout the 19th century.

In 1906, the estate was acquired by Captain Ronald Greville and his wife Margaret, the daughter of a Scottish brewing magnate and a celebrated high society hostess. Over the following three decades, they invited a succession of rich and influential guests to Polesden Lacey whose number included Edward VII and George VI and Queen Elizabeth (now the Queen Mother) who spent part of their honeymoon here in 1923. The Grevilles carried out a number of alterations of their own during this period and the extravagant Edwardian–Louis XVI internal decoration remains as a testimony to Margaret Greville's taste (or, some may say, the lack of it).

Whatever the perspective, the house contains an undeniably fine collection of furniture, paintings, tapestries, porcelain and silver which the Grevilles accumulated over 40 years, and Margaret's personal collection of photographs provides a fascinating record of British high society at play during the early part of the century. The surrounding grounds amount to over 1000 acres and incorporate a walled rose garden, open lawns, a YHA youth hostel and a large area of natural woodland; there is also a charming open-air theatre which holds an annual season of events in late June and early July.

ALBURY   *Map 6 ref N21*

Dating largely from the last century, Albury was constructed in fanciful neo-Gothic style as an estate village for nearby **Albury Park**. This large country mansion was built on the site of a Tudor manor house in the early 18th century and was much altered by Pugin in the 1840s. The most eccentric feature of the house is its collection of chimneys, 63 of them built for only 60 rooms in an amazing variety of shapes and sizes. Although the mansion has now been converted into flats, the estate gardens are open to visitors and are well worth a look. They were laid out by the diarist John Evelyn at the turn of the 18th century and feature a series of terraced orchards which rise above the house to the north.

Set in the very heart of the village is **Stream Cottage**, a period beamed cottage which offers its guest a warm and friendly welcome and allows them the time to relax and recuperate in a homely and cosy atmosphere. All of the double and twin bedded rooms have alarm clock radios, hair dryers, complimentary tea and coffee making trays, colour televisions and en-suite facilities, whilst the family

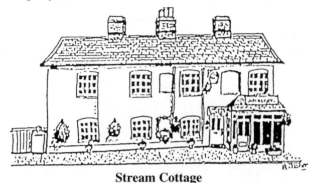

Stream Cottage

suite boasts a lounge complete with a sofa bed and fridge. The traditional English breakfast is served in the light and airy dining room and there is also an attractive residents' lounge with satellite television, pay-phone, music centre and writing desk. Stream Cottage is also ideally located close to the Drummond Arms Inn which is the perfect place for an evening meal or a cool glass of wine, before returning to the comfortable bedrooms and a blissful nights sleep.

Stream Cottage, The Street, Albury, Surrey GU5 9AG Tel: 01483 202228 Fax: 01483 202793

GODALMING   *Map 6 ref N22*

This old market town was once an important staging post between London and Portsmouth and a number of elegant 17th and 18th century shops and coaching inns can still be found in the High Street. A market was established here in 1300 and the town later became a centre for the local wool and textile industries. Perhaps the most interesting building in the old centre is **The Pepperpot**, the former town hall which was built at the western end of the High Street in 1814. Now surrounded on all sides by heavy traffic, this unusual arcaded building once contained an interesting **Museum of Local History** which has recently moved to new premises at 109a High Street.

Godalming's part Norman parish church of St Peter and St Paul is built of Bargate stone, a locally quarried hard brown sandstone that was much loved by the Victorians. This material was also used extensively to build **Charterhouse School**, the famous public school which moved from London to a hillside site on the northern side of Godalming in 1872. Among its most striking features are the 150 foot Founder's Tower and the chapel designed by Sir Giles Gilbert Scott as a memorial to those killed in World War I.

The timber framed house once belonging to Gertrude Jekyll can be found in dense woodland on the southern side of town; it was designed for her by Edwin Lutyens in characteristic rural vernacular style and is partially constructed of Bargate stone.

The renowned **Winkworth Arboretum**, just outside Godalming, is a 95 acre area of wooded hillside which was presented to the National Trust in 1952. The grounds contain two lakes and a magnificent collection of rare trees and shrubs, many of them native to other continents.

The King Alfred

On leaving Godalming on the A3100 towards Milford, it's worth taking a detour by turning right into Eashing Lane and again into Quarry Lane to discover **The King Alfred** public house. Run by licensees and welcoming hosts Alain and Sylvie Chedru, this local has just been refurbished and is fast becoming the popular place to be out of town. Serving good food with a French flavour, it is well worth calling in and sampling the interesting dishes. There's a beer garden and pub games to enjoy as well as excellent ales on tap. No facilities for children and pets. Easy car parking.

The King Alfred, 18 Quarry Hill, (off Eashing lane), Godalming, Surrey GU7 2NW Tel: 01483 421467

CHIDDINGFOLD   *Map 6 ref N22*

With its three sided green, waterlily filled pond, part 13th century church, medieval pub and handsome collection of Georgian cottages, this attractive settlement contains all the features of a quintessential English village. During the 13th and 14th centuries, it was an important centre of the glass-making industry, a once flourishing trade which utilised local sand as its main ingredient, timber for fuel, and employed skilled craftspeople from across northern Europe. Some fragments of medieval Chiddingfold glass can be seen in the small lancet window in **St Mary's Church**, below which a brass plaque can be seen which is inscribed with the names of several early glass-makers. The church itself was much altered during the 1860s; however, its west tower is 17th century and contains a peal of eight bells, one of which is believed to be around 500 years old. The churchyard is entered through an exceptionally fine lych gate, a covered gateway with a wide timber slab which was used to shelter coffins awaiting burial.

Of the many handsome buildings standing around Chiddingfold's village green, the **Crown Inn** is perhaps the most impressive. One of several hostelries which claim to be the oldest in England, its existence was first recorded in 1383. The structure is half-timbered and incorporates a medieval great hall; Edward VI is reported to have stayed here in the 15th century. Other buildings in the village worthy of note are Chantry House, Manor House and Glebe House, the last two of which have elegant Georgian façades. An 18th century façade is all that remains of **Shillinglee Park**, a once imposing country mansion which stood in the village until the end of World War II. The remainder of the house was destroyed, not by enemy action but by a party of Canadian service personnel who accidentally set the building on fire during a party to celebrate the allied victory.

HASLEMERE   *Map 6 ref N22*

This genteel Surrey town is now a quiet and comfortable home for well-to-do commuters. The central streets are filled with handsome Georgian and Victorian buildings, most of which were constructed following the arrival of the railway in 1859. The building styles, including stucco, redbrick and tile-hung, combine to form an attractive and harmonious architectural mix.

Towards the end of the last century, Haslemere became something of a centre for the arts. Alfred Lord Tennyson settled nearby and a group, known as the Haslemere Society of Artists, was formed whose number included Birket Foster and the landscape painter, Helen Allingham. At the end of World War I, the French born musician and enthusiastic exponent of early music, Arnold Dolmetsch, founded what has become a world famous musical instrument workshop here. Present day visitors can make an appointment to view the intricately handcrafted harpsichords, lutes and other authentic early instruments being made. Dolmetsch's family went on to establish the Haslemere Festival of Early Music in 1925 which is still held each year in July.

Another of Haslemere's attractions is the **Educational Museum** in the High Street, an establishment founded in 1888 by local surgeon and Quaker, Sir James Hutchinson, and which now contains an imaginative series of displays on local birds, botany, zoology, geology and history.

HINDHEAD   *Map 6 ref N22*

The **Devil's Punch Bowl** is a steep-sided natural sandstone amphitheatre through which the busy A3 Guildford to Petersfield road passes. Hindhead itself stands near the top of the nearby ridge and, at 850 feet above sea level, is the highest village in Surrey; perhaps surprisingly, it has only been in existence since the late 19th century. The National Trust owns 1400 acres of local wood and heathland which incorporates the Devil's Punch Bowl and nearby **Gibbet Hill**. At almost 900 feet, the latter offers spectacular views to the north as far as the Chilterns and to the south across the Weald to the South Downs. In 1786, the hill was the scene a notorious murder, the perpetrators of which were hanged and chained near the Punch Bowl. Today, an inscribed stone commemorates the incident which is also remembered in a series of paintings in the nearby Royal Huts Hotel.

FRENSHAM   *Map 5 ref M22*

St Mary's Church contains a large medieval copper cauldron whose history is surrounded in legend. According to one story, it was lent by the fairies to a human who held onto it for longer than was agreed; when it was finally returned, the fairies refused to accept it, vowing never again to lend anything to human beings. Another story tells how the cauldron once belonged to Mother Ludlam, a local witch-like character who inhabited a cave near Waverley Abbey.

The A287 to the south of the village runs between Frensham's **Great and Little Ponds**, two sizable National Trust owned lakes which provide good bird-watching and other recreational facilities including sailing and walking. These are now contained with a 1000 acre country park which incorporates four prehistoric bowl barrows and the Devil's Jumps, three irregularly shaped hills whose origin, like many other unusual natural features, is attributed to Satan.

The Mariners Hotel is an established family run hotel which caters for all the differing requirements of families, businessmen, tourists and disabled guests, all of who receive a warm and friendly welcome, together with a professional and high quality level of service. With 21 bedrooms, bistro-style restaurant, lounge bar and function room, the hotel offers comprehensive facilities to all who stay.

Situated in a pleasant and tranquil setting by the River Wey, The Mariners Hotel offers comfortable and spacious rooms at very competitive prices. Each room is fully equipped with en-suite bathroom, colour television, direct dial telephone and complimentary tea and coffee making facilities. Disabled guest can be accommodated in ground floor bedrooms which have easy access and an outlook over the picturesque gardens. For newlyweds, a deluxe Bridal Suite is available with four poster bed fitted with luxurious drapes; a superb setting for the occasion. Parents with young children will find the family rooms ideal, enhanced by the baby sitting and listening services which can be arranged.

Diners in the bistro-style restaurant are offered an excellent range of speciality Italian pizza and pasta, as well as an extensive daily buffet and à la carte menu. Food is also served in the very comfortable lounge bar which, with its relaxed atmosphere, offers a wide selection of real ales and fine wines together with a cosy log fire for those chilly evenings. The River View function room has its own dance floor and a tempting choice of table d'hôte and à la carte menus making it the perfect venue for wedding receptions, banquets, dinner dances and special parties.

The Mariners Hotel

Set amidst some of Surrey's most beautiful countryside, there are opportunities to participate in numerous outdoor activities, including walking, riding, fishing and shooting, whilst for golfers there are several excellent courses within a few miles. The Mariners Hotel is situated on the A287 between Farnham and Hindhead.

The Mariners Hotel, Millbridge, Frensham, near Farnham, Surrey
GU10 3DJ Tel: 01252 792050/794745 Fax: 01252 792649

FARNHAM   *Map 5 ref M21*

This fine old settlement stands at the point where the old Pilgrims' Way from Winchester to Canterbury crosses the River Wey and it has long been an important staging post on the busy trading route between Southampton and London. The town first became a residence of the Bishops of Winchester during Saxon times and, following the Norman Conquest, the new Norman bishop built himself a castle on a pleasant tree-covered rise above the centre of the town. This impressive structure underwent a number of alterations, most notably in the 15th century when the decorated brick-built tower was added, and it remained in the hands of the Bishops of Winchester until 1927.

Farnham Castle has been visited on a number of occasions by the reigning English monarch and was besieged during the English Civil War. Today, it is approached along Castle Street, a delightful wide thoroughfare of Georgian and neo-Georgian buildings which was laid out to accommodate a traditional street market. The old Norman keep including the Great Hall is now owned by English Heritage.

Farnham contains a number of other interesting historic buildings, including a row of 17th century gabled almshouses and Willmer House in West Street, a handsome Georgian-fronted structure which now houses the informative **Farnham Museum**. As well as some fine wood panelling, carvings and period furniture, the museum contains some interesting archeological exhibits and a unique collection of 19th century glass paperweights.

To the southeast of the town are the atmospheric ruins of **Waverley Abbey**. Dating from the 12th century, this was the first Cistercian abbey to be built in England. The abbey remains are open during daylight hours and are said to have provided the inspiration for Sir Walter Scott's romantic novel, *Waverley*, published in 1814.

For a plant nursery that offers its customers the very best in service and expertise, then look no further than **The Oaks Nursery**. Situated just off of the main road through **Ash**, to the northeast of Farnham and near Aldershot, this attractive nursery offers a wide range of plants, shrubs and gardening equipment at very reasonable prices. Owned and run by Jim and Cindy for the past 50 years, visitors can guarantee that most of their gardening queries can be sorted out by just chatting to this charming couple whose half a century of experience is given freely to those who seek their advice. Cindy also carries a locally renowned reputation for producing superb flower arrangements and is kept very busy throughout the year producing floral works of art for both visitors and

The Oaks Nursery

locals alike. So visitors to Ash should make sure they pay a visit to Jim and Cindy at The Oaks Nursery, an establishment just blooming with quality and charm. *The Oaks Nursery, Foreman Road, Ash, Surrey Tel: 01252 28590*

COMPTON   *Map 5 ref N21*

This historic community was once an important stopping place on the old Pilgrims' Way and the village possesses an exceptional part Saxon **St Nicholas's Church** with some remarkable internal features, including a series of 12th century murals which were only rediscovered in 1966, an ancient hermit's, or anchorite's, cell, and a unique two storey Romanesque sanctuary which is thought to have once contained an early Christian relic.

Compton is also renowned for being the home of the 19th century artist GF Watts, a chiefly self-taught painter and sculptor whose most famous work, *Physical Energy*, stands in London's Kensington Gardens. At the age of 47, Watts married the actress Ellen Terry but the couple separated a year later; then at the age of 69, he successfully remarried, this time to Mary Fraser-Tytler, a painter and potter 33 years his junior who went on to design **Watts' Memorial Gallery**, which today contains over 200 pieces of the artist's work, along with the Watts Mortuary Chapel, an extraordinary building which was completed in 1904 and is decorated in exuberant Art Nouveau style.

To the east of Compton lies **Loseley Park**, a handsome Elizabethan country estate, built in 1562 of Bargate stone, some of which was taken from the ruins of Waverley Abbey. **Loseley House** is the former home of the Elizabethan statesman, Sir William More. Both Elizabeth I and James I are known to have stayed here and the interior is decorated with a series of outstanding period features, including hand-painted panelling, woodcarving, delicate plasterwork ceilings, and a unique chimney-piece carved from a massive piece of chalk. The walled garden is a beautiful place to take a stroll, the surrounding gardens contain a terrace and a moat walk, and the nearby fields are home to Loseley's famous herd of pedigree Jersey cattle. Visitors can take a trailer ride to the traditional working dairy farm, where you can see the Jersey herd being milked every afternoon and discover the history of the estate.

Berkshire

INTRODUCTION

This county is the only one in England which can proudly call itself Royal, due to the location of Windsor Castle, the Royal family's principal residence outside London, within its boundaries. The massive castle, which attracts many visitors each year, is, perhaps Berkshire's greatest attraction but there are many others.

The eastern part of the county is, now, very much commuterland with excellent road and rail links with London. The county town of Reading, famous as being place where Oscar Wilde was jailed for two years, also lies at the confluence of Berkshire's two rivers, the Thames and the Kennet. The Thames is very popular and though there are some pleasant walks along its banks in and around the town, Reading is also most riverboat holidaymakers starting point.

To the west of Reading the county becomes increasingly more rural as the links with London lessen. In the north are the rolling grassland slopes of the Berkshire Downs and the famous racehorse training town of Lambourn. Southwest of Lambourn is the town of Newbury which has lost none of its old character and is also home to a first class racecourse.

READING   *Map 5 ref M20*

Despite being a modern business community and thriving shopping centre, Reading still features many buildings of historic and architectural interest. In the centre of the town, the **Forbury Gardens** were formerly the grounds of **Reading**

Abbey and today provide an attractive oasis for the public to enjoy, with the dominant feature being the famous Maiwand Lion, an enormous stone sculpture weighing some 16 tons! To the southeast of the lion, a smaller yet very important memorial is the Celtic Cross which was erected in 1901 in memory of King Henry I, founder, in 1121, of the abbey. Today only the ruined shell of the abbey can be seen including the remains of the church's south transept, the Chapter House, Refectory and Dormitory.

Housed within the restored Town Hall, the **Museum of Reading** is well worth a visit. It provides a detailed history of the town from Saxon times to the present day with various exhibitions and galleries including one housing a facsimile of the Bayeux Tapestry. It is also noted for the display of Roman remains from the abandoned town of Silchester, or Calleva. However, the most famous building in Reading is probably old **Town Gaol**, where Oscar Wilde languished and wrote his famous *Ballad of Reading Gaol* during his two year sentence to hard labour.

Straddling the River Thames, which is busy for much of its course with all manner of pleasure craft, Reading is also the home of the **Blake's Lock Museum**. Refurbished in recent years this interesting museum tells the story of inland waterways in the area.

COOKHAM
Map 5 ref N20

Anyone familiar with the paintings of Stanley Spencer may recognise parts of the village: he was born here and based much of his work on local scenes. The **Stanley Spencer Gallery** and the house where he was born stand in the High Street.

The ancient ceremony of Swan Upping, the annual marking of the Queen's swans, starts here in early July, and the boatyard by the bridge belongs to the Queen's Swan Master.

ETON
Map 5 ref N20

The famous **Eton College** was founded in 1440 as a Collegiate Church with a Grammar School. Still seen today as the epitome of the public school, it has educated a string of famous people and still retains many, now anachronistic, traditions that have added to its fame. Of the original school only the College Hall and the kitchen survive with most of the rest dating from the 15th century. The west range of the cloisters, the great gatehouse, and Lupton's Tower were added in the early 16th century and the Upper School was built in about 1690.

WINDSOR
Map 5 ref N20

This beautiful Royal town is most notable for its **Castle** which covers 13 acres and is the largest in Britain. A popular tourist spot, magnificent Windsor boasts a wealth of delightful pubs and restaurants and shopping here is a sheer delight, with a variety of wonderful shops set inside beautiful buildings and dotted down narrow cobbled streets and pedestrianised walkways. From the castle the long tree-lined walk offers magnificent views of the town and its surroundings. The changing of the castle guard is a daily event during the summer months.

The town, which has given its name to the Royal Family, owes its existence to this fortress which dominates the area from its high hill above the Thames and remains the largest inhabited castle in the world. The settlement of Windelsora was used for centuries by Saxon kings hunting in the forest and the conquering Normans followed suit, building the first fortress four miles upstream from the Saxon settlement. The site was chosen by William the Conqueror, who built a fort of earthworks and wooden defences. It soon became an important castle, with a town growing around it. Henry I held court here, its defensive position giving him protection from the hostile Saxons but not until Henry II's reign were the first stone buildings built; providing a home for kings and queens for nearly 900 years.

Open to the public are the Precincts, the State Apartments and Queen Mary's Doll's House, and they attract visitors from the world over. The 16 magnificent **State Apartments** hold a remarkable collection of furniture, porcelain and armour. The carvings of Grinling Gibbons are everywhere, the walls adorned with a plethora of masterpieces, especially those by Van Dyck and Rembrandt. In the amazing **Doll's House**, built by Sir Edwin Lutyens, everything works, right down to the dewdrop sized lightbulbs. Built to a scale of one inch to one foot famous artists, craftsmen and writers all contributed to this gift to Queen Mary, presented in 1924. The detail is breathtaking, linen in the pantry is initialled and the cars in the garage can manage 20,000 mpg!

St George's Chapel, the Chapel of the Order of the Garter, was begun in the reign of Edward IV and completed by Henry VIII. Until the recent devastating fire it was the setting of the ceremonious annual service of the Sovereign and Knights Companion of the Order. Restoration has, of course, begun but it will be the turn of the millennium before this marvel of medieval architecture can be fully admired once again.

Today's town of Windsor is largely Georgian and Victorian, though there are far older buildings. Windsor **Parish Church** dates from 1168, though it was rebuilt in 1820, and its register records the burial of Charles I. The **Three Tuns Hotel** was built in 1518 and, in St Albans Street, is the 17th century home of Nell Gwynne, mistress of Charles II. **The Guildhall**, begun in 1689 by Sir Thomas Fitz and finished by Wren, today houses an exhibition of local history from the palaeolithic period to the present day. There is also a notable collection of royal portraits from the time of Elizabeth I and a series of dioramas showing historical events at Windsor from earliest times to the celebration of George III's Jubilee celebrations of 1809.

In the old buildings of Central Station is a firm visitors' favourite, Madame Tussaud's **Royalty and Empire Exhibition**. Undoubtedly the most impressive display here depicts Queen Victoria's Diamond Jubilee celebrations with a full sized replica of the Royal Train and a theatre presentation! For those with an interest in the military the **Household Cavalry Museum**, at Combermore Barracks, is considered one of the finest in the country. Exhibits, including uniforms, weapons, horse furniture and armour, help trace the history of the regiment from the Monmouth Rebellion of 1685 right up to the present day.

To the south of the castle is **Windsor Great Park**, 4800 acres of Royal Park that include parkland, woods and magnificent gardens. The Long Walk stretches from the towers of Windsor to Snow Hill, a distance of some three miles. Up on Snow Hill stands a huge bronze of George III on horseback, erected in 1831. During his reign Thomas Sandby and his brother laid out the two mile long lake of **Virginia Water**, with its fine cascade. On the banks of the lake stand a group of Roman columns brought from Tripoli. During her reign Queen Anne added the three mile ride to Ascot.

ASCOT   *Map 5 ref N21*

The town is most famous for its horse racing and, in particular, for the Royal Ascot meeting held each summer. For four days, the magnificent thoroughbreds on the race course are over shadowed by the spectacular outfits and hats of the spectators. Each afternoon, the Royal party travel, by carriage, from Windsor Castle along the driveway laided out by Queen Anne. The fifth day of the meeting, a Saturday, however, is not 'Royal' and the outfits tend to be somewhat more relaxed.

ALDERMASTON   *Map 5 ref L21*

It was in this tranquil village that the William pear was first propagated in 1840 by the village schoolmaster John Staid, although it was then known as the Aldermaston pear. A cutting of this plant is believed to have been given to Australia where it is called the Bartlett pear.

Aldermaston's **Church of St Mary the Virgin** still retains much of its original 12th century structure and has a splendid Norman door. This lovely church provides the setting for the York Mystery Cycle, nativity plays dating from the 14th century which are performed annually in beautiful contemporary costume with period music including a piece written by William Byrd. Lasting a week, the plays attract visitors from far and wide. Outside under the yew tree in the churchyard lies the grave of Maria Hale, formerly known as the Aldermaston witch. She was said to turn herself into a large brown hare and, although the hare was never caught or killed, at one time a local keeper wounded it in the leg and from then on it was noticed that Maria Hale had become lame!

Close to the village there is a delightful canalside walk along Aldermaston Wharf leading to **Aldermaston Lock**, a Grade II listed structure of beautifully restored 18th century scalloped brickwork. More recent history has seen the famous protest marches of the 1950s outside the Atomic Research Establishment, which, rather mysteriously, is not to be found on Ordnance Survey maps.

NEWBURY
Map 5 ref L21

Now a major business centre renowned for its horse racing and famous for Civil War battles, this bustling town is very much a mixture of the old and the new. The Kennet Centre with its modern shopping mall contrasts strongly with the old market town atmosphere which still prevails. The best place to stop is the conveniently placed car park, which lies just off the main road into the town, close to **Newbury Museum**. The museum is housed within a magnificent 17th century Cloth Hall and 18th century Granary.

Another interesting feature in the town is the central **Clock Tower** which was built in 1929 with three clocks facing each road above a hexagonal roof. From one of the old canal wharves, West Mills, there is a pleasant walk where beautiful 18th century houses can be seen to contrast with the almshouses for the poor. **Newbury Lock**, which dates back to 1796, was the first lock to be built on the Kennet and Avon Canal and is the only lock to have lever-operated ground paddles (sluices that let in the water), known as Jack Cloughs.

LAMBOURN
Map 5 ref L20

Set in the heart of the beautiful west Berkshire Downs, Lambourn is one of the most celebrated racehorse training centres in Europe. The immediate area is home to over 30 trainers, as well as to a concentration of related services, including veterinary surgeons, laser and solarium facilities, saddlers and race-horse transporters.

In recent years, members of the **Lambourn Trainers Association** have been opening their yards to visitors at certain times and offering guided tours. Trainers are on hand to answer questions on the training of thoroughbred racehorses and visitors are able to see the horses in their stables, at exercise on the gallops, or perhaps even having a swim in an equine pool. On Good Friday, the Association holds its annual open day, when over 30 training stables throw open their gates to visitors. As well as tours of the stables, there are a number of ancillary attractions, including live music, refreshments and a number of horse-related events. For further information on the activities of the Lambourn Trainers Association, please contact the office of Peter Walwyn on 01488 71347.

Although the village is dominated by horse racing, there is also plenty to keep the less equine minded visitor happy. There is a fine medieval church, for example, and do look out for the old almshouses and the ancient village cross.

Buckinghamshire

INTRODUCTION

Like many of the counties surrounding Greater London, the towns and villages closest to the capital are home to many commuters and, though there may be much 20th century development, many still retain their original charm and character. The River Thames, still reasonably wide, passes through the part of Buckinghamshire and here also is Marlow, a typical Thames river town. Further to the east lies the famous beauty spot of Burnham Beeches.

The county is, essentially, a farming county which prospered through its ability to meet the needs of the ever expanding population of London quickly and easily. Buckingham, the ancient county town, dates back to the time of the Saxons and, though its importance in some areas has been relinquished to places nearer London, it is still an interesting place to visit. Buckinghamshire is too famous for its new town—Milton Keynes. An extension of the garden city movement from earlier this century, the town was development in the 1960s with the help of fast road and rail links. However, Milton Keynes' most well known feature are the imitation cows standing in a field beside the main rail line.

MARLOW
Map 5 ref M20

This was the Thames river town where Jerome K Jerome wrote his amusing masterpiece *Three Men in a Boat* at the Two Brewers pub in St Peter Street. He obviously enjoyed being there, for he wrote: "Marlow is one of the pleasantest river centres I know of. It is a bustling, lively little town; not very picturesque on the whole, it is true, but there are many quaint nooks and corners to be found in it, nevertheless—standing arches in the shattered bridge of Time, over which our fancy travels back to the days when Marlow Manor owned Saxon Algar for its lord, ere conquering William seized it to give it to Queen Matilda, ere it passed to the Earls of Warwick....."

In fact, it seems to be a good place for writing, for Mary Shelley, wife of the poet, finished writing her novel *Frankenstein* after the newly married couple moved to the town in 1817. Thomas Love Peacock, a novelist and poet nowadays almost completely forgotten outside examination syllabi, lived in West Street while writing one of his works, *Nightmare Abbey*, published in 1818.

The architectural feature by which the town is best known is its **Suspension Bridge**, finished in 1836 and designed by the same architect who was responsible for the famous bridge which connects Buda and Pest, the two halves of the Hungarian capital. Other interesting buildings are the **Old Parsonage**, part of a 14th century house; **Marlow Place**, built in 1720 with, as Pevsner puts it, "the oddest details on its facade"; and **Remnantz**, in West Street, a curiously named house of the early 18th century.

However, Marlow is probably best known for its annual Regatta, held in June, but all year round there is activity on the river, with pleasure boats giving rides as well as canoes and rowing boats for hire.

BURNHAM
Map 5 ref N20

This community has grown a little since it was named 'homestead by a stream', though it still retains a rural air. To the south lies **Dorney Court**, a lovely pink brick and timbered house built about 1440 that has managed to kept much its original appearance, as a many gabled Tudor house with tall brick chimneys. Inside is a feast of furniture, oak from the 15th and 16th centuries and examples of lacquered furniture from the 17th. In addition there are 400 years of family portraits.

The house, which has been in the ownership of the same family since 1542, has associations with Barbara Lady Castlemaine, for many years the mistress of Charles II, who married into the family about 1659. She was beautiful and, according to Count Grammont's memoirs of the court, "a woman lively and discerning". She was also extremely elegant. Pepys admitted, in his diary for 21st May 1662, ogling the washing in her garden: "saw the finest smocks and linen petticoats of my Lady Castlemaine's, with rich lace at the bottom, that ever I saw; and did me good to look at them". She also managed to scandalise the unshockable Restoration court with her other liaisons, particularly one involving a tightrope walker!

Just to the north are **Burnham Beeches**, which have long been a place of rest and recreation for Londoners. How the area has survived to the late 20th century as an open space is an early example of a successful effort to save a stretch of well loved landscape for the general public. In 1879 it was put up for sale by public auction. There were fears that the trees would be cut down and the land developed as London expanded. One of the earliest pieces of legislation by which countryside could be protected from development allowed the City of London Corporation to purchase open land in order to preserve it for public access. The problem in the case of Burnham Beeches was that it was included in a lot with some arable land, which, under the legislation, the City Corporation could not buy. However an MP called Sir Henry Peek bought the whole lot and sold the Burnham Beeches part to the Corporation. It was then dedicated to be kept as an open space for ever for the recreation and enjoyment of the public.

CHALFONT ST GILES
Map 5 ref N20

A fascinating time is guaranteed at **The Chiltern Open Air Museum**, which rescues buildings of historic or architectural importance from across the Chilterns region and re-erects them on its 45 acre site of beautiful natural meadow and woodland. Offers of buildings come from many sources and the museum will only accept one if it is to be demolished, always preferring to see a building remain where it was originally built. Over 30 buildings are now on display, including an Iron Age House and cast iron Edwardian Conveniences. There is a complete Victorian farmyard, with appropriate livestock including a shire horse, Aylesbury ducks, chickens, geese, turkeys, Jersey cattle, Oxford Down sheep and goats. Other buildings include a blacksmith's forge, a toll house, 18th century thatched cottages, a 1940s prefab and a Victorian Vicarage room. Three acres of fields are farmed in a medieval method, organically growing historic crop varieties including woad, from which indigo dye is extracted and used in dyeing demonstrations.

In a 19th century barn rescued from Skippings Farm in Chalfont St Peter is the **Hawk and Owl Trust's National Education and Exhibition Centre**. The Trust is dedicated to conserving wild birds of prey in their natural habitats through practical research, creative conservation and imaginative education.

Chalfont St Giles itself is a pretty village with several interesting houses, including **Milton's Cottage**, where the blind poet John Milton wrote *Paradise Lost* and began work on its sequel, *Paradise Regained*. He moved to this cottage, found for him by a former pupil, another Quaker named Thomas Ellwood, in 1665 to escape the plague which was raging in London. He returned to London in 1666 but this is the only one of his homes to survive. The 16th century timber framed building has been preserved as it was at the time Milton lived here, complete with a cottage garden. There is a display of rare books, including first editions of *Paradise Lost* and *Paradise Regained* as well as other items of interest on Milton's life and the area.

CHESHAM   *Map 5 ref N19*

Chesham is a pleasant town among wooded hills with a number of interesting houses of the 18th and 19th centuries and a large church with a wall painting of St Christopher wading through the water. Its growth from a sleepy market town has been due to the 'Metroland' factor: it is one of the termini of the Metropolitan Line of the London Underground system. The Metropolitan Railway Company began by operating the first urban underground railway in the world from 1863, running trains from Paddington to Farringdon Street in central London. However, the company was never content with being only an urban or even, later, suburban railway and pushed its main line ambitions through a policy of acquiring other lines to link into its system as well as building its own. At its high point the Metropolitan operated trains as far into Buckinghamshire as Quainton Road and Aylesbury.

BUCKINGHAM   *Map 10 ref M18*

The old town centre is contained in a loop of the Great Ouse which, at this point, is not very great at all. Buckingham was the county town of Buckinghamshire in Saxon times, though many of the functions of a county town seem to have been performed by the more centrally placed Aylesbury from quite an early date. It is a pleasant town, with many interesting old buildings. The **Town Hall** is on the south side of the Market Place and dates from the late 17th century though the brick façade was added about 1780. It is a pleasingly simple building with a clock turret on top.

A disastrous fire in 1725 destroyed many of the houses in the town. Some of the replacements are very fine Georgian houses and, of these, **Castle House**, in West Street, is the best. One notable, recent addition to the town is the University of Buckingham which was granted its Royal Charter in 1983, seven years after it first opened its doors to students. Unlike most British universities, it receives no direct state funding and also has a four term year which allows students to complete their degrees in two years rather than the more usual three.

MILTON KEYNES   *Map 10 ref M18*

Studies carried out in the early 1960s favoured the dispersal of the population concentrated in London out into new towns, of which Milton Keynes was one. The Development Corporation which was charged with bringing it into being was set up in 1967 and, since then, the population of the borough has gone up from 60,000 to about 180,000. It is a modern town, proud of its new housing, high-tech industries, modern leisure facilities and its shopping centre with over 140 shops, a creche, 12,000 free parking places, public transport facilities and racks for cycles.

However, Milton Keynes has not turned its back on the past. A fascinating **Museum of Industry and Rural Life**, with a large collection of industrial, domestic and agricultural bygones, is devoted to the lives of the people who lived in the area in the 200 years before the new town was a gleam in a planner's eye. Exhibitions on art, crafts, local history and social life can be seen at the Exhibition Gallery, next to the library.

The new town of Milton Keynes absorbed several older villages, taking its name from one of them. In **Willen** is the Church of St Mary Magdalene; an elegant jewel of a church, built 1679-80 to designs drawn up by Robert Hooke. He used a pleasing red brick with details highlighted in stone. Also in Willen is the **Peace Pagoda and Buddhist Temple**, opened in 1980. It was built by the monks and nuns of the Nipponsan Myohoji, the first in the western hemisphere and it is a place of great peace and beauty. A thousand cherry trees and cedars donated by the ancient Japanese town of Yoshino, famous for the beauty of its cherry blossom, have been planted on the hill surrounding the Pagoda.

NEWPORT PAGNELL   *Map 10 ref N18*

In spite of having expanded a good deal in recent years, the centre has managed to retain the atmosphere of a market town. At first sight the name is a bit of a puzzle; by no stretch of the imagination can this ever have been a 'new port', so far from the sea, and even though it is sited where the river Lovat meets the Great Ouse it seems unlikely that water-borne traffic here could ever have been important. The answer is that 'port' sometimes mean 'a place to which goods are transported and where they are sold', that is, a market town. Pagnell refers to a 12th century Norman Lord of the Manor, Fulc Paganel (paganel being a nickname meaning 'little pagan'), whose family had a castle here at the junction of the two rivers. In spite of the pagan association of the name, Newport Pagnell's **Church** is a fine building, a large and impressive, mostly of the 15th century. The west tower is late medieval, built 1542-48 but the pinnacles date only from the 19th century restoration.

The town has been known for many years as 'the town that built the M1' and later famed for the motorway service station with its unique cuisine. Newport Pagnell's famous car manufacturer, Aston Martin, must have welcomed the new highway back in the days when there was no speed limit and, today, they still hand-build cars that would test the mettle of the most law-abiding driver.

Just to the east of Newport Pagnell is **Chicheley Hall**, a beautiful baroque house built in the early 18th century for Sir John Chester. His curious library is in the attic storey, with all the bookshelves hidden away behind mock panelling which must reduce the problem of keeping the books dusted. Inside there is also a museum devoted to Admiral Lord Beatty, hero of World War I and containing memorabilia of his naval campaigns. He was the son of a cavalry officer who joined the Navy as a cadet at the age of 13. In the opening days of the Great War in 1914 he commanded a battlecruiser squadron which sank two German cruisers and went on to show equal initiative in the most important naval battle of the war, at Jutland in 1916, though the losses to his battle cruiser squadron were heavy.

CHAPTER TWO
Southern England

Stonehenge

2
Southern England

Hampshire

INTRODUCTION

Hampshire has much to offer both resident and casual visitor alike. Its eastern regions lie close enough to London to be influenced by the city and to provide comfortable housing within easy commuting distance whilst it stretches down to the south coast and to the great naval base at Portsmouth. Still a busy harbour city, Portsmouth's connections with the sea and the defence of England go back many centuries. Here too can be seen both Nelson's flagship *HMS Victory* and Henry VIII's *Mary Rose*. Back in the east, a little under 150 years ago, Aldershot was nothing more than a quiet rural village and then the army moved here. The army is still here and a number of military museums can be found in and around the barracks. Nearby, Farnborough is home to the Royal Aircraft Establishment, the host of the huge, annual Air Show.

However, the county is not all barracks, hangars and dockyards. The ancient county town of Winchester, with its exceptional cathedral, was the capital of King Alfred's kingdom of Wessex. While for centuries the New Forest was a favourite haunt of English kings and famous for its wandering ponies. Nova Foresta, as it was named by William the Conqueror, is still subject to the special laws which he created to protect his sport of the forest's Red Deer. Over 900 years later, the ancient forest and heathland that is a unique survivor of England's royal hunting forests can still be explored and enjoyed.

It comes as a surprise to many people that the forest is not just mile upon mile of trees and that much of it is, and always has been, heathland. The word forest derives from the Latin 'foris' which was formerly used to denote a royal hunting ground, an unenclosed tract of land, rather than a distinct wooded area. The forest of Bowland in Lancashire has hardly a tree to its name and never has had. For walkers, the South Downs Way, a 99 mile footpath from Winchester to Eastbourne and the 24 mile Clarendon Way linking Winchester with Salisbury provide the ideal opportunity for either day rambles or longer treks.

PORTSMOUTH   *Map 5 ref M23*

Most of Portsmouth is built on the flat **Portsea Island** surrounded by Langstone and Portsmouth Harbour. It is the only British city on an island site—at one time it was linked to the mainland by a single bridge road, hard to believe today. As the city fathers have attracted more businesses into the area they have had to purchase land outside Portsea Island to house the working people. This has been carefully carried out and well planned but it is Old Portsmouth and its resort, Southsea, that attract visitors together with the wealth of places of historical interest and importance.

Those who would prefer to sit on the beach or enjoy sporting activities will be in their element. Portsmouth offers miles of foreshore for keen anglers as well as quiet waters for relaxing. For sailing and windsurfing enthusiasts there are several very good marinas and, at the Eastney end of the beach, a special area, close to a windsurfing shop, has been designed for windsurfers. Cricketers are not forgotten: the United Services ground is used for matches to first class standard. Though all these pleasurable activities make a stay here very enjoyable, it is the city's great history that makes it so attractive. Portsmouth's strategic situation, with its safe and sheltered anchorage, was ideal for the departure and return of the troops in the days of the great Crusades. Richard I used the port so often that he had a little house built here in which he lived whilst he was fitting out his fleet for the Crusade. He came back to Portsmouth after his imprisonment in Austria and no doubt sat in his little house plotting revenge.

In about 1418 the **Round and Square Towers** were begun to defend the harbour entrance from determined enemies and these two stone bastions are still here today. The Square Tower was finally completed in 1494 and, standing on the corner of High Street and Broad Street, it was originally a residence for the Governor. Later on it became a storehouse for supplying both gunpowder and victuals for the fleet which would lie off Spithead. From both the Round Tower and Square Tower naval wives have waved to their husbands on passing ships. The Round Tower, in particular, is a great vantage point from which to watch warships and merchantmen sailing by at close quarters. A gilded bust of Charles I, set in a circular recess of the Round Tower's north wall, looks down at passers-by. His Majesty gave the bust to Portsmouth in 1635 and the inscription states: "After his travels through all France and Spain both by sea and land, he arrived here on the 5th day of October 1623."

The Saluting Platform which adjoins the Square Tower and from which ceremonial gun salutes are fired is still in use when the occasion demands. Behind the grim walls the unfortunate convicts who were to be shipped to Australia as the first settlers were herded awaiting transportation.

The **High Street** is unique in history because over the last 800 years every English monarch, with the exception of Mary Tudor, has walked down this ancient street. At one time it was the site of the Guildhall and a theatre which was mentioned by Charles Dickens in *Nicholas Nickleby*. Incidentally, Dickens was born in Portsmouth, in 1812, in a smart terraced house near the docks. His father, John, was a pay clerk in the Navy Pay Office but the family left Portsmouth when the young Charles was just two years old. In later years on his return to Portsmouth to give readings of his work, he went back to his old home at 393 Commercial Road. Subsequently it has become the **Charles Dickens Birthplace Museum**; well worth a visit to see the kind of life style into which he was born.

Nelson spent his last night alive on English soil at the Old George Hotel in the High Street. He was astonished at the large crowds waiting to wish him well as he left in the morning and he tried to get away from them by leaving through a rear entrance of the hotel in Penny Street but still the crowds caught up with him. He was so touched by their demonstration of affection that he said, "I wish I had two hands then I could accommodate more of you." A house that Nelson would have passed as he went along The Hard at Portsmouth Point would have been the white timbered **Quebec House**, built in 1754 as a bath house. It was to this house that General Wolfe's body was brought home after the Battle of Quebec. Another piece of history happened here too in May 1845 when a captain of Dragoons was shot dead in a duel with a Royal Marine. He is recorded as the last man to die in England as a result of a duel—officially that is.

There is so much character in this part of Old Portsmouth, especially in the historic Royal Naval Dockyard, home of the British Navy for 500 years. The **Royal Naval Museum** here recreates Nelson's great life in a panoramic scene which takes the visitor from the first shot being fired at Trafalgar to his death from a sniper's bullet at the height of the battle in which England was victorious. In the accompanying sound track the cannon's roar can be heard, together with the shouts and screams of the men on deck. The museum also includes 20th century naval history and brings the story up-to-date with mementoes of the Falklands Campaign.

As might be expected, there are several ships to be visited at Portsmouth and none is more famous than ***HMS Victory***. A first rate 104 gun ship of the line, she was, of course, Vice-Admiral Nelson's Flagship at Trafalgar and the ship that flew the famous signal, "England expects that every man should do his duty", before engaging the French and Spanish fleets. Now safe in a dry dock, a tour of the battleship gives a very vivid impression of life in the Navy of George III. Today the *Victory* is the flagship of the Commander-in-Chief Naval Home Command, manned by officers and ratings of the Royal Navy. Though now performing only a ceremonial role she is still the oldest commissioned warship in the world.

Right next door to *Victory* is the ***Mary Rose***, which lies in a special dry dock workshop in Portsmouth's Naval Base. She presents a breathtaking spectacle as the hull can be seen as a giant cutaway model, with the ship's structural detail exposed. Nearby in a Georgian timber boat house is an exhibition which features fascinating displays of historical treasures of the ship, the everyday objects she was carrying on the fateful day in July 1545 when she sank. The climax of the operation to rescue the Mary Rose came on October 11th 1982 when the hull was raised to the surface in the Solent and the story of the *Mary Rose*, her loss and her dramatic recovery is told in an exciting audiovisual presentation.

The third great ship at Portsmouth Naval Dockyard is **HMS Warrior**, rescued from Pembroke Dock where she was being used as a fuelling pontoon. Victorian seafaring history is brought to life aboard this sleek black battleship. Her four decks have been beautifully and minutely restored to their former glory, each portraying an aspect of life in the 19th century Navy. The pride of Queen Victoria's navy, the battleship was the largest, fastest and most powerful warship in the world. These docks are not just museum pieces and all around here the work of the Navy goes on.

Portsmouth came under heavy bombardment from the German warplanes in World War II and one of the many buildings that were destroyed by the bombs was the **Royal Garrison Church** which is still in ruins today except for the chancel, which miraculously escaped. It has a nice history, originally serving as a hospital known as the Domus Dei or God's House. It was a place of refuge for pilgrims and strangers entering the country as far back as the 13th century. It was also to this chapel, dedicated to St Nicholas, the guardian of sailors, that Catherine of Braganza came for her marriage with Charles II in 1662. The poor soul was kept waiting for several days after her arrival in this country before her future husband deigned to put in an appearance, in spite of the fact that she brought with her some £300,000 as a dowry for which the King was desperate.

Portsmouth became a city in 1927 and the town's Mother Church of St Thomas Becket was chosen to become the **Cathedral**. It is a mixture of architecture starting from the last quarter of the 12th century, with a central tower over which has been raised a cupola-top. One special feature is the D-Day memorial window. A plaque nearby recalls the visit of Queen Elizabeth the Queen Mother on the 3rd June 1984 for the dedication of the window by the Archbishop of Canterbury. The window depicts the arms of all the Allied countries and the badges of the units that took part in the landings.

Up on **Southsea Common** stands a statue of Nelson looking out over the sea; there are reminders of this great man all over the city. For example on **Portsdown Hill** there is a tall obelisk paid for by contributions from the men who fought with him in his last action "to perpetuate his triumph and their regret".

HAVANT   *Map 5 ref M23*

This is a pleasant small town with a large church that stands at the centre where four roads meet. Havant was once renowned for its parchment making and it is claimed that the Magna Carta was written on Havant parchment. Even though this is not proven the parchment was used for the 1919 Treaty of Versailles certainly came from here.

PETERSFIELD   *Map 5 ref M22*

In the main square of this delightful country town stands a **Statue of William III**, for some strange reason in Roman costume, presides on horseback. The statue once stood in the grounds of Petersfield House, the home of the Joliffe family which stood in the square until its demolition in 1793, after which the family presented the statue to the town.

Petersfield was once an important coaching station with nine inns to cater for the 30 or so coaches that passed through daily between London and Portsmouth. Samuel Pepys, the diarist and Secretary to the Admiralty, used to stay here on his way to the dockyard. There are also many fine houses in Petersfield, one of the best known belonging to the actor Sir Alec Guinness.

ALDERSHOT   *Map 6 ref M21*

Before the army came to Aldershot in 1854, it was a village of about 800 inhabitants. Hundreds of artisans poured into the village from all over the country when news got around that the army were going to build a large camp here and a town of camp followers soon grew up. When the building had been finished many stayed on to become the tradesmen and shopkeepers of the new Aldershot. Naturally, they built their shops as close to the military camp as possible and they inadvertently created the only one-sided High Street in the country.

The story of how Aldershot became the home of the British Army is told at the **Military Museum**, which stands in the centre of the camp, and it is a must for anyone with an interest in military, social or local history. Housed in the last two surviving Victorian barrack blocks, its tiny appearance from the outside belies the wealth of fascinating information and interest found inside. Military museums usually abound with stories of great battles and deeds of valour but this museum is one of the few that set out to describe what life was like for a soldier in peacetime, which was after all most of his service. During World War II, the camps in and around Aldershot were taken over by the Canadian Army and the museum has the only gallery in the country devoted to their exploits both in Aldershot and throughout the European campaigns.

Not far from the Military Museum stands a famous Dakota aircraft, the largest exhibit at the **Airborne Forces Museum**. Inside the history of those who fought as part of Airborne is told. The British 6th Airborne Division had a vital role to play in the D-Day invasion, landing by parachute and glider to secure the canal crossings northeast of Caen. Their story is told with the help of the original model used to plan the seizure of Pegasus Bridge, the first place in mainland Europe to be liberated from the Nazis. The story of Operation Market Garden and the failed attempt to secure the bridge at Arnhem, immortalised in the book and the film *A Bridge Too Far*, is also told.

In Manor Park there is **The Heroes Shrine**, which is dedicated to the dead of World War I. Close by is a walled and sunken garden, sheltered by a huge deodar tree, which is Aldershot's memorial and that of the Nation to those who fell in the Battle of Britain and in the civil bombing. The stones used in its construction came from such war devastated buildings as Coventry Cathedral, the Guard's Chapel in London, York's Guildhall and the church in Portsmouth Dockyard.

On **Round Hill** there is a bronze statue of the Duke of Wellington gazing down on the world from his favourite horse, Copenhagen. It once stood on top of the Triumphal Arch at Hyde Park Corner in London but was brought to Aldershot in 1885.

FARNBOROUGH   *Map 5 ref N21*

The town is situated in northeastern Hampshire where the combination of chalk downlands, heathland and forest provides a rich variety of natural beauty whatever the season. Since 1906 the town has been the home of the **Royal Aircraft Establishment**, the laboratory of British Aviation. It is here that examinations are carried out not only on service aircraft that have crashed but also on civil aircraft; the pieces of aircraft are brought here for intensive research to see if the cause of the accident can be pinned down. The Royal Aircraft Establishment is also home to the famous Farnborough Air Show which brings people and planes from all over the world.

Today Farnborough almost merges into Aldershot but it was also a village before the coming of the army. Its earliest claim to fame is perhaps that it witnessed the end of the long story of Napoleon. The ex-Imperial family, including the Empress and the Prince Imperial, took refuge in Chislehurst in Kent (where the Emperor died in 1873) after the crushing defeat at Sedan in 1870, at the hands of the Prussians. Six years later the Prince was killed in the Zulu wars and the Empress could no longer bear to be in Chislehurst so she bought **Farnborough Hill** and lived there until her death in 1920 aged 94. Just off the A325 is the **Benedictine Abbey of St Michael**. The Empress had this built to serve the chapel above a mausoleum containing Napoleon III and the Prince Imperial which was presented to her by Queen Victoria. It now contains the sarcophagus of the Empress as well. The mausoleum is rather flamboyant and very French; the abbey too has a strong French influence, parts of it modelled on part of the Abbey of Solesmes in Normandy.

It is hard to imagine that this bustling town was once such a backwater that it was a haven for smugglers and highwaymen. Though right on the border with Surrey,

Tumble Down Dick is actually in Hampshire. Sited by the Clock House, this inn is thought to date from the Restoration period and its name is believed to refer either to its links with Dick Turpin, the highwayman, or to Richard Cromwell and his fall from office of Lord Protector. Whatever the story behind the name it is a fine hostelry well worth the visit.

ODIHAM   *Map 5 ref M21*

Dating from Saxon times, Odiham was listed in the Domesday Book as the largest holding of the King in Hampshire. King John had a favourite hunting lodge here and he built a castle in the grounds of the manor around which the present town grew. The High Street is a lovely mixture of Georgian houses but, like all the old towns of the area, is Tudor behind the Georgian facades. It was from the castle that King John set out to Runnymede to sign the Magna Carta in 1215; his barons, aided and abetted by the French, besieged the castle the next year.

Just a few hundred yards from the High Street at Colts Hill lies the **Basingstoke Canal**. John Pinkerton was responsible for building the canal some 200 years ago and it has thankfully been restored to its former glory. The beauty of the canal can also be enjoyed by strolling along the tow path or perhaps by hiring a rowing boat at Colt Hill.

Situated in this historic and picturesque village, **The Grapevine Bistro Restaurant** is ideally located only a few miles from the M3, London to Basingstoke road, perfect for an impromptu break. This superb restaurant is run by its owners Matthew and Penny Fleet whose constant aim for excellence has been rewarded by a continual stream of customers throughout the week, with booking essential at weekends to avoid disappointment. The restaurant was opened in 1994 and can be found on the ground floor of an elegant Georgian building at the end of

The Grapevine Bistro Restaurant

England

Odiham High Street, with a pleasantly relaxed and informal atmosphere that proves popular with shoppers who flock to sample the two course lunch time special. The menus are mainly on blackboards and change on a regular basis, offering a wide variety of high quality food, simply cooked and sensibly priced. Dishes range from the exotic tastes of tea smoked duck breast with a chicory and orange salad to the more rustic pan fried calves liver with a pea, mustard and tarragon cream sauce with a good selection of home-made puddings for dessert. Vegetarian food is always available and children are given the choice of dishes from their very own kid's menu, with high chairs supplied for those younger customers. The restaurant is fully air-conditioned and is now listed in the 1997 *Good Food Guide* and *The Michelin Guide*.
The Grapevine Bistro Restaurant, 121 High Street, Odiham, Hampshire, RG29 1LA Tel: 01256 701122

SILCHESTER   *Map 5 ref M21*

The Iron Age and Roman settlement of **Calleva Atrebatum** lies in the parish of Silchester. Unlike many other Roman towns in Britain which have survived and grown, Roman Silchester has no successor and remained deserted (the modern town has grown up on a separate site). Only large sections of its walls of flint bonded with blocks of chalk survive above the ground. The site was excavated in the late 19th century and the network of roads, defensive works and siting of buildings, including the earliest Christian temple in Britain, were recorded before being covered up again with earth. A hollow in the ground marks the site of the former amphitheatre and there is a small display in the nearby scout hut.

The site of the Roman town is now farmland but beside a portion of the lost town stands the Church of medieval origins, **St Mary's**. The Jacobean pulpit with its domed canopy and the 15th century screen have survived a Victorian restoration that unfortunately removed box pews and dormer windows. There is also a beautiful 14th century effigy of a lady and a delightful frieze of genuflecting angels on an oak screen.

KINGSCLERE   *Map 5 ref L21*

Charming and sleepy, Kingsclere has a weather vane of a bug on its Church of St Mary, placed there by order of King John in the 13th century, when he remonstrated against a bug-infested bed in which he had slept in the local inn. The church also has some fine Norman work.

Burghclere, nearby, also has a church with Norman elements but its most notable building is the **Sandham Memorial Chapel**, built between 1923 and 1927 specifically for the artist Stanley Spencer, who over a period of six years painted scenes from the Salonika front of World War I. The paintings cover the walls and dramatically convey the horror and futility of war, whilst emphasising the human companionship of the troops.

HIGHCLERE   *Map 5 ref L21*

Once **Highclere Castle** was a Georgian home and it proved to be too plain for the 3rd Earl of Caernarvon who wanted his house to be a mansion that would impress the world. Queen Victoria was new to the throne when the Earl invited Sir Charles Barry to alter Highclere and Sir Charles set about his task with relish, much preferring it to the building of the Houses of Parliament, which he was undertaking at the same time. The result is a huge, ornate and typically Victorian mansion which its architect called Anglo-Italian.

It was the 4th Earl who finished what had been started by his predecessor. He commissioned Thomas Allen to complete the interiors, working from some of Sir Charles Barry's original designs but adding ideas of his own. The final result is a wonderful mixture of all the styles of the past in superbly contrasting rooms which reflect the Victorian gentleman's desire to create an effect larger than life.

Outside, the gardens were originally laid out by Rupert Herbert with a series of vistas, but afterwards Capability Brown had a hand in part of the design and landscaped the gardens in a more naturalistic manner.

ANDOVER   *Map 5 ref L21*

Much of old Andover has disappeared to make room for large housing estates and industry but one outstanding landmark that remains is the **Church of St Mary the Virgin** which is strikingly situated on a hill overlooking the new central area. It was built in 1840 at the expense of a retired headmaster of Winchester College and has a soaring vaulted interior inspired by Salisbury Cathedral which is quite magnificent. In fact it is quite a remarkable building altogether with a very impressive if slightly austere exterior.

For those interested in prehistory, the town boasts a splendid **Museum of the Iron Age** on Church Close. The exhibits come from the excavations of Professor Barry Cunliffe and his team, who for a long time have excavated Danebury Ring, an Iron Age hillfort. Their endeavours have resulted in the largest excavation on a prehistoric site in Britain and revealed an unparalleled view of what life was like in the Iron Age during the period 600 BC to AD 50.

Andover Museum is based in the same old Grammar School building but it is separate. Built about 1750 in red brick, it is believed the doorcase is the original. Jane Austen knew this house well as she often visited the headmaster and his family. The displays here tell the story of the town from Saxon times right through to the massive development in the 1960s and are well worth visiting.

A rather unusual drinking tradition has been observed in the town for many years. It was the job of the ancient, and recently honorary, Ale Taster to taste the local brew and to report beer which was below standard as well as any local publicans who were selling short measure. At one time the Ale Taster was provided with a pair of leather breeches and one of the tests he had to carry out was to pour some ale on to a wooden seat and sit in it. If he stuck to the seat at all the ale was below standard but if he rose freely it was fit to drink!

WINCHESTER   *Map 5 ref L22*

The Romans used the prehistoric ford here to cross the River Itchen and founded a walled city called **Venta Belgarum**, a regional capital with some 6000 inhabitants, which also featured many fine villas with intricate mosaic floors and ingenious underfloor heating, though sadly little sign remains as the modern city was built right on top of it. Down by the river, set back behind a grille, a small portion of Roman Wall does remain and from the footpath along the river bank, the medieval walls, still following the line of Roman walls, are also visible. The stone which forms the greater part of the city wall is flint or Hampshire Diamond as it is often called. The stone of the great buildings such as the Cathedral had to come all the way from the Isle of Wight or from Beer, in Devon, and some of the finer limestone used for carving was imported from Caen in Normandy.

The city was restored after the Dark Ages by King Alfred the Great, King of Wessex, who drove back the invading Danes. Winchester was his capital and his statue dominates Broadway. He died and was buried here and his descendants became the first kings of England. For 400 years, beginning in the days of Alfred, Winchester was the principal city of England. **Winchester Heritage Centre**, on Upper Brook Street, is run by the Winchester Preservation Trust and its audiovisual and permanent displays tell the 2000 year old story of the city. For those who want to immerse themselves more deeply in how life was lived in Roman and Medieval times, **The Brook Experience** is based on actual excavated remains and tells the story of the city in an exciting, action-packed drama suitable for all the family.

The **Statue of Alfred** himself, sculpted by Sir Hamo Thorneycroft, stands at the lower end of the town, gazing up the High Street, the line of which, even in his day, was the main street of the Saxon town. A story is told of the difficulties experienced when manoeuvring into position the enormous blocks of Cornish granite which form the base of the statue. In order to allow them to be positioned, one accurately on the top of the other, cubed sugar was spread on the lower one. As the top one was hauled into place, the sugar was crushed to powder but gave them a second's breathing space in which the blocks could be lined up.

William the Conqueror came to Winchester to claim the Crown of England and the Domesday Book, begun at William's order, was written here. Of the Norman **Castle** that William began and Henry III rebuilt, only the Great Hall escaped Oliver Cromwell's attentions during the Civil War. Inside hangs the mysterious Round Table, often said to be the very one of Arthurian legend. Undoubtedly one of the country's finest medieval buildings, no visit to the city would be complete without taking in its splendour.

The city's crown jewel, however, must be the **Cathedral**, which was begun in Saxon times and rebuilt soon after the Norman Conquest. Bishop William Wakelin, a relative of William the Conqueror, had seen the start of this work in 1079 and, by 1093, enough of the cathedral was built for the monks of St Swithun's Monastery to move into their new premises from their former ones, those of the Old Minster, the first cathedral. The Saxon building was then knocked down and the stone reused in the nave of the Norman cathedral. At 556 feet from east to west it is the longest medieval cathedral in Europe and, perhaps, one of the most beautiful. The interior is simply stunning and has, like all great churches, a very peaceful atmosphere. Here, Henry III was baptised, Henry VI was married and Mary Tudor married Philip of Spain. William Rufus and the Anglo-Saxon kings of England lie buried in the choir. This is truly a place of history. Jane Austen spent the last six weeks of her life in the town while a local doctor tried in vain to save her life. Her tombstone can be seen in the North Aisle.

Winchester Cathedral

Everyone will have heard of St Swithun but not many people know that he was a Bishop of Winchester. When he died, his wishes were that he be buried outside the West Door of the cathedral but when the minster was enlarged the grave was opened in order to move the remains. Unfortunately that day it rained, giving rise to the legend that if it rains on St Swithun's Day it will rain for a further 40 days.

Nearby is the area known as Wolvesey, where the Bishop's Palace now stands—smaller than it was but quite big enough to live in these days. In the background are the ruins of the huge **Wolvesey Castle**, the fortified palace where, from Norman to Stuart times, the bishops lived. Bishop Henry of Blois was responsible for fortifying the palace in 1141 during the fighting between Stephen and Matilda which destroyed most of the city. He also founded the **Hospital of St Cross** in 1136. It is the oldest charitable institution still occupied in England and people can still get their Wayfarer's Dole on request from the gateman as a legacy from Bishop Henry.

The great range of buildings across College Street from Wolvesey is **Winchester College**, one of the oldest boys' boarding schools in the country. It was founded in 1383 by William of Wykeham, Bishop of Winchester and Chancellor to Edward III and Richard II. He gave the college its now famous motto, "Manners Makyth Man", embracing the moral and spiritual attributes he believed to be essential to a young man's education. The great Chamber Court is bounded on one side by the Chapel while on the other sides live the 70 boys who are the Scholars of the original foundation. Nowadays there are over 500 other boys, Commoners as they are called, who live scattered around this part of the town in school boarding houses. From April to September guided tours of the college leave the Porter's Lodge on a daily basis.

Though it might not strike the visitor immediately, Winchester has, for centuries, been a military town and close to the cathedral there are five regimental museums at the **Peninsula Barracks** and nearby **Serle's House**. Displays at the Royal Green Jackets Museum include a diorama of the battlefield of Waterloo, with over 22,000 model soldiers, as well as no less than 33 of the Green Jackets 55 Victoria Crosses. The famous Gurkhas of Nepal have served the British Crown since 1815 and heroic exploits of this famous jungle fighting regiment are told in their museum. The history of the 10th and 11th Hussars cavalry regiments, formed in 1715, is lavishly illustrated with paintings, pictures and uniforms and covers the regiment's exploits in the Crimean War and involvement in Charge of the Light Brigade. The Light Infantry displays concentrate on events of modern times and include a piece of The Berlin Wall and the chronicle of the regiment's service in the Gulf War. These museums are all in the barracks, whilst next door in Serle's House is told the story of the Hampshire Regiment, first raised in 1705.

The military do not hold a monopoly on museums though. **City Museum** is a small but nonetheless interesting museum that houses important exhibits illustrating both the archeological and social history of the great city. Its sister, **Westgate Museum**, is situated in a fortified medieval gateway on the High Street which has, in the past, served as a debtors' prison. Today it houses a number of fascinating displays including weights and measures and a fine painted ceiling from Winchester College. **The Red Cross Museum** illustrates the history of Red Cross Service in Hampshire. Finally, the **Winchester City Mill**, built over the river in 1744 and now owned by the National Trust, has an impressive millrace with a restored waterwheel as well as timbered and raftered ceilings, a delightful small island garden and a shop selling local crafts.

Many famous people have lived in or visited Winchester and have left their mark on the city, such as Izaak Walton, author of *The Compleat Angler*; Jane Austen, whose grave and memorial are in the Cathedral; the poet John Keats and composer Samuel Sebastian Wesley, who was organist at the Cathedral. Sir Walter Raleigh was tried for treason in the Great Hall in 1603 but was later reprieved from his sentence of death. Another frequent visitor to Winchester was King Charles II, but Nell Gwynn was not so welcome and had to lodge in different accommodation from the King.

ROMSEY   *Map 5 ref L22*

This bustling market town has always been very much associated with **Broadlands**, which lies on the southern outskirts. It was the birthplace of Lord Palmerston, whose statue stands in the market square. He loved his home and whenever he could get away from the affairs of state he went to Broadlands for a run with the New Forest hounds or a day's shooting. Today the house is, perhaps, more closely associated with the Mountbatten family whose home it still is. Lord and Lady Romsey, Mountbatten's grandson and his wife are the present residents after the murder of Earl Mountbatten. Visitors may view the house with its treasures and mementoes that include many of Mountbatten's personal things. The Mountbatten Exhibition chronicles the life of this most extraordinary man and in the grounds there are the magnificent riverside lawns.

Broadlands, Romsey

The town itself is dominated by its splendid Abbey. The **Abbey Church of St Mary and Ethelflaeda** was founded at the start of the 10th century and rebuilt in the 12th and 13th centuries on a magnificent scale, making it the finest church in Hampshire if not in the whole of southern England. It became the parish church at the Dissolution of the Monasteries in 1539. The original deed of sale to the people of Romsey shows it was sold for £100. The south side of the choir is very special, one of the best examples of Norman architecture anywhere. A marvellous effigy to a lady in Purbeck marble stands beneath an ogee canopy in the south transept together with the 17th century St Barbe monument and the much more recent tomb of Earl Mountbatten.

Also in the town is the wonderful medieval **King John's Hunting Lodge**, said to be the house where his daughter Joanna lived with her governess before she married the King of Scotland.

LYNDHURST   *Map 5 ref K23*

Often described as the capital of the New Forest, Lyndhurst is still an attractive place and a good central point for exploring the Forest, though sadly its tranquillity has long gone because of the through traffic. In the churchyard of the splendid mid-Victorian parish church lies the grave of Mrs Reginald Hargreaves, born Alice Liddell, a daughter of the Dean of Christ Church Oxford, for whom his friend, Charles Dodgson, wrote *Alice in Wonderland* under the pen name of Lewis Carroll.

There is much more to the New Forest than ponies and deer and the **New Forest Museum and Visitors Centre** is the place to come to find out more. As well as The Changing Forest audiovisual show, which reflects the beauty of the forest through the seasons, there are displays on how the forest came into being and details of the area's particular customs and laws.

BEAULIEU   *Map 5 ref L23*

It is as the result of an enormous amount of careful planning that **Beaulieu** (the famous attraction not the village) has become one of the most popular stately homes in the country. Lord Montagu, who inherited the estate from his father in 1952, is a man of great sensitivity and vision. Originally Lord Montagu just organised a display of early motor vehicles in the front hall of Palace House in memory of his father who was one of the leading pioneers of motoring in Great Britain. He certainly did not envisage that it would become the now world famous **National Motor Museum**. Tracing the story of motoring from 1894 to the present day, this is a fascinating exhibition for young and old alike. There are special displays, over 250 cars, commercial vehicles and motor cycles and a monorail which takes visitors around the grounds and passes the museum at roof top level. Perhaps the most interesting of all the exhibits are the four cars that have all, at one time, broken the land speed record. As if all this was not enough in a day, there is also a very good **Maritime Museum**.

Back in the village, the parish church of the Blessed Virgin and Child can be found situated in the refectory of a great Cistercian **Abbey**. It is Early English architecture seen at its best: the abbey was founded in 1204 and, although most of the buildings were destroyed during the 16th century, much of the beauty remains.

Leading south from the village, a footpath follows the path of the Beaulieu river. With thickly wooded banks on either side, this is a birdwatcher's paradise. At the end of the path is the little hamlet of **Bucklers Hard**, which consists of only one main street, which slopes down to the river. It was conceived by an 18th century Duke of Montagu (a title no longer in use) who saw it as the first stage in the development of a new port where he could land cargoes of sugar from his vast estates in the Caribbean. The little community did thrive as a shipbuilding yard, able to use the plentiful supply of oak from the New Forest.

Many ships of the fleet were built here for Nelson's Navy, the most famous of these was the *Agamemnon*, in 1781, which he used as his flagship at the battle of Copenhagen and as part of his fleet at Trafalgar. For some reason or other, the shipyard was dilatory in delivering commissioned ships on time and, instead of growing into a thriving port, time stood still in Bucklers Hard and the whole hamlet has become a museum.

The museum that tells the story of the Hard adjoins the old New Inn, which vividly recreates the pub interior as it would been in 1793 and then runs into an example of a labourer's cottage and the deprivations they lived with. Across the street is a shipwright's cottage, its relative comfort contrasting strongly with that of the labourers. Nearest the water, overlooking the slipways, is the former 18th century home of Henry Adams, the master ship builder and now a hotel.

Even the peace of Bucklers Hard was broken during the war when it was a base for Motor Torpedo Boats or MTBs and the Special Operations Executive trained in and around the Beaulieu Estate. These men and women undertook some of the bravest and most hazardous missions of the war, working behind enemy lines, risking torture and certain death as spies.

Dorset

INTRODUCTION

This county covers a land that encompasses the rolling chalk downs, the dark heathland so beloved of Thomas Hardy, the long ridge of the Purbeck Hills and the incomparable Dorset coast with its wealth of magnificent rock formations sculpted by the sea. It is often said that Dorset is England in miniature, the variations in its underlying rock producing almost all of the different landscapes, lacking only high mountains. There is also a fine mixture of charming towns, from the ancient county town of Dorchester to the sedate resort of Bournemouth.

Nearly all of west Dorset's 417 square miles are designated an Area of Outstanding Natural Beauty. The coastline, which is part of the Dorset Heritage Coast, goes through dramatic changes from the spectacular Chesil Bank, the 18 mile pebble bank which joins the Isle of Portland to the mainland, through the sandstone headland, known as Golden Cap and finally on to the fossil encrusted cliffs of Lyme Regis and Charmouth. Inland, as John Fowles once wrote, "villages hide around corners and in dips in the gentle slopes of the hills, towns remain small and neat, not one daring to emulate another".

DORCHESTER   *Map 4 ref I24*

The Romans were largely responsible for the way the town is laid out today. During the reign of Queen Anne, the beautiful tree-lined avenues, known as the Walks, were laid out following the lines of the old Roman walls which circled the town. Many of the artefacts discovered from recent excavations are on display in the **County Museum** and one of the more interesting finds was the remains of a Roman town house close to the County Hall. This revealed evidence of Roman-style central heating, together with mosaics, a bathroom and a covered verandah. The Romans themselves discovered the ancient stone circle, now know as **Maumbury Rings**, in the southern outskirts of the town. They transformed it into an amphitheatre and it was later to be used for all manner of public displays throughout medieval times, with jousting and May Day celebrations being performed here.

In addition to the County Museum, Dorchester has a number of other good museums well worth taking the time to see. Also in High West Street is **Tutankhamun, The Exhibition**. Visitors who missed the great London exhibition will thoroughly enjoy the marvellous recreations here of the boy Pharaoh's tomb and treasures, including his famous golden mask. The **Dorset Military Museum** is housed in the original keep of the Dorset Regiment Depot on Bridport Road. It provides a history of the Queen's Own Dorset Yeomanry, the Militia Volunteers and the Dorset Regiment itself; there are also displays of uniforms, medals and firearms down the ages. Most interesting of the exhibits is, perhaps, Adolf Hitler's writing desk! One exhibition that is sure to fascinate children is the **Dinosaur Museum** on Icen Way. With fossils, skeletons, superb exhibits and computerised displays, it makes for a interesting, enjoyable and educational trip through prehistoric times. Somewhat surprisingly, it is Britain's only museum dedicated exclusively to dinosaurs.

Those familiar with the novels of Thomas Hardy will know Dorchester as 'Casterbridge' and, also on Icen Way, is another exhibition which no fan of the novelist will want to miss. **Hardy's Wessex** depicts typical scenes of old Dorset country life and offers a realistic glimpse of the past as it would have been known to Hardy. There is a typical Victorian village setting with an inn and shops and many of the displays and exhibitions include moving models.

WEYMOUTH   *Map 4 ref I24*

Having always had a good reputation for sea bathing, Weymouth was, in 1748, one of the first resorts to put up bathing huts. Two distinct settlements originally developed here at the mouth of the River Wey—Melcombe Regis to the north and Weymouth to the south. They were officially united in 1571 and, although Melcombe Regis was the larger of the two, Weymouth gradually began to dominate.

In 1780 the Duke of Gloucester decided to spend the winter at Melcombe Regis and was so impressed by the area and its beaches that he built a great house on the front and persuaded his brother, George III, to visit too. The King most definitely approved and took his summer holidays here for many years thereafter. His royal patronage soon put the town on the map as a fashionable resort. George III also has the dubious distinction of being the first monarch ever to have used a bathing machine and his personal model—a solid octagonal box mounted on cartwheels—can be seen at **Weymouth Museum**.

Once Society got the message that Weymouth was the place to be seen, a building boom ensued, giving rise to the fine Georgian and Regency houses that continue to add such elegance to the town today. The beach and promenade are overlooked by two gloriously ornate works of art. The first is an unashamedly elaborate statue of George III, erected in 1810 to commemorate the King's golden jubilee, and the other is the red, blue and gold painted clock tower which followed in 1887 to celebrate Queen Victoria's 50 years on the throne. When the railway arrived, closely followed by the cross Channel and Channel Island ferry services, the continuing prosperity of Weymouth was assured.

The old harbour area of the town has been transformed in recent years and now features a host of shops, pubs, restaurants and places to visit. Amongst them is **Nothe Fort**: built, in 1860, as part of the defences of Portland Harbour, it was designed and constructed by the Royal Engineers to house a 12 gun battery of massive cannons. Later adapted for modern guns it remained in service until 1956 when Coastal Defence was abandoned. Today it is home a multitude of displays that chronicle everything from the life of the Victorian soldier to Weymouth at War, as well as having on display many of the old guns on which the fort depended.

The **Deep Sea Adventure** is perhaps one of Weymouth's most unusual attractions. Situated in a listed Victorian grain warehouse in the beautiful old harbour area, it offers visitors the opportunity to discover and explore the exciting and mysterious undersea world. There are many displays that tell the story of undersea exploration from the contraptions of the 18th century to today's divers working in the oilfields of the North Sea.

Alongside displays of items from shipwrecks along the Dorset coast are the famous stories of the ocean depths, such as the discovery and recovery of £40,000,000 worth of gold bullion from *HMS Edinburgh* (which sank in the freezing Barents Sea on her way to Russia in World War II) and the most famous disaster of all, the *Titanic*, which sank after hitting an iceberg in 1912 with the loss of over 1500 souls.

CORFE CASTLE   *Map 4 ref J24*

This picturesque little town, with its charming grey stone houses and cottages, is dominated by the ruins of the fortress from which it takes its name. The **Castle** stands on a hill at a narrow pass in the Purbeck Hills and the fact that so much of it still stands today is proof of its great strength. It was on this site that Elfrida, mother of Ethelred the Unready, had a hunting lodge in 978 before she took holy vows and retired to the Priory at Wherwell. After the Norman Conquest, the great walls and the towering keep were built. The castle's formidable strength caused it to be used both as a prison and as a royal residence and it had its fair share of notable occupants, some more willing than others. Purchased, in 1635, Sir John Bankes, Corfe Castle was successfully defended by Lady Bankes and her household through two sieges during the Civil War while her husband was away fighting with the King. It eventually fell into Parliamentarian hands through treachery in 1646 and a month later its demolition was ordered by Parliament.

Although Corfe Castle now stands in splendid ruin, a smaller, intact version, can be seen at the model village just off the square in West Street. This superbly accurate replica is built from the same Purbeck stone as the real thing and the details of the miniature medieval folk about their daily business are wonderful. Situated in beautiful gardens, it makes a real treat for anyone with a penchant for the little things in life!

POOLE   *Map 4 ref J24*

Once the largest town in Dorset, this is now a pleasant, bustling harbour town. Its natural harbour is said to be one of the largest in the world and is a perfect haven for all types of watercraft. It seems appropriate that the town should be the headquarters of the Royal National Lifeboat Institution. The **Maritime Museum** tells all there is to know about the seafaring history of the town, while the **Waterfront and Scalpen's Court Museum** is the place to visit to view the local archaeological finds.

The old town, which is now a conservation area, lies behind the Quay and a stroll round its narrow streets is like stepping back into the Georgian era. Poole is also, of course, a major holiday destination and the great attraction for many visitors is the stretch of golden sand at the entrance to the harbour. Sandbanks is considered to be one of the finest bathing spots on the south coast and it is made even more attractive by the fact that Poole benefits from a double high tide, providing around 14 hours of high water every day. Ferries travel back and forth across Poole Harbour from Poole Quay and Sandbanks, taking visitors to **Brownsea Island** and its 500 acres of heath and woodland. Owned by the National Trust since 1962, the island has a nature reserve and bird sanctuary on its northeastern side, while to the southeast lies **Branksea Castle**, built by Henry VIII to defend the harbour. Brownsea Island is also the place where the first Boy Scout camp was held by Lord Baden Powell in 1907.

On Canford Cliffs to the east of the town is **Compton Acres**; the gardens have a reputation as being some of Europe's finest. Planning began in 1919 but it took several years for the gardens to evolve. They feature many rare plants, both tropical and subtropical, enhanced with the collection of statues in bronze and marble, together with lead figures from all over the world. The Japanese Garden is reputed to be the only completely genuine Japanese garden in Europe and equally delightful are the Italian Garden, Woodland Walk and Glen, Palm Court, Rock and Water Gardens and the Heather Dell.

BOURNEMOUTH   *Map 4 ref K24*

This is a sophisticated town well used to pleasing visitors on a grand scale. With fine hotels, sandy beaches, excellent quality entertainment and superb shopping facilities, this is very much a five star resort. Queen Victoria enjoyed her vacations here and the town retains an air of 19th century grandeur to this day. It was the coming of the railway in 1870 that allowed Bournemouth to develop its potential as a holiday centre and the town is famous for the three deep valleys, or chines, that cut through the cliffs and provide shady pine-filled groves through which there are pleasant strolls down to the beach.

Bournemouth has a number of excellent museums covering a wide range of subjects that should appeal to a variety of tastes: the **Rusell-Cotes Art Gallery and Museum** features the diverse collection of artefacts built up by Sir Merton Rusell-Cotes during his extensive travels, and includes the last remaining Bath chair in the town, Buddhist shrines, an aquarium and a fascinating assortment of sculptures. The **Rothesay Museum** has a mainly nautical theme, but also includes the **British Typewriter Museum** with over 300 typewriters going back as far as 1864. The **Casa Magni Shelley Museum** is the only museum in the world entirely devoted to the life and works of Percy Bysshe Shelley and it is housed in Shelley House where the poet's son lived from 1849 to 1889. Shelley's wife, Mary—the gentle English rose who somehow managed to dream up the Gothic horror of *Frankenstein*—lies buried in the parish church.

BLANDFORD FORUM   *Map 4 ref J23*

Beautifully situated in the wooded valley of the River Stour, this has been a crossing point for many centuries. It is an interesting town and, considering that it had to suffer the trauma of a great fire in 1731, there is still a lot of pleasing architecture (albeit now mainly Georgian) to be seen. The fire was said to have started in the tallow-chandler's cottage and rapidly spread, the burning thatch being carried on the breeze to the neighbouring villages of Bryanston and Blandford St Mary. Two brothers, the local architects John and William Bastard sought to repair the damage and undertook large scale rebuilding programme. Some buildings, however, managed to survive the inferno including the Ryves Almshouses, the Corn Exchange and the splendid Old House in the Close.

Over Blandford bridge, on the opposite bank of the Stour, are the wooded slopes of **Bryanston Park**. The great mansion that was built here in 1890 for Viscount Portman is now a public school. Local legend insists that the family's fall in fortune was partly due to the fact that in demolishing the original house to build the new one, they inadvertently disturbed the spirit of Aunt Charlotte and brought bad luck upon their own heads. Another superstition which they unwisely ignored decreed that were the resident peacocks to vacate the premises the family would do so too. Lo and behold, the peacocks were sold, the 3rd Viscount died and the Portmans sold the house and part of the estate!

BEAMINSTER   *Map 4 ref H23*

In Hardy's novel when Tess arrived in Beaminster, or Emminster as it was to her, she found a delightful little market town. Nothing much has changed: the 17th century almshouse, the fine hamstone church with its ornamented tower and the charming Market Square with its stone roofed market cross are now much the same as they were more than a century ago. Rope and sailcloth, embroidered buttons, shoes, wrought ironwork and clockmaking are just some of the industries that once thrived here.

The Greyhound Inn

The Greyhound Inn is a fine example of a town pub, excellently situated in the town's historic square. Originally a cottage, this establishment now ranks with the very best of English public houses, not only because of the warmth of welcome which all visitors receive, but also because of the wide variety of ales which are served. Food is also available and is of an excellent standard. Be sure to try one of the fish dishes for which the Greyhound is locally renowned. A hidden place not to be missed.

The Greyhound Inn, The Square, Beaminster, Dorset DT8 3AW
Tel: 01308 862496

Conveniently located on Hogshill Street, close to the Square, is **Jenny Wren's**, a bed and breakfast establishment and tea shop of the highest calibre. The comfortable guest rooms are well appointed, one has a four poster bed, and have en-suite facilities. All rooms have colour television and tea and coffee making facilities. The 17th century tea shop offers a fine range of light meals, teas and snacks and is just the place to stop for refreshments whilst exploring this delightful town.

Jenny Wren's

Jenny Wren's, 1 Hogshill Street, Beaminster, Dorsest DT8 3AE
Tel: 01308 862814

Whilst in the area be sure to call in at **The New Inn**, a fine pub with a wonderful atmosphere. Nestling about six miles from the coast at **Stoke Abbott**, this friendly 17th century thatched inn is the ideal centre for walks in the surrounding rolling countryside. The bar has around 200 horse brasses covering its beams, as well as wheelback chairs and cushioned built in settles around simple wooden tables, and settles built into snug stripped stone alcoves on either side of the big log fireplace. A fine selection of well kept ales can be enjoyed in these relaxing surroundings. There is a nonsmoking dining room serving excellent food which is very good value for money. The inn is closed on Mondays except for Bank Holidays. This truly is a hidden place not to be missed.

The New Inn

The New Inn, Stoke Abbott, near Beaminster, Dorset DT8 3JW
Tel: 01308 868333

BROADWINDSOR   *Map 4 ref H23*

A plaque on the wall of a house in the Square commemorates the fact that Charles II, disguised as an ostler, stopped off here for an overnight stay in 1651 as he fled from Worcester to Charmouth.

The Broadwindsor Craft and Design Centre

Situated on the edge of this delightful village, in the rolling countryside of west Dorset, the **Broadwindsor Craft and Design Centre** has been developed from what were once farm buildings into a range of shops, workshops and studios for local artists and craftsmen. This is the ideal place to purchase a gift or stop for a delicious meal or snack. The award winning restaurant serves a bewildering choice of pastries and cakes—Dorset cream teas are a speciality that should not be missed.

The Broadwindsor Craft and Design Centre, Broadwindsor, Dorset DT8 3PX Tel: 01308 868362

FORDE ABBEY   *Map 4 ref H23*

Situated in the beautiful valley of the River Axe, right on the Somerset border, **Forde Abbey** dates back to 1138 but was completed much later in the 15th century. A Cistercian order was founded here and the building survived the Dissolution surprisingly intact, losing only the great abbey church. The abbey was converted to a private house in 1650 by Sir Edward Prideaux, Cromwell's Attorney General, and is still privately owned today. Virtually unaltered since its conversion, the house contains a superb collection of furniture, tapestries and pictures and deserves several hours out of a busy schedule to absorb all that is here. Not only is the house, gardens, lakes and magnificent parkland open to the public but there is also Forde Abbey Fruit Gardens where visitors can pick their own fruit.

LYME REGIS   *Map 4 ref H24*

The importance of Lyme Regis as a port is entirely due to the **Cobb**, a dog-leg breakwater which was built in the 13th century to provide safe harbour for ships along this otherwise dangerous part of the coast. The Cobb is a place with romantic associations and is described in the famous novel *The French Lieutenant's Woman* as being the most beautiful sea rampart on the south coast because of its long and illustrious history (it is from here that English ships sailed to meet the Spanish Armada) and because it is a superb example of folk art. Another writer who fell in love with Lyme was Jane Austen, who visited the town from Bath. In her novel *Persuasion*, the character Louisa Musgrove fell off the steeply slopping Cobb into the sea.

The beach at Lyme is well known for its fossils but do remember that the cliffs are dangerous and are liable to constant subsidence, especially after bad weather. The **Philpot Museum** near the Guildhall has a comprehensive display of local fossils and, in the parish church, there is a window dedicated to Mary Anning. Mary was born in 1799 and, at the age of 11, she discovered in the blue limestone around Lyme the first complete skeleton of an ichthyosaurus which can now be seen in the Natural History Museum, London. Later on she found the first plesiosaur and the flying reptile. Another place to find out about the local fossils is at Peter Langham's **Dinosaurland** in Coombe Street. The exhibitions are mainly devoted to the Jurassic period of 195 million years ago, when the cliffs of Lyme were being formed.

The town is quite charming with its colourful seafront cottages and most visitors quickly fall under its spell. August is the month when the locals pull out all the stops with the Regatta and Carnival and various sporting events and races are held on sea and sand. Today's visitors may be surprised to learn that Lyme was, at one time, one of the most important ports in England. Five ships sailed from here in 1588 to join the battle against the Spanish Armada and, in 1685, the Duke of Monmouth landed on what is now called Monmouth Beach, announcing his intention to take the throne. Lyme's decline as a port came with the silting up of the harbour and the increasing size of seagoing vessels. Today it is far better suited to yachtsmen and fishing boats and seems quite happy to prosper as a place for visitors to enjoy a relaxing holiday.

St Michael's Hotel is an elegant Georgian house which retains all of the charm and atmosphere of a bygone age. This delightful hidden place is ideally situated

St Michael's Hotel

England

for a holiday or short break in this part of the country. The hotel enjoys panoramic views of the coastal scenery of Lyme Bay and is within walking distance of the famous Cobb, the town and the beach. The accommodation is of a commendably high standard and many rooms have en-suite facilities.
St Michael's Hotel, Pound Street, Lyme Regis, Dorset DT7 3HZ
Tel: 01297 442503

Just to the north lies **Uplyme** and the **Devon Hotel**, Uplyme's old Rectory, with early records dating back to AD 774. The hotel stands in its own landscaped gardens and is situated in this picturesque village, only five minutes drive from the coast. Records show that this historic manor house began as a monastery until 938 when King Athelston granted Uplyme Manor to Glastonbury Abbey and is later referred to in The Glebe Terriers of 1680 as The Parsonage House. In the latter period the manor became Uplyme's Rectory, with its ornate 16 foot fireplace and hammer vaulted ceiling bearing heraldic shields.

The Devon Hotel

This exquisite hotel has been owned and personally run by Richard and Fiona for over two decades and it is down to their expertise and commitment that a stay here will be a relaxing and enjoyable one. All of the individually decorated and furnished bedrooms have full en-suite facilities and offer all the modern conveniences including colour television, telephone and complimentary beverage tray. Guests can also enjoy the solarium, gymnasium, games room and putting green, relax in the elegant and ornately decorated lounges, or sunbathe beside the swimming pool situated in the hotel's extensive grounds. Nothing has been overlooked to make a stay here memorable, tasteful decor, beautiful gardens, excellent cuisine and superb service, the Devon Hotel offers a unique chance to experience tranquillity amidst the most historic surroundings.
The Devon Hotel, Uplyme, near Lyme Regis, Dorset DT7 3TQ
Tel: 01297 443231 Fax: 01297 445836

Situated close to the famous fossil beach, **Lydwell Guest House** offers a high standard of bed and breakfast accommodation at the most affordable prices. This is a picturesque old house set in a superb garden which features its own well. The atmosphere is both warm and friendly and the standard of food served is of the highest order. All of the letting rooms are comfortable, spacious and well equipped and en-suite facilities are available.

Lydwell Guest House

Lydwell Guest House, Lyme Road, Uplyme, near Lyme Regis, Dorset DT7 3TQ Tel: 01227 443522

CHARMOUTH   *Map 4 ref H24*

This village marks the beginning of fossil country and a visit to the **Fossils and Country Life Museum** is recommended. This is a pleasant coastal village with a fine sandy beach at low tide and it was one of Jane Austen's favourite places. When Charles II eventually reached Charmouth on his flight from Worcester, he stayed for a time at the Queen's Arms Inn. His intention to escape from here by boat to France was foiled when Cromwell's spies learnt of his presence in the village and he was forced to flee on horseback instead.

This is understandably one of the most popular parts of the country to base a holiday. The unspoilt countryside is ideal for walking and the many places of interest and the fine beaches all make for a very varied and interesting vacation. For those looking for high class accommodation, well placed for all of these attractions, then look no further than **Dolphins River Park**.

Situated on the banks of the River Char, close to the famous fossil beach, this fine park offers luxury fully self-contained holiday caravans, all equipped to a very high standard and attractively sited. The park has its own small, but well stocked shop, a fully equipped laundry room, a public telephone, a table tennis room and

Dolphins River Park

a children's play area. The park is very well kept and efficiently run, with a friendly, happy atmosphere—be sure to put it at the top of the list when deciding on a holiday location. Situated just off the A35 between Bridport and Lyme Regis.

Dolphins River Park, Berne Lane, Charmouth, Dorset DT6 6RD
Tel: 01297 560022 or 01308 868180

Enjoying magnificent views from the Chard valley to the sea at Lyme Bay is **Higher Pound Farm**. Offering a very high standard of holiday accommodation in seven self-contained cottages which have recently been converted from what were farm buildings. The cottages vary in size and are able to accommodate groups as large as six, thus making them ideal for families. Each cottage has gas

Higher Pound Holiday Cottages

central heating, a lounge, colour television and well equipped modern kitchen complete with refrigerator, microwave and cooker. Children will particularly enjoy the safe play area which has swings, a Wendy house and an adventure climbing frame. Tame sheep, Kunekune pigs and Shetland ponies graze fields over which visitors may wander.

The farm also boasts a superb riding centre. The **Higher Pound Riding Centre** has a range of horses from Shetlands to Shires which cater for riders and would-be riders of all ages and abilities. In addition to some of the most beautiful countryside in the area which is suitable for horse riding, indoor tuition is available. Whether 'starting from scratch' or already an experienced rider, everyone can be sure of helpful expert advice and encouragement. For further information or to book rides please contact 01297 678747 or fax 01297 678730. *Higher Pound Holiday Cottages, Monkton Wylde, Charmouth, Dorset DT6 6DD Tel: 01297 678345 Fax: 01297 678730*

Higher Spence

Situated on the edge of Charmouth Forest at **Wootton Fitzpaine**, stands **Higher Spence**, an attractive bed and breakfast establishment that boasts spectacular sea and country views. This recently restored 300 year old farm cottage is set in its own expansive gardens, which occasionally attracts visits from wild deer, foxes and badgers who have wandered from the seclusion of the surrounding forest. There are two well appointed rooms available in this family home and the hosts, Christine and Peter, pride themselves on the warm welcome that they extend to all their guests. No smoking. Pets welcomed. *Higher Spence, Wootton Fitzpaine, near Charmouth, Dorset DT6 6DF Tel: 01297 560556*

CHIDEOCK   *Map 4 ref H24*

Mentioned in the Domesday Book, this village was home to the Chideock Martyrs; a group of Catholics who refused to conform to the new Church of England and were tried and sentenced to death. Chideock was also the headquarters of Colonel Fairfax, Cromwell's general during the Civil War. Of the 14th century castle only the moat remains, the rest being destroyed during the Civil War.

Situated in the picturesque, mainly thatched cob village of Chideock in an outstanding area of west Dorset stands **Betchworth House**. This charming 17th century house is owned and personally run by Ann and Bob and offers its guests a choice of six en-suite double, twin and single rooms, each offering excellent facilities and attractive views. The house is furnished throughout with antique and traditional furniture and Ann and Bob's warm welcome will guarantee that

Betchworth House

their guest's break will be a comfortable and relaxing one. All guests are greeted by a freshly prepared and cooked English breakfast which is served in the attractive dining room, whilst in the pretty cottage garden and attractive tea rooms morning coffee, vegetarian specials and Dorset cream teas are served throughout the day.

Betchworth House, Main Street, Chideock, Dorset DT6 6JW
Tel: 01297 489478

Situated in the centre of Chideock is **Chimneys Guest House**, one of the best places to base a stay in the area. A lovely 17th century cottage, with a thatched roof and period decor, all guests can be sure of a warm welcome and a relaxing stay. A choice of five rooms is available and all are well appointed and very

Chimneys Guest House

comfortable. There is also a Bridal Suite with a four poster bed. This is a lovely part of the country in which to spend a romantic break and Chimneys is a delightful hidden place with much to recommend it.

Chimneys Guest House, Main Street, Chideock, Dorset BT6 6JH
Tel: 01297 489368

BRIDPORT   *Map 4 ref H24*

The pleasant town is famous for the Bridport dagger, otherwise known as the hangman's noose! The rope-making industry was a vital part of the town's economy and nets are still made there today. Flax and hemp flourished in the Marshwood Vale and the origins of the industry here go back as far as the early 13th century. The ropes were not just used for executions but also for the navy and fishing fleets—so famous were Bridport's cordage ropes and twine that Newfoundland fishermen requested it specifically. The streets of the town are noticeably broad and this is said to be a direct result of the space required to make rope in the old-fashioned way—ropewalks were laid out where the lengths of hemp could be twisted to make the finished product. The **Bridport Museum** has a large section on this fascinating subject.

Bridport bustles as all good hard working coastal towns should do and, in addition to its lively street market, it has some interesting backstreets and hidden alleyways to explore.

The West Point Tavern, standing on the magnificent Esplanade and facing the sandy west beach, has become one of the most popular places in this secluded bay. Owned and personally run by Bea and Don Slade, visitors can enjoy a tasty

bar snack and beers from the newly constructed cellar which are kept in superb condition. The restaurant seats over 60 and offers everything from snacks to substantial meals. Be sure to try the fine steak or chicken dishes, for they are a great speciality. Musical entertainment is provided throughout the year on Saturday nights and also on Fridays during July and August.

Accommodation of a commendably high standard is available here; there are five double or twin rooms, all lavishly appointed and enjoying magnificent sea views through wall-to-wall double glazed windows. There is also a fully self-contained flat which is able to

The West Point Tavern

accommodate six people and is the ideal base for a fulfilling family holiday.

The West Point Tavern, The Esplanade, West Bay, Bridport, Dorset
DT6 4HG Tel: 01308 423636

Situated in a secluded and peaceful spot just to the north of Bridport in the village of **Symondsbury**, where nearly every building is of the local golden sandstone, is **The Ilchester Arms**; a traditional English pub with a fascinating history and a fine reputation. Its exact date of construction is difficult to ascertain but

The Ilchester Arms

evidence points to 1325 as being a likely date for the original building. Much has altered since then, of course, but one thing which can always be relied upon is the warmth of welcome and quality of ale which is served. A high standard of food is available and, for those who wish to take a short break in the area, bed and breakfast accommodation is available. A hidden place not to be missed.
The Ilchester Arms, Symondsbury, near Bridport, Dorset DT6 6HD
Tel: 01308 422600

The New Inn

Situated in the centre of the lovely village of **Shipton Gorge**, to the south of Bridport, is a very pleasant country pub which offers a good choice of beers and fine food. **The New Inn** is managed and run by Susan and Keith and together they have turned it into one of the best pubs in the area. The food is all home-cooked and offers very good value for money, the atmosphere is warm and welcoming and anyone visiting will certainly not be disappointed.
The New Inn, Shipton Lane, Shipton Gorge, near Bridport, Dorset DT6 4LT
Tel: 01308 897302

ABBOTSBURY
Map 4 ref I24

Lying at the western tip of **Chesil Beach**, this is one of the county's most popular tourist spots and, by any standards, one of the loveliest villages in England. The village is truly ancient, predating even the Domesday Book and, until the Dissolution, it was the site of a thriving Benedictine Abbey. All that remains of the abbey today is the splendid **Tithe Barn** which measures 272 feet by 31 feet, making it one of the largest of its kind in the country.

Abbotsbury is associated in old tales with St Catherine and a 14th century chapel dedicated to her stands high above the village on a hill. Those women with a burning desire to be married would climb the hill and seek assistance from their patron saint by chanting the following lines: "Sweet, St Catherine; A Husband, St Catherine; Handsome, St Catherine; Rich, St Catherine; Soon, St Catherine."

Perhaps the main attraction of Abbotsbury is the unique **Swannery** that lies to the south of the village. It is the only nesting colony of mute swans in Britain, providing a safe habitat for up to 500 in summer and twice as many in winter. Once bred for the Abbot's table, these distinguished birds have nested here for hundreds of years, sharing their habitat with many other varieties of birds and waterfowl.

Close by are the **Subtropical Gardens**, the original walled gardens of Abbotsbury Castle, which itself no longer stands. They are situated in a hollow away from the rigorous winds that sweep Lyme Bay. This is a massive collection, comprising over 7000 species of exotic plants and trees, many of which have grown to phenomenal size. It is amazing to see certain varieties of plants thriving here that would be expected to grow only in greenhouse conditions. However, the Chesil Bank and surrounding oak trees keep the frost at bay and rhododendrons, camellias and azaleas flourish.

Three miles northeast of the village is the gorse and heather-covered summit of **Black Down**, which rises 777 feet above sea level and affords splendid views in all directions. The summit is crowned by a rather unprepossessing octagonal tower, looking for all the world like a giant chimney. It is dedicated to Thomas Masterman Hardy—no relation to his literary namesake—for it was in his arms that our great seafaring hero, Lord Nelson, expired. The monument stands 70 feet high above Black Down and acts as a landmark to sailors, a fitting tribute to Hardy who was to become an Admiral towards the end of his career. He was born at Kingston Russell House to the west and lived as a boy in his "beloved Possum", or Portesham, at the foot of the hill.

There are many standing stones and prehistoric tumuli in the immediate area. **Kingston Russell** stone circle is not particularly spectacular in itself, though it is quite unusual to find a site like this so near the sea, and it is worth a visit for the pleasant and undemanding walk across the downs.

Somerset

INTRODUCTION

On the northernmost boundary of the county lies Bristol, the largest town of southwest England and a busy industrial and commercial centre. Just a few miles to the southeast lies Bath, a peaceful place of elegant Georgian architecture, whose history as a spa town goes back to Roman times. Separating these two centres from much of the rest of the county are the Mendip Hills. As they are limestone, the hills are full of holes, with caves and potholes and streams that disappear underground.

The Mendips are also home to the well known caves at Wookey Hole and the spectacular Cheddar Gorge which carves a path through them as well as lending its name to the cheese. The city of Wells, below the hills, is a charming old town and from here the county's plain stretches out to Glastonbury and on to Taunton near the boundary with Devon. Somerset also has a long coastline with many popular seaside resorts such as Weston-Super-Mare and Watchet.

In the far northwest corner of the county, and straddling the border with Devon, can be found the smallest national park in the country—**Exmoor**. With dramatic coastal cliffs, rolling heather moorland and secluded wooded valleys, Exmoor, though often overlooked for its larger neighbour, Dartmoor, has a character and charm all its own. This was once wild hunting country and its abundance of prehistoric sites, ancient packhorse bridges and wild deer and ponies, easily makes it one of the more romantic and mysterious parts of the country. Not surprisingly, this countryside inspired the writer RD Blackmoor and fans of his novel, *Lorna Doone*, are drawn to the area to visit the places he describes.

BRISTOL   *Map 3 ref I20*

The city was founded during Saxon times at the point where the River Frome curved to join the River Avon. This strategically important bridging point, at the head of the Avon gorge, soon became a prominent port and market centre and, by the early 11th century, it had its own mint and was trading with other ports throughout western England, Wales and Ireland. In 1067, the Normans began work on a massive stone keep which stood between the present day floating harbour and Newgate, a site which is still known as **Castle Park** despite the almost total demolition of the structure at the end of the Civil War. The heart of the old city lies to the west of here around the point where Corn, Broad, Wine and High streets converge.

A third of a mile further west, Bristol's **Anglican Cathedral** stands on College Green. Founded in the 12th century as the great church of an Augustinian abbey, several original Norman features remain, including the southeast transept walls, the chapter house, the gatehouse, and the eastern side of the delightful enclosed cloisters. Elsewhere there is some good 14th century stained glass and a series of striking roof bosses in the north transept. Following the Dissolution of the Monasteries in 1539, Henry VIII took the unusual step of elevating the church to the status of a cathedral and, soon after, the richly carved choir stalls were added; the superb organ case was carved by Grinling Gibbons over a century later. The building was not fully completed until the 19th century when a nave was built to match the choir in sympathetic style. This area contains some exceptional monuments and tombs, as well as a pair of unusual candlesticks which were donated in 1712 by the rescuers of Alexander Selkirk, the actual castaway on whom Daniel Defoe's character, Robinson Crusoe, was modelled.

Bristol expanded enormously as a trading centre during the medieval period and, at one time, it was second only to London as a seaport. Its trade was based largely on the export of raw wool and woollen cloth from the Mendip and Cotswold hills and the import of wines from Spain and southwest France. The city's first major wharf development was carried out during this period: the diverting of the River Frome from its original course into the wide artificial channel now known as St Augustine's Reach.

A stroll around Bristol city centre reveals an unusual number of interesting historical buildings. Queen Square, to the northwest of Redcliffe Bridge, is lined with handsome early 18th century buildings, although two sides had to be rebuilt following their destruction in a riot in 1831. The **Theatre Royal** in King Street is the home of the Bristol Old Vic theatre company and is said to be the oldest theatre in the country still in regular use; it was built in the 1760s with a semicircular auditorium, a rare feature for the time. At the end of the street stands a timber framed merchant's house of 1669 known as **Llandoger Trow** and, continuing northwards into the area once contained within the city walls, **The Exchange** in Corn Street was built in the 1740s by the architect, John Wood the Elder, whose work is much in evidence at Bath.

Other noteworthy buildings include **The Red Lodge** in Park Row, a house containing the only remaining 16th century domestic interior in Bristol. Part of the Bristol Museums and Art Gallery, The Red Lodge was built for a wealthy gentleman, Sir John Younge, together with a similar building called the White Lodge. With few alterations made during its lifetime, today it boasts one of the finest Tudor oak panelled rooms in the whole of the West Country.

The impressive **Melbourne's Restaurant** is situated in Bristol's famous Park Street, not far from the City Museum and Art Gallery. As might be expected from its name, this lively eating place offers the best in Australian-style cooking. It has come a long way in the few years since Tony and Nick took it over and most days it is filled with enthusiastic diners wanting a change from the usual restaurant atmosphere. The stylish interior is decorated with Australiana in every direction and there is a pleasant feeling of space, with seating for up to 100 diners. The bar serves exclusive Red Back beer, brewed and shipped directly from Freemantle, Western Australia. (A redback is an Australian spider which, like the beer, packs quite a bite.) A glance at the menu soon starts the taste buds tingling. The choice is superb, with unusual starters like warm tartlet of broccoli, leeks and vegetarian cheese or house-style gravadlax marinated in fresh lime juice and fennel. Main courses include a selection of lamb, pork and chicken

Melbourne's Restaurant

dishes, and the mouthwatering desserts include profiteroles with cream and hot chocolate sauce. An excellent opportunity to taste fine national cooking without obvious stereotypes, Melbourne's is open every lunchtime and evening (except Sunday evening and Monday lunch).

Melbourne's Restaurant, 74 Park Street, Bristol, Somerset BS1 5JX
Tel: 0117 922 6996

BATH   *Map 3 ref I21*

One of the most remarkable cities in Britain, Bath is a glorious assembly of architectural set pieces and less spectacular buildings which have been constructed since the time of the ancient Romans around the only thermal springs in the country. Since time immemorial, over half a million gallons of water a day have bubbled to the surface here at the constant temperature of 46°C. The Celts believed that the mysterious steaming spring which emerged from within a great curve of the River Avon was the domain of the goddess Sulis, and it is likely that they were aware of its healing properties long before the arrival of the Romans in AD 43. However, it was the new arrivals who first enclosed the spring and created the spectacular health resort known as Aquae Sulis, a name coined as a diplomatic gesture to the local population they now controlled.

With the possible exception of Hadrian's Wall, the great **Roman Baths** are the most outstanding monument to the Roman Empire to survive in Britain. After remaining buried under seven feet of mud for centuries they were only rediscovered in the late 19th century and their full extent did not become apparent until the 1920s. (Ironically, they had remained hidden throughout the whole of Bath's 18th century renaissance as a spa town.) The complex of buildings which can be visited today is centred around the Great Bath, a lead lined rectangular pool which is surrounded by steps and the truncated remains of a colonnaded quadrangle.

The population of Bath fell away during the Dark Ages, and it was not until the 8th century that the Saxons founded a nunnery. This was later elevated to monastic statues when King Edgar of Wessex chose to be crowned here in 973. The present great church of **Bath Abbey** was begun in 1499 after its Norman predecessor had been destroyed by fire. However, the new building was not finished before the Dissolution halted work in 1539. The building then remained without a roof for 75 years and it was not fully completed until 1901.

Roman Baths, Bath

One tablet in the abbey stands as a memorial to Richard 'Beau' Nash, a legendary Bath figure who was one of the three people generally considered to be responsible for creating the fashionable Georgian spa town. Prior to Nash's arrival in the early 1700s, Bath had been a squalid community of around 2000 inhabitants whose former prosperity as a medieval wool town had all but disappeared. Even so, small numbers of the rich and aristocratic continued to be attracted to Bath for its curative hot spring and, in the mid-17th century, the corporation finally took action to improve sanitary conditions, an initiative which was rewarded in 1702 by a visit from Queen Anne.

Nash, a man of great elegance and style, took on the job of cleaning up the city. Despite having been something of a reprobate himself—he only came to Bath in an attempt to earn his living as a gambler—he rose to become Bath's Master of

Ceremonies, an unpaid yet highly influential position to which he ascended when the previous MC was killed in a duel. He pressurised the authorities into paving, cleaning and lighting the streets, he outlawed duelling and the wearing of swords and he set about creating a relaxed social atmosphere in which the gentry (the landed middle-class) could mix on equal terms with their social superiors (the aristocracy). Under his guidance, Bath became elegant and fashionable and soon began to attract significant numbers of the 'right people', not only patrons, but also the architects and entrepreneurs who shared Nash's grand vision for the city. The **Assembly Rooms** was one of the places where polite 18th century society congregated to dance, play cards or just be seen. After having been severely damaged by World War II bombs, the building was reopened in 1963 and now incorporates an interesting **Museum of Costume**.

Among those sharing Nash's enthusiasm was architect John Wood who, along with his son (also called John), was responsible for designing most of the city's finest neoclassical squares and terraces. These include North and South Parades, Queen Square, The Circus, and most notably, **Royal Crescent**; John Wood the Younger's Palladian masterpiece was the first terrace in Britain to be built to an elliptical design. The Royal Crescent was built between 1767 and 1774 in a style which is both majestic and conservative. The huge sweep of the Crescent comprises 30 houses of three or four bays, each of which are divided by a giant Ionic half column. The Crescent when first built looked out over unspoilt countryside which was later developed as part of the expanding 19th century city. At the beginning of the last century many of the windows in the crescent were enlarged and glazing bars replaced by plate glass windows. Number One, however, provides an opportunity to see how the correctly proportioned windows would have been before these changes. It was scrupulously restored by the Bath Preservation Trust in the late 1960s, both outside and inside and subsequently opened to the public in 1970.

Bath's third 18th century founding father was Ralph Allen, an entrepreneur who made his first fortune developing an efficient postal system for the provinces and who then went on to make a second one as the owner of the local quarries which supplied most of the honey-coloured Bath stone to the city's Georgian building sites. One final building worth of note is the magnificent **Pulteney Bridge**, the only example of the work of Robert Adam in Bath. Inspired by Florence's Ponte Vecchio, it is the only bridge in Britain to incorporate a terrace of buildings.

Bath also contains several specialist museums and galleries. The **Victorian Art Gallery**, near Pulteney Bridge, is the city's principal venue for major touring exhibitions; there is also a permanent collection of classical paintings and a smaller gallery displaying work from the area. The **British Folk Art Collection**, in the Paragon, is an exceptional collection of 18th and 19th century paintings which show a 'direct simplicity'. On the same site is the **Building of Bath Museum**, a fascinating display of models and illustrations which bring to life the city's unique architectural evolution. The first known mailing of a Penny Black postage stamp was made in 1840 at No 8 Broad Street, now the site of the **Bath Postal Museum**; exhibits include a reconstruction of a Victorian sorting office and a children's activity room. The **Bath Industrial Heritage Centre**, in Julian Road, is a recreation of an aerated water manufactory which provides an insight into the city's traditional industries.

On the northern edge of the city, Lansdown Road leads up to the summit of Lansdown, the location of one of the most remarkable follies in Britain. **Beckford's Tower** was built in the 1820s for the wealthy and eccentric scholar, William Beckford, to house his extensive collection of works of art. Visitors climbing the 156 steps to the belvedere are rewarded with a magnificent view stretching from the Black Mountains of Wales to the Wiltshire Downs.

The Wife of Bath is one of Chaucer's most colourful characters in The Canterbury Tales and, here, can be found her namesake, the delightful **Wife of Bath Restaurant**. It is located in a spacious basement converted from the cellars of a building dating from around 1740 which was constructed on the site of the abbey orchard. Mr and Mrs Ensom have been in business here since 1972 and, over the years, the Wife of Bath has certainly lost none of her character and charm!

The Wife of Bath Restaurant

The 80 seater restaurant is beautifully decorated, with a magnificent feature mirror which immediately draws the attention. There is also a small patio area which is perfect for sitting out on a warm day or summer's evening. The menu offers an impressive range of meat, fish and vegetarian dishes, including such delights as fresh shellfish au gratin, and Madeira and mushroom pasta, a vegetarian option that will appeal to all. There is also an impressive range of drinks, including wines, cocktails, draught beers and elderflower pressé. A popular eating place with visitors and residents alike, this is a restaurant to seek out when visiting the city.

The Wife of Bath Restaurant, 12 Pierrepont Street, Bath, Somerset BA1 1LA Tel: 01225 461745

SHEPTON MALLET   *Map 3 ref I22*

An important centre of communications since pre-Roman times, this old market town lies on the River Sheppey, a little to the west of the Fosse Way, the old Roman route which at this point comprises a stretch of the modern A37. The settlement's Saxon name, which means simply 'sheep town', reveals its main commercial activity during the pre-Norman and medieval periods, originally as a centre of wool production and later as a weaving town. The industry reached its peak in the 15th century and it was then that Shepton Mallet's magnificent parish church was constructed.

Perhaps Shepton Mallet's most characteristic structure, however, is its 50 foot **Market Cross**. Built around 1500 and restored in 1841, it has been the town's civic and commercial hub for almost 500 years. Indeed, a lively modern market continues to be held here every Friday. Several participants in the Duke of Monmouth's ill-fated Pitchfork Rebellion were executed at the cross in 1685 on the orders of the infamous Judge Jeffreys.

WELLS   *Map 3 ref I21*

This ancient ecclesiastical centre, with a population of under 10,000, is the smallest city in England and, were it not for its cathedral and neighbouring bishop's palace, it would be unlikely to be more than an attractive small market town. However, the magnificent **Cathedral of St Andrew**, the first entirely Gothic structure of its kind in Britain and its adjacent cathedral close undoubtedly make this one of the gems of north Somerset.

Deriving its name from a line of springs which rises from the base of the Mendips, King Ine of the West Saxons is believed to have founded the first church at Wells around AD 700. After a diocesan tussle with Bath, the present cathedral was begun in the 12th century and took over three centuries to complete.

The 52 acre cathedral close is a tranquil city within a city. Indeed for many centuries, Wells functioned as two distinct entities: the ecclesiastical city and civic city. At that time, the parishioners were not welcomed into the cathedral and instead had to listen to the choir through strategically placed holes in the cathedral walls. Similarly, the clergymen who died in the Black Death were buried under the cathedral green rather than in the town graveyard. The green itself is surrounded by a high wall which is breached at only three castellated entrance points. The **Vicars' Close**, one of the oldest planned streets in Europe, lies on the northern side of the cathedral green. This remarkable cobbled thoroughfare was built in the mid 14th century, although the ornate chimneys were added a century later. Originally intended for cathedral choristers, it is still occupied by officers of the cathedral.

The fortified **Bishop's Palace** is situated in an adjoining site to the south of the cathedral cloisters. This remarkable medieval building is surrounded by a moat which is fed by the springs which give the city its name. The palace is enclosed within a high stone wall and, in order to gain access from the Market Place, it is necessary to pass under a 13th century arch known as the Bishop's Eye and then cross a drawbridge which was last raised for defensive purposes in 1831. For those keen to find out more about the history of the locality, **Wells Museum**, near the west front of the cathedral, contains an interesting collection of locally found artefacts.

WOOKEY HOLE   *Map 3 ref I21*

Throughout the centuries, the carboniferous limestone core of the Mendip Hills has been gradually dissolved by the small amount of carbonic acid in rainwater, an effect which has turned cracks into fissures, fissures into underground rivers and, on rare occasions, underground rivers into immense subterranean caverns such as these. During the Palaeolithic and subsequent eras, Wookey Hole was lived in by wild animals such as lions, bears and woolly mammoths. Evidence of their occupation is supported by the large cache of prehistoric mammals' bones which was discovered in a recess known as the Hyena's Den, many of them showing the animals' teeth marks. There is also evidence of human occupation during the Iron Age. In total, there are over 25 caverns, although only the largest half dozen are open to visitors. The Great Cave contains a rock formation known as the Witch of Wookey which casts a ghostly shadow and is associated with gruesome legends of child-eating.

The river emerging from Wookey Hole, the Axe, has been harnessed to provide power for industrial use since the 16th century. Originally constructed in the mid-1800s as a paper mill, the present building on the site was acquired in 1973 by Madame Tussaud's who have installed a number of popular visitor attractions. These include an exhibition on the **History of Waxworks**, a **Museum of Fairground Equipment**, and a workshop where paper continues to be produced by hand.

GLASTONBURY   *Map 3 ref I22*

An ancient ecclesiastical centre and a small town with an immense history, Glastonbury is a mecca for those encompassing such diverse beliefs as paganism, Christianity, Arthurian legend and the existence of UFOs. Before the surrounding Somerset Levels were drained in the 18th century, the dramatic form of **Glastonbury Tor** stood out above a great expanse of mist-covered marshland. Known throughout the region as the Isle of Avalon, one of the first outsiders to sail up the River Brue and land at this distinctive conical hill was the early Christian trader, Joseph of Arimathea, who arrived from the Holy Land around AD 60.

According to local legend, Joseph was walking one day on nearby Wearyall Hill when he plunged his staff into the ground. Miraculously, the stick took root and burst into leaf and this he took as a sign he should found a church. A wattle and daub structure was duly erected at the spot which later became the site of the great Glastonbury Abbey. Joseph's staff is reputed to have grown into the celebrated Christmas-flowering Glastonbury hawthorn and, although the original is believed to have been felled during Cromwellian times by an overzealous Puritan (he was blinded by a flying shard of wood in the process, no doubt as a gesture of retribution), one of its windswept ancestors can still be seen on the crest of Wearyall Hill. In an extended version of the legend, Joseph was accompanied on one of his visits to Glastonbury by his nephew, the young Jesus Christ, an occurrence which is reputed to have provided William Blake with the inspiration for his hymn, *Jerusalem*.

Glastonbury Abbey

Along with mystical energy, the tor offers a magnificent panorama across Somerset to Wells, the Mendips, the Quantocks and the Bristol Channel. The view from the top is most breathtaking on a misty day when the tor is surrounded by a sea of silver cloud. The striking tower at the summit is all that remains of the 15th century Church of St Michael, an offshoot of Glastonbury Abbey which fell into disrepair following the Dissolution. In that turbulent year, the tor became a place of execution when the last abbot of Glastonbury, Richard Whiting, and two of his monks were hanged near the summit for opposing the will of Henry VIII.

The wooded rise standing between Glastonbury Tor and the town centre is known as **Chalice Hill**. During one of his visits in the 1st century, Joseph of Arimathea is supposed to have buried the Holy Grail (the cup used by Christ at the Last Supper) beneath a spring which emerges from the foot of the hill's southern slope. The spring forms a natural well which was partially enclosed within a masonry structure during medieval times. This is now situated in an attractive garden maintained by the Chalice Well Trust.

The dramatic remains of **Glastonbury Abbey** can be found to the northwest of Chalice Hill in the heart of the old town. If the legend of Joseph of Arimathea is to be believed, this is the site of the earliest Christian foundation in the British Isles. The abbey is thought to have been founded by King Ine around AD 700 and, under St Dunstan, the 10th century abbot who went on to become the Archbishop of Canterbury, it grew in influence so that by the time of the Norman invasion, it owned estates covering an eighth of the county of Somerset. The abbey continued to grow under the guidance of the Benedictines until a disastrous fire destroyed most of the abbey buildings in 1184.

When the foundations of the replacement great church were being excavated seven years later, a wooden sarcophagus was discovered between the shafts of two ancient crosses. Inside were found the bones of a large man and a slender woman, and one story tells of how the woman's long golden hair seemed in a perfect state of preservation until a monk touched it, transforming it to dust. A lead cross found nearby convinced the abbot that he had discovered the remains of King Arthur and Queen Guinevere, although it was known at the time that this was the burial place of at least three kings from the later, Saxon period. The abbey continued to wield considerable power until Henry VIII's Dissolution of the Monasteries of 1539 forced it to close. The building was abandoned and soon fell into disrepair: its walls were plundered for building stone and Arthur's tomb was destroyed.

The abbey's principal **Tithe Barn** stands on its own to the southeast of the main monastic buildings. Although it is relatively small for such a great estate, it incorporates some fine sculptured detail, notably the carved heads on the corner buttresses and emblems of the four Evangelists on the gables. The barn is now the home of the **Somerset Rural Life Museum**, an imaginatively presented exhibition dedicated to the era of premechanised farming. As well as a collection of historic farm implements, there are special displays devoted to cider making, willow shoot (or withy) cutting, peat digging and thatching.

TAUNTON   *Map 3 ref H22*

The county town of Somerset, Taunton has only been its sole centre of administration since 1936, previous county towns having been Ilchester and Somerton. The settlement was founded as a military camp by the Saxon King Ine in the 8th century and, by Norman times, it had grown to have its own Augustinian monastery, minster and castle. An extensive structure whose purpose has always been more administrative than military, the **Castle** was nevertheless the focus of two important sieges during the English Civil War. A few years later, over 150 followers of the Duke of Monmouth were sentenced to death here by the infamous Judge Jeffreys during the Bloody Autumn Assizes which followed the Pitchfork Rebellion of 1685. Even now, the judge's ghost is said to haunt the castle grounds on September nights.

Today, the much-altered castle houses the **Somerset County Museum**, an informative local museum containing a large collection of exhibits on the archeology and natural history of the county. There is also a special display chronicling the colourful history of the Somerset Light Infantry.

Somerset's famous County Cricket Ground occupies part of the old priory grounds which once stretched down to the river. A section of the old monastic gatehouse known as the Priory Barn can still be seen beside the cricket ground. Now restored, this medieval stone building houses the fascinating **Somerset County Cricket Museum**.

In common with many other towns and villages in the West Country, Taunton was a thriving wool, cloth-making, and later silk, centre during the late Middle Ages. The profits earned by the medieval clothiers went to build not one, but two huge churches: St James' and St Mary's. The town centre is scattered with other fine buildings, most notably the timber-framed Tudor House in Fore Street and the 17th century almshouses.

DUNSTER   *Map 3 ref G22*

This ancient fortified settlement has an almost fairy tale appearance when approached from the southeast, with its huge turreted castle rising above the trees and distinctive ruined folly on nearby Conygar hill. **Dunster Castle** was founded by William de Mohun on a natural promontory above the River Avill a few years before the Domesday Book was compiled in 1086. In 1404, it passed to the Luttrells for the then colossal sum of 5000 marks (about £3300) in whose family it remained until Lt Col GF Luttrell presented the property to the National Trust in 1975.

During the English Civil War, Dunster Castle was one of the last Royalist strongholds in the West Country to fall, the garrison finally surrendering after a siege lasting 160 days. The castle underwent some major alterations during the latter part of the 17th century and some of its finest internal features date from this period. Further changes to the building by Anthony Salvin in the 19th century completed the transformation from castle to country mansion.

Work on the steeply terraced garden with its striking collection of rare shrubs and subtropical plants was also carried out at this time. Dunster Castle is surrounded by an attractive 28 acre park containing an 18th century flour mill which was built on the site of a Norman predecessor. Restored to working order in 1979, **Dunster Working Water Mill** continues to produce flour and other cereals for wholesale and retail sale.

The old feudal settlement of Dunster has a wide main street which is dominated by the castle. At the northern end stands the former Yarn Market, a small octagonal building erected by the Luttrells in around 1600 when the village was a centre of the cloth trade. Indeed, such was its importance that, at one time, Dunster gave its name to a type of woollen cloth which was renowned for its quality and strength. On the southern edge of the village, the River Avill is spanned by the ancient **Gallox Bridge**, a medieval packhorse bridge which is now under the care of English Heritage.

The characteristic heartland of the **Exmoor National Park**, 70 per cent of which lies within Somerset, is a high treeless plateau of hard wearing Devonian shale which has been carved into a series of steep-sided valleys by the prolonged action of the moor's many fast flowing streams. Whereas the upland vegetation is mostly heather, gorse and bracken, the more sheltered valleys are carpeted with grassy meadows and pockets of woodland. The deep wooded combes also provide shelter for herds of shy red deer which roam at will but are seldom seen. Easier to spot are the hardy Exmoor ponies, now almost all cross-breeds, which often congregate at roadside parking areas where there can be rich pickings from holidaymakers.

Exmoor is crisscrossed by a network of paths and bridleways which provide some superb opportunities for walking and pony-trekking. Many follow the routes of the ancient ridgeways across the high moor and pass close to the numerous hut circles, standing stones, barrows and other Bronze and Iron Age remains which litter the landscape. Among the finest examples are the stone circle on **Porlock Hill**, **Alderman's Barrow** north of Exford, and the delightfully named **Cow Castle** near Simonsbath. The remarkable medieval packhorse bridge known as **Tarr Steps** lies to the north of the village of **Hawkridge**, near Dulverton. A superb example of a West Country clapper bridge, it is composed of massive flat stones placed across solidly-built dry stone uprights.

WATCHET   *Map 3 ref G22*

This small town has been a port since Saxon times and, in the 6th century, St Decuman is reputed to have landed here from Wales. The settlement was important enough, by the 9th century, to have been sacked by the Vikings on at least three occasions. By the 17th century, Watchet had become an important paper manufacturing centre and, by the mid 19th century, around 30,000 tons of iron ore from the Brendon Hills were being exported each year through its docks. Coleridge's imaginary crew set sail from here in *The Rime Of The Ancient Mariner*.

Unlike many similar sized ports which fell into disuse following the arrival of the railways, Watchet docks has somehow managed to survive. Despite the total decline in the iron ore trade, sizable cargo vessels continue to tie up here to be loaded with goods bound for the Iberian peninsula and elsewhere.

England

WESTON-SUPER-MARE   *Map 3 ref H21*

This popular seaside resort has, in recent years, developed as a centre of light
industry though, by many standard it developed relatively belatedly as a seaside
resort. In 1811, it was still a fishing hamlet with only 170 inhabitants; however,
within the next 100 years it had grown to become the second largest town in
Somerset. Despite its relatively modern character, the locality has been inhabited since prehistoric times. The wooded promontory at the northern end of
Weston Bay was the site of a sizable Iron Age hill settlement known as
Worlebury Camp.

Weston-Super-Mare has little of the grandiose architecture which characterises
earlier seaside resorts such as Brighton or Torquay. Instead, it developed on a
more comfortable scale with plenty of wide boulevards, leafy parks and open
spaces. The town's greatest resource is its long safe sandy beach which is ideal
for paddling, sunbathing and ball games. However, its gentle incline means that
swimmers have to wade out long way to find water deep enough to take the
plunge.

The **Woodspring Museum** in Burlington Street contains a series of fascinating
displays on the social and natural history of the area, including the Victorian
seaside holiday, royal potteries, early bicycles and period costume. It also
incorporates an art gallery which offers a constantly changing programme of
exhibitions. Situated adjacent to the museum, **Clara's Cottage** is a typical
Victorian dwelling furnished in the style of 1900.

The narrow coastroad to the north of Weston-Super-Mare passes along the beach
at Sand Bay before terminating at Middle Hope, a high ridge jutting out into the
Severn Channel whose western end, **Sand Point**, provides another fine viewpoint. The ridge overlooks a lonely salt marsh which is home to a wide variety
of wading birds, including shelduck and oystercatchers. To the east, a path leads
down to the Landmark Trust owned **Woodspring Priory**, a surprisingly intact
medieval monastery which was founded around 1220 by a grandson of one of
Thomas Becket's murderers, William de Courtenay. The priory fell into
disrepair following the Dissolution and its buildings were given over to agricultural use for many years. However, the church, tower, refectory and tithe barn
have all survived, and the outline of the cloister can also be made out.

CHEDDAR   *Map 3 ref H21*

One of the most famous and often visited natural attractions in Britain, **Cheddar
Gorge** is characterised by towering cliffs of weathered limestone and precari-
ously rooted bands of undergrowth. As well as being known for its gorge, this
sprawling village is internationally renowned for its caves and, of course, its
cheese. Although much embellished by modern tourist paraphernalia, its two
main show caverns, **Gough's Cave** and **Cox's Cave**, are worth seeing for their

sheer scale and spectacular calcite formations. An almost complete skeleton dubbed 'Cheddar Man' was discovered in Gough's Cave in 1903. This can now be seen in a nearby museum along with further evidence of human occupation of the caves, including flint and bone tools dating from the last Ice Age and artefacts from the Iron Age and the Romano-British period.

Wiltshire

INTRODUCTION

This essentially rural county is dominated by the great central high plateau of Salisbury Plain, parts of which are reserved for military use. Ringed by towns and villages the plain is virtually uninhabited and it was not until after World War I that some of the grassy downland was cultivated. The plain though is home to the most famous prehistoric monument in the country, Stonehenge, which remains an impressive sight even with the main road passing close by. In fact, Stonehenge is not alone, as Wiltshire boasts the highest concentration of leading prehistoric sights in the country.

Many of towns and villages of the county also date back many, many years and though a lot has been lost over the centuries there is still much to see for those interested in history and architecture. With plenty of grazing land sheep have been a feature of the landscape in Wiltshire for many centuries and, during the Middle Ages and later, the wool trade flourished here. Many towns prospered but one, Wilton, has become world famous after the town lent its name to a particular type of carpet. Among the other towns worthy of a visit there is Salisbury, with its beautiful, tall spired cathedral, the ancient market town and river crossing of Bradford-on-Avon, and Malmesbury, the oldest borough in England.

SALISBURY   *Map 4 ref K22*

This beautiful medieval city stands at the confluence of the rivers Avon, Wylye, Bourne and Nadder. Originally called New Sarum, the settlement grew up around the present **Cathedral** which was erected between 1220 and 1258 in a sheltered position two miles to the south of its Norman predecessor at Old Sarum. Over the centuries, the townspeople followed the clergy down from the wind-swept hilltop site on the edge of Salisbury Plain and the new settlement developed into a flourishing ecclesiastical and market centre which continues to host a twice weekly open air market every Tuesday and Saturday.

The new cathedral was the inspiration of Bishop Herbert Poole who wanted to distance the church from the military authorities occupying the great castle at Old Sarum. Sadly, the bishop died before his dream could be realised and it fell to his brother Richard to see the project through to completion. Work began on Easter Monday 1220 and continued for 38 years, a remarkably short time considering the scale of the building and construction methods of the day. As a result, this is the only medieval cathedral in England to be built entirely in Early English style. The soaring spire rises to a height of 404 feet, also making it the tallest in the country.

A brass plate set into the floor beneath the spire bears the inscription, "AD 1737 Centre of the Tower". This commemorates the fact that 50 years before, Sir Christopher Wren had been brought in by the cathedral authorities who were concerned the spire may topple over. He calculated the structure was indeed leaning almost two and a half feet off centre and his answer was to attach iron tie-rods to certain parts of it. When these were replaced in the 1950s, it was discovered Wren's efforts had been successful and the lean had not worsened in over 250 years.

Salisbury Cathedral

The cathedral is said to contain a door for each month, a window for each day and a column for each hour of the year (making 8760 columns in all). A small statue of Salisbury's 17th century 'Boy Bishop' stands inside the cathedral's west door. It was a custom at that time for the choristers to elect one of their number 'bishop' for a period lasting from St Nicholas Day to Holy Innocents' Day (6–28 December). One year, however, the incumbent is reputed to have been literally 'tickled to death' by the other choirboys and, as a result of him having died in office, a statue was erected showing him in full bishop's regalia. The oldest working clock in Britain, and possibly in the world, is situated in the cathedral's fan-vaulted north transept. It was built in 1386 to strike the hour and has no clock face.

As the cathedral was built before the town, new accommodation had to be built to house the clergy and ancillary staff. This was constructed around a walled square which is now considered to be the finest cathedral close in the country. Just to the south of the cathedral lies the **Bishop's Palace** which dates from the 13th century and now houses the cathedral choir school. During the Great Plague of 1665, Charles II based his court here for several months in order to steer clear of the pestilence which was sweeping London. The bishop's residence was also made famous by John Constable who painted his renowned landscape of Salisbury Cathedral in the palace gardens.

The award winning **Salisbury and South Wiltshire Museum** is situated in the 17th century King's House on the western side of the cathedral close. This absorbing museum contains a large collection of historic artefacts, including relics from Stonehenge, pottery fragments from Old Sarum and sections of an ancient Roman mosaic. A few doors away, the **Royal Gloucestershire, Berkshire and Wiltshire Regiment's Museum** is housed in the splendid Bishop's Wardrobe, a building dating from the mid-13th century which was originally used to store the bishop's clothes and documents.

One of the most elegant buildings in the cathedral close can be found on the northern side of Choristers' Green. A superb example of Queen Anne architecture, **Mompesson House** was constructed for the wealthy Wiltshire merchant, Charles Mompesson, around 1701. Now owned by the National Trust, the property contains a delicately carved oak staircase, a splendid collection of period furniture and some fine overmantels and plaster ceilings which were installed by Charles Longeville around 1740.

Originally a 13th century canonry, **Malmesbury House** on the northwestern side of the cathedral close was enlarged in the 14th century and again in the late 17th century when the west façade was added by Sir Christopher Wren to accommodate rooms displaying magnificent rococo plasterwork. The many famous visitors to the house include King Charles II and Handel who used to give recitals in the chapel above St Ann's Gate. The house contains some fine 18th century furnishings and is now the residence of the Cordle family.

WILTON   *Map 4 ref K22*

The third oldest borough in England, this 2000 year old settlement was once the capital of Saxon Wessex. In more recent times, it has become internationally renowned for its carpets which continue to be made at the **Wilton Carpet Factory**, an enterprise which was given a royal charter by William III in 1699.

Carpets are still woven here from local wool using traditional methods and visitors can join a guided tour which takes in an attractive garden and a museum celebrating 300 years of carpet-making history.

The old part of Wilton is centred around the Market Square, a bustling shopping area which contains an interesting collection of early buildings, including the 18th century town hall and the part-ruined medieval church of St Mary. Wilton's famous Italianate church lies a short walk away and, for those wanting to venture a little further afield, there is an attractive riverside walk along the Wylye.

The magnificent **Wilton House** stands on the southeastern edge of the town on a site originally occupied by a nunnery founded by Alfred the Great in the 9th century. The nunnery was eventually dissolved by Henry VIII in 1539 and the land given to Sir William Herbert, the future Earl of Pembroke, in whose family it has remained ever since. When the original building was destroyed by fire in 1647, the celebrated architect Inigo Jones was commissioned to build its replacement. The house was further remodelled at the beginning of the 19th century by James Wyatt, who designed the present north and west fronts and the cloisters.

Today, Wilton House contains an outstanding collection of art and furniture. There are also famous collections of model soldiers and miniature teddy bears, a magnificent Tudor kitchen, and a Victorian laundry. The 21 acre grounds are also well worth investigating. During World War II, Wilton House was used as an operations centre for southern command and the Normandy landings are believed to have been planned here.

BRADFORD-ON-AVON   *Map 4 ref J21*

This historic market town is situated at an ancient bridging point on the River Avon; a settlement has stood on this important riverside site since the time of the Saxons. Indeed, the town's oldest building, the **Church of St Lawrence**, is believed to have been founded by St Aldhelm around AD 700. Once part of a monastery which was largely destroyed by the Danes, the building 'disappeared' for over a thousand years, during which time the townspeople used it as a school, a charnel house for storing the bones of the dead, and a residential dwelling. The building was only rediscovered in 1858, when a clergyman looking down from the hill above the town spied the cruciform shape of a church. Further investigations on the site revealed two carved angels and confirmed the structure as the Saxon place of worship which had been 'missing' for over ten centuries. The surrounding buildings were gradually removed to reveal the present gem which, at only 38 feet long and with a chancel arch only three feet wide, is one of the smallest churches in the country.

Perhaps the town's best known feature is the superb nine-arch **Bridge** which spans the River Avon. Originally constructed in the 13th century for packhorse traffic, it was extensively rebuilt in the 17th century. The small, domed building near its southern end is a tiny former chapel which subsequently became the town lock-up. John Wesley is said to have spent an uncomfortable night here; however, the two cells were more often employed to house local drunks, a use which led to the building being dubbed the Blind House.

Another of Bradford's outstanding buildings, the **Tithe Barn**, dates from the time the town was under the administration of the nuns of Shaftesbury Abbey. By the 14th century, the increased output from the surrounding farms had created such a problem in storing the tithes—one tenth of the local farmers' annual produce—that a new storehouse had to be built near the river. The result was the gigantic tithe barn 164 feet long and 33 feet wide which had 14 bays, four projecting porches and a roof consisting of 30,000 stone tiles weighing an estimated 100 tons. Today, this magnificent stone building houses an interesting collection of antique farm implements and agricultural machinery.

In the heart of Bradford-on-Avon is the fine establishment **The Bunch of Grapes** which dates back to the 18th century; the building was originally used as a Porters Store where wines were stored before being exported.

Today visitors will find it the location of one of the finest restaurants in the area. The home-cooked dishes feature fresh local ingredients and all meals are prepared to order. To accompany a meal, a traditional glass of ale is to be recommended with all the beers sourced from local breweries.

The Bunch of Grapes, 14 Silver Street, Bradford-on-Avon, Wiltshire BA15 1JY

The Bunch of Grapes   *Tel: 01225 863877*

LACOCK   *Map 4 ref J21*

Preserved as only an estate village can be and owned by the National Trust, the buildings here are all reputed to be 18th century or older. A stroll around the quadrangle of streets reveals a delightful assortment of mellow stone buildings, including the famous Red Lion Hotel in the High Street. Another inn worth mentioning is the George, one of the oldest continuously licensed premises in the country. The village is regularly used as a period film location and, with this in mind, the Trust have taken steps to ensure that all cables run underground and all references to the modern era are kept well out of sight.

In the heart of the village is the **Sign of the Angel**, a 15th century, former wool merchant's house. Run by the Levis family since 1953, the Sign of the Angel is the quintessential English pub today offering fine food and pleasant accommodation. Always relaxed and comfortable there are log fires and oak panelling, low beams and squeaky floorboards; and the hosts are always on hand to offer friendly and informal service. The restaurant, lit by candlelight in the evenings, has become renowned for its traditional English style of cooking. The four course lunches and dinners centre round a roast main course—with a fish or vegetarian alternative—served with fresh locally grown vegetables. All the puddings, including the ice creams, are made on the premises and meals are rounded off with truckles of Stilton and Cheddar.

Sign of the Angel

The 10 comfortable bedrooms are furnished with antiques collected by the family over many years. One of the few concessions to the 20th century has been the sensitive introduction of private bathrooms for all the bedrooms. Another feature of the rooms are the painted wall decorations, the work of a local artist, which reflect the hand-crafted fabrics used in the soft furnishings. The oak panelled lounge, for the use of guests, demonstrates perfectly the warm and relaxed atmosphere of this old family house, while outside the pretty gardens are best enjoyed on warm summer evenings.

Sign of the Angel, Church Street, Lacock, Wiltshire Tel: 01249 730230

MALMESBURY   *Map 4 ref J20*

The oldest borough in England and still one of its most attractive places, this historic settlement stands around the site of an ancient hill fort on the southern margin of the Cotswolds. The Benedictine **Malmesbury Abbey** was founded here in the 7th century by St Aldhelm, then in 880 Alfred the Great granted the town a charter.

In the 10th century, King Athelstan, Alfred's grandson and the first Saxon monarch to unite the whole of England, granted 500 acres of land to the townspeople of Malmesbury after they had helped him resist a Norse invasion. The area is still known as **King's Heath** and continues to be owned by around 200 residents of the town who can trace their ancestry back to the men who fought for the Saxon king over 1000 years ago.

One of the first attempts at human powered flight was made from the abbey tower by a monk early in the 11th century. Brother Elmer (who is sometimes known as Oliver) strapped a pair of home-made wings to his arms and, flapping wildly, flew for some 200 yards before returning to earth, breaking both his legs in the process and crippling himself for life. Despite this mishap, he lived on for another 50 years and is said to have predicted the Norman invasion following a sighting of Halley's comet. Elmer's pioneering flight is commemorated in one of the abbey's stained glass windows.

Following the Dissolution in 1539, Malmesbury Abbey was sold to a wealthy local wool merchant, William Stumpe, for the sum of £1517 15s 2d. Stumpe proceeded to set up cloth-weaving workshops in the abbey buildings; however, the great church survived this indignity and was presented to the town as its new parish church in 1541.

The **Old Bell Hotel**, situated adjacent to the abbey, is thought to be one of the oldest hostelries in England. Established by an early abbot of Malmesbury at a time when scholars came from all over Europe to study in the abbey's famous library, the inn was mentioned in the Domesday Book and is now a Grade I listed building.

Just out of the main town centre is **The Three Cups** public house. This 18th century inn was originally established when stones were being brought down the River Avon to build the abbey. Three hundred years later the abbey at

The Three Cups

England

Malmesbury is being restored to its former beauty and worthy of a visit. The inn is also thought to be the site, in earlier years, of a meeting place of the Worshipful Company of Salters, producers and sellers of seasalt. The present day hosts, John and Diana, offer a warm welcome to visitors whether local or just passing through the area. They also offer a fine choice of ales and a good selection of bar food. The menu is traditional pub fayre, all freshly cooked to order.

The Three Cups, 90 The Triangle, Malmesbury, Wiltshire SN16 0AH
Tel: 01666 923278

AVEBURY   *Map 4 ref K21*

This ancient settlement is situated at the heart of one of the most extraordinary megalithic monuments in Europe. Now designated a World Heritage Site, the village stands on a 28 acre area which is surrounded by a ring of sarsen stones almost a mile in circumference. This in turn is enclosed by a ditch and a raised bank which encircle almost 100 standing stones which are thought to date from around 2300 BC. These are believed to have been erected by the Beaker people, immigrants from Europe who brought with them sophisticated pottery-making skills. Ceramic fragments have been discovered throughout the locality and some exceptional undamaged pieces have been found in the graves of their former chieftains.

A remarkable feat for its time, stones weighing as much as 40 tons were dragged down from the Marlborough Downs and erected in three circles. The megaliths come in two basic shapes: tall narrow ones, which are believed to represent the male form, and broad diamond-shaped ones, which represent the female form. These characteristics have led archeologists to conclude the site was principally used for the observance of fertility rituals. Sadly, only 27 stones in the most central area remain, the others having been removed over the centuries largely to provide the village with building materials. The positions of the missing megaliths have been marked by a series of modern concrete piers.

Avebury Stone Circle was extensively excavated by Alexander Keiller during the 1930s and a museum bearing his name is located just outside the earthwork perimeter near the part-Saxon, part-Norman village church of St James. Administered by English Heritage, the **Alexander Keiller Museum** houses a fascinating collection of artefacts discovered at Avebury and, at nearby Windmill Hill, a Neolithic hill fort and Bronze Age burial ground which lies in the downs a mile to the northwest.

Another interesting attraction is the **Great Barn Museum**, an exhibition of Wiltshire rural life which is housed in a magnificently restored 17th century thatched barn. The history of such long established rural skills as blacksmithing, thatching, cheese-making, saddlery and shepherding is documented in a unique collection of old photographs, tools and other related exhibits. Regular demonstrations of rural crafts take place throughout the season.

AMESBURY   *Map 4 ref K22*

According to Mallory, Queen Guinevere withdrew to a priory in the village on
hearing of King Arthur's death (when she herself died, her body was taken back
to Glastonbury by Sir Launcelot to be buried beside the King). A more verifiable
account records Queen Elfrida as having founded the abbey in around 979 in
reparation for her part in the murder of her son-in-law, Edward the Martyr, at
Corfe Castle. Sadly none of original buildings remain above ground, except for
the old church of St Mary. The present day abbey buildings were completed in
1840 and are not open to the public.

To the west of the village lies the most famous Magalithic site in Europe,
Stonehenge. Dwarfed by the vast open expanse of Salisbury Plain, only by
walking up to the great Bronze Age monument does the true scale of this
spectacular monument become clear. In fact, some of its great stones stand over
20 feet high and are embedded up to eight feet in the ground. The central area
consists of an inner horseshoe and an outer ring of massive sarsen (or foreign)
stones with lintels which are thought to have been brought all the way from the
Marlborough Downs. The double outer circle of 80 bluestones was erected
earlier and they are believed to have been quarried some 200 miles away in the
Preseli Hills in Dyfed.

The largest bluestone, the Altar Stone, is set at the very centre of the formation
and, from here, the Heel Stone can be seen some 256 feet away. On the longest
day of the year, the sun rises over this stone leading experts to conclude that the
site was constructed for the purpose of observing ancient sun worshipping
rituals.

Oxfordshire

INTRODUCTION

Oxford, the county town, is also the only town of any notable size and, naturally,
it receives most attention. As well as being the great university town, it also lies
on the River Thames, which by this point is becoming rather narrow and, just
upstream from the city, can be found one of the main tributaries, the Cherwell.
From this point onwards the Thames is also referred to as the Isis. To the north
of Oxford is the charming town of Woodstock, often bypassed by those who visit
one of the country's most famous stately homes, Blenheim Palace. Further north
again can by found Banbury, well known for its Cross of the nursery rhyme but
which also boasts a busy livestock market.

The River Thames forms the southeastern boundary of the county and here
Oxfordshire is crossed by the Chiltern Hills. Further west lies the Vale of the
White Horse and also the oldest of the Iron Age hill figures in the country.
Known as the White Horse of Uffington it has been connected with King Alfred.

Almost completely dominated by the University, it is to the wonderful college buildings that hundreds of thousands of tourists flock each year. All the University colleges have their own special interest but one that should not be missed is **St Edmund Hall**, part of which is the only surviving medieval academic hall. It also has a Norman crypt and a 17th century dining hall. Many greatly enjoy the charm of the quadrangle, especially the north range with its mullioned windows and sundial, contrasting vividly with the classical library and chapel entrance which adjoins it.

Corpus Christi College

For those who would like to find out more about the University, without walking around all the colleges, there is the innovative **Oxford Story Museum**, on Broad Street. Here visitors sit in a scholars' desks and are transported through time to discover its 800 year history through its characters, sounds and, not least, its smells. A visit to the **Museum of Oxford** where there are permanent displays showing the archaeology and history of the city from the earliest times to the present is also worth a visit.

The **Ashmolean Museum** is the oldest museum in the country, having first opened in 1683, although the present building dates back only to 1845. There are archaeological collections from Britain, Europe, the Mediterranean, Egypt and the Middle East, a very fine coin and medal collection and Italian, Dutch, Flemish, French and English old masters as well as more modern paintings and prints. There are also collections of far eastern art, ceramics and lacquer work, Islamic pottery and Chinese bronzes.

One museum which would captivate many who are not particularly interested in art is the **Museum of the History of Science**, which has the largest collection of astrolabes in the world and is housed in the original Ashmolean building in Broad Street. In the same vein, the **Curioxity**, in the Old Fire Station in George Street, is a new 'hands-on' science gallery where adults and children can explore the world of science and technology and have fun at the same time.

Then there is the **Oxford University Museum**, housed in a splendid high Victorian-Gothic building on Parks Road. Here can be seen the remains of the dodo, extinct since about 1680, as well as fossilised dinosaur remains and much else. Another section of the same museum, where visitors can listen to recordings of musical instruments from all over the world on display there, is to be found at the Balfour Building, Banbury Road.

Finally, those in Oxford on a summer Sunday afternoon also have the opportunity to see the **Rotunda Museum of Antique Dolls' Houses** and their contents. The exhibits date from 1700 to 1900. As well as the many museums, a wondrous collection of antique prints, maps and books can be found in several specialist shops, the sort of places where people are encouraged to spend hours just browsing and digging into the piles of stock—sometimes still priced in shillings rather than decimal money.

ABINGDON   *Map 9 ref L19*

The town owes its origin to a monastery, which was founded in 675, and Abingdon grew up around a market held immediately in front of the **Abbey** gateway. And it is this gateway which is the most impressive remaining monument to what was once a thriving religious community. It was built in the late 15th century, though of the three arches seen today the southern one is a 19th century reconstruction. Above the middle arch is a niche which originally held a statue of the Virgin Mary. Built on to the gateway is the Church of St Nicholas, which retains some Norman features although there is a lot of later work. Not much is left of the abbey considering its original extent but some of the secular buildings have survived and can be visited. The Long Gallery, partly built of stone and partly timber-framed, dates from about 1500, while the Checker Hall is a 13th Century stone building with an unusual chimney.

Apart from the remnants of the abbey, Abingdon has many interesting buildings. The **County Hall** in the Market Place impressed even Sir Nickolaus Pevsner who commented "Of the free-standing town halls of England with open ground floors this is the grandest." It was built from 1678–82 and makes for a very harmonious whole, with its warm brown stone and hipped roof topped off with balustrade and cupola. It was built to house the local market (at street level), while upstairs was the court. Inside there is now a museum devoted to local history and archaeology, well worth a visit. Abingdon is a place which amply repays time spent simply wandering about the streets, soaking up the atmosphere. There are many attractive houses to be seen, particularly Stratton House, in Bath Street, built in red brick about 1722 featuring a handsome doorway with doric pilasters. The view of the town from the bridge should also not be missed. The bridge itself dates from 1416, though it was extensively rebuilt in 1927.

Abingdon was the birthplace of Dorothy Miller Richardson, whose novels, written between 1915 and 1938, pioneered the 'stream of consciousness' method. Another literary association is with John Ruskin, who lodged at the Crown and Thistle Inn on Bridge Street. He lived there in 1871 after having been appointed Slade Professor of Art at Oxford, before moving into rooms at Corpus Christi College. Ruskin was an interesting character, little read nowadays, but immensely influential and controversial in his time.

In more recent times Abingdon has been home to the MG car factory, which turned out thousands of open topped sports cars and sporting saloons until its demise in the early 1980s.

FARINGDON   *Map 5 ref K20*

The attractive name comes from the Old English for Fern Hill and this is a pleasant market town with an old market hall and some picturesque inns. The **Church** is in a very prominent position at the top of the market place and at one time it had a steeple but this was destroyed during the Civil War; however, the ironwork on the main door has survived intact for 700 years. The beautiful 18th century **Faringdon Hall**, to the west of the church, was built by George III's poet laureate, Henry James Pye, some of whose family have memorials in the Church.

Pye's main claim to fame seems to have been that he was universally ridiculed by the rest of the literary scene. He was also forced to sell the house after becoming an MP, partly due to election expenses. Political campaigning at the time was largely a question of how many voters the candidate could afford to bribe, so it was perhaps hardly surprising that he got into debt.

The house has other literary associations, one of them derived from a rather more chilling spisode in the history of the famiy, which had lived in an earlier house on the same site. Legend had it that the headless ghost of Hampden Pye haunts the grounds. He was serving in the Navy as a midshipman when his stepmother, who wanted her own son to inherit, plotted with his captain to make sure he did not return alive. Hampden was indeed killed in action at sea during which his head was blown off. This does not seem to have been a result of his stepmother's plot but all the same he is said to have returned to haunt her.

To the south lies one of Oxfordshire's better known attractions, the **Uffington White Horse**. Found on a hillside, this mysteriously abstract and very beautiful figure of a horse some 400 feet long has been created by removing the turf to expose the gleaming white chalk beneath. Popular tradition links the horse with the victory of King Alfred over the Danes at the battle of Ashdown, which was fought somewhere on these Downs in 871. However, modern scholars now considers it to date from around 100 BC. Above the horse is the Iron Age camp known as **Uffington Castle**. To one side is the knoll known as Dragon's Hill where, according to legend, St George killed the dragon.

Buscot, to the west of Faringdon, is a National Trust village and here can also be found **Buscot Village Shop and Tea Rooms**, just three minutes from the Thames path, weir and lock. The well stocked shop has, amongst other things, an interesting range of dried flowers, paintings and costume jewellery. Owned by Gerald and Brenda for the past two years, it has become a popular stopping

Buscot Village Shop and Tea Rooms

point for many visitors to the area. Brenda does most of the home-cooking and her cakes, pastries, soups, sandwiches and baguettes are to be recommended. In the summer, cream teas are served al fresco in the garden and home grown vegetables and plants are available for purchase. Suitable access is available for disabled visitors.

Buscot Village Shop and Tea Rooms, Buscot, near Faringdon, Oxfordshire SN7 8DA Tel: 01367 252142

HENLEY-ON-THAMES   *Map 5 ref M20*

The town is renowned in society circles for its prestigious annual Regatta, held in July. The first inter-varsity race took place here in 1829 and within a decade the event was enjoying royal patronage. The graceful 18th century bridge in Henley is appropriately decorated with faces of Father Thames and the goddess Isis. Apart from the boating available throughout the summer and the pleasant walks along the tow paths, there are lots of interesting shops, inns and tea shops in the town. Most of the inns are old coaching houses with yards that were once the scene of bull and bear fights.

Since opening in 1995, **Henley Needlecrafts** has established itself as a comprehensive one stop supplier of tapestry, cross-stitch and embroidery kits, fabrics, threads, ribbons and sewing accessories of every description. With over 100 different suppliers, the shop tries to have everything anyone might need for embroidersy, cross-stitch and canvas work. It also offers friendly helpful service in an Aladdin's Cave atmosphere where customers are welcome to browse. The staff are happy to order items that are not in stock and offer a postal forwarding service. Henley Needlecrafts also run special classes for those keen to improve their skill or learn new techniques, and regularly hold exhibitions of well known designers' work.

Henley Needlecrafts, 13 Reading Road, Henley-on-Thames, Oxfordshire
RG9 1AB Tel & Fax: 01491 410840

Henley Needlecrafts

Close to Henley-on-Thames lies the small village of **Sonning**. The 11 arch brick bridge over the river here is one of the oldest on the upper Thames and is so narrow that traffic has to cross it in single file. The ground climbs steeply away from the bridge on this side of the river and, close by, is the famous Sonning Cutting, a deep and steep man-made gorge through which runs the main Paddington to Bristol railway line.

WOODSTOCK *Map 9 ref L19*

John Churchill, 1st Duke of Marlborough, was a brave soldier, skilful general and he also had an eye on the main chance. At the height of his power after the victory at Blenheim during the War of the Spanish Succession, he was received in London as a hero and Queen Anne proposed that he should be rewarded with a palace. She gave him her manor at Woodstock as the site, but there the national gratitude seems to have run out of steam, for he paid for most of it himself in the end.

As his architect, Marlborough chose Sir John Vanbrugh whose life was even more colourful than that of his patron. He was at the same time both an architect (although at the time he was relatively unknown) and a playwright, and had the distinction of having been imprisoned in the Bastille. The result of his work was the Continental looking baroque **Blenheim Palace**, which is now seen set in a very English park laid out later by Capability Brown. The new house did not meet with universal approval. It was ridiculed by Jonathan Swift and Alexander Pope; Duchess Sarah, who seems to have held the family purse strings, delayed paying Vanbrugh as long as possible. But recently its international importance has been recognised by inclusion in the World Heritage List. It is a magnificent palace, both inside and out, and, after marvelling at the treasures and the more intimate souvenirs of Marlborough's descendant, Sir Winston Churchill, there is much to see the grounds.

The Blenheim Orange apple got its name from here. It was first grown by George Kempster, a tailor from Old Woodstock, though the exact date of the first apple is unknown. Kempster himself died in 1773 and the original tree blew down in 1853. A plaque in Old Woodstock marks its site and so famous did the spot become that it is said London-bound coaches and horses used to slow down so that passengers might gaze upon it.

Woodstock itself is a relaxed, unpretentious place giving no hint of the grandeur of its most famous building, which is approached through the main street. Formerly the centre of the glove-making industry, the town was also the site of one of the most splendid of the medieval royal palaces, the scene of Henry II's courtship of Rosamond and birthplace of the Black Prince; Elizabeth I was imprisoned there in 1554 by her sister, Mary Tudor. The old palace was damaged during the Civil War, when it served as a Royalist garrison and the last remains were demolished in 1710.

BANBURY   *Map 9 ref L18*

The **Cross** at Banbury, known to many who heard the nursery rhyme as children, can be found in Horsefair. It was built in 1859 to commemorate a previous one which was demolished during the Civil War by the Puritans, for whom Banbury also used to be famous. The ever so slightly comic figures around the base of the present cross, of Queen Victoria, Edward VII and George V, were added in 1914.

Banbury was also at one time famous for its cheeses which were only about an inch thick and this gave rise to the expression "thin as a Banbury cheese". The town's other legendary claim to fame is its cakes, made of spicy fruit pastry. These can still be bought and very good they are too.

A wander round Banbury's streets is very varied and rewarding. There are also lots of interesting old houses and shops to linger over. The **Museum**, also in Horsefair, tells the story of the development of Banbury and district.

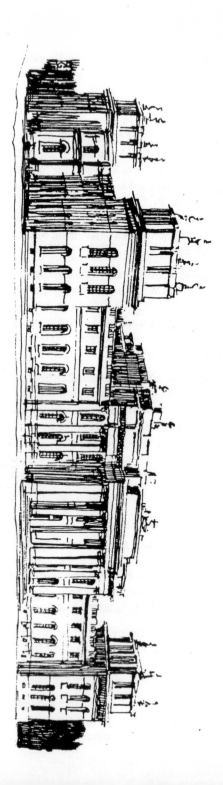

Blenheim Palace, Woodstock

CHAPTER THREE
Devon

St Mary's Steps, Exeter

3
Devon

Southeast Devon

INTRODUCTION

Devon is the third largest county in England, only Yorkshire and Cumbria are larger, and it is well known for both its spectacular scenery and its long tradition of sea faring. This southeastern corner of the county, bounded by the River Exe in the west, the Dorset county border in the east and the M5 motorway to the north, is usually most peoples' entry point into the county.

The county town and cathedral city of Exeter has dominated the area for many centuries. Dating from before the Roman occupation, the city has an interesting and varied history and, though much was destroyed by enemy bombing during World War II, the magnificent Norman cathedral and the 19th century Quay both withstood the bombardment.

Many of the ancient fishing villages along Devon's southeast coast saw a period of growth and development during the late 18th and early 19th centuries when the Napoleonic Wars prevented those seeking fresh air and sea bathing from travelling to France. Essentially Regency in style, these resorts maintain a genteel and refined atmosphere today and few, if any, have been spoilt by more recent, less stylish, development. The mix of sand and shingle beaches remains popular with holidaymakers seeking to avoid the bright lights, funfairs and candyfloss of many English seaside resorts.

Inland can be found delightful villages, hidden away in charming and secluded valleys. The ancient market towns of Honiton, Ottery St Mary and Axminster still provide focal points for the local, rural communities.

EXETER
Map 3 ref G24

The city stands on a rise above the River Exe at what was once its lowest fording point. Protected by valleys to the north and south and by the Haldon Hills to the west, a settlement has existed on this important strategic site since the days of the

Celts. The ancient Romans made Isca their southwestern stronghold, capturing it in around AD 56 and constructing a military fort which they expanded into a city over the next century. Around this new regional capital, they built a massive defensive wall in the shape of an irregular rectangle within which the city remained right up until the 18th century.

During the Dark Ages that followed the departure of the Roman legions in the 5th century, Exeter was twice occupied by the Vikings. William I then captured the city in 1086 following a siege which lasted 18 days. To defend their new conquest, the Normans built **Rougemont Castle**, the gatehouse and tower of which can still be seen in Rougemont Gardens to the north of the city centre.

The finest Norman legacy in Exeter, however, is undoubtedly **St Peter's Cathedral** which stands within its own attractive close to the west of Southernhay Gardens. The original structure was built in the 11th and 12th centuries; however, with the exception of the two sturdy towers, the body of the cathedral was demolished in 1260 and rebuilt over the next 90 years. A remarkable astronomical clock can be found on the north wall of the transept. Dating from around 1400, its twin blue and gold faces indicate the phases of the moon as well as the time of day; its inscription, translated from the Latin, reads "The hours perish and are reckoned to our account".

In addition to the cathedral, the centre of Exeter once contained over 30 churches, seven monasteries and several other ecclesiastical institutions. **St Nicholas's Priory**, an exceptional example of a small Norman priory, is now an interesting museum where visitors can view the original prior's cell, the 15th century kitchens and the imposing central hall with its vaulted ceiling and solid Norman pillars. One of Exeter's most rewarding attractions is its unique labyrinth of **Underground Passages** which were built by the cathedral clergy in medieval times to regulate the water supply and provide safe passage between the city's many ecclesiastical houses. Guided tours around this fascinating subterranean world are available all year round and are strongly recommended.

Exeter's most impressive non-ecclesiastical medieval building can be found in the partly pedestrianised High Street. The **Guildhall** was built by the powerful craftsmen's guilds in the late 15th century, its splendid portico having been added a century later. On occasion, the main chamber is still used for formal meetings of the city burgers, making this one of the oldest municipal buildings in Britain still in use. On a smaller scale, the **Tucker's Hall** was built in 1471 for one of the city's most powerful wool guilds—the Company of Weavers, Fullers and Shearmen. Inside, there is some exceptional carved panelling, a collection of rare silver, and a remarkable pair of fulling shears weighing over 25 lbs and measuring almost 4 feet.

Exeter's importance as a centre of the wool trade developed throughout the Tudor and Elizabethan periods, with raw fleeces, spun yarn and finished cloth being traded in the market in considerable quantities. Woollen products of all kinds were exported to the major cities of Europe, initially through Topsham downstream on the Exe, then later through a quay in the heart of the city.

Following a long period of decline which began in the mid-19th century, Exeter Quay underwent a dramatic revival in the 1980s when many of its old warehouses and maritime buildings were renovated and reopened as restaurants, shops and commercial units. The **Custom House**, one of the most handsome 17th century buildings in Exeter (and one of the first to be constructed of brick), can be found here. By the time it was completed in 1681, large quantities of sugar, rice, tea and other commodities were being landed at the quay, requiring an official presence of some consequence. The Custom House was therefore constructed to an impressive standard, with fine plasterwork ceilings and balustraded staircases which are worth seeing. Visitors are admitted by arrangement with HM Customs and Excise, though casual visitors are generally welcomed. Exeter Quay is also the location of the internationally renowned **Maritime Museum**, the world's largest collection of boats. Exhibits include an Arab dhow, a reed boat from Lake Titicaca in South America, and the *Cygnet*, an eccentric rowing dinghy which was used to ferry guests to wild parties on her even more eccentric sister vessel, the *Swan*.

The character of modern Exeter was much altered by the effects of World War II bombing, carried out, it was claimed, in revenge for the Allied attacks on the historic city of Lübeck. The devastating raids of May 1942 destroyed much of the medieval and Georgian city. Large areas of the old city had to be rebuilt in the 1950s, often in the form of modern shopping centres, though it is amazing that so many buildings did survive the raids.

The **Hotel Gledhills** presents a very smart appearance and is situated conveniently close to the shops, leisure centre, Exeter's famous quay and riverside walks. It is easily reached by leaving the M5 motorway at junction 31. David

Hotel Gledhills

England

and Suzanne Greening have been the owners of this hotel for 10 years and are justifiably proud of their QQQ AA and RAC Acclaimed status. The couple offer modern facilities with old fashioned service in a relaxed and friendly atmosphere. All rooms have private facilities, colour television with movie channel and beverage tray. A comfortable residents' lounge has TV and separate well stocked bar. Very pleasant gardens and a good size car park to the rear.
Hotel Gledhills, 32 Alphington Road, Exeter, Devon EX2 8HN
Tel: 01392 271439 Tel & Fax: 01392 430469

TOPSHAM   *Map 3 ref G24*

Lying at the head of the Exe estuary and four miles south of Exeter, Topsham was the city's gateway to the sea and, at one time, a place of great importance. A port has existed on this ancient site since the days when the Celts and the Romans used it as a main landing point, building a direct road to connect it with their royal forum in Exeter.

Topsham continued to grow in importance throughout the medieval upsurge in the wool trade, especially when a series of weirs prevented any kind of tidal access to the city. The later construction of a ship canal inland failed to herald the decline which was predicted and the town continued to prosper; a fact borne out by some of the fine early 18th century buildings found here.

Once a thriving tangle of wharves, boatyards and chandleries, today the narrow lanes running down to the shore from the main street are filled with historic buildings of all descriptions. Indeed, the entire old town has been designated a conservation area. The view across the broad estuary from the churchyard is outstanding, especially at high tide, and the old maritime inns are delightful places to visit.

The **Georgian Tea Rooms and Restaurant**, on the High Street, is one of those splendid places that are few and far between. An impressive Georgian house is the location and, within, the owner, Heather Knee, is busy organising and

Georgian Tea Rooms & Restaurant

140

looking after her customers. Heather is a farmer's daughter and knows all about home-cooking and really delicious food. She also serves the cream tea to end all cream teas! With plenty of awards for her excellence, anyone coming here will certainly be spoilt for choice, so it is always a good idea to allow plenty of time to enjoy the delights of her cooking and baking. The perfect tea rooms!

Georgian Tea Rooms & Restaurant, Broadway House, 33 High Street, Topsham, Devon EX3 0ED Tel: 01392 873465

Just to the south of Topsham lies **Exton**, the location of **The Puffing Billy Inn**. John Crompton recently acquired the establishment and as chef–patron, with a wide experience in top grade hotels and country clubs, offers a menu of quality food, all home prepared and cooked to order. The emphasis is on good English fare with a touch of Continental flavouring. Attended by lively friendly staff, the food arrives well presented and in good measure. There are many favourites on the menu and making the choice is not easy. There's a nonsmoking area in the restaurant where children are very welcome. Well behaved pets are allowed in the general rooms. The inn has also undergone a total refurbishment bringing it in line with the excellent facilities offered.

The Puffing Billy Inn, Station Road, Exton, Devon Tel: 01392 873152

LYMPSTONE   *Map 3 ref G24*

This is a pleasant and quiet backwater nestling between two low red sandstone cliffs on the eastern shores of the Exe estuary. Shipbuilding has been an important activity here for centuries; whalers from Newfoundland and Greenland would put in here for the winter months. However, competition from the ship yards at Topsham proved too much and the industry closed in Lympstone in the early 19th century. The people of Lympstone then turned to fishing for oysters and mussels and today fresh seafood is a local speciality.

One of the very best pubs in the area can be found here on The Strand. Justifiably popular with locals and visitors alike, **The Swan Inn and Restaurant** is an Irish theme pub. Run by an Irishman, Seamus O'Neill, this warm, welcoming pub

The Swan Inn and Restaurant

serves the very best cask beers, fine wines and wonderful food in a lively atmosphere with live music and a good craic. The food is excellent, all prepared using only the very best ingredients, locally produced wherever possible. Be sure to try a seafood dish, this restaurant is locally renowned for them. Visitors to this gem can be assured of Céad-Mile Fáilte—a hundred thousand welcomes! *The Swan Inn and Restaurant, The Strand, Lympstone, Devon EX8 5ET Tel: 01395 270403/272284*

EXMOUTH   *Map 3 ref G24*

Exmouth with its two miles long seafront and its sandy beaches has attracted visitors from Exeter and beyond since the early 18th century. The oldest seaside resort in Devon, even before the arrival of the railway in 1861, the wealthy and fashionable have been coming here in large numbers to reap the benefits of the sea air and saltwater bathing.

Originally a small fishing port formed from the parishes of Littleham and Withycombe Regis, the population of Exmouth rose dramatically between 1800 and 1900. Much of this development was inspired by the Rolle family, owners of Littleham Manor, who were responsible for constructing some of the town's most elegant late Georgian terraces.

One of the finest seafront promenades on the south coast runs along the great sea wall, which was built in stages between 1840 and 1915. Somewhat surprisingly, the town was a target for enemy bombers during World War II; maybe because it was mistaken for Exeter or perhaps it was an easy target.

Just outside Exmouth, in the centre of the picturesque village of **Withycombe** nestles **The Holly Tree**, a traditional English inn that has been personally run by Chris and Maria for the past 14 years. Originally built in the 1600s, this attractive pub has lost none of its charm and character. Around the walls inside the bar area

The Holly Tree

are displayed an amazing collection of World War II RAF photographs, many depict the historic Battle of Britain and were inherited by Chris many years ago. Visitors will find plenty to amuse them in the games room including pool, bar billiards and darts, whilst the excellent real ale has been known to coax many a local out on a cold winter night. The Holly Tree is the perfect example of what can be achieved when committed to good old fashioned hospitality and a warm and friendly welcome.

The Holly Tree, Withycombe Village Road, Withycombe, near Exmouth, Devon Tel: 01395 273440

Tythe Cottage Tea Rooms

Situated just to the east of Exmouth, the church at **Littleham**, which overlooks the village, has a memorial window to Nelson's wife who died in Exmouth in 1831. Close by the **Tythe Cottage Tea Rooms** are a traditional English tea rooms and restaurant located within a charming thatched building in the heart of village. There is a good selection of drinks and snacks on offer with the cream teas a particular speciality. All the scones and cakes are home-made and all dishes are freshly prepared. The restaurant additionally serves hot meals from a daily special board. The three course Sunday lunches are very popular so advance booking is recommended.

Tythe Cottage Tea Rooms, Littleham, near Exmouth, Devon EX8 2AQ Tel: 01395 271627

BUDLEIGH SALTERTON   *Map 3 ref G24*

This pleasant seaside resort to the east of Exmouth takes its name from the salt-pans, or salterns, which were constructed near the mouth of the River Otter over 1000 years ago. Despite its early foundation, the town, as seen today, developed in the last two centuries as a peaceful residential and holiday centre which is popular with those preferring the local cobbles to the sandy beach at Exmouth.

England

Several elegant late Georgian and Regency buildings survive, and visitors should look out for **The Octagon** at the west end of the Parade which for a time was used as a studio by the painter, John Millais, the co-founder of the Pre-Raphaelite Brotherhood. An excellent view over Lyme Bay can be had from the summit of nearby West Down Beacon.

The Cosy Teapot

Situated at the end of the main street is **The Cosy Teapot**, a Victorian style tea room with a friendly, welcoming atmosphere and a range of teas and snacks second to none. The very highest standards are maintained and all teas and snacks are served on bone china. Pat and Norman, the owners, are members of The Tea Council, such is their enthusiasm for tea. Be sure to call in for a refreshing snack—a treat is in store.

The Cosy Teapot, 13 Fore Street, Budleigh Salterton, Devon
Tel: 01395 444016

The Feathers, situated on the busy High Street, is a fine public house with much to recommend it. It is understandably popular with locals and visitors alike, and families are made most welcome. This is the ideal place to call in for a snack and

The Feathers

refreshing drink and do sample one of the many real ales which are kept on tap. The pub boasts its own skittle alley and beer garden—the perfect place to while away the warm summer evenings. This is a hidden place which is well worth a visit and should be near the top of everyone's list.

The Feathers, 35 High Street, Budleigh Salterton, Devon Tel: 01395 442042

SIDMOUTH   *Map 3 ref G24*

This genteel seaside resort to the south of Ottery St Mary lies at the point where the small River Sid breaches the soft local sandstone and reaches the sea. On either side, the bright red cliffs rise dramatically to over 500 feet, creating a spectacular backdrop to the white Georgian and Victorian buildings of the town. Prior to the 1780s, Sidmouth was an attractive, but struggling, fishing village which faced annihilation following a series of unsuccessful attempts to build an effective harbour. However, this decline was reversed when the new fashion for bathing in the bracing waters of the sea arrived at the end of the 18th century, a time when members of the leisured classes were unable to travel to the Continent because of the Napoleonic Wars.

Between 1800 and 1820, Sidmouth's population doubled as the aristocratic and well-to-do built substantial cottages in and around the town. A number of less extravagant developments were constructed during the same period and given such flamboyant names as Elysian Fields and Fortified Terrace. In total, there are now almost 500 listed buildings in the town and a stroll around the centre is likely to prove very rewarding for those interested in Georgian and early Victorian architecture.

With its shingle beach, handsome buildings and refined atmosphere, Sidmouth provides an excellent base for a relaxing seaside break. Bear in mind, however, that the mood changes out of all recognition when the annual Sidmouth International Folk Festival comes to town. For one week in early August, the streets and pubs teem with singers, dancers, musicians and enthusiastic onlookers, and the atmosphere transforms from polite gentility to good humoured revelry.

Just a short walk from the sea and in the heart of this floral town stands **Southcombe Guest House**, a charming bed and breakfast establishment that is owned and run by Richard and Diana Dann. Elegantly furnished throughout, Southcombe offers excellent guest bedrooms, one of which is on the ground floor and all have full en-suite facilities, satellite TV and complimentary tea and coffee maker. The hearty English breakfast is guaranteed to set guests up for the day and the four course evening dinner is really something to look forward to on their return.

Richard and Diana have collected many prizes for both the back and front garden displays, the colourful herbaceous borders fill the air with the scent of summer

Southcombe Guest House

whilst the attractive fishpond creates fascination and interest. It would almost be worth visiting Southcombe Guest House for the garden alone; stretching down to the River Sid, it has a soothing quality brought about by its proximity to the water and the summer house and lawns are the perfect place to sit and relax. *Southcombe Guest House, Vicarage Road, Sidmouth, Devon EX10 8UQ* *Tel: 01395 513861*

The very pleasant **Browns Wine Bar and Bistro** can be found in the heart of Sidmouth near the seafront. Hospitality is the keyword at Browns and the owner, Richard Houghton-Brown, extends a warm welcome to all whether they call in for morning coffee or an evening meal. Browns has been established for over eight years. Richard has an excellent wine cellar and will be pleased to advise

Browns Wine Bar & Bistro

on selection. Try a glass of house wine for example whilst choosing from the varied and interesting menu. Fish is, not surprisingly, a house speciality though there are many other dishes to tempt the palate. Good parking nearby—a big plus in Sidmouth!

Browns Wine Bar & Bistro, Fore Street, Sidmouth, Devon EX10 8AQ
Tel: 01395 516724

The Abbeydale Hotel

Built around the turn of the century as a private residence for a military general, **The Abbeydale Hotel** today offers accommodation of a high standard at very affordable prices. Situated in sheltered grounds and enjoying spectacular views of the sea, this family run hotel has to be one of the very best places in the area to stay. All rooms have en-suite facilities and are extremely well equipped. A lift provides easy access to all floors. The food and service are second to none and, being just 300 yards from The Esplanade, it is a perfect place to stay.

The Abbeydale Hotel, Manor Road, Sidmouth, Devon EX10 8RP
Tel: 01395 512060 Fax: 01395 515566

For an authentic taste of Indian cuisine with excellent service at very affordable prices, be sure to call for a meal at **Sidmouth Tandoori**. This fine restaurant is situated within easy reach of the town centre on the Sidford road, near the High Street.

Sidmouth Tandoori Restaurant & Takeaway, 7 Radway Place, Sidmouth, Devon Tel: 01395 579944

Whilst shopping or sightseeing in Sidmouth, a visit to **The Willow Tree** is well worth making. This delightful tea shop offers a very varied choice of food, from roast beef to cream teas, all nicely served by pleasant staff in happy surroundings. The Knickerbocker Glory is a particular speciality, served in the traditional way

The Willow Tree

with all of the old fashioned ingredients—lovely! Whether calling in for a refreshing cup of tea or a wonderful Sunday lunch, nobody will be disappointed. *The Willow Tree, Church Street, Sidmouth, Devon Tel: 01395 514890*

Situated just two miles northwest of Sidmouth is the small and ancient settlement of **Bowd**. Here too is **The Barn and Pinn Cottage**, a picturesque 14th century listed building which offers a high standard of accommodation for those wishing to stay in this delightful area. The building is full of character and historic interest and guests can be assured of a warm welcome and a relaxing stay. The rooms are all different but very well appointed; ground floor rooms suitable for disabled guests are also available. The food too is excellent, all home-cooked and using home-grown produce wherever possible. There is also a bar with a log fire for those cold evenings. This is a wonderful hidden place that guests return to time and time again.

The Barn and Pinn Cottage

The Barn and Pinn Cottage, Bowd Cross, Sidmouth, Devon EX10 0ND Tel: 01395 513613

To the north of Sidmouth and in the small village of **Sidford** lies **Boswell Farm**. In the secluded Sweetcombe Valley in an Area of Outstanding Natural Beauty, this farm offers superior self-catering family holiday accommodation in a range of beautifully restored and renovated farm buildings. The name 'Boswell' was mentioned in the Domesday Book and the site certainly dates back to the pre-Norman days. The farmhouse, Boswell House, was built in the 17th century and is a Grade II listed building as is the threshing barn. Becoming a working farm in 1860, it remains so today and holiday guests have access to the 45 acres of farmland.

Boswell Farm

Each of the seven holiday cottages has its own story to tell—Mill House was used for processing the milk from the farm, Cider Lodge was the pressing house and some of the original equipment has been preserved and The Loft was the farm's hay loft. Sympathetically designed, decorated and furnished to a high standard each cottage offers fully self-contained accommodation in peaceful and tranquil surroundings. The kitchens are modern and fully equipped, the sitting rooms are spacious and one cottage even has a four poster bed. With individual and enclosed private gardens as well as a large children's play area, all weather tennis court and well stocked trout pond, there is plenty to occupy the family at the farm. No visitor, after seeing this wonderful place, will be surprised to learn that Boswell Farm has a well deserved English Tourist Board 4 to 5 Keys Highly Commended rating.
Boswell Farm, Sidford, near Sidmouth, Devon EX10 0P Tel: 01395 514162

The Rising Sun lies very much at the heart of Sidford, both geographically and culturally as a meeting place for the local people, many of whom make use of the pub's skittle alley. A busy, traditional pub, the landlady, Andrea Broadhurst, ensures that everyone who visits receives a warm and friendly welcome as well as fine hospitality. There are two bars and a restaurant at The Rising Sun and, as well as serving real ale, bar snacks are available throughout the day whilst there is a full menu served in the restaurant. Renowned local butchers supply the

The Rising Sun

inn with its meat and the tasty vegetables are all grown in the area so a real taste of Devon is assured. Bed and breakfast accommodation is also offered, for those wishing to linger, in four en-suite bedrooms.

The Rising Sun, School Street, Sidford, Sidmouth, Devon EX10 9PF
Tel: 01395 513722

The tiny village of **Salcombe Regis** is perfectly situated in a beautiful valley, to the southeast of Sidford, set back from the sea and with red sandstone cliffs on the shore. For those touring the area, a good place to stay is the **Salcombe Regis Caravan and Camping Park**. This very pleasant site has plenty of room and enjoys some truly spectacular views. Luxury, well equipped mobile homes are also available to let and these provide the ideal base for a family holiday. The site has its own, well stocked shop and off licence, together with an amenities block which includes a launderette and ironing facilities, a washing-up area, hairdryers, a family/disabled bathroom and free hot water to all showers and basins. The site is well signposted from the A3052.

Salcombe Regis Caravan & Camping Park

Salcombe Regis Caravan & Camping Park, Salcombe Regis, near Sidmouth, Devon EX10 0JH Tel & Fax: 01395 514303

OTTERY ST MARY

Map 3 ref G24

Despite some devastating outbreaks of fire, Ottery St Mary still contains some fine Georgian buildings, including an old wool manufactory by the River Otter which is a striking example of early industrial architecture. The town is famous for its Guy Fawkes celebrations which take place each year on the Saturday closest to November 5; these include the time-honoured tradition of rolling barrels of flaming tar through the narrow streets.

One of the most impressive parish churches in the whole of the southwest can be found in this pleasant, ancient market town. Built in the 14th century by Bishop Grandisson, who at the time was supervising the final touches to the refurbishment of Exeter Cathedral, it was constructed as the **Collegiate Church** for a small school for secular priests. The interior is unusually light and airy and contains some exceptional features, including a square-faced clock believed to have been made around 1340 which once showed the phases of the moon as well as the time of day. The vicar here for over 60 years during the 18th century was John Coleridge whose youngest son, Samuel Taylor Coleridge, went on to become one of Devon's few prominent literary figures, with such works to his name as the *Rime Of The Ancient Mariner* and *Kubla Khan*.

One of the few remaining Tudor mansions in the county, **Cadhay**, lies one mile to the northwest. This remarkable house is constructed around a rectangular quadrangle known as the Court of the Kings whose four entrances are guarded by figures of Henry VIII and his offspring, Edward VI, Mary I and Elizabeth I.

The Lamb and Flag is a pink washed, cosy Devon pub, built on the site of an old pilgrim hospital in this beautiful town. Situated close to the river, it is reputed to be the oldest pub in the town. Sally and Gordon have been the established licensees for over 30 years and are well known for their menu of very tasty home-

The Lamb and Flag

made bar snacks—the scampi is a must! The pub has a small function room as well as a skittle alley, which is very popular in the area. Caught at the right time of year, the exterior is bedecked with a mass of floral colour cascading from hanging baskets and window boxes. Disabled visitors are made welcome and assisted. Well behaved pets are also welcome.

The Lamb and Flag, Bats Lane, Ottery St Mary, Devon EX11 1EY
Tel: 01404 812616

Just south of Ottery St Mary lies **Fluxton Farm Hotel**, a charming 16th century Devon longhouse with wonderful views over the Otter Valley owned and run by Ann and Maurice Forth. The farmhouse is delightful and full of character, with beams, open log fires and comfortable furnishings creating a cosy and relaxing atmosphere. The 12 guest bedrooms are all centrally heated and provide tea and coffee making facilities, and all but one are en-suite. With the full English breakfast guests can enjoy free range eggs—indeed, all the cooking makes use of the best of fresh local produce. As the hotel is licensed guests can also enjoy a bottle of wine with their four-course evening meal.

Fluxton Farm Hotel

The large lawned gardens are the perfect place to relax and they feature a putting green and a small trout stream and pond. There is also a miniature railway line running round the garden. This is Maurice's great passion and guests of like mind are welcome to bring their own engines with them. Ann's abiding interest is cats, lots of them, most rescued by the Cats Protection League. These days they naturally form part of the Fluxton Farm scene. A great place for an informal relaxed holiday.

Fluxton Farm Hotel, Ottery St Mary, Devon EX11 1RJ Tel: 01404 812818

Many people dash up and down the motorway to and from the West Country but few venture off to find a more pleasant and quieter route for their journey. The quiet village of **Southerton**, to the southwest of Ottery St Mary is one such place that is easily missed. The village is the home of **The Coach House Hotel**, where delightful walks may be enjoyed by guests in the evening through a glade of rhododendrons leading to a stream in a secluded corner of the hotel grounds. The hotel offers its guests this quiet seclusion and many other joys in the tranquil setting of its 2.5 acres of garden. Nearby is Aylesbeare Common, one of the RSPB bird sanctuaries where many unusual species can be seen and enjoyed. Fishing, hunting, golfing and sea fishing are all at hand.

The Coach House Hotel

The Coach House was transformed from the former Southerton House estate and has been acclaimed by many, including Ashley Courtenay, as a great discovery for discerning people. The rooms are airy and light, in true country house fashion, with views over the lawns and flower beds. All bedrooms are en-suite with television and hot drink facilities; two have four-poster beds and some are situated on the ground floor for easy access. The restaurant maintains a high standard of cuisine and a fine wine list is available to complement the meal. The Coach House is undoubtedly a perfect place for a relaxing break or a quiet holiday in the beautiful valley of the River Otter. ETB 3 Crown Highly Commended.

The Coach House Hotel, Southerton, near Ottery St Mary, Devon EX11 1SE Tel: 01395 568577

SEATON   *Map 3 ref H24*

This is a small seaside town which, before it developed as a resort, lay half a mile inland. Attractively framed by some impressive coastal scenery, much of the architecture is Victorian and Edwardian though the parish church of St Gregory dates from the 14th century. However, perhaps the most noteworthy feature of the town is the **Seaton Tramway**, a three mile stretch of track running along the western bank of the River Axe to Colyton. Operated by an enthusiastic team of devotees, many of them volunteers, the open tramcars are popular with holiday-makers in summer and bird-watchers in winter; the latter benefit from being able to glide along the estuary, seemingly without causing disturbance to the local feathered population.

Set close to the shops in this busy holiday town is the **Beaumont Guest House** which offers a high standard of accommodation at affordable prices. The ideal place for a relaxing short break or longer stay, this family run establishment has a friendly, welcoming atmosphere. The rooms are well appointed and spacious

Beaumont Guest House

and each has en-suite facilities. The food is of a commendably high standard and the views of the sea from the dining room are excellent. Children and pets are welcome and private parking is available.

Beaumont Guest House, Castle Hill, Seaton, Devon EX12 2QW
Tel: 01297 20832

For a relaxing, 'go as you please' holiday in Devon, the **Axevale Caravan Park** is the ideal base. With a combination of beautiful rural views, first class facilities and its proximity to the town and beach, this surely has to be one of the premier sites in the area. The modern range of mobile homes are well appointed and scrupulously clean and all have colour TV with satellite reception. The park is fenced and has a range of play areas, so the children will love it; adults will too, for a reliable baby sitting service provides the opportunity for a romantic evening out. Follow the Seaton road from the A3052 at Colyford Post Office.

Axevale Caravan Park

Axevale Caravan Park, Colyford Road, Seaton, Devon EX12 2DF
Tel: 01297 21342 Fax: 01297 21712

Just to the east of Seaton lies the small village of **Rousdon**, home to the famous **All Hallows School** which occupies a striking Victorian mock-Tudor mansion. **The Orchard**, a newly refurbished fine country hotel, is situated just outside the village, three miles west of Lyme Regis. Perfectly located in beautiful countryside popular with walkers, this is the ideal place for a relaxing break spent exploring the area.

The Orchard

Many things at The Orchard encourage guests to return: the fine food, the warm welcome and friendly atmosphere will all stick in the memory. All 12 guest rooms are very comfortable and well equipped with en-suite facilities, colour TV and tea and coffee making facilities. The extensive menu changes daily but guests can be assured that a meal here will be of the very highest quality, enjoyed in pleasant surroundings. The hotel boasts its own bar and the south facing reception rooms provide a good place to relax and chat with friends at the end of a full day.

The Orchard, Rousdon, Devon DT7 3XW Tel: 01297 442972

Boasting a quiet, level site covering about 10 acres, **Shrubbery Caravan Park**, near Lyme Regis and Seaton, has to be top of the list for those who are touring the area or looking for a well placed holiday base. The park is within easy travelling distance of the many local places of interest including Pecorama, Farway Countryside Park, The Donkey Sanctuary, Seaton Tramway and Bicton

Shrubbery Caravan Park

Park, to name but a few. Shrubbery Caravan Park is fortunate in having a well stocked general store and petrol pump situated adjacent to the site. Additionally, there are shower and toilet facilities, electrical hook-ups on many of the pitches and laundry facilities are also available. Children will enjoy their own safe play area; pets are made welcome and may be exercised in an adjoining field. This is the ideal caravan site, one which is difficult to fault.

Shrubbery Caravan Park, Rousdon, near Lyme Regis, Devon DT7 3XW
Tel: 01297 442227

AXMINSTER   *Map 3 ref H23*

Close to the Dorset border, this former monastic town now benefits from a much needed bypass. Founded in the 7th century above an important crossing on the River Axe, the town has had a long and eventful history as a commercial centre. A Sunday market was founded here in the 12th century which continued until the 19th and two popular one day agricultural fairs still take place today: one on the first Tuesday after 25 April and the other on the first Wednesday after 10 October.

However, Axminster is perhaps best known for having given its name to a type of high quality carpet, although these were made in the town for a period of only 80 years between 1755 and 1835 (the old factory still stands to the northeast of the parish church). At one time, a church bell was rung every time a new carpet was completed, perhaps an indication of the poor productivity which led to the eventual downfall of the business. In recent years, efforts have been make to revive the carpet-making industry in Axminster with some success. The town also contains a surprising number of elegant 18th century buildings, including a handsome coaching inn, the George Hotel.

Situated on the main A35 road at Axminster is the famous **Hunters Lodge Inn**, a coaching inn which dates from the 16th century, a hidden place that is steeped in history. It is said that Judge Jeffries, the Hanging Judge, once used the lodge as one of his courts, sentencing criminals and sending them to the dungeons below, later to be taken to the hanging tree that stood across the road. It is reputed that The Hunters Lodge has its own resident ghost, a criminal who was refused a last drink before being hanged.

The Hunters Lodge Inn

This certainly is a public house which is well worth a visit, a place to relax and enjoy a meal and a quiet drink in warm, friendly surroundings. There is a fine selection of well kept ales and wines together with and extensive selection of superbly prepared home-cooked food. As might be imagined, the pub is a popular one and is apt to get booked-up well in advance, so be sure to make a reservation during peak times. This public house has much to recommend it.

The Hunters Lodge Inn, Raymond's Hill, near Axminster, Devon EX13 5SZ Tel: 01297 33286 Fax: 01297 35061

HONITON   *Map 3 ref G23*

The main centre of east Devon, Honiton is a delightful little town in the valley of the River Otter which could be described as the 'gateway to the far southwest'. The settlement was once a stopping place on Fosse Way, one of the Romans' four royal roads of Britain, which connected Exeter with Bath, Cirencester and the east coast at Lincoln. Honiton's long association with overland travel has had a significant effect on its character; the main feature of the town is its wide, ribbon-like High Street which for centuries carried horse-drawn coaches.

In the late medieval period, Honiton was an important market town and centre of the woollen industry; indeed, the first serge cloth in Devon is said to have been manufactured here. However, it is for another material that the town is perhaps best known: Honiton lace. Lace-making is thought to have been introduced to the area by Flemish immigrants at the time of Elizabeth I. By the end of the 17th century, the industry employed around 5000 people, most of whom worked in their own homes making fine bone lace by hand. (At that time, local children from the age of five went to lace schools where, along with a basic education, they were instructed in the intricacies of lace-making.) The introduction of cheaper machine-made alternatives towards the end of the 18th century almost wiped out demand for the traditionally made fabric until a lifeline was thrown to the industry by Queen Victoria when she insisted upon Honiton lace for her wedding dress. This ensured a small but enduring revival and, today, traditional, hand-made lace can still be found in local shops.

A series of devastating fires in the mid-18th century destroyed most of the older buildings in Honiton, with the result that the town now has the pleasant, unhurried atmosphere of a Georgian coaching town. One pre-Georgian building in the town is **Marwood House**, at the northeastern end of the High Street. It was built in 1619 by the second son of Thomas Marwood, one of Queen Elizabeth I's many physicians who achieved notoriety by curing the Earl of Essex when all others had failed. Marwood Senior then lived on to the extraordinary age of 105 and was buried in St Michael's, Honiton's former parish church.

A couple of buildings on the outskirts of the town also are worth a mention: **St Margaret's Hospital**, to the west, was founded in the Middle Ages as a refuge for lepers who were refused entry to the town. In the 16th century, this attractive thatched building was reconstructed as an almshouse. To the east, an early 19th century castellated toll house, known as **Copper Castle**, can be seen with its original iron toll gates.

Allhallows Museum is a registered museum housed in the 13th century Allhallows Chapel with its decorated ceiling, and the Allhallows School dining hall of the 18th century and its galleries provide an interesting insight into the history and culture of Honiton. The museum is open Monday to Saturday, 10 am to 5 pm, from the Monday before Easter until the last Saturday in October.

Allhallows Museum

The Murch Gallery has a local history from prehistoric to modern times. The displays show how rotten the Borough was, where the first Governor of Upper Canada lived, how Joe Kennedy, the American President's brother, gave his life, and where the German bombs landed in the surrounding area. Honiton's contribution to the art and craft of the world was the development of its lace and the Nichol Gallery is devoted to displays of comparative lace; from June to August (and at other times by arrangement) there are demonstrations of lace-making. The Norman Gallery holds the world's most comprehensive collection of Honiton Lace, an attraction of great fascination for tourists, students and connoisseurs.

Allhallows Museum, High Street, Honiton, Devon EX14 8PE
Tel: 01404 44966

The New Dolphin Hotel, a typical old coaching inn found in Honiton's High Street, is the ideal place for visitors to call in to for refreshment but many will leave without knowing anything of the hotel's colourful past. In 1377, the manor of Honiton was inherited by Sir Philip Courtenay of Powderham, fifth son of the 2nd Earl of Devon, and it was this manor house which became the present Dolphin Hotel. To this day, on one of the hotel walls, is a shield of arms similar to ones that would have been borne by the Courtenay's in the 14th century and this design has been taken as the sign for the inn. The earliest authentic record of the Dolphin as an inn was found in the will of Tristram Stoneinge of Honiton, dated January 20th, 1688, in which he gives his son-in-law, Richard Minify, "all that my messuage with its appurtenances called the Dolphin."

Also in 1688, according to the memoirs of James II, the momentous events that occurred in Honiton "were the turning point of his fortunes" and the Dolphin was the backdrop. The inn was being used as the headquarters of Colonel Tollemache, the commanding officer of the advance guard of the army of William of Orange. One November's night, Lord Cornbury and several other senior officers of James II's advance guard rode to Honiton where they were received by Tollemache. The Colonel gave the men until the morning to decide whether they would desert James II and join his army or whether they would remain loyal to their King and be taken prisoner. The majority of the men switched allegiance and, as a result of their desertion, James II, in a panic, fled to the Continent.

The New Dolphin Hotel

Other visitors have included George III, who in 1789 received the homage of the people of Honiton from the Market Cross near the inn, and, in 1833, Princess Victoria changed horses here. The present proprietor, Alan Tyson, lays claim to an actual sighting of the resident ghost, the mother of a soldier who, according to the burial register of the parish for the 17th century, records that on 23rd June 1685 there was buried "Rice Ward, a Souldier, who died at ye Dolphin".

Today, the Dolphin offers a warm and friendly welcome where good ale may be enjoyed and where a full à la carte menu is available for residents and diners. The front lounge with its warm toned walls is a sunny area where tea and coffee are served all day. The 16 guest bedrooms are of good size and tastefully decorated, most having en-suite bathrooms. As well as a comfortable lounge bar the hotel has a large newly refurbished theme bar, serving a good variety of draft and bottled beers. Food is served in either bars or in the intimate atmosphere of the candlelit restaurant and ranges from reasonably priced bar snacks to the full menu.

The New Dolphin Hotel, 115 High Street, Honiton, Devon EX14 8LS
Tel: 01404 42377 Fax: 01404 47662

Located in the small village of **Weston**, just off the Honiton bypass and situated in its own beautiful gardens by the side of the River Otter is the aptly named **Otter Inn**. This is a delightfully unspoilt country pub offering a welcome to the whole family, no matter what their age, where visitors can sit and enjoy a meal or a drink in the cosy and relaxing atmosphere that is created by the low, heavily beamed ceilings and large log fire that burns from September through to the warmer

The Otter Inn

spring months. Open seven days a week, food is served everyday except Christmas Day with an extensive menu that offers a good selection of home-cooked dishes and specialities, including a menu just for the kids. Babies in high chairs eat for free! The Otter Inn has been awarded *The Good Pub Guide –* Family Pub of the Year 1997, a great relief for those who have children in tow. *The Otter Inn, Weston, near Honiton, Devon EX14 0NZ Tel: 01404 42594*

The village of **Dunkeswell**, to the north of Honiton, lies in the heart of the Blackdown plateau. Its **St Nicholas' Church** contains a carved Norman font depicting what is believed to be one of the earliest representations of an elephant in England. The remains of a 13th century Cistercian abbey can be found to the north of the village on a site now occupied by the Victorian Church of the Holy Trinity. Before rising to the crest of the Blackdown Hills on the Somerset border, the land here descends into the valley of the River Culm. Though it seems unlikely today, this was once a major centre of the woollen industry.

Originally a cottage built in 1201, all the panelling and woodwork for **Fishponds House** was taken from oak cut from the estate. The ponds used to supply the carp for the Cistercian monks at Dunkeswell Abbey up until the Reformation when many of the church buildings were destroyed. Fishponds House is a country inn which provides the ideal setting for weddings and functions within 45 acres of grounds ideal for fishing, camping and caravanning. The inn provides excellent cuisine and traditional hospitality in comfortable and relaxing surroundings, with an à la carte menu each evening in the restaurant. Bar meals are available every lunchtime and evening with a carvery on Sunday. The added facility of first class en-suite accommodation and an outdoor heated swimming pool makes Fishponds House the perfect choice for all occasions.

Fishponds House

Fishponds House, Dunkeswell, Devon EX14 0SH Tel: 01404 891287/ 891358 Fax: 01404 891109

To the west of Honiton lies **Gittisham**, a typical Devonshire village of pretty thatched flint and cob cottages with a central village green. The magnificent stately Elizabethan mansion of Combe House has been the home of John and Thérèse Boswell since 1970. Tucked away from the noise of modern day living amongst the sloping lawns, rhododendrons, magnolias and cherry trees of its 3,000 acre estate, one can enjoy peace and quiet, lovely walks, and even private fishing. **Combe House Hotel** is absolutely stunning: a hotel within a stately home, affording a rare chance to participate in the history and splendour of Britain's heritage.

A remarkable sense of occasion passes over guests as they move through the gloriously panelled drawing room hung with portraits of 18th century ancestors

Combe House Hotel

and filled with the morning sun. In the dining rooms, one with its fine carved pine doorcases and remarkable mirrored overmantle and the other with a fine Italian fireplace and mural by Thérèse Boswell, dinner is served by candlelight. Photographs of the family's horse racing successes are displayed in the cosy bar, an interesting place to gather for an aperitif at any time of the day. John Boswell has had a lifetime involvement with racehorses in India and this country and many of the photographs feature old friends such as Young Inca, Roman Prose, Pride of Britain and many more.

Improvements to the house are undertaken every year but the basic concept of the family run hotel has not changed, that of creating the kind of hotel that the family themselves would like to stay in. The intimate atmosphere of Combe is enhanced by the fact that there are only 15 bedrooms—one suite and two rooms with four-poster beds, all of which have their own bathrooms, colour television, direct dial telephone and hair dryer. Here again, the timeless elegance of Combe may be enjoyed in these spacious and comfortable rooms with their lovely views over the estate. The passage of time has left many noteworthy relics of Combe's illustrious owners, perhaps from as far back as the 14th century. Antique lovers will enjoy the fine architecture, furniture and decor which echoes their taste through the centuries. The hotel is an excellent centre from which to tour east Devon and is conveniently situated less than two miles from the main A30 London to Exeter road.

Combe House Hotel, Gittisham, near Honiton, Devon EX14 0AD
Tel: 01404 42756 Fax: 01404 46004

Just off the main A30 at **Fenny Bridges** lies **Little Ash Farmhouse** which is at least 200 years old and was once part of the Escot estate. Robert and Sadie Reid moved here in 1990 when Robert was looking for a suitable place to set up a workshop. He designs and makes individual pieces of furniture. They have created a comfortable and friendly home where they welcome guests for bed and breakfast and evening meals by arrangement (do try Sadie's Haddock in Stilton sauce, its a must). All bedrooms have a radio, tea maker and colour TV and two overlook the ancient cobbled yard where a former cob stable has been converted

Little Ash Farmhouse

into a two bedroom luxury cottage with magnificent views over the Otter Vale. The large garden offers outdoor relaxation and Sadie's home-cooking is truly something to look forward to!

Little Ash Farmhouse, Fenny Bridges, near Honiton, Devon EX14 0BL
Tel: 01404 850271

Undiscovered by the masses, yet very accessible to those in the know, **Colestocks Country House Hotel** is situated about two miles north of the A30 between Fenny Bridges and **Payhembury**. This 16th century thatched hotel has glorious country views and a particular style for those appreciating the good things in life. Elegant furnishings, marvellous food and an evening tipple served in cut glass are some of the pleasures Colestocks has in store. Ten individual and attractive bedrooms with en-suite bath and shower are provided with the personal comforts of television, central heating and hot drinks facilities. The country style dining

Colestocks Country House Hotel

room has a menu with a wide choice of tasty English and Continental dishes supported by personally selected wines imported by the proprietor. Add to this the many antiques, log fires in the inglenook, home-cooking and intimate bar and it is easy to see why those in the know want to keep Colestocks a secret haven.

Colestocks Country House Hotel, Payhembury, near Honiton, Devon
EX14 0JR Tel: 01404 850633 Fax: 01404 850901

From Junction 28 off the M5 motorway take the former B1376 and follow the sign to **Clyst Hydon**. Just before entering the village, turn right at the sign to the village hall and swimming pool and down this road can be found the quaint **Five**

Five Bells Inn

Bells Inn. Robin, Mark, Angela and Charles extend a warm welcome to all visitors to their 16th century thatched inn, nestling in large award winning picturesque gardens in the beautiful Devon countryside. This well known inn offers a very large selection of home-made meals in the bars, garden and the more formal à la carte restaurant. Spacious car park.
Five Bells Inn, Clyst Hydon, near Cullompton, Devon EX15 2NT
Tel: 01884 277288

Southwest Devon

INTRODUCTION

This area of Devon is dominated by two very different landscapes: the coastal area with towns such as Plymouth, Dartmouth and Torquay and the vast empty and lonely moorland of Dartmoor National Park. The town of Plymouth will forever be remembered as the place where Sir Francis Drake insisted on completing his game of bowls before setting sail to meet the invading forces of the Spanish Fleet. The fine natural deep water harbour here has also been the starting point for many famous voyages of discovery and perhaps the best remembered is the journey made to the east coast of America by the Pilgrim Fathers. The base of Queen Elizabeth I's fleet, the town, along with neighbouring Devonport, is still closely linked to the Royal Navy.

Dartmouth too has strong naval links which go back many hundreds of years and, though its importance as a seafaring town has declined, the construction of the Royal Naval College here has retained its ties with the past.

Inland the wild expanses of Dartmoor contrast strongly with the gently bays, coves and inlets of the coast. The moor's most characteristic topographical features are its tors, the great chunks of fragmented granite which have stood up to the centuries of ice, rain and wind better than the less resistent rock which once surrounded them. Some of the most spectacular and most visited are Hay Tor and Hound Tor near Ilsington in the east and the Great Mis Tor and Vixen Tor near Merrivale in the west. Those walking on the moor should also take great care to avoid the mires and, in particular, the featherbeds, the deep poles of saturated moss which heave up and down when disturbed.

PLYMOUTH
Map 2 ref E25

With around a quarter-of-a-million inhabitants, Plymouth is the largest centre of population in this southwest peninsula. Compared to many settlements here, however, its development has been relatively recent. It was not until the end of the 12th century that the site was recognised as having any potential as a military and commercial port and even then it was not until the 1500s that Plymouth established itself as the main base for the English fleet guarding the western Channel against a seaborne attack from Spain.

The best way of becoming acquainted with this historic city is to approach **Plymouth Hoe** on foot; this is also the most famous part of the town. As the grassy thoroughfare rises onto a broad limestone ridge, a magnificent vista opens up across Plymouth Sound, one of the finest natural deep water harbours in Europe. The Hoe itself is a wide, partly-paved open space which combines the functions of promenade, public park and parade ground. It was here, in 1588, that Sir Francis Drake completed his leisurely game of bowls before sailing out to defeat the Spanish Armada; his statue, a copy of the one by Boehm at Tavistock, looks proudly towards the horizon.

Just offshore, the striking shape of **Drake's Island** rises like Alcatraz from the deep swirling waters at the mouth of the River Tamar. In its time, this stark fortified islet has been used as a gunpowder repository (it is said to be riddled with underground tunnels where the powder was stored), a prison and a youth adventure centre.

Two miles from the Hoe, Plymouth's remarkable **Breakwater** protects the Sound from the destructive effects of the prevailing southwesterly winds. Built between 1812 and 1840, this massive mile long construction required around four million tons of limestone which was ferried out in barges from quarries on the mainland. Twelve miles out to sea and visible on a clear day, the famous **Eddystone Lighthouse** warns shipping of the treacherous group of rocks which rise up from the floor of the English Channel. The present lighthouse is the fourth to be built here: the first, a fragile timber structure, was swept away in a huge storm in 1703 taking with it its builder, the shipowner Winstanley. The third was built in 1759 by John Smeaton to a revolutionary design using dovetail-jointed blocks of granite. It lasted for 120 years before the rocks on which it stood began to collapse and the lighthouse had to be dismantled. However, it was soon rebuilt on Plymouth Hoe and today, it is still one of the city's most rewarding tourist attractions.

The view to the west from the top of Smeaton's Tower takes in **Millbay Docks**, Plymouth's busy commercial port which was once a terminus for transatlantic passenger liners; today, the docks handle a variety of merchant shipping, including the Continental ferry services to Brittany and northern Spain. The view to the east is dominated by **The Citadel**, a massive fortification which was built by Charles II to guard the seaward approaches to Plymouth. Although ostensibly built as a defence against seaborne attack, the presence of gun ports facing the town suggest an ulterior motive. During the English Civil War, the town declared for Parliament and held out for four years against the forces of Charles' ill-fated father.

Plymouth's oldest quarter, **The Barbican**, lies below and a short distance to the northeast of the Citadel. Now a lively entertainment area filled with restaurants, pubs and an innovative small theatre, it was here that 15th century merchants began trading in wine and wool with their opposite numbers in Continental

Europe. The influence of Drake helped to establish the port as a naval base in Elizabethan times and, in 1620, the Pilgrim Fathers set out from the **Mayflower Steps** on their historic voyage to Massachusetts; the names of the Mayflower's company are listed on a board on nearby Island House, now the tourist information office. Plymouth's **Sutton Harbour** became a major departure point for migrants seeking their fortune in the colonies and as a result, there are now around 40 Plymouths in the English-speaking world. A number of interesting old buildings around the Barbican have survived the combined ravages of time and the Luftwaffe, including the **Elizabethan House** in New Street, the **Merchant's House** in St Andrew's Street, and **Prysten House**, a 15th century priest's house which is hidden behind St Andrew's church, off Royal Parade; all now contain delightful specialist museums.

The increased threat from France which came at the end of the 17th century prompted the Admiralty to build a new naval dockyard at the western end of the Channel. Plymouth was chosen but, instead of extending the existing port at the mouth of the Plym, a new deep-water site was developed on the Tamar estuary, which here is known as the Hamoaze (pronounced Ham-oys). Over the following two centuries, the **Devonport Dockyard** grew to cover 240 acres along a two mile stretch of riverside and the surrounding town grew to outstrip its parent to the east. The massive **Royal William Victualling Yard** was added in the early 19th century on a partially reclaimed site at the end of Durnford Street in Stonehouse; here, all the foodstuffs and supplies required by the western fleet were manufactured and packed in watertight barrels.

Although the Barbican area managed to escape serious damage during the Blitz, much of the rest of Plymouth was devastated by a succession of enemy air raids during the spring of 1941. The naval base and dockyard at Devonport made the city an important strategic target and its location on the southwest peninsula meant that it was both difficult to defend and easy to reach from northern France. On the night of 21 March, the entire centre of the city was razed to the ground by the combined effects of high explosive and incendiary bombs.

Many of the city's most important civic and residential buildings were destroyed, including much of the early 19th century work of John Foulston, the architect who was to Plymouth what Nash was to London. The 15th century parish church of St Andrew had to be almost totally rebuilt; however, it was decided that the nearby **Charles' Church** would be left as a burned out shell as a memorial to the 1000 who died and 5000 who were injured in air raids during the course of World War II. A powerful and poignant audiovisual presentation on Plymouth's Blitz can be seen at **The Dome**, an award winning museum which is located on the southern side of the Hoe.

Even before the end of the War, plans were being drawn up for Plymouth's resurrection. The renowned town planner, Sir Patrick Abercrombie, was commissioned to come up with a bold scheme which would sweep away the largely Victorian street plan and create a modern and vibrant city centre. Despite most of the rebuilding being carried out in the 1950s (not the most celebrated era for architecture) his scheme has gradually taken on a pleasant distinguished air, and today Plymouth has the character of a prosperous regional capital.

For a wide variety of snacks in the daytime and Greek food and fun at night time, **The Country Kitchen & Zorba's Taverna** is the place to head for. Located in Bretonside, this duel purpose café and restaurant meets the varied needs of city life. During shopping hours the Country Kitchen serves a wide variety of pastries, sandwiches, cakes and other snacks, teas, coffees, milk shakes and soft drinks. The staff are welcoming and helpful.

Zorba's Taverna & Country Kitchen

At night some changes are made and the taverna opens for business. Zorba's is a busy restaurant used by many individuals and companies for fun nights out. The 70 foot long room has tables running the full length of it. A great place for partying, where guests can indulge in some traditional Greek dancing, plate throwing and table dancing—yes, it's all here; all the ingredients for a fun night out. For those who prefer to just sit and enjoy the interesting Greek food, there is plenty to choose from on Zorba's menu. Stop by and have some fun! Two minutes from the Barbican Centre.

Zorba's Taverna & Country Kitchen, Bretonside, Plymouth, Devon
PL4 0BG Tel: 01752 662481

Set in the heart of Plymouth's historic Barbican district, **Piermasters** is renowned as one of the finest restaurants in the southwest. This handsome listed building stands within a few yards of Sutton Harbour, where ships have set out around the world since the time of Sir Francis Drake and the Pilgrim Fathers and where modern fishing boats tie up to this day. Easily found at the eastern end of

Southside Street, the restaurant enjoys the benefits of a private car park, a bonus in this sometimes congested area. Proprietor Stephen Williams has successfully created a relaxed bistro atmosphere, enhanced by natural wood and exposed brickwork and lit by candles and discreet spotlights. Although the setting is delightfully informal, this is a place for serious food and wine. An enthusiast for over 25 years, Stephen offers a breathtaking list of wines, each of which has been personally selected. The major strength of the menu is seafood, but it also features local game, venison, Cornish poultry and prime south Devon beef and lamb, along with an imaginative range of vegetarian dishes. Cooking in a modern British style which combines traditional English ingredients with influences from northern Europe and the Mediterranean, chef Peter Constable juxtaposes old favourites, new ideas and sudden inspirations. His range

Piermasters Restaurant

of home-made patisseries and desserts is also superb. One of the regulars to be found taking advantage of the excellent cuisine is larger-than-life local artist, Robert Lenkiewicz. Advance booking is advised.

Piermasters Restaurant, 33 Southside Street, The Barbican, Plymouth, Devon Tel: 01752 229345

For many The Platters are remembered as a chart-topping group from the States, but in Plymouth **Platters** is synonymous with the best in seafood in town. Renowned for its lobster, dressed crab and other imaginative fish dishes, the restaurant is very well patronised. All produce is bought fresh each day from the local fish merchants and carefully prepared to create mouthwatering and delicate

Platters Restaurant

flavours in fish cuisine. Guests can enjoy their meal at a private table or with other diners on longer bench-type tables and seating. The interior plaster decor was executed by local artist Ginger Keaton who literally throws the plaster on to the wall to create the seascapes! Platters is a family business with a comfortable and friendly atmosphere, though more importantly, it offers first class food. It is fully licensed and booking is advisable.

Platters Restaurant, 12 The Barbican, Plymouth, Devon PL1 2LS
Tel: 01752 227262

WEMBURY   *Map 2 ref E25*

The **Great Mew Stone** (presumably so called to distinguish it from the much smaller rock known simply as The Mew Stone, near Bayard's Cove) stands a mile offshore in Wembury Bay, to the south of Plymouth. This lonely islet was, apparently, once inhabited but is now the home of seabirds and is also used for training purposes by the *HMS Cambridge* gunnery school on Wembury Point. Wembury church makes a dramatic landmark as it stands isolated on the edge of the cliff and the coastal path offers spectacular views of the Yealm estuary to the east and Plymouth Sound to the west. The path is, however, occasionally closed to walkers when the firing range is in use, so look out for the red warning flags.

Located beside the main road when entering this picturesque seaside village, **The Odd Wheel** is a traditional inn that offers its visitors a taste of true Devonshire hospitality. Owned and personally run by Allan and Nada Gordon, this attractive pub has two wooden beamed bar areas complete with dark mahogany furniture

The Odd Wheel

and embroidered upholstery. Serving some excellent, traditional real ales The Odd Wheel is also locally renowned for its delicious home-cooked meals. The menu is a varied one and includes such delicacies as Beef in Guinness, Somerset Pork and the generously sized Odd Wheel Mixed Grill with an ever changing selection of daily specials. The dessert menu is like stepping into a seriously sinful heaven with Death by Chocolate and Chocolate Trufito—a sublime concoction consisting of a hard chocolate case encrusted with chopped nuts, filled with soft chocolate ice cream and a truffle centre—perfection. Animal lovers will enjoy Nada's collection of unusual pets, which includes a large Vietnamese pot-bellied pig and a collection of goats, geese and a very friendly pony. With live jazz every Thursday evening and a games area for pool and darts, the Odd Wheel is a cosy inn that truly offers something for everyone.

The Odd Wheel, Wembury, Devon PL9 0EA Tel: 01752 862287

IVYBRIDGE
Map 2 ref F25

Lying below the beautiful Erme Valley, the town grew rapidly from a small village as a result of the development of its paper industry in the 19th century. Located in the heart of this bustling town and only 10 miles east of Plymouth, **The Old Smithy** offers a welcome resting place for those travelling through this attractive part of Devon. Serving hot and cold lunches from Monday through to Friday, the ceilings are heavily beamed and the walls are panelled in attractive

The Old Smithy

wood and adorned with old farming tools and general countryside memorabilia. This large and airy inn has traditional Georgian leaded windows that let in plenty of light and a large log burner warms the bar area on those long winter nights. The hosts, Pat and Paul Pritchard, serve some excellent St Austell real ales as well as a good range of lagers, stouts and spirits which can be enjoyed either inside or out in the pretty walled beer garden. This summer suntrap proves very popular amongst all sun worshippers and also has a safe play area for the children.

The Old Smithy, Fore Street, Ivybridge, Devon PL21 9AE
Tel: 01752 892490

SALCOMBE
Map 2 ref F26

This delightful former fishing village, which is now a yachting centre, occupies one of the loveliest coastal settings in the West Country. The resort lies a mile inland from the sandy bar at the mouth of the Kingsbridge estuary and is sheltered from the prevailing west winds by a steep hillside. As a result, it has one of the mildest climates in the country and it is not unusual to see mimosa, palms and even orange trees in the terraced gardens which rise from the water's edge. Salcombe's long association with the sea is brought to life at the **Museum of Maritime and Local History** on the Custom House Quay.

Cars are banned from the central area and, in summer, the narrow streets throng with visitors, many of whom arrive by yacht or pleasure craft from the marinas of southeast England and Europe. A plethora of small shops and eating places have sprung up to satisfy their demand for the modish and expensive and, at certain times of the year, the town takes on the atmosphere of an exclusive resort which has more in common with the south of France than the South Hams.

On a rock beside North Sands stand the remains of **Salcombe Castle**, or Fort Charles, a fortification which was built in Tudor times as part of Henry VIII's Channel coast defences. During the English Civil War, its Royalist garrison was the last in Devon to hold out against the Parliamentarians (indeed, it is claimed the Royalists only agreed to surrender in return for the castle being renamed Fort Charles). Sadly, the structure has since fallen into disrepair and now only a tower and some shattered walls remain.

Originally an Admiralty coastal lookout, **Rickham Coastguard Station** at Gara Rock has a long and interesting history. Constructed in 1847, its original purpose was to safeguard shipping from the infamous smugglers and wreckers operating in the area. In 1909 the station was disbanded and the building was purchased to begin its career as a private hotel. At the outbreak of World War II, however, Gara Rock was requisitioned by the armed forces and occupied as a headquarters for the nearby West Prawle radar station. Following the war Gara Rock returned to private ownership.

The striking promontory known as Sharpitor is the location of a charming National Trust owned museum and garden, **Overbecks**. This handsome Edwardian house stands in a breathtaking position above the Kingsbridge estuary and enjoys one of the finest views in south Devon. The six acre gardens are famous for their collection of rare and tender plants which thrive in these mild coastal conditions. The museum contains a secret children's room, an exhibition on the natural history of Sharpitor, and a room devoted to the clipper schooner, Salcombe's traditional sailing ship. Also on show are special collections of shipbuilding tools, model boats, toys and old photographs.

The coastline to the south and west of Salcombe, some of the most magnificent in Britain, is now largely owned by the National Trust. Here, great slanting chunks of gneiss and schist tower above the coastal path to form a breathtaking, if somewhat demanding, clifftop walk. At Bolt Head, the rock forms a jagged promontory which protrudes into the western approaches to the Kingsbridge

England

estuary, and further west, the spectacular cliffs between Bolt Head and Bolt Tail are interrupted by a steep descent at Soar Mill Cove. After rounding Bolt Tail, the footpath drops down to the sheltered sandy beach and tourist shops of Hope Cove.

DARTMOUTH   *Map 3 ref F25*

This ancient nautical town stands in a dramatic position on the steeply sloping west bank of the Dart estuary, a mile inland from its mouth. This sheltered deep water port has long been used as an assembly point for departing naval forces: the Second and Third Crusades set sail from here in the 12th century and, in more recent times, part of the D-Day invasion force congregated here before setting out for the beaches of Normandy in 1944.

During the late Middle Ages, Dartmouth grew rapidly to become the fourth largest town in the county (after Exeter, Plymouth and Barnstaple), partly as a result of Henry II's marriage to Eleanor of Aquitaine in 1152. This link with southwestern France led to a dramatic upturn in the wine trade, an activity which was balanced with the export of woollen cloth from Totnes and Ashburton.

Dartmouth's subsequent rise as a commercial port was largely due to one man, John Hawley, an enterprising merchant and seafarer who was elected mayor seven times during the 14th century. Geoffrey Chaucer met Hawley in 1373 when visiting the town in his official capacity as a customs' inspector, an encounter which is thought to have provided the inspiration for the character of the Shipman in *The Canterbury Tales*. Hawley was also responsible for building **Dartmouth Castle**, the imposing fortification guarding the entrance to the Dart estuary which was specifically constructed as an artillery emplacement. Most of the present remains date from the 15th century when a special winding mechanism was added to provide the harbour with a second line of defence: a heavy chain stretched across the estuary to Kingswear Castle.

Standing within the castle grounds, the church of St Petrock was built in the 17th century on the site of an early Christian minster; inside there is a Norman font and some good monumental brasses. The remains of a 17th century Civil War redoubt known as **Gallants Bower** can be seen further up the hillside.

Another ruined fortification, one built as part of Henry VIII's coastal defences, can be seen near the site of the Old Quay on the southern edge of Dartmouth town centre. Also situated here is the old **Custom House**, a handsome building of 1739 which has some fine internal plasterwork ceilings. Before the New Quay was constructed in the late 16th century, on land reclaimed from the estuary, ships used to tie up against the wall of **St Saviour's Parish Church**, a part 14th century building with an impressive stone pulpit and a striking monumental brass to John Hawley and his two wives; the south door also features some remarkable early ironwork in the design of a tree and two leopards.

For nearly two centuries, Dartmouth's fleet of ocean-going trawlers departed from the New Quay for the rich cod fishing grounds off Newfoundland. However, when the fishing and textile industries started to decline at the end of the 17th century, Dartmouth also began to declined. A further blow was dealt in 1689 when the Admiralty decided to locate its new naval dockyard at Devonport, thanks to the greater availability of land. In the 19th century it was hoped that Dartmouth would become a terminus for transatlantic steamers; however, the lack of a main line railway meant this also came to nothing. The one major development which did go Dartmouth's way was the construction of the mighty **Britannia Royal Naval College** between 1899 and 1905; this sprawling red and white building continues to dominate the town from its position on the hillside to the north.

The centre of present day Dartmouth is a very attractive combination of narrow lanes, historic buildings and picturesque waterfront parades. The particularly fine 17th century **Butterwalk** is home to a museum which houses an engine designed by Thomas Newcomen, a native of Dartmouth who began as a local blacksmith and ironmonger, and went on to invent an early version of the industrial steam engine in 1712.

TORQUAY   *Map 3 ref F25*

The origins of Torquay date back to the end of the 12th century when **Torre Abbey** was founded on a site a quarter-of-a-mile inland from the northern end of Tor Bay. By Tudor times, the abbey had grown to become the wealthiest Premonstratensian monastery in England; however, it was forced into non-ecclesiastical ownership in 1539 and fell into disrepair. The site then changed hands several times before it was acquired by the Careys in 1662, a family whose descendants built the present house of Torre Abbey in Georgian times and who continued to own the property until shortly after World War II. It was then acquired by Torquay Corporation for use as a museum and art gallery. Over 25 rooms are now open to the public, one of which is devoted to the Torquay born mystery writer, Agatha Christie; many contain superb pieces of period furniture and works of art.

Several impressive medieval remains can still be seen in the abbey grounds, including the late 12th century entrance to the Chapter House, the gatehouse of 1320, a section of the Abbot's tower, and the great Spanish barn, a massive 124 foot long tithe barn which was later used to house prisoners-of-war from the Armada. The grounds now form one of the many public open spaces in the town and are open daily, all year round; admission free.

As a fashionable watering place, Torquay was a relatively late developer and it was not until the early 19th century that wealthy patrons began to arrive in significant numbers after they were denied access to the Continent by the Napoleonic Wars. The expansion of the town was strictly controlled by two families (the Careys of Torre Abbey and the Palks of Haldon House, near Exeter) and together, they set about creating a select resort which would appeal to the rich and aristocratic. The only resistance to this expansion came from Torquay's third landed family, the Mallocks of Cockington, who refused to grant building leases on their land until the 1860s, and then only very sparingly. Instead, they went to great lengths to preserve their estate, with its part-Elizabethan manor house, 15th century red sandstone church, forge and immaculate thatched village. After seeming to be suspended in time for several centuries, **Cockington** was eventually sold to Torquay Corporation in 1935 for £50,000, and it is now a fascinating outdoor museum and public open space which can be found a mile from the sea on the western edge of the built up area.

Kent's Cavern is a series of caves which is believed to be one of the oldest inhabited sites in the British Isles. When the caves were excavated in the early 19th century, they were found to contain primitive tools of the sort used by neolithic man around 5000 years ago; they also contained the bones of animals which have long been extinct. Now easily accessible and clearly lit, they provide an interesting all weather attraction.

To the north of Torquay, the ancient village of **Maidencombe** dates back to the days before the Norman Conquest. Its name, which is derived from Anglo-Saxon, means Valley of Water and, indeed, numerous springs are to be found nearby. A quiet and peaceful community today, in the 18th and 19th centuries things were a little different as the local people took to smuggling to supplement their meagre income from farming and fishing. The coast line around this area is dotted with secluded coves and here the contraband would be stored until it could be hauled up the cliffs and distributed inland by river.

Bowden Close is a delightful country house hotel situated in this peaceful village with panoramic sea and coastal views. The hotel is found along the B3199 coast road midway between Teignmouth and Torquay. The south facing hotel is set in spacious grounds where guests can sit out and soak up the sun and enjoy the tranquil surroundings and views over Lyme Bay. Most of the bedrooms are en-suite and all are equipped with colour television and hot drink facilities. The

Bowden Close Hotel

licensed restaurant, which overlooks the garden and sea, is open each evening and offers a good variety of dishes including vegetarian, prepared using home grown or local produce where possible. During the day, the Garden Tea Room is open for morning coffee, light lunches and afternoon teas. Children of any age are welcome and pets can generally be accepted by arrangement. The hotel is open all year round. ETB 3 Crown.

Bowden Close Hotel, Teignmouth Road, Maidencombe, near Torquay, Devon TQ1 4TJ Tel: 01803 328029

BOVEY TRACEY   *Map 3 ref F24*

This pleasant old market town is a good base from which to explore the eastern fringes of Dartmoor. A settlement was founded at this ancient crossing point on the River Bovey in pre-Norman times and, by the 13th century, it had grown sufficiently to be granted its own weekly market and an annual three day festival.

The Parish **Church of St Thomas of Canterbury** stands high above the north bank of the river. An imposing building with a 14th century tower, it contains a number of impressive internal features, most notably its eleven bay rood screen of 1427 which was sympathetically restored by the Victorians. Several of the church's finest treasures were hidden away by the vicar following the execution of Charles I in 1649. He did not return them until the Restoration, when he put up notices voicing his disapproval at the events of the previous 11 years (these in turn have become treasures in their own right).

At the foot of the town, the present day bridge over the Bovey was built in 1643 and widened two centuries later. The water wheel on the nearby mill was originally used to raise water to a tank in the little tower above. (This building has never, in fact, been a mill, rather it was the stables and domestics' quarters of nearby Riverside House.)

Two miles to the west, the National Nature Reserve at **Yarner Wood** is a protected breeding ground for several uncommon species of birds. The road then continues northwestwards past the prominent viewpoint on Trendlebere Down before dropping down to the impressive, if well visited, beauty spot of **Becka Falls**.

The headquarters of **Dartmoor National Park** are located at **Parke**, a handsome late Georgian house standing beside the B3387 Widecombe road on the western edge of Bovey Tracey. The house stands within beautiful 200 acre grounds which also contain an interesting privately run rare breeds farm and a delightful nature trail which descends through the woods to the river.

During the late Neolithic and Bronze Age periods, Dartmoor was relatively densely populated and the moorland is strewn with many remains. Dozens of Bronze Age burial mounds have been identified, many of which have been found to contain stone caskets (keasts) where the ashes or crouched bodies of ancient tribal leaders were placed. The most impressive of all is **Grimspound**, a complex settlement of around 25 dwellings dating from around 1000 BC which can be found on Hamel Down to the north of Widecombe-in-the-Moor.

During the Middle Ages, Dartmoor became the focus of large scale open cast tin mining and, though it is hard to imagine today, at one time the moor was one of the largest tin producing areas in the world. Evidence of this early industrial activity can still be seen in the overgrown spoil heaps and ruined smelting houses with litter the valleys running off the high moor. The medieval tinners were also responsible for building Dartmoor's famous clapper bridges, a design in which vertical stone pillars were linked together by great unmorticed slabs of granite. They were built to enable packhorses loaded with smelted tin make their way down to the four Stannary towns of Ashburton, Chagford, Tavistock and Plympton where the tin was weighed and stamped. The best example still remaining can be seen beside the B3213 at Postbridge. Mining activity on Dartmoor reached its peak in the 16th century, by which time shaft mining had replaced open cast working. The industry then began a long and slow period of decline, interspersed with spells of revival, until the last mine closed in the 1930s.

Those interested in undertaking the demanding hikes which can be made across the moor might also be interested in looking out for some of Dartmoor's many letterboxes; small weatherproof boxes containing a rubber stamp and an ink pad which are concealed at selected sites throughout the National Park. The idea began in around 1850 when walkers reaching remote **Cranmere Pool** on the northern moor got into the habit of leaving a visiting card in a proscribed place. Later, it became the practice to leave a self-addressed postcard which the next walker would take and post from home. There are an estimated 350 letterboxes scattered throughout the moor.

Once a Mission House built in the 1930s, **Courtenay House** offers a multiplicity of functions. It is primarily an Antique and Craft Centre displaying furniture,

Courtenay House

linens, jewellery, silver, china, dried flowers, local crafts and bric-a-brac. The owner, Tina Richardson, also caters in the tea rooms and garden with a wide range of food, from snacks to a full lunch. Sunday Lunch is especially popular and booking is essential. The tea rooms are strongly supported by local people and Tina offers a special lunch for senior citizens on Mondays. For those who decide to stay a while in the area, then bed and breakfast accommodation is also available. What more could anyone ask for?

Courtenay House, Fore Street, Bovey Tracey, Devon Tel: 01626 835363

The Old Cottage Tea Shop

About 100 yards over the bridge in the town centre, is **The Old Cottage Tea Shop**, owned by Louise Pawson for the past 11 years. Well known for her home-cooked lunches, cakes and scones, Louise offers a great variety of hot and cold dishes throughout the day which include toasted sandwiches, jacket potatoes with tasty fillings, omelettes, fish dishes, soups and salads. Cream teas are, of course, a favourite, as are the many home-made sweets on offer—Devon Farmhouse ice cream served in many flavours is particularly tempting. The fully carpeted interior and many paintings by local artists add to the cosy cottage atmosphere. Well worth taking a refreshment break here.

The Old Cottage Tea Shop, 20 Fore Street, Bovey Tracey, Devon TQ13 9BE Tel: 01626 833430

The splendid **Dartmoor Inn** as seen today has evolved over a long period, the available adjoining cottages being gradually acquired and added. During the last 10 years it has reached proportions whereby the original inn now forms part of a beautiful lounge and dining area. Around the inn, old beams and open fireplaces have maintained the character from earlier years. Ten fully fitted guest bedrooms are available all with en-suite bathrooms and modern amenities. Meals are served during normal opening hours and diners will find generous

The Dartmoor Inn

portions and quality food. The Dartmoor is well known for its wonderful breakfasts. Good parking and easy to find on the High Street.

The Dartmoor Inn, High Street, Bovey Tracey, Devon TQ13 9AL
Tel: 01626 832211

Chudleigh, to the east of Bovey Tracey and ideal for those travelling along the A38 south of Exeter, is the location of a good stopping point at **The Bishop Lacy Inn**, a Grade II listed building that was a Devon church house. There existed a secret tunnel to the nearby church which is sadly now filled in due to subsidence. The pub is reputedly haunted by a monk and a white lady. The great fire of Chudleigh in 1807 ended at the east wall of the inn, charring some of its timbers. Robin and Wendy are the resident proprietors of this free house and offer a friendly welcome to the all who come here to enjoy the good home-cooked food and the gravity fed real ales. A super place, just call in and sample the hospitality.

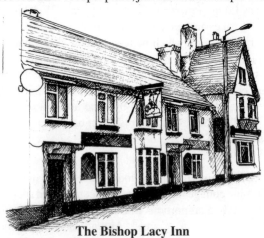

The Bishop Lacy Inn

The Bishop Lacy Inn, Fore Street, Chudleigh, Devon TQ13 0HY
Tel: 01626 854585

BUCKFASTLEIGH

Map 2 ref F25

Buckfastleigh, an old mill village with narrow street and quaint mews cottages, once stood on the Totnes-Ashburton railway line, a branch which ran alongside the beautiful River Dart for most of its length. Although the line was closed in the 1960s, it was given a new lease of life in 1969 when the Dart Valley Railway Company purchased the track and began operating a steam train service between Buckfastleigh and Totnes.

The line has since changed its name to the **South Devon Railway** and operates regular services throughout the summer. With its carefully chosen advertisements and railway memorabilia, Buckfastleigh station is now a delightful reminder of the heyday of the Great Western Railway. An interesting butterfly farm is also located on the same site.

The part 13th century **Parish Church of the Holy Trinity** is set away from the village centre in an impressive position on a limestone rock overlooking the Dart valley. Unfortunately the church's unusual red sandstone Norman font was lost in a devastating fire in 1992 which also left this historic church little more than a blackened shell. Although the tower and spire have been rebuilt and the exterior walls renovated, the roof has not been replaced and it remains open to the elements. The 200 step climb up from the village is well worth the effort.

However, another of the church's interesting features, a rare penthouse tomb, still remains. The last resting place for members of the Cabell family, it was Sir Richard Cabell who inspired Sir Arthur Conan Doyle to write his best known Sherlock Holmes novel *The Hound of the Baskervilles*. Sir Richard, who died in 1677, was a notorious man in the area and was known to hunt the nearby moors with a pack of hounds. The iron grille seen around his tomb was erected to prevent his ghost escaping onto Dartmoor.

The Singing Kettle

The Singing Kettle Tea Rooms with its pretty green washed frontage and bow windows can easily be found in the main street and is a well kept 17th century building with large open fireplaces.

This is a traditional English tea room, with comfort and ambience, serving home-made cakes and scones from an extensive and varied menu. Delicious Devon cream teas are a speciality with home-made jam and clotted cream. Awarded the Heartbeat Award.

The Singing Kettle, 54 Fore Street, Buckfastleigh, Devon TQ11 0BS
Tel: 01364 642383

TAVISTOCK   *Map 2 ref E24*

This is a busy little town situated on the western edge of Dartmoor which
continues to fulfil its traditional function as a market serving a large area of rural
west Devon. Although there is some evidence of Celtic and Saxon occupation,
the town is essentially the creation of two institutions: Tavistock Abbey, which
was founded in 974 and dominated the town until the Dissolution of the
Monasteries in 1539, and the Russell family who, as the dukes and earls of
Bedford, owned much of the town until 1911.

Tavistock's Benedictine **Abbey**, one of the grandest in the West Country, had its
own great church, cloisters and chapter house and was surrounded by an
immense castellated wall. The abbey soon gave rise to a prosperous lay
community which, in 1105, was granted permission to hold a weekly market and
an annual three day fair. The weekly market still takes place on Fridays in the
pannier market, and the annual event has evolved into the Goose Fair, a
wonderful traditional street fair which is held on the second Wednesday in
October. When the expansion in tin mining on Dartmoor began at the end of the
12th century, Tavistock was established as a Stannary town.

For centuries, smelted ore was transported here by packhorse from all over the
western sector of the moor to be weighed and stamped, before being sold on to
merchants and metalworkers. The effects of the industry's eventual decline was
tempered by the expansion of the woollen industry in the 16th century when
Tavistock became known for the manufacture of fine serge. When this industry
also began to decline during the 1700s, the discovery of rich deposits of copper
around Mary Tavy heralded a new era of prosperity which lasted until the end of
the 19th century.

The Russell family acquired the site and estates of Tavistock abbey following the
Dissolution and, after demolishing most of the abbey buildings (a few discon-
nected remains can still be seen between the river and the parish church), they
created the town plan seen today. During the 1840s, the Dukes of Bedford, as
they subsequently became, built the Guildhall and several other civic buildings,
remodelled the Bedford Hotel and constructed the model estate of artisans'
cottages on the western side of town.

Hidden amongst rolling farmland on the edge of the tiny hamlet of **Ottery** but
only two miles from historic Tavistock is **The Old Coach House Hotel**.
Originally built in 1857 for the Duke of Bedford, it was sympathetically
renovated in 1989. By retaining many old timber beams and the granite open
fireplace in the dining room, the character of this lovely old building has been
preserved. The bedrooms are of a good size with cottage style furnishings, en-
suite bathrooms and are equipped with television, radio/alarm, telephone and tea
and coffee making facilities. The meals are superb with a selection and standard
equal to any quality restaurant. A small bar is available for hotel guests only. For

The Old Coach House

those who prefer a little activity during their stay, fishing tuition, natural history guided tours, riding and golf can be arranged. ETB 3 Crowns.
The Old Coach House, Ottery, near Tavistock, Devon PL19 8NS
Tel: 01822 617515

To the southeast of Tavistock close to the pretty village of **Walkhampton** lies **Burrator Reservoir**, a picturesque artificial lake which was built in 1898 to hold Plymouth's water supply; it is held back behind a dam made of six ton blocks of granite which were quarried locally. A magnificent view of the reservoir and the surrounding countryside can be had from the top of **Sheeps Tor**, a typical Dartmoor tor which also gives its name to the hamlet lying at its base.

Situated in the very centre of Walkhampton, the **Walkhampton Inn** is the oldest inhabited building in the surrounding three valleys. Built back in 1381, the building was originally used as a lodging house for tinners, stonemasons, shepherds and monks who regularly travelled the weary road from Buckfastleigh to Tavistock Abbey. This attractive inn became a free house in 1991 and has been

The Walkhampton Inn

owned and personally run by Morgan and Nikki for the past two years. Home of the award winning Jail Ale (as sampled by Prince Charles during a visit to Devon), the Walkhampton Inn prides itself on supplying its thirsty guests with some of the very best real ales. Beer festivals are a regular occurrence within these natural stone walls and prove very popular amongst locals and visitors alike, with people travelling many miles just to sample some of the imaginatively named cask beers that Morgan stocks.

The food being served within this cosy pub proves to be excellent value for money, there is the usual home-cooked pub fayre which rubs shoulders with a superbly varied à la carte menu for evening dining. The steaks and beef dishes prove very popular amongst the diners for they comprise only the best locally produced organic meat and all dishes are produced using only the freshest seasonal ingredients. In the winter visitors can toast their feet in front of one of three crackling open fires, cosy beneath wooden beamed ceilings and rough stone walls, but in the summer the beer garden is definitely the place to be. This south facing suntrap is the perfect spot to relax and catch a few rays whilst sipping on a long, cool drink.

The Walkhampton Inn, Walkhampton, Devon PL20 6JY Tel: 01822 855556

North Devon

INTRODUCTION

North Devon too has a splendid coastline with high cliffs along the Bristol Channel near Lynton and fine sandy beaches around Appledore. Between the coast and the dramatic scenery of Dartmoor is a land of green hills, thatched cottages and the valleys of the Torridge and Taw.

Barnstaple stands at the midpoint of the **Tarka Trail**, a 180 mile long-distance walk in the shape of a great figure of eight. The northern circle takes in parts of Exmoor and the North Devon coastal path. The trail takes its name from Henry Williamson's enchanting *Tarka The Otter* stories which were set in the valleys of the Taw and Torridge.

ILFRACOMBE   *Map 2 ref E21*

The largest seaside resort on the North Devon coast prior to 1800, Ilfracombe was a small fishing and market town which totally relied on the sea, not only for its living, but as its principal means of communication. The boundaries of the old town are marked by a sheltered natural harbour to the north and a part Norman parish church half-a-mile away to the south.

The entrance to the harbour is guarded by **Lantern Hill**, a steep sided conical rock which is crowned by the restored medieval chapel of St Nicholas. For centuries, this highly conspicuous former fishermen's chapel doubled as a lighthouse, the light being placed in a lantern at the west end of the building. Today, Lantern Hill provides a spectacular view of Ilfracombe's old street plan, boat-filled harbour and craggy coastline.

The town first expanded with the arrival of the new fashion for sea-bathing in the first few decades of the 19th century. The **Tunnel Baths**, with their extravagant Doric façade, were opened in Bath Place in 1836, by which time a number of elegant residential terraces had been built on the hillside to the south of the old town. However, it was not until later in the century that Ilfracombe became popular with holidaymakers of all backgrounds; the railway arrived in 1874 and the harbour was significantly enlarged to take the paddle steamers which ferried trippers from Bristol and South Wales.

Like many British seaside resorts, Ilfracombe is a place of contrasts. The part-Norman parish church of the Holy Trinity, whose unique wagon roof braces are guarded by a series of unusual carved angels and gargoyles, lies within a half-mile radius of the Pavilion theatre, Winter Gardens, discos, bars and a modern pleasure park. For those who prefer to expend their energy exploring the coastal path, there is some spectacular walking along the cliffs to Capstone Point to the west and Hillsborough Hill to the east. In summer, the *MS Oldenburg* sails from Ilfracombe to Lundy island.

Turn into the drive of the **Epchris Hotel** where, in past times horse drawn carriages would have entered, and arrive at the oldest building on the Torrs. Set in two acres of terraced grounds, guests will discover, tucked into discreet sunny corners, the superb heated swimming pool and paddling pool, a putting green, play area and games chalet. This former country residence offers the comfort and charm of yesteryear whilst satisfying the modern needs of today's expectations. Guests can enjoy satisfying, home-cooking in the elegant dining room and gather in the cosy bar or residents lounge at any time for pleasant relaxation. All but one

Epchris Hotel

of the 10 bedrooms have en-suite facilities; they are spacious, comfortable and have TVs and hot drink facilities. There is enough to keep everyone occupied without the need for driving—so take a break and enjoy Ilfracombe and this lovely hotel.

Epchris Hotel, Torrs Park, Ilfracombe, Devon EX34 8AZ
Tel: 01271 862751

A warm and friendly greeting awaits all guests in the three hotels of the Devonia Hotels Group, which are centrally situated for all of Ilfracombe's many amenities and offer an ideal base from which to explore the West Country. **The Arlington Hotel** is registered with the ETB as a 4 Crown Hotel and is perfectly positioned overlooking the sea and surrounding views. The cuisine is excellent and offers a full English breakfast and five course evening meals, whilst the heated outdoor swimming pool proves very popular place to relax in the long, summer months.

Arlington Hotel, Sommers Crescent, Ilfracombe, Devon EX34 9DP Tel: 01271 862002

Next is **The Granville Hotel** that is located very close to the beautiful National Trust Torrs Walk, and only a short distance from the promenade. With impressive views from most of the guest rooms, the personal service and homely atmosphere make the Granville Hotel ideal for a memorable holiday, relaxing break or a successful business seminar.

The Granville Hotel, Granville Road, Ilfracombe, Devon EX34 8AT Tel: 01271 862002

Last but by no means least is **The Wildersmouth Hotel**, a friendly hotel that makes all its guests feel at home from the moment that they walk through the doors. Offering a traditional full English breakfast and four course evening meal,

The Wildersmouth Hotel

the Wildersmouth has varied entertainment most nights, sauna and solarium and, as in all the hotels, colour satellite TV and tea making facilities in all of its bedrooms. All hotels offer business accommodation at very competitive rates during the cooler months and have flexible arrangements are available for meeting rooms and conferences with a full choice of facilities. The Devonia Hotels Group also offer a large range of Special Weekend and Price Cutting breaks ranging from the popular Champagne Weekends at the Arlington to the exciting Murder-Mystery Weekends which take place at the Granville. Having stayed in any one of these three wonderful hotels, guests find that they want to come back for more again and again.

The Wildersmouth Hotel, Sommers Crescent, Ilfracombe, Devon EX34 9DP Tel: 01271 862002

LYNTON and LYNMOUTH   *Map 3 ref F21*

These two small resorts are often mentioned in the same breath but they are very different in character. The older settlement, Lynmouth, is a former herring fishing village whose decline was halted when visitors began arriving to sample the delights of the north Devon coast at the time of the Napoleonic wars. Coleridge and Wordsworth were among its early visitors, arriving here on foot in the 1790s, and Shelley wrote fondly of the place when he visited in 1812.

As its name suggests, the town stands at the point where the steep sided valleys of the Rivers East and West Lyn reach the Bristol Channel, a dramatic location whose rugged beauty conceals a dormant threat. During the night of 15 August 1952, nine inches of rain fell onto an already rain-saturated Exmoor; as a result, an immense surge of surface rainwater cascaded into the Lyn valleys, bursting the riverbanks and sweeping away everything in its path on its journey to the sea. Several upstream communities were devastated; however, it was in Lynmouth that the damage was most acute. Power lines were severed, and in the thundering darkness, dozens of houses were destroyed, the harbour was damaged, cars were swept out to sea, and 31 people lost their lives.

Lynmouth was soon repaired, thankfully with much improved flood control measures, but the memory of the disaster lives on to this day. Among the structures to be rebuilt after the flood was the **Rhenish Tower**, a 19th century affectation which was originally constructed to store seawater for the medical baths of its eccentric owner, General Rawdon.

The town is connected to its more recent sister, Lynton, by an ingenious cliff railway, the first of its kind in Britain when it was opened on Easter Monday, 1890. With a vertical height of 450 feet and a gradient of 1:1.75, the railway is powered by gravitational force: twin cars are connected to each other by a looped cable. Each has a 700 gallon water tank which, when full, weighs around three tons; when the tank at the top is filled and the one on the bottom emptied, the brakes are released and the cars change places.

Passengers alighting at the top find themselves in Lynton, a small resort which expanded around the Lynton to Barnstaple railway terminus. With its magnificent setting, it is well worth a visit, and there is a well established local museum containing some worthwhile background information on Exmoor and the Lyn valleys. One of the most popular beauty spots in the area lies at the confluence of the East Lyn and Hoar Oak Water, one mile to the east of Lynton. The wooded gorge at **Watersmeet** is now under the ownership of the National Trust and a restored 19th century Gothic fishing lodge on the site has been made into a visitor centre and tea garden.

A toll road to the west of Lynton leads to the spectacular **Valley of the Rocks**, a dry scarified valley which may once have been the ancient course of the West Lyn. The great rocky outcrops have been given such names as Chimney Rock, Rugged Jack, the White Lady and the Devil's Cheese Ring, and occasionally the valley's resident population of wild goats can be seen frolicking amongst them. A little further on, **Lee Abbey** is now a conference and study centre run by the Anglican church; never actually a monastic house, it was built in the mid-19th century on the site of an ancient manor farm referred to in *Lorna Doone*.

Ideally situated towards the picturesque Valley of the Rocks and overlooked by Hollerday Hill, **Longmead House Hotel** offers its guests good old fashioned hospitality in pleasantly informal surroundings. This family run hotel offers excellent bed and breakfast accommodation in this beautiful, old Lynton house that has a large, peaceful garden that boasts stunning views of the local beauty spots. The excellent cuisine is supplied courtesy of Bryony, who with the help of her husband Brian, will endeavour to provide guests with everything they require to make their stay at Longmead a memorable one.

The attractively oak panelled dining room, complete with large open fireplace, is where residents can sit and enjoy Bryony's superb home-cooking. The menu is a varied one, combining the delights of Continental and traditional English cuisine using only the freshest local produce and supported by a good selection

Longmead House Hotel

of wines to accompany the evening meal. Most of the eight delightful and individually decorated bedrooms have full en-suite facilities, with the large family room sleeping up to four people in comfort. There is also a cosy TV lounge which comes complete with a fully licensed, well stocked bar, the perfect place to sit and contemplate the next days exploring over a warming glass of brandy.

Longmead House Hotel, Longmead, Lynton, Devon EX35 6DQ Tel & Fax: 01598 752523

Superbly positioned, at **Barbrook**, and overlooking picturesque Lynton and Lynmouth, **Channel View Park** is a family run caravan site that is surrounded by some of the finest scenery in England. Owned and personally run by Robbie and Pat Wren, this welcoming couple are only too willing to ensure that their guests' stay at this superb park is a successful and memorable one. The facilities available to campers and caravanners alike is superb, with a well stocked self-service shop, modern toilet block with free showers, hairdryers and razor points, and an excellent launderette complete with washer, tumble dryer, spin dryer and ironing facilities. There are also plenty of electric hook-ups and a large children's play area where the young ones can let off some steam in a safe

Channel View Caravan Park

environment. All of the superb caravans are fully equipped to meet every need and are personally cleaned and maintained by the proprietors, all holidaymakers will need to bring is their own linen. Each comes complete with colour television, refrigerator, gas cooker and bathroom with shower and WC, whilst all electricity and gas being included in the price. Walking in this enchanting area is very popular and campers will find plenty of trails through green, scented woods to local Lynmouth, Lynbridge and Lynton and rambling cliff paths that lead you to Watersmeet Valley, Valley of the Rocks and Lee Bay. For those who prefer to do their sightseeing in a less demanding fashion, there are three local stables for trekking and a nearby golf course can be found at either Saunton or Ilfracombe.

Channel View Caravan Park, Manor Farm, Barbrook, near Lynton, Devon EX35 6LD Tel: 01598 753349

MESHAW   *Map 3 ref F23*

Set amidst the peaceful, rolling countryside of North Devon, **Bournebridge Country Cottages** offers excellent self-catering accommodation in a relaxing and tranquil environment. The hosts are John and Celia Hughes, who have personally ensured that each cottage is equipped with everything guests should need to make their stay a special and memorable one. Beech Cottage offers spacious accommodation for up to five people and combines many original features including exposed beams and stonework. Attractively furnished and decorated throughout, Beech Cottage has a relaxing and comfortable lounge/diner and shares a large courtyard garden.

Bournebridge Cottages

Bramble Cottage is a cosy single storey dwelling which comfortably accommodates five guests. Perfect for those not wishing to tackle stairs, this cottage offers three bedrooms, lounge/diner and a private garden to the rear that overlooks lush green fields. Hazel Cottage offers a high standard of convenience and comfort for four. Superbly decorated throughout, the original features such as exposed beams add an air of history to this pretty home. The kitchenette is well equipped and the one double and one twin bedroom are both on the ground floor level. Each cottage has a patio area and garden furniture and bed linen is provided throughout with the beds being made-up prior to arrival.
Bournebridge Cottages, Meshaw, South Molton, Devon EX36 4NL
Tel: 01884 860134

BAMPTON   *Map 3 ref G22*

The pleasant community of Bampton, lying in the Exe Valley, was once a small market town whose economy relied on the wool trade. Now a quiet backwater, it possesses the remnants of an old castle and a much altered 14th century church with a wagon roof and some interesting tombs and internal detailing. The village is liveliest during the last week in October when the streets are closed off, and sheep and cattle (though no longer Exmoor ponies) are brought down from the moor to be bought and sold at the autumn fair.

The **Seahorse Inn** is a large country pub with a crisp white and black exterior and it is easy to find, situated on the corner and junction of Ford Road and Briton Street. This well decorated pub has good facilities and, in addition to the main bar, it has a function room with a separate bar, a conservatory and games which include skittles, darts and pool. John and Helga Brown offer a friendly welcome to visitors to the Seahorse Inn where those in the know gravitate for good cooking

Seahorse Inn

and real ales. There's an extensive menu with a selection of good value home-cooked meals catering for many different tastes. About 10 options to start, including Breaded Brie, Battered calamari and Smoked trout, and a huge selection of main courses. Bar snacks are available and the Carvery is especially popular, booking is strongly recommended on Sundays. The conversion of an old stone barn into a children's play area provides an excellent, safe area to keep the youngsters happy. Special theme evenings are also a feature of the pub where parties and functions for all occasions are catered for. Open seven days a week.
Seahorse Inn, Briton Street, Bampton, Devon EX16 9LN Tel: 01398 331480

TIVERTON   *Map 3 ref G23*

A settlement had been founded by the Saxons on the wedge of land between the rivers Exe and Loman in the 7th century which, two centuries later, King Alfred made reference to in his will. By the time of the Domesday Book, the local agriculture-based economy had become well established; however, it was not until the wool manufacturing industry was founded in the late 1400s that the town really began to grow, reaching its zenith in the 17th and 18th centuries, when locally produced cloth was much in demand throughout Europe. During Tiverton's golden age of wool-based prosperity, it became a fashion for local merchants and manufacturers to make extravagant charitable endowments, often in ways which would ensure their names lived on in perpetuity. Several such 16th and 17th century almshouses can still be seen around the town, including George Slee's in St Peter's Street, John Waldron's in Welbrook Street, and John Greenway's with its Tudor chapel in Gold Street.

Peter Blundell, another rich clothier from this period, chose to endow a school; **Blundell's Old School** was built in 1604 at the southeastern end of town near the bridge over the River Loman, but was converted into residential dwellings when the school moved to a new location on the edge of town in 1880. Among the many influential people educated here was the author RD Blackmore, creator of the character John Ridd, whose education at Blundell's he describes in the opening chapter of *Lorna Doone*.

A great deal of damage was done to the older buildings in Tiverton by the great town fire of 1731. The Norman **Castle**, however, suffered a different fate, having been deliberately dismantled by Parliamentarian forces following its surrender in 1645. Notwithstanding, several 14th century remains have survived, including the main gateway, banqueting hall, round tower and section of the old chapel, and these have now been incorporated into a striking privately owned residence. The castle and the parish church, with its striking red sandstone tower, stand on a rise above the river at the northwest end of town. One of Devon's few noteworthy Georgian churches, **St George's**, can be found in the town centre. Consecrated two years after the great fire in 1733, it contains some fine period ceilings, galleries and other fixtures, although the pulpit and pews are Victorian. Elsewhere in the centre, there are a considerable number of handsome Georgian and Regency town houses, some made of brick.

The last of the great woollen mills of Tiverton was established in 1816 by John Heathcoat, a Midlands entrepreneur who had been driven south from Leicestershire by Luddites. Heathcoat founded a thriving and enduring textiles business which he passed on to his grandson, John Heathcoat-Amory. An entrepreneur like his grandfather, Heathcoat-Amory built a large country mansion just to the north of Tiverton on a magnificent hillside site which was selected to give an uninterrupted view of the factory from the drawing room window.

A quay on the southeastern edge of town marks the western end of the now-disused **Grand Western Canal**, the inland waterway which was built in a brave attempt to connect Topsham and the River Exe with Bridgewater and the Bristol Channel. Never fully completed, sections of the canal remained open for over 100 years until the 1920s. An attractive stretch running for 12 miles from Tiverton to the Somerset border has now been restored.

CHERITON FITZPAINE   *Map 3 ref F23*

This is a pretty village of thatched cottages which also retains some almshouses dating back to 1594. **Jellicoe's** is a most friendly bed and breakfast establishment which has been totally refurbished to capture the country flavour of the house and its surroundings. There are most enjoyable views from all around the property and those requiring peace and quiet will surely enjoy their stay here. It is very convenient for several National Trust properties and good for rambling and birdwatching.

Jellicoe's

Two doubles and one family room are available with modern en-suite facilities; children are very welcome. Apart from a variety of breakfasts, exceptional evening meals prepared from local fresh produce are offered at modest cost; vegetarian or omnivore. No smoking please and sorry, no pets.

Jellicoe's, Higher Holn, Upham, Cheriton Fitzpaine, Crediton, Devon EX17 4HN Tel: 01363 866165

CASTLE DROGO   *Map 2 ref F24*

The extraordinary granite house was built to the castle-like designs of Lutyens in 1911–30. Standing on a granite bluff to the southwest of **Drewsteignton**, the countryside around is as striking as the building.

Built in the 18th century, the **Old Inn Restaurant and Guest House** was originally a village inn serving the local community and travellers alike. Now transformed into a licenced restaurant with bedroom accommodation, the hosts are Maureen and Clive Gribble. Situated in the village square of Drewsteignton, the restaurant serves à la carte and table d'hôte menus to satisfy all tastes. Twin or double bedded en-suite rooms are comfortably furnished and have tea/coffee makers and colour television. Hair dryers and ironing facilities are available upon request. A resident's bar and private lounge make a comfortable place in which to relax.

The whole of the surrounding area is one of outstanding natural beauty, one mile from Castle Drogo with numerous natural walks through woodland and river

England

Old Inn Restaurant & Guest House

banks. Permits are available locally for fishing in the River Teign whilst golf
courses and riding facilities are within a short distance.
*Old Inn Restaurant & Guest House, Drewsteignton, Devon EX6 6QR
Tel: 01647 281276*

OKEHAMPTON   *Map 2 ref E24*

This ancient market town stands at the foot of the soaring north Dartmoor ridge,
on the main east–west route through mid-Devon. The Saxons were the first to
found a settlement here, on a hill half-a-mile west of the current town centre. The
parish **Church of All Saints** still occupies this site; however, the present
building is largely Victorian thanks to a fire in 1842 which totally destroyed the
previous structure except for its 15th century granite tower. The 19th century
church windows were designed by William Morris, the founder of the Arts and
Crafts movement.

The Normans were soon to recognise Okehampton's strategic importance and
built a sizable double keep on the raised strip of land between the east and west
Okement rivers, a mile to the southwest of the present town centre. The castle
was extended by Hugh Courtenay, Earl of Devon, in the 14th century, but was
partially dismantled two centuries later after one of his heirs was tried and
convicted of treason. The remains are nevertheless impressive, standing on top
of a substantial earthwork mound (or motte) which dominates the surrounding
valley. **Okehampton Castle** is now under the ownership of English Heritage.

Present day Okehampton is a quiet old fashioned town which offers visitors the
opportunity to relax and enjoy the 365 square miles of Dartmoor which towers
above it to the south and the **Museum of Dartmoor Life** which is open from
April to October is an excellent place to learn about the area. Walking on the
fringes of the moor is a joy, or for those who would rather see the scenery from
the back of a horse, there are some excellent riding stables nearby.

ASHWATER

Map 2 ref D23

This a picturesque hamlet of mostly late Victorian farm workers' cottages is set around a triangular green. Overlooking the green is the **Church of St Peter in Chains**, which contains some striking features, including an unusually wide wagon roof, a collection of early bench ends, a delicate looking plasterwork coat of arms of Charles I and a vast 15th century chest tomb which incorporates the reclining figures of Thomas Carminow and his wife. However, perhaps the most exceptional feature is the massive Norman font, one of the largest in Devon, which stands on four semicircular stone panels and is carved with lions, dragons, salamanders and other exotic creatures.

Blagdon Manor Country Hotel lies off the beaten track and nestles in eight acres of superb rolling countryside. A 17th century manor which has been beautifully restored by the owners Tim and Gill Casey to a very high quality, this surely will become one of the West Country's leading and much sought after hotels. Seven delightfully decorated and welcoming rooms contain high quality furnishings, with bathrooms that have really been designed for guest comfort, and the fluffiest of towels. There is nothing more a guest could wish for as far as courtesy, comfort and hospitality are concerned. The ambience of the house-party style of dining is only surpassed by the cuisine that comes from the kitchen of Gill Casey. The carefully prepared daily menus and extensive wine list would delight the most discerning dinner guests from any part of the world. The relaxed and easy manner displayed by the charming owners is reflected by the many years living and working in Hong Kong and travelling widely. Blagdon Manor unquestionably provides its guests with perfect relaxation and personal attention. ETB 3 Crown Highly Commended, AA 2 Star and 2 Rosettes for cuisine.

Blagdon Manor Country Hotel

The old dovecot of Blagdon Manor, known as **Dovecot Cottage**, has recently been converted and is now a pretty and charming cottage. It is situated across the courtyard from the hotel and offers accommodation for up to four guests. It is well equipped, decorated in a fresh county style and offers a private sitting out area and full use of the hotel grounds and facilities.

Blagdon Manor Country Hotel, Ashwater, Devon EX21 5DF
Tel: 01409 211224 Fax: 01409 211634 E-mail:
Blagdon_Manor@compuserve.com

BRIDGERULE   *Map 2 ref D23*

Hedley Wood Caravan and Camping Park offers a relaxing holiday with a laid back atmosphere amid 16 acres of woodland with outstanding views. This family run site has many facilities and caters for all age groups. Children have a wonderful adventure playground, pets corner and a special area in the family licensed bar. Bar meals are readily available which include breakfasts and Sunday lunches. Apart from the other splendid domestic amenities, there are dog walks and daily kennelling facilities, a Woodland Nature Trail, clay pigeon sport shoots for novices and lots more. Modern static caravans can be hired at very reasonable cost or private caravans can be sited and stored here. Hedley Wood is open all year round and, being only three and a half miles from the coastal resort of Bude and other sandy beach areas, it is a popular holiday spot at any season of the year. Brochure on request. AA, RAC and CCC.

Hedley Wood Caravan & Camping Park

Hedley Wood Caravan & Camping Park, Bridgerule, near Bude, Devon EX22 7ED Tel & Fax: 01288 381404

HARTLAND   *Map 2 ref D22*

Hartland Point marks the place where the Bristol Channel becomes the Atlantic and, here, the sea is characterised by a savage tidal race which rips along the coastline in all weathers. High above the waterline, a grim cliff rises untidily to nearly 350 feet, and about half way up, a lighthouse built in 1874 warns vessels to stay clear. To the east of Hartland Point, the shingle beach at Shipload Bay can be reached by descending over 250 steps, and to the west, the coastline turns sharply southwards and turns into the stark, yet spectacular, stretch known as the iron coast.

APPLEDORE   *Map 2 ref E22*

This delightful old seafaring community overlooks the treacherous bar at the mouth of the Taw estuary and, surprisingly, it has remained an unspoilt village of narrow winding lanes and solid 18th and 19th century fishermen's cottages. Appledore's nautical tradition has not been preserved merely for the benefit of the tourist: it is also the location of one the largest boat building yards in the region. The yard is capable of constructing and refitting quite sizable ships, and has managed to survive in the face of harsh economic conditions. It seems appropriate that the **North Devon Maritime Museum** should also be situated in this truly nautical setting. Besides the wealth of nautical memorabilia, the museum also houses a unique collection of historical records and maps.

There is a wonderful riverside patio with views of the boats and wildlife, where one can relax with a cool drink and peruse the tantalising dishes on offer at **The Beaver Inn**. What a splendid place—panoramic views, friendly service, wonderful home-cooked food and the choice from a well kept cellar. The owners and charming hosts are Graham and Alison Stone who have certainly built an excellent reputation for fine food and hospitality.

Their menu offers a great deal of variety, away from the usual, although that said, there are some old favourites too, such as Barbecued rack of ribs with ranch fries and juicy steak with all the trimmings cooked in a special sauce. A wide variety of fresh fish is available in season which includes: wild Torridge salmon, skate wing, Lundy Island plaice, lemon sole, Clovelly crab and lobster. Have a try at the Seafood and seaweed lasagne with warm French bread or how about Enchiladas, Deluxe nachos or Sizzling fajitas; then there are the puddings!

The Beaver Inn, Irsha Street, Appledore, Devon EX39 1RY
Tel: 01237 474822

CHAPTER FOUR
Cornwall

Polperro

4
Cornwall

East Cornwall

INTRODUCTION

This county of narrow, winding lanes and small villages of granite houses is separated from the rest of Britain by the River Tamar which rises just behind the north coast, to the northeast of Bude and forms the boundary with Devon right down to its estuary on the south coast. This natural barrier has, over many centuries, preserved the Celtic heritage of Cornwall which is still very much in evidence today. The Cornish place names beginning with 'Tre', 'Pol' and 'Pen' are the most common reminders. There are also more substantial reminders of the past with numerous ancient crosses, holy wells and prehistoric sites littered around the countryside.

Nowhere in Cornwall is more than 20 miles from the sea but the north and the south coasts are very different: the north coast and, in particular around Boscastle and Tintagel, is dominated by high cliffs whilst the south is a series of secluded rocky coves and bays. Naturally, the sea has played an important part in the life of the villages of Cornwall and, although pilchard fishing was once important, incomes were supplemented by dealing in contraband. The magnificent coastline making it easy to hid even the largest haul of legal wine or brandy.

However, this eastern area of Cornwall is dominated by the bleak expanse of **Bodmin Moor** which covers some 80 square miles. The two highest peaks on the exposed moorland are both lie in the north; at 1370 foot **Brown Willy** is the highest point in the county and, close by and almost as high, is **Rough Tor**. Standing on National Trust owned land, Rough Tor, as well as being a magnificent viewing point, is also the site of a memorial to the men of the Wessex Regiment who died in World War II. Bodmin moor is covered in prehistoric remains and typical of many are the scattered Bronze Age hut circles and field enclosures which can be seen on the side of Rough Tor. A little to the south lies the **Fernacre Stone Circle**: also Bronze Age, it contains over 30 standing stones and is the largest example of its kind on the moor.

England

Evidence of earlier occupation can be seen between the A30 and Hawks Tor, the site of the Neolithic henge monument known as the **Stripple Stones**, but most impressive of all is **Hurlers Stone Circle**, a Bronze Age temple consisting of three stone circles arranged in a line which can be found near the exposed former mining community of **Minions** on the moor's southeastern fringe. According to Cornish legend, the circles were formed when teams of local men were turned to stone for playing hurling, a Celtic form of hockey, on the Sabbath.

Half-a-mile away to the north stands the spectacular natural granite formation known as **The Cheesewring**. Another local legend states that this was the haunt of a druid who possessed a golden cup which never ran dry and provided thirsty passers-by with an endless supply of water. The story was partially borne out in 1818 when archeologists excavating a nearby burial chamber discovered a skeleton clutching a golden chalice; dubbed the Rillaton Cup, it is now kept in the British Museum.

LAUNCESTON   *Map 2 ref D24*

Pronounced locally as Lawn-son, this is one of the most pleasant inland towns in Cornwall. For centuries, it was an important regional capital which guarded the main land route into the county and, shortly after the Norman invasion, William the Conqueror's half-brother, Robert of Mortain, built a massive **Castle** here on an elevated site above the River Kensey from where subsequent Earls of Cornwall attempted to govern the defiant Cornish people. An excellent example of a motte and bailey castle, it features an outer bailey, now a public park, and a round double keep whose outer wall is 12 feet thick in places. Towards the end of its working life, the decaying structure was used as a gaol: a fearsome place where prisoners were kept in appalling conditions, its inmates included George Fox, the founder of the Quakers.

Some of the most impressive stonework in the area can be found on the **Church of St Mary Magdalene**, a granite structure which was built in the early 16th century by a local landowner following the tragic death of his wife and son. In their memory, he assembled the finest stonemasons in Cornwall to create a remarkable cornucopia of ornamental carving which covers nearly every surface of the building.

Elsewhere in Launceston, the streets around the castle are filled with handsome Georgian and earlier buildings, including the National Trust owned **Lawrence House** in Castle Street. Built in 1753, it has some fine plasterwork ceilings and now houses an interesting town museum. There is also an art gallery near the medieval **South Gate**, the last remnant of Launceston's town walls, and for railway enthusiasts, a steam railway runs along the Kensey valley to the west of the town.

BUDE

Map 2 ref D23

The town's late Victorian and Edwardian centre is sheltered from the worst Atlantic extremes by a low cliff which separates the shallow valley of the River Neet from the ocean. The character of the place seems to change with every change in the weather; a winter gale can make it seem like a remote outpost clinging to the edge of the world, while, a warm summer breeze transforms it into a genial holiday town with some excellent facilities for beach-lovers, surfers and coastal walkers.

Bude stood at the northern end of the now disused **Bude Canal**, an ambitious early 19th century inland waterway which was intended to connect the Atlantic with English Channel by way of the River Tamar. The only stretch to be completed, that between Bude and Launceston, was largely used for transporting seaweed, sand and other fertiliser to inland farms. Finally abandoned when the railway arrived in the 1890s, the two mile long section at the northern end has now been restored for use as a recreational amenity. The small fort guarding the northern entrance to the canal was built in the 1840s as an eccentric private residence and the old forge on the canalside has been converted into an interesting **Museum** on Bude's maritime heritage.

The Edgcumbe Hotel forms part of a row of substantial houses in Summerleaze Crescent which overlooks the Bay in Bude. It certainly has an unrivalled position with panoramic views of the beach and breakwater. The Edgcumbe offers a good standard of facilities with bar lounge complete with pool table, TV sun lounge, baby listening service, laundry and private car parking. The 15 bedrooms are comfortably furnished and most have private facilities. All have hand basins, shaver points, bedside lights, colour television, and hot drinks facilities. Children are very welcome and reductions are offered. Cynthia and John are the

The Edgcumbe Hotel

resident owners and take pride in offering varied and interesting food with a choice of menu at all meals.

The Edgcumbe Hotel, Summerleaze Crescent, Bude, Cornwall EX23 8HJ
Tel: 01288 353846 Fax: 01288 355256

The **Maer Lodge Hotel** is an AA/RAC 2 star country house style hotel which has been owned by the same family for 38 years. Situated in two acres of grounds near the beach, it overlooks an 18 hole golf course, with countryside views to the rear. The hotel restaurant enjoys a reputation for fine food and excellent service. There are 18 bedrooms all with en-suite WC and bath or shower, TV, telephone, radio and hot drink facilities. Other amenities include a bar, games room, pool room, lounge with resident pianist and putting green. Close to the town centre yet private and peaceful.

Maer Lodge Hotel

Maer Lodge Hotel, Maer Down Road, Crooklets Beach, Bude, Cornwall
EX23 8NG Tel: 01288 353306 Fax: 01288 354005

Just to the north of Bude, at **Poughill**, those who enjoy caravanning and holiday homes need look no further than **Wooda Farm**. Here, holidaymakers have the choice of siting their own van in beautifully laid out areas or selecting one of 54 luxury caravan holiday homes set in landscaped gardens with plenty of open space for young children to play safely. The holiday homes are six-berth featuring two bedrooms and are exceptionally well equipped. The touring and camping pitches are mostly level, closely mown and very generous in size. Many have electric hook-ups while individually screened pitches are available with

Wooda Farm Park

water, electricity and drainage. All site facilities and amenities including a shop are of a very high standard. The Farm itself is five minutes walk from the Park and here visitors will find Linney Larder providing excellent home-cooked food and Cornish ales. Throughout the Park there are plenty of activities taking place—though one thing not found here is a noisy nightclub! An excellent brochure is available on request.

Wooda Farm Park, Poughill, near Bude, Cornwall EX23 9HJ
Tel: 01288 352069

To the east of Bude lies **Stratton** which is believed to have been founded by the ancient Romans. The steeply sloping main street is lined with fine Georgian houses and cottages many of which are thatched. The town's early 14th century parish church contains a Norman font and some striking early memorials and monumental brasses. During the English Civil War, the **Tree Inn** was used as a centre of operations by the Royalist general, Sir Bevil Grenville, before he led his troops to victory at nearby **Stamford Hill** in May 1643. The Iron Age earthwork which had been held by the Parliamentarians can be seen a mile away to the northwest. After the battle, the dead from both sides were buried in unmarked graves in Stratton churchyard. The Tree Inn was also the birthplace of the legendary Anthony Payne, a 7 foot giant who fought for the Royalist cause and was offered a post in Sir Bevil's household as a reward.

Stratton Gardens Hotel and Restaurant is the lovely 16th century home of Tony and Sandra Dixon. Tucked away in the village near the church, it was formerly owned by the church and used as a Christian retreat for monks and nuns. Built in 1542 and Grade II listed, the building is steeped in history and has a relaxing and peaceful atmosphere complete with its resident friendly ghost, Clarissa.

Stratton Gardens Hotel

Pretty terraced gardens to the rear of the hotel are the perfect spot to enjoy a pre-dinner drink or cream tea in the summer. Lovely home-cooked food and a selection of fine wines are served in the licensed restaurant and the three course table d'hôte menu offers a choice of at least four dishes on each course, always with fresh fish and a vegetarian option. Special dishes can be prepared to order with notice and small parties can be catered for in the restaurant or the newly refurbished function room. As Sandra uses fresh produce, purchased daily, it is essential that tables are booked in advance.

The hotel has five charming bedrooms, all with en-suite facilities and most overlooking the well stocked gardens which extend to about an acre. The rooms are individual in style and furnishing, one has a four poster bed and another is a canopied room. Residents have a choice of two lounges which have roaring log fires in the winter creating a warmth and ambience reflecting the general atmosphere of the hotel. Awarded 3 Crown Commended rating by ETB. Private car park.

Stratton Gardens Hotel, Cot Hill, Stratton, Bude, Cornwall EX23 9DN
Tel & Fax: 01288 352500

Just to the north of Stratton, **Willow Valley Holiday Park**, at **Bush**, offers holiday accommodation in Wooden Lodges which sleep up to six people. They are very spacious and are equipped to a high standard which includes colour television and microwave oven. All bedding is provided and gas and electricity are not metered. Well behaved pets are very welcome and there are seven acres of land for them (and their owners) to exercise in. The lodges all have their own garden areas and to help guests relax, there's a sauna and spa bath available. Camping and caravanning is also available on an adjoining field where there is a children's playground.

Willow Valley Holiday Park

Willow Valley is only 10 minutes drive away from the sandy, surfing beaches of Bude with its open air sea water pool, with Widemouth Bay only another five minutes from there.

Willow Valley Holiday Park, Willow Valley, Bush, Bude, Cornwall EX23 9LB Tel: 01288 353104

Further north and close to the coast, the agricultural income of the tiny settlement of **Morwenstow** has long been supplemented by ill-gotten gains from the sea and it is also a good access point to this dramatic stretch of coastline. The part-

Norman church has some impressive wagon roofs, a richly carved Norman font and a medieval wall painting of St Morwenna, the Celtic saint to whom the building is dedicated.

Morwenstow's most renowned former inhabitant is the eccentric vicar and poet, Robert Stephen Hawker, who arrived here in 1834 and remained amongst his congregation of 'smugglers, wreckers and dissenters' until his death 41 years later. A colourful figure dressed in a purple cloak and long fisherman's boots, Hawker would spend much of his time striding across the clifftops, or writing verse and smoking (some accounts say opium) in a tiny driftwood hut he built for himself on the cliff. He was among the first to show concern about the number of merchant vessels which were coming to grief on this perilous stretch of coastline. (Prior to his intervention, is was a common custom for the locals to use lights to lure passing ships onto the rocks.) He would often climb down to rescue shipwrecked crews from shore or to carry back the bodies of drowned mariners so they could be given a Christian burial. A distinctive ship's figurehead in the churchyard marks the final resting place of the crew of the *Caledonia* which went down in 1842.

Hideaway Farm Holidays is run by a small, selected group of farmer's wives offering peaceful, relaxing holidays on their working farms. These wonderful retreats are tucked away amidst rolling countryside and dramatic coastal locations in west Devon and north Cornwall.

Hideaway Farm Holidays

For those who enjoy exploring on foot, Hideaway Holidays offer the unique facility of walking from farm to farm, whilst guests' luggage is transported for them. All the locations are ideal for peaceful and safe holidays with the distinct advantage of traditional farmhouse breakfasts and evening meals prepared with good, fresh food, home grown vegetables and freshly baked bread. All the accommodation is ETB inspected and many of the bedrooms are en-suite or have private bathrooms.

The many facilities collectively offered include: involvement and space for children around the farms, play facilities, coarse fishing lakes, vineyards, woods and orchards to wander in, nature walks, fishing in the River Tamar, games rooms and, of course, outstanding views. There are many local towns, villages and beaches to visit. For further information and brochure telephone 01288 381264.

Hideaway Farm Holidays, Woodford, Morwenstow, Bude, Cornwall EX23 9HY Tel: 01288 331222

BOSCASTLE   *Map 2 ref C24*

Lying on a delightful, unspoilt stretch of the north Cornwall coastline, this was a thriving seaport up to the 19th century and is now used by local inshore fishermen and visitors. The National Trust own and protect the harbour area as well as a considerable amount of land and coastline in north Cornwall.

Two miles to the southwest of Boscastle, the B3263 crosses the mile long **Rocky Valley**, a curious rock strewn cleft in the landscape which has a character all of its own. In the wooded upper reaches can be found the impressive 40 foot waterfall known as **St Nectan's Kieve**. St Nectan was a Celtic hermit whose cell is believed to have stood beside the basin, or kieve, at the foot of the cascade and whose grave is said to lie beneath it.

Tolcarne House is a pleasing late Victorian House set in an acre of lawned and sloping gardens situated in the upper coastal village of Boscastle. Lovingly cared for, it is the home of Margaret and Graham Crown who are welcoming hosts combining high standards with a very friendly atmosphere. All the rooms in Tolcarne House are brightly presented and carefully furnished. There is a comfortable residents lounge and also a snug lounge bar. Guests have a choice of table d'hôte or à la carte menus which for a hotel of this size is pleasing indeed. The eight guest bedrooms have en-suite bathrooms or shower, television and hot drink making facilities. Dogs are welcome by prior arrangement. ETB 3 Crown Highly Commended.

Tolcarne House

Tolcarne House, Boscastle, Cornwall PL35 0AS Tel & Fax: 01840 250654

Lower Meadows House, situated about 350 yards from the historic harbour, is the immaculate home of Brian and Sandra Abraham and their two young children. The house offers modern, well appointed bed and breakfast facilities in seven guest rooms. Two doubles and a family room are en-suite. Children are

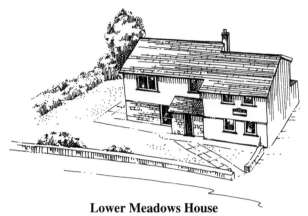

Lower Meadows House

very welcome and a cot and high chair are available on request. A full English breakfast is provided though special diets can be catered for. A wide choice for lunch or evening meal exists within a short walking distance at the nearby inn which has a restaurant and children's room. Guest car parking. No smoking or pets please.
Lower Meadows House, Penally Hill, Boscastle, Cornwall PL35 0HF
Tel: 01840 250570

TINTAGEL   *Map 2 ref C24*

The village owes much of its popularity to the Arthurian connection and one of its most noteworthy attractions is **King Arthur's Halls**. These were built in the 1930s by devotees of the legend and include the Hall of Chivalry, a room with over 70 stained glass windows depicting the coats of arms of the Knights of the Round Table.

The **Parish Church** is set some distance away from the village centre on an exposed cliff. Norman in origin, it retains substantial fragments of its original fabric, including the font, windows and sections of the walls. There is also a good early 15th century monumental brass and a rare Roman tinners' milestone from the 4th century which is one of only five surviving examples in Cornwall.

Perhaps the finest building in the Tintagel is the **Old Post Office**, a small 14th century slate-built manor house which, in the 19th century, found new life as a letter receiving station. Now owned by the National Trust, this charming and strangely organic looking structure has recently been carefully restored to its Victorian livery.

The romantic remains of **Tintagel Castle** stand on top of Tintagel Head, to the west of the village. Prior to a series of rock falls in the 19th century, this formidable headland was connected to the mainland by a natural stone bridge; now only a narrow isthmus remains. Many like to believe that this was the birthplace of the legendary King Arthur, or even that it was the site of Camelot, the mythical headquarters of the Knights of the Round Table (other candidates are Caerleon in Wales and South Cadbury in Somerset). Fragments of a Celtic monastic house dating from the 6th century have been uncovered on the headland whose origins coincide with the activities of the Welsh military leader the Arthurian legends are thought to be based upon. However, the fortification seen today was founded by Reginald Earl of Cornwall, the illegitimate son of Henry I, in the 12th century, over 600 years after Arthur would have died. Whatever the true heritage of Tintagel castle, the scramble down towards the sea and back up to its clifftop site 250 feet above the Atlantic is a breathtaking experience.

The Wootons Country Hotel is situated in an Area of Outstanding Natural Beauty overlooking the Vale of Avalon and part of Tintagel Castle. The hotel has been completely refurbished and discerning guests will appreciate the very high standards offered here. With just 11 en-suite bedrooms, the owners are able to provide a very personal service for their guests. All the rooms have high quality traditional furniture and special attention has been paid to the provision of luxury beds, remote control television and video systems, direct dial telephone, radio, trouser press and hospitality tray; all have the benefit of well appointed en-suite bathrooms. For special occasions, the hotel has a Bridal Suite with four poster and sumptuous whirlpool bath.

The Wootons Country Hotel

Guests have a choice of dining in the à la carte restaurant or taking lighter meals in the Servery. As well as a large lounge and bar, there is a separate billiard room complete with full size snooker table. The sun lounge affords a comfortable place to relax or guests can curl up with a book in the resident's lounge. There are many activities and places of interest to be enjoyed using The Wottons as a base. Awarded 4 Crown Commended by ETB.

The Wootons Country Hotel, Atlantic Road, Tintagel, Cornwall
Tel: 01840 770170 Fax: 01840 770978

After five years in construction, **King Arthur's Castle Hotel** opened in 1899 as was reported in a newspaper of the day—"By invitation of the Directors a representative gathering from various parts of Cornwall attended the opening. On arrival at Camelford the visitors were conveyed by waggonettes to Tintagel some five miles distant." The rooms were reported to be "lofty and commodious and lighted throughout by electricity generated on the premises, sumptuously furnished and fitted with every requisite for a modern first class hotel."

King Arthur's Castle Hotel

The substantial castellated hotel perched on a rocky promontory, occupies a magnificent and unique position overlooking the sea and Tintagel Castle with uninterrupted views of the coastline. The hotel, which is privately owned and personally run by the proprietors, has been in the same family since 1953 and its spacious hall, from which a wide staircase leads, makes an imposing entrance to this grand building. A lift transports guests to all floor levels where the spacious en-suite bedrooms look out to a land of great legends. All rooms have TVs, tea and coffee facilities, hair dryers and a computerised telephone system. Over-looking the magnificent Castle ruins, the dining room offers guests an excellent choice of cuisine, expertly prepared from local and home-grown produce. Live entertainment is provided in the Dance Hall whilst those preferring to relax will find the Arthurian bar a welcoming refuge.

King Arthur's Castle Hotel, Atlantic Road, Tintagel, Cornwall
Tel: 01840 770202 Fax: 01840 770978

PORT ISAAC   *Map 2 ref C24*

This is a most attractive old fishing community of stone and slate houses divided by narrow alleyways, or drangs, one of which goes by the charming name of Squeeze-Belly Alley. At one time, huge quantities of herring were landed here and, after the arrival of the railway, these were gutted and packed in the village's many fish cellars before being despatched by train to Britain's inland centres of population. One of the old cellars is now an inshore lifeboat station, and others are used as boathouses or retail outlets.

Just half a mile away in a small sheltered cove, is the early 17th century inn and hotel of **Port Gaverne** which has been gently restored retaining all of its original character. Since 1969 the proprietors have welcomed many thousands of resident guests from all over the world. Their policy being to provide pleasant comfortable accommodation, good food prepared from the best ingredients available, complemented by a wine cellar of repute. All this is achieved with a staff who know how to care and an ambience which draws you into the relaxed Cornish pace of life. Bedrooms are all en-suite and comfortably furnished with all amenities.

Port Gaverne Hotel

Additionally, the hotel has six splendidly restored 18th century fishermen's cottages which are convenient to the hotel. Each is completely and attractively furnished with simply everything provided from central heating and a completely equipped fitted kitchen, to the towels, duvets and electricity; here guests's comfort is assured. Comprehensive brochures are available upon request. Simply the best of everything! ETB 4 Crown Commended. AA Rosette.

Port Gaverne Hotel, near Port Isaac, Cornwall PL29 3SQ
Tel: 01208 880244 Fax: 01208 880151

Rogues' Retreat is a beautifully situated 19th century slate and stone built house which has been tastefully converted into three luxury self-catering apartments. Entirely self-contained, they enjoy a superb position overlooking Port Isaac and from their sitting room windows there are far reaching views of the Cornish coastline and the fishing boats entering the harbour between the cliffs below.

All the apartments are heated and have newly fitted kitchens; The Top Deck provides accommodation for four to five people, whilst on the first floor Smugglers Rest will sleep two to four and the Pirate's Den is for two guests. The position of the apartments, at the top of a no through road above the village,

Rogues' Retreat

provides a peaceful retreat yet has easy access to the attractions around the harbour below. Close by are the pretty cove villages of Port Gaverne and Port Quin. Available throughout the year with three day breaks out of season.
Frank & Jill Gadman, Rogues' Retreat, Roscarrock Hill, Port Isaac, Cornwall PL29 3RG Tel: 01208 880566

Trevathan Farm has been farmed by the Symons family since 1850. The farm buildings which proved unsuitable for modern farming, have been restored and converted into high quality Holiday Cottages. All the family is involved in the running of the farm and helping hands are always welcome. All age groups enjoy feeding the animals and, with goats, hens, ducks, rabbits, Shetland ponies and the pot bellied pig, there's plenty to go at.

Trevathan Farm

The cottages are certainly a credit to the family, beautifully restored, equipped with every convenience and all heated and snug. There's TV, video, microwave, cooker, fridge/freezer, food processor, slow cook pot, washer/dryer and the list goes on. Each cottage has its own garden with furniture and barbecue. On the farm there is a tennis and volley ball court, play area, a great games room and even a fitness room to work off the cream teas! Awarded up to 5 keys and Highly Commended by ETB, Trevathan Farm is something special and proprietors Henry and Shirley Symons are "waiting to greet you". Open all year.
Trevathan Farm, St Endellion, Port Isaac, Cornwall PL29 3TT Tel & Fax: 01208 880248

England

Named after one of the oldest stone crosses in Cornwall, **The Long Cross Hotel**, in **Trelights**, to the south of Port Isaac, began its life as a late Victorian country house and thankfully, has retained many of its original features. Owned by Dave and Dorothy Crawford for the past four years, this family run hotel has 12 en-suite bedrooms, each being individually decorated and furnished to a high standard. Each guest room has its own colour television, complimentary tea and coffee facilities and is fully central heated with many of the rooms boasting panoramic sea views.

Located adjacent to the hotel is the Long Cross Victorian Gardens, the only public gardens on the north Cornwall coast and recently the subject of a television feature because of the gardens unusual aspects. Still laid out in their original Victorian style with a maze-like layout which is created by the hedges and shrubs that protect the colourful borders from the brisk sea air. Also to be found in these extensive grounds is the Tregenna Tavern, a free house which is locally renowned for its excellent real ales and delicious home-made meals. The Tea Gardens are considered by many as the finest in north Cornwall due to their spectacular views and tranquil location whilst the Long Cross pets' corner proves very popular amongst both the young and old alike.

Long Cross Hotel

Long Cross Hotel, Trelights, near Port Isaac, Cornwall PL29 3TF
Tel: 01208 880243

BODMIN   *Map 1 ref C25*

Bustling by day, yet quiet by night, this historic former county town lies midway between Cornwall's north and south coasts at the junction of two ancient cross-county trading routes. For many centuries, traders between Wales, Ireland and northern France preferred the overland route between the Camel and Fowey estuaries to the hazardous sea journey around Land's End. **Castle Canyke**, to the southeast of the town, was built during the Iron Age to defend this important trade route and, a few centuries later, the Romans erected a fort on a site above the River Camel to the west of the town, one of a string they built in the southwest to defend strategic river crossings; the remains of a quadrilateral earthwork can still be made out today. The ancient cross-country route is now a waymarked footpath known as **The Saints' Way**.

Perhaps Bodmin's most famous early visitor was St Petroc, one of the most influential of the early Welsh missionary saints who landed in Cornwall in the 6th century. The monastery he founded near Padstow was moved to Bodmin in the 10th century to protect it from seaborne Viking raids; although it survived until the Dissolution of the Monasteries in 1539, little of it remains today. Bodmin's parish **Church**, perhaps the most impressive in Cornwall, is dedicated to St Petroc. Rebuilt in the 15th century and renovated in the 19th, it contains a magnificent Norman font whose immense bowl is supported on five finely carved columns and a priceless ivory casket in which the remains of the saint were placed in 1177 after they had been recovered from a light-fingered Augustinian monk. Bodmin is also renowned for its holy wells—11 in all. Some, such as **Eye Water Well**, are known for their restorative properties, and others, such as **St Guron's Well** opposite the church, for being ancient places of baptism.

Bodmin was the only market town in Cornwall to be mentioned in the Domesday Book and, at one time, it boasted its own mint and, later, the county assizes. However, the 19th century rise of Truro as Cornwall's cathedral city stripped Bodmin of its county town status. Bodmin also contains two first-rate museums: the recently refurbished **Town Museum**, and the **Duke of Cornwall Light Infantry Museum** which is housed in the old regimental headquarters.

The spectacular National Trust owned property, **Lanhydrock House**, lies two miles to the south of Bodmin. Prior to the Dissolution of the Monasteries, the 400 acre estate belonged to Bodmin's Augustinian priory of St Petroc, then in 1620 it was acquired by the Robartes family in whose possession it remained until it passed to the National Trust in 1953. The house is set in a superb position in the valley of the River Fowey and is approached along an avenue of sycamore and beech trees, some of which were originally planted over three centuries ago. Visitors pass through an imposing 17th century gatehouse which, along with the north wing, is one of the few parts of the original structure to have escaped the fire which swept through the building in 1881. The grounds contain an attractive woodland shrubbery and a much photographed formal garden and parterre which is overlooked by the small estate church of St Hyderoc.

In recent years, **Rock**, on the banks of the River Camel to the northwest of Bodmin, has become renowned as a watersports centre, with its own sailing and wind-surfing school. In common with the church at St Enodoc, St Michael's church at nearby Porthilly has had to be regularly retrieved from unwelcome sand drifts.

Originally built at the turn of the century as a gentleman's residence, **Gleneglos Hotel and Restaurant** has been personally owned and run by Michael and Pauline Burton for the past nine years. This comfortable and tastefully furnished country style hotel lends itself readily to anyone looking for a peaceful and relaxing break away from the hustle and bustle of everyday life. Each of the six well appointed guest bedrooms have full facilities including a child listening service, whilst offering superb views over the surrounding countryside and

The Gleneglos Hotel and Restaurant

Camel estuary. Guests can enjoy a quiet drink in the well stocked bar before sitting down to their evening meal which is served in the attractive dining room. All of the food served has been freshly prepared using only the finest local ingredients, much of which is taken from Michael and Pauline's own vegetable garden, which is situated in the large gardens that surround this quiet retreat. Both the à la carte and table d'hôte menus offer a comprehensive selection of dishes ranging from the traditional to the more unusual, whilst those guests with special diets can be catered for with prior notice.

The Gleneglos Hotel and Restaurant, Trewint Lane, Rock, Wadebridge, Cornwall PL27 6LU Tel: 01208 862369

LOOE   *Map 2 ref D25*

At the mouth of the rivers East and West Looe stands the bustling coastal resort and fishing port of Looe. Originally two separate towns facing each other across the estuary, **East** and **West Looe** were first connected by a bridge in the early 15th century and officially incorporated in 1883. (The present seven arch bridge dates from the 19th century and is wide enough to carry the A387 Polperro road.) In common with many other Cornish coastal settlements which have had to scratch a living by whatever means available, Looe has always been something of a jack-of-all-trades. As well as having a long established pilchard fishing fleet, it has also served the mineral extractors of Bodmin moor as a port for exporting tin and, later, copper ore.

As early as 1800, a bathing machine was constructed at the top of Looe's sandy beach and, when visitors began to arrive in numbers with the coming of the railway in 1859, the town began to develop as a resort. More recently, Looe has established itself as Britain's premier shark fishing centre which regularly hosts an International Sea Angling Festival.

Over the years, Looe has evolved into a small seaside resort which has managed to retain a good deal of its original character, despite the annual invasion of holiday-makers. The old quarters on either side of the river are mazes of narrow lanes lined with old stone fishermen's cottages and inns, some of which are partially constructed from old ships' timbers. The 16th century guildhall in East Looe is now an impressive local **Museum** and there is also an interesting **Cornish Folk Museum** in Lower Street.

In summer, pleasure boats depart from the quay for trips along the coast to Polperro and Fowey and boat trips can also be taken to **St George's Island** half-a-mile offshore. Now a privately run bird sanctuary, this was once the refuge of the notorious pirate and smuggler, Black Joan, who along with her brother Fyn, terrorised the population of this lonely stretch of coast.

Anchor Lights is another delightful B&B with a quayside location and views across Looe and out to sea—the fishing boats are almost on the doorstep. The resident proprietors, Richard and Rachel Essam, have owned this comfortable establishment for 14 years, extend a real welcome and personal service to both new and returning guests.

All rooms are neatly decorated and well appointed, with aspects over the river and harbour. Suites are doubles with private bathrooms and include: television,

Anchor Lights

England

hair dryer, radio alarm, tea and coffee facilities, payphone, central heating and fresh towels every day. A sizeable English breakfast is served to set guests up for the day.

Anchor Lights, The Quay, West Looe, Cornwall PL13 2BU
Tel: 01503 262334

Hiding its delights and tucked away in Church Street, is **Tidal Court**, a delightful cottage providing bed and breakfast with en-suite bedrooms. Just 100 feet from the quayside where fishing boats still ply their trade in a town with lots to offer especially out of season. Tidal Court is one of the few popular residences open all year round.

Tidal Court, 3 Church Street, West Looe, Cornwall PL13 2EX Tel: 01503
263695

For those who appreciate the peace, tranquillity and beauty of the Cornish countryside, **Catherine Park** is ideally placed for a family holiday. Eight comfortably furnished bungalows are sited in a designated Area of Outstanding Natural Beauty yet only two mile from the picturesque fishing villages of Looe and Polperro.

The bungalows are solidly constructed, double glazed and have either two or three bedrooms, a spacious lounge/diner, kitchen and shower room; four to six people can easily be accommodated. Each bungalow is fully carpeted and well equipped, including remote control television, direct dial telephones and fire safety equipment; outside a seating area to the front has flower tubs, hanging baskets clematis and pergolas, this area is suitable for barbecues or leisurely meals in the summer. Level parking is a few yards from the front doors making it easy for the those who may have difficulty in walking and disabled guests, who are most welcome.

Catherine Park Holiday Bungalows

In a sheltered position and surrounded by lush foliage, is a superb heated swimming pool which is open from May through to September. It's a real suntrap and a wonderful place to have fun or laze away the hours. The grounds of Catherine Park extend to some four acres of well stocked informal gardens with an enclosed children's play area and paddocks. Ponies, goats and friendly dogs, cats and ducks await attention and make friends with their visitors. With extensive woodlands two minutes walk away, coastal footpaths close at hand and numerous pastimes to occupy young and old, Catherine Park has a lot to offer—and a great atmosphere!

Catherine Park Holiday Bungalows, Trelawne Cross, West Looe, Cornwall PL13 2NA Tel & Fax: 01530 272570

The Monkey Sanctuary, to the east of Looe, has been home to a natural colony of Woolly monkeys since 1964. It was established to provide a stable setting for Woolly monkeys rescued from lives of isolation in zoos and as pets. Today, four generations, all born here, form a strong colony living in an extensive territory spread over several outdoor grassed enclosures linked together with heated indoor rooms.

The Monkey Sanctuary

Visitors are able to see them in their territory and may see mother monkeys and youngsters foraging in the grounds; and hear informal talks about individuals and their families within the colony. A new enclosure, built over the winter, provides more bad weather viewing for visitors as well as an exciting new area for the adult male monkeys to patrol.

Regular talks and indoor displays explain more about monkey life and their natural habitat, the Amazon Rainforest, as well as detailing plans to establish a rehabilitation site in South America in order to allow the monkeys the chance to live in their natural habitat. The beautiful gardens provide a home for native wildlife encouraging environmental awareness closer to home.

The Monkey Sanctuary, Looe, Cornwall PL13 1NZ
Tel & Fax: 01503 262532

West of Looe, the scattered village of **Lansallos** stands on rocky cliffs overlooking Lantivet Bay. Through careful and progressive restoration carried out since 1978 on what was once farmworkers cottages, **Valleybrook** has become a well established holiday venue for many returning guests and families year after year. Valleybrook has lodges, cottages, apartments and caravans available, offering a really wide choice to suit every requirement. The characterful cottages with beamed ceilings and Cornish stone fireplaces, have all the modern facilities with cosy centrally heated rooms and well equipped kitchens. Duvets, pillows and bed linen are provided. Outside, bordered by a stream, private lawns with garden furniture are for the exclusive use of cottage residents.

Valleybrook

The recently constructed Scandinavian style timber lodges which are extremely comfortable with a high degree of insulation and central heating, are recommended for winter as well as summer holidays. The interiors are carpeted throughout and attractive verandas lead off at two floor levels. Many facilities are provided especially for children's play.

Valleybrook, Peakswater, Lansallos, Looe, Cornwall PL13 2QE
Tel: 01503 220493 Fax: 01503 220455

Closer to Looe, the lovely old fishing community of **Polperro** is many people's idea of the archetypal Cornish village. It stands at the point where a steep-sided wooded combe converges with a narrow tidal inlet from the sea. Its steep narrow streets and alleyways are piled high with white-painted fishermen's cottages.

All routes seem to lead down to Polperro's highly photogenic double harbour, a working fishing port which normally contains an assortment of attractive inshore fishing vessels. The mouth of the inner harbour was fitted with movable timber gates after a southeasterly storm destroyed over 20 boats which were sheltering here in the early 19th century (they have now been replaced by a modern tidal floodgate). At one time, the smell of Polperro pilchards was so overwhelming that outsiders renamed the village Polstink!

Polperro has a long association with smuggling: the practice was so rife in the 18th century that almost everyone in the village was involved in shipping, storing or transporting contraband goods. To combat the problem, HM Customs and Excise established the first preventive station in Cornwall here in the early 1800s. The atmosphere and events of those days are brought to life in a fascinating **Smugglers' Museum** which can be found near the inner harbour.

Situated in the centre of Polperro **The Old Mill House Hotel** is a well appointed traditional hotel that offers its guests the opportunity to escape from their busy lives, sit back and relax. All of the eight individually decorated and furnished bedrooms have full en-suite facilities with colour TV and complimentary tea and coffee maker. The fully licensed bar and bistro style restaurant provide superb

The Old Mill House Hotel

local ales and good home-cooked food, including fresh fish dishes from the Catch of the Day board. Families are catered for in the both the hotel and bar area, whilst the children can enjoy the patio and garden areas and their very own spacious family room. Those visiting this historic part of Cornwall should be sure to pay a visit to the Old Mill House Hotel and experience true Cornish hospitality at its best.

The Old Mill House Hotel, Polperro, Cornwall PL13 2RP
Tel: 01503 272362

The village of **Pelynt**, to the north of Polperro, is well known for its quaint architecture (including the church which has an unusual classical aisle dating from 1680), narrow streets, Banjo Pier and location as a splendid holiday centre. This area of Cornwall also has many National Trust properties, farm parks, gardens and activity centres.

Along a quiet leafy country lane one mile from the village are **Cartole Cottages**, a small select group of seven cottages converted from the barns of Cartole Farm, which has been part of the local countryside for at least 300 years. Many original features were left intact and each cottage has a shape and identity entirely its own. The award winning country gardens and surrounding patchwork fields, make it hard to imagine a more peaceful setting.

All the cottages are spotlessly clean, heated, very well equipped and have fitted carpets throughout. The furnishing are comfortable and well presented and beds

Cartole Cottages

are made ready for guests' arrivals. Pets are welcome. Looe and Polperro are only eight minutes by car and the market town of Liskeard with its leisure centre and swimming pool is about 20 minutes drive.

Cartole Cottages, Pelynt, near Looe, Cornwall PL13 2QH Tel: 01503 220956

At the entrance to Pelynt is the 16th century **Jubilee Inn**, once a medieval farmhouse the inn has been family owned for over 20 years and offers its guests a casual but comfortable atmosphere. Inside this attractive building are oak beamed ceilings, fresh flowers in the summer, roaring log fires in the winter and the promise of good food and wine. All of the nine bedrooms have been individually decorated and furnished with full en-suite facilities, colour television, radio and direct dial telephone. There are three special family rooms and

a beautiful bridal suite complete with a four poster bed overlooking a quiet courtyard and a spiral staircase designed by Stuart Armfield, the well known West Country artist. The dining room is light and spacious, full of antique furniture, gleaming glass and silver and an extensive menu that could liven up even the most jaded of palates. Fresh crabs, lobster, scallops, mackerel, sole and cod come straight from the brightly coloured boats in nearby Looe to the Jubilee's spotless kitchens, here they are turned into dishes ranging from the simplest of bar snacks to the most sophisticated banquet. Real ales, afternoon teas, summer barbecues, coastal walks—the Jubilee Inn really does offer its guests the very best in Cornish hospitality.

The Jubilee Inn, Penlynt, near Looe, Cornwall PL13 2JZ Tel: 01503 220312 Fax: 01503 220920

To the north of Looe, **Polraen Country House Hotel** is in a quiet position at **Sandplace**, in the beautiful Looe Valley at the junction of the A387 and the B3254 roads. Set in two and a half acres of landscaped gardens, the house was built of Cornish stone in the early 1700s and is reputed to have been a coaching inn. It nestles in a hollow, facing south, which makes the garden ideal for relaxing and enjoying the mild climate.

Polraen Country House Hotel

Inside guests will discover the friendly service of a private hotel, together with the personal comfort of a private house. The bedrooms all have their own private showers and toilets, are equipped with tea and coffee making facilities, colour television, radio alarm and hair dryers, and the hotel is centrally heated through-out. There is a comfortable sunny lounge with French windows opening on to the patio and garden. In the dining room, with its old fashioned range, guests are invited to enjoy a wealth of home-cooked food. An excellent selection of wine is available together with a cosy well stocked bar where they can meet some of the local characters.

Joyce and Peter Allcroft have been the resident owners of Polraen for 14 years and certainly provide their guests with all the comforts for an enjoyable holiday. *Polraen Country House Hotel, Sandplace, near Looe, Cornwall PL13 1PJ Tel: 01503 263956*

LISKEARD   *Map 2 ref D25*

Standing on an undulating site between the valleys of the East Looe and Seaton rivers, Liskeard is a pleasant old market town which was one of Cornwall's five medieval Stannary towns (the others are Bodmin, Lostwithiel, Truro and Helston). The town has a long history as a centre for mineral extraction: for centuries, the medieval Cornish tinners brought their smelted tin down from Bodmin Moor for weighing, stamping and taxing. Then, in the early 19th century, great quantities of copper ore from the nearby Caradon mines and granite from the Cheesewring quarries were loaded onto barges here and despatched to the coast along the newly constructed Looe canal. In the 1850s, the canal was replaced by the Looe valley branch of the Great Western Railway, a scenic stretch of line which still operates today although its industrial cargoes have long been replaced by passenger holiday traffic.

Perhaps Liskeard's most unusual feature can be found in Well Lane where an arched grotto marks the site of **Pipe Well**, a medieval spring which is reputed to have curative powers.

To the north of Liskeard, in the peaceful moorland village of **Henwood** and surrounded by the famous peaks of Sharptor and the Cheesewring, a group of 200 year old farm buildings has been converted into three distinctive self-catering holiday cottages, known as **Henwood Barns**. There is a stunning panorama across the valley all the way to Dartmoor on the horizon. One could easily spend hours quietly contemplating this view, watching the buzzards hovering and soaring overhead, and musing over how different it all must have felt just a hundred or so years ago, when the copper mines and granite quarries were in full production and steam locomotives made their way to the Prince of Wales engine house across the valley on Caradon Hill. It is easy to see how the author EV Thompson, who lived just outside Henwood, must have drawn inspiration from his surroundings for his bestselling tales of historic Cornwall.

Henwood Barns

The three converted barns provide a range of accommodation; the smallest has been designed as a retreat for busy couples while the largest, sleeping six, is ideal for families. An added advantage is that all kinds of groups can be accommodated by renting more than one cottage. The friendly owners Michelle and Joe, who live next door, report that three generation bookings are quite popular; parents and children stay in one cottage while grandparents staying in another can enjoy their company—and still have their own place in which to hide when necessary!

The barns, which are built of local granite with slate roofs, have been tastefully and imaginatively converted, retaining the rustic character of the original while providing very comfortable facilities for today's visitors. All three cottages have wood-burning stoves.

Henwood Barns, Henwood, Liskeard, Cornwall PL14 5BP
Tel: 01579 363576

In the small village of Tideford, to the southeast of Liskeard, is **Heskyn Mill Restaurant** which has the look of a large country home. This unique stone building (now Grade II listed) was originally built as a corn mill and part of the Eliot Estate. It remained a working mill into the 1950s and became a restaurant 18 years ago. Within the restaurant are two waterwheels, gearing and other large items of machinery, still intact and seemingly still in working order. Heskyn Mill is highly acclaimed for its excellent cuisine and is open at lunch times and evenings from Tuesday to Saturday. A wood burning stove gives off a nice

Heskyn Mill Restaurant

warmth as guests enter the cosy bar where a smaller menu is available for lunchtimes. Upstairs, amongst the machinery, is the restaurant, where a full à la carte menu is served. Imaginative dishes tempt one to linger over choice and the selection of a complementary wine from countries worldwide, adds to the pleasure. Game, fish, seafood, poultry and vegetarian dishes all feature on the à la carte or specials' menu. The whole atmosphere and ambience is mellow and relaxing and the dining experience one to savour and remember. Behind the restaurant is a Craft Shop where pottery, jewellery and paintings from local artists and crafts people are sold.

Heskyn Mill Restaurant, Tideford, Saltash, Cornwall PL12 5JS
Tel: 01752 851481

West Cornwall

INTRODUCTION

This, the most southwesterly area of mainland Britain, juts out into the Atlantic and, as a result, experiences a mild climate with the help of the warm flowing waters of the Gulf Stream. The southern coast, the Cornish Riviera, is characterised by the small fishing harbours built in quiet natural coves and the strange village names of Mevagissey and Mullion. Legends abound in the area, with tales of ship wrecks, smugglers and exotic sea creatures featuring heavily.

Whilst fishing, obviously, was the mainstay of the local economy, the remains of the Cornish tin mining industry can still be seen. As can the great conical spoil heaps built out of the waste material from the china clay pits. The great beauty and isolation of this wonderful county has been an inspiration to many artists over the years and Newlyn, near Penzance, attracted a well known school of artists at the beginning of the 20th century.

Today, tourist and visitors still flock to Cornwall. The home of Britain's surfing fraternity, both the sea and the inland countryside have much to offer those who enjoy the outdoor life.

TRURO   *Map 1 ref C26*

This elegant small town has grown to become the administrative capital of Cornwall. Its site at the head of a branch of the Fal estuary has been occupied for thousands of years, but it was not until large scale mineral extraction began in medieval times that the settlement took on any significance. One of the first Cornish towns to be granted rights of Stannary, huge quantities of smelted tin ore and other metals were brought here for weighing, taxing and shipping until the industry went into decline in 17th century. By this time, the estuary had also begun to silt up, allowing Falmouth to take over as the area's principal seaport. A number of picturesque alleyways or opes (pronounced opps) have survived from Truro's heyday as a port, many of which have colourful names such as Tippet's Backlet, Burton's Ope or Squeezeguts Alley.

An increase in metal prices during the 18th century led to a revival in Truro's fortunes; wealthy merchants and banks moved in and the town became a centre for fashionable society with a reputation to rival Bath. This Georgian renaissance has left a distinctive mark on the town's architecture, particularly around Pydar Street, with its handsome Assembly Rooms and Theatre, Walsingham Place, and Lemon Street, one of the finest complete Georgian streets in the country.

The arrival of the railway in 1859 confirmed Truro's status as regional capital and, in 1877, it became a city in its own right when the diocese of Exeter was divided into two and Cornwall was granted its own bishop. Three years later, the foundation stone of the new **Cathedral**, the first to be built in Britain since Wren's St Paul's, was laid by the future Edward VII. Constructed over the next 30 years to the designs of architect John Loughborough Pearson, the cathedral was finished in locally sourced granite. A graceful, three spired building, it incorporates the early 16th century south aisle of St Mary's Church which originally occupied part of the site.

To the southwest of Truro, the village of **Devoran** sits beside a quiet estuary which runs into the River Fal. As well as the many footpaths leading into the surrounding countryside, the area around the village is well known as a birdwatchers paradise.

The Old Quay Inn lies secluded, overlooking a creek which runs into the River Fal. Sitting outside in the beer garden having lunch in this delightful little inn, glass in hand—is a pleasure indeed. A traditional village pub, The Old Quay has more than its fair share of characters and many have stories to tell over a few whiskies! The inn has a number of pub activities ranging from darts tournaments and euchre nights to gig rowing and juggling. However, all customers are more than welcome to sit and have a quiet drink in the very comfortable atmosphere of the bar. For those who want to extend their visit to take in some birdwatching and enjoy this area rich in wildlife, or simply relax in the wonderful countryside, then book in for bed and breakfast and enjoy more fine hospitality at The Old Quay Inn.

The Old Quay Inn

The Old Quay Inn, Devoran, Truro, Cornwall TR3 6NE Tel: 01872 863142

MEVAGISSEY   *Map 1 ref C26*

Once aptly known as Porthilly, the village was renamed in late medieval times after the Welsh and Irish saints, Meva and Itha. Renowned for its fishing, this was once an important centre of the pilchard industry and, each year, during the 18th and 19th centuries thousands of tons of the oily fish were landed here for salting, packing or processing into lamp oil. The need to process the catch within easy reach of the harbour created a labyrinth of buildings separated by steep sloping alleyways, some of which were so narrow that the baskets of fish sometimes had to be carried on poles between people walking one behind the other. There are also a number of more modern indoor attractions including a **Museum**, which contains an interesting assortment of fishing and agricultural equipment, and a model village.

The Ship Inn, a traditional and charming pub, was built in the reign of Elizabeth I and it still retains many of its original features. Personally run by Amanda and David for the past 2 years, as well as offering a good range of beers and spirits, the pub also serves a comprehensive selection of tasty bar meals throughout the day.

The Ship Inn

The Ship Inn also offers exceedingly comfortable accommodation with all modern amenities including hot and cold water, colour television, and tea and coffee making facilities in all six bedrooms. Bed and breakfast is available on a nightly or weekly basis, giving guests the perfect opportunity to explore the historic town or visit the safe sandy beaches that are located only a few minutes walk from the Inns front door.

The Ship Inn, Mevagissey, Cornwall Tel: 01726 843324

Capture the uninterrupted views of the Cornish countryside and Mevagissey Bay from the welcoming **Steep House**. Owned and personally run by David Youlden for the past 18 years, this attractive guest house provides its guests with pleasantly furnished, comfortable rooms which provide lots of facilities and pleasing views at moderate costs. The large seaside garden tempts visitors to relax and enjoy the fabulous coastal view from the southerly sunny lawn or they may even find the time for a swim in the large swimming pool. All guests can be sure of a warm welcome all year round. Old fashioned Mevagissey has plenty

Steep House

of places to visit including a super museum, aquarium and model railway. Many guests visit the Lost Gardens of Heligan which are only a 10 minute drive away. *Steep House, Portmellon Cove, Mevagissey, Cornwall Tel: 01726 843732*

Seapoint House Hotel enjoys a magnificent position on the south-facing cliffs of Mevagissey. This fantastic location provides spectacular views over the harbour and coastline from most of the bedrooms, the dining room and the gardens of this delightful hotel. Owned and run by Penny and Michael, visitors are always made more than welcome. The bedrooms are comfortably furnished and all have en-suite facilities, hots drinks bar, colour TVs and private telephones. Excellent home-cooked food can be enjoyed in the dining room, and there is also a games room and bar for residents' use. The luxurious lounge is ideal for a relaxing pre-dinner drink or for a quiet chat with friends and in warm weather the sun terrace and lawns are a delightful spot to settle with the papers or a good book. Special break rates are available throughout the year and the week-long 'Great Gardens' breaks are ideal for garden lovers. Phone or fax for full details.

Seapoint House Hotel

Seapoint House Hotel, Battery Terrace, Mevagissey, Cornwall PL26 6QS
Tel: 01726 842684 Fax: 01726 842266

ST AUSTELL

Map 1 ref C25

This sprawling former market and mining town was transformed in the second half of the 18th century when William Cookworthy discovered large deposits of china clay, or kaolin, here in 1755. Over the years, waste material from the clay pits has been piled into great conical spoil heaps which dominate the landscape to the north and west of the town. These bare bleached uplands are sometimes referred to as the Cornish Alps, although in recent years steps have been taken to landscape their surface and seed them with grass.

This part of Cornwall is still one of the world's largest producers of china clay, a surprisingly versatile material which, as well as being the basic ingredient of porcelain, is used in the manufacture of paper, paint and pharmaceuticals.

The narrow streets of old St Austell create an atmosphere more befitting a market town than a mining community. The central thoroughfares radiate from the parish church of the Holy Trinity, an imposing structure with a tall 15th century tower which is decorated on all four sides with carved figures and topped by impressive pinnacles and crenelations. The granite facing stones were brought from the famous Pentewan quarries, three miles to the south. Elsewhere in the town centre there are some notable old buildings, including the Town Hall, Quaker Meeting House and White Hart Hotel, as well as a good modern shopping precinct.

FOWEY

Map 2 ref D25

The lovely old port of Fowey (pronounced Foy) guards the western entrance to the river from which it takes its name. The narrow lanes and alleyways of the old town rise abruptly from the water's edge in a pleasant mixture of architectural styles from Elizabethan to Edwardian.

The deep water harbour has been used as an anchorage for seagoing vessels since the time of the ancient Romans and china clay continues to be exported from the whitened jetties which lie half-a-mile or so upstream. The town's long history is closely linked with its maritime tradition. During the Hundred Years War, local mariners recruited to fight the French became known as the Fowey Gallants; some refused to disband and instead formed a notorious gang of pirates who would attack any vessel straying too close to this stretch of coast. Following a devastating French raid in 1457, a chain was stretched across the estuary mouth at night to deter hostile ships from entering the harbour.

Present day Fowey is a peaceful community which is connected by vehicle ferry to Bodinnick on the eastern bank and by passenger ferry to Polruan. The harbour is filled with pleasure craft from all over Britain and Continental Europe and there are a number of fine old buildings which are worth a closer inspection, for example the **Noah's Ark Museum**, which is housed one of the oldest structures in Fowey, the medieval Town Hall in Trafalgar Square, which is occupied by another interesting local museum, and **The Ship Inn**, a part 15th century building with a Victorian façade which was once the town house of the Rashleigh family. Their family seat, Menabilly, lies to the southeast of the town and was subsequently the home of Daphne du Maurier who used the setting, rechristened as 'Manderley', in her famous novel, *Rebecca*. Another of Fowey's literary residents was the Cornish novelist, Sir Arthur Quiller-Couch, who lived for over 50 years at the Haven on the Esplanade.

Penhale Caravan and Camping Park is small, family run park just one and a half miles away from the bustling town of Fowey and with many lovely coastal and riverside walks only minutes away. Each of the static caravans for hire is fully connected to mains water and electricity and has a shower, toilet, gas cooker, refrigerator and colour TV for visitors' convenience. The touring caravans, campervans and tents have their own separate area with level and

Penhale

gently sloping pitches and plenty of space so overcrowding is not a problem. The shower blocks have hot showers, flush toilets, wash basins, hair dryer and electrical shaving points whilst the laundry room offers a washing machine, tumble dryer and sinks with free hot water for both dishes and clothes. This attractive camping park is ideally situated for exploring picturesque Cornwall and enjoying the many different aspects of this lovely county.
Penhale, Fowey, Cornwall PL23 1JU Tel: 01726 833425

Ideally situated for visiting every corner of Cornwall, **The Cormorant Hotel** is located close to, and high above, the very beautiful Fowey Estuary. All of the 11 attractively furnished bedrooms have spectacular views over the river and offer their guests the very best in home comforts including full en-suite facilities, colour TV, radio and direct dial telephone.

Guests can sit and relax in the comfortable lounge, warm themselves in front of the real log fire and gaze out of the full length picture windows onto one of the loveliest views in all of England. Enjoy a drink in the newly decorated bar area and then move into the candle lit dining room, where two extensive menus are offered with the accent on dishes created using only the freshest local fish caught that day. For those who fancy a little exercise after all this indulgence then the hotel's heated swimming pool is the place to head for. Situated even higher than the hotel, the pool is covered by a sliding roof and offers some fantastic views

The Cormorant Hotel

over the estuary and creeks. The Cormorant Hotel offers its guests the very best in Cornish hospitality and the opportunity to escape the hurly burly of modern life and relax in the warm and welcoming atmosphere that permeates through this superb establishment.

The Cormorant Hotel, Golant by Fowey, Cornwall PL23 1LL
Tel: 01726 833426

LOSTWITHIEL   *Map 2 ref C25*

This attractive small market town stands at the head of the Fowey estuary at the historic lowest bridging point on the river. One of Cornwall's medieval Stannary towns, tin and other raw metals were brought here for assaying and onward shipping until upstream mining activity caused the anchorage to silt up, forcing the port to move down river to the estuary mouth. Present day Lostwithiel is an atmospheric touring and angling centre whose long history has left it with a legacy of interesting old buildings, many of which are set in characteristic narrow alleyways, or opes.

The remains of the 13th century great hall which served as the treasury and stannary offices can be seen in Quay Street and, in Fore Street, there is a fine example of an early 18th century arcaded Guildhall, which now serves as the civic **Museum**. The nearby municipal offices date from later in the century, as does the old grammar school in Queen Street, and elsewhere in the town there are some fine Georgian residences and shop fronts.

On the outskirts of Lostwithiel the imposing Norman keep of **Restormel Castle** stands on a promontory overlooking the wooded valley of the River Fowey. The fortress was built early in the 12th century by Edmund, Earl of Cornwall and is remarkably well preserved for its age. The walls of the massive circular shell are 30 feet high in places and the whole structure is surrounded by a deep dry moat which is lined with flowers in spring. The castle was in use until the 16th century, and was reoccupied for a time by Parliamentarian forces during the English Civil War. Now under the care of English Heritage, visitors can climb a series of walkways onto the ramparts.

Situated in this charming town near the old Duchy Palace and River Fowey, **Trewithen Restaurant** is a cosy converted 300 year old dwelling catering for those who enjoy something special. The restaurant was established in 1980 by

Lorraine and Brian Rolls and is very neatly presented and full of character with old stone walls, cast iron range and interesting objects d'art. Featured in many guides and, in 1996, awarded Les Routiers Casserole Award in recognition of its high standards of cuisine. The à la carte menu specialities vary according to season but typically offer south coast lobster during the summer months and local venison and game in the winter. A variety of fish dishes, local scallops and monkfish feature regularly alongside crispy duckling and prime fillet steak. Special evenings have become an established part of the restaurant calendar which have included Indian, Cajun, Italian and French delights.

Trewithen Restaurant

The menu is supplemented by extra selections on the blackboard whilst in the summer holidays a set Cornish menu is also offered. Vegetarians will also find a variety of creative dishes available including the very appealing vegetarian platter. Highly recommended.

Trewithen Restaurant, 3 Fore Street, Lostwithiel, Cornwall PL22 0BP
Tel: 01208 872373

The small and historic town of Lostwithiel, once the capital of Cornwall, is the home of the **Restormel Lodge Hotel**. This well appointed hotel has been owned and managed by the Hanson family for over 30 years and offers its guests a relaxed and friendly atmosphere with good old fashioned hospitality. All of the 33 bedrooms have en-suite facilities and are fully equipped for comfort, whilst the family suite welcomes children of all ages and has superb facilities including a baby-listening service so parents can go out and enjoy a meal or a drink with total peace of mind. The restaurant is popular with locals and visitors alike, the chef has a professional commitment to using only the freshest and finest Cornish farm and sea produce to create the menus many varied and interesting dishes.

Restormel Lodge Hotel

The south facing swimming pool and patio area is a secluded haven with pool side service available and on those warmer summer evenings the patio makes the ideal location for the chef's superb barbecues. It is not hard to see why the Restormel Lodge Hotel has achieved such a reputation with visitors from home and abroad as one of the best centres for exploring the Duchy of Cornwall.
Restormel Lodge Hotel, Castle Hill, Lostwithiel, Cornwall PL22 0DD
Tel: 01208 872223

To the west of Lostwithiel and an excellent place to stop on the A391 St Austell to Bodmin road is the **Bugle Inn**, a handsome former coaching inn which stands at the main crossroads in the village of **Bugle**. In 1840, the newly constructed inn was named by local miners and clay workers as a tribute to the bugler on the *Regulator*, one of the coach lines which, like the *Quicksilver Mail*, passed daily along this route. Today, the Bugle is a pleasant inn which provides a warm welcome to visitors and locals alike. Along with a full range of St Austell ales, hosts Pam and Simon Rodger serve an extensive range of excellent value food, including sandwiches, salads, basket meals, steaks and daily specials; they also offer traditional roast lunches on Sundays.

Bugle Inn

Bugle Inn, Fore Street, Bugle, Cornwall PL26 9PB Tel: 01726 850307

NEWQUAY *Map 1 ref C25*

A settlement since ancient times, evidence of an Iron Age coastal fort can be seen among the cliffs and caves of **Porth Island** a detached outcrop which is connected to the mainland by an elegant suspended footbridge and which lies to the northeast of the town centre. In common with many Cornish coastal communities, this was an important pilchard fishing centre in the centuries leading up to the industry's decline early in the 20th century. An original huer's hut can still be seen on the headland to the west of the harbour; this was where a local man would keep a look out for shoals of red pilchards and alert the fishing crews when one was sighted close to shore by calling "hevva" through a long loud hailer. He would then guide the seine boats towards their quarry with semaphore-style signals using a pair of bats known as bushes.

The town takes its name from the new harbour which was built in the 1830s by Joseph Treffry of Fowey for exporting china clay, a trade which continued for several decades until the purpose built port facility was completed on the south coast at Par. The decline of Newquay as a port was tempered by the arrival of the railway in 1875 and, before long, train loads of visitors were arriving to enjoy the town's extensive sandy beaches, scenic position and mild climate. Over the years, a number of popular attractions have been constructed to satisfy tourist demand, including **Trenance Garden** with its boating lake, miniature railway and zoo. Towan Beach is a good sheltered beach with a tidal paddling pool which is ideal for children; this can be found at the base of the Porth Island. In recent decades, Newquay has also acquired a reputation as one of the finest surfing centres in the British Isles. Throughout the year, thousands of keen surfers arrive in Volkswagen campers and the like to catch the waves of **Fistral Beach** or to watch the increasing number of national and international competitions which are held here each season.

Along the coast, to the north of Newquay, lies the small village of **Porthcothan**. Much of the cliffscape around this former smugglers' haunt is owned by the National Trust, and further north, the view of the Atlantic is particularly dramatic around Constantine Bay and Trevose Head.

Bay House Hotel, the only hotel in Porthcothan, overlooks one of the finest unspoilt beaches on the north Cornwall coast. Only 50 yards from the beach, this family run hotel offers a personal and friendly service in clean, comfortable and relaxing surroundings. The hotel is an ideal resting place for coastal path walkers and offers a quiet, away from it all location for those who enjoy the scenic views and lazing on the beach. The Bay House is located on the scenic coastal road (B3276) which runs between the picturesque fishing port of Padstow and the vibrant surfing town of Newquay.

The hotel is open all year round and offers special mid-week, long weekend, golfing and walking breaks in the low season and a fun four day Christmas holiday. Padstow holds a special May Day celebration which draws people from all over the world and the Bay House Hotel makes a comfortable base for such a visit.

Recent refurbishment of the hotel's kitchen has brought new standards to the licensed restaurant which now offers freshly prepared and varied cuisine to suit most tastes, including vegetarian, and can now offer meals from breakfast through to evening dinner for hotel and self-catering residents, and visitors to the bay during the day and evening.

Bay House Hotel

Thirteen guest bedrooms offer a range of accommodation which includes family rooms, some en-suite and most with magnificent sea views. Three self-contained holiday flats which have been upgraded, can accommodate four to six persons. The tariff varies during the seasons, and there are some good deals to be had especially in the low season. Telephone for further details.
Bay House Hotel, Porthcothan Bay, near Padstow, Cornwall PL28 8LW
Tel: 01841 520472

ST AGNES
Map 1 ref B25

Once known as the source of the finest tin in Cornwall, this old mining community lies at the head of a steep valley. Despite having been subjected to 200 years of mineral extraction and almost 100 years of tourism, it still manages to retain its original character, especially around the narrow spired parish church and nearby terrace of stepped miners' cottages which are known locally as the Stippy-Stappy. The village is also renowned as the birthplace of the Georgian society painter, John Opie, and is known to thousands of readers of Winston Graham's *Poldark* novels as 'St Ann'. A good local **Museum** can be found near the church and there is also a popular leisure park to the south of the village which features a model of Cornwall in miniature and a number of themed areas, all set in seven acres of attractive landscaped grounds.

Porthvean Hotel is the original hotel in St Agnes village, with a history of well over 200 years. Today, it provides all one would expect from a small, personally run hotel—and much more. At the front of the hotel is a small sunny terrace providing an ideal vantage point to watch the world go by. Once inside, guests will discover a really cosy atmosphere where Geoff and Frin, resident proprietors for 19 years, have created a most attractive and carefully presented interior. The seven bedrooms are beautifully appointed and have their own en-suite shower rooms. All are equipped with TV, hot drinks facilities, hair dryer and telephone.

Porthvean Hotel

Good food holds pride of place in this hotel—the breakfast menu being one of the most comprehensive ever seen! In the evening Frins Restaurant caters for all tastes and budgets, simple or lavish; there's a good choice for vegetarians and vegans too. There is a wonderful ambience and service to match and guests should be prepared to be spoilt and pampered at Porthvean. ETB 3 Crown Commended.

Porthvean Hotel, Churchtown, St Agnes, Cornwall TR5 0QP
Tel: 01872 552581 Fax: 01872 553773

Lying in the very heart of St Agnes, **The Railway Inn** dates back to 1804 when it was known as the Smith's Arms, because it was originally a blacksmith's shop. The inn has been personally managed by Julie for the past five years and visitors will find good home-made food and plenty of real ale being served in the wood panelled bar that is home to the second largest collection of horse brasses in the country. These rub shoulders with an unusual collection of famous memorabilia which includes a pair of Tommy Cooper's shoes and Lilian Board's Mexico Olympic running shoes!

The Railway Inn, St Agnes, Cornwall TR5 0TJ Tel: 01872 552310

In **Trevaunance Cove** near St Agnes, which incidentally is one of the best surfing beaches in Cornwall, is a gem of a place called, rather oddly, **The Driftwood Spars**. This first class free house run by Gordon and Jill Treleaven takes its name from the fact that part of its construction is of huge wooden ships spars which were used in the building of what was, at one time, a mine warehouse and a sail loft before its conversion to the hotel and inn seen today. It has lost nothing of its earlier character, however, and there is even a wreckers tunnel which can be seen through a porthole set into one of the walls. With something for everyone, there a three cosy bars with one particularly suitable for children, a separate restaurant upstairs and with the added bonus of overnight accommodation this is an ideal place to stop, be it by car or for those who are using the coastal footpath for Perranporth which passes the front door. Also of interest to those travelling through the area is the local craft workshop that is situated only five minutes walk away and proves very popular with those looking for a different or unusual gift.

The Driftwood Spars

The Driftwood Spars, Trevaunance Cove, St Agnes, Cornwall TR5 0RT
Tel: 01872 552428

REDRUTH   *Map 1 ref B26*

In the mid-19th century, the surrounding area was the most intensely mined in the world and the district is still littered with evidence of this lost era. In the 1850s, Cornwall had well over 300 mines which together produced two-thirds of the world's copper and employed around 50,000 workers. However, most had to close in the first few decades of the 20th century when the discovery of extensive mineral deposits in the Americas, South Africa and Australia rendered the local industry uneconomic.

Now combined with **Camborne** to form the largest urban centre of population in the county, Redruth and Camborne have much to offer those with an interest in industrial archeology. Midway between the two, at **Pool**, the National Trust have acquired a pair of massive old high pressure beam engines, one of which has a cylinder over seven feet in diameter. One was built by Holmans of Camborne in 1887 as a winding engine for raising ore and delivering workers into the mine; the other was built by Harveys of Hayle in 1892 for pumping water from depths of up to 1700 feet. The Trust's Norris Collection of minerals can be seen in the **Geological Museum** of the old Camborne School of Mines, half-a-mile to the west. Still one of the foremost institutes of mining technology, the School moved to new premises in Redruth in the 1970s.

The home of pioneer Cornish engineer Richard Trevithick can be seen at **Penponds** on the southwestern outskirts of Camborne. This little known inventor was responsible for developing the high pressure steam engine, the screw propeller and an early locomotive which predated Stephenson's *Rocket* by 12 years, yet he died penniless and was buried in an unmarked grave in Dartford, Kent. Known locally as the Cornish Giant, a statue of this underrated genius and accomplished amateur wrestler can be seen outside Camborne Library; he is also commemorated in the colourful Trevithick Day procession which is held in the last week of April. Another inventor who settled in the area was Scotsman William Murdock. Responsible for such innovations as coal-gas lighting and the vacuum-powered tubes which were once a common feature in most department stores, his home in **Cross Street**, Redruth is now open to the public.

To the northwest of Redruth leads past the **Tolgus Tin Mill**, an 18th century streaming mill where tin deposits were extracted from the river bed by a process of sifting and stamping. Prior to a quay being constructed at **Portreath** in 1760, copper ore from the mines around Redruth and St Day had to be loaded onto ships from the beach, a slow and dangerous task. Built by Francis Basset, the man whose monument stands on **Carn Brea**, the harbour was connected to the mines in 1809 by the first railway in Cornwall. The remains of the inclined plane which was used to lower ore laden wagons down the final 1 in 10 gradient to the quay can still be made out.

ST IVES   *Map 1 ref A26*

With its five sandy beaches, maze of narrow streets, and picturesque harbour and headland, this attractive fishing and former mining centre manages to retain a special atmosphere, despite being deluged with visitors throughout the summer. The settlement takes its name from the 6th century missionary saint, St Ia, who is said to have landed here having sailed across from Ireland on an ivy leaf. The 15th century **Parish Church** near the harbour's shorter west pier bears her name. An impressive building with a soaring pinnacled tower, it contains an unusual granite font carved with stylised angels and lions.

St Ives was one of Cornwall's most important pilchard fishing centres until the industry went into decline in the early 20th century. The town holds a record dating back to 1868 for the greatest number of fish caught in a single seine net. Once the pilchards were brought ashore, they were compressed to release fish oil before being salted and packed into barrels for despatch to southern Europe where the Catholic code for avoiding meat on Fridays guaranteed a steady demand. At such times, the streets of St Ives would stream with the oily residue of these once plentiful fish and the air would be filled with an appalling smell which would drive away all but the most determined outsiders. A local speciality, heavy, or hevva, cake was traditionally made for the seiners returning with their catch.

As well as providing shelter for the fishing fleet, St Ives' harbour was built for exporting locally mined metal ores. The sturdy main pier was built by John Smeaton, the 18th century marine architect who was responsible for designing the famous Eddystone lighthouse which now stands on Plymouth Hoe. Like many parts of western Cornwall, the surrounding valley was once rich in veins of tin, copper and other minerals, and indeed the building which now houses **St Ives Museum** began life as Wheal Dream copper mine. The town's labyrinth of narrow streets was once divided into two communities: Downalong, where the fishing families lived and Upalong, which was inhabited by the mining community. There was much tension between the two and fights would often break out between gangs of young rivals, a practice which ended with the closing of the mines and the steady reduction in the fishing fleet.

St Ives' decline as a mining and fishing centre has been offset by its rise as an artists' colony. The painter William Turner visited the town towards the end of his life and both Whistler and Sickert are known to have been attracted here by the special light of west Cornwall. In the first half of the 20th century, Barbara Hepworth, Ben Nicholson and others began to convert the disused pilchard cellars and sail lofts around the harbour into artists' studios, and a St Ives School was established which gained an international reputation.

One of the highlights of any stay in St Ives is a visit to the **Barbara Hepworth Sculpture Garden** and **Museum** in Barnoon Hill. After she died in a fire at the premises in 1975, the sculptor's living quarters, studio and garden were turned into a museum and gallery dedicated to her life and work. The garden is packed with a remarkable concentration of her work and two particularly poignant features are the little summerhouse where she used to rest in the afternoons. Barbara Hepworth's studio is now administered by the **Tate Gallery**, the London-based institution which has also opened a large scale annexe in the town which is dedicated to the work of the St Ives School. An imposing white-painted building which uses Porthmeor Beach as a stunning backdrop, the architecture is considered by some to dwarf the quality of the work inside!

PENZANCE   *Map 1 ref A26*

For centuries, this was a remote market town which made its living from fishing, mining and smuggling. It was sacked by the Spanish in 1595, then, at the end of the English Civil War, it suffered a similar fate for being such a staunch supporter of the Royalist cause. However, the fortunes of the town were transformed by the arrival of the railway in 1859, a development which permitted the direct despatch of early flowers, vegetables and locally caught fish to the urban centres of Britain and which also allowed increasing numbers of holidaymakers to be carried in the opposite direction.

The main broad thoroughfare of Penzance, **Market Jew Street**, takes its name from the Cornish term for Thursday market; it has a high stepped pavement on one side and, at its southwestern end, there is a domed neoclassical **Market House** of 1837. In front of this stands the statue of Penzance born, Humphry Davy, the 19th century scientist who is remembered for inventing the miners' safety lamp. A number of interesting buildings are located in Chapel Street and the most unexpected is the **Egyptian House**, with its exotic 1830s façade, which has recently been restored by the Landmark Trust; the National Trust occupy the ground floor shop.

The **Maritime Museum** contains a unique collection of artefacts recovered from shipwrecks around the Cornish coast. Marie Branwell, the mother of the Brontë sisters, was brought up at No 25 Chapel Street, and at its lower end, the early 19th century St Mary's church stands on a ledge above the harbour and Customs House, a reassuring landmark for returning sailors. Elsewhere in Penzance, there is an interesting **Geological Museum** in Alverton Street, a good local history museum and exhibition of paintings by the Newlyn School in Penlee Memorial Gardens, and a striking collection of subtropical trees and flowers in **Morrab Gardens**.

Penmorvah Hotel

Situated in a tree lined avenue and only a short walk from the Promenade, **Penmorvah Hotel** is the ideal base from which to explore Cornwall's magnificent countryside. This Victorian town hotel has been personally owned and managed by Colin and Mary William's for the past 14 years and has been 3 Crown approved by the local Tourist Board. Although the hotel is small by international standards, having only eight bedrooms, Colin and Mary have aimed to provide a relaxed and friendly atmosphere that has been successfully blended with an extremely high level of service and quality. All of the eight bedrooms have full en-suite facilities and offer their guests a colour television and complimentary tea and coffee making facilities, with children and well behaved pets welcomed at all times.

Penmorvah Hotel, Alexandra Road, Penzance, Cornwall TR18 4LZ Tel: 01736 363711

The isolated granite hamlet of **Lamorna** lies in a rocky cove at the end of a beautiful wooded valley to the south of Penzance. Once only licensed to sell beer, its pub, **The Wink**, got its name from the old custom of winking to the landlord to obtain something stronger from under the counter.

An exceptional Bronze Age stone circle can be seen near here. Known as the **Merry Maidens**, its standing stones are reputed to be all that remain of 19 young women who were turned to granite for daring to dance on the Sabbath. The nearby **Pipers**, two large menhirs 100 yards apart, are rumoured to be the accompanying musicians who suffered the same fate.

Lamorna Cove, the haunt of local families, has, for many years, been the secret find of tourists and visitors who returned year after year to enjoy the seclusion of this delightful and peaceful cove. Perhaps the ideal setting in the mind's eye of so many stories featuring the sandy coves along the rugged Cornish coast, intimate cottages with proliferating garden greenery and steep narrow lanes with their high hedges. **The Lamorna Cove Hotel** is the perfect haven from which

The Lamorna Cove Hotel

to enjoy this and many other southerly parts of Cornwall, with Penzance and Lands End in near reach. Set peacefully amidst the terraced gardens overlooking Lamorna Cove, immortalised by so many famous artists, this 19th century house was once the home of Sir Alfred Munnings. It has an atmosphere of warmth and privacy, antiques and family heirlooms giving this country hotel a unique reputation. For the summer days between May and September, the outdoor heated swimming pool adds a further dimension to the pleasure of your stay. Bookings need to be made early!

The Lamorna Cove Hotel, Lamorna Cove, near Penzance, Cornwall
TR19 6XH Tel: 01736 731411

HELSTON *Map 1 ref B26*

The westernmost of Cornwall's five medieval Stannary towns, during the early Middle Ages streamed tin was brought here for assaying and taxing before being despatched throughout southern Britain and Europe. Although difficult to imagine today, this was a busy port until the 13th century when a shingle bar formed across the mouth of the River Cober preventing access to the sea. Goods were then transported to a new quay at Gweek until further silting and a decline in tin extraction brought an end to the trade.

Helston's long and colourful history has left it with a legacy of interesting old buildings. The **Blue Anchor Inn**, a hostel for monks in the 15th century, can be found at the lower end of the main Coinagehall Street, and further up, the part 16th century **Angel Hotel** is the former town house of the Godolphin family. In the 1750s, the Earl of Godolphin was responsible for rebuilding the Parish **Church of St Michael** at the back of the town with its imposing exterior, fine plaster ceiling in the chancel, and impressive internal gallery on three sides of the nave. The churchyard contains a memorial to Henry Trengrouse, the Helston man responsible for inventing the rocket-propelled safety line which saved so many lives around the British coast. He dedicated himself to developing the device after the frigate *Anson* ran aground on nearby Loe Bar in 1807, resulting in the unnecessary loss of 100 lives. An exhibit devoted to his life's work can be found in Helston's **Folk Museum**, a fascinating collection of historical artefacts which is housed in the old Butter Market.

However, Helston is perhaps best known for its Furry Fair which takes place each year in early May. This ancient pagan celebration of spring takes its name from the Cornish 'fer', meaning feast day, although in the 18th century, it was given Roman roots and renamed after the goddess, Flora. According to local legend, what is now often referred to as the Floral Dance is performed in commemoration of St Michael's victory over the Devil who tried to claim possession of the town. (The final boulder thrown by Satan is claimed to have missed its target, ending up in the garden of the Angel Hotel where it remained until 1783.) Every May 8, the town is closed to traffic and formally dressed couples and pairs of children dance through the streets, and in and out of people's houses, to the strains of traditional folk melodies.

The view from **Mullion**, which lies to the south of Helston, is enhanced by the sight of St Michael's Mount, a dozen miles away across Mount's Bay.

Campden House is a splendid place in which to stay, located as it is in this lovely old village and with the coves of Poldhu, Polurian and Mullion easily reached close by. Comfortable beds await in the eight bedrooms some of which have en-suite showers. There's a large sun lounge, dining room, bar and television lounge available to guests at all times. Dinner is served at 6.30 pm although hot snacks, tea and coffee are always available during the day and evening. The owners

Campden House

Brian and Joan Hyde grow most of their own vegetables giving their home-cooking that special taste. The Campden House Cornish Cream Tea is something special—not to be missed! From Helston, take the A3083 towards the Lizard and follow the Mullion Golf Course signpost.

Campden House, The Commons, Mullion, Cornwall TR12 7HZ
Tel: 01326 240365

FALMOUTH   *Map 1 ref B26*

Although a settlement has existed here for many hundreds of years, it was not until the 17th century that the port was properly developed as a mail packet station which subsequently became the communications' hub for the British empire. During its heyday in the early 19th century, Falmouth was the base for almost 40 sailing ships which carried documents, personal effects and cargo to almost every corner of the globe. A few decades later, however, the introduction of steam-powered vessels heralded the end for Falmouth and by the 1850s, the packet service had moved to Southampton.

Three centuries before, Henry VIII built a pair of fortresses on either side of the estuary mouth to protect the strategically important deep-water anchorage from attack by forces loyal to the Catholic faith. **Pendennis Castle** on the western side is superbly sited on a 200 foot promontory overlooking the entrance to the Carrick Roads. Its low circular keep has immensely thick walls and stands within a 16-sided enclosure; the outer curtain wall was added during Elizabethan times in response to the threat of a second Spanish Armada. One of the last Royalist strongholds to fall during the English Civil War, Pendennis only succumbed to the Parliamentarians following a grim siege lasting five months. The castle remained in use as a coastal defence station until the end of the Second World War and is now under the ownership of English Heritage. The spectacular viewpoint of **Pendennis Point** is also the location of the Maritime Rescue Centre, the operational headquarters which was opened in 1981 to coordinate all search and rescue operations around the British coastline.

That Falmouth was developed as a port at all was due to Sir Walter Raleigh, a man whose early vision was later realised by the influential local buccaneering family, the Killigrews. A monument to the family erected in 1737 can be seen in Grove Place, a short distance from the remains of their once splendid Tudor mansion, **Arwenack House**. Falmouth's Royalist sympathies are demonstrated in the 17th century parish church which is dedicated to 'King Charles the Martyr'; much altered, it retains its curious rectangular tower and arcades with Ionic plaster capitals. Elsewhere in the town there are some handsome early 19th century buildings, including the **Falmouth Arts Centre**, in Church Street, which began life as a Quaker institute 'to promote useful arts'. A curious chimney near the Custom House was used for burning contraband tobacco and is still referred to as the **King's Pipe**. The area around Custom House Quay has been made into a conservation area, the centrepiece of which is the tall funnelled steam tug, the *St Denys*; this fascinating little ship forms part of Falmouth's **Maritime Museum**.

Tudor Court Hotel is a strikingly stylish mock Tudor building set in pleasant gardens and convenient to all Falmouth's main beaches and the famous Princess Pavilion. The hotel has 11 bedrooms with en-suite bathrooms/shower; all rooms have television and hot drinks facilities and are double glazed and are centrally

Tudor Court Hotel

heated. The dining room affords pleasant views over the gardens which gained the hotel Britain in Bloom Award 1996. Menus offer a wide choice of dishes available at all meals with special diets also catered for. Guests can relax in the intimate lounge bar after their evening meal. Unfortunately children under six years cannot be catered for, nor can family pets. This is a comfortable and relaxing hotel. RAC Listed.

Tudor Court Hotel, 55 Melvill Road, Falmouth, Cornwall TR11 4DF Tel & Fax: 01326 312807

Castleton Guest House is a pretty, well presented terrace-style house forming part of an attractive row of cottages close to the centre of Falmouth, the Pier and only five minutes from the beach. Run by Molly and Peter Appleton for 14 years, Castleton has a lovely warm feeling where guests are well cared for. Rooms have colour television, hot drinks facilities and are pleasantly decorated—most have en suite facilities. A ground floor bedroom is suitable for disabled guests. Full English breakfast is served unless a special diet is arranged. There are some facilities for children but check in advance. Pets are accommodated by arrangement.

Castleton Guest House

Castleton Guest House, 68 Killigrew Street, Falmouth, Cornwall TR11 3PR
Tel: 01326 311072

CHAPTER FIVE
Central England

Nottingham Street, Melton Mowbray

5
Central England

Gloucestershire

INTRODUCTION

This essentially rural county divides into three very distinct areas: the Forest of Dean, the Vale of Berkeley and the Cotswold Hills. The River Severn separates the Forest of Dean from the rest of Gloucestershire and this area still remains remote though it is not nearly as densely forested as it once was. On the eastern banks of the Severn are the flat and fertile lands of the Vale of Berkeley. The Severn, which dominates this area, is the longest river in Britain; also the most dangerous, it is well known for its strange reverse tidal wave called the bore.

The county, however, is probably best known for the many quaint villages and ancient market towns all built of the subtle Cotswold limestone. Although Cheltenham is the county's second town, it is perhaps the best known. Not only is it the home of National Hunt Racing but this former spa town has retained much of the elegance and gentility of Regency age which saw its great expansion. To the south of the great escarpment of the Cotswold Hills can also be found the charming and thriving market town of Cirencester.

CHELTENHAM   *Map 9 ref J18*

Cheltenham is a superb Georgian town and also one of the largest centres of population in Gloucestershire, though its history is relatively short. Indeed, the only surviving medieval building here is the parish Church of St Mary in Clarence Street, which has parts dating back to the 12th century.

Prior to the 18th century, Cheltenham was a small market town with a single main street. However in 1715, a local farmer accidentally discovered a saline spring in one of his fields, an occurrence which began a sequence of events which was to change the character of Cheltenham out of all recognition. Twenty years later, his son-in-law, the retired privateer Captain Henry Skillicorne, saw the potential of the discovery and built an enclosure around the spring, along with a meeting room, a ballroom, and a network of walks and rides which now form the tree-lined Promenade. Later, he added a stylish Long Room to the complex of buildings.

As the reputation of Cheltenham Spa grew, a number of other springs were discovered, including one in the High Street around which the first Assembly Rooms were constructed. In 1788, the prosperity of the town was assured following the visit of George III who, along with his queen and daughters, spent five weeks in Cheltenham taking the waters. This royal endorsement made the town a highly fashionable resort and a period of spectacular development followed. A team of eminent architects were commissioned to plan an entirely new town which would incorporate the best features of neoclassical Regency architecture.

This golden era of architecture reached its high point in the late 1820s with the completion of two unique structures. The Promenade is noted for its superb fountain of Neptune, and the Pittville Pump Room is an extravagant masterpiece which stands within spacious parkland to the north of the town centre. The latter was designed by John Forbes and features a great hall fronted by a colonnade of Ionic columns and topped by a domed gallery. It was built by Joseph Pitt MP as a place to entertain his circle of friends, though by the time of his death in 1842, the cost of its construction had left him heavily in debt. Today, the building houses the **Pittville Pump Room Museum**, an imaginative museum of original period costume which brings to life Cheltenham's past from its Regency renaissance to the swinging 1960s.

Also in the centre of Cheltenham are the **Gustav Holst Birthplace Museum**, in Clarence Road, housed in the terraced Regency house where the famous composer of the *Planets Suite* was born in 1874, and the **Cheltenham Art Gallery and Museum**. The museum has a fine collection of Cotswold-made pieces inspired by William Morris, the artist and poet who founded the much respected Arts and Crafts Movement in the 19th century. There is also a fascinating collection of personal items belonging to Edward Wilson, a member of Captain Scott's ill-fated team of Antarctic explorers.

A popular Cricket Festival has been held in Cheltenham each August since 1877, and the town also hosts one of the nation's premier horse racing events, the Cheltenham National Hunt Festival, which takes place in March. **Cheltenham Racecourse**, Britain's top steeplechasing venue, is situated at Prestbury Park, two miles north of the town centre and a little to the east of the A435.

The **Axiom Centre for the Arts** is housed in a refurbished grain warehouse dating from the 1840s and leased from Cheltenham Borough Council for a peppercorn rent. The Centre offers a host of projects and activities ranging from workshops and live music to visual arts and theatre. This worthy establishment is predominantly staffed by volunteers and operates as a registered charity, with

Axiom Art Centre

membership schemes and exhibitions helping to fund the centre. Housed at the front of the art centre is **Café Axiom**, the perfect place to relax, listen to live music and meet friends. The café staff offer their visitors an inspired and freshly cooked selection of vegan and vegetarian foods with daily menus including budget special, an exciting range of salads, delicious Continental dishes, tempting cakes and a wide range of beverages including fresh fruit yoghurt drinks and kombucha tea.

Axiom Art Centre, 57-59 Winchcombe Street, Cheltenham, Gloucestershire GL52 2NE Tel: 01242 690243

In the centre of the town of Cheltenham is the delightful **Cotswold Grange Hotel**. Built from mellow Cotswold limestone, the building is a fine example of Georgian architecture which bears testament to the style and luxury of the grand old days when Cheltenham was a popular spa town. Originally the country house of a London solicitor, the Cotswold Grange is now one of the longest established

Cotswold Grange Hotel

family run hotels in Cheltenham, offering the warmth and personal touch of the family and staff which has made the hotel a favourite with guests who return year after year.

The 25 well equipped en-suite bedrooms are all tastefully decorated and furnished to a high standard. Fine food and good service can be enjoyed in the comfortable surroundings of the dining room, one of the fine rooms of the original house. The menus offer a wide variety of dishes, carefully prepared from the freshest produce and are complemented by the modestly priced and well stocked wine cellar. The hotel is perfect for that well earned break. It is within walking distance of the town centre and makes an ideal base for touring the surrounding Cotswold towns and villages.

Cotswold Grange Hotel, Pittville Circus Road, Cheltenham, Gloucestershire GL52 2QH Tel: 01242 515119

TEWKESBURY
Map 9 ref J18

This historic and strategically important town stands at the confluence of the rivers Severn and Avon. Because its position between the two rivers prevented it from expanding outwards, Tewkesbury's narrow streets became densely packed with unusually tall buildings, many of which were constructed during a time of prosperity in the 15th and 16th centuries. Thanks to the period of relative decline which followed, a great many handsome black and white timber framed structures remain.

Tewkesbury's three main thoroughfares, the High Street, Church Street and Barton Street, form a 'Y' shape, and the area between is filled with narrow alleyways and hidden courtyards which contain some wonderful old pubs and medieval cottages. At the centre of the 'Y' stands the spectacular **Tewkesbury Abbey**, a parish church of cathedral-like proportions which was founded in the 8th century and completely rebuilt at the end of the 11th century. It was once the church of the mighty Benedictine Abbey of Tewkesbury and was one of the last monasteries to be dissolved by Henry VIII. In 1540, it was saved from destruction by the town burghers who bought it from the crown for just £453.

At 132 feet high and 46 feet square, the abbey's colossal main tower is believed to be the largest Norman church tower still in existence. Those making the climb to the top will be rewarded with a breathtaking view of the town and the surrounding landscape. Indeed, the tower was used as a lookout position during one of the bloodiest and most decisive confrontations of the Wars of the Roses, the Battle of Tewkesbury.

The battle took place on Saturday 4 May 1471 in a field to the south of the town which ever since has been known as Bloody Meadow. Following the Lancastrian defeat, those who had not been slaughtered on the battlefield fled to the abbey where they were pursued by the victorious Yorkist army. A further massacre began, but this was halted by timely intervention of Abbot Strensham. Two days later, however, the refugees, who included the Duke of Somerset, were handed over to the King and executed at the town's Market Cross. The 17 year old son of Henry VI, Edward Prince of Wales, was also killed during the conflict and a plaque marking his final resting place can be seen in the abbey.

Almost two centuries later, Tewkesbury was again the scene of military action, this time during the English Civil War. The town changed hands several times during the conflict and on one occasion, Charles I began his siege of Gloucester by requisitioning every pick, mattock, spade and shovel in Tewkesbury. Those keen on finding out more about the town's turbulent military history should follow the Tewkesbury's Battle Trail. Alternatively, there is an impressive model of the battlefield in the **Tewkesbury Town Museum**. This excellent museum occupies a medieval timber-framed building in Barton Street and contains a number of displays on the social history and archeology of Tewkesbury and its environs. Two specialist museums can be found almost adjacent to each other in Church Street. The **Little Museum** is situated in a timber-framed merchant's house dating from around 1450. The building was fully restored in 1971 and is laid out as a typical Tewkesbury merchant's home and workplace of the late medieval period. The nearby **John Moore Countryside Museum** contains a wide variety of artefacts relating to the Gloucestershire countryside, past and present.

Tewkesbury also has some renowned literary associations. Charles Dickens set part of *The Pickwick Papers* in the town's Royal Hop Pole Hotel, and the Victorian romantic writer, Mrs Craik, based her novel *John Halifax, Gentleman* on the people and places of the borough.

FOREST OF DEAN   *Map 8 ref I19*

Throughout its history, this ancient forest has been a wild wood, a royal hunting ground, an important mining and industrial area and a naval timber reserve and, because its geographical location effectively isolated it from the rest of England and Wales, it has developed its own unique character that endures today.

As early as 4000 BC the forest was being cleared for crop cultivation and the timber was used as building materials and as fuel. It was around this time that the practice of coppicing was devised where the new shoots growing from the bases of felled trees were cultivated for periodical cutting. Many species of animals and birds inhabited the forest and it was the presence of deer which led to it being designated a royal hunting forest by King Edmund Ironside early in the 11th century.

As well as being rich in wood, the forest was found to contain iron ore deposits over 2500 years ago. Although they were exploited by the Romans it was not until the Crown allowed areas of the forest to be leased to commercially motivated entrepreneurs in the 1600s that mineral extraction began to take place on a grand scale. Far more devastating, however, was the demand for timber to fuel the iron-smelting process and such was the scale of the requirement that, by the 1660s, the once vast forest had been reduced to a few hundred trees. Serious concern about the shortage of mature oaks for naval shipbuilding led the government to pass one of the first examples of conservation legislation in 1668 which cancelled all the mineral leases. By 1840, nearly 20,000 acres had been replanted and by the time these trees reached maturity steel had taken over as the major shipbuilding material and they were never needed. The **Cannop Valley Nature Reserve** is one excellent example of this early 19th century replanting programme.

During the Victorian era, coal began to be extracted in large quantities, rising to over one million tons a year. Large scale mining ceased in the 1930s but there are still a few seams being worked by groups of 'free miners', the individuals who exercise their traditional right to extract minerals from the forest. Today, the forest is one of the Forestry Commission's most successfully managed areas and the organisation has opened up a large number of waymarked woodland walks.

The Belfry is situated on the edge of the Forest of Dean in the village of **Littledean** and originates from early mining days. It was then known as The George and was used by local people after a hard nights work down the mines—in fact the pub was frequently full at 4.00 in the morning! However The George, like the mining industry, fell on hard times and was eventually closed by its brewery owner. It was purchased in 1991 by the Bell family who, with the help of local people, have created The Belfry Hotel.

The Belfry Hotel

Now run by Mr Strain, The Belfry is a traditional public house with restaurant and gardens as well as accommodation. The establishment also offers traditional beers, skittles, pool and darts as well as a children's room, play area, satellite TV and afternoon teas. The tastefully furnished accommodation available comprises five double rooms and two family rooms all en-suite.

The Belfry offers an impressive variety of food—children's selections, bar snacks and an à la carte—plenty of choice to suit all tastes and pockets. Choose from mouthwatering dishes such as Stilton parcels, Garlic prawns, Venison with cranberries and bacon, Dover sole, Broccoli pithiver and Lemon chicken, all cooked on the premises and fresh to order. The Belfry is ideal for a weekend break or as a base for a longer visit to the area. A very pleasant and relaxing atmosphere with families well catered for.

The Belfry Hotel, Broad Street, Littledean, near Cinderford, Gloucestershire GL14 3JS Tel: 015944 827858

BERKELEY   *Map 4 ref I19*

The low lying **Vale of Berkeley** is bounded to the north by the River Severn and to the south by the M5. This fertile coastal strip takes its name from the peaceful little town of Berkeley, an ancient settlement with a largely Georgian centre which is dominated by its imposing Norman **Castle**. Said to be the oldest castle in England still be inhabited, it was built between 1117 and 1153 on the site of a Saxon fort and has remained in the Berkeley family for over 800 years.

Great Hall, Berkeley Castle

It was here that, in 1215, the barons of the West congregated before setting out to witness the sealing of the Magna Carta by King John at Runnymede. The incident which gave Berkeley Castle its greatest notoriety, however, was the gruesome murder of King Edward II in 1327. Years of ineffectual rule, made worse by his ill judged choice of friends, led to Edward being usurped from the throne by his wife and her lover. He was imprisoned at Berkeley for several months, before being made to suffer a literally terrible end by way of 'a hoot brooche put into the secret place posteriale'. Subsequent monarchs appear to have received rather better treatment when visiting the castle. Richard II was well entertained here and Elizabeth I is known to have stayed on a number of occasions.

Over the centuries Berkeley Castle has been magnificently maintained by the various Lords and Earls of Berkeley. Now open to the public, visitors enter this impressive stronghold by way of a bridge over a moat. The castle is surrounded by an Elizabethan terraced garden which contains a number of interesting features, including a medieval bowling alley and a beautiful lily pond which was formerly a swimming pool.

Memorials to several members of the Berkeley family can be seen in the parish **Church of St Mary**. This impressive building also has a fine Norman doorway, a detached tower which was added in 1783, and a striking east window with nine lights depicting scenes of Christ healing the sick. The churchyard contains the grave of pioneer immunologist Edward Jenner (1749-1823), who spent much of his life in the town.

The son of a local parson, Jenner was apprenticed to a surgeon in Chipping Sodbury in 1763 at the age of 14. Seven years later he moved to London to become a student at St George's Hospital, before he eventually returned to Berkeley to practice as a country doctor and to continue his pioneering work in immunology.

While still an apprentice, Jenner had become aware of the link between cowpox and smallpox, noticing that exposure to one protected against infection from the other. His work over several decades led to the first vaccination against smallpox, a disease which is thought to have killed as many as 60 million people worldwide in the preceding century. Thanks to Jenner's pioneering work, the disease has now been effectively eradicated from the planet.

Jenner's former home, a splendid Georgian house in Church Lane known as the Chantry, was purchased in the early 1980s by a trust who converted it into the **Jenner Museum** and Immunology Conference Centre, thanks in part to a donation from the Japanese philanthropist Ryoichi Sasakawa. A thatched rustic hut where Jenner used to vaccinate the poor free of charge and which he named the Temple of Vaccinia still stands in the grounds.

In the centre of the village of **Wanswell**, to the north of Berkeley, is the delightful **Salmon Inn**. This lovely old country inn offers a warm and friendly welcome to locals and visitors alike. It is well worth travelling out of the way to sample the home-cooked food on offer. The menu is wide ranging, with the specialities being the seafood and steaks, and vegetarians will also find a good selection. The dishes are all well priced and the servings more than generous. For those with large appetites there is also a tempting selection of yummy desserts. To accompany a meal the Salmon Inn has an excellent choice of beers and wines.

The Salmon Inn

Outside there is a large garden for the children to play in and keep them entertained, while the parents enjoy a quiet drink.
The Salmon Inn, Wanswell, Berkeley, Gloucestershire GL11 9SE
Tel: 01453 811306

The village of **Breadstone** is located just off the A38 between Slimbridge, home of the famous Slimbridge Wildfowl Trust, and Newport. It lies within the Vale of Berkeley and not far from the town of Berkeley itself which has much to offer visitors. The area is very beautiful and there are many interesting walks along the banks of the canals. Alternatively, the Cotswold Way, to the east, provides some stunning views of the Vale and the River Severn.

Within the village of Breadstone is a well established guest house, **Green Acres Farm**. Run by Barbara Evans, this is a quality bed and breakfast establishment with four en-suite rooms. The house is well furnished and attractively decorated and the atmosphere is warm and friendly. There is a large garden and there are some lovely views of the surrounding countryside. Facilities for guests include a dining room where they can book to have dinner, a TV lounge and a sauna for

Green Acres Farm

England

the ultimate in relaxation! There is plenty of excellent walking in the area and Barbara is always happy to help plan a route. If this sounds a little too strenuous, Barbara's husband owns a small pine furniture factory offering high quality pieces where visitors are welcome to browse. All in all, this is a delightful place to stay, within easy reach of all that the area has to offer.

Green Acres Farm, Breadstone, Berkeley, Gloucestershire GL12 9HF
Tel: 01453 810348

THORNBURY   *Map 4 ref I20*

This bustling market town lies between the River Severn and the M5, in the part of southern Gloucestershire which used to fall within the county of Avon. A prosperous dormitory settlement with many recent housing developments, its old centre still possesses a surprising number of Georgian and earlier buildings. The original main streets of the Plane, the High Street and Castle Street form a characteristic medieval 'Y' pattern which converges on the old marketplace, now a frequent bottleneck. Not far away, two giant creatures, a lion and a swan, stare out at each other across the High Street from their positions above the main entrances to the White Lion and Swan hotels; two handsome former coaching inns which have been rivals since the 18th century.

On the northern edge of this attractive small town lies **Thornbury Castle**. The building of the castle began in 1511 after Edward Stafford, the 3rd Duke of Buckingham and Constable of England, received a licence from Henry VIII. Building came to a halt just 10 years later, however, when the Duke was accused of treason and subsequently executed. The Duke's lands were confiscated and the castle was appropriated by Henry VIII who retained it as a Royal Demesne for 33 years. In 1535 the King stayed at the castle for 10 days with Anne Boleyn, and later his daughter, Mary Tudor, lived here as a princess. She returned when she became Queen and passed the castle back into the hands of the family of the late Duke of Buckingham in 1554. Unable to afford the upkeep of so magnificent

Thornbury Castle

a home neither Henry, the Duke's son, nor his descendants were to settle here. Over two centuries of neglect reduced the castle to a picturesque ruin, described as "well-known to admirers of ancient architecture for the elaborate and beautiful style of the windows, chimneys and other ornaments."

Though unfinished by its founder and virtually neglected by subsequent owners, Buckingham's concept of a sumptuous castle in the late medieval style is abundantly clear. Major renovation did not take place until the mid-19th century when Anthony Salvin re-roofed the state apartments and restored the interiors to his own designs. The work was completed in 1854 and, for the first time since the 16th century, the castle became, in part, what Buckingham had intended: a splendid and comfortable residence. The castle was ultimately purchased by the present owner, Maurice CR Taylor, in 1986.

Today Thornbury Castle stands in 15 acres, surrounded by its vineyards, gardens and high walls, with distant views over the Severn Estuary and the hills of south Gloucestershire and Wales. Renowned for its fine food and the recipient of many awards, the restaurant has three intimate dining rooms which are baronial in style with panelled walls, heraldic shields and large open fires. The main apartments have been carefully restored to provide 21 bedchambers. Each is individually decorated with private bathroom and retains original features. Most overlook the gardens or vineyard and many have sumptuous four-poster beds and huge Tudor fireplaces.

Thornbury is an ideal base from which to discover the many historic sites, villages and towns located within an hour's drive of the castle.
Thornbury Castle, Thornbury, Gloucestershire BS12 1HH
Tel: 01454 281181 Fax: 01454 416188

At **Buckover**, on the main A38 road near Thornbury, is **The White Horse** public house and restaurant. This family run establishment is well situated overlooking the Severn estuary. The warm and friendly atmosphere makes this is ideal place to stop for a drink or a bite to eat. The traditional bar food is served every lunch and evening, with dishes cooked freshly to order and the desserts are to be highly recommended. For those who need somewhere to stay in the area, bed and breakfast accommodation is also available. Outside the floral displays are quite spectacular with the White Horse being a regular winner of awards in the Britain in Bloom competition.

The White Horse, Buckover, near Thornbury, Gloucestershire GL12 8DX
Tel: 01454 413361

To the northeast of Thornbury at **Falfield**, **The Gables Inn**, on the A38, is conveniently situated for the city of Bristol and for exploring the Cotswold countryside. Whether staying for just one night or looking for a longer break, a warm and friendly welcome awaits all guests, who can relax in style and experience a quality of service that will ensure they enjoy a restful stay. The well appointed, spacious bedrooms are all fitted with modern conveniences including colour TV, hairdryers, tea and coffee making facilities and telephone. For that special occasion a selection of individually designed bedrooms are available.

The Gables Inn

The best of modern and traditional English country house cuisine can be enjoyed in the attractively styled Tyndale Restaurant. Warmth and comfort with relaxed, yet attentive service, combine to ensure the best value for money. Additionally there is the Charfield Bar which offers an more informal atmosphere. It is ideal for a relaxing drink over conversation with friends and is also a delightful place to unwind. Within the hotel there is a well-equipped multi-gym which is available for guests' use at no additional charge. All in all, The Gables is a quality alternative to expensive hotels.

The Gables Inn, Bristol Road, Falfield, Gloucestershire GL12 8DL
Tel: 01454 260502 Fax: 01454 261821

To the southwest of Thornbury and close to the banks of the River Severn, lies **Northwick**. Situated near to this picturesque village in the heart of the south Gloucestershire countryside, stands **The White Horse**. This 18th century coaching inn still retains all of its original features including heavy oak beams and open log fires that crackle and burn in the cold winter months. The inn comprises a separate bar and lounge which contains a comfortable restaurant area where meals are served everyday from 12–2.00 pm and again in the evening from 6.30–9.30 pm. There is an extensive menu, with all dishes having been freshly prepared using only the finest local ingredients with real chips being a house speciality. There is a daily specials board and selection of vegetarian dishes always available whilst the traditional Sunday Roast offers a wide choice of meat and vegetables.

The White Horse

In the bar there is a large selection of real ales with a visiting guest ale changing weekly and there is also a good range of speciality coffees and house wines to tempt the palate. This family pub has large and colourful gardens complete with ducks, hens, chipmunks, swings, slide and a small football pitch to keep the youngsters happy whilst the adults sit back and relax. The White Horse is ideally located for visiting Wales and the West Country and a warm welcome is guaranteed from hosts Gary, Sara and the triplets!
The White Horse, Northwick Road, Northwick, Pilning, Gloucestershire BS12 3HA Tel: 01454 632349

CHIPPING SODBURY

Map 4 ref I20

This pleasant former market town is one of the earliest examples of town planning in Britain; the settlement was laid out in narrow strips on either side of the broad main street in the 12th century. Although the market has long since disappeared, the main street, which is wide enough for cars to park end-on, remains an attractive thoroughfare of 17th to 19th century buildings whose contrasting styles and materials combine to form a delightful whole.

In the village of **Coalpit Heath**, southwest of Chipping Sodbury, Lady Val and Lord Roy welcome one and all to ye old medieval **Horseshoe Inn**. Although a little off the beaten track, this traditional village pub thankfully retains much of its original character. There have been a few additions in the form of a bouncy castle and some animals to help entertain the children while the adults enjoy a quiet drink. Medieval children's parties can even be arranged—just ring for details. Food is served and the Sunday lunches are a speciality. Real ale drinkers take note; this is a free house with two real ales always available on tap.

The Horseshoe Inn, The Causeway, Coalpit Heath, near Bristol, Gloucestershire BS17 2PF Tel: 01454 772272

Situated further south and east of Chipping Sodbury, in this sleepy village of **Hinton**, the **Bull Inn** is the quintessential English pub. It was originally built as a farmhouse in the 16th century and then converted to an inn in 1650. Despite being located only two miles from junction 18 on the M4, it has a delightful rural feel. It is set in four acres of grounds and has its own attractive beer garden and plenty of off-road parking. The interior retains its traditional character, with beamed ceilings, inglenook fireplaces and stone floors, creating a cosy and welcoming atmosphere which is enhanced by some interesting historic memorabilia. The old milking parlour and creamery have been tastefully converted into a 50 seater restaurant, the Bull Ring, which offers a delicious à la carte menu

Bull Inn

on weekdays and a carvery on Sundays. As well as for its food, the Bull is renowned for its fine ale. It is listed in the *Good Beer Guide* and always offers at least three real ales, along with guest beers and ciders. To the rear of the pub is another room, the pantry, which can be hired for small meetings and functions. The restaurant can be popular at weekends, so advance booking is advisable.

Bull Inn, Hinton, near Dyrham, Gloucestershire SN14 8HG
Tel: 0117 937 2332

DURSLEY   *Map 4 ref I19*

The impressive 18th century Market House has an interesting bell turret on the roof and overhanging upper storeys which are supported on pillars. Inside, there is a statue of Queen Anne and the distinctive coat of arms of the Estcourt family. Dursley also possesses a fine parish church which was constructed in the 14th and 15th centuries. William Shakespeare is rumoured to have spent some months laying low in the town after having been spotted poaching Thomas Lacy's deer at Charlecote. One legacy of his stay is a reference in *Henry IV* to a bailiff from Dursley.

Located in the centre of Dursley, close to the local church stands the magnificent **Old Bell Hotel**, a 14th century coaching inn with a very chequered history. Over the centuries it has been occupied by monks when it was built as a monastery and later by judges when it was used as a court, where criminals were sentenced to

hang. This historic building has also had its fair share of hauntings and has been used as a base for psychic research for many years, whilst also being featured in numerous books and television programmes. As well as being visited by the apparitions of two monks and an old man, the most famous ghost is that of a young chambermaid who became pregnant by her soldier lover and on being rejected committed suicide in the hotel. Her restless soul is still said to walk the darkened corridors late at night, mourning her lost love.

But there is nothing cold or supernatural about the warm greeting that guests receive when they visit this most welcoming

The Old Bell Hotel

of family run hotels. Hostess Sonia Praki prides herself in ensuring that all her guests enjoy a stay that is both relaxing and invigorating. Guests can choose from seven en-suite bedrooms, each offering all the usual home comforts including some personal touches that will make their stay a memorable one. Many guests travel from all over the world to sample Sonia's unique style of hospitality, whilst Capone's, the Hotels own night club, ensures that the party atmosphere continues well into the night.

The Old Bell Hotel, Long Street, Dursley Gloucestershire GL11 4HL
Tel: 01453 542821

To the southwest of Dursley at **Charfield**, the old parish churchyard, which lies to the south of the village at Churchend, contains the common grave of 14 unfortunate victims of a railway accident which took place near here early one morning in 1928. The disaster happened in thick fog when a freight train failed to clear the main line in time. A passenger express travelling at full speed smashed into the goods train and the force of the collision piled the carriages against the road bridge in Charfield. To make matters worse, a second freight train travelling in the opposite direction collided with the first, causing a consignment of gas canisters to explode and setting the wreckage on fire. Of the 14 casualties, two were thought to be children, although they may have been jockeys as some were known to have been on the train. Strangely, the two small bodies were never claimed by their relatives, although for years after a mysterious woman dressed in black was seen from time to time kneeling by their memorial in the churchyard. The identity of all three remains a mystery to this day.

Huntingford Mill

For those looking to get away from the hustle and bustle should head for **Huntingford Mill**, situated in a quiet spot by a mill stream and surrounded by unspoilt countryside. This hotel with restaurant is charming and, although undergoing a programme of refurbishment, much of the original character will be preserved. The accommodation on offer is four bedrooms, two en-suite, all comfortably furnished. The bright and pleasant restaurant has an excellent reputation and serves fresh, home-cooked food.

Huntingford Mill, Charfield, near Wotton-under-Edge, Gloucestershire GL12 8EX Tel: 01453 843431

Lying between Dursley and Charfield, the village of **North Nibley** was the birthplace of the early biblical translator, William Tyndale. Born here around 1494, he is reputed to be the first scholar to translate the New Testament into English and it is upon his work that the authorised version of the Bible was based. Instead of using the approved Latin texts, Tyndale chose to use original Greek and Hebrew sources, a choice which eventually led to him being accused of heresy. In 1536, he was arrested and taken to Vilvorde near Brussels where he was convicted and burned at the stake.

Some 330 years later, the impressive **Tyndale Monument** was erected on the ridge above North Nibley to commemorate the life and work of this pioneering scholar. From its position on top of the 700 foot Cotswold escarpment, the 111 foot structure can be seen from miles around, making it one of the most prominent landmarks on the Cotswold Way. North Nibley is also renowned as the site of the last private battle in England which took place in 1471 between rival barons William Lord Berkeley and the Viscount De Lisle.

The Black Horse Inn

Nestled amongst the slopes of the Cotswold escarpment in this small Gloucestershire village stands **The Black Horse Inn**. This 16th century coaching inn is renowned for its welcoming warmth and friendly old world charm, which has made it popular with visitors from all around the world. The bar and restaurant have an intimate atmosphere with low ceilings, a profusion of oak beams, inglenooks and brass works which combine to create traditional warmth and comfort. Extensive lunchtime and evening menus are designed to cater for all tastes ranging from light bar snacks to full à la carte meals prepared to order and created using only the freshest local ingredients. The Black Horse Inn also offers six comfortable rooms, four with en-suite facilities and all offering colour television, telephone and beverage making facilities with all prices fully inclusive of a substantial full English breakfast.

For those wishing to explore the area or just wanting to get away from it all and relax, special weekend breaks are available commencing with a candle lit dinner on Friday evening and rounding off with a traditional Sunday lunch prior to departure. With the main commercial centres of Avon and Gloucestershire only a short distance from the inn's doorstep, the Black Horse is also an ideal location for a business base.

The Black Horse Inn, North Nibley, Gloucestershire GL11 6DT
Tel: 01453 546841

North of Dursley, the ancient village of **Cam**, despite its modern urban appearance, dates from the 11th century when its manor, then known as Camma, formed part of the huge Berkeley estate. The village has been a cloth-making centre for centuries and today, Cam Mill carries on the tradition which began on the site in 1522. Cam's Hopton Manor School was founded in 1730 and is thought to be one of the oldest primary schools in the country.

The small, uniformly shaped hill on the edge of the village is known as **Cam Long Down**. This strange, isolated peak is steeped in local mythology. It is said that the Devil, thinking the landscape too much God's country, decided to cart away the Cotswolds to dam the Severn. After loading up his first barrow and setting out towards the river, he met a cobbler laden with shoes. "How far is it to the river?" asked Satan. The cobbler showed him one of the shoes he was taking home to mend and replied, "Do you see this sole? Well, I've worn it out walking from the Severn." At this point, the Devil abandoned his task and tipped out his barrow, leaving behind the unusual formation that can be seen today.

An ideal place to stop for a snack or cup of tea is **The Cottage Bakery and Coffee Shop**. A family run bakery, it is Rosemary Ward who runs the shop while her

The Cottage Bakery & Coffee Shop

husband does the baking. For many years they have supplied the locals and surrounding trade with their fresh bread which, along with many other tasty snacks, is on sale in the shop. The country style coffee shop serves these home-baked goodies along with a good selection of beverages.

The Cottage Bakery & Coffee Shop, 7/9 Chapel Street, Cam, near Dursley, Gloucestershire Tel: 01453 545814

TETBURY   *Map 4 ref J20*

This delightful Elizabethan market town was another important centre of the once prosperous Cotswold wool trade. At one time fleeces were weighed and sold amongst the stone pillars of the 17th century Market House in the heart of the town. Today, this striking colonnaded building hosts a popular antiques market and the immediate area is filled with market stalls offering a wide range of produce from fresh fruit and vegetables to handmade local crafts. Chipping Lane connects the Market House to The Chipping, a word meaning market or trading centre in Old English, via the famous Chipping Steps. This ancient stairway descends past a collection of charming stepped houses which are among the most handsome in Tetbury.

Standing adjacent to the tourist information office in Long Street, Tetbury's Old Court House and police station now house the **Police Bygones Museum**, an interesting collection of historic artefacts, uniforms and memorabilia from the archives of the Gloucestershire Constabulary.

Ormond's Head Coaching Inn

The Ormond's Head Coaching Inn, which dates back to the 16th century, is situated in the centre of Tetbury. It is an excellent base from which to explore the town itself and the beautiful surrounding Cotswold countryside. The hotel has 20 bedrooms which provide all the comforts today's traveller demands.

However, the original charm of the coaching has been retained and can be enjoyed at its best in the Hotel Lounge and the Lounge Bar. The bar offers a fine selection of real ales and a large open log fire in the winter. The Courtyard restaurant is well known locally for its fine cuisine and offers both à la carte and table d'hôte menus featuring fresh local produce. A less formal dining alternative is available in the Wine Bar and Creperie. Outside, the secluded Cotswold stone walled garden is the perfect setting for relaxing in the summer evenings. *Ormond's Head Coaching Inn, Long Street, Tetbury, Gloucestershire GL8 8AA Tel: 01666 505690*

Imagine an ideal country hideaway, the perfect place for a peaceful week or two, a long weekend break or a home from home base during a business trip; it would probably be just like the much loved **Folly Farm Cottages**. These lovely old Cotswold stone cottages have been converted from the time-mellowed workshops, byres and wool stores of the original Folly Farm, which dates back hundreds of years. Their names reflect a fascinating past with the huge Tythe Barn providing full conference facilities. The resident host welcomes all guests to Folly Farm which is a working farm with a large herd of dairy cattle, situated just five minutes walk from historic Royal Tetbury, an authentic Cotswold town famous for its wool trade. Today, it is an antique hunter's Mecca with many antique shops and regular fairs in the vicinity. Just a few miles away is Westonbirt Arborcium, one of the greatest collections of rare trees and shrubs in Europe. The elegant Regency cities of Bath and Cheltenham, Shakespeare's Stratford, several castles, cathedrals, Slimbridge Wildfowl Trust and Roman remains all make pleasant day trips from Folly Farm Cottages.

Folly Farm Cottages

Tetbury district also boasts some fine restaurants and gourmet pubs offering excellent lunch and dinner menus. Between meals available close by are excellent golf courses, fishing, gliding, sailing, horse riding, polo, hang gliding, jet-skiing and many other activities on which to work up an appetite.

Churn Cottage is a recently converted cosy little cottage which is situated on its own. Downstairs it has a living room with a log stove and French doors overlooking the main farm courtyard, separate kitchen, bathroom with bath, overhead shower and WC. Upstairs to a small double bedroom and a small child's room with a full size bed.

Kiln Cottage is probably the most popular secluded retreat, a light and cosy cottage with log burning stove and private corner garden. It has one double bedroom, a bathroom with WC, open plan living with spacious sitting/dining/kitchen area and is especially suitable for the disabled. Middleyard, Cowbyres and Barn End are south facing, traditional Cotswold cowbyres with high vaulted ceilings and many original features, proving popular for adults with children. Downstairs there is one twin bedroom, a bathroom with WC and an open plan living/dining/kitchen room with large glazed doors leading to a private suntrap patio overlooking the courtyard. Upstairs the galleried sleeping area has twin full-sized beds suitable for children

Standing side by side, the Weigh House and Wheelwrights are two open beamed character cottages with log burning stoves and their own patio access and gardens. Downstairs is a spacious open plan living area and upstairs there are two bedrooms, both with twin beds and a bathroom with full facilities. The Cider Loft has many of its original features including beams, pulley hoists and log burning stove and adjoins the huge Tythe Barn. Downstairs is a double, four poster bedroom and a bathroom, an open plan living area with sliding doors that lead out to the patio area. Upstairs there are two twin bedrooms with full sized beds and a shower room with another WC.

The Bull Pen is the largest and most spacious cottage with vaulted beams and log burning stove. The hall leads to a cloakroom with shower and WC, one twin bedroom with en-suite facilities and an open plan living/dining/kitchen area with trench doors leading to a partly covered patio area. Upstairs the galleried landing leads to one double bedroom, bathroom and two further twin bedded bedrooms. Mrs Tiggy Winkle would have liked Folly Cottage, an 18th century detached cottage standing in mature gardens with its country views, situated some 150 yards from Folly Farm. Downstairs is a fitted kitchen with laundry facilities, a dining room and sitting room complete with log stove, one twin bedroom and one single and a bathroom with WC. Upstairs there are a further two double bedrooms, one single and a bathroom with second WC. It also offers off road parking for four cars and a private and secure garden, though the property is not considered suitable for the disabled.

Folly Farm Cottages are close to the M4/M5 motorways and are only one and a half hours from Heathrow.

Folly Farm Cottages, Tetbury, Gloucestershire GL8 8XA
Tel: 01666 502475 Fax: 01666 502358 e-mail: follyandtythe2enterprise.net

NAILSWORTH

Map 4 ref J19

Once a centre of the wool trade, there are some fine Jacobean and Georgian merchants' houses to be found in the town centre. An unusual 17th century building on Cossack Square known as Stokescroft is also referred to locally as 'the barracks': graffiti uncovered during restoration work in 1972 suggests that local troops were billeted here in 1812 and 1815. It was also used to house Russian prisoners during the Crimean War, an episode which is commemorated in the unusual name of the square.

Several of Nailsworth's original mills have been modernised and continue in a manufacturing role. Others have been given a new life, for example Egypt Mill, a former grain and logging mill with two working water wheels, has been converted to a popular family pub. **Ruskin Mill** is a 19th century former woollen mill which has been rejuvenated as a thriving craft centre. Inspired by the principles of William Morris, John Ruskin and Rudolph Steiner, this vibrant place incorporates an exhibition gallery, a vegetarian café, and a series of traditional craft workshops covering such skills as cobbling, woodworking and stained glass.

Tipputs Inn

Set deep in the Gloustershire countryside and standing adjacent to the main A46 Nailsworth to Bath road is the attractive **Tipputs Inn**. This traditionally English pub has been owned and personally run by Kevin Bratchell for the past three years and is a true credit to his obvious attention to detail and high standards. Delicious food is served throughout the day and real ales can be enjoyed at a leisurely pace in the bar area which has been decorated and furnished in a country style. Kevin also offers his visitors four comfortable letting rooms which all offer full en-suite facilities and have been recently refurbished throughout. On those long, hot summer days, the beer garden proves very popular with children and those wishing to enjoy their refreshment al fresco, though for those wishing to dine it is best to book a table, as Tipputs Inn can become very popular at weekends.

Tipputs Inn, Bath Road, Nailsworth, Gloucestershire GL6 0QE
Tel: 01453 832466

Just a short distance from the centre of Nailsworth is the **Jovial Foresters** public house. This friendly pub, run by Colin and Jean Castree, is one of the oldest in the area and offers a warm traditional welcome to all its visitors. It is well situated with some breathtaking views over the surrounding countryside and a beer garden to enjoy in warm weather. The house speciality is home-made curry, with the menu providing a good selection of curries and baltis to suit all palates.

The Jovial Foresters

The Jovial Foresters, Northfield Road, Nailsworth, Gloucestershire GL6 0NH Tel: 01453 832254

To the northeast of Nailsworth, the picturesque community of **Chalfont** is spread over the steep northern slope of the Golden Valley in a maze of narrow lanes. Lying just three miles to the southeast of Stroud, this is the centre of the area known as the Alpine Cotswolds and, at one time, food and fuel had to be delivered up the steep gradient by donkey. Today, Chalford is best explored on foot, its tight thoroughfares being filled with interesting shops and pubs.

In the heart of the village is the welcoming establishment of **The Old Neighbourhood Inn**. The pub provides a good range of ales including Tetleys, 6X and

The Old Neighbourhood Inn

Archers Best. Visitors can enjoy their drinks in the attractive beer garden or on the patio, which offer views over the Golden Valley. Home-made food is served each day with vegetarian options also available, with a roast served at Sunday lunch. Families are welcome.

The Old Neighbourhood Inn, Chalford Hill, Chalford, near Stroud, Gloucestershire GL6 8EN Tel: 01453 883385

The village of **France Lynch** is signposted from Chalford Hill, just outside Chalford. Here, Pat and Mike Duff extend a warm welcome to customers old and new to their delightful public house **The Kings Head**. Set in a secluded valley the pub has a lovely beer garden with superb views and a children's play area to keep the smaller visitors entertained. Featured in the Good Beer Guide, here visitors can enjoy real ales and a good selection of hot and cold food.

The Kings Head

The Kings Head, France Lynch, near Stroud, Gloucestershire GL6 8LT Tel: 01453 883225

CIRENCESTER   *Map 4 ref J19*

Often referred to as the capital of the Cotswolds, this ancient market town has a history dating back to the Roman occupation of Britain. In AD 47, the Romans built the Fosse Way, one of four major roads in Britain, to link the prosperous wool-based centres of southwest England with Lincoln and the military garrisons of the north. A series of defensive fortifications were constructed along its length, including one which was sited at the junction with Ermin Street and Akeman Street, two other Roman highways. This fort quickly grew to become Corinium Dobunnorum, the second most important Roman settlement in Britain after Londinium. It was named after a conquered tribe, the Dobunni, who inhabited much of the Southwest.

Little evidence of Cirencester's Roman roots can be seen in situ today. However, the award winning **Corinium Museum** in Park Street houses one of the finest collections of ancient Roman antiquities in the country. Exhibits include superb sculptures, domestic items and two remarkable floor mosaics: the four seasons and the hunting dogs. There is also a life-size reconstruction of a Roman garden, dining room and kitchen, as well as a cutaway section of a surprisingly sophisticated central heating system.

After a prolonged period of decline which lasted until the Norman Invasion, Cirencester eventually came under the influence of William FitzOrbern, the Earl of Hereford. In 1117, King Henry I founded the Augustinian Abbey of St Mary here which survived until Henry VIII's Dissolution of the Monasteries in the mid-16th century. Little of this now remains except for a single Norman arch which can be seen in the northeastern corner of the **Abbey Grounds**. The grounds now form an attractive park containing a lake, trees and a lively population of wildfowl. An outline of the original abbey walls can also be seen here, along with the only surviving section of the old Roman fortifications.

Cirencester's **Church of St John the Baptist** was built in the 15th and 16th centuries and is perhaps the finest example of a Cotswold 'wool' church. Like many other churches in the area, its construction was financed by the wealthy wool merchants who prospered during that period. (Such churches can often be identified by the fact they were built to a grander scale than befits the size of the community they now serve.) The famous silver and gilt Boleyn Cup can be found in the south aisle. This was made for Henry VIII's second wife in 1535, the year before she was executed for alleged adultery. Anne's personal insignia—a rose tree and a falcon holding a sceptre—can be seen on the lid. Look out also for the depiction of a cat chasing a mouse, a medieval craftsmen's joke which can be seen in the Lady Chapel.

Cirencester House stands at the top of Cecily Hill on the western edge of town and, although not open to the public, its grounds are. Walkers and horse riders are permitted to roam freely over the 3000 acre **Cirencester Park** which has pathways stretching almost as far as Sapperton, five miles to the west. The park was laid out in the 18th century by the First Earl Bathurst with the assistance of his friend, Alexander Pope. Pope's Seat, an elegant summerhouse standing at the point where ten pathways meet, was one of the poet's favourite places of contemplation.

The remains of the **Bull Ring**, a once glorious Roman amphitheatre which is perhaps the largest and best preserved example of its kind in Britain, can be found on a site to the west of Cirencester. Best approached from Querns Hill and Cotswold Avenue, the remains consist of an oval arena with twin entrances and a series of sloping earth banks which would have supported rows of timber seating.

Hereford and Worcester

INTRODUCTION

The two counties of Herefordshire and Worcestershire, which lay side by side with Herefordshire to the west, were joined in 1974. Sharing the shapely Malvern Hills, with there many prehistoric hillforts and dramatic views the two areas still retain their own character.

Herefordshire is quiet and remarkably unspoilt given that it is within easy reach of the vast industrial centre of the Midlands. Famous for its red cattle, the county is also a prolific maker of cider. To the east lies Worcester, the cathedral city and also the birthplace of Edward Elgar. Best known for its Royal Worcester porcelain, this is also the home of the spicy bottled sauce.

HEREFORD   *Map 8 ref I18*

Founded in around AD 700 on the banks of the River Wye, Hereford was, in Saxon times, the capital of West Mercia. The city is full of legends and, perhaps, the best one concerns **Hereford Cathedral**, which is, externally at least, a relatively plain and stalwart building. Ethelbert is the cathedral's patron saint and it was built on his shrine. Ethelbert was supposed to wed Offa's daughter and he arrived at court only to be decapitated. In the tale, the King had great trouble disposing of Ethelbert's remains as, whenever they were interred, a strange light shone above the spot. So great was Offa's guilt over the terrible deed that he set off to Rome to confess and hopefully be forgiven. Ethelbert's remains were removed from the graveyard at Marden and brought to Hereford and, apparently, when his head rested on the ground here, a gush of water appeared which became known as St Ethelbert's Well.

Perhaps Hereford Cathedral's most interesting features lie in the **Chained Library**, where there are a staggering 1400 chained books and around 224 medieval manuscripts dating from as far back as the 8th century. Two of Thomas Caxton's books are here and the library houses the largest collection of printed and handwritten books in the world. However, the cathedral's greatest treasure is undoubtedly the **Mappa Mundi**. This beautiful world map dating back to 1290 may not be geographically accurate, with Jerusalem at its centre, but as an historical and religious artefact it is quite unsurpassed.

Hereford Castle also has a legend associated with it, in this case a romantic one concerning the Governor's daughter, Isobel Chandos. She apparently fell in love with Hugh Despenser, Edward II's favourite. He did not, however, reveal his royal connections but warned her of an impending attack upon the castle. Presumably, he was hoping that she would flee with him but, loyal to her family, Isobel hastened to her father to warn him. Despenser led the attack himself and when the battle turned against him, he was captured and hanged. The tragedy continued for, when poor Isobel saw her beloved hanging high, her sanity was destroyed. They say that she only found brief solace after this by taking short river trips alone towards Ross-on-Wye but, on one such occasion, the boat overturned and she drowned. Isobel's spirit is said to still haunt that stretch of the Wye today.

Cider is still this city's principal product and the **Cider Museum and Distillery** is well worth a visit. The museum is housed in a former cider works and, along with exhibitions showing how cider has been processed throughout the centuries, visitors are able to see a travelling cider brandy maker's still. Housed in a wonderful timber framed building dating from 1621, is **The Old House Museum**. Furnished in the style of the 17th century, the three floors include a kitchen, hall and bedrooms.

Just to the west of Hereford, **Breinton Court Lodge** is conveniently situated in the village **Breinton**, thus offering the perfect base for touring this popular area. Attractions such as the Wye Valley Walk, Elgar's House, the Cider Museum and the towns of Malvern and Hay are easily reached. Hazel and Gerald Williams offer comfortable bed and breakfast accommodation in their attractive detached house which is pleasantly surrounded by established trees and neat hedges, in a country setting. Hazel offers a very genuine welcome and is anxious to make everyone's stay a happy one. Although established only three years, many guests have already returned on several occasions—which speaks for itself. A good area for walking and bird-watching. Children are welcome and pets by arrangement.

Breinton Court Lodge

Breinton Court Lodge, Lower Breinton, Herefordshire HR4 7PG
Tel: 01432 274523

WORCESTER   *Map 8 ref J17*

A bustling county capital and a cathedral city, Worcester is especially known for its fine porcelain, its aromatic sauce, gloves and the internationally famous cricket ground. The crypt at **Worcester Cathedral** is the oldest surviving building in the city and is a relic of the cathedral begun in 1084 by St Wulston. The masonry from which the crypt was built came originally from St Oswald's Benedictine priory which was founded in 961 and records show that a church must have existed as early as 680 when the first Bishop of Worcester was enthroned. Though the building was begun in the 11th century, a fire in 1203 destroyed much of it and it was not until the 14th century that the nave was rebuilt. Other parts of the building had to wait much longer to be rebuilt. Prior to his death in 1216, King John requested that he be buried in the cathedral choir and his tomb is to be found before the High Altar. A masterpiece of medieval sculpture, it is reputed to be the oldest royal effigy in England.

The town centre and major shopping area have a wealth of interesting features and attractive shops. In particular, there is a marvellous bronze statue of one of Worcester's most respected citizens, Edward Elgar. Dominating the High Street is the imposing **Guildhall**, a wonderful example of Queen Anne architecture designed by a local man, Thomas White. Built between 1721 and 1723, the sumptuous interior contains an elegant Assembly Room

The **Commandery Civil War Centre**, housed in a delightful 15th century timber framed building, contains a dramatic museum dedicated to England's turbulent Civil War. The Commandery was established as the Hospital of St Wulstan in the late 11th century and it contained a monastic order who ministered to the sick and poor of the city. After the dissolution of the monasteries, the hospital was suppressed and then sold to the Royalist Wylde family who made The Commandery their home for 200 years. Worcester witnessed the final battle of the Civil War in 1651 and The Commandery became the Royalists' headquarters. Amongst the many interesting exhibits is a reconstruction of the trial of Charles I, where members of the public become jurors and seal the King's fate.

Whilst in the city, most visitors make for **Royal Worcester Porcelain** and the **Dyson Perrins Museum**: Royal Worcester is Britain's oldest continuous producer of porcelain and they are known the world over for their exquisite fine bone china. The factory was founded in 1751 by Dr John Wall with the intention "to create a ware of a form so precise as to be easily distinguished from other English porcelain." Today, this tradition still flourishes and Royal Worcester's unique range of fine chine and porcelain remains unsurpassed throughout the world. In the magnificent collection at the Dyson Perrins Museum some of the finest treasures from this unique artistic heritage can be seen.

To the south of Worcester is where, in the Roman Catholic Church of St Wulstan at **Little Malvern**, Sir Edward Elgar and his wife Caroline are buried. It's a popular little church and receives many visitors. Not far from the church is Craiglea, which was Elgar's home between 1899 and 1904.

Warwickshire

INTRODUCTION

Leafy Warwickshire, Shakespeare's county, is probably everyone's idea of the very best of England and the area's attractions draw an influx of tourists from all over the world. The county has much to offer with delightful contrasts from the rich vein of Tudor history at the heart of Warwickshire to post war reconstruction of Coventry. Rugby home of the famous public school which introduced the game Rugby is close by. There are also the romantic ruins of Kenilworth Castle, Warwick Castle and a wealth of beautiful National Trust properties.

The Warwickshire heritage spans many generations and the final battle between the Roman Army and British troops led by Queen Bodicea in AD 60 took place at Mancetter, to the north of Coventry. The Norman Conquest saw the establishment of Warwick Castle as a royal stronghold. In order to keep the local population under control, a number of smaller castles were also erected and a fine example can still be seen at Brinklow. The county has seen the hatching and subsequent discovery of the Gunpowder Plot of 1605 and the first major battle of the Civil War was at Edgehill in 1645.

During the Commonwealth, when Oliver Cromwell ruled England as Lord Protector, there was a period of relative prosperity. Country houses such as Ragley, Farnborough, Upton and Compton Verney were built or extended, symbols of good taste, power and wealth. The 18th century saw the redesign of country estates, including Capability Brown's work at Warwick Castle. At the close of the century Leamington Priors began to develop as a spa. At the other end of the social scale, Joseph Arch was born in 1826 at Barford. A pioneer of the farm workers union movement and later an MP, the Joseph Arch Inn at Barford must be one of the few pubs in England to be named after a trade union leader.

Even people living in Warwickshire may not be aware of the history they drive over; the hump back bridge can hide an altogether different world when seen from below. Waterways form an important and extensive part of the two thousand miles of Britain's inland network. The Oxford and Grand Union Canals pass through the county as do restored lengths of the Stratford canal and the upper Avon.

WARWICK

Map 9 ref K17

The **Castle** which dominates Warwick is surely everyone's ideal of a medieval building and it is also one of the few that still serves as a home as well as retaining the greater part of its original masonry. Standing by the River Avon, Warwick is in a good defensive position and became part of Crown lands as recorded in the Domesday Book in 1086. Much of the castle was destroyed during the baron's revolt in 1264 by troops led by Simon de Montfort and the majority of the present castle dates from the 14th century. The towers at each end are very impressive, one known as Caesar's Tower is shaped rather like a clover leaf. The armoury houses one of the best private collections in the country and, in the state apartments, are some superb art treasures including work by Holbein, Rubens and Velasquez. The 60 acres of landscaped gardens were by Capability Brown with a famous display of peacocks.

A strong link with the castle is found in the **Collegiate Church of St Mary**, a fine landmark towering over the town. Of pre-Conquest origin, the church contains the Beauchamp Chapel, built in the 18th century to house the monuments of Richard Beauchamp, Earl of Warwick and his family. History of a different kind can be seen at **Oken's House**, an ancient building owned by Thomas Oken, a self-made businessman who died childless in 1573 and left his fortune to found almshouses for the poor. Today his home houses **The Doll Museum**, literally 100 yards from the Castle.

One of the most important buildings in Warwick is **St John's House**, dating from 1666 and considered a very good example of the period. Today the building houses a museum where visitors can find out how people lived in the past. The displays include a gallery of costume, a kitchen full of drawers to open and cupboards to explore, a parlour, and a schoolroom just waiting for Victorian children. Upstairs there is the **Museum of the Royal Warwickshire Regiment**.

One of the most outstanding bed and breakfast establishments in the country can be found in the heart of Warwick, within easy walking distance of the castle and the many shops, restaurants and cultural facilities of the town centre. **Charter House** is a superb Grade II listed timber framed building dating from the 15th century which has been immaculately restored to retain its medieval character. Hostess Sheila Penon offers the warmest of welcomes and a superb gourmet breakfast. Her three large guest bedrooms are all beautifully appointed and equipped with private facilities, colour televisions and a number of thoughtful extras. Charter House is rated 2 Crowns Highly Commended by the ETB and is a nonsmoking establishment.

Charter House

Charter House, West Street, Warwick, Warwicksshire CV34 6AH
Tel: 01926 496965 Fax: 01926 411910

To the northwest of Warwick, **Shrewley** is situated on the **Grand Union Canal** and its well known landmark is the Hatton flight of 21 locks that stretches for two and a half miles up Hatton Hill.

Be in no doubt that **Shrewley House** offers the highest standard of accommodation—it's simply wonderful! Set quietly in this small village surrounded by the beautiful Warwickshire countryside, this Georgian farmhouse and home which dates from the 17th century is superbly furnished and a joy to behold. The delightful bedrooms all have en-suite bathrooms and showers as well as all the modern facilities one would expect in such a fine home. For that special occasion, choose one of the deluxe bedrooms with beautifully draped king sized four poster beds.

Shrewley House

The elegant drawing room opens on to the lawned gardens, whilst within the adjacent dining room traditional English fayre is served. Set in the grounds overlooking the gardens, Shrewley cottages offer equally perfect accommodation for the businessman or visitor. Each centrally heated cottage has been delightfully furnished with all the comforts of home. Really first class.
Shrewley House, Shrewley, near Warwick, Warwickshire CV35 7AT
Tel: 01926 842549

STRATFORD-UPON-AVON   *Map 9 ref K17*

After London, for many visitors to England, Stratford-upon-Avon is the next place on their itinerary and all because of one man, William Shakespeare. He was born here, found fame in London and retired here to die in 1616 and some 500,000 people each year visit Shakespeare's birthplace alone. This place, where he was born and where he died, is dominated by the great playwright and poet. In the very centre of the town, in Henley Street, is the house in which he was born. The timber framed building contains the **William Shakespeare Museum** in the east half whilst the west half is furnished in the style of a 16th century home.

Further along on Chapel Street stands New Place and **Nash's House**. This half -timbered building was inherited by Shakespeare's granddaughter, Elizabeth Hall, from her first husband, Thomas Nash. It now contains a **Museum of Local History** and beside it can be found gardens on the foundations of New Place, the house that Shakespeare bought and retired to in 1611. The house was torn down by Reverend Francis Gatrell in 1759 after a dispute over rates with the Corporation.

However, Shakespeare is not the only famous person to have associations with the town and **Harvard House**, in the High Street and dating from 1596, was the childhood home of Katherine Rogers. Her son, John Harvard, went to America and the famous university is named after him. The building was restored and presented to Harvard University in 1909.

In fact, there are many fascinating old buildings in Stratford. The old market site in Rother Street has a history dating from 1196, when a weekly market was granted by King John. In the square is an ornate fountain-cum-clock tower, a gift from GW Childs from Philadelphia in the jubilee year of Queen Victoria. It was unveiled by the famous actor Henry Irving who, when knighted in 1895, became the first ever "Sir of the Stage". Stratford has become the Mecca of theatre lovers and they flock to enjoy an evening at one of the three theatres. On the walls of a pub called **The Dirty Duck** is a gallery of glossy signed photographs of familiar faces. These are of some of the actors and actresses who have appeared at the Royal Shakespeare Theatre just across the road and popped in for a drink there. This attractive pub with its famous customers sums up Stratford; it manages to go about its busy life with thousands of visitors arriving from all over the world each year.

William Shakespeare

The Royal Shakespeare Company has a marvellous reputation both in the UK and abroad. To see Shakespeare performed at the Royal Shakespeare Theatre is quite possibly every theatre lovers dream; however, wherever the RSC perform, the audience are certain of witnessing performances of a high standard. The company has operated in its present manner since 1961, but the history of Stratford and theatres goes beyond that. The first permanent theatre was built as a result of local brewer, Charles Edward Flower, who gave a two acre site on which to build a theatre in Shakespeare's birthplace in 1875 and then launched an appeal for funds.

This theatre opened in 1879 with a performance of *Much Ado about Nothing* starring Ellen Terry and Beerbohm Tree. The season was limited to one week as part of the summer festival. It was so successful that under the direction of FR Benson it grew to spring and summer seasons and toured Britain in between. In 1925, because of the excellence of the performances and direction, the company was granted a Royal Charter. Sadly, a year later the theatre perished in a fire. The company, not deterred, continued by giving performances in cinemas whilst a worldwide campaign was launched to build a new theatre, which was opened on April 23rd, 1932, traditionally thought of as the Bards birthday.

A theatre tour gives visitors the opportunity to discover what is going on behind the curtains. The itinerary for the tours varies according to rehearsal schedules and the incidence of technical work on stage but they are great value and usually include the **RSC Collection** as well as both the Royal Shakespeare and Swan Theatre.

A short walk from the centre of the town are the Bancroft Gardens near to the 14 arch Clopton Bridge. This delightful leisure area contains the great **Shakespeare Memorial** which was designed by Lord Ronald Gower and built in Paris. The work took 12 years to complete and was finally presented to the town in 1888. Only a few yards away is a preserved industrial tram, employed on the horse-drawn tramway connecting wharfs in Stratford with those in Shipston-on-Stour and Moreton-in-the-Marsh in Gloucestershire. The canal was completed in 1816 but fell into disuse with the advance of the railways.

East Bank Guest House

Set within a picturesque conservation area close to the Royal Shakespeare Theatre and just 350 yards from Stratford-upon-Avon town centre, **East Bank Guest House** is ideally located to enjoy all that this vibrant and interesting town has to offer. Owned and personally run by Andrew Marsh for the past 10 years, this elegant Victorian residence has 11 well appointed guest rooms with the choice of en-suite shower-rooms or a standard room with shared bath and shower room. All of the light and airy rooms are equipped with a colour TV, tea and coffee making facilities and attractive furnishings and decor, with two of the bedrooms being ground floor offering easy access for the elderly or disabled. Guests will find a large, comfortable and quiet lounge where they can relax and the attractive dining room, containing period Victorian pine furniture, is the place to enjoy a hearty breakfast before setting out to explore the scenic surroundings. Stratford-upon-Avon is situated in the Heart of England and is an ideal base from which to explore. Those new to the area can visit the Cotswold villages, numerous historic houses and castles are clustered in the surrounding countryside and there are always plenty of restaurants and pubs in which to relax after a hard day.

East Bank Guest House, 19 Warwick Road, Stratford-upon-Avon, Warwickshire CV37 6YW Tel & Fax: 01789 292758

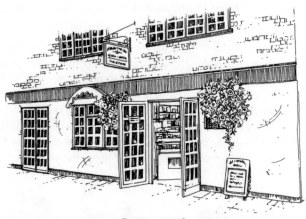

Jaquenetta's

Nestled amongst half-timbered, character properties in a quiet courtyard away from the hustle and bustle of Stratford town centre, **Jaquenetta's** is an attractive café offering light refreshments throughout the day. The unusual name comes from the Shakespearian play *Love Labour Lost* and was the name of a young country wench who featured in the drama. There is plenty of Continental style patio seating outside in the sunshine, where visitors can sit and enjoy some of the fine selection of cakes, pastries and scones that are on offer. All of the food has been home-made and prepared daily including filled sandwiches and light lunches, whilst the smell of the French baguettes, which are baked on the premises, has been known to drive the hungry into a small frenzy! As well as cappucchino, fine teas and filter coffee, Jaquenetta's is also licenced so guests can enjoy a glass of wine with their meal if they so choose. Owned and very personally run by Mike and Jackie Brown, this delightful café is open every day

except Mondays and is surrounded by interesting shops where visitors can browse their afternoon away in relaxing peace.
Jaquenetta's, Unit 3, The Minories, Rother Street, Stratford-upon-Avon, Warwickshire CV37 6NT Tel: 01789 294471

Situated beside the scenic River Avon in the centre of this celebrated town, the **Arena Restaurant** offers its visitors a true taste of Mexican and Texan dishes, in attractive surroundings. The staff are welcoming and the service is fast and efficient with a menu that is guaranteed not to break the bank. For a true taste of America, the Texan dishes range from large 16oz steaks and whole rack of ribs in barbecue sauce to Gulf Bay prawns—King prawns pan fried in garlic, butter, wine and fresh cream; sounds heavenly. Or for those who fancy something a little more spicy, the Mexican menu offers something for everyone, why not try a Chimichanga, some Enchiladas or maybe a deliciously authentic Chilli Con Carne topped with sour cream and onion. Whatever the diners' preference, the Arena Restaurant will provide them with all the right ingredients for the perfect evening out.

The Arena Restaurant

The Arena Restaurant, Swans Nest Lane, Stratford-upon-Avon, Warwickshire CV37 7LS Tel: 01789 292121 Fax: 01789 295359

Positioned at the very heart of historic Stratford upon Avon, **Thai Kingdom** is a restaurant that combines traditional Thai hospitality and impeccable service with sumptuous cuisine and tranquil surroundings. On entering this beautiful restaurant guests will be warmly greeted by the beautiful waiting staff in traditional Thai costume who, with charm and courtesy, will show them to their table set amidst tropical plants, hand carved statues and jewelled tapestries.

The menu at Thai Kingdom is a varied and extensive and whether visitors came for a light lunch or a Royal Banquet, they will feast like a King. All of the mouthwatering dishes are prepared using only the freshest herbs and spices flown in from Thailand and range from extravagant and beautifully garnished dishes to the more rustic style of Thai cooking but it will be an eating experience never to be forgotten. Also available is the recently refurbished conference room

Thai Kingdom

which provides the ideal venue for business meetings or conferences, seating up to 50 delegates in comfort business can be mixed with pleasure and the exotic tastes of Thailand enjoyed in the heart of England.

Thai Kingdom, 11 Warwick Road, Stratford-upon-Avon, Warwickshire
Tel: 01789 261103 Fax: 01789 261103

In the picturesque town centre location of Guild Street, a short distance from Shakespeare's birthplace, **Courtland Hotel** provides an excellent base from which to explore this historic area. Guests will receive a warm welcome from their host Bridget Johnson, who has owned and run this attractive bed and breakfast for over a decade and knows how to make everyone feel at home. Bridget is also a very well travelled lady, with particular knowledge of South America where she lived for a number of years.

The building itself is Victorian and has numerous special features including original antique furniture and attractive decor, whilst each of the seven guest rooms have a colour television and tea and coffee making facilities. Because Courtland Hotel charges such reasonable rates for its bed and breakfast, it is essential to book ahead to avoid any disappointment.

Courtland Hotel

Courtland Hotel, 12 Guild Street, Stratford-upon-Avon, Warwickshire
CV37 6RE Tel: 01789 292401

Located just 100 yards from the birthplace of Shakespeare in Henley Street, **Greek Connection** is a restaurant that can bring memories of that heavenly holiday in Corfu flooding back. The restaurant is situated in a converted church, which creates a wonderfully unusual atmosphere, whilst the attractive decor and furnishings evoke a sense of luxury. A great place to hold a party, the Greek Connection is open every night of the week with live music and some energetic Greek dancing to be enjoyed at all times. The food is quite superb with the house specialities ranging from Kleftico—slowly roasted English lamb seasoned with mountain herbs—to the more adventurous Kota Methismeni or drunken chicken as its known in English! So for a lively time in Stratford-upon-Avon pay a visit to the Greek Connection.

Greek Connection

Greek Connection, 1 Shakespeare Street, Stratford-upon-Avon, Warwickshire CV37 6RN Tel: 01789 292214 Fax: 01789 266999

Just to the south of Stratford-upon-Avon and set in the heart of Shakespeare country, **Winton House**, a historic Victorian farmhouse built in 1856, lies in an Area of Outstanding Natural Beauty in the village of **Upper Quinton**. The house overlooks Meon Hill which is partly owned by Oxford University and is steeped in witchcraft and folklore. Comfortable accommodation is found in the bedrooms which are tastefully decorated in traditional fashion. All beds are antique featuring a canopy four poster, a wrought iron half tester, and a pine box bed. They are all complemented with hand-made quilts, old lace and embroidery. Each bedroom has an en-suite or private bathroom and there are tea and coffee making facilities. All the rooms have fine views overlooking Meon Hill or a country garden. An old pine staircase leads residents to a private guest lounge, where they can enjoy a crackling log fire and relax after their day's adventure. Breakfast is a hearty choice of local specialities served with home-made jams and fruit from the orchard. There is also a Winton House Special which is an unusual dish that changes daily. Should guests prefer something more self-contained then a self-catering cottage is available with a four poster bed.

Winton House

Winton House is ideally situated for visiting a wide variety of interesting places. The world famous Cotswold villages are just a short drive away. There is an abundance of cycle paths and walks—the most famous being the Cotswold Way which runs eventually to Bath. Bicycles are available and guests can ride on a disused railway track into Stratford. The village of Lower Quinton boasts two olde worlde pubs, which serve local ales and traditional fayre. The local church with its tall steeple is a landmark for miles around and represents many styles of architecture. It has a rare Royal Arms board of Queen Elizabeth I. A delightful house with a real atmosphere of English tradition.

Winton House, The Green, Upper Quinton, Stratford-upon-Avon,
Warwickshire CV37 8SX Tel: 01789 720500

KENILWORTH   *Map 9 ref K16*

This town was made famous by its **Castle** and also, in some part, by Sir Walter Scott's romantic novel *Kenilworth*. Although the town was here before the Domesday Book was compiled, Kenilworth's name is invariably linked with its castle. The keep, the oldest part of the ruins, was built between 1150 and 1175. After Simon de Montfort's death at the Battle of Evesham in 1265, Kenilworth was held by his son. At that time the castle was surrounded by the Kenilworth Great Pool; a lake covering about 120 acres.

About 300 years later Elizabeth I visited Kenilworth, then held by her favourite the Earl of Leicester. He laid on celebrations that cost around £60,000, in which the Queen was welcomed by the Lady of the Lake, floating on the lake.

The remains of the abbey can be seen in the churchyard of the parish church St Nicholas in the High Street. Much of interest was discovered during excavations and there are many relics on display in the church, including a pig made of lead. It is said that this formed part of the roof at the time of Dissolution but was then melted down and stamped by the Commissioners of Henry VIII.

Abbey Guest House

The **Abbey Guest House** is ideal for those seeking a comfortable base within easy driving distance of Warwick, Stratford-upon-Avon, Coventry and the National Exhibition Centre at Birmingham. Situated just six miles from junction 15 on the M40, this imposing late Victorian residence stands in a quiet location a few hundred yards from Kenilworth town centre. Resident proprietors Angela and Trevor Jefferies are charming hosts who provide a warm welcome, first rate accommodation and a delicious English breakfast. Their seven guest bedrooms are equipped with colour TVs, electric shaver points and tea and coffee making facilities, and three have the added benefit of en-suite bathrooms. Unsuitable for smokers.
Abbey Guest House, 41 Station Road, Kenilworth, Warwickshire
Tel: 01926 512707 Fax: 01926 859148

Kenilworth is a town steeped in history dating back to the 12th century and is an ideal location from which to explore the Heart of England. Visitors and business

Castle Laurels Hotel

people too will find a warm welcome upon arrival at **Castle Laurels Hotel**, a lovely detached Victorian house opposite the castle ruins and just around the corner from old Kenilworth. A high standard is maintained by the resident owners Pam and Nick Moore, as will be seen in the tastefully decorated en-suite bedrooms which are well equipped with all facilities. Freshly prepared evening meals are served accompanied by a small yet interesting wine list. A very comfortable hotel. ETB 3 Crown Commended with private car park.
Castle Laurels Hotel, 22 Castle Road, Kenilworth, Warwickshire CV8 1NG
Tel 01926 856179 Fax: 01926 854954

RUGBY   *Map 9 ref L16*

The only town of any great size in northeastern Warwickshire, Rugby's market place is surrounded by old buildings which act as reminders of the town's origins during the reign of Henry III. The Church of St Andrew was built by the Rokeby family after their castle had been destroyed by Henry II and its unusual tower look more like a fortress with its battlements and 3 feet thick walls.

Rugby, however, is probably most famous for its public **School**, founded in 1567. There are many fine buildings, largely by Butterfield, housing such treasure as stained glass, believed to be the work of Albrecht Durer, the 15th century German artist and engraver. The game of Rugby originated here when William Webb Ellis broke the rules during a football match in 1823 by picking up and running with the ball. The town is also the setting for Thomas Hughes' *Tom Brown's School Days*. Some of the school's illustrious pupils include Rupert Brooke, the World War I poet, Charles Lutwidge Dodgson, better known as Lewis Carroll, and the writer Matthew Arnold.

Rugby School

The school has not always been the calm and peaceful seat of learning that it is today. In November 1797, the Riot Act was read to a group of rebellious pupils who made a bonfire of books, pictures ad other school property before retreating to the moated island in the school grounds. They were eventually captured by a large force of soldiers, school masters and volunteer civilians who waded through the water to the island. Rugby is also the home of the **James Gilbert Rugby Museum**; housed in a building which, since 1842, the Gilberts have been making their world famous footballs.

The town is also as far inland as it is possible to get in the British Isles, yet Rugby is an excellent centre of all kinds of water based activities. The Oxford Canal winds its way through the borough and the Rivers Avon, Leam and Swift provide good angling, pleasant walks and places to picnic.

To the west of Rugby can be found **The Woodhouse Hotel and Restaurant** in the small village of **Princethorpe**. It is privately owned by a Swiss trained Chef who, together with his team of dedicated staff, provides an unpretentious relaxing base from which to explore historic Warwick, Leamington Spa or the more contemporary Coventry. The Woodhouse offers residential accommodation in individually styled rooms in the main building or cottages adjacent to it. Rooms are generously equipped with all comforts and residents have the advantage of a choice of excellent dining rooms for their lunch or dinner as the main business of the Woodhouse is as a restaurant. The Orchard Room offers

The Woodhouse

full Silver Service and a choice of competitively priced three course Chef Recommends Menu or a Specialities à la carte. In the relaxed ambience of The Walnut Tree Room diners can enjoy a superb hot carvery or cold buffet designed for informal meals or choose from a varied menu. An attractive 18th century barn is just the place for private parties. Its mellow brickwork, timbered roof and original Minstrels Gallery create the perfect atmosphere. Needless to say, with all these facilities, all manner of occasions are catered for both business and pleasure. The Woodhouse at Princethorpe is well worth a visit.

The Woodhouse, Leamington Road, Princethorpe, near Rugby, Warwickshire CV23 9PZ Tel & Fax: 01926 632131

Situated to the north of the A428, midway between Rugby and Coventry, the **Old Smithy**, in **Church Lawford**, is an outstanding pub and eating place which can be found in the heart of this village. A charming free house which is full of traditional character, the interior is renowned for its highly polished bars and woodwork. Proprietors Kathy and John O'Neill have created an atmosphere which is truly inviting, with warming open fires in winter and a range of traditional ales which is kept to perfection. The food menu has to be seen to be believed. The extensive choice of starters includes such items as royal dim sum and spinach and feta goujons, and the main courses include succulent steaks,

Old Smithy

grills, country pies, fresh fish, curries, salads, pizzas and pasta—a choice of around 50 dishes in all. There is also a mouthwatering selection of desserts and specialist coffees, a special children's menu, and an impressive list of wines to accompany the meal. On Sundays, a traditional three course lunch is served for which advance booking is advised. With its fine ale, good food and welcoming atmosphere, it is no wonder that the Old Smithy was a regional finalist in a recent Good Pub competition.

Old Smithy, Green Lane, Church Lawford, near Rugby, Warwickshire
Tel: 01203 542333

COVENTRY   *Map 9 ref L16*

Although on the fringe of the West Midlands conurbation, Coventry is surrounded by some of the finest scenery and heritage in the country. It claims amongst many of its famous residents, George Eliot, who attended boarding school in Warwick Row and lived with her father between 1841–49 in Floeshill Road; more recently the controversial poet Philip Larkin was born in the city in 1922.

Standing in the ruins of the old 14th century **Coventry Cathedral**, destroyed by fire in the savage bombing of the city in World War II, can be a strange and moving experience. The altar is made of broken stones gathered from the night of horror on the 15th November 1940. It is surmounted by a cross of charred roof beams and a cross of medieval nails, behind which are inscribed the words from Calvary, "Father Forgive."

The new Cathedral stands by its side and together they symbolise sacrifice and resurrection. It is not only in the two cathedrals that Coventry has shown its indomitable spirit. It is hard to imagine that in the space of one night in November the city centre was gutted, 46,000 homes severely damaged and nearly 75 per cent of the industrial area was almost destroyed. The Cathedral Visitor Centre, in the Undercroft, tells the story of the historical events which took place in Coventry, including the Blitz and its aftermath and the cathedral's role in reconciliation world wide through the Community of the Cross of Nails.

The city's most famous legend tells of the story of Lady Godiva who rode the streets naked to reduce taxation on the 11th century town dwellers. A bronze statue in Broadgate has been erected to her memory. It was Leofric who started commerce and industry in Coventry as early as 1043, when he chose the small Saxon township as the site for a Benedictine monastery. He gave the monks land on which to raise sheep, laying the basis for the wool trade which made Coventry prosperous for over 500 years. The story has it though, that this hard hearted man taxed the people too heavily and Godiva begged him to lessen the burden. She apparently took the precaution of sending her messengers to ask everyone to stay indoors behind closed shutters before she rode. Peeping Tom disregarded the request and was struck blind. The Earl, duly chastened, relented and the taxes were cut.

There are still many old buildings to be seen in this modern city; **Bond's Hospital** and **Ford's Hospital** are delightful half-timbered Tudor almshouses still very much in use. Another half-timbered building, **Cheylesmore Manor House** was once owned by the Black Prince. Close by is the Toy Museum, which houses a collection of toys dating from the 18th century and, on London Road, stands **Whitefriars**, a renovated Carmelite friary dating from 1342 which plays host to art exhibitions, theatre productions and concerts. Near to the cathedral is the **Herbert Art Gallery and Museum**, which includes the story of Coventry and reconstructed rooms showing weaving and other skills that became associated with the city.

The traditional industries of the city, clockmaking and silk weaving, came under threat from Switzerland and France respectively, and during the rapid slump in the city's fortunes many families emigrated to America. It was cycle making and engineering that started the new wave of prosperity and, by 1896, Daimler and Humber had opened Coventry's first car factories. It was not long before they were joined by other companies and Coventry became a magnet for labour from all over Britain. The **Museum of British Road Transport** portrays the enormous contribution made by the city to the industry.

For those who are looking for a different kind of a holiday, why not get afloat? With ever increasing popularity, narrow boats are seen plying the many canals of this country. **Club Line Cruisers**, based at **Stoke Heath** in Coventry, is a family run business with over 25 years experience, their reputation is solidly built on value for money holidays. For the inexperienced and beginner, there are many miles of lock free cruising and, taking a weekend break, is an ideal way of getting

Club Line Cruisers

to know the canals and experiencing the pleasures of narrow boat cruising, perhaps prior to deciding on a longer duration holiday. All year round, from their base at Swan Lane Wharf in Coventry, Club Line luxury narrow boats may be hired for the weekend departing Fridays at 3.00 pm and returning on Sundays at 4.00 pm. All Club Line staff attend industry training courses and are efficient and informed on all modern and traditional procedures. An excellent colour brochure is available showing detailed layout plans of all the different boats and includes suggested one, two and three week cruises encompassing many famous locations. The narrow boats offer a surprising degree of comfort and this style of holiday is worth considering by active people of all ages.

Club Line Cruisers, Swan Lane Wharf, Stoke Heath, Coventry, Warwickshire Tel: 01203 258864

Set in attractive wooded grounds near **Meriden** to the west of Coventry, the **Somers Wood Caravan and Camping Park** is a delightful family run facility which is open all year round. Conveniently located midway between Coventry and Birmingham, it is easily accessible from the A45, and from junction 6 on the M42 and junction 4 on the M6. The park offers 48 pitches and is well provided with electric hook-ups, water points

Somers Wood Caravan and Camping Park

and a clean and well appointed shower and toilet block. Welcoming to all, it stands adjacent to the Stonebridge Golf Centre and the Somers Coarse Fishery, with the Pakington Trout Fishery only a short distance away and is especially suitable for golfing and angling enthusiasts.
Somers Wood Caravan and Camping Park, Somers Road, Meriden, West Midlands Tel: 01676 522978

Northamptonshire

INTRODUCTION

This is a smallish county in the quiet and unspectacular landscape of the East Midlands. Primarily farming country, Northamptonshire is also at the heart of the country's shoe manufacturing industry. Up on high ground, near to the Civil War battlefield of Naseby, is one of the country's great watersheds, where the Rivers Avon, Nene and Welland all rise. The county is also traversed by the M1 motorway, Watling Street, the Grand Union Canal and the main London to Birmingham rail track. This gives the impression that Northamptonshire is a county to be travelled through on the way to somewhere else and though this might often be the case due to its geographical position there is plenty to take the traveller off the major routes and into the countryside.

WELLINGBOROUGH   *Map 10 ref M16*

Wellingborough sits near the point where the River Ise joins the Nene and its medieval church spire can be seen for many miles. There are fine avenues of trees leading to the town which has, over the years, swallowed up the smaller villages surrounding it. Wellingborough is noted for its industry of iron mills, flour mills and tanneries.

In and around the Market Square there are several interesting old buildings. The **Hind Hotel** with its gabled roof and handsome windows looks out on the square. It has a 17th century oak staircase, a fine stone fireplace and a room furnished in oak which is called the Cromwell Room because it was being constructed whilst the Battle of Naseby was being fought.

There is another fine old house called Croyland Abbey, with dormer windows in the 500 year old roof. Near to it, in public grounds, stands an old **Tithe Barn**, stone walled and thatched, 70 feet long and 22 feet wide. It was built in the 15th century and has two great doorways at either side, one of which is 13 feet high. All these buildings escaped a great fire which razed most of the town to the ground in four hours in 1738. The handsome 13th century tower and spire of the parish church of All Hallows rises amongst the trees in the centre of town. The great tower seen from across the Nene is that of St Mary's, a modern church built between 1906 and 1930.

DESBOROUGH   *Map 10 ref M16*

This is a small town with old ironstone houses; it used to be a Saxon settlement and many treasures have come to light in recent years. Three massive stones have been unearthed in the Rectory gardens, the biggest carved on two sides with Saxon scrollwork and a crude picture thought to represent Daniel in the lion's den. Also found here was the grave of a Saxon lady still wearing a beautiful necklace of 37 gold beads with a pendant cross of gold. It is one of the earliest Christian crosses in the country and is now in the British Museum. In another grave a Celtic bronze mirror exquisitely engraved with a spiral design, and an elaborate handle six inches long was found. The church has been here for 700 years, though its pinnacled tower with a fine spire is early 16th century. The church house dates from about 1700 and the Market Cross, at the north end of the High Street, was built in the 18th century.

Leicestershire

INTRODUCTION

The county is at the geographical centre of England and it is well known for its Red Leicester and Stilton cheese, Melton Mowbray pork pies and fox hunting. The old market town of Melton Mowbray, in the 19th century, gained its fame with the making of pies as the ideal hunting snack. In fact, it is not surprising that fox hunting is almost synonymous with the county as there are vast expanses of fertile farming land and also plenty of cover for the foxes. It is the Vale of Belvoir (pronounced beaver), in the north of the county that lends its name to one of the oldest and most well known hunts.

With the industrial centres of Nottinghamshire and Derbyshire to the north and the Midlands to the west, Leicestershire provides an excellent contrast. The county also has, with in its boundaries, the smallest of all English counties, Rutland which joined with Leicestershire in 1974. Famous for being home to the largest man-made lake in Europe, Rutland Water, the county dates back to the 12th century and still retains a great air of independence.

MELTON MOWBRAY   *Map 10 ref M14*

The Tuesday market (there is also one on a Saturday) was recorded as a profitable concern in 1077 and certainly dates from Saxon times. The Old English settled here as early as the 5th century and one of their pagan cemeteries has been discovered on the outskirts of the town. Melton takes the second part of its name from the great Norman family of Mowbray who owned the manor by 1125.

There are several notable buildings here including the so called **Anne of Cleves House**; though now used as a restaurant it is basically 15th century and was either a Chantry House belonging to the church or perhaps the dwelling house of one of the rich wool merchants, who must have subscribed to the magnificent enlargement of the once Norman Church of St Mary in the late 15th century. Opposite the church is the Masion Dieu founded as an almshouse in 1640 and, in the market place, the former Swan Inn retains a fine porch over the pavement. Melton became the hunting metropolis of England; the meeting place of the Quorn, Cottesmore and Belvoir hunts and was frequented by the nobility and gentry from all parts of the country. As late as 1939 it was said that, at the beginning of the season, a thousand fine hunters were stabled in the town. Many of the stables have now been converted into flats, but a number of the larger houses belonging to the wealthy, are still to be seen.

COALVILLE

Map 9 ref L14

Originally called Long Lane, Coalville sprang up on a bleak common when Whitwick Colliery was opened in 1824. George Stephenson was responsible for establishing the early railway here in 1832 as well as erecting the churches.

To the south of Coalville, lies **Market Bosworth** and it is from this small 700 year old market town that the Battle of Bosworth took its name. It is a village of no great size but its former grammar school had a high reputation in the Midlands. Originally founded in early Tudor times, in 1601, it was given a new lease of life by Sir Wolstan Dixie. It was to this school that Samuel Johnson came to teach after leaving university. He hated it so much that even Boswell failed to induce him to talk about his time here.

Further south, at **Sutton Cheney**, the place where, traditionally, Richard III took communion just before he went to battle, a mile away, on Bosworth field. This lovely village houses some fine examples of Jacobean architecture: The Almshouse is one such example.

Further south still lies **Burbage**, on the outskirts of Hinckley. The name Burbage was originally Burbach and evidently came from the bur thistle which grew abundantly in its fields. It was a stylish and prosperous village at one time and one of its earliest incumbents was the 9th Earl of Kent who was rector here for 50 years. Burbage has a fine large common and a wood which attract people from far and wide. The River Soar rises here to begin its winding journey to the Trent and the church of St Catherine has a spire which can be seen for miles.

Situated in rural splendour on the borders of Leicestershire and Warwickshire is the prestigious, family owned **Sketchley Grange Hotel**. Perfectly located for business or pleasure, the hotel is close to all major routes and mainline railway stations. Thirty eight well appointed bedrooms offer the traveller a high degree of comfort with quality furnishings, en-suite and all modern facilities including satellite TV. Four poster suites and superb executive rooms, all with spa baths, offer a further level of luxury. The Willow Restaurant which overlooks the garden, offers a very pleasant dining experience. Awarded the coveted AA

Rosette for its high standard of cuisine, guests are sure to enjoy their choice from the à la carte menu and fine wine list. The cocktail bar is always a popular venue where business lunches are served throughout the week. Sketchley Grange offers extensive facilities for conferences and functions of all types, whatever the requirements, professional service is at hand.

Sketchley Grange

Sketchley Grange, Sketchley Lane, Burbage, Hinckley, Leics LE10 3HU
Tel: 01455 251133 Fax: 01455 631384

LUTTERWORTH   *Map 9 ref L16*

The town of Lutterworth is notable in that Wycliffe was rector here, under the protection of John of Gaunt. His widespread opposition to papal abuses was bad enough but when he instigated the translation of the Bible into English he became totally persona non grata. He died in 1384 and was buried in the Lutterworth church but, when he was excommunicated in 1428, his body was exhumed, burned and his ashes scattered on the River Swift.

Known by the Romans as Venonae, the present day community of **Highcross** stands at the point to the west of Lutterworth where the two ancient roads of Watling Street and Fosse Way meet. Now the junction of the A5 and B4455, this scenic yet unassuming place once represented the Roman heart of Britain. Today, it is the site of **Highcross House**, an outstanding small hotel which offers some of the most delightful food, accommodation and hospitality in the region. Originally a 16th century coaching inn known as the Sun, the grounds of this beautiful listed building still contain the historic remains of the Earl of Denbigh's monument which was erected in 1712 to commemorate the end of the Hundred Years' War. The interior has been tastefully renovated and now offers superb accommodation with the finest up-to-date facilities. The guest rooms are beautifully appointed, individually decorated and furnished with antique furniture. One room has a stately four poster bed, another a half tester bed and there are even rooms with Jacuzzis. Proprietor Jain Galliford is also renowned for her

Highcross House

fine cuisine; patrons come from miles around to dine at Highcross House which is also a popular venue for private parties, business functions, wedding receptions and other special celebrations.

61Highcross House, Highcross, near Lutterworth, Leicestershire LE17 5AT Tel: 01455 220840

SWINFORD   *Map 9 ref L16*

Mentioned in the Domesday Book, the parish of Stanford to the south of Lutterworth, in which this village lies, is an ancient one. Some years after it was given to the Benedictine Abbey of Selby by a Norman companion of the Conqueror in 1069, another grant of Stanford land was made in 1140 to the Abbey by King Stephen. When the dissolution of the monasteries took place, Sir Thomas Cave purchased the original manor of **Stanford Hall**, just outside the village, from Henry VIII in 1540. The present building dates from the reign of William and Mary, around 1690, and has a majestic facade that adds to the its pleasing design. Inside, the rooms contain interesting collections of Stuart and Jacobite paintings, costumes and furniture. The stables house a motor museum and a replica of an 1898 flying machine.

When travelling near the intersection of the M1 and M6, it's well worth making a detour to find the **Chequers Inn**, a delightful pub and eating place which is

Chequers Inn

situated in this peaceful community, half-a-mile northeast of junction 19. This sprawling village inn is run by Chris and Brian Priest, charming hosts who provide a warm welcome to visitors and locals alike. Along with an impressive selection of traditional ales, they offer a delicious range of snacks and bar meals, both at lunchtime and in the evening. The inn also has plenty of parking and a lawned garden to the rear which contains an attractive children's play area.
Chequers Inn, High Street, Swinford, Leicestershire LE17 6BL
Tel: 01788 860318

Shropshire

INTRODUCTION

At first appearances Shropshire seems a quiet and peaceful, rural county that has been relatively unspoilt and, indeed, it has not. But, paradoxically, Shropshire was the place where the Industrial Revolution, which changed so many other landscapes, began. The famous Iron Bridge, built in 1779, in the picturesque Ironbridge Gorge on the River Severn, now lies at the centre of an interesting complex of industrial museums. The county is also home to a new town, Telford, developed in the 1960s amid the exhausted coal mines of the southern region of Shropshire.

The great River Severn, which rises in mid-Wales and reaches the sea at Bristol, flows right across the county, under the Iron Bridge and around Shrewsbury (creating almost an island), leaving Shropshire after passing by Bridgnorth.

BRIDGNORTH   *Map 8 ref I15*

The main part of the town stands on a high ridge above the River Severn and is known as High Town while below the ridge and across the river is known as Low Town. The two towns are linked by a six arch road bridge, built in 1823 and the only other ways to get between the two are by cliff railway or by a steep flight of steps.

Little remains of **Bridgnorth Castle** but the ruined Norman keep is still standing—just! It leans at 17 degrees from the perpendicular because it was undermined during the Civil War. The Castle Walk, adjoining the castle grounds, provides the loveliest views of this delightful town. Near to the grounds is the Church of St mary Magdalene, which is the third church to be built on the site. It was designed by Thomas Telford and built in 1792; although most people connect Telford with bridges and canals, rather than churches, he has certainly created a lovely building in the Italianate style.

The oldest house in Bridgnorth is Bishop Percy's House. It is an attractive timbered building of 1580 and was later the birthplace of Thomas Percy, who became Bishop of Dromore. The house stands on Cartway, which leads down from the High Street to the river and has caves along its sides cut into the sandstone which were used as dwellings in Victorian times. One, The Hermitage, is said to have been the home of Ethelred, brother of King Athelstan, in the 10th century.

Although it lies in the heart of rural Shropshire, Bridgnorth is only 15 minutes from the motorway network and a short drive from the commercial centres of Telford and Wolverhampton. In this delightful and historic town is **The Falcon Hotel** with its distinctive original character retained in parts from the 17th century. The hotel has 15 attractively designed bedrooms, each with private bathroom, TV, telephone, hospitality tray and the occasional ghost! The

The Falcon Hotel

comfortable oak beamed bar and restaurant have welcoming open fires and a collection of unusual curios and souvenirs; look particularly at the display case of miniature wine and whisky bottles. The Falcon's menu features good, fresh wholesome food, including a range of char grilled steaks, game pie, fish and vegetarian dishes. Wines are represented from Europe and the New World offering a good choice while the dessert menu invites further indulgence! A wonderful blend of old character and modern comfort. Egon Ronay recommended. 2 Star AA and RAC.

The Falcon Hotel, St John Street, Lowtown, Bridgnorth, Shropshire WV15 6AG Tel: 01746 763134 Fax: 01746 765401

LUDLOW   *Map 8 ref H16*

Ludlow is one of the most beautiful country towns in England and it was from here, being so close to the Welsh border, that a fortress was constructed and the unruly Welsh tribes were kept at bay. The fine **Norman Castle** was the home of the Lord President of the Council of the Marches of Wales and it was a regular occurrence for the English monarch to take up residence at the castle. Indeed, the people of Ludlow treated the arrival of the monarch as a perfectly normal happening.

Ludlow Castle

The castle was built between 1086 and 1094 by a Norman knight named Robert de Lacy. The outer bailey is the size of a sports field and may well have been used as a place of refuge for the townspeople when the Welsh were marauding. The massive keep was built up from the original gatehouse tower in the early 12th century and the domestic buildings were added in the late 13th and early 14th centuries by the Mortimer family who inherited the castle from the de Lacys.

The Mortimers were an ambitious family; one managed to get himself made Duke of York and another became Edward IV. The doomed Little Princes grew up here and it was probably the happiest times of their short lives. Prince Arthur brought his bride, Catherine of Aragon here for their honeymoon but it ended, sadly, in his death from pneumonia.

In the summer, Ludlow holds a festival of music, drama and art. Among its highlights is an open air production of a Shakespeare play staged in the castle.

Number Twenty Eight is a listed house of charm and character situated on Lower Broad Street, half way between the old Broad Gate and Ludford Bridge.

Number Twenty Eight

Patricia Ross is a professional hotelier who couldn't retire—she enjoys it too much! So Number Twenty Eight is well run, yet friendly and with a great welcome and hospitality. The guest bedrooms are all en-suite and equipped to a very high standard. The food is scrumptious, with fine wines to match and after dinner, guests can relax in the lounge looking out into the walled garden and browse amongst the many books, which are there for their enjoyment. ETB 4 Crown Highly Commended.

Number Twenty Eight, 28 Lower Broad Street, Ludlow, Shropshire SY8 1PQ
Tel & Fax: 01584 876996

To the east of Ludlow and for those who like to take their holiday far from the crowds spending time walking in beautiful areas and exploring and visiting historic places of interest, then **Corndene** country holiday accommodation could be idyllic. Once a rectory, the house dates, in part, from the late 18th century; it retains all the charm and atmosphere of a place much loved and long inhabited. Surrounded by six and a half acres of gardens where there is a large pond, hay meadow, a small wood and many mature trees, the area is rich in wildlife.

Corndene

Inside, guests find a charming sitting room with books, maps, games, a log fire and doors leading on to the terrace. The three ground floor twin bedrooms can also be used as singles or family rooms, children of all ages being welcome. All rooms have en-suite facilities, central heating, drinks tray, television and pleasant views. Breakfast offers a wonderful selection and, although evening meals are not provided, there is a fully equipped visitors' kitchen for guests wishing to make meals or snacks whenever they wish—what a wonderful idea! Disabled visitors will find Corndene ideal, with specially adapted rooms and Category 1 and 2 certificates from the National Accessible Scheme. Ask for further details and precise directions.

Corndene, Coreley, Ludlow, Shropshire SY8 3AW Tel: 01584 890324

CHURCH STRETTON

Map 8 ref H15

There has been a market in the town since King John first granted a charter in 1214 and it is still held here on a Thursday. Though Church Stretton is undoubtedly old, many of the black and white timbered buildings are, in fact, not medieval but were built around the turn of this century when the town had ideas of becoming a health resort.

One ancient building here is the **Church of St Laurence** which was constructed on a Saxon foundation and has a Norman nave; the tower was added around 1200. Over the aisle is a memorial to a tragic event that happened in 1968 when three boys died in a hotel fire. The memorial takes the form of a gridiron with twisted flakes of copper simulating flames. The gridiron is the symbol of St Laurence who was burnt to death in AD 258.

The origins of **Willowfield Country Guest House** date from the 17th century and a mixture of architectural styles from Elizabethan to the present create a house of interesting character. Situated just to the northwest of Church Stretton in the foothills of Long Mynd, with wonderful open aspects away from the traffic and main roads, guests can enjoy the lovely gardens and panoramic views of rural England.

Willowfield

The Elizabethan dining rooms provide the perfect setting for a three course candlelit dinner with a glass of wine or two! With many surprises each evening the traditional home-cooking is highly commended; fresh produce grown at Willowfield is complemented by local meats. Vegetarian dishes and special requirements are catered for too. The bedrooms are individual in character with attractive decor and lovely views. All are en-suite with lounge seating area, colour TV, radio, telephone and beverage tray. The breakfast menu caters for all palates with midday packed lunches available to fill in between. A no smoking policy operates and regrettably pets cannot be accommodated in the house. ETB 3 Crowns.

Willowfield, Lower Wood, Church Stretton, Shropshire SY6 6LF
Tel: 01694 751471

All Stretton, just to the north of Church Stretton, is said to have got its name because James I needed to distinguish between the three Strettons when he was visiting the area. He is supposed to have arrived at Little Stretton and given it that name; then he went on to name Church Stretton because of its Norman church and, when he finally arrived here, he remarked "It's all Stretton hereabouts."

Jinlye is reputedly claimed to be one of the most beautifully situated guest houses in England and it is also the winner of the Heart of England Tourist Board Bed and Breakfast of the Year 1997. Standing in 15 acres of grounds at 1400 feet, the house immediately adjoins the Long Mynd and 6000 acres of National Trust land. This delightful 16th century stone built house must be many peoples' idea of heaven. The colourful cascading flowers and shrubs which surround the house are a welcoming spectacle.

Jinlye

Jinlye has been totally refurbished and offers luxury accommodation. There's a wealth of old beams, open log fires and leaded light windows, which instantly make guests feel welcome. The superb reading lounge, once a barn, now has a large inglenook fireplace and makes for a very comfortable evening, whilst the cosy television lounge and Victorian conservatory overlook an acre of garden. The spacious en-suite bedrooms all have magnificent views. They are delightfully furnished in period style each with an individual character. For that special occasion, book the wedding suite, furnished around a splendidly carved 17th century French wedding bed and overlooking the wild windswept moors of the Long Mynd; shades of Wuthering Heights! Two guest rooms are at ground floor level one of which is suitable for the disabled visitor. Excellent home-cooking is served with an abundance of fresh local produce but, be warned, deserts are a speciality! There is an enormous variety of wild life almost on the door step and many recreational activities can be enjoyed in the area.

Jinlye, Castle Hill, All Stretton, Church Stretton, Shropshire SY6 6JP
Tel & Fax: 01694 723243

England

SHREWSBURY   *Map 8 ref H15*

The River Severn winds around this lively, beautiful county town in a horseshoe
bend, making it almost an island site. It would be hard not to love this town as
it is so rich in picturesque half-timbered houses of the 16th century and the later,
more elegant Queen Anne, Georgian and Victorian architecture. There is a sense
of history everywhere and several of the houses are associated with famous
historical figures, such as the house where Mary Tudor lodged.

There are some 30 churches in Shrewsbury, all of which seem to have some
feature of architectural or historical note. One in particular, is **Holy Trinity
Church** which has some wonderful stained glass windows by William Morris.
However, perhaps the town's favourite church is **Holy Cross Abbey**. The west
front is superb with a fine stained glass window, sumptuously traceried and
extends up to a statue of Edward II, in whose reign the building of the tower was
begun.

Another building in the town well worth visiting is **Clive House**, in the Georgian
area of Shrewsbury. Clive of India lived here in 1762 while he was Mayor of
Shrewsbury and there are one or two mementoes of this great man to be seen. The
house is built of 18th century brick and is quite splendid and, inside, several of
the rooms show period settings, mostly as a background to a magnificent
collection of Shropshire ceramics.

Dating from 1083, **Shrewsbury Castle** was built by the Norman, Earl Roger de
Montgomery and last saw action during the Civil War. It was later converted into
a private residence by Telford, the great engineer. Today the castle houses the
regimental collections of the Kings Shropshire Yeomanry Cavalry and the
Shropshire Royal Horse Artillery. There are relics on display from the last War
and uniforms dating back to the Napoleonic invasion scare at the beginning of
the 19th century.

TELFORD   *Map 8 ref I15*

Described as Britain's brightest and newest town, Telford is certainly an
imaginative blend of old and new in which the developers have linked together
several existing towns and created a modern purpose-designed town centre.

Immense care has also been taken to make sure Telford is a green and pleasant
place and a million trees and shrubs were planted to achieve this. Certainly,
Telford Park, which is right in the town centre, is an expansive area of
landscaped countryside featuring a miniature steam railway, lakeside amphitheatre, sports arena and children's fortress.

Just north of Telford is **Oakengates**, which, as all horse racing buffs will know,
is the birthplace of the incomparable jockey and trainer Sir Gordon Richards. He
first learned to ride on pit ponies because his father was a miner. It must have

been an excellent training as Sir Gordon, when he retired from the saddle after 33 years riding, had 4827 wins to his credit and had been champion jockey for 20 years.

To the south of Telford lies the village of **Ironbridge**, home of the first iron bridge ever constructed and the cradle of the Industrial Revolution. This remarkable valley is now home to a unique series of industrial monuments and museums and it has also been designated a World Heritage Site. Visiting all the museums that make up the **Ironbridge Gorge Museum** might, at first, seem a daunting task but it is a very rewarding experience.

The **Museum of Iron**, in the nearby village of **Coalbrookdale**, is where the whole industry began back in 1709 when Abraham Darby invented a revolutionary technique that enable cheap cast iron to be mass produced. The smelting furnace used by Darby is still here and it is the centrepiece of a collection that traces the history of iron-making and the fortunes of the Darby family. Situated on the banks of the River Severn, in the tranquil surroundings of Riverside Park, the **Museum of the River** presents the history of Ironbridge Gorge.

To the east of Telford, just outside Shifnal, **The Hundred House Hotel**, in the village of **Norton**, is one of those very rare gems, unusual, idiosyncratic and yet luxurious. After all there can be few places to stay that offer not only four poster beds, but swings in some of the bedrooms! The hotel's name stems from medieval days when subdivisions of the shires of England were known as 'hundreds'. The oldest remaining part of this Hundred House is the delightful 14th century half-timbered, thatched courthouse barn in the hotel courtyard. Wood panelling, red quarry tiles, open log fires and bunches of dried flowers and herbs all serve to enhance the unique character and welcoming ambience of this

The Hundred House Hotel

super establishment. Dining is an absolute delight, with a bar menu far above average and an à la carte restaurant that caters for the most discerning gastronome. With all this and more, staying at the Hundred House is truly a memorable experience.

The Hundred House Hotel, Bridgnorth Road, Norton, near Shifnal, Shropshire TF11 9EE Tel: 01952 730353 Fax: 01952 730355

Staffordshire

INTRODUCTION

The area around Stoke-on-Trent is famous the world over for its pottery industry. Originally centred on the five towns of Stoke, Tunstall, Burslem, Hanley and Longton, The Potteries were at the heart of the Industrial Revolution. Still very much an industrial area, the countryside, towns and villages around Stoke-on-Trent are often overlooked as travellers motor up and down the M6. However, behind the Victorian and industrial architecture there are some much older buildings to be found. After visiting the industrial districts of Stoke-on-Trent, it is worth remembering that, just a short drive away, there is the wonderful 17th century cottage that was the home of Sir Izaak Walton.

Staffordshire encompasses many changing landscapes, from the busy, industrial towns of Stafford and Burton upon Trent to the peace and quiet of Cannock Chase. Along with the Hednesford Hills, the Chase provides a wonderful open area of woodland and moorland that is one of the county's great recreational centres. Well supported by an interesting and informative visitors' centre, the Chase is a must for anyone visiting this part of Staffordshire.

Finally, Lichfield, a cathedral city, Stafford, the county town, and Tamworth have roots which date back well beyond the Industrial Revolution and, behind the modern city offices, medieval buildings can still be found.

STAFFORD

Map 9 ref J14

The county town of Staffordshire is Saxon in origin though little of its early history is visible except the extensive earthworks close to the Castle and the foundations of a tiny Saxon Chapel in the grounds of St Mary's Church. Like many old towns around Britain, Stafford originally had a medieval town wall and evidence of it can still be seen today in the names of the town's main streets. However, it is only East Gate that remains of the structure. This was where Elizabeth I met with the town councillors on her visit here in 1575 and the Gate can be found at the top of the appropriately named Queensgate.

Stafford lies on the banks of the River Sow and Green Bridge marks the site of the ancient ford across the river. There has been a bridge on this spot since the late 13th century but the gate in the town's medieval walls that was also at this point was demolished in 1777. A place well worth visiting during any stay in Stafford is The **Ancient High House**, a beautiful Elizabethan house built in 1595 that is in fact the largest timber-framed town house in England. Through painstaking efforts over several years, Stafford Borough Council have restored this amazing piece of architecture to its former glory and, today, the building houses the **Museum of the Staffordshire Yeomanry** and the Tourist Information Centre. The Ancient High House's varied history can be followed through the permanent displays in the period room settings taking the visitor through the 17th, 18th and 19th centuries and telling the life stories of people who came to know this House so intimately. Not surprisingly, the House has Royal connections with both King Charles I and Prince Rupert having stayed here in 1642.

Close to the High House is the Collegiate **Church of St Mary**, an unusual building which dates, in part, from the late 12th century, but has received additions in the early English, Gothic and Victorian styles. The huge tower arches in the nave seem to divide the building into two, which is, in fact, exactly what they were intended to do, as St Mary's is two churches under one roof. The nave was the Parish Church of Stafford with its own altar whilst the chancel beyond was used by the Deans of the College of St Mary, whose duty it was to pray for deceased members of the Royal family. Sir Izaak Walton was baptized here on 21st September 1593 and his bust can be seen on the north wall of the nave. Each year, at a civic service, a wreath is placed around the bust to commemorate his supposed birthday (9th August). Those interested in ecclesiastical architecture will, however, prefer to visit the little Norman and medieval Church of St Chad.

Situated high up above the town, one Stafford landmark that is viewed by countless travellers along the M6 are the impressive earthworks of the Norman **Castle** which can be reached via the A518 Newport Road, about a mile and a half from the town centre. Set within 20 acres, the remains of this splendid fortress are open to the public and visitors can follow an illustrated trail which leads from the outer bailey to the site of a medieval settlement.

Best known today for his work *The Compleat Angler*, throughout his lifetime, Sir Izaak Walton was famous as a writer of biographies. However, the story of his own life is somewhat obscure: it is certain that he was born in Stafford, in 1593, though the date is less certain. From humble origins, Walton became accepted in the intellectual and ecclesiastical circles of the day and, during the Civil War, he remained a staunch Royalist and stayed in the Stafford area.

As might be expected Walton is associated with several buildings in the town though the house of his birth, in Eastgate Street, was demolished in 1888 and the site is now occupied by the Stafford Police Station. Also in Eastgate Street, is the **William Salt Library**, which houses a sizable collection of interesting local history documents, including several relating to Sir Izaak.

To the north of Stafford lies **Shallowford** and Shallowford Brook, which forms part of the River Meece and runs by Walton's Cottage. Set in beautiful grounds in this tiny hamlet, **Izaak Walton's Cottage** is a pretty 17th century half timbered cottage which was once owned by Izaak Walton, famous biographer and author of *The Compleat Angler*. Walton bequeathed the cottage to Stafford Borough Council and it was subsequently transformed into the Museum found today. Within the grounds there is an authentic 17th century herb garden, a lovely picnic area and orchard.

Izaak Walton's Cottage

CANNOCK CHASE

Map 9 ref J15

Though near to areas of dense population, Cannock Chase is a surprisingly wild place of heath and woodland that has been designated an Area of Outstanding Natural Beauty. Covering some 20,000 acres, the Chase was once the hunting ground of Norman kings and, later, the Bishops of Lichfield and deer are still plentiful. Sherbrook Valley is a good starting point from which to find these timid creatures. Now chiefly planted with conifers it is still possible to find the remains of the ancient oak forest and, in the less well walked marshy grounds, many rare species survive.

A popular place for leisurely strolls, the Chase is also ideal for more strenuous walking and other outdoor recreational activities. Excellent view points can be found at Coppice Hill and Brereton Spurs whilst Castle Ring, an impressive Iron Age hillfort, is well worth the effort to find.

Amid all this natural beauty, there are also reminders of the 20th century and, in particular, the unique military cemeteries near Broadhurst Green, where some 5,000 German soldiers from the Great War lie buried. Cannock Chase was used as a training ground during the First World War and was the last billet for many thousands of soldiers before they left for France. The remnants of the training area can still be seen as can the prisoner of war camp. The use of the Chase as a training ground was not a new idea, in 1873, there were extensive manoeuvres here with one army base at Etching Hill and the other army at Hednesford Hills, where the battle took place.

The **Museum of Cannock Chase** at the Valley Heritage Centre is only one of the many wonderful parts of Cannock Chase. The Council have encouraged visitors by helping in the conservation of areas of beauty. Opened in May 1989, the Centre is a new concept in the world of museums, arts and crafts and its galleries provide different exhibitions, with rooms dedicated to the natural history of the Hednesford Hills and Castle Ring hillfort. Subjects covered in these galleries change every six months to deal with as many aspects of the area's history as possible.

LICHFIELD   *Map 9 ref K15*

During the 18th century Lichfield was a prominent city but it failed to compete with other towns in extensive rebuilding programmes and consequently it still retains its medieval grid pattern streets with elegant Georgian houses and, mixed in amongst them, black and white Tudor cottages. Little alleyways, such as Tudor Row, invite shoppers to visit specialist boutiques and a 16th century café—so different from the usual high streets found in today's cities and towns.

The first cathedral was built here in 669 but no traces of this building, or the later Norman structure, remain. The **Lichfield Cathedral** seen today dates from the 12th century and is particularly famous for its magnificent three spires which dominate the City skyline. Inside there are many treasures including the beautiful 8th century illuminated manuscript *The Lichfield Gospels* and Sir Francis Chantrey's famous sculpture *The Sleeping Children*.

The surrounding Cathedral Close, regarded as the most unspoilt in the country, is particularly fine and, as the Close is separated from the rest of the city by Stowe and Minster Pools, it is also a peaceful haven of calm. These two wonderful pools, Stowe and Minster, are used for fishing and sailing as well as being the site of the Festival fireworks display each July. The Minster Pool is particularly beautiful, it was landscaped in the late 18th century by Anna Seward and is now a haven for wildfowl.

The City has been a place of pilgrims and travellers for centuries and, in 1135, **St John's Hospital** opened to offer shelter to those passing through Lichfield. One of the finest Tudor brick buildings in the country, the Hospital is now a home for the elderly. The Hospital Chapel, with its magnificent stained glass window by the designer of the celebrated east window at Coventry Cathedral, John Piper, is open daily.

Lichfield's most famous son is Dr Samuel Johnson, the poet, novelist and author of the first comprehensive English dictionary. The son of a bookseller, Johnson was born in 1709, in Breadmarket Street, and the house is now home to the **Samuel Johnson Birthplace Museum**. Open every day except Sundays, the Museum, as well as exhibiting artefacts relating to his life and works, also has a series of tableaux showing how the house looked in the early 18th century.

BURTON UPON TRENT   *Map 9 ref K14*

The 'capital' of East Staffordshire, Burton upon Trent is famous for its brewing industry. However, the industry began long before the Victorian Age and even the monks of the Benedictine Abbey, founded here in 1100, were not the first to realise that the Burton well water was specially suited to brewing. Today, the town is dominated by beer and ale and it was William Worthington and William Bass (names familiar to those who enjoy a pint or two) who first began commercial production here in the mid-18th century.

Today, Bass Charrington dominates and the **Bass Museum of Brewing**, in Horninglow Street, is well worth a visit. As well as being offered the opportunity of seeing, sniffing and sampling the traditionally brewed beer, visitors can tour the machinery, inspect the fleet of old vehicles and admire the famous Bass shire horses.

A Benedictine Abbey, founded by a Saxon earl called Wulfric Spot, was established on the banks of the River Trent, where the Market Place now stands. The focus of Burton, it was from here that the town grew and, in the 12th century, the monks constructed a large stone bridge of some 36 arches across the River Trent. Today's bridge replaced the medieval structure in 1864. The area along the banks of the Trent, between Burton Bridge and the later structure of Ferry Bridge, which opened in 1889, is known as the Washlands. Rich in native wildlife, the Washlands is a haven for all manner of birds, small mammals, trees and plants.

STOKE-ON-TRENT   *Map 9 ref J13*

The city was established as late as 1910 when Fenton joined the five towns (Tunstall, Burslem, Hanley, Longton and Stoke) immortalized by the novels of Arnold Bennett. Once fiercely independent, the towns became progressively involved with each other as improvements in roads, water supplies and other amenities forced them towards amalgamation. The new city's crest, of an ancient Egyptian potter at his wheel in one quarter, sums up the fortune on which the wealth of the area was created. Each of the old towns is also represented in the crest and the joint motto translates to "Strength is stronger for unity".

It was the presence of the essential raw materials for the manufacture and decoration of ceramics, in particular marl clay, coal and water, that led to the concentration of pottery manufacture in this area. Though production started in the 17th century it was the entrepreneurial skills of Josiah Wedgwood and Thomas Minton, who brought the individual potters together in factory-style workplaces, that caused the massive leap forward in production that took place in the 18th century. Their factories were large but there were also hundreds of small establishments producing a whole range of more utilitarian chinaware. Production in The Potteries reached its height towards the end of the 19th century and it was at this time that the area was described as being the most unhealthy in the country. The Trent and Mersey Canal, flowing right through the city, is home to the industry that has made the fortune of the area. The Royal Doulton factory lines both banks and from here the Stoke flight of locks lifts the Canal some 50 feet into Etruria.

For those interested in industrial and Victorian architecture, Stoke-on-Trent is a wonderful place to visit, with many museums and factories opening to the public to tell the story of the wealth of the city. For many though, Stoke-on-Trent will always be remembered for its football team, Stoke City, and the local hero, Sir Stanley Matthews.

Derbyshire

INTRODUCTION

Derbyshire was at the forefront of modern thinking at the beginning of the Industrial Revolution. The chief inheritor of this legacy was Derby and the city, still a busy industrial centre, is also home to the Industrial Museum. There are plenty of other places to visit in Derby, which is not, as is often supposed, the county town (that title belongs to Matlock).

In the valley of the River Trent, which runs through the southern part of the county, can be found many splendid stately homes, including Kedleston Hall and the eccentric Calke Abbey. Though the scenery is less dramatic than the popular Peak District, in which most of north Derbyshire lies, there are ample opportunities to enjoy pleasant walks in the extensive grounds of many of the estates.

The **Peak District**, in which most of north Derbyshire lies, was the first of Britain's ten National Parks and it covers an area of over 540 square miles. Its situation, close to the large industrial conurbations of Manchester, Sheffield, Derby, Nottingham and Staffordshire, have meant that this region of high, windswept moorland and charming river valleys has always been popular. From the time of the first railways into the area, in the mid-19th century, the Peak District has been a Mecca for walkers and those wishing to discover its many hidden secrets.

The National Park is littered with the remains of ancient settlements and the origin of the word peak probably comes from the Pecsaetans, or hill people, a primitive tribe who are thought to have settle here in around the 7th century. At most of the crossings into the Park there are millstones standing on stone plinths at the side of the road. These are used as boundary markers by the Park Authority, which has also adopted the millstone symbol as its logo.

Referred to as the Dark Peak and also High Peak, the northern area of the Peak District National Park is not as foreboding as might be imagined from its name. These high moors are ripe for exploring on foot, and a walk from the Kinder

Reservoir will eventually lead to the western edge of Kinder Scout. This whole area of the Dark Peak is really a series of plateaux, rather than mountains and valleys, and the highest point on Kinder Scout is some 2,088 feet above sea level.

The central area of the Peak District National Park is less wild and isolated than the remote High Peak area. The two main Rivers, the Wye and the Derwent, which both have their source further north, are, in this region, at a more gentle stage of their course. Over the centuries, the fast flowing waters were harnessed to provide power to drive mills situated on the riverbanks and any walk taken along the riverbanks will not only give the opportunity to discover a wide range of plant and animal life but also provide the opportunity to see the remains of buildings that once played an important part in the economy of north Derbyshire.

Bakewell, the largest town in the Peak District, dominates the area and close to it are two of the most magnificent stately homes in Britain, Chatsworth House and Haddon Hall. Hardly a hidden place, the vast Chatsworth estate straddles the River Derwent, east of Bakewell, but the influence of the Cavendish family extends much further and few villages in the surrounding area have escaped.

DERBY   *Map 9 ref L14*

Essentially a commercial and industrial city, Derby's position, historically and geographically, has ensured that it has remained one of the most important and interesting cities in the area and, consequently, there is much for the visitor to see, whether from an architectural or historical point of view. There are, however, two things almost everyone, whether they have been to the city before or not, known of Derby: Rolls-Royce engines and Royal Crown Derby porcelain. When in 1906, Sir Henry Royce and the Hon CS Rolls joined forces and built the first Rolls-Royce, a Silver Ghost, at Derby they built much more than just a motorcar. Considered by many to be the best cars in the world, it is often said that the noisiest moving part in any Rolls-Royce is the dashboard clock!

The home of **Royal Crown Derby**, a visit to the city would not be complete without a trip to the factory and its museum and shop. The guided tours offering an intriguing insight into the high level of skill required to create the delicate flower petals, hand gild the plates and hand paint the Derby Dwarves.

The city's **Cathedral** possesses a fine 16th century tower though the airy building was actually built in the 1720s by James Gibbs. Inside is a beautiful wrought-iron screen by Robert Bakewell and among the splendid monuments lies the tomb of Bess of Hardwick Hall. Originally Derby's Parish Church it was given Cathedral status in 1927. In the late 1960s, the building was extended eastwards and the retrochoir, baldacchino and sacristy were added along with the screen.

One of Derby's newest of museums is **Pickford House**, situated on the city's finest Georgian street at number 41. It is a Grade I listed building, erected in 1770 by the architect Joseph Pickford as a combined family home and place of work. Pickford House varies from the majority of grand stately homes; unlike most it does not have a wealth of priceless furnishings and works of art. Instead, visitors are able to gain an insight into everyday middle class life during the 1830s. Pickford House is the epitome of a late, Georgian professional man's residence.

Just a short walk from Pickford House is the **Industrial Museum**. What better place to house a museum devoted to the preservation of Derby's industrial heritage than the beautiful old **Silk Mill**; a building which stands on one of the most interesting sites in the country and which preceded Richard Arkwright's first cotton mill by over 50 years. The Silk Mill was badly damaged by fire in 1910 and had to be substantially rebuilt, however it still gives an impression of Lombe's original mill and tower. The whole of the ground floor galleries are devoted to the Rolls Royce aero engine collection and illustrate the importance the aeronautical industry has played in the history of the city.

The **City Museum and Art Gallery** is also well worth visiting. Opened in 1879, it is the oldest of Derby's museums and the displays include, natural history, archaeology and social history. One section of the Museum is devoted to a Military Gallery and relates to Derby's local historical regiments. A relatively new feature is the walk-in World War I trench scene which captures the experience of a night at the front. A ground floor gallery houses the city's superb collection of fine porcelain, manufactured in Derby from the mid-18th century. The museum is also home to a collection of portraits, landscapes, scientific and industrial scenes by the local painter Joseph Wright, ARA.

Well dressing is an ancient custom, recently revived, that is more commonly associated with the villages and towns of northern Derbyshire and the Peak District. However, two wells in Derby have been dressed since 1982, on the Saturday before the late Spring Bank Holiday. Possibly dating from the 3rd century, the wells were built by the Romans near the walls of their fort, Derventio. In 1929, excavations discovered one of the wells, which was rediscovered again in 1967, while the second well was discovered in 1978. On the opposite bank of the River Derwent is a third well, the holy well where St Alkmund's coffin was rested whilst on its journey to Lilleshall in Shropshire. Though not dressed at present, the well has been dressed spasmodically since the 1850s.

ELVASTON   *Map 9 ref L14*

The village is gathered around the edge of the **Elvaston Castle** estate, the home of the Earls of Harrington. The magnificent Gothic Castle seen today replaced a 17th century brick and gabled manor house and part of the original structure can be seen on the end of the south front. Designed by James Wyatt, the Castle was finished in the early 19th century but, unfortunately, the 3rd Earl died in 1829 and had little time to enjoy his new home.

It is, perhaps, the grounds which make Elvaston Castle famous today; they were original laid out and designed for the 4th Earl by William Barron. Barron, who was born in Berwickshire in 1805, started work in 1830 on what, at first, appeared to be an impossible task. The 4th Earl wanted a garden "second to none" but the land available, which had never been landscaped, was flat, water logged and uninspiring with just two avenues of trees and a walled kitchen garden (but no hot houses). Firstly, draining the land, Barron then planted trees, to offer shelter to more tender plants and from there the project grew. In order to stock the gardens, Barron began a programme of propagation of rarer tree species and, along with the tree planting methods he developed specially to deal with Elvaston's problems, his fame spread. The gardens became a showcase of rare and interesting trees, many to be found nowhere else in Britain. Barron continued to work for the 5th Earl but resigned in 1865 to live in nearby Borrowash and set up his own nursery.

Elvaston Castle

Now owned by Derby County Council, the gardens, after years of neglect, have been completely restored and the delights of the formal gardens, with their fine topiary, the avenues and the kitchen garden can be enjoyed by all visitors to the grounds which are now a Country Park.

As well as fine formal gardens and the walled kitchen garden there are gentle woodland walks and, of course, the man-made lake. However, no visit to Elvaston would be complete without a walk down to the Golden Gates. Erected in 1819 at the southern end of the formal gardens, the gates were brought from the Palace of Versailles by the 3rd Earl of Harrington. Little is known of the Gates' history but they remain a fine monument and are the symbol of Elvaston. Around the courtyard of the Castle can be found a restaurant as well as an information centre and well stocked gift shop. All manner of activities take place from the Castle and details can be found here.

ASHBOURNE

Map 9 K13

Featuring as Esseburne in the Domesday Book, the town was originally a small settlement lying in the northern bank of Henmore Brook which already had a church. It was a 13th century lord of the manor who laid out the new town to the east around its unusual shaped market place. Many of the town's traders, in order to continue to enjoy the benefits without paying the town's tolls, built themselves houses on the south side of the Brook. The area became known as Compton and it was slowly absorbed into the town. When writing *Adam Bede*, George Eliot based 'Oakbourne' on the town.

Often called The Gateway to the North, today, this is a pretty town that is a pleasure to visit with plenty of shop-filled streets to potter up and down. The triangular cobbled Market Square, in the heart of Ashbourne, was part of a new development that started in the 13th century and shifted the town to the east, away from the Church. It was from this market place, that used to be lined with ale houses, that Bonnie Prince Charlie proclaimed his father King of England and so started the Jacobite Rebellions. Though the old bull ring no longer exists, here can be found many fine examples of 18th century architecture as well as some older buildings, notably the Gingerbread Shop which is timber framed and probably dates from the 15th century. Traditional Ashbourne gingerbread is said to be made from a recipe that was acquired from French prisoners of war who were kept in the town during the Napoleonic Wars.

Also worthy of a second glance is the **Green Man and Black's Head Royal Hotel**. The inn sign stretches over the St John's Street and was put up when the Blackamoor Inn joined with the Green Man in 1825. Though the Blackamoor is no more the sign remains and it claims to be the longest hotel name in the country. Of Georgian origin, the amalgamated Hotel played host to James Boswell, Dr Johnson and the young Princess Victoria. Ashbourne was, in fact, one of Dr Johnson's favourite places and he came to the town on several occasions between 1737 and 1784. He also visited the Hotel so often that he had his own chair, with his name on it! The chair can still be seen at the Green Man.

A stroll down Church Street, described by Pevsner as one of the finest streets in Derbyshire, takes the walker passed many interesting Georgian houses including the Grey House which stands next to The **Grammar School**. Founded by Queen Elizabeth I in 1585, the school was visited on its 400th anniversary by the present Queen. Almost opposite the Grey House is The Mansion, the late 17th century home of the Rev Dr John Taylor, oldest friend of Dr Johnson. As well as walking the main streets, Ashbourne retains many of its narrow alleyways and, in particular, there is Lovatt's Yard where the town lock-up can be seen.

Ashbourne is also home of the famous Shrovetide football game played on Shrove Tuesday and Ash Wednesday. The two teams, the Up'ards (those born north of the Henmore Brook) and the Down'ards (those born south of it) begin their match at 2 pm behind the Green Man Hotel and the game continues until well into the evening. The two goals are situated three miles apart, along the Brook, on the site of the old mills at Clifton and Sturston and it is rare for more than one goal to be scored in this slow moving game.

BAKEWELL
Map 9 ref K12

The only true town in the Peak District National Park, Bakewell attracts many day trippers, walkers and campers as well as locals who come to take advantage of its many amenities. The beautiful medieval five-arched bridge spanning the River Wye is still in use today as the main crossing point for traffic.

However, for most people it is a dessert that has made the name of Bakewell so famous, but please remember it is referred to locally as a pudding and most definitely not a tart! Its invention is said to have been an accident when what was supposed to have been a strawberry tart turned into something all together different. The cooking mishap took place in the kitchens of the Rutland Arms Hotel which was built in 1804 on the site of a coaching inn. One of the Hotel's more famous guests was the novelist Jane Austen, who stayed there in 1811. The Rutland Arms featured in her book *Pride and Prejudice*, while Bakewell itself appeared as the town of Lambton.

Bakewell's situation has always made it the ideal place for a settlement and, as well as being home to the Romans, an Iron Age fort has been discovered close by. Another reason for the popularity of the town was the existence of 12 fresh water springs and they also gave the town its name—Bad kwell means bath spring.

The market town for this whole central area of the Peak District, markets were held here well before the granting of a charter in 1330. In fact, its importance during the 11th century was such that, as recorded in the Domesday Book of 1086, Bakewell had two priests. Monday is now Bakewell's market day and the cattle market, one of the largest in Derbyshire, is an important part on the area's farming life. The annual Bakewell Show, held every August, started in 1819 and has gone on to become one of the foremost agricultural shows in the country.

The lovely **Old House Museum** is housed in a building which dates back to 1534. Originally the Parsonage House, this beautiful building escaped demolition and has been lovingly restored by the Bakewell Historical Society and now displays its original wattle and daub interior walls. It was extended during the early 17th century and, at one time, the building was converted into tenements by the industrialist Richard Arkwright. Now established as a folk museum, it houses a fascinating collection of rural bygones.

The town is full of delightful, mellow stone buildings many of which date from the early 17th century and are still in use today. The Old Town Hall, famous as the scene of the Bakewell riots, is now the Tourist Information Centre of the Peak

District. Few buildings remain from the days when Bakewell was a minor spa town but the **Bath House**, on Bath Street, is one such building. Built in 1697 for the Duke of Rutland, it contained a large bath which was filled with the spa water and kept at a constant temperature of 59 degrees Fahrenheit. At the nearby Bath Gardens a Roman bath was discovered near the British Legion's Garden of Remembrance.

Traditionally well dressing flourished in the town in the 18th century when Bakewell had aspirations to become a fashionable spa. However, the recent revival only dates back to the 1970s when the British Legion, with the help of the well dressers of Ashford in the Water, dressed the warm well at Bath House. Today all five wells, in the same room, are dressed on the last Saturday in June.

There is little evidence of industry in the town, which is not very surprising considering Bakewell is surrounded by farming country, but the remnants of **Lumsford Mill** can still be seen. Originally built in 1778 by Sir Richard Arkwright as a cotton spinning mill, over 300 hands, mainly women and children, were employed here. Badly damaged by fire in 1868, the Mill has been rebuilt and it used as offices today.

Only a mile to the south of Bakewell is **Haddon Hall**, hidden from the road by a beech hedge. The Hall is thought by many to have been the first fortified house in the country although the turrets and battlements were actually put on purely for show. The home of the Dukes of Rutland for over 800 years, the Hall has enjoyed a fairly peaceful existence and, as with all good ancestral homes, it has a family legend. In this case the story dates from the 16th century when Lady Dorothy Vernon eloped with Sir John Manners. A small museum by the gatehouse tells of their romantic journey as well as the history of the Hall.

Little construction work has been carried out on the Hall since the days of Henry VIII and it remains one of the best examples of a medieval and Tudor manor house. The 16th century terraced gardens are one of the chief delights of the Hall and are thought by many to be the most romantic in the England. The Halls's splendour and charm has led it to be used as a backdrop to television and film productions including *Jane Eyre*, *Moll Flanders* and *The Prince and the Pauper*.

The home of the Dukes of Devonshire, **Chatsworth House** is without doubt one of the finest of the great houses in Britain. The origins of the House as a great showpiece must be attributable to Bess of Hardwick, whose marriage into the Cavendish family helped to secure the future of the palace.

Bess's husband, Sir William Cavendish, bought the estate for £600 in 1549 and it was Bess who completed the new House after his death. Over the years, the Cavendish fortune continued to pour into Chatsworth, making it an almost unparalleled showcase for art treasures. Every aspect of the fine arts is here, ranging from old masterpieces, furniture, tapestries, porcelain and some magnificent alabaster carvings.

The gardens of this stately home also have some marvellous features, including the Emperor Fountain, which dominates the Canal Pond, and is said to reach a height of 290 feet. There is a maze and a Laburnam Tunnel and, behind the house, are the famous Cascades. The overall appearance of the park as it is seen today is chiefly due to the talents of Capability' Brown, who was first consulted in 1761. However, the name perhaps most strongly associated with Chatsworth is Joseph Paxton. His experiments in glasshouse design led him eventually to his masterpiece, the Crystal Palace, built to house the Great Exhibition of 1851.

BUXTON   *Map 9 ref J12*

Referred to as the heart of the Peak District, Buxton, England's highest market town, provides a wealth of things to do. The current popularity of the town can be attributed to the 5th Duke of Devonshire, however, it was the Romans who first discovered the waters here and named the place Aquae Arnemetiae—The Spa of the Goddess of the Grove. With waters maintained at constant temperature of 82 degrees Fahrenheit, Buxton soon became a place of pilgrimage particularly for sufferers of rheumatism. St Anne's Well still provides water and many people coming to the town make a point of trying the tepid waters. The people of Buxton also say that it makes the best cup of tea possible and collect bottles of it to take home.

In the 18th century, the Duke of Devonshire, with the intention that Buxton would rival Bath as a spa town, commissioned the building of **The Crescent** to ensured that visitors would flock here. Designed by John Carr, the building is similar to the architecture found in Bath and, after suffering from neglect, has undergone a huge restoration programme. As with many places, the coming of the railway, to Buxton in 1863, marked the height of the popularity of the town. Nothing, however, could be done to alter the harsh climate and the incessant rain fall meant that the Duke of Devonshire's wish, to make Buxton a 'Bath of the North', was never truly realised.

Originally built in 1905, the attractive **Opera House** was restored, in 1979, to its grand Edwardian style. After being used as a cinema for many years, it is once again the host the live performances and, as well as offering a comprehensive and popular programme throughout the year, it also has one of the largest stages in England. The octagonal **Pump Room**, a marvellous construction in glass and iron where visitors can discover the **Micrarium**, the only exhibition of its kind which uses microscopes to view the amazing structures that abound in the natural world.

With such a long and varied history, the story of Buxton and the surrounding area is an interesting one and more can be discovered at the **Buxton Museum**. As well as housing an important local archaeology collection, the Museum also has a fine collection of Ashford Marble, Blue John ornaments, paintings, prints, pottery and glassware.

To the west of the town lies **Axe Edge**, the highest point of which rises to 1,807 feet above sea level. From this spot, on a clear day (and the weather here is notorious), the panoramic views of Derbyshire are overwhelming. Just beyond stands, at 1,690 feet above sea level, the **Cat and Fiddle Inn**, the second highest pub in England. Axe Edge Moor, which receives an average annual rainfall of over 4 feet, is strictly for hardened walkers.

NEW MILLS   *Map 13 ref J12*

Situated by the River Sett, New Mills takes its name from the Tudor corn mills that once stood on the riverbanks. Later, in the 18th and 19th centuries water power was used to drive several cotton-spinning mills in the town and, as New Mills grew, the textile industry was joined by engineering industries and the confectionery trade.

The town is also the start of the **Sett Valley Trail** which follows the line of the old branch railway to Hayfield some three miles away. Opened in 1868, the single track line carried passengers and freight for over 100 years. However, by the late 1960s much of the trade had ceased and the line close soon afterwards. In 1973, the line was reopened as a trail and it is still well used by walkers, cyclists and horse riders and it takes in the remains of buildings that were once part of the prosperous textile industry.

Masons Arms

Those looking for a traditional Derbyshire inn on the edge of the High Peak should make a point of finding the **Masons Arms**. This pleasant meeting place is situated in the High Street, off Market Street, and is one of only two pubs in the road to survive from the five which once stood here. Over the years, Masons has grown from small beginnings by incorporating a neighbouring house and barber's shop. Today, it is a popular inn with a relaxed homely atmosphere which is welcoming to visitors and locals alike. Julie and Vic Chappell are friendly hosts who provide charming hospitality, fine ales and a range of appetising

snacks and sandwiches. A blazing coal fire welcomes visitors on colder days and most of the time the bar is filled with lively conversation and local colour. A range of traditional pub games, including pool, is also available. The Masons Arms is open from 11 am to 11 pm Mondays to Saturdays and from 12 noon to 10.30 pm on Sundays. Plenty of parking is available in the large car park.
Masons Arms, High Street, New Mills, Derbyshire SK22 4BR
Tel: 01663 744292

GLOSSOP   *Map 13 ref J11*

At the foot of Snake Pass, Glossop is an interesting mix of styles: the industrial town of the 19th century with its towering Victorian mills and the 17th century village with its charming old cottages standing in the cobble streets. Further back in time, the Romans came here and established a fort now known as **Melandra Castle** but probably then called Zerdotalia (or Ardotalia). Built to guard the entrance to Longdendale, little of survives today but the stone foundations. The settlement developed further, as part of the monastic estates of Basingwerk Abbey in north Wales, and the village received its market charter in 1290 but, subsequently, there was a decline in its importance. Little remains of Old Glossop except the medieval parish Church of All Saints.

Planned as a new town in the 19th century by the Duke of Norfolk, the original village stood on the banks of the Glossop Brook at the crossing point of three turnpike roads. The brook had already been harnessed to provide power for the cotton mills as this was one of the most easterly town's of the booming Lancashire cotton industry. Many still refer to the older Glossop as Old Glossop and the Victorian settlement as Howard Town, named after the Duke, Bernard Edward Howard.

From Glossop, the A57 east is an exhilarating stretch of road, with hair-raising bends, that is known as **Snake Pass**. The road is frequently made impassable by landslides, heavy mist and massive snowfalls in winter but, weather permitting, it is an experience not to be missed. At the top of the Pass stands **The Snake Inn**, built in 1821 by the 6th Duke of Devonshire and still offering hospitality to weary travellers. The Cavendish family, whose main seat is at Chatsworth House, have a coat of arms depicting a serpent and the Duke presumably felt that the name would be appropriate for the Inn.

For much of the length of the turnpike road that Thomas Telford built across Snake Pass in 1821, the route follows the line of an ancient Roman road, known as **Doctor's Gate**, which ran between Glossop and a fort at Brough. The route was so named after it was rediscovered, in the 16th century, by Dr Talbot, a vicar from Glossop. The illegitimate son of the Earl of Shrewsbury, Talbot used the road with great frequency as he travelled from Glossop to his father's castle at Sheffield.

Nottinghamshire

INTRODUCTION

For most people the county of Nottinghamshire is the home of the legendary outlaw Robin Hood. Stories of his battles with the wicked Sheriff of Nottingham have been told in films from the beginning of the 20th century whilst the romance of his home, Sherwood Forest, can still be explored. Once covering much of the north of the county, only a few remnants remain the Major Oak can still be seen, much supported, near Edwinstowe.

North Nottinghamshire is the land of the Pilgrim Fathers while the central area is home to the great Dukeries, the collective name for the four estates governed by the dukes who owned these lands. There are lovely houses to discover throughout the county, like Newstead Abbey, Hodsock Priory, and the beautiful Wollaton Hall, as well as large tracts of parkland to explore.

Nottinghamshire is also an industrial county, where coal mining and industry blend with arable and livestock farming. To the west, near the Derbyshire border, are the industrial towns and, in particular, there is Eastwood, the birthplace of DH Lawrence and the home of a museum dedicated to the novelists life and works. Nottingham, situated on the banks of the River Trent, is by far the largest town. The home of Boot's the Chemist, this is also a lace town but the town also offers many leisure facilities including the famous Trent Cricket Ground and the National Watersports Centre. To the east lies Southwell, home to one of England's smallest cathedrals and the famous Saracen's Head inn.

NOTTINGHAM

Map 10 ref L13

Nottingham, self-proclaimed Queen of the Midlands, is justifiably said to be one of England's finest cities. It is ripe for exploration but visitors are regaled with the Robin Hood theme wherever they go. However, once they begin to discover the city, it becomes perfectly obvious that Nottingham has plenty going for it without having to rely upon its associations with the popular folk hero.

The settlement of Nottingham was founded by the unfortunately named Snot, chief of a 6th century Anglo-Saxon tribe. He and his people carved out dwellings in the soft local sandstone, and the settlement thrived to become Snottingaham, 'home of the followers of Snot'. The name changed into its current more acceptable form at some stage in Nottingham's ancient history but when that was has never been established.

Those visiting **Nottingham Castle**, the place so closely associated with the Sheriff, the wicked Prince, and the brave and faithful outlaw, Robin Hood, and expecting to see crossbow tournaments and siege towers will be in for a great disappointment. The current building could not be described as a 'castle' in the popular sense of the word at all. In fact, this 17th century mansion belies its spectacular position on its massive sandstone rock, standing plain and rather disappointingly lacking in majesty. However, a castle of one sort or another has occupied the site since the Middle Ages, although today only a few ruins of the original can be seen. In 1831, the castle fell victim to an angry mob who set it ablaze whilst petitioning for the Reform Bill to go through. It remained a virtual shell until 1875, when it was taken over by the Corporation and converted into a museum for public use. It was in fact the first municipal museum in England outside London. Inside there are displays of ceramic, local history, and the picture gallery contains works by Rossetti, Spencer, Crome and others .

The castle sits on top of a monstrous beehive of pale golden sandstone, a rock formation quite riddled with caves. Some 400 have been discovered throughout the city and guided tours through some of the eerie passageways start from the top of Castle Rock. At the base of Castle Rock, is the **Trip to Jerusalem** where Crusaders are said to have stopped for a pint to fortify themselves before their journey to the Holy Land. Dating back to around 1189, it is said to be the oldest pub in England. Set back into the rock, it was once the brewhouse for the Castle. Another pub in the area which oozes with ancient charm is the **Salutation Inn**, with its heavy beams and hints that robbers such as Turpin may have dropped in for an ale.

The **Tales of Robin Hood** which is located along Maid Marian Way is definitely worth taking the time to visit. It may not strictly be called a hidden place but the exhibition has won awards, and quite justifiably, as it is well produced and should please anyone with a romantic notion or two!

Nottingham is of course famous for its lace, and **The Lace Centre** in a 16th century half timbered building on Castle Road offers a selection of beautiful lace designs for sale. For a further insight into the lace making process, then **The Lace Hall**, in High Pavement, is the place to go. Situated in a lovely row of 18th century houses, a wonderful setting for the beautiful clothes on display, is the **Museum of Costume and Textiles**. One of the most important study centres for textile design in this country, clothing dating from 1790 to the 1960s can be seen here along with the unique Eyre map tapestries of 1632.

Nottingham's waterways and canals have played a major part in the life of the city. **The Canal Museum** is situated in an old warehouse on the banks of the Nottingham to Beeston canal and trips on canal boats can be enjoyed during the Summer season. The big names of Raleigh, Players and Boots have their massive factories in this city.

The oldest fair in England, possibly going back 1000 years, is Nottingham's Goose Fair. Once a wonderful place for the showman, it is held in October and attracts enormous crowds. Originally a glorified goose market, it became, at its peak, a 15 day event with all the side shows imaginable: dancing bears, human oddities, merry-go-rounds and swingboats.

This elegant market town boasts a cathedral which may sound implausible to the uninitiated, but the lovely 12th century Minster was elevated to the status of **Cathedral** in 1884, when the new Diocese of Southwell was created. This has given rise to the building often being referred to as the 'village cathedral'.

The choir screen is quite stunning, bearing no less than 200 human carvings, while the Chapter House has 13th century carvings of the most beautiful natural objects. The two west towers with their pyramidal roofs make quite a striking note as they stand proud, dominating the cathedral green. The Eagle lectern which stands in the choir was salvaged from the lake at Newstead Abbey in 1750. It had been thrown there by the monks to protect it from the looting that occurred during the Dissolution, and was presented to the Minster in 1805.

Southwell has many other fine buildings and a wealth of fascinating places to discover. Among these are the Prebendal houses where the secular canons resided, the ruins of the Archbishop's palace, sequestered alleyways, and charming coaching inns like the **Saracen's Head** where Charles I spent his last hours of freedom before his final surrender.

The young Lord Byron often stayed at Burgage Manor while on vacation from Harrow and Cambridge. He was a member of the local theatrical group and it was his friends in the town who convinced him to publish his first set of poems. One of his earlier collections, *Hours of Idleness*, was published by Ridges of Newark and was to bring him great acclaim.

Southwell can also be credited as the birthplace of the Bramley apple. The story goes that in the early 19th century, two ladies planted some apple pips in their cottage garden in Easthorpe. Nature took its course and one of the seedlings grew into a tree. By this time, one Matthew Bramley owned the cottage, and the quality of the tree's fruit began to excite public interest.

Mr Henry Merryweather, a local nurseryman, persuaded Bramley to let him take a cutting, which he consequently propagated with enormous success. Permission had been granted on the condition that the apples took Mr Bramley's name and not the two ladies'! Mr Merryweather's descendants still operate a nursery today just outside the town, and here visitors can enjoy an exhibition about the famous apple.

EDWINSTOWE   *Map 9 ref L12*

The church here dates back to the 12th century and, it is said, that Robin and Maid Marian were married here. King Edwin, who gave the village its name, died in battle in 633 and his burial place is close by. The village became the most important settlement in the forest and as one of the main routes to Sherwood passes through it, Edwinstowe still attracts a fair number of 'pilgrims' today.

A little way out of the centre of the village is the **Sherwood Forest Visitor Centre**: the Shire Wood was once a great woodland mass, stretching from Nottingham to Worksop. Although only relatively small pockets of the original forest remain today, it is still possible to get lost amongst the trees, both figuratively and literally! Arguments still rage as to which particular historical figure gave rise to the legend of the famous outlaw. Records from the 12th century suggest a number of possible candidates, including the Earl of Huntingdon.

Undeterred by the vague foundations upon which the legend is built, visitors still flock to see the great hollow tree which the outlaws purportedly used as a meeting place and as a cache for their supplies. **The Major Oak** is located about 10 minutes walk along the main track in the heart of the forest. This huge tree, which is not so much tall as broad, with its massive wooden crutches and supportive iron corsets presents a rather forlorn sight. There is no denying that it is at least 500 years old and some sources would claim it to be more than double that figure. Yet despite its appearance, the tree is still alive thanks to careful preservation. Recent tests have established that some parts of the tree have successfully taken to grafting, and one hopes that at some stage a whole colony of minor oaks may be produced.

EAST RETFORD   *Map 14 ref M12*

The town has grown in importance over the centuries, from the granting of its charter by Henry III in 1246, to the prosperity bought to it by the railway and canal links. Retford has a typical market square which is the hub of the town, and is dominated by the magnificent Town Hall. One of the town's most infamous visitors was the highwayman Dick Turpin and several historic inns still stand as a reminder of the old coaching days. Another man who 'stood and delivered' here in a more respectable fashion was John Wesley, who conducted many of his open air meetings in East Retford.

CHAPTER SIX
Eastern England

Guildhall, Lavenham

6

Eastern England

Essex

INTRODUCTION

Originally the land of the East Saxons, much of the southwest corner of Essex has now been engulfed by the London; indeed, the influence of the capital can be felt all over the county and it is now the home of many commuters. The northern bank of the Thames, which forms the county's southern boundary, and, in particular, Canvey Island are home to a formidable array of gas and oil installations and container ports. This somewhat dismal landscape gives a rather false impression of the rest of the county.

Although Chelmsford is the county town, it is Colchester, which proclaims to be the earliest recorded English town, that has the greater character. The old town of Harwich, now a major container port for northern Europe is well worth a visit and, in north Essex, there is the rather genteel Saffron Walden. Anyone exploring inland Essex should also take in the Stour Valley which has become known as Constable country.

Much of east Essex, around the banks of the rivers Crouch, Blackwater and Colne, is marshland and the sole preserve of waterfowl and small-boat sailors. There are also sandy beaches, particularly around Clacton-on-Sea, Frinton-on-Sea and Walton on the Naze, where there can also be found donkey rides and the usual seaside amusements.

COLCHESTER   *Map 11 ref Q18*

The ancient garrison and market town stands in the midst of rolling East Anglian countryside. Colchester is England's oldest recorded town, a settlement being established here as far back as the 7th century BC. To the west of the town are the remains of the massive earthworks which protected pre-Roman Colchester. During the 1st century the town was the capital of the southeast and an obvious target for the invading Romans. In AD 60 Queen Bodicea carved her name in the annals of history by sacking the town and destroying its glorious temple before her uprising was crushed; an attack that led to the building of the town walls. The oldest part of the town is still surrounded by those Roman walls, which include the huge **Balkerne Gate**, the west gate of the Roman town, magnificent to this day.

When the Normans arrived, Colchester (a name coined by the Saxons) was an important borough and they built their tremendous castle on the foundations of the Roman temple of Claudius. Later occupations are marked by the houses of the Flemish weavers in the Dutch Quarter to the west of the castle and the Civil War scars visible on the walls of Siege House on East Street. Today, the town is presided over by its lofty town hall and an enormous Victorian **Water Tower** nicknamed Jumbo. Jumbo was the name of London Zoo's first African elephant controversially sold to circus owner, Phineas Barnum, in 1882. The tower, its four massive pillars made of one and a quarter million bricks, 369 tons of stone and 142 tons of iron supporting a 230,000 gallon tank, was named in his honour.

Colchester was once famed for its oysters and roses. There is still an annual Oyster Feast, a civic banquet worthy of Royal patronage, and the annual Colchester Rose Show. The famous Colchester Oysters are still cultivated on beds in the lower reaches of the River Colne, which skirts the northern edge of the town

There is plenty to see and explore in the town and there can be no better place to start than the **Castle** and its museum. The Normans built the castle on the site of the temple of the Emperor Claudius using many Roman bricks in its construction. The keep, the largest ever built in Europe, is the only part still standing and now houses the **Castle Museum**, which contains an interesting collection of Iron Age, Roman and medieval relics.

Behind the High Street, to the west of the castle, is the Dutch Quarter, a charming and quiet corner of this bustling town. Dutch Protestants arrived here in the 16th century, forced to flee the Spanish rule in the Netherlands, and revitalised the local cloth industry and creating their own prosperous corner of the town.

Close to the castle, on East Hill, is **Hollytrees Museum**, which is a fine Georgian House that houses a wonderful collection of costumes and antiquities. It opened as a museum after it was purchased for the town by Viscount Cowdray in 1920. Almost across the road from Hollytrees is the **Natural History Museum**, whose exhibits illustrate the natural history of Essex and which is situated in the former All Saints' Church. Housing the museum here saved the church, with its fine flint tower, from demolition in 1958. Another former church houses the **Museum of Social History**. This interesting museum contains historical displays of rural crafts and country life. Its home, the historic church of Holy Trinity in Trinity Street, is the only Saxon building left in the town. An arch opposite the church leads to Tymperleys, once the home of William Gilberd, who entertained Elizabeth I with experiments in electricity, and today houses a magnificent collection of antique clocks; nearby in West Stockwell Street lived the Taylor sisters, writers of *Twinkle, Twinkle, Little Star*.

Close to Colchester Town railway station are the ruins of **St Botolph's Priory**. The priory was a victim of the long siege of Colchester during the Civil War, when the Royalists, who held out for 11 weeks, were finally starved into submission. On Bourne Road to the south of the town centre is Bourne Mill. This rather striking stepped and curved gabled building is constructed of stone taken from the nearby St John's Abbeygate and was built in 1591. Originally a fishing lodge, it was converted into a mill in the 19th century and is still in working order.

Colchester Zoo, just off the A12 outside the town, stands in the 40 acre park of Stanway Hall, with its 16th century mansion and church dating from the 14th century. Founded in 1963, it has a wide and exciting variety of attractions including an aquarium, birdland, all the breeds of big cat and a model railway, as well as the opportunity to meet the penguins and, for the brave, the chance to wear a snake!

HARWICH

Map 11 ref R18

The town's name probably originates from the time of King Alfred, when 'Here' meant army and 'Wic' a camp. This attractive old town was built in the 13th century by the Earls of Norfolk to exploit its strategic position on the Stour and Orwell estuary and the town has an important seafaring history which continues today. During the 14th and 15th century French campaigns it was an important naval base. The ship which carried the Pilgrim Fathers to America in 1620, *The Mayflower*, was a frequent visitor and its Captain Christopher Jones lived in Kings Head Street. The famous diarist Samuel Pepys was MP for the town in the 1660s.

High Lighthouse

With all this rich history it's perhaps no surprise that the town has a fascinating maritime heritage trail which takes visitors around the old town. Highlights of the trail include the **High** and **Low Lighthouses** dating from 1818; when in line they indicated the safe shipping channel into the harbour. They replaced wooden structures and, in 1862, were themselves replaced when the shifting sandbanks altered the channel. Both are rather unusual designs; the Low lighthouse is now the town's **Maritime Museum**, and the 90 foot and nine sided High lighthouse is now a private residence. These two were replaced by iron structures, one of which still stands on the front at Dovercourt just along the coast. Shipping now relies on light buoys to find its way.

Today the **Treadwheel Crane** stands on Harwich Green, but for over 250 years it was sited in the Naval Shipyard. It is worked by two men walking in two 16 foot diameter wheels and is the only known example. Amazingly it only fell into disuse in the 1920s. The importance of the port during the 19th century is confirmed by **The Redoubt**, a huge grey fort that was built between 1808 and 1810. Its design is an enlarged version of the Martello towers which dotted the English coast awaiting a Napoleonic invasion which never came. Today the Harwich Society has largely restored it and it is open as a museum.

The old town also contains many ancient buildings, including the Guildhall which was rebuilt in 1769 and has graffiti, probably carved by prisoners when it was used as a gaol, and is well worth putting an afternoon aside to explore. Another fascinating piece of the town's history is the **Electric Palace Cinema**, built in 1911, and now the oldest unaltered purpose built cinema in Britain. It was restored by a trust and re-opened in 1981.

WALTON ON THE NAZE   *Map 11 ref R18*

The town's seafront was developed in the 1800s and provides a fine illustration of the character of an early Victorian seaside resort. The shape of the Naze is constantly changing, eroded by wind, water and tide: 1796 saw the demise of the medieval church and somewhere beyond the 800 foot pier lies medieval Walton and much of the naze or headland. Inhabitants have been enjoying the bracing sea air at Walton since before Neolithic times, flint-shaping instruments have been found here, and fossil teeth and ears of sharks and whales have been discovered in the red crag cliffs.

During the 19th century Walton was a source of seaholly for making love potions but, today, offers donkeys, deckchairs and amusements on the pier. The large, windowless and rather grim looking edifice on the highest point of the Naze is **Trinity House Tower**, built in 1720 to warn shipping of the treacherous offshore West Rocks.

CHELMSFORD   *Map 7 ref P19*

Roman workmen cutting their great road linking London with Colchester built a fort at what is today called Chelmsford. Then called Caesaromagus, it stands at the confluence of the Rivers Chelmer and Can. The town has always been an important market centre and is now the bustling county town of Essex. It is also directly descended from a new town planned by the Bishop of London in 1199. At its centre are the principal inn, the Royal Saracen's Head, and the elegant Shire Hall of 1792.

It was John Johnson, the distinguished local architect who designed both the Shire Hall and the bridge over the River Can and who also rebuilt the parish Church of St Mary when most of its 15th century tower fell down. The church became a **Cathedral** when the new diocese of Chelmsford was created in 1913.

The Marconi Company, pioneers in the manufacture of wireless equipment, set up the first radio company in the world here in 1899. Exhibits of those pioneering days of wireless can be seen in the **Chelmsford and Essex Museum** in Oaklands Park, as can interesting displays of Roman remains and local history.

SAFFRON WALDEN   *Map 10 ref P18*

The town was named after the Saffron crocus, which was grown in the area to make dyestuffs in the Middle Ages. A great deal of the street plan of the town from those times survives as do hundreds of fine buildings, many timbered with overhanging upper floors and decorative plastering (pargeting). Gog and Magog (or perhaps folk hero Tom Hickathrift and the Wisbech Giant) battle in plaster forever on the gable of the Old Sun Inn, where, legend has it, Oliver Cromwell and General Fairfax both lodged during the Civil War.

On the local Common, once Castle Green, is the largest surviving turf maze in England. Only eight ancient turf mazes survive in England: though there were many more in the Middle Ages, but if they are not looked after they soon become overgrown and lost.

Though many miles from the sea Henry Winstanley, born here in 1644, is said to have held trials with a wooden lantern in the lavishly decorated 15th–16th century church, before building the first Eddystone Lighthouse; which was lost with him in a fierce storm in 1703. At the **Town Museum**, as well as the gloves worn by Mary Queen of Scots on the day she died, is a piece of human skin which once coated the church door at Hadstock.

The town was also famous for its resident Cockatrice, which was hatched from a cock's egg by a toad or serpent and could kill its victims with a glance. The Cockatrice was blamed for any inexplicable disasters in the town. Like Perseus and Medusa the Gorgon, a Cockatrice could be destroyed by making it see its own reflection thereby turning it to stone. The Saffron Walden Cockatrice's slayer was said to be a knight in a coat of 'cristal glass'.

Audley End House was, at one time, home of the 1st Earl of Suffolk and the original house, with its two large courtyards, had a magnificence claimed to match Hampton Court. Unfortunately the subsequent earls lacked his financial acumen and much of the house was demolished as it fell into disrepair. Today it still remains one of England's most impressive Jacobean mansions; its distinguished stone façade set off perfectly by Capability Brown's lake. The remaining state rooms still retain their palatial magnificence and the exquisite state bed in the Neville Room is still hung with the original embroidered drapes.

In the rolling parkland grounds are several elegant outbuildings, some of which were designed by Robert Adam. Amongst these are an icehouse, a circular temple and a Springwood Column. A popular miniature steam railway runs in the grounds and certainly anyone visiting this corner of Essex should make time to stop and take in this wonderful house which reflects the rise and fall of the aristocratic country mansion perfectly.

Just to the north of Saffron Walden lies **Hadstock** and, as well as claiming to have the oldest church door in England, this village also has a macabre tale to tell. The church's north door was once covered with a piece of human skin, now to be seen in Saffron Walden Museum. Local legend says it is a 'Daneskin', from a Viking flayed alive.

Lining doors with animal leather was common in the Middle Ages and many so called 'Daneskins' are just that. However, the skins at Hadstock and at Copford also in Essex are almost certainly human, the poor wretch at Hadstock undoubtedly having his hide nailed there as a warning to others. The door itself is Saxon, as are the 11th century carvings, windows and arches, rare survivors that predates the Norman Conquest.

Hertfordshire

INTRODUCTION

Hertfordshire has for many years been dominated by London which lies to the south. Supplying the capital with food and the space for fine country residences for centuries, in the 20th century, the influence of London has become even greater. Few can approach the capital from the north without passing through Hertfordshire as not only does the M1 motorway traverse the county so does the A1, Watling Street, the A10 to Cambridgeshire and the Grand Union Canal to say nothing of the railway links.

At the turn of this century, London was expanding to such a degree that the need for further housing, and the space for it, was becoming acute. Hertfordshire was chosen as the site for the famous 'garden cities' of Letchworth and Welwyn Garden City, the forerunners of today's 'new towns' of which the county has three; Stevenage, Hemel Hempstead and Hatfield. The county town of St Albans, with its cathedral and many Roman sites, is quite a contrast to the planned towns of the 20th century.

ST ALBANS   *Map 6 ref N19*

Dominating the skyline from every direction, the magnificent Norman Abbey stands proudly above the city. A wonderful blend of the old with the new, it was built on the site of a Saxon abbey and was designated as a **Cathedral** in 1877.

There is much to see and do in this lovely city and the **Verulamium Museum** is an excellent place to start. Standing on the site of one of Roman Britain's major cities, the museum provides a fascinating insight into life during Roman times, with ceramics, mosaic walls and personal possessions displayed in an authentic Roman setting. On Hatfield Road, the **Museum of St Albans** relates the interesting history of the city from Roman times to present day. Among the exhibits is the famous Salaman Collection of trade and craft tools, considered the finest of its kind in Britain. At **St Albans Organ Museum** visitors can enjoy the stirring sounds of an amazing collection of working mechanical musical instruments including two theatre organs, musical boxes and reproducing pianos all lovingly restored.

The remains of the Roman Walls, the hypocaust and the site of the London Gate to the city can all be seen in the peaceful oasis of **Verulamium Park**.

BERKHAMSTEAD   *Map 6 ref N19*

It was here, two months after that Battle of Hastings, that the Saxons finally submitted to William of Normandy and it was shortly afterwards that building work began on the Norman **Castle**. Built close to the river, the ruins are still visible today. Although not many of the original buildings of the town remain, one that is particularly attractive is Dean John Incent's jettied house, an impressive black and white timbered building situated on the High Street. Dean Incent was the founder of the original Grammar School built in 1554 which has since been incorporated into Berkhamstead School.

HITCHIN   *Map 10 ref O18*

This medieval market town still retains many old buildings among the newer developments. One such building is the **Priory** which was built in 1770–7 by Robert Adam for the Radcliffe family. Also worth of a mention is **The Biggin**, a building erected during the 17th century on the site of a Gilbertine Priory. Having been successively a private residence and a school, in 1723 it became an almshouse for "poore auncient or middle aged women", a function which in modern terms it still performs today.

During medieval times Hitchin had a vast market area where straw was purchased for the local cottage industry of straw plaiting and where completed plaits were sold. Gradually the area was reduced, giving way to more permanent premises and today only a small market place west of the Parish Church remains.

BISHOP'S STORTFORD   *Map 10 ref P18*

During the 18th century this delightful rural town prospered as a market centre. A major coaching town on the route from London to Norwich, its two main industries were malting and brewing. Its name is believed to have been derived from two sources: the River Stort provides the 'Stortford' and the 'Bishop' was added in Norman times, the Domesday Book recording that the Bishop of London was Lord of the Manor here in 1087.

There is a wealth of history within the town and it was here, in 1853, that Cecil Rhodes was born. After leaving in 1870, Rhodes went to South Africa where he found fame and fortune as the founder of the famous Kimberley Diamond Mines. One of Bishop Stortford's most famous inhabitants, his former home Nettleswell House has now become the **Rhodes Memorial Museum** with displays detailing his life story.

HATFIELD   *Map 10 ref O19*

This historic old town grew up around the gateway to the Palace of the Abbot and Bishop of Ely. This is now the site of **Hatfield House**, an impressive Jacobean house built between 1607 and 1611 by Robert Cecil, 1st Earl of Salisbury who was Chief Minister to James I. The elaborate architecture of the building is equalled by the exquisite interior, with a world famous collection of beautiful tapestries and paintings complementing ornate wood panelling and splendid antique furniture.

The new town, created after World War II, was built to help solve the acute housing shortage in London following the destruction of much of the capital by German bombers.

Bedfordshire

INTRODUCTION

One of England's smaller counties, Bedfordshire is essentially arable farming country although it also lies within easy commuting distance from London. The Great Ouse winds its way across the northern area of Bedfordshire, looping around many ancient villages, and it was in the river valley that a lace industry was developed in the 16th century.

The county town, Bedford, also sits on the banks of the river and is proud of its links with John Bunyan who used many places in the county in his great work Pilgrim's Progress. To the west of Bedford lies the seat of the Dukes of Bedford, Woburn Abbey which is now also home to Europe's largest drive-in safari park.

To the south, and close to the M1 motorway, are the industrial towns of Luton and Dunstable. Both were once important centres for the manufacture of straw hats and they, and the surrounding area, are very different from the rural northern half of the county.

BEDFORD   *Map 10 ref N17*

This bustling county town is very proud of its most famous son, John Bunyan, whose statue stands at the northern end of the High Street. Bunyan was born in Elstow, just to the south, and he followed his father to become a tinsmith. During the Civil War, at the age of 16, he was drafted into the Parliamentarian Army and was very much affected by the ferment of religious ideas characteristic of those unsettled times. In the 1650s, Bunyan met John Gifford, who had been appointed pastor of an independent congregation, which Bunyan joined. Gifford is commonly taken to be the model for Evangelist, in *Pilgrim's Progress*, who asks Christian, "Do you see yonder shining light?" and sends him off to "keep that light in your eye".

Bunyan was baptised by Gifford in the River Ouse and later became a preacher, travelling round the villages of Bedfordshire. This brought him into conflict with the authorities and he was imprisoned in Bedford for 12 years. The successor of the barn in which Bunyan preached to his congregation is the **Bunyan Meeting House**, in Mill Street. It was built in 1850 and the interior has been restored and remodelled; the bronze doors making an impressive entrance. In the Church buildings is the **Bunyan Museum**, which has collections of Bunyan's personal belongings, relics associated with his life and a collection of some 200 copies of *Pilgrim's Progress* in many translations.

WOBURN   *Map 10 ref N18*

The village has retained many Georgian houses and attractive shop fronts, built in warm red brick which gives the streets a cheerful air. The church is a grand Victorian building that was constructed in a 12th century French style in 1868. Part of the old church still stands in the High Street and is now used as a visitors centre.

The Abbey from which **Woburn Abbey** takes its name was a daughter community of the Cistercian Abbey at Fountains in Yorkshire, founded in 1145. After the dissolution of the monasteries under Henry VIII it was granted, in 1547, to the 1st Earl of Bedford. Elements of the present house go back to about 1630, but what is seen today is almost all 18th century. The house contains an extremely important art collection, English and French 18th century furniture and a famous dinner service made at Sevres. The 3000 acres deer park was landscaped by Sir Humphrey Repton and within it some 300 acres are set aside as a **Wild Animal Kingdom and Leisure Park**.

Suffolk

INTRODUCTION

Although some of the county has become the preserve of the London commuter, much of Suffolk is still the beautiful farming countryside that is associated with the wonderful Suffolk Punch breed of heavy horse. The coastline, home to many idyllic seaside resorts of character and charm, also has a commercial side with Felixstowe, a busy container port as well as a seaside resort, and the fishing port of Lowestoft. The northern coast is studded with Martello towers, marshes and numerous bird sanctuaries.

England

Although there is some splendid scenery in the county, in particular the area around the Stour valley and the heathland of Breckland, Suffolk has some wonderful, old towns that are well worth taking the time to visit. The jewel in the crown is most certainly Lavenham, a former wool town that has changed little since it was built in medieval times. The three mile long High Street in Long Melford follows the route of an ancient Roman road passed a particularly beautiful church. Bury St Edmunds is also attractive and its ruined abbey can be found in lovely gardens and, of course, Suffolk is also home to the headquarters of British horse racing. Newmarket is a town like no other, though not especially attractive overall, it is totally dominated by the horse and there are even special walks for the strings which take the horses from the many stables in the town to the open heathland and the gallops.

BURY ST EDMUNDS   *Map 11 ref Q13*

Widely held to be a jewel of Suffolk's towns, Bury St Edmunds is rich in archaeological treasures and places of great historical interest. It has long been known as one of the least spoilt towns in England; a reputation that has been greatly enhanced by the building of the A45 by-pass.

The town takes its name from St Edmund, who was born in Nuremberg in 841 and arrived on these shores 14 years later to become King of East Anglia. He was a renowned soldier and a fervent Christian. The latter was to prove his undoing, for when he was captured by the Danes in 870 he refused to deny his Christianity and was brutally murdered by being tied to a tree, shot full of arrows and beheaded. At this point, legend mingles with fact, for it is said that although his body was recovered, his head could not be found. His men searched desperately for it for 40 days, then heard his voice directing them to it from the depths of a wood, where they discovered it lying protected between the paws of a wolf. When the head was taken back to his body they were miraculously joined, with no apparent signs of damage. To commemorate the wolf's benign influence, the crest of the town's armorial bearings depicts a wolf with a man's head.

Edmund was buried first at Hoxne, the site of his martyrdom, but when he was canonised some 30 years later his remains were transferred to the monastery at what was then called Beodricksworth. The town changed its name to St Edmundsbury and a shrine was built here in his honour, later to be incorporated into the Normans' Abbey Church after the monastery was granted abbey status by King Canute in 1032.

All that remains of the abbey and its church today are the romantic ruins which stand within the beautiful municipal park known as the **Abbey Gardens**. These can be reached from the broad thoroughfare (or medieval 'square') called Angel Hill by going through the superb Abbey Gate. This was originally built for defensive purposes and once led into the monastery courtyard.

Angel Hill itself is full of interest. Firstly, there is the impressive Norman Tower, the original gateway to the Abbey Church which was built by Abbot Anselm in the 12th century. It now serves as a belfry for the cathedral church of St James which stands alongside. St James's was rebuilt in the 16th century and was elevated to the status of cathedral when the diocese of St Edmundsbury and Ipswich was created in 1914. To the south on Crown Street is the 15th century St Mary's Church, renowned for its wonderful oak roof and famous as the burial place of Henry VIII's sister, Mary Tudor. To the west is the **Athenaeum**, the centre of Bury's social life in Regency times, and the place where Charles Dickens gave two of his stirring public readings. He also stayed at the adjacent Angel Hotel, which was to be immortalised as the place where Mr Pickwick learns of the intended lawsuit against him by the 'spurned' Mrs Bardell.

The lovely Abbey Gardens were created in 1831, their central feature being a one acre circle filled with flower beds, set out along the lines of the Royal Botanic Gardens in Brussels. This had been transferred to its new site from Nathaniel Hodson's original garden to the east of the Abbey Churchyard, and it is estimated that some 2,000 plants were used. This botanic garden was conceived strictly as a scientific establishment, with native flowers and herbs laid out in their botanical orders; but ornamental plants were later introduced so that the fee-paying public could take over the financing of the project.

No visitor should miss the opportunity of taking a leisurely stroll along Abbeygate Street, which leads up from Angel Hill and features a fascinating and diverse variety of old shop fronts. Past the Victorian Corn Exchange on The Traverse is the charming Nutshell which claims to be the smallest pub in England and belies its name by offering large-scale hospitality. Further along is the handsome Cupola House, a fine old inn that was built in 1693 and reputedly numbered Daniel Defoe amongst its guests. At the end of The Traverse and facing Cornhill is the Market Cross, originally built as a market hall and theatre combined (note the telltale masks of tragedy and comedy), later to become the town hall, and now housing an art gallery on its upper storey.

Moyses Hall Museum in the Butter Market is said to be the oldest stone domestic building in England. Although its precise origins are unclear, it is thought to have been built sometime around 1180; of flint and limestone in a town whose secular buildings were strictly made of wood. The fact that these materials would have been transported from quarries more than 70 miles away implies that whoever it was built for must have been a person of no small distinction. The Hall has served various functions over the centuries; it has been a prison and a workhouse, a police station and a railway office, and in 1899 it became the Borough museum—which it remains to this day.

For horologists, the **Manor House Museum** on Honey Hill is devoted to timepieces of all shapes and sizes; from clocks and watches to sundials and a replica of a 15th century planetarium. Around 200 exhibits from the Gershom

Parkington Collection are displayed, formerly housed at the Clock Museum on Angel Hill, and, in addition, there are some fine works of art by such painters as James Tissot and Joshua Reynolds.

Not far from here, at the junction of Crown Street and Westgate Street, evidence of Regency patronage can be seen in the handsome architecture of the **Theatre Royal**, now in the care of the National Trust, though still a working theatre. It was built in 1819 by William Wilkins (also the architect of the National Gallery) and can claim the distinction of being the first theatre in the world to premiere *Charley's Aunt*, apparently before an audience of five!

NEWMARKET   *Map 11 ref P17*

This is, of course, the headquarters of British horse racing and bloodstock breeding, with two of the most famous racecourses in the world. On either side of the town are four square miles of land used to train the horses who have such vast amounts of cash hanging on their performances. There are something like 60 training stables and 50 stud farms within the area, and Newmarket is without doubt the premier place to purchase pure bred racehorses in Britain.

It is said that Bodicea herself enjoyed the spirit of horse racing, although the shaggy ponies that pulled the ancient Iceni chariots are a far cry from the long-legged equine beauties that grace the paddocks of Newmarket today. The **National Horse Racing Museum** in the High Street is a tribute to the men and the rules that have fashioned this modern 300 year old sport, and most importantly to the horses themselves—without whom none of it would be possible. Founded in 1752, the **Jockey Club** building (erected in 1882) stands in the High Street. The governing body of horse racing in Britain, the Club is next to the museum.

It is likely that Newmarket has the only racecourse in the world which is haunted. A phantom rider has often been spotted joining his colleagues on the turf, occasionally making the other horses shy. Jockeys say that the spirit is obviously taking part in the races, as it tends to keep well up in front with the leaders! Some reckon that it could be the ghost of Fred Archer, who won the Derby on four occasions before his tragic death in 1886 at the age of 29.

James I is thought to have been the first monarch to enjoy the sporting grounds of the heathland surrounding the town; he was so taken by it that he chose to revisit the town on many occasions to watch the hare coursing events. But it was Charles II who firmly established Newmarket as the place for horse racing, taking part in many races himself. His mistress Nell Gwynne used to stay at a house in Palace Street which can still be seen today. Newmarket's largest racecourse is called The Rowley Mile, a tribute to Charles whose favourite horse was a stallion called Old Rowley—a name also used by the king himself when he went off on his nocturnal adventures! Another famous lady associated with

Newmarket was the actress who dominated the Victorian stage, Lillie Langtry. She owned the house in Gazeley Road which is now the Langtry Hotel.

LAVENHAM

Map 11 ref Q17

This jewel in Suffolk's crown proudly claims to be the finest surviving medieval town in England. Considerable care has been taken to ensure that the medieval character of this lovely wool trading town has remained unspoiled by modern developments. From the 14th to 16th centuries, Lavenham flourished as one of the foremost and wealthiest wool and cloth making centres in the country, specialising in blue broadcloth. The demise of this industry and the steady decline in the town's fortunes began in the second half of the 16th century and, ironically, it is largely due to the fact that Lavenham never found another industry to reverse its fall from prosperity that it remains such an attractive and fascinating town today. Unlike other places in Suffolk that saw an energetic programme of rebuilding and redevelopment during the 18th century, there is no sweeping evidence of a Georgian invasion as far as Lavenham's architecture is concerned—it was simply not rich enough at that time to make such a thing possible.

And so, centuries later, it stays a delightful medieval and Tudor town which has remained almost untouched by later styles; firmly rooted in its ancient traditions, yet at the same time no mouldering museum piece but a thriving little town with much to offer today's visitors. The residents here have gone to great lengths to maintain the original character of the town: telegraph poles were removed in 1967 and cables buried underground, and even such familiar sights as television aerials have been hidden away in the attics of the houses!

Lavenham's medieval street pattern is still in existence today, complete with the market place and market cross; erected in 1501 and thought to have originally been a preaching cross. This was used as a setting in that wonderful old horror film: *Witchfinder General*. Although the market place is almost entirely surrounded by timber-framed buildings (Lavenham has more than 300 buildings which are officially listed as being of architectural and historical interest) perhaps the finest of them all is the **Guildhall**. Dating from the early part of the 16th century, this was originally the meeting hall of the Guild of Corpus Christi, an organisation that regulated the production of local wool. It has since served many purposes, and has at various times been a prison, workhouse, almshouse and woolstore. It is now owned by the National Trust and houses a museum of local history, with a fascinating exhibition covering seven centuries of the cloth industry.

Also in the market place is the **Little Hall**, a 15th century former Hall House and now headquarters of the Suffolk Preservation Society. Both the house and its lovely enclosed garden are open to the public during the summer. Dating back originally to the 13th century, **The Priory**, in Water Street, was first the home of Benedictine monks, and was bought by a wealthy clothier after the Dissolution. The entire building as seen today was completed by 1600. It contains medieval and Jacobean staircases, a Tudor brick fireplace, mullioned windows and the best examples of pargeting to be found anywhere in the town.

Across the road, the **Wool Hall** was built in 1464 and was originally the hall of Our Lady's Guild. It now forms part of the splendid Swan Hotel, but was nearly lost altogether in 1911 when the Duchess of Argyll decided to up timbers, dismantle the entire building and remove it to Ascot. Local feeling ran so high that the plan was abandoned and the hall was returned to the town and re-erected in its rightful place. Lavenham also has its connections with the Arts: John Constable attended the Old Grammar School in Barn Street and Shilling Grange in Shilling Street was once the home of Jane Taylor. Her name may not ring any bells at first, until you learn that she wrote that immortal nursery rhyme, familiar to us all, *Twinkle Twinkle Little Star*.

LONG MELFORD   *Map 11 ref Q17*

This small town could not be more aptly named; its tree-lined main street seems to go on and on, covering a distance of 3 miles in all. A lot of visitors come here specifically to browse around Melford's surprisingly large number of antique shops, most of which lie dotted about the main street with its timber-framed and Georgian houses.

Overlooking the green is **Melford Hall**, built during the 1570s and once used by the Abbot of Bury St Edmunds as his country retreat, where he could enjoy venison from the deer park. Now a National Trust property, this mellow red-brick house with its 'pepperpot' towers is full of fine paintings, furniture and porcelain for the public to enjoy; but what interested us especially was the charming collection of water colours by Beatrix Potter. She was related to the Parker family who bought the house in the 18th century and somehow her pictures seem more quintessentially English than those of our greatest landscape painters!

EAST BERGHOLT   *Map 11 ref R18*

John Constable was born in this pretty, scattered village in 1776, and if it has now geared itself ever so slightly to cater for Constable-mania, who can blame it? The actual house in which the painter was born no longer stands, but its site is marked by a plaque on the fence of its successor, now a private house called Constables. A little further along Church Street is the tiny Moss Cottage, which Constable once used as a studio.

It was at the Old Rectory that he first met his future wife, Maria Bicknell. There is a memorial to her at **St Mary's Church**, together with a somewhat garish stained glass memorial window to Constable himself, and his parents and his old friend Willy Lott are buried in the churchyard. The unusual timber-framed structure in the churchyard is a bell-cage, built in 1531 and a memorial of sorts to Cardinal Wolsey. He had apparently pledged money to the church for a bell tower and the cage was intended as a temporary resting place for the bells until its completion. When Wolsey fell from grace and the funds were not forthcoming, the tower was left unfinished and the bells have been in their cage ever since. They hang upside-down and are rung by hand by pulling on the wooden shoulder stocks; no mean feat, as these five bells are said to be the heaviest in England.

Flatford Mill

A leafy lane leads south of the village to the River Stour, where two of Constable's best known subjects still stand today, looking just as they did when he first painted them. The first is **Flatford Mill**, the brick watermill owned by Constable's father, built in 1733 and now owned by the National Trust and run as a residential field study centre. A little way downstream is the charming **Willy Lott's Cottage**, subject of Constable's most famous work, *The Haywain*, and also maintained by the National Trust. Neither is open to the casual visitor, but there is a way-marked trail laid out by the Trust along the banks of the river for memorable views of cottage, mill, lock and weir. Under Flatford Bridge, a replacement for the bridge that Constable painted many times, is Bridge Cottage, with a National Trust shop, a tea garden and a permanent exhibition of the painter's life and works. There are also facilities for boating and fishing.

Exploring this delightful area around the banks of the willow-lined river, it is with the knowledge that here, too, Constable walked, sketchbook in hand, drawing constant inspiration from the idyllic riverside scenery. He would return here many times after he had moved to London to become a student at the Royal Academy, and much of his greatest work was done in this rural setting.

Also at East Bergholt are **Stour Gardens**, where sweeping lawns, colourful flower beds and small ponds are laid out neatly below Stour House, former home of the journalist and author Randolph Churchill, son of Sir Winston. The gardens are open daily.

Norfolk

INTRODUCTION

Relatively isolated from the rest of the country, Norfolk is as close to Amsterdam as it is to London, this flat county is given over, in the most part, to efficient and prosperous arable farming. To the west lie the fenlands of Cambridgeshire and in the north there is the great inland port of King's Lynn on the Great Ouse. Here, too is the royal estate of Sandringham. The coastline is dotted with small harbours, saltmarshes and mudflats and at one small village, Burnham Thorpe, one of the country's greatest naval heroes, Lord Nelson, was born and brought up.

The county is also well know for its **Broads**, a fascinating area with a wide variety of wildlife that offers remoteness and tranquillity. This landscape has developed over the years and is a delicate balance between man's use of the land and changing natural conditions. In medieval Norfolk, the thriving peat digging industry left huge pits in the land and, as the sea level rose, these pits flooded and created the shallow lakes, known today as the Broads.

Two thirds of Norfolk is drained by the main Broads' rivers and, with over 120 miles of waterways, boats have always been an important form of transport. Each village here has a staithe, or quay, for mooring and the Broads even had its own style of boat: the single-sailed wherries. These shallow-draught boats, specially built for the shallow waters of the area delivered their cargoes of corn, coal, reed and sedge to the villagers.

There are few towns of any size in Norfolk but **Norwich**, the county town, is a lively and exciting city whose unique character has, in the main, been sensitively preserved. The earliest reference to Norwich is on coins struck during the reign of King Athelstan, as far back as AD 930. By the time of the Norman Conquest, some 130 years later, it was one of the largest towns in England. The great 12th century Norman **Castle** is one of the city's landmarks and the **Cathedral** is the other. Dating from the 11th century, the cathedral's history is a turbulent one, with fires, riots and natural disasters all inflicting damage to one degree or another. Fortunately, it has survived and remains today one of England's finest cathedrals.

KING'S LYNN   *Map 10 ref P14*

Situated on the eastern bank of the River Great Ouse at the southernmost end of The Wash, King's Lynn is Norfolk's third largest town. For centuries this ancient seaport was the gateway to the Midlands and an important trade-link with the Continent. First mentioned in the Domesday Book as the harbour of Lena (from the Celtic word 'lindo', meaning lake), it became known as Lynn Episcopi or Bishop's Lynn during the Middle Ages when the town was officially founded by Herbert de Losinga, the first bishop of Norwich. In 1537, after the Dissolution of the Monasteries, Henry VIII firmly quashed this ecclesiastical association by granting it a charter and it took on its present name of Lynn Regis, or King's Lynn.

A previous charter had been granted by King John who visited the town in 1205 and it was on the occasion of his later visit in 1216, prior to his final trip to Newark, that he 'lost his jewels in the Wash'. When travelling between his estates King John tended to take many of his personal treasures with him and, after enjoying the local hospitality here in September of 1216, he decided to carry on to Swineshead. As his convoy traversed the estuary between Cross Keys and Long Sutton, the tide swept in unexpectedly quickly and the royal wagons became embroiled in the treacherous quicksands. An historical event that has caused much merriment in history lessons at school, sounding as it does like an unfortunate mishap in the launderette.

Over on the Lincolnshire border, the King must have lost much of his spirit as he witnessed his beloved treasure sinking below the waters. The Crown Jewels, his formal regalia, goblets and candelabra, his coronation robe and the Sword of Tristram given to him by his grandmother all disappeared within a matter of minutes. Presumably, these treasures still lie out at sea waiting for some lucky diver to recover them and, to add insult to injury, poor John contracted dysentery whilst in the town and later died at Newark. An alternative story claims that he fell ill at Swineshead after being given a dish of peaches and new ale and some believe he was poisoned by a monk who had heard that the King intended to raise the price of bread.

The heart of King's Lynn encapsulates the Georgian era with many charming houses from that period but it retains the feel of a much older harbour town. Architectural treasures such as the National Trust owned **St George's Guildhall** can be seen in King Street; it is distinctively built of flint in a chequer-board design and is reputedly the oldest hall in England, built around 1406. Shakespeare is said to have performed here and this splendid building is still used for civic functions today.

Other architectural highlights to look out for include the handsome Custom House, built in 1683 on the banks of the Purfleet, and the magnificent 15th century South Gates which stand proud at the entrance to the town. Buildings such as these, together with its many fascinating warehouses and narrow streets, all add to the charm of King's Lynn. Though it is by no means a pretty town, thanks to the efforts of the King's Lynn Preservation Trust, many of the town's more interesting buildings have been saved.

Just to the north of King's Lynn, in the village of **Dersingham**, the Church of St Nicholas has some impressive tombs and a remarkable carved chest of great antiquity, decorated with the symbols of the Evangelists. The ancient gabled tithe barn opposite the church dates back to 1671 and is now used by the county council as a storehouse for fragments from historic buildings.

The Gamekeeper's Lodge and **Dersingham Hotel**, in Chapel Road, is a truly charming establishment with plenty of character and a friendly, relaxed atmosphere. Refurbished in the last few years, the Lodge has a wonderful countrified feel, making it a splendid place to stop off for a drink and a meal. Since coming here six years ago, Margaret, Dick, their daughter Mandy and son Allan, have established an excellent reputation. The five separate restaurants, including a magnificent carvery restaurant that can seat over 300 diners, offer an excellent

Gamekeepers Lodge and Dersingham Hotel

international menu featuring a superb range of fish, meat, poultry and vegetarian dishes. Interesting and imaginative, there is always something to catch the eye and tickle the tastebuds. In addition to the restaurant fare, bar snacks and daily specials are also available and even though all the food is distinctly upmarket, the prices are very reasonable, though booking is advised at the weekends to avoid disappointment. There is a fine selection of wines to accompany the meal and for those looking for somewhere special to eat out as the highlight of the holiday, there is no need look further. To make things even better there are excellent facilities for the disabled and accommodation is available in six individually styled and decorated en-suite guest bedrooms and there is no doubt that these facilities are of the same high standard as the rest of this superb establishment. *Gamekeepers Lodge and Dersingham Hotel, Chapel Road, Dersingham, Norfolk PE31 6PJ Tel: 01485 543514*

Further east lies **Great Bircham** and while in the village, situated on the edge of the Sandringham Estate, it is certainly worth taking time out to visit **Bircham Windmill**, which can be found on the B1155 about half a mile outside the village heading towards Snettisham. This is undoubtedly one of Norfolk's finest corn mills and surrounded as it is by acres of unspoilt countryside, no one could not wish for a more beautiful setting. The mill has been in use since the 1700s and for those who are not afraid of heights, it is well worth climbing the five floors to see the milling machinery in action. It is certainly a long way to the top (and seems even further to the bottom!) but as the ascent is made there is something interesting to look at on every level.

Bircham Windmill

On the ground floor, there are video displays and plenty of information on the history of the mill and the working of the machinery. After scaling the heights of the mill, it is good to come back to earth and enjoy a pot of tea with home-made cakes in the tea rooms. No ordinary tea room either, but Egon Ronay recommended; and as they are separate from the mill they can be enjoyed at any time. While here, visitors can also peruse the Gift shop and choose from a fascinating selection of items connected with milling and baking. This is an ideal opportunity to pick up an unusual present for a friend or relative. In the old days, horse and cart was the mode of transport used by the miller and baker for their deliveries and two ponies are still kept in the stables today. A marvellous way of enjoying this peaceful countryside is by bike and cycle hire is available from the mill at hourly, daily and weekly rates. Day routes and traffic-free green lane routes are provided together with a range of bikes to suit all ages and requirements. Bircham Mill is open daily from Easter until the end of September. Free parking is available and coach parties are welcome by prior arrangement. There are numerous walks from the Mill itself with a guide that can be borrowed from the Bakery.

Bircham Windmill, Great Bircham, near King's Lynn, Norfolk PE31 6SJ
Tel: 01485 578393

HUNSTANTON *Map 11 P14*

Pronounced "Hunston", this is a charming Victorian seaside resort (the only one in East Anglia to face west, incidentally) with a fine sandy beach and rock pools and distinctive candy-striped cliffs. A layer of red chalk, then white and, finally, brown and yellow stone make these 60 foot high cliffs particularly interesting to geologists. At the northern end of the Promenade, next to the 1830 disused lighthouse, are the ruins of St Edmund's Chapel where Edmund, King of East Anglia, is reputed to have landed in AD 850.

The **Sea Life Centre** on the Promenade is a super place for children. The Ocean Tunnel gives visitors a unique opportunity to watch the varied and often weird forms of life that inhabit the British Isles without even getting wet! Many of these creatures can be observed and handled in the 'Living Touch' rock pools and there is also an exciting audiovisual presentation which tells the story of man's involvement with the oceans. The Centre is open throughout the year and will appeal to young and old alike.

Elegant villas overlook Hunstanton's green and, even though past glories such as the pier, the railway and the impressive Sandringham Hotel have disappeared, visitors are still left with a very pleasing impression of this gracious town. For hundreds of years the local gentry were the Le Strange family who did much to develop the town. Their residence was the handsome moated Tudor Hall to the south of St Mary's church in Old Hunstanton. The family's hereditary title was Lord High Admirals of The Wash, giving them the rights to anything washed up on the shore or found out to sea as far as they could ride a horse at low tide and throw a spear. No doubt they kept their fingers crossed that King John's jewels might reappear at some time!

Entertainment at Hunstanton is plentiful and varied; catering for visitors of all ages. During the summer months you can take a boat trip out to the sandbank in The Wash known as **Seal Island**, where seals can sometimes be spotted sunbathing at low tide.

Standing within its own attractive grounds beside Hunstanton golf links, the **Linksway Country House Hotel** enjoys one of the finest views in North Norfolk. English Tourist Board 3 Crowns Commended, the hotel has been owned and personally run by Margaret and John for the past four years and has 15 beautifully appointed bedrooms, two of which can be found on the ground floor and are convenient for those who have trouble with stairs. Each of the bedrooms have full en-suite facilities, colour TV, hair dryer and tea and coffee maker, whilst the hotel also has a four poster bedroom and two spacious family

The Linksway Country House Hotel

rooms. For guests' enjoyment there is an indoor heated swimming pool, comfortable and quiet lounge and a cosy licensed lounge bar. As well as magnificent views over the links, the restaurant offers first class cuisine, all freshly prepared using only the finest local ingredients by the excellent in-house chef. The hotel is open all year round and stands adjacent to the coastal Heritage walk and is within a two minutes walk of a beautiful sandy beach.

The Linksway Country House Hotel, Golf Course Road, Old Hunstanton, Norfolk PE36 6JE Tel: 01485 532209/532653

WELLS-NEXT-THE-SEA   *Map 11 ref Q13*

Very much a seaside town that has kept firmly to its origins, its working harbour gives it great character. The town's name, however, is something of a misnomer as the harbour now stands a mile from the sea beside a creek! The mile-long 'Embankment' was built in 1859 to prevent the harbour from silting up altogether and it provides a pleasant walk down to the sea. In addition to being the largest of North Norfolk's ports, Wells is also a popular resort.

Just to the east of the town the **Wells and Walsingham Steam Railway** takes passengers on a particularly lovely ride along the former Great Eastern Line with halts at Warham St Mary and Wighton. The Old Station for the Great Eastern Line at Wells has a charming restored signal box which now sells souvenirs and refreshments and the 1986 Garratt locomotive was built specifically for this railway.

One of the most interesting craft workshops in the area can be found in the Old Station at Wells-next-the-Sea, the home of the famous **Burnham Pottery**. Jan and Thom Borthwick started their pottery business in Burnham over a decade ago, but moved here as things expanded. They now produce a unique range of hand-made domestic and decorative pottery, including vases, large terracotta pots for the patio or garden and a delightful variety of animal figures including the immensely popular Burnham Colourful Cats. These charming feline characters have names like Ambrose, Bertram, Claudia and Amelia and are made

Burnham Pottery

in a variety of colours and poses. (One favourite is Everard, captured with a cheeky expression that all cat lovers will recognise). Another speciality of Burnham Pottery is their selection of hand-thrown items with a splash glaze; for collectors, they also produce a range of studio pottery with an attractive spongeware finish in limited edition. The Borthwicks have also managed to indulge their love of old and rare books, especially those with an emphasis on the eccentric and the humorous. Over the years they have accumulated a superb collection of secondhand titles which visitors are welcome to browse through and purchase.

Burnham Pottery, The Old Station, 2-4 Maryland Wells-next-the-Sea, Norfolk NR23 1LX Tel: 01328 710847

Burnham Market, to the west of Wells-next-the-Sea, is the largest of the, in all, seven Burnhams situated along the Burn valley, Burnham Market, encompassing Westgate, Sutton and Ulph, has some elegant 18th century houses.

Fishes Restaurant

The delightful **Fishes Restaurant** can be found in the Market Place, Burnham Market. This superb eating place specialises in fresh local seafood, including shellfish, shrimps from the Wash, lobster (when available), and fish landed on the beach at Holkham Bay. Starters include crab soup, smoked fish pate and oysters, as well as non-seafood dishes. There is also an impressive list of carefully selected wines. In the 24 years that proprietor Gillian Cape has run Fishes, she has built an enviable reputation for fine food and service. Her restaurant has a charming atmosphere, with comfortable cane furniture, attractive prints and paintings on the walls, and a fascinating collection of books. Do note that the restaurant is closed on Sunday evenings and all day Monday and it is advisable to book when in season or at weekends to avoid disappointment.

Fishes Restaurant, Market Place, Burnham Market, Norfolk PE31 8HE Tel: 01328 738588

Close by, **Burnham Overy Staithe** is a delightful place almost solely concerned with sailing: there is an annual regatta and facilities for windsurfing too. There is a restored tower mill, now a private residence, standing to the side of the main road just before entering the village. The attractive harbour, where boat trips to Scolt Head Island are available, lies in a creek some distance from the sea. Indeed, it could be said to have followed the sea northwards in a manner of speaking, as Overy Staithe was built after the sea receded from the original port of Burnham Overy. This lies a mile to the south on the B1155 and is now referred to as Burnham Overy Town.

A good stopping place for walkers and bird watchers, the impressive **Hero Inn** can be found on the main A149 at Burnham Overy Staithe, near the junction with East Harbour Way. This first rate pub and eating place has a warm friendly atmosphere, with old fashioned brasses and traditional hospitality. Owners Annie and Pat only purchased the Hero and the nearby caravan park after spending many years holidaying in the area. Since then they have built up an enviable reputation for serving the finest real ales and pub food in the district. Food is served from 12–2.30 pm and from 7–9 pm each day and is produced using only the freshest local ingredients with the house speciality being a magnificent Crab Salad that has always proved very popular with visitors. They also have a well appointed standing caravan available to let which sleeps six.

The Hero Inn

The Hero Inn, Wells Road, Burnham Overy Staithe, near King's Lynn, Norfolk PE31 8JE Tel: 01328 738334

South of Burnham lies **South Creake**, a pretty village of flint cottages with the River Burn flowing quietly alongside the main street. Some of the residents have to cross their own little wooden footbridges when entering and leaving their homes! Towering above the cottages in the centre of the village is one of South Creake's most interesting and incongruous sights: a truly hideous collection of dilapidated buildings that were originally built in the 1920s as a razor blade factory. The factory owner was George Theophilus Money, a London-born entrepreneur, whose business sense failed to live up to the expectations of his name. Though the key to success in selling razor blades lies in their inherent disposability, George would have none of this and, instead, he offered to sharpen his customers' old ones! Needless to say, his factory was not in business for very long.

A delightful place to eat can be found overlooking the green in the heart of the village. **Cartwrights Restaurant** is an impressive 17th century structure which originally formed one side of a square, set around a courtyard. The building incorporates a post office and general store, a beautiful walled garden and a renowned eating place serving delicious lunches and evening meals from the excellent and very comprehensive menu. The interior is traditionally decorated, with low beamed ceilings, exposed timbers and attractive framed pictures by local artists. However, it is the food that customers come for miles around, all home-cooked by the manageress Anita Woodget. For lunch there are dishes such as Hot Smoked Mackerel served with fresh horseradish sauce or diners can make

Cartwrights Restaurant

their choice from the ever changing daily specials board. In the evening diners are in for a real culinary treat with dishes ranging from a Selection of deep-fried breaded cheeses served with a raspberry sauce to the very substantial Lamb chops cooked with spicy lemon and honey. They also serve an excellent traditional Sunday lunch for which advanced bookings are advisable. The proprietors Jacqueline and Michael Seaman also have three well appointed holiday cottages to let, sleeping from two to six people, these are available throughout the year and are set amidst the beautiful secluded gardens adjacent to the village green.

Cartwrights Restaurant, The Green South, Creake, near Fakenham, Norfolk NR21 9AB Tel: 01328 823564 Fax: 01328 823335

SHERINGHAM   *Map 11 ref R13*

A pleasant, bustling town, Sheringham has undergone the transition from quiet fishing village to small-scale resort quite gracefully. It is not a resort in the unattractive sense of the word but simply a place where everyone will find something to enjoy. The beach here is markedly different from the shingle beaches elsewhere on this part of the coast, consisting mainly of gently sloping sand; it is excellent for bathing and its adequate quota of lifeguards makes it ideal for families with children. Gorse flourishes along the cliff path and the tiny yellow flowers give out a perfume reminiscent of coconut.

A small fleet of fishing boats still operates from here and several original fishermen's cottages remain, some with lofts where the nets were mended, and baited pots for catching crabs are still set along the seafront as they would have been in bygone days. Like so many other former fishing villages in England, Sheringham owes its transformation into a popular seaside resort to the coming of the railway which, in this instance, arrived in 1887. And a ride on an authentic full-sized passenger steam railway ride can still be enjoyed at the **North Norfolk Railway**. The company runs steam locomotives between Sheringham, Weybourne and a new station at Holt, where there are plans to develop a museum and buildings on the site.

Locals and visitors alike should give thanks to the National Trust for their policy of acquiring large parts of the heath and woodland that lie to the south of Sheringham, thereby halting the spread of suburbia so beloved by our town planners. The land here rises steeply to a sand and gravel ridge which runs parallel to the coastline from Cromer to Holt and reaches a height of more than 300 feet in places.

EAST DEREHAM   *Map 11 ref Q15*

Geographically, East Dereham is at the centre of the county and, although there is a West Dereham village near Downham Market, it is usually called Dereham. The town's origins go way back to 654 AD, when St Withburga, a daughter of Anna, King of the East Angles, founded a convent here. Local legend has it that the nuns were kept alive during a famine by the milk of two deer, who providently appeared in response to Withburga's prayers.

It is thought that Dereham derives its name from this miraculous event and the legend was quickly seized upon by Harry Carter as the theme of the town sign; spanning the High Street, it is the largest and perhaps most ambitious of his works. Withburga was buried in the churchyard of **St Nicholas's Church** and her shrine was said to have been the scene of a number of miracles. Unscrupulous monks removed her bones several hundred years later to lay them next to those of her sister, Etheldreda, who had founded their own community at Ely. The intention was, of course, to divert the steady stream of pilgrims from Dereham to Ely, but the monks' plan backfired: the desecrated grave filled with water which was discovered to have miraculous properties. It was promptly dubbed 'St Withburga's Well' and Dereham became even more popular than before despite its recently vacated resident!

Another resident of the churchyard is the poet, William Cowper. Known for his deeply melancholic nature, he attempted suicide at one stage before eventually dying here of natural causes in 1800. He left a legacy of several much-loved hymns, poems such as the brilliant 'Castaway' and 'The Task' which looks at the everyday life of rural folk, and a number of translations of Milton and the works of Homer.

Another local writer was George Borrow, who was born in the nearby hamlet of Dumpling Green in 1803. His great love of travelling led to such works as *The Zencali*, or an account of the Gypsies in Spain, *The Romany Rye* and *The Wordbook of the English-Gypsy Language*.

To the east of St Nicholas' Church is an exquisite row of thatched cottages called **Bishop Bonner's Cottages**, named after the 16th century rector who resided there and later became Bishop of London. The cottages now house a museum, and the delightful pargetry work which forms a frieze of flower and fruit designs below the eaves is extremely rare in Norfolk. Such beauty is in fact completely at odds with Bishop Bonner's character: 'Bloody Bonner', they called him, as he was responsible for sending many unfortunate Protestants to the stake during Mary Tudor's reign.

The attractive market place at **Foulsham**, to the north of East Dereham, was rebuilt after a devastating fire in 1771 and the village's imposing Georgian houses are dominated by the 15th century tower of Holy Innocents' Church.

The Queens Head

The Queens Head dates back in parts to the 17th century and is full of character, both inside and out. Colin Rowe and his partner Dorothy Deadman have been here for 17 years and have worked hard to produce a truly outstanding establishment. The interior is charming, with low beams, feature fireplaces and a pleasant clutter of antiques and knick-knacks giving it a cosy and intriguing atmosphere.

All meals are prepared using fresh local produce and the menu offers an excellent range. Guests can choose from sandwiches with great fillings, to juicy steaks and some interesting vegetarian dishes such as the tasty cauliflower cheese with a dash of white wine. A children's menu is available too and all prices are extremely reasonable. The large garden is a superb place to sit out and relax when the weather permits and there is a bowling green for grown ups, and every May Day the pub plays host to an annual Fun Run—not to be missed!

One of Colin and Dorothy's latest improvements has been to refurbish an old stable block to a very high standard; and this now provides a comfortable function room for meetings and parties of all kinds. A wide range of buffet menus is available here to suit different occasions, and a television is provided. The Queens Head is also a great place to visit over the festive season, for what could be better than enjoying traditional Christmas Fayre next to a roaring log fire in the friendly atmosphere of a lively pub?
The Queens Head, High Street, Foulsham, Norfolk NR20 5AD
Tel: 01362 683339

Northwest of Foulsham lies the small village of **Barney**. It is always a pleasure to come across a caravan and camping park which is not only attractive but has all the required amenities too, and **The Old Brick Kilns** park at Little Barney is one such place. Owners Alan and Pam Greenhalgh have set their seven acre park on two levels, where the pleasant combination of wooded areas and open spaces creates a wonderfully peaceful atmosphere. The natural pond is a perfect habitat for many types of wildlife and for nature lovers, the wild bird reserves and beautiful beaches of the North Norfolk coast are only eight miles away.

The Old Brick Kilns

There are 60 pitches in all, each has an electrical supply. The old brick drying shed has been converted to modern standards to provide all the main facilities of the park; and here visitors will find the reception area, a first aid room and the shop, which operates a gas exchange and will supply all basic food needs as well as home-made produce, crafts and gifts and a wide range of caravan accessories. There are luxury showers and toilets, including excellent facilities for the disabled and other amenities including fishing, a giant chess board and garden games including croquet. In addition, there is a safe children's play area, and there are also cycles for hire for those who want to take off for an hour or two along the country lanes. Bearing in mind the pleasant aspect of the park and the high standard of facilities provided, it came as no surprise to discover that this fine park has won the David Bellamy Award for Conservation 1996, Top Touring Park in North Norfolk 1996/97 and the Tourist Board Award for Excellence. All these recognition's are richly deserved and for those who would like to discover the pleasures of staying here for themselves, the park is open from the beginning of March to the end of October.

The Greenlaghs also offer superb bed and breakfast facilities throughout the year in their lovely family home, which has been converted from three brickworker's cottages. The accommodation comprises one twin, one double and one single room, all have en-suite facilities and are well appointed and tastefully decorated. The house is comfortable and spacious and guests will be made to feel most welcome in the peaceful, relaxing atmosphere that pervades. The atmosphere is enhanced by the log fire in the winter and in the summer there is the sunny, sheltered garden to enjoy. Guests also have access to all the facilities in the park and the newly opened restaurant that serves a full à la carte menu on selected evenings. The standard and attention to detail in both the park and B&B accommodation are extremely high, this is one of the very best places from which to base an exploration of this rewarding area.

The Old Brick Kilns, Little Barney Lane, Barney, near Fakenham, Norfolk NR21 0NL Tel: 01328 878305 Fax: 01328 878948

No one visiting East Anglia should miss the extraordinary exhibition, **The Thursford Collection** at the village of **Thursford**, just to the north of Barney. Thursford might not seem the most likely place for a museum of fairground rides and steam engines but, in fact, East Anglia has many connections with the history of festival and its trappings, and the real Norfolk traditional art is not watercolour painting but the practice of festival. There have been many fairs all over Norfolk for over a thousand years. Norfolk is full of folk history in which fairs were significant events for isolated communities. It is hard for us to imagine now the effects which the visit of a fair would have had on the isolated villages in Norfolk, in the late 19th and early 20th centuries.

Out of the plain landscape came these exuberant vehicles and their mechanical mysteries with carved monsters and swinging chairs, all of them painted and polished in a style of power and colour. The cinema too had its beginnings in the fair, with the huge bioscopes which travelled between 1896 and 1914, some of them able to seat 1,000 people. Above all else, the fairs brought electricity with them, at a time when most towns and villages themselves would have had only gas lighting! For many people, therefore, this would have been their first glimpse of electric light. Families would walk miles to see these things, because in a pre-television era this was the place where the truly spectacular could be experienced and, more importantly shared. Among the scattered groups who went to the fair was one small boy, George Cushing, who instinctively understood these things and has retained the image of its all his life to make the Thursford Collection a show for all of us to see and enjoy.

The Thursford Collection

George Cushing was caring for and collecting steam engines when most men would not have given five pounds for one. Without his perceptive honesty the museum would not exist. All the exhibits have one thing in common, which is that they are beautiful objects made by craftsmen who knew their work. George Cushing's real love for these things has a countryman's sense of the intrinsic value of the objects, to bring together this collection, to see through the blindness or carelessness which allowed traction engines, for example to go for scrap, and to remake for all of us, one of the best arrangements of steam engines and organs in the world. More that the skill, more than the money which it has taken to finance the museum, it has required his vision and enthusiasm. Thursford: it is not just a museum but a total experience. Music: live music shows starring Robert Wolfe in the Wurlitzer show, plus music from nine mechanical organs. Shops: housed in renovated farm buildings, offering a wide and varied selection of goods, many locally made. Food: cream teas on the lawn, light snacks and delicious home-cooked lunches in the genuine Norfolk barn, home-made ice-cream from the parlour. And to top it all there are enough activities, including a Savage Venetian Gondola ride to complete the visit.

The Thursford Collection, Thursford Green, Thursford, near Fakenham, Norfolk NR21 0AS Tel: 01328 878477 Fax: 01328 878415

Just the other side of Fakenham lies the village of **Colkirk**. From its ostentatious, though well kept exterior, people might ordinarily pass by **The Colkirk Crown** in the village, between the B1146 and A1065, but what a mistake that would be! This local village pub is definitely not one to be missed. On this spot has stood a pub for over 300 years and licensees Pat and Rosemary Whitmore have been resident here for 18 of them, all the while building business and attracting customers to the Crown for their delicious food, expertise and knowledge of wine and most pleasant and convivial atmosphere. Pat, who makes regular buying trips to French vineyards says, "I always make a point of selling wine by the glass, which means its easier to try more wines than would be possible by buying a bottle every time."

The Colkirk Crown

Rosemary's strength lies behind the scenes creating interesting traditional menus which offer a wide choice for everyone's taste, including vegetarian dishes, salads, local fresh fish, chicken and grills, not to mention the fateful hot puddings and desserts. The food is cooked to perfection and the portions are generous with many daily specials available, find it at all costs!

The Colkirk Crown, Colkirk, near Fakenham, Norfolk NR21 7AA
Tel: 01328 862172

Further south and half way along the Peddars Way long-distance footpath stands the spectacular hillside village of **Castle Acre**, set around a green and standing within the outer bailey of a ruined Norman **Castle**. The original castle, on a hill to the east of the village, was founded by William de Warenne, the Earl of Surrey, shortly after the Norman Conquest. Nothing more than a robust private dwelling, it was not seriously fortified until the middle of the 12th century.

Castle Acre is generally considered to be the 'jewel' of Norfolk's many picturesque villages. The approach road from the south leads through a narrow stone gateway (built in the 13th century to defend the northern entrance to the castle) and on to the village green. Many of the attractive cottages are of local flint, much of it taken from the castle when it was abandoned, and modern building work is largely sympathetic.

In a grassy hollow to the west of the village is Castle Acre's other fascinating historic building, **Castle Acre Priory**, now in the care of English Heritage. Now in ruins, this superb 12th century priory still creates an imposing atmosphere. Many of the original priory buildings came through the Dissolution surprisingly intact, including large parts of the church, the Prior's Lodging, various agricultural buildings and the gatehouse.

It was at Castle Acre that the Peddars Way crossed the River Nar via a ford, taking travellers on to Holme-next-the-Sea. Unlikely as it may seem today, this little stream was, incidentally, once large enough for boats to navigate from the Wash.

Eating out in Castle Acre presents no problem thanks to the wonderful **Castlegate Restaurant** in Stocks Green. Commanding one of the best positions in the village, this delightful eating place can seat up to 34 diners and stands overlooking the green near the 18th century Ostrich Inn. It could be said that owners Rex and Alan have their fingers in a lot of pies, as they sell a tempting range of these along with an impressive selection of more elaborate English and continental dishes. All of the bread, scones and pies are home-made and all dishes are prepared using only the freshest local ingredients. They are open seven days a week for breakfast, morning coffee, lunch and afternoon tea, with evening meals served from Wednesday to Saturday, though booking is advisable for the Castlegate Sunday lunch as it proves very popular with locals and visitors alike.

Castlegate Restaurant

Castlegate Restaurant, Stocks Green, Castle Acre, near King's Lynn, Norfolk PE32 2AE Tel: 01760 755340

SWAFFHAM   *Map 11 ref Q15*

A charming, but increasingly busy, market town, Swaffham's centre piece is the large wedge-shaped market place, surrounded by many fine Georgian houses. The main gathering place, and the heart of the town's social life in the early 19th century, was the Assembly Room at the northern end of the market place, which dates back to 1817. Nearby is the former Headmaster's House (now the Sixth Form Centre), Oakley House, the Corn Exchange and Plowright Place, a collection of old workshops now transformed into a delightful shopping precinct.

The main focus of the market place is the so-called **Butter Cross** (from the fact that beneath it, butter-sellers once displayed their wares), which was presented to the town by the Earl of Orford in 1783. It is not a cross at all but a classical lead-covered dome standing on eight pillars, surmounted by a life-sized statue of Ceres, the Roman goddess of agriculture. An appropriate symbol for a market town that has long relied upon the rewards which a good harvest would bring!

In contrast to Ceres and her pagan associations, the quite magnificent 15th century **Church of St Peter and St Paul** lies to the east of the market place. Its tower dates back to the early 1500s and features a fine lead and timber Georgian spire crowned by a copper ball. Inside is one of the very best double hammerbeam roofs in the county, strikingly embellished with many angels. Here too are some carved bench-ends representing a little man and a dog on a chain, a figure that has also been incorporated into the town's coat of arms. This is a reference to John Chapman, the legendary 'Pedlar of Swaffham', whose change in fortune was to prove so beneficial to the church.

The story goes that Chapman, an impoverished tinker who lived in Swaffham some time during the 15th century, had a dream which foretold that if he made his way to London Bridge he would meet a man who would make him rich. So, he set off with his faithful dog and tramped all the way to London to find his fortune. There, on London Bridge, he met a shopkeeper who told him that he too had had a strange dream—in which a pedlar from Swaffham discovered gold buried in his garden! Returning back home post-haste, Chapman was amply rewarded for his long journey when he unearthed two large pots of gold coins beneath a tree in his garden. In thanks, Chapman donated a generous part of his fortune to the church and the north aisle was built as a consequence.

John Chapman and his dog are further commemorated in the town sign which stands just beyond the market place. The sign here was carved by the same talented craftsman, who carved the 'Bishop Beaver' featured in the village sign at Babingley, a schoolmaster called Harry Carter who was a Swaffham man. Harry rose to prominence during the 1950s when the villages of Norfolk felt the need to commemorate the Queen's Coronation in a way that would be both visually striking and permanent. Today, beautifully carved and brightly painted signs can be found all over the county; many of them created by Harry himself and others by the craftsmen of the Queen's Carving School at Sandringham who carried on his good work. As well as the name of the village or town in which it stands, each sign depicts the history of the place by reference to a local personality or legend.

Saturday is market day in Swaffham and the famous open-air market and public auction held here each week has attracted thousands of visitors over the years. Nearby is the **Swaffham Museum**, at the Town Hall in London Street, which offers a fascinating insight into the life and history of the town.

To the southwest of Swaffham, **St Mary's Church** at **Beechamwell** is a delightful thatched church with a round Saxon tower to which an octagonal top was later added. During the 14th century, when the church was being rebuilt, the stonemasons scratched the figures of a demon and a woman on one of the columns—they can still be seen today. To the north of the village is part of the **Devil's Dyke**, an ancient earthwork which is generally thought to be a territorial boundary dating back to Saxon times.

The Great Dane's Head pub is charmingly situated overlooking the village green and was originally built back in 1840, though the cellars are said to be much older. The inn was originally known as the Coopers Arms until 15 years ago when the previous owner changed the name due to his passion for Great Dane dogs. Jenny and Frank White, the able hosts, came to the inn over five years ago from Derbyshire and have created a typical English pub where good food, excellent ales and friendly hospitality are guaranteed.

The Great Dane's Head

The restaurant here is cosy and intimate and can seat up to 20 diners whilst the menu, prepared by Jenny, features fresh local produce and specialises in game and locally caught fish. An interesting and imaginative wine list, supplied by a wine merchant, has something to suit all tastes and there is always a range of excellent beers and ales on tap. Food or drinks can be enjoyed in the spacious gardens to the rear of the property on those long summer days, but do remember that booking for the restaurant is advisable at weekends to avoid disappointment. *The Great Dane's Head, The Green, Beachamwell, near Swaffham Norfolk PE37 8BG Tel: 01366 328443*

Just to the west, standing in the picturesque Norfolk village of **Barton Bendish**, is the well known and very popular **Spread Eagle Country Inn**, personally run for the past five years by Carole and Roger Gransden. Dating back to the 1700s, the inn is still the hub of the village, but it and the village offer much more to the local and visitor alike. At the front of the pub is a well stocked cottage garden filled with colourful and fragrant flowers and shrubs.

Inside the atmosphere is cosy and welcoming with an attractive lounge bar and restaurant. Carole and Roger offer a comprehensive menu that includes such

The Spread Eagle Country Inn

dishes as the traditional Ploughman's to the home-baked Steak, Kidney and Ale pie with a wide range of sandwiches, filled baguettes and jacket potatoes also available. The Spread Eagle also offers four spacious bedrooms with full facilities, all year round, so no one will find an excuse for not visiting this charming village inn set in its picture postcard surroundings.

The Spread Eagle Country Inn, Church Road, Barton Bendish, near King's Lynn, Norfolk PE33 9DP Tel: 01366 347295

Cambridgeshire

INTRODUCTION

This large county, which includes the old county of Huntingdon, forms the western marches of East Anglia. Cambridgeshire is also home to much of the fenland, a land of marshes and bogs that has been successfully drained over the centuries by the Romans, the medieval monasteries, 17th century Dutch engineers and, finally, by the sophisticated equipment available in the late 20th century.

The regained land is rich and fertile and both fruit and vegetables are grown here with great success. Amidst this flat plain, the great towers of Ely Cathedral can be seen for many miles around. Another splendid city is the county town of Cambridge, situated on the banks of the River Cam and in the chalk downland of southern Cambridgeshire.

The principle river is the Great Ouse which runs through the middle of the county while, on the River Nene can by found the inland port of Wisbech. To the west lies Huntingdon, the birthplace of Oliver Cromwell and for many years the county town of another of England's lost counties. Situated on the old Roman road of Ermine Street, this was a coaching town and many of the old inns survive today.

CAMBRIDGE

Map 10 ref P17

This city really needs no introduction as it is, without doubt, one of the great centres of learning, with a unique history and reputation known throughout the world. The growth of the city began in 1284 when the oldest college, Peterhouse, was founded by the Bishop of Ely. The 14th and 15th centuries saw rapid expansion with a cluster of buildings springing up along the River Cam. As much of the early learning was based on theological work the churches and chapels formed an integral part of the colleges and the jewel in this architectural crown is **King's College Chapel**. Best viewed from the River, this is a stunning building started in 1446 by Henry VI with a similarly spectacular interior. Of particular note is the fan vaulted ceiling, built 1512–15 and the stained glass windows added just after. More recently, the Rubens masterpiece *The Adoration of the Magi* was donated. Although well used by the world famous choir, the chapel is open to the public from 9 am to 3.45 pm during term time and until 5 pm in the vacations on Mondays to Saturdays.

Punting on the River Cam

Among the many famous people who have studied at Cambridge, Trinity College boasts a host of poets including Byron, Dryden and Tennyson whilst Newton, Bacon and Rutherford, all with scientific leanings, also spent time there. John Harvard, the founder of the American university of that name, studied at Emmanuel.

The colleges themselves are also surprisingly visitor friendly and visitors can at least walk into most of the central courtyards and chapels. Please remember, however, that the colleges are closed to visitors during the exam period from May to mid June and that, being private property, there is no automatic right of way.

The **Bridge of Sighs**, over the River Cam at St John's College, resembles the bridge in Venice and was constructed in 1831, while the **Mathematical Bridge** at Queen's is built on physical principles and uses no bolts to maintain its construction.

A visit to the **Fitzwilliam Museum**, on Trumpington Street, conveniently placed in the centre near Peterhouse College, is well worthwhile. Dating back to 1816, the Fitzwilliam is one of the oldest museums in the country and its fine art treasures are particularly impressive with works from van Dyke to Monet and Matisse. Also in this area, it will be of particular interest to American readers that the chapel to Peterhouse, originally called St Peter's and dating back to the 12th century, has a memorial tablet to Godfrey Washington showing the family crest of stars and stripes. Near to the bulk of the colleges but an antidote to the academic is the **Cambridge Folk Museum** which is full of artefacts showing how domestic life and local trades have developed over the centuries. There is also, on Lensfield Road, the **Scott Polar Research Institute** which displays memorabilia from Polar expeditions.

Cambridge is blessed with a large number of open spaces, most notably **The Backs** which stretch along the banks of the River Cam. Still very central and a short walk from the railway station is the **University Botanic Garden**. The gardens contain many rare species and are open to the public from 8.30 am to 6.30 pm with reduced hours on Sundays opening at 2.30 pm.

HUNTINGDON

Map 10 ref O16

An ancient town, first settled by the Romans, the street plan, laid down sometime later by the Danes who sailed up the River Great Ouse, is still recognisable today. During the 13th century there were as many as 13 churches in the town though only two survive today. One of these, **All Saints'** in the market square, displays several architectural styles from medieval to Victorian times. A great wealth of Georgian building can also be found here including the fine, three-storey **Town Hall**.

Famous today for its local MP, John Major the former Prime Minister, Huntingdon was also the birthplace of Oliver Cromwell in 1599. Rising to power as a Military Commander in the Civil War, Cromwell raised his troops from this area and the Falcon Inn was used as his headquarters. Appointed Lord Protector of England in 1653, Cromwell was never crowned King though he ruled until his death in 1658. Educated at Huntingdon Grammar School, which was also attended by the famous diarist, Samuel Pepys, who lived at nearby Brampton, the building is now a museum dedicated to the Civil War.

The Cromwell Museum houses the only public collection which specifically relates to Oliver Cromwell and it is open throughout the year though closed on Mondays.

WISBECH

Map 10 ref P15

Wisbech is one of the larger Fenland towns and it was not far from here that the luckless King John lost his baggage train together with a King's fortune in The Wash in 1216. There was once a Norman castle in Wisbech, built in 1086, complete with moat and drawbridge. The castle is long gone but its impact is felt today. On the old fortress site now stands The Castle, a Regency villa, and the whole of the centre of town has a circular layout. Two crescents of fine Georgian houses run to the north and south of the Castle grounds. Also many houses built where the castle moat once was are now suffering from severe subsidence.

Wisbech has had a **Museum** for over 150 years and the present building was opened in 1847. There is a large collection of Continental and British pottery and porcelain, including a Sevres breakfast service once owned by Napoleon and a Burmese Buddha. The anti-slavery campaigner, Thomas Clarkson, came from Wisbech and the museum includes material gathered by him as evidence against the trade, as well as objects collected by a local man on the first European expedition up the Niger. A memorial to Clarkson stands beside the old bridge.

On the other side of the River Nene is the Old Market, now a neat garden laid out on the site of former shops which were demolished after the disastrous flood of 1978. The Old Market describes this triangular space surrounded by fine Georgian buildings which testify to the golden days of the river trade. **North Brink**, along the river from Old Market, is considered by many to be Wisbech's most outstanding feature and it is described by Pevsner as one of the finest Georgian brick streets in England. The buildings form a beautiful composition of Georgian designs which tend to be less grand as one gets further from the town. Among these buildings is the North Brink Brewery. Built in 1790, the frontage of this classical Georgian brewery has remained almost unchanged to the present day. The Brewery was purchased by its present owners, Elgoods, in 1878 and still supplies fifty public houses in the Wisbech area.

Further along the river bank, a little further away from the town centre, is **Peckover House**. This National Trust property has well furnished rooms, a fine staircase and an ornate garden containing an orangery and many rare specimens, for which it is justly famous. The house also contains an excellent collection of Cornwallis family portraits and an exhibition on the life and work of Wisbech-born Octavia Hill, a co-founder of the National Trust. Built in 1722, Peckover House is a Grade I listed building which makes it of outstanding national importance.

ELY

Map 10 ref P16

The city of Ely is the jewel in the Fen's crown. Not only a great place to pick up loads of information on what to see and where to go in this part of Cambridgeshire, but the Tourist Information Centre is a tourist attraction in its own right.

The pretty black and white timbered building is the only remaining house, other than Hampton Court, where Oliver Cromwell and his family are known to have lived. The present east wing represents what is left of the original 13th century building. Some 750 years old, the house has a varied history. In the 1840s it was a public house aptly called The Cromwell Arms and from 1905 to 1986 it was the vicarage for the adjoining St Mary's Church. Inside, several rooms have been refurbished in Cromwellian style and an audiovisual presentation gives an insight into the domestic, military and political aspects of his life.

Both the Cathedral and the surrounding fens have played a major role in the history of Ely. The fens' influence is even reflected in the city's name: Ely was once known as Elg or Elig because of the large number of eels which could be caught in the surrounding fenland (Elig meaning eel island).

Ely, however, owes its existence to St Etheldreda who founded a religious community on the hill-top site in the 7th century but it was not until 1081 that building of the present **Cathedral** was begun by the Normans. Undoubtedly, the most outstanding feature of this fine example of Romanesque architecture is the Octagon and Lantern, built to replace the Norman tower which collapsed in 1322. They took 30 years and 8 huge oaks to build! Its framework is unique in the world, estimated to weigh 400 tons, and once included a set of bells. It is a medieval engineering feat still much admired by modern architects and builders. Also in the Cathedral are the **Brass Rubbing Centre** and **Stained Glass Museum**.

Near the river is **The Maltings**, a building which dates back to 1868 when it was constructed for malting barley (using high temperatures to cause the barley to sprout before it could be taken to the brewery). In 1971 it was converted into the delightful, attractive building seen today and is used as a public exhibition and conference centre, cinema and serves drinks, meals and snacks. The riverside walk in front of The Maltings is known as Quai D'Orsay, and was named shortly after the twinning of East Cambridgeshire District with the town of Orsay in France in the early 1980s.

Lincolnshire

INTRODUCTION

The Danes began their campaign in England sometime before AD 800 and they broached this part of the country through the Humber and the Wash. The village place names ending with 'ing' and 'by', so common in Lincolnshire, can be traced back to the Danish settlements. Under their rule, this area of the country became known as The Danelaw and Lincoln, Stamford, Nottingham, Derby and Leicester were the five Burghs or administrative centres of the region. The Danes were to stay in England for some three hundred years before being routed during the Norman Conquest under William the Conqueror around 1066.

Today, Lincolnshire is one of the country's larger counties and it is rich in both agricultural and horticultural land. The area around Spalding is particularly colourful as this is a major bulb-growing centre and, in May, the town holds a magnificent Tulip Parade. Lincolnshire's landscape and geographical position was also the reason it has gained a rich aviation heritage. The county's connections with the RAF date from the Great War and by 1945 there were 49 airfields here, 28 of them bomber bases; more than any other county in Britain. RAF Coningsby is the base of the **Battle of Britain Memorial Flight**, a team of five Spitfires, a Hurricane and a Lancaster, which regularly tour major airshows in memory of the RAF crews who gave their lives during the World War II.

However, Lincolnshire is not all fields and old market towns. On the eastern side lie the Lincolnshire Wolds which rise up to 550 feet whilst, in the southeast, there is the Holland area, a continuation of the Cambridgeshire fenland. The quiet of the low lying, solitary North Sea coastline is broken by Skegness, a brash and loud seaside resort that is the home of the first Butlin's holiday camp which opened in the 1930s.

LINCOLN   *Map 14 ref N12*

A simple, but inadequate description of the city, would be that 'historic' Lincoln sits high on a hill, dominated by the cathedral and castle, while the modern city lies on the valley floor 200 feet below, with the River Witham flowing through it on its way to Boston. Lincoln certainly has all the conveniences of a modern city centre but it also has its fair share of fine buildings and historic associations too.

St Catherine's Hotel was once the site of a most important and interesting religious houses, the **Gilbertine Priory**. It was founded about 1148 for canons, that is, religious men who lived together in a community but who also acted as parish priests in the parishes belonging to the house. Lay sisters, or religious women, who had not taken the vows of a nun, were soon introduced to look after the sick and the children in the hospital of St Sepulchre, which was attached to the priory.

It was here that Queen Eleanor's body was prepared for burial in 1290, and the first of the famous Eleanor Crosses was erected just outside the priory on Swine Green. King Henry VII once stayed here and, after the Dissolution, the house became known as **St Catherine's Hall**. It was used as a residence by its various owners and as a place of entertainment for distinguished guests. On one occasion James I stayed there and, among the guests was a young man, John Hutchinson, who later signed the death warrant of James' son Charles. In the 18th century the building was allowed to fall into ruin and was pulled down.

In the ancient heart of the city and near the bottom of Steep Hill, is the **Jews House**. The building itself is a fine example of a Norman house, which as the name suggests was originally the property of one of the members of the Jewish community in Lincoln and indeed it is reputed to be the oldest inhabited domestic dwelling in Britain.

At the top of the aptly named Steep Hill, is the delightful cobbled Castle Square with the Cathedral on the right the eastern gateway to the Castle on the left. **Lincoln Castle** is steeped in history: commissioned by William the Conqueror in 1068, it was built on the site of a former Roman fort. Originally very primitive with earth banks and a timber stockade, the castle was eventually rebuilt of stone. It has often been under siege, first in the 1140s when the Empress Matilda invaded England and disputed King Stephen's throne, and later during the Civil War. In 1644, the Parliamentarians took the castle and the Royalists were thrown out of the city. The castle's main role from then on was as a seat of law and within the walls is Lincoln County Gaol and a Prison Chapel. Near the prison buildings is another cross commemorating Queen Eleanor, who died nearby in the small village of Harby.

Lincoln Cathedral is said by many to be the finest in the country and it is certainly most impressive. Over 900 years old, the massive front tower stands proud, while the two towers at the southern end are splendid monuments to man's ability to put heart and soul into these ecclesiastical buildings.

Finally, another fascinating place to visit whilst here is the **National Cycle Museum**, Britain's premier collection of cycles and associated artefacts. Here the changes in cycle design from 1820 onwards—from old-fashioned boneshakers to modern racers and mountain bikes—can be discovered and this is certainly a place that will appeal to the whole family.

The **Museum of Lincolnshire Life**, on Burton Road, is housed in a listed building that was once home to the Royal North Lincoln Militia. This award winning museum gives the visitor the opportunity to gain a comprehensive insight into life in the past. Displays cover areas of transport, agriculture and industrial life as well as the recreation of homes and shops from bygone times.

GAINSBOROUGH
Map 14 ref M11

Its name is derived from the earliest settlers who were known as the Gainas and came here in the 6th century. The Danish king, Svein Forkbeard, took the town in 1013 and although he died soon after, his son Canute took control. Already ruler of Denmark and Norway, the succession to England's rule was the final prize needed to make Canute the most politically important ruler in the northern kingdoms.

There is an interesting local anecdote regarding Canute, who is generally remembered as the king who tried to hold back the sea. Gainsborough folk reckon that history has got it wrong and that it was, in fact, the River Trent which he attempted to master. The Trent here is well known for its tidal wave that rises with the spring tides. The bore, or Aegir as it is known by the locals, rolls down the river several feet above the normal level. They say that Canute sat on the bank of the river and commanded the tidal wave not to splash his royal personage. Nevertheless the tide swept by and drenched him, and he leapt back with the immortal words, "Let all the world know that the power of monarchs is vain."

From the 17th to the 18th century, Gainsborough prospered mainly through its river trade, together with ship and boatbuilding and allied trades. As an inland port, it was conveniently situated to import and export goods to Hull and inland to Nottinghamshire and Derbyshire. With the advent of the railways the river trade fell off considerably, but the town survived and prospered thanks to its connections with agriculture and engineering.

CLEETHORPES   *Map 14 ref O11*

Developed as a resort in the mid 19th century along with the growth of the railways, Cleethorpes is now more a suburb of Grimsby. This was certainly an improvement on earlier Cleethorpes history when the area was known for piracy and aggressive competition, particularly with it neighbour. The pier was completed in 1873 and opened on August Bank Holiday. Ten years later the promenade and gardens were laid out as more people came to enjoy its safe beaches and other holiday attractions; these include golf, boating, fresh and sea water fishing. There are shops to satisfy most needs and weekly markets are held on Wednesdays with occasional Sunday markets.

SPALDING   *Map 10 ref O14*

A strong Dutch influence can be seen in some of the architecture of the county but there is another feature of Lincolnshire quite startling in its associations with the Dutch—tulips. Not simply a few garden centres that specialise in the flower, but acres and acres of vibrant colour have gone to make Spalding the tulip capital of Britain. This area is said to be the largest bulb growing centre in the world, with 2,500 acres devoted to their cultivation.

May is the month for the flower parades and the floats decorated with millions of flower heads are a sight worth seeing. The parade is led by a float with 'Miss Tulip Land' waving gaily to the visitors and, for those who are wondering why only the flower heads are used, it is done for good reason. The growers remove the heads to ensure good strong growth for the bulbs which will be ready to sell in Autumn.

GRANTHAM   *Map 10 ref N14*

This pleasant town has, in recent times, become well known through its links with Margaret Thatcher, who was born here. Its most famous son, however, is Sir Isaac Newton and, in front of the Guildhall, stands a large bronze statue of the renowned scientist to remind all of this great man's influence. He was born on Christmas Day 1642 at Woolsthorpe Manor, in the village of **Woolsthorpe**, seven miles south of Grantham. He attended King's School in Grantham, where his name can still be seen carved into one of the window sills. It was at Woolsthorpe Manor that he is said to have had his inspirational encounter with a falling apple! The **Grantham Museum**, near the statue, houses local archaeological finds and a Newton collection.

Grantham's coaching inns were used as a stopping place for those travelling on the Great North Road. One of the oldest inns in Britain is said to be the Angel and Royal Hotel, found in the High Street. King Richard III reputedly signed the death warrant for the Duke of Buckingham here in 1483.

CHAPTER SEVEN
Yorkshire

Whitby Abbey

7
Yorkshire

South Yorkshire

INTRODUCTION

Primarily an industrial county dominated by Sheffield, England's fourth largest city, this was the principal coal mining area in the north of England. It was also these mines which provided the fuel to develop Sheffield into the booming steel town of the 19th century.

However, though heavy industry still, in many ways, dominates South Yorkshire the county is also home to many historic treasures and it also lies close to, and partly in, the **Peak District National Park**. Some of the most dramatic scenery in the Park can be found on its border with South Yorkshire and this area provides the opportunity for many outdoor recreations including rock climbing and hill walking. The 250 mile long **Pennine Way** also passes through the county, following the line of the 'backbone of England', from north Derbyshire to the Scottish borders.

SHEFFIELD   *Map 13 ref L12*

This was once the greatest steel-making town in the world and it does not, on the surface, seem a likely prospect for the sightseer. There is nowhere in the world where some item made of Sheffield steel will not be found and such a heritage has made a deep mark indeed. The tradition of working with metals goes back many years and it was Geoffrey Chaucer, in his *Canterbury Tales*, who, by mentioning "Sheffield Thwittle" gave the city its immortal link with cutlery. By the end of the 18th century, Sheffield had more than 150 water powered cutlery and tool-grinding workshops and, some 100 years later, further expansion and the full force of the Industrial Revolution had turned Sheffield into the foremost cutlery making centre in the world. The same could also be said of its steel, tool and silverware industries. The production of silverware products became so important that, in 1773, the city was granted its own Assay Office and hallmark which are still in use today. It was the development of the crucible steel process, invented by Benjamin Huntsman, that secured the city's world wide reputation and the oldest surviving crucible furnace in the world is preserved as part of Sheffield's Abbeydale Industrial Hamlet.

Dating back to the 18th century, **Abbeydale Industrial Hamlet** is a delightful restored courtyard with surrounding buildings which lies just four miles from the city centre. In this peaceful, rural setting it is hard, now, to believe that Abbeydale was, during Victorian times, a major industrial complex. As well as the crucible furnace, visitors here can see a water-driven tilt forge and grinding wheel, handsmiths' forges, workshops and warehouses. Today, traditional craftsmen and women can be seen at work whilst, at the exhibition centre, films of the old tool-making processes show how the place might have looked in its heyday.

Sheffield is not often credited with the fact that it contains more parks within its boundaries than any other European city except Glasgow—the rich steel barons of the town needed somewhere to promenade their ladies after all! At Weston Park, is the **City Museum**, with the world's greatest collection of cutlery, dating from the Palaeolithic Age to the present day. Nearby, is one of the few buildings of national importance left unused in Sheffield, the **Globe Works**. It was built in 1825 by cutlery and tool manufacturers Henry and William Ibbotson. Here is an unusual example of an industrial building which also incorporates a domestic residence. The interior includes a magnificent circular staircase and fine plaster mouldings, which have now been adapted to provide prestigious office accommodation. The original factory areas have been given over as craft workshops, and other additions, such as a visitor centre, restaurant and public house help to make this beautiful building a busy visitor attraction as well. Also close by is the **Kelham Island Museum** which displays products made in the city over the past 300 years, including a ten ton bomb and the silver-plated penny farthing bicycle that was made for a Russian Tzar. The whole of this Kelham Island area has, in fact been designated a conservation site by Sheffield City Council.

Most of the buildings seen today in the centre of the city were built during the prosperous Victorian age. The Grade I listed **Town Hall**, opened by Queen Victoria in 1897, has a magnificent entrance hall and a sculptured frieze which represents all of Sheffield's industries. Nearby, in Church Street, is the headquarters of the Company of Cutlers in Hallamshire, **Cutlers Hall**. This distinguished columned building, constructed in 1832, is the home of the one of the few livery companies outside London and the annual Cutlers' Feast is the highlight of the city's social calendar and is often attended by the Prime Minister and senior Cabinet Ministers. Opposite the hall is Sheffield's **Anglican Cathedral** of St Peter and St Paul. Founded in the 12th century, the church was rebuilt in the 15th century but did not become a cathedral until the start of the 20th century.

Finally, in a timber-framed Tudor yeoman's house, built on high ground commanding a panoramic view over Sheffield, is the **Bishop's House Museum**. Developed to include fine examples of 17th century oak panelling and plasterwork, there are furnished rooms, displays of Sheffield during Tudor and Stuart times, and a programme of ever changing exhibitions.

The village of **Chapeltown**, to the north of Sheffield, developed following the arrival of the railway and the building of its own station. In 1897 the line was extended to Barnsley and the station is still used today by commuters.

Ivy clad **Staindrop Lodge** was built in 1806 as the family home of George Newton, a founding father of the famous Yorkshire firm Newton Chambers, but was later sympathetically converted into a country house style hotel with all modern day conveniences. Ideally situated within easy reach of Sheffield city centre and within two miles of junctions 35 and 36 of the M1, Staindrop Lodge is the perfect place for a quick stopover or a longer, more leisurely break being only 10 minutes from Meadowhall and the Sheffield Arena and 20 minutes from the Peak District National Park, where the world famous Chatsworth House is situated. Family owned and run by the Baileys for the past 12 years, this classic hotel is surrounded by secluded mature gardens and offers its guests the very best

Staindrop Lodge Hotel and Restaurant

in hospitality and comfort. Each of the 13 en-suite bedrooms have been individually designed and furnished to offer its discerning visitor every comfort, including direct-dial telephone, colour television and tea and coffee making facilities. The light and airy restaurant has a justly earned reputation for serving fine modern English cuisine blended with traditional and classical French influences. An aperitif can be enjoyed in the elegant cocktail bar or in the conservatory style lounge and the substantial wine cellar offers an excellent range of wines from around the globe, a perfect complement to an evening meal.

Staindrop Lodge Hotel and Restaurant, Lane End, Chapeltown, near
Sheffield, South Yorkshire S35 3UH Tel: 0114 284 6727
Fax: 0114 284 6783

Northwest of Sheffield on the A616, in the small, peaceful village of **Crow Edge**, stands **Pratty Flowers**, a popular inn and restaurant. Originally built back in the 1800s as a coaching inn, this unusually named pub is owned and personally run by Richard and Paul, with their willing families always ready to lend a hand if needed. Inside the inn the decor is reminiscent of days gone by, with a traditional country feel permeating throughout and with the warm and friendly atmosphere that greets all guests, everyone is guaranteed to feel welcome. Richard and Paul

Pratty Flowers

also offer the weary traveller the opportunity of bed and breakfast accommodation. There is a choice of 10 attractive bedrooms, each offering its guests full en-suite facilities, tea and coffee maker, colour TV and rustic antique pine furniture. The recently refurbished restaurant can seat up to 100 people and offers a full menu as well as a daily specials board which includes home-cooked speciality dishes and a good range of vegetarian meals. In the bar area there is a good selection of traditionally casked regular and guest ales, whilst the light and airy function room offers the perfect location to hold a party, anniversary or disco.

Pratty Flowers, Whams Road, Crow Edge, near Sheffield, South Yorkshire S30 5HT Tel: 01226 761692

BARNSLEY   *Map 13 ref L11*

It was the wealth of coal that shaped the town and its mines were of vital importance to the iron and steelworks of its neighbours. This industrial town was founded in Saxon times and its markets, which date back many years, are still busy and popular. **Cannon Hall**, built in the 17th century, was remodelled in the 18th century by John Carr of York and its great parkland is a particular favourite with children. The Hall is now a museum and the rooms are furnished in a variety of styles from Jacobean to Victorian. There is an interesting glassware collection which, amongst other things, contains such oddities as glass rolling pins and walking sticks. The **Regimental Museum** of the 13th and 18th Royal Hussars is also here and their part in the Charge of the Light Brigade in 1854 is recalled in a series of stirring displays. Art lovers will appreciate the **Cooper Gallery**, which, as well as hosting a lively programme of contemporary exhibitions also houses a fine collection of British watercolours.

Visitors to the town should also make a point of trying the famous local delicacy, the Barnsley Chop, a double sided lamb steak.

To the south of the town centre lies **Worsbrough Country Park**, a haven for wildlife which also operates a programme of guided country walks. Here to can be found the **Worsbrough Mill**, a finely preserved example of the area's industrial heritage which displays the corn grinding processes.

To the east of Barnsley can be seen the ruined **Monk Bretton Priory**, the only remaining settlement of the Cluniac Order of monks. Started in 1154 and colonised from the wealthy Pontefract Priory, Monk Bretton achieved independence in 1281. The plan of the priory, which includes the foundations of both the infirmary and the guest house, is unusually complete. The Prior's lodgings, based on the first floor of the west claustral stage are particularly interesting due to the fine detailed chimney piece.

DONCASTER   *Map 13 ref L11*

An important Roman town, known as Danum, this site was chosen because it was the lowest crossing point on the River Don. Budding archaeologists may be interested to know that there is a well preserved piece of Roman road, just west of Ardwick le Street ,and that many of the churches in the area have Saxon connections.

Doncaster and its surrounding districts have strong roots in several nonconformist religions—the **Quaker Meeting House** at Warmsworth was one of the earliest in the district. George Fox visited it and held rallies at nearby Balby. It is also worth noting that John Wesley came from Epworth and William Bradford, one of the Pilgrim Fathers who sailed with the Mayflower, was baptised at Austerfield.

The town also has some impressive public buildings, including the Mansion House, the Parish Church and the Corn Exchange. The **Mansion House** was built in 1748, designed by James Paine, and was to be the only civic mansion house outside London and York. The Parish Church was rebuilt in 1858 by Sir Giles Gilbert Scott as an outstanding example of Gothic revival architecture. The lively shopping centre is enhanced by a stately Corn Exchange building and a market which takes place every Tuesday, Friday and Saturday.

The town has a wealth of galleries and museums for people seeking more aesthetic pleasures. The **Doncaster Museum and Art Gallery** is based in Chequer Road, in a modern building it has used since 1964, although the actual gallery was founded in 1909. It houses impressive collections of archaeology, regional natural history, geology, local history, European fine art, paintings and sculpture, costumes, militaria and special exhibitions. Within the gallery is the collection of the King's Own Yorkshire Light Infantry, introduced in 1987, including uniforms, medals and equipment.

England

The **Museum of South Yorkshire Life** at Cusworth Hall appeals to a wide range of ages and tastes. Cedar and strawberry trees, larches, cypress, fig, yew and bamboo all grow in the pleasure gardens around this imposing mansion while the Hall sports fine ornamental doors, windows and palladian pavilions, in one of the finest examples of early Georgian architecture. The interior is adorned with elaborate plasterwork, panelling and carved marble chimney pieces.

Doncaster is also a railway town and was one of the most important centres for the production of steam engines. Thousands were built here, including both the Flying Scotsman and the Mallard, two of the fastest and most advanced engines of their day.

There is no-one connected with the racing fraternity that has not heard of the St Leger, one of the oldest classic races, which has been held at Doncaster since 1776. Doncaster, in that Yorkshire tradition, provides a magnet for all horse racing enthusiasts and there are a total of twenty-six meetings held here a year.

West Yorkshire

INTRODUCTION

The county of West Yorkshire is very much a mixture of industrial and beautiful rural countryside. The Industrial Revolution turned this area into a great wool manufacturing district with Bradford as its leading town. Today, much of the textile industry has gone, though the many of the mills and the associated millworkers' terraced housing can still be seen. Many of the towns, including Bradford, Wakefield and Leeds, have had to adjust to the new industries of the late 20th century and turn to engineering, electronics and the service industries.

The west of the county is dominated by the Pennine Hills and the enchanting scenery that can be found there. Beautiful and remote in many areas, the long winter nights lead the Bronte sisters to invent their own imaginary world and then to write their moving books. Haworth, and the surrounding moorland, still draws many visitors interesting in seeing the setting that inspired *Wuthering Heights*.

LEEDS   *Map 13 ref K10*

This city can certainly lay claim to being the economic capital of the county of West Yorkshire. Leeds developed rapidly in the early 19th century as the inland port on the Leeds–Liverpool and Aire and Calder Navigation canals. The city formed a central link between Liverpool and Hull, from where goods were exported world wide. The Canal Basin, which formed the link, rapidly grew, providing extensive wharves, warehouses, boat building yards and wet and dry docks where boats could be repaired. Although the water based trade sadly declined, as first the railways then the roadways took over as the trade routes, interest in the long neglected warehouses and waterways, with their rich and historical tradition, has been rekindled. The **Canal Basin** has been designated a Conservation Area and the once derelict buildings redeveloped into sought after offices and shopping areas, as well as providing a venue for street shows, markets and landscaped waterside areas. The canal itself is also enjoying a new lease of life with a wide variety of leisure craft increasingly evident on its waters. In response to the enormous interest in the site, a trail with an environmental theme is being developed, which is available to disabled visitors, and a Visitor Centre is now housed in the former Canal Office.

Another excellent way to discover Leeds' remarkable early industrial heritage is to follow the Museum of Leeds Trail along the towpath of the canal through the Kirkstall Valley. This takes the visitor from the Canal Basin past warehouses and mills, bridges, locks and canal architecture, to the **Leeds Industrial Museum** at **Armley Mill**, once the largest textile mill in the world. It now houses a museum of the textile, clothing and engineering industries of which Leeds is still a major centre.

Leeds city centre offers a great deal to occupy its visitors as well as offering some of the most beautiful baroque civic architecture in the north of England. There is plenty of shopping available, with wonderful arcades and a large market and other attractions include a regional theatre, the Opera House and the **City Museum and Art Gallery**. The latter houses the **Henry Moore Sculpture Gallery**, founded by the late sculptor who was born in nearby Castleford. The museum has been in existence for over 170 years and its collections are among the finest outside London.

Kirkstall Abbey, to the northwest of the city, is one of the most complete ruins in this part of Yorkshire. Building started in 1152 by the Cistercians and was finished within a generation, thus Kirkstall is regarded by many to reflect Cistercian architecture at its most monumental. It was executed with the typical early Cistercian austerity, as can be seen in the simplicity of the outer domestic buildings but the bell tower, a 16th century addition, was in contravention of the rule that there were to be no stone bell towers as they were considered an unnecessary vanity.

To the east of Leeds, set back off the A63, is **Temple Newsam House**. There has been a mansion here of sorts since a couple of Anglo-Saxon thanes, Dunstan and Glunier, set their claim to the land. The house has had a great many owners, including the Earl of Pembroke, the Darcy family, the Ingrams and the Marchioness of Hertford. It was purchased in 1922 by Leeds City Council. In its time such names as John Carr, the Adam brothers, Chippendale and Capability Brown have contributed to its improvement and it houses some incomparable collections of antiques within its walls. The view of the house is impressive, set amidst huge expanses of rolling grassland. The grounds cover 1200 acres, and include the Home Farm, where there is a rare breeds centre.

England

The Crown Hotel lies in the urban area of Leeds which is located within walking distance of the Royal Armouries and the Tetley Brewery Museum. This pleasant family orientated pub and eating place offers a range of popular dishes including giant Yorkshire pudding with different fillings, burger with chips, spicy Tortilla, and pancakes both savoury and sweet. Sandwiches, jacket potatoes and other snacks can also be ordered. Bed and breakfast accommodation is available in clean and tidy rooms at most reasonable prices. The bedrooms cater for single, double or family accommodation. Chris is the recent owner of The Crown and offers a friendly welcome in this Victorian hotel which retains much of its original character. Open fires create a cheerful atmosphere and the home-cooked food is available at both dinner times and evenings.

The Crown Hotel

The Crown Hotel, Crown Point Road, Hunslet, Leeds, West Yorkshire LS10 1EX Tel: 0113 2451901

BOSTON SPA   *Map 13 ref L9*

This is a gracious, inviting place, whose growth began in 1744, through the discovery of its spring by a labourer called John Shires. A guidebook of 1853 tells of the "pure and bracing air to be had at Boston Spa, where one might either drink or bathe in the waters, by visiting one of the pump-rooms and variety of baths." Nowadays, it no longer functions as a spa town and is better known as a popular fishing ground.

The town's main activity focuses on the High Street which is also where the **Crown Hotel** can be found. No doubt with quite a history from its days as a coaching inn, the Crown has a mellow stone exterior, typical of many buildings in Boston Spa. Today, its activities include live music every Friday and the live jazz club featuring national and international artists every Saturday night and Bank Holidays. An economically priced menu offers traditional and popular pub

376

The Crown Hotel

food and bar snacks. The Crown also has a Petanque league for those who fancy a game of French bowls. There are seven guest bedrooms and Boston Spa is a very well placed area to stay for visits to York, Harrogate, Leeds and the Dales. *The Crown Hotel, 128 High Street, Boston Spa, West Yorkshire LS23 6BW Tel: 01937 842608*

WETHERBY   *Map 13 ref L9*

Completely unspoilt by industry, the town is situated on the Great North Road at a point nearly midway between Edinburgh and London. Hence it is renowned for its coaching inns, of which the two most famous were The Angel and The Swan and Talbot. It is rumoured that serving positions at these inns were considered so lucrative that employees had to pay for the privilege of employment in them!

The town has a quaint appearance and, in the centre, is a market place that was first granted to the Knights' Templar, who were allowed to hold a market here every Thursday and an annual fair lasting three days. Many of the houses in the town are Georgian, Regency or early Victorian. Apart from its shops, galleries, old pubs and cafés, there is also a popular racecourse nearby. Another feature is the renowned 18th century **Bridge** with a long weir which once provided power for Wetherby's corn mill and possibly dates from medieval times.

The Bay Tree is a family run café and tearooms conveniently located in the pedestrian area of the arched Shambles off Market Square and 50 yards from the Town Hall. However, it is a perfect diversion from the A1 route which is only a quarter of a mile away and it is also centrally placed between York and Harrogate. David Gill and his son Jim provide good food and service in their busy café where a variety of home-cooked food is offered on the menu with a daily changing specials blackboard. Patrons can start their day here with a full English breakfast, choose from the all day bakery, enjoy one of the home-made soups, take a glass of wine with their lunch, order freshly prepared sandwiches

The Bay Tree

or salad or call in for a cafetiere of speciality coffee and perhaps one of the wonderful home-made scones. After that, make time for a stroll alongside the nearby river and weir.

The Bay Tree, 9 The Shambles, Wetherby, West Yorkshire LS22 6NG
Tel: 01937 586031

ILKLEY   *Map 13 ref K9*

One of the most famous West Yorkshire attractions has to be **Ilkley Moor**, immortalised in the well known song, and a visit is a must. Like any of the Yorkshire moors, Ilkley Moor can look inviting and attractive on a sunny day but ominous and forbidding when the weather takes a turn for the worse. The River Wharfe runs along the edge of the moor and through the town, which is clustered within a narrow section of the valley, in the midst of heather moorland, craggy gritstone and wooded hillside.

Originally an Iron Age settlement, Ilkley was eventually occupied by the Romans, who built a camp here to protect their crossing of the River Wharfe, and who named the town that sprang up Olicana, giving rise to the present name, with the familiar ley (Anglo Saxon for pasture) added. Behind the medieval church is a grassy mound where a little fort was built and in the town's museum are altars carved in gritstone, dedicated to the Roman gods.

The spring at White Wells brought more visitors in the 18th century and a small bath house was built, where genteel and elderly patients were encouraged to take a dip in the healing waters of the 'heather spa', as it was known. Early Victorian times saw the development of the hydros–hydropathic treatment hotels, providing hot and cold treatments based on the ideas of Dr Preissnitz of Austria who, in 1843, opened Britain's first hydro at nearby Ben Rhydding.

The coming of the railway lines from Leeds and Bradford in the 1860s and 70s, during a period of growth in the Yorkshire woollen industry, saw Ilkley take on a new role as a fashionable commuter town. Wool manufacturers and their better paid employees came, not only to enjoy the superb amenities, but to build handsome villas of West Riding gritstone. If Bradford and Leeds was where people made their 'brass', then it was usually Ilkley where they spent it. Ilkley's patrons and well-to-do citizens gave the town a splendid Town Hall, library, Winter Gardens, and King's Hall and a sense of elegance is still present along the Grove. It is still a delight to have morning coffee in the famous **Betty's Coffee House**, and discerning shoppers will find a wealth of choice, some in a perfectly preserved Victorian arcade, complete with beautiful potted palms and balconies.

Promenade Tea Room

Originally used as a dress shop, the **Promenade Tea Room** was converted in 1992 and has been popular with tourists and locals alike ever since. Owned and run by the aptly named Geoff and Margaret Kettlewell, the tea rooms have seating for up to 36 people and are open from 10 am until 5 pm Monday to Saturday. The decor and furnishings are reminiscent of a country cottage, with attractive pine tables and chairs, pretty wallpaper, paintings and traditional all-white china tea sets. The Promenade Tea Room can be found on Grove Promenade which runs just off Brook Street at the top of the main car park in Ilkley.

Promenade Tea Room, 27 Grove Promenade, Ilkley, West Yorkshire
LS29 8AF Tel: 01943 817387

Ben Rydding is the close neighbour of Ilkley, well known for its shops, hotels and Ilkley Moor. But Ben Rydding has its own character, and **Gracefields** is a very pleasant guest house in which to stay. An Edwardian house, it forms part of a substantial row of large houses common to this part. The three double guest rooms are spacious and are furnished with a mixture of antique and comfortable furniture. The three rooms share two bathrooms. The guest lounge has an open fire and is a comfortable place to relax at the end of the day. Between them, the owners Mr and Mrs Weinert speak French, German and English so most visitors

Gracefields

should be able to communicate. The terrace patio and conservatory have splendid views of the Wharfe Valley, a pleasant place to be on those bright days. Registered with the Tourist Board.

Gracefields, 133 Bolling Road, Ben Rydding, Ilkley, West Yorkshire LS29 8PN Tel: 01943 600960

KEIGHLEY   *Map 13 ref J9*

At the junction of the rivers Worth and Aire lies this bustling textile and engineering town which, despite its modern redevelopment, still retains a strangely nostalgic air of the Victorian Industrial Revolution. It was that era that created the town seen today, beginning at **Low Mill** in 1780, when cotton spinning on a factory scale was first introduced. Despite being reminders of hardship, the labyrinth of ginnels and terraces amid the many elaborately decorated mills hold a great deal of exploration potential. There are delightful carvings and on one early mill chimney are three heads, one wearing a top hat; in contrast is the classical French styled **Dalton Mill** in Dalton Lane with its ornate viewing gallery.

The centre of Keighley is dominated by impressive Victorian civic buildings and a beautifully set out covered shopping precinct, where the statue of legendary local giant Rombald stands. The parish church, also in the centre, is famous as the site where Patrick Brontë often officiated at marriages. The graveyard contains 15th century headstones, as well as a crude cross made from four carved heads which is believed to be Saxon in origin.

Outside the town centre is **Cliffe Castle** which, despite its deceptive name, is in fact a grand late 19th century mansion complete with a tower, battlements and parkland, which once belonged to local mill owners, the Butterfields. It now houses a natural history museum, with fascinating information on the local topography and geology of Airedale. A short way down the valley is **East Riddlesden Hall**, a National Trust Property with parts dating back to Saxon times. The main building was constructed in the 1630s by James Murgatroyd, a wealthy Halifax clothier and merchant. It is a gabled house built of dark stone with mullioned windows, original central hall, superb period fireplaces, oak panelling and plaster ceilings. The house is furnished in Jacobean style, which is complemented by carved likenesses of Charles Stuart and Henrietta Maria. East Riddlesden Hall also has one of the largest and most impressive timber-framed barns in the North of England, which now houses a collection of farm waggons and agricultural equipment.

Only five miles from Brontë country and just north of Keighley, **Silsden** is a well contained stone built industrial town which spreads uphill from the Leeds–Liverpool canal. Rows of stone built terraced cottages and houses lie on the steep hill sides and there is newer housing on the outskirts of the town. Silsden owes its development to the textile industry and some textile companies remain in the original mill buildings.

Opposite the park in Bolton Road is a truly exceptional restaurant which is located in a converted stone cottage. **Merlin's** is owned and personally run by Chris and Cynthia Sykes and their son Howard who over the years have accumulated a wealth of training and experience in catering to the highest standard. Today, they offer their customers the very best in food and wine, both in the relaxed atmosphere of the bar and in the more formal surroundings of the restaurant.

Merlin's Restaurant

Howard is responsible for selecting Merlin's first class wine list which features examples from some of the world's finest but lesser known vineyards. He also chooses the daily menu for Merlin's first-class à la carte restaurant which features a variety of English, Continental and International dishes, carefully prepared from top quality ingredients including fresh fish, game in season and meat supplied by a celebrated local butcher. Meals are individually cooked to order and may take a little time to prepare, but the results are well worth waiting for. For those requiring a lighter, more straightforward meal, these are provided in the bar every evening except Saturdays. Each month the Sykes also organise excellent value gourmet wine-tasting evenings which typically feature a six course meal accompanied by up to seven specially selected wines. Open Monday to Saturday, 7 pm to midnight and for lunch, Thursday to Saturday, 12 noon to 2 pm.

Merlin's Restaurant, 7 Bolton Road, Silsden, near Keighley, West Yorkshire BD20 0JY Tel: 01535 655995

Also just north of Keighley, in the small village of **Utley**, is a charming family run hotel and restaurant, the **Dalesgate Hotel**, which is under the personal management and supervision of Stephen and Jane Atha. Originally, the hotel was the residence of the minister to the chapel which stood on the site of the new extension to the hotel. Situated on the very edge of Dales and Brontë country, the Dalesgate is only 10 minutes drive from Skipton, the gateway to the dales,

Dalesgate Hotel

and therefore is an ideal base for touring and exploring this much loved area of Yorkshire. Business travellers will appreciate the convenience of easy access to the major towns and cities of the region whilst enjoying the retreat to the countryside setting at the close of day. The 20 bedrooms are centrally heated and have double glazing; all luxury fittings are provided as are en-suite facilities. The restaurant is open Monday–Saturday evenings and both à la carte and table d'hôte menus offer excellent fare. Ask for details on special weekend breaks.

Dalesgate Hotel, 406 Skipton Road, Utley, near Keighley, West Yorkshire BD20 6HP Tel: 01535 664930 Fax: 01535 611253

BRADFORD   *Map 13 ref K10*

The growth which this town experienced during the first 50 years of the 19th century can only be considered as phenomenal: in 1801 Bradford was a quiet market town of 13,000 inhabitants but by 1830 the population had grown to

103,000. The cause of such an explosion was the introduction of the textile industry factory system to the town and, by the end of the century, Bradford was handling 90 per cent of the world's wool trade. All claims which the town has to having been the Wool Capital of the World are, therefore, justly founded.

The prosperity which the wool brought to the town can still be seen in many of the grand Victorian buildings which the wealthy manufacturers had constructed from the local Pennine stone. An area well worth exploring is **Little Germany**, the historic wool merchants' quarter where ornate warehouses were built. Many of the mills too were constructed in elaborate style and some resemble Italian palaces rather than places of intense labour. All in all, today Bradford has over 4000 buildings in its area that are listed for their architectural or historical importance. One of these is **Lister's Mill**, whose huge ornate chimney dominates the city's skyline and which, according to legend, is wide enough at the top to drive a horse and cart around. A rather quirkier sign of the city's former riches is **Undercliffe Cemetery**. Here the wool barons were buried, each in a more opulent gothic mausoleum than the last.

The fact that Bradford has a **Cathedral** is an indication of its historical importance as a city. The first evidence of worship on the site comes from the remains of a Saxon preaching cross and today the cathedral contains many items of interest, including beautiful stained glass windows, some of which were designed by William Morris.

Naturally, the textile heritage of the city is one the great features of Bradford's museums and two of particular interest are the **Industrial Museum**, which tells the history of the textile manufacturing here, and the **Colour Museum**, which shows how colour was and is used in textiles and printing. Right in the centre of the city is the **National Museum of Film, Photography and Television**; home to Britain's only permanent IMAX screen which stands five storeys high.

West of Bradford, off the A629, and midway between Thornton, famous as the birthplace of the Brontë sisters, and **Denholme**, is **The Brown Cow**. An 18th century Grade II listed building, it retains its delightful character with many original features having been preserved. Owners Alan and Carol have retained it old English style with appropriate furnishings and created a very friendly

The Brown Cow

atmosphere. There is a spacious restaurant where a goodly selection of home-cooked dishes are served and diners have additional daily specials from which to choose. Customers can enjoy a pleasant drink in the large beer garden which is also has a children's play area. Large car parking area.

The Brown Cow, 1370 Thornton Road, Denholme, West Yorkshire
BD13 4HQ Tel: 01274 833077

HALIFAX   *Map 13 ref K10*

The town of Halifax has one of Yorkshire's most impressive examples of municipal architecture, the large and beautiful **Piece Hall**. It possesses a large quadrangle, where regular markets are held, surrounded by colonnades and balconies, behind which is a host of interesting shops and commercial outlets. There is also an art gallery with a varied programme of contemporary exhibitions and workshops. Built in the 17th century, the hall was originally utilised for the selling of cloth or pieces and, in the 18th century, after having been allowed to fall into disrepair, was renovated with the permission of Lord Ingram.

The Town Hall is another notable building, designed by Sir Charles Barry, who also designed the Houses of Parliament, and there is an attractive Borough Market, constructed in cast-iron and glass, with an ornate central clock. In Gibbet Street stands a grisly reminder of the past—a replica of a guillotine—the original blade being kept in the **Piece Hall Museum**. There are a lot of hidden places in old Halifax to explore; from Shear's Inn, an old weavers' inn below the centre, one can walk up the cobbled Boy's Lane, very little changed from Victorian times; or trace out the ancient **Magna Via**, a medieval path to the summit of Breacon Hill.

Halifax also has the largest **Parish Church** in England, of almost cathedral sized proportions, which dates from the 12th and 13th centuries, although most of the present building is from the 15th century. There is a lovely wooden ceiling which was constructed in 1635, and visitors should look out for Old Tristram, a life-sized wooden effigy of a beggar, reputedly based on a local character, which was once the church poor box.

The **Calderdale Industrial Museum**, which houses still-working looms and mill-machinery, the **Horses at Work Museum** at Dobbin's Yard and the **Bankfield Museum** are all worthy of a visit. A new addition is **Eureka!**, which introduces children of all ages to science with a host of hands on exhibits and do-it-yourself experiments.

Shibden Hall and Park, about two miles out of town, is somewhere very special that should not be missed. The Old hall itself lies in a valley on the outskirts of the town and is situated in 90 acres of parkland. The distinctive timber framed house dates from 1420 and is deliberately furnished to reflect the various periods of its history. The 17th century barn behind the hall houses a fine collection of horse-drawn vehicles and the original buildings have been transformed into a 19th century village centre with a pub, estate-worker's cottage, and saddler's, blacksmith's, wheelwright's and potter's workshops.

The town centre has recently been enhanced by an interesting retailing idea; **Spinnies** which is located in Woolshops—just above Sainsburys facing the walkway to the historic Piece Hall. The concept is a shop that has been designed specifically with the customer in mind. In the ground floor gift shop, Spinnies offer a wide selection of hand-made English and Belgian chocolates, beautifully displayed and hard to resist. Unusual cards for every occasion and ornate silver photo frames, jewellery and other gift items offer great present ideas.

Spinnies

The first floor coffee shop provides a much needed haven of refinement from the hustle and bustle of town centre shopping. The attention to detail is immediately striking and customers will find it a pleasure to be treated with care and consideration by friendly waitresses in traditional blouses and lace pinnies. The aroma of freshly ground coffee is always a draw and customers will be tempted by the traditional coffee shop menu with its tempting array of salads and garnished sandwiches. Only the finest fresh food is served and great care is given to the presentation. For morning coffee, lunch or afternoon tea, there could be no better venue. Don't miss Spinnies!

Spinnies, 23 Woolshops, Halifax, West Yorkshire HX1 1RU
Tel: 01422 349377

Nestling in the picturesque village of **Luddenden**, just to the west of Halifax, and steeped in Brontë history, **The Lord Nelson Inn** dates back to 1634 and has very strong links with the Brontë family. This traditional old pub is located opposite the historic church of St Mary's and the River Ludd and has retained many of its original features including heavy oak beams and a large inglenook fireplace. In years gone by the inn was regularly frequented by Patrick Branwell Brontë, brother of the famous sisters of Haworth, who once wrote "I would rather give my hand than undergo again the malignant yet cold debauchery which too often marked my conduct there."

The Lord Nelson Inn

Today the pub is owned and personally run by Paul and Bronwen, a very welcoming couple who have ensured that all their customers will leave the Lord Nelson Inn feeling rested and relaxed. In the warmer weather visitors can sit and enjoy traditional ales in the pleasant cottage beer garden, but in the colder months the open fireplace proves popular amongst the inn's many patrons. For those who feel a little more active, there are numerous gentle walks in the local area so that a good thirst can be built up before returning to The Lord Nelson Inn for a cool drink.

The Lord Nelson Inn, 15 High Street, Luddenden, near Halifax, West Yorkshire HX2 6PX Tel: 01422 882176

HUDDERSFIELD   *Map 13 ref K11*

This town has a gritty, industrial atmosphere with steep, often cobbled streets, a mixture of terraced houses, older millstone grit cottages and larger Victorian dwellings, some interesting pubs and a skyline dominated by the scars and marks of its industrialisation. The wealthy lords of the manor hereabouts were the Ramsdens and much of the grand architecture in the centre is due to their efforts. There is a very impressive railway station, designed by James Pigott of York and built between 1846–50. Other buildings of interest include the Italianate Town Hall, the neo-Gothic parish Church of St Peter and Bryam Arcade. The Brook Street market is another pleasant place to wander around.

The outskirts of the town are interesting, and many visitors may decide to head towards the highest point in the area, **Castle Hill**, about two miles south of Huddersfield. It is considered one of the most important archaeological sites in Yorkshire. The hill, a high moorland ridge overlooking the Colne and Holme Valleys has been occupied as a place of defence since Stone Age times, circa

20,000 BC, by what are believed to be Neolithic herdsmen from mainland Europe—simple tools, flints, bone needles, combs and pottery have been unearthed to substantiate this. The magnificent ramparts of an Iron Age Fort, built here in 600 BC and later destroyed by fire, can also still be seen. In 1147 the Normans restored the earthworks, building a motte and bailey castle here which was apparently used as a base for hunting. The hill was also used as a beacon during the times of the Armada and also during the Napoleonic wars. At present it is crowned with the Jubilee Tower, built in 1897, to celebrate Queen Victoria's reign. It stands at just under 1000 feet above sea level and apart from offering wonderful panoramic views of the valleys, it also houses an exhibition of the hill's long history.

Huddersfield Christian Fellowship, in the heart of the town, is a lively nondenominational church where people from all cultural backgrounds with the same belief in the basic truth of the Bible can come together. Run by church leader Colin Cooper and his wife Sue, there is a main church service held every Sunday morning to which all are welcome.

Huddersfield Christian Fellowship

The Fellowship Centre also offers a full range of activities and social group events for people of every age. Open from Monday to Saturday, the centre has pool, snooker and table tennis as part of the activities and, for the more energetic, there is also a gym. Music and drama play an important part in the life of the Fellowship centre and there are several discussion groups which meet to consider the principles of church life and the wider Christian message. Finally, the centre has a well stocked craft and bookshop as well as a coffee shop where many people come to enjoy a drink and a hot meal. The excellent crèche facilities are also a feature of this family church.

Huddersfield Christian Fellowship, 5a Northumberland Street, Huddersfield HD1 1RL Tel: 01484 426344

The White Horse Inn, two miles outside of Huddersfield, has been family owned and run by father and daughter team Michael and Clare for just over a year. The warm and friendly welcome on arrival sets the homely tone, whilst the natural stone floors and large fireplaces add an air of tradition and history. The pub was totally refurbished in January 1997 and has a host of attractive features including plenty of good pine furnishings and quality modern decor. Visitors will find a good range of beers and lagers and the extensive food menu is a credit to the Clare, who is a fully qualified chef and partner in this family business. There is live entertainment and quiz nights on various evenings and many international sporting events are shown on the pub's big screen TV.

The White Horse Inn

The White Horse Inn, 761 Leeds Road, Huddersfield, West Yorkshire HD2 1YZ Tel: 01484 423899

HOLMFIRTH   *Map 13 ref K11*

While in this area, many will no doubt feel compelled to visit this town, best known as the location of the television series *Last Of The Summer Wine*, and despite the commercialisation, their trip will not be disappointing. Visitors can take a trip to the real Sid's Café, Nora Batty's cottage and sit in the famous pub. The rest of the town offers a network of side lanes, courts and alleyways with some interesting shops and cafés besides. The terraces of weavers' cottages are typical of a town famous for its production of wool textiles. As with so many of these moors villages, there is a lot of water surrounding and in its time, Holmfirth has suffered three major floods; of which the flood of 1852 was the worst. The nearby Bilbury Reservoir burst its banks, killing 81 people and destroying mills, cottages and farms at the cost of 7,000 jobs. A pillar near the church records the height of the waters.

The lovely Georgian church was built in 1777–8 in neo-classical style to the designs of Joseph Jagger. The gable faces the street and the tower is constructed at the eastern end against a steep hillside. Also in Holmfirth is the delightful **Holmfirth Postcard Museum** (above the library), based on nearby Balmforth's— the country's leading publishers of the traditional saucy seaside postcard. The displays also include cards from over nearly a century, including patriotic cards from World War I, less sentimental ones from World War II and a moving audiovisual documentary presentation of the 1852 flood.

Spring Lodge affords visitors to Holmfirth the opportunity to stay in a refined Victorian period residence which harks back to an era before the days of *Last of the Summer Wine*. This bright and beautiful house is delightfully and charmingly furnished in period, with quality furniture and decor. The decorative fanlight entrance door is original as are all the internal doors. The polished floor in the

Spring Lodge

dining room adds a further touch of the style and manner for which this house was intended. There are five guest rooms—two double, one twin and two single rooms serviced by three Victorian bathrooms; all rooms have television and tea and coffee making facilities. The house is in an elevated position and overlooks tennis courts and bowling greens. Car parking. Ideal for sightseeing and walking.

Spring Lodge, 1 Calf Hill Road, Thongsbright, Holmfirth, West Yorkshire HD7 2UB Tel: 01484 685705

To the southeast of Holmfirth lies **Denby Dale**, a village famous for its production of gigantic meat pies. The tradition was started in the village to celebrate King George III's recovery from mental illness. Several have been produced since then, to celebrate such occasions as the Battle of Waterloo and the repeal of the Corn Laws. One of the most recent was in 1964, when the pie measured 18 feet in length and weighed six and a half tons. The last one was made in 1987 and the dish used is now on display just outside the village.

The Dunkirk Inn occupies an imposing position in the hamlet of Dunkirk at Denby Dale with breathtaking open views over rural West Yorkshire making it a popular stopping point for country walkers. Formerly three cottages with stabling, it was converted into a free house in 1912 though the buildings date from the 1880s. The atmosphere is comfortable and traditional with beamed ceilings and a wealth of old timber with glowing open fires for those cold winter nights. Paul and Michelle Tugwell are attentive hosts who extend a warm welcome to all.

The Dunkirk has an excellent menu of popular dishes which includes a vegetarian choice and children's meals. They also offer a traditional Sunday lunch. Each order is individually prepared using fresh produce whenever possible. The first ales to be served from this stone built inn were local from the Cudley Brewery at Thurlstone, approximately six miles away, today a wide variety of beers, lagers and spirits are served and a choice from the range of selected wines make a fine accompaniment to a meal. Bed and breakfast accommodation is now offered at the inn.

The Dunkirk Inn

The Dunkirk Inn, Barnsley Road, Denby Dale, near Huddersfield, West Yorkshire HD8 8TX Tel: 01484 862646

Situated on the A636 Wakefield road, just past the village of Denby Dale, stands **The Travellers Rest**, a traditional inn that was built around 1700. Owned and run by Paul and Judith for the past 15 months, the pub is split into three rooms, two lounges and an attractive dining room which is attached to a small patio area outside for al fresco eating. The inn is filled with character and has many original features including large wooden beams over head and open stone fireplaces that crackle and blaze in those cold, wintry months. Home-cooking is order of the day at the Travellers Rest and food is served from Monday to Sunday from 12 pm until 3 pm and Monday to Saturday 6 pm until 8.30 pm, so visitors can always be sure of a hot snack or meal. Also available is a function room that is large enough to handle most events and occasions, with Paul and Judith giving a hand with the catering if needed.

The Travellers Rest

The Travellers Rest, 250 Wakefield Road, Denby Dale, near Huddersfield, West Yorkshire HD8 8SU Tel: 01484 867440

WAKEFIELD *Map13 ref K10*

This is one of the oldest towns in Yorkshire and it has been a focal point for the surrounding area from as far back as Anglo-Saxon times. Standing on a hill guarding an important crossing of the River Calder, its defensive position has always been important and, indeed, it was the Battle of Wakefield, in 1460, when the Duke of York was defeated, that gave rise to the song *The Grand Old Duke of York*. There are also some strong arguments that Robin Hood came from this area—according to the Court Rolls, a Robin Hode lived here in the 14th century with his wife Matilda before fleeing to become an outlaw.

The city centre is dominated by its 13th century **Cathedral** with its 247 foot spire—the highest in Yorkshire. Wakefield is also well known for its cycle of medieval miracle plays, which explore New and Old Testament stories in vivid language. The cycle is performed on the precinct in front of the cathedral as part of the city's annual festival.

There are three main streets in the city, Westgate, Northgate and Kirkgate, which still follow their original medieval route. The tiny **Chantry Chapel**, on Chantry Bridge (the old Wakefield Bridge) dates from the mid-14th century and is the best of only four such examples of bridge chapels in England. It was believed to have been built by Edward IV to commemorate the brutal murder of his brother Edmund.

Wakefield Museum, located in an 1820s building in Wood Street, was originally a music saloon and then a Mechanics Institute before becoming a museum. It now houses collections on the history and archaeology of the city and its people from prehistoric times to the present day. Other museums worthy of a visit are the **Stephen G Beaumont Museum**, which houses an unusual exhibition of medical memorabilia, and the **Yorkshire Mining Museum**.

The Railway Hotel

Conveniently located only three miles from Junction 35 on the A1–A638 to Wakefield road, in the village of **South Elmsall**, stands **The Railway Hotel**, a traditional railway inn that is today home to Tim, Dave, Roger and their ever welcoming dog Hamish. All of the nine en-suite guest bedrooms have excellent facilities, with a full English breakfast being served at a time that is convenient for the guest, now there's a rarity! The restaurant is open for dining from 11.30 am until 10.30 pm and, if the chef has 24 hours notice, guests can dine on any dish of their choosing, regardless as to whether it is included in the hotel's comprehensive menu. The bar is open all day, every day, with Tim, Dave and Roger regularly sitting down to enjoy a late drink and a chat with their guests. The Railway Hotel displays a level of service that is seldom seen today and those who are visiting this picturesque area should do drop in and for a most memorable and relaxing break.

The Railway Hotel, Station Road, South Elmsall, West Yorkshire WF9 2HP
Tel: 01977 642839

At **Horbury**, three miles from Wakefield on the A642, is **The Quarry Inn**, an interesting old stone building formerly a quarry masters house shared with his employees. The lounge wall of the inn is built from the last original stone to be quarried locally before the quarry's closure at the turn of the century. Tools and memorabilia decorate the walls and some of the original cutting blades are displayed. Owners Mike and Cybil Bennett have created a warm and very friendly atmosphere and old quarry lights surrounding the Westmorland slate bar give it a cosy feel. An à la carte menu offers traditional home-cooked food prepared by son and chef, Terry. There are four pleasant guest bedrooms which have en-suite facilities, hospitality tray and colour television. Leeds and Bradford centres are easily reached as is the National Coalmining Museum.

The Quarry Inn

The Quarry Inn, Horbury, near Wakefield, West Yorkshire WF4 5NF
Tel: 01924 272523

When travelling along the A648 between Wakefield and Rothwell, be sure to look out for **The Spindle Tree** at **Stanley**, an attractive pub set on the side of the road. Owned and run by Pauline and Graham, this family style inn was once a coaching house at the time when roads were frequented by horse and carriage rather than cars and the pace of life was a slower one. Today the interior is smart and modern, with attractive wallpaper and teak style tables and chairs throughout. The welcome is a warm one and Pauline is a qualified Cordon Bleu Chef who has trained at Bradford College and Trusthouse Forte, so visitors can be guaranteed a good meal if they decide to stay and eat. Food is served from Tuesday–Saturday 6.30 pm until 9.30 pm and lunchtimes from 12–2 pm, with some guests travelling from as far afield as Chorley, Liverpool and Leeds to sample Pauline's culinary delights.

The Spindle Tree

The Spindle Tree, 46 Taberford Road, Stanley, near Wakefield, West Yorkshire WF3 4AJ Tel: 01924 826353

DEWSBURY   *Map 13 ref K10*

This is an extremely old town which once had considerable influence and it remains the centre of Yorkshire's heavy woollen industry, filled as it is with old mills and warehouses. It has one of the region's oldest town centres with an imposing Town Hall designed by Henry Ashton and George Fox. It also has a number of other notable public and commercial buildings and a substantial shopping centre with a famous market.

The **Church of All Saints** is situated, according to legend, at the point where Saint Paulinus baptised converts in the river Calder. It dates from the 12th century although the tower was designed by the eminent York architect John Carr in 1767. The interior is interesting with several intriguing features, including fragments of an Anglo-Saxon Cross and coffin lids. It is, however, best known for its custom of tolling the Devil's Knell on Christmas Eve to ward off evil spirits with the bell that is known as Black Tom. Patrick Brontë was the curate of Dewsbury between 1809–11 and Charlotte taught at Wealds House School nearby which was run by Miss Wooler, who later gave her away when she married.

One place of interest to visit while in the town is Crow Nest Park, a landscaped park with a Victorian mansion which contains the **Dewsbury Museum of Childhood**, including a reconstructed classroom and a wonderful display of toys and dolls. Dewsbury is also famous as the home of Betty Boothroyd, Stan Laurel and Eddie Waring.

Just off the main Dewsbury to Wakefield road lies **The Spangled Bull** pub, a delightful oasis where visitors are guaranteed a warm welcome by hosts Beryl and Malcolm Flowers. The pub building dates back to the 17th century and was formerly Home Farm House where, later, beer was brewed. The interior houses a fine collection of gleaming brasses which can be enjoyed while relaxing on the

The Spangled Bull

traditional wooden settle seating. A visit at lunch time will enable guests to sample the delights of honest Yorkshire home-cooking, including Yorkshire pudding, accompanied by one of the fine ales from the bar. In summer, Malcolm decorates the exterior with hanging baskets which ensure that the picturesque pub is a sight worth visiting.

The Spangled Bull, 6 Town Street, Earlsheaton, Dewsbury, West Yorkshire
Tel: 01924 462949

Northwest Yorkshire

INTRODUCTION

This northwestern area of the county of North Yorkshire is home to some of the most breathtaking scenery in England. The **Yorkshire Dales National Park**, which encompasses a large section of the Pennines, is an area rich in contrast: there is wild rugged moorland and, in the shelter of the dales, lush green pasture and unspoilt rural villages. There are some 20 dales in all and, though they have been inhabited for over 10,000 years, for much of this time the communities led isolated lives and each developed its own distinct character. In many of the dales the handknitting industry thrived and, of course, the area is also famous for Wensleydale cheese. Produced over 700 years ago by the monks of Jervaulx Abbey, it is still made in the dale today.

However, though the area is rich in pretty, unspoilt villages and small market towns, it is the wealth of the dales natural wonders that draws people here. The grandeur of **Malham Cove**, a magnificent 300 foot limestone amphitheatre is certainly one great natural features not to be missed. Whilst, nearby, **Gordale**

Scar, a huge gorge carved out by glacial melt water, is also well worth a visit. Throughout the whole area, the action of glaciers on limestone has given rise to a whole range of interesting and unusual features that make the Dale so loved by many.

HARROGATE   *Map 13 ref K9*

One of England's most attractive towns and a frequent winner of Britain in Bloom; a great feature of the town are its acres of gardens with an array of colour throughout the year, open spaces and broad tree lined boulevards. Following the discovery of the first mineral water by William Slingsby over 400 years ago, their healing properties have been drawing the well-to-do ever since. The town's reputation reached a peak at the beginning of this century resulting in considerable expansion and leaving a rich legacy of Victorian and Edwardian architecture. Though the waters no longer attract the rich and influential the gentile town created around them still holds great appeal for the discerning tourist.

The many old-fashioned shops are typified by **Montpelier Parade**, a crescent of shops surrounded by trees and flower-beds. **The Stray**, which is unique to Harrogate, virtually encircles the town centre. The 200 acres of open space are protected by ancient law to ensure that the residents of the town and visitors always have access for sports, events and walking. The spacious lawns are at their most picturesque during the spring when edged with crocus and daffodils.

The **Royal Pump Room Museum** was built in 1842 to enclose the old sulphur well and it has now been painstakingly restored to illustrate all the aspects of Harrogate's history. Beneath the building sulphur water still rises to the surface and can be sampled. There will be few Harrogate residents who have not heard of Betty Lupton, the almost legendary Queen of the Wells who, for over 50 years, dispensed the spa waters, dishing out cupfuls to paying visitors, who were then encouraged to walk off the dubious effects of the medicine by taking a trip around the Bogs Fields, known today as Valley Gardens. She conducted her business in the ostentatiously named Royal Baths which, in their heyday, were full of rich visitors sampling the waters. Today, the buildings have been restored to house the **Turkish Baths** where visitors can enjoy a sauna and solarium, and are open to the public daily.

Surrounded by beautifully laid out grounds, the attractive Regency house, **Rudding Park**, contains a wealth of paintings, tapestries and antiques inside and captures the atmosphere of the town admirably. Also on the outskirts of the town are the **Harlow Car Botanical Gardens**. The gardens belong to the Northern Horticultural Society and include a wide range of plants, trees and shrubs in 68 acres. There is also a museum of gardening, model village and shop.

Situated in a quiet, tree-lined avenue only a short walk from the Valley Gardens and Royal Pump Room Museum, stands **Acorn Lodge Hotel**, an elegant

Edwardian residence that offers both quality and value. Owned and run for the past eight years by Sue Tinker, this attractive hotel offers seven tastefully and individually decorated bedrooms with colour television, alarm clock radio and tea and coffee making facilities. En-suite bedrooms with shower and toilet are also available and the hotel is centrally heated throughout, so even in the coldest months guests will be cosy and comfortable. Sue is noted for her excellent home-

Acorn Lodge Hotel

cooking and as well as the hearty English breakfast, visitors can enjoy an optional four course dinner that is served in the delightful dining room. The Acorn Lodge also has a full residential license and a good selection of wines are available to compliment the evening meal. For those who prefer to eat out, then they have a lot of restaurants to choose from, 64 in fact and all within easy walking distance of the hotel—Harrogate is considered to be the "Paris of the North". So whether visiting Harrogate on holiday or business be sure to stay at the Acorn Lodge Hotel, the small hotel with a growing reputation.

Acorn Lodge Hotel, 1 Studley Road, Harrogate, North Yorkshire HG1 5JU
Tel: 01423 525630

The elegance of England's leading floral resort is matched only by the warmth and comfort of the long established award winning **Scotia House Hotel**, the home of Gilly and Graeme Everett for the past eight years. This attractive Victorian house was originally built in 1895 and offers its visitors the very best in traditional English hospitality. All of the 14 delightful bedrooms have been individually styled and furnished and offer en-suite facilities, colour TV, direct dialling telephone, radio and a complimentary beverage tray. The light and airy dining room is where guests will be served one of the best British breakfasts around, freshly cooked and guaranteed to keep them going until dinnertime. Gilly and Graeme are also pleased to accept reservations for their traditional home-cooked dinners, prepared using only the freshest local ingredients; vegetarian and vegan dishes are available with prior notice. To complement the meal, why not select a wine from the good selection available and, also for guests' enjoyment Graeme serves a wide range of aperitifs, liqueurs, beers and spirits at the bar. All of this and much, much more is at hand when staying at Scotia House where hospitality means that guests will linger longer and return again soon. Awarded ETB 3 Crowns, AA 1 Star and RAC 1 Star.

Scotia House Hotel

Scotia House Hotel, 66/68 Kings Road, Harrogate, North Yorkshire HG1 5JR Tel: 01423 504361 Fax: 01423 526578

Spring Lodge Guest House is a comfortable town house dating from the Edwardian period and situated in a quiet cul-de-sac close to Harrogate town

Spring Lodge Guest House

centre. This attractive establishment is ideally situated for the business and tourist visitor alike, being just a short walk from the Royal Hall, Conference Centre and Exhibition Halls, and close to the centre of town with its many restaurants and attractions. All of the six individually decorated and furnished guest bedrooms have either en-suite, shower or shared bathroom facilities and come complete with full central heating, baby listening service and a complimentary beverage tray. Owned and personally run by Carol and Derek for the past three years, Spring Lodge also offers its guests two or three course evening meals on request as well as the generous full English breakfast that is served every morning in the dining room.

Spring Lodge Guest House, 22 Spring Mount, Harrogate, North Yorkshire HG1 2 HX Tel: 01423 506036

The lovely village of **Kettlesing** in Nidderdale, just off the A59 west of Harrogate, is the home of **Harrogate Holiday Cottages**, a friendly family run efficient business offering self-catering apartments and country cottages within a 25 mile radius of Harrogate. Their specialist knowledge of the area and of the properties featured in their brochure, takes the hassle out of choosing the ideal holiday and gives visitors complete peace of mind. For the business man, Harrogate Holiday Cottages offer excellent town-based properties with easy access to motorways, and yet just a stroll away from Harrogate's Conference Centre and Exhibition Halls. For the family, the versatility of Harrogate as a

Harrogate Holiday Cottages

touring base is without comparison, from the beauty of its breathtaking scenery, to the warmth and character of its people; Yorkshire has an individuality all of its own. Accommodation ranges from small, character filled cottages and flats sleeping two, to large, former coach houses and village schools sleeping up to nine. All of the holiday cottages are in lovely locations and are sensibly priced, offering their guests the very best value for money. Harrogate Holiday Cottages is based near to the American Airforce Base of Menwith Hill, home of the large white "golf balls" and many Americans whilst working in the area. Why not contact the local specialist for a country cottage or apartment in Harrogate for the freedom and enjoyment of a self-catering holiday with a difference. Visit the rugged moors, the picturesque dales and the many attractions the area has to offer. Escape for a break in spring, autumn or winter, celebrate the Festive seasons at Christmas, New Year and Easter, book a break with Harrogate Holiday Cottages and an unforgettable holiday is guaranteed.
Harrogate Holiday Cottages, The Old Post Office, Kettlesing, near Harrogate, North Yorkshire HG3 2LB Tel: 01423 772700 Fax: 01423 772359

Set in the picturesque village of **Bishop Monkton**, found between Harrogate and Ripon and in the heart of North Yorkshire's rustic backwaters, stands the delightful country inn, The Lamb and Flag. This attractive pub has been owned and personally run by Carol and Trevor for the past five years and has become very popular with tourists, locals and ramblers alike. The name itself comes from the crusade based upon the sacrificial lamb and the flag of St George whilst the atmosphere is a warm and friendly one, with blazing open fires and plenty of local memorabilia and old photographs covering the walls. Any walker's appetite will be seriously challenged by the infamous "Flag Fry", whilst the blackboard menu offers a whole host of delicious freshly prepared and home-cooked meals using local vegetables, meat and fish. Ideally situated only eight miles from Harrogate on the Boroughbridge Road, The Lamb and Flag is an ideal meeting place for those visiting Ripon races and historic Fountains Abbey. With its large car park, green and spacious beer garden, good food and excellent beers, this traditional inn is the perfect place to rest and relax before exploring the beautiful surrounding countryside.

The Lamb and Flag

The Lamb and Flag, Boroughbridge Road, Bishop Monkton, North Yorkshire HG3 3QN Tel: 01765 677322

MASHAM   *Map 13 ref K8*

Situated beside the River Ure, this a very picturesque place with old buildings and narrow roads with, at the heart of the town, a wonderfully spacious partly cobbled market place. The ancient church of St Mary stands at one corner, the school founded in 1760 at another and at its centre is the market cross amid trees and flowers.

Masham is home to **Theakston's Brewery**, famed for its Old Peculier brew. The brothers Thomas and Robert first practised their craft 150 years ago and the brewery is now a major employer of the town. Adjoining the brewery is a new visitor centre where the some of the secrets of the process of brewing and cooperage are told. Interestingly, the name of the famous brew commemorates the fact that Masham was a 'peculier' from Roger de Mowbray's time, when the

Archbishop of York freed it to have its own Peculier Court—an ecclesiastical body with wide powers.

Black Sheep Brewery

Are you looking for something different? For those looking for a gift for that special occasion, for family and friends both young and old, then look no further than **Black Sheep Brewery Visitors Centre**. They stock a wide and interesting range of gifts, such as Black Sheep wear T-shirts, Rugby shirts, ties and a whole host of sheepy fits, tankards and lots more. The Black Sheep Bistro offers a welcoming atmosphere with cheerful, friendly service. Using their own beers and local produce, the menu is varied and interesting from a simple cup of freshly brewed coffee to a delicious Riggwelter casserole, everyone's needs will be satisfied.

For those looking for somewhere totally different to hold their birthday party, wedding celebration or Christmas party then the Bistro is the perfect place. The 'shepherded' brewery tours take approximately one hour and involve a fascinating trip around the traditional brewhouse and fermenting room. Visitors can experience the brewing process from the aroma and taste of English hops, malted barley and pure, clear Dale water to the end product, a glass of their award winning Black Sheep ales.

Black Sheep Brewery, Wellgarth, Masham, North Yorkshire HG4 4EN
Tel: 01765 689227 Fax: 0118 982 0077

MIDDLEHAM   *Map 13 ref K8*

The entrance to this historic town is via a fascinating castellated bridge, similar to those normally seen spanning a castle's moat. The famous **Castle** here was once the stronghold of the powerful Kingmaker Neville family, and favourite home of Richard III. However, on the death of Richard at Bosworth Field, the great castle fell into to decay, much of its stone being used to create buildings for the town below. The recent discovery of the Middleham Jewel near the ruins, which was sold for £1.3 million, brought new interest in the castle and its history.

Middleham itself has two market places, some splendid Georgian and Victorian buildings, and a profusion of racing stables, for which the town is renowned (three Grand National winners have been trained here). There is also an old stepped cross in the main market, known as the Swine Cross, which once bore the White Boar emblem of Richard III, hence the name. The lovely parish church is outside the town, with an inscription over the door informing visitors that the church was built by Thomas, Lord of Aylesbury. This spot is quiet and idyllic, with sheep grazing in the graveyard on the brow of the hill that sweeps down to the Coverdale valley.

Overlooked by the castle in Middleham's market place is the **Richard III Hotel**. This beautiful establishment is named after King Richard III who had strong links with the town. For those who are looking for a hotel that is well placed for a short break in the area, perhaps whilst visiting the local racecourse, then this must surely be at the top of the list.

The hotel has a cosy candlelit restaurant which seats 24 and the menu is wide and varied, but features many traditional dishes. All are of the highest quality and offer excellent value for money. The restaurant is always popular, so be sure to book in advance. The rooms are well appointed and have TVs, drinks making facilities and en-suite bathrooms. Particularly attractive is the Honeymoon Suite, which with its fine Georgian style furniture and four-poster bed provides the ideal location for a romantic break.

Richard III Hotel

Richard III Hotel, Market Place, Middleham, North Yorkshire
Tel: 01969 623240

RICHMOND   *Map 13 ref K7*

This is yet another place with a rich and fascinating history. The former county of Richmondshire (which locals still refer to) of which this town was the capital, once occupied a third of the North Riding. Alan Rufus, the first Earl of Richmond, built the original **Castle** here in 1071. The site, 100 feet up on a rocky promontory with the River Swale passing below, is imposing indeed, and well-chosen. The keep rises to 109 feet in height with walls 11 feet thick, while the other side is afforded an impregnable defence by means of the cliff and the river.

With such an inspiring setting, it is hardly surprising that there is a legend that King Arthur himself is buried here, reputedly in a cave beneath the castle. The story goes that a simple potter called Thompson stumbled across an underground passage which led to a chamber where he discovered the King and his knights lying in an enchanted sleep, surrounded by priceless treasures. A voice warned him not to disturb the sleepers and he fled, predictably, unable to locate the passage again.

The **Regimental Museum of the Green Howards**, the North Riding's infantry regiment, is based in the old Trinity Church in the centre of the cobbled market square. The regiment dates back to 1688, when it was founded, and the displays and collections illustrate its history with war relics, weapons, uniforms, medals and regimental silver. Also housed in the museum is the town's silver.

Easby Abbey, situated outside the town's boundaries, on a minor road off the B6271, is a low built monastic ruin which looks down to the River Swale. Founded in 1155, its order of monks were of more modest leanings than the Cistercians, and the building certainly possesses none of the grandiose lines of Rievaulx and Fountains, although the riverside setting is typically in common. The Abbey can be reached by a pleasant riverside walk which is well sign-posted.

The Old Brewery Guest House

The Old Brewery Guest House is conveniently situated in Richmond, nestling in a quiet, secluded corner, near the castle. This 17th century inn has now been fully refurbished in a luxurious Victorian style, capturing the essence of a bygone age whilst retaining all of the modern comforts required by today's travellers.

All of the bedrooms are en-suite and have many other amenities such as beverage making facilities and hair dryers. The Honeymoon Suite is particularly attractive and features a four-poster bed. Packed lunches and three course dinners are available to order in advance. All guests can be sure of a warm welcome and a relaxed stay. This is the ideal base for a break in this fascinating part of England. *The Old Brewery Guest House, 29 The Green, Richmond, North Yorkshire DL10 4RG Tel: 01748 822460 Fax: 01748 825561*

Take the opportunity to explore the wild, remote dale of Arkengarthdale, where one can see the bridge at Langthwaite which featured in the title sequence of the TV series *All Creatures Great and Small*. There are villages here that were established long before lead mining dominated the area, with such wonderful Nordic names as Booze, Eskeleth and Wham.

Arkle Town is another and here can be found a delightful hidden place which is ideally placed to serve as a base for a rewarding stay in this spectacular part of the country. **The Ghyll**, a farmhouse which dates from around 1800, is now a fine guest house which enjoys panoramic views of the dale and offers quality bed and breakfast accommodation. There is a choice of one or two twin rooms or a double room, all have en-suite facilities, shaver points, hairdryers, tea and coffee facilities and colour TV. The delicious full English breakfast which is served sets everyone up for a busy day's exploration and vegetarian choices are also available. Dogs are made welcome with prior request and packed lunches are available if ordered the previous night. No smoking. ETB 2 crowns. A member of the Yorkshire Tourist Board.

The Ghyll

The Ghyll, Arkle Town, Arkengarthdale, near Richmond, North Yorkshire DL11 6EU Tel: 01748 884353 Fax: 01748 884015 Internet: www.yorkshirenet.co.uk/accgde/ghyll

Northeast Yorkshire

INTRODUCTION

Lovers of beautiful architecture, archaeology and ancient churches will find no end of such commodities in and around the great city of York. The Vale of York to the east of the city and running almost to the coast is famed for its agriculture and this flat and highly fertile land is ideal for those who wish to explore the countryside on foot and by bicycle.

To the north lie the great moorland expanses of the North York Moors National Park while the coastline also offers some spectacular scenery. To the north it is rugged and from here the great whaling ships of the 19th century set out on their dangerous journeys. The many, and sometimes grim, tales that were told by the seafarers helped to inspire Bram Stoker to write his famous novel *Dracula*, parts of which are set in Whitby.

YORK   *Map 13 ref L9*

The Romans came here first in AD 71, when the Roman governor, Quintus Petilius Cerealis chose it as the best military strong point for his invasion of Brigantia. He called the new fortress city Eboracum and it was soon to become the capital of Lower Britain and a major city within the Roman Empire. The Legions occupied Eboracum until AD 410, their headquarters standing on the site where York Minster is today. Parts of their building are evident in the foundations that are on view to the public, and a 31 foot Roman pillar, part of the garrison, can be seen near the south entrance.

The withdrawal of the Romans left the way clear for the invading Anglo-Saxons, who occupied the city and set it up as Eoferwic. The arrival of Christianity also brought learning to the North and, by the 8th century, Eoferwic was the most important centre of learning in this part of Britain. The Vikings invaded in the 9th century—naming the city Jorvik—and remains of their settlement can be viewed at the **Jorvik Centre**. This a fascinating experience for museum-goers of all ages., where visitors are required to step aboard a time-car and travel back through representations of real life Viking Age Britain.

The area was in constant turmoil throughout the 11th century and so troublesome were these Northern lands that William I embarked on a terrible solution to the problem and began the dreaded harrowing of the North (laying the land barren) driving the Northerners into submission by means of starvation. York eventually re-established itself as a major centre, which was helped by the birth of William's son, Henry I, at nearby Selby. By the Middle Ages over a hundred crafts were being practised here, bringing about the founding of the many guilds, the wealthiest of which were the Company of Merchant Adventurers, or overseas traders.

York was by now the second largest and most important city in England. The bars, or gates were built at this time, and many kings and queens were frequent visitors. In 1397, a Royal Performance of the York Mystery Plays was staged, an event which has since taken place every four years. Richard III was the monarch most closely associated with the city. The long standing Wars of the Roses centred on the houses of York and Lancaster, only being resolved through the marriage of Henry VII and Elizabeth of York. The city, however, suffered during the Reformation of Henry VIII, losing its Abbey, priories and friaries; countless treasures were lost. Paradoxically, though, it was the Tudor monarch who did York its greatest favour by setting up the Council of the North, which brought back power to the region. The Council increased York's importance to such a degree that it became the centre for so many of the battles between the Royalists and the Parliamentarians in the Civil War almost a century later. The turning point of the war happened at the battle of Marston Moor, just to the west of York, after which Prince Rupert was forced to hide within the city walls until the surrender to Sir Thomas Fairfax in 1644.

The historical events connected with York are numerous and many are centred around **York Minster**, the city's cathedral that dominates the skyline from most of the town's streets—a splendid vision of great ecclesiastical influence and power. The origins of the Minster stretch back so far that it has always been in contention with Canterbury itself for ecclesiastical precedence. One should be prepared to spend some time here, as there is a lot to see, from the substantial foundations, right up to the guided tour of the Great Tower which gives breathtaking (not to mention dizzy) views of the city.

Sadly, the Minster has suffered from three major fires in its long history. The first was caused deliberately by a madman, Jonathan Martin, in 1829. The second fire occurred only 11 years after the first and was a result of a careless handyman leaving a candle burning. The third, and most recent fire, took place in July 1984 and was probable caused by lightning. It destroyed the central vault of the south transept and all but two of its carved bosses.

The medieval **Shambles** is probably York's most famous street deriving its name from 'Fleshammels', the street of butchers and slaughter houses. The houses on either side were built so as to keep the street out of direct sunlight. The meat carcasses were hung from hooks outside the houses, many of which can still be seen.

The black and white timbered **Merchant Adventurers' Hall** on Fossgate is another magnet for tourists, who are drawn by the history that is associated with this powerful guild. It comprises the Great Hall where all their affairs were transacted, a hospital or almshouse and their own chapel of worship. The guild controlled the trade in all "goods bought and sold foreign", and indeed, is still in operation today. The building with its beautiful and complex timbered roof exhibits the many colourful banners of York's Medieval guilds. In a similar vein, there is also the Merchant Taylors' Hall on Aldwalk, originally constructed by the Confraternity of St John the Baptist.

The ARC (Archaeological Research Centre) is located in a beautifully restored church close to the Shambles, and is an award winning hands-on exploration of archaeology for visitors of all ages. Here one can meet practising archaeologists who offer advice on how to sort and identify genuine finds and to try out ancient crafts. For the more technically minded, there are a series of inter-active computer displays which demonstrate the value of modern technology in uncovering the past.

Railway enthusiasts will be similarly drawn to the **National Railway Museum**, on Leeman Road, where 200 years of technical and social changes brought about by the invention of railways and their contribution to the civilisation are celebrated. Here the story of Britain's railways, from Stephenson's Rocket right through to the Channel Tunnel and beyond, is told. Seekers of information on anything to do with railways can also use the extensive reference library here, with a reading room attached

The definition of automata is 'man-made objects that imitate the movement of living things through a mechanism that is concealed, so as to make them appear to move spontaneously' and the **Automata Museum** traces the history of such objects. From the simple articulated figurines from ancient civilisations, through to the displays of modern robotics there is plenty to see. While **the York Castle Museum** is a goldmine of nostalgic memorabilia and reconstructions not to be missed. It was opened in 1938, based on the collections of Dr John Kirk, a country doctor from Pickering, who acquired the objects to represent a way of life that was fast disappearing. Today, the Museum has extended to fill the former Female and Debtor's prisons that used to be here.

Located in a quiet and secluded area of York stands **Tyburn House Hotel**, this elegant Victorian town house boasts superb views over the famous York

Tyburn House Hotel

racecourse and yet is only a 10 minute walk from the City centre. This attractive hotel has been owned and personally run by David and Eileen for over 20 years and it is their commitment to high standards that has given them a well earned reputation for comfort and value for money. All 12 of the bedrooms have full en-suite facilities and each is individually decorated and furnished in traditional Victorian style, with the Honeymoon suite coming complete with a romantic four poster bed. Some of the comforts of the hotel include TV lounge, central heating, residential licence, personal attention from the hosts and a warm and friendly welcome is always guaranteed. Open all year, Tyburn House Hotel has full facilities for children and pets and their Winter Bargain Breaks prove very popular with many out of season travellers wishing to experience the delights of York, without the crowds.

Tyburn House Hotel, Albermarle Road, The Mount, York, North Yorkshire YO2 1EN Tel: 01904 655069

For the taste of traditional British food at its best then pay a visit to one of **Russells Restaurants**. Both are housed in historic listed buildings conveniently situated in the heart of the city and are ideal for that special treat while shopping or sight-seeing. Choose either the Victorian elegance of **Russells of Stonegate** in York's most picturesque streets leading to the Minster or enjoy the rustic atmosphere of **Russells of Coppergate**, a 16th century timbered building, formerly a coaching inn. After a warm personal welcome from the friendly staff guests can relax in

Russells Restaurant

style and savour the pleasure of the Russells experience—quality food, wine and service—offering true value for money at affordable prices. First choose from a wide selection of appetising, freshly prepared starters. Then the highlight of the meal is a visit to the carving table with succulent roasts and other main dishes with fresh local vegetables and cool refreshing salads. Everyone will definitely be spoilt for choice! For dessert try their famous bread and butter pudding or any one of the other tempting array of home-made sweets. Finally for the perfect ending, there are the Russells speciality liqueur coffees. Russells Restaurants are

open all day serving coffees, lunches, afternoon teas and evening dinners.
Russells Restaurant, 26 Coppergate, York, North Yorkshire
Tel: 01904 644330
Russells Restaurant, 34 Stonegate, York, North Yorkshire Tel: 01904 641432

Tucked away off Bootham, one of the main roads into the city centre, is **Brentwood Guest House**, a substantial and attractive Victorian house with colourful tubs and window boxes, creeper, and a neat frontage. Brentwood is certainly well situated for exploring this historic city: York Minster, the theatre, museums, river and city walls are an easy walk away with many other places of interest within the city a comfortable walking distance.

Brentwood Guest House

Brentwood is a family run guest house providing very clean and comfortable accommodation, centrally heated throughout. Bedrooms are light and pleasantly decorated, neatly furnished and with hand basins—some rooms have private facilities. The dining room has a large display of decorative plates where a first class breakfast will give guests a good start for the day. Evening meals can also be provided. 2 Crowns Commended by ETB.
Brentwood Guest House, 54 Bootham Crescent, Bootham, York, North Yorkshire YO3 7AH Tel: 01904 636419

The Judges Lodging is certainly one of the most centrally located hotels in the city of York. Originally built as a private house around 1710, it became the official residence for Assize Court Judges in 1806. It is now a privately owned and family run hotel. A Grade I listed building retaining many of the Georgian features—panelled walls, high ceilings with elaborate cornicing and a grand oak staircase.

The Judges Brasserie serves excellent food to suit all tastes, both lunch time and evening. Guests will find the elegant surroundings of the residents' lounge an ideal setting for an aperitif or for relaxing with coffee after dinner. The individually furnished guest rooms are en-suite and have satellite TV, radio, telephone and tea and coffee making facilities. Four poster beds, suites, spa baths and impressive views of York Minster are all available, but the hotel's main attribute has to be its central location. Guests can leave their cars in the secure on-site car park and explore the city on foot.

The Judges Lodging

The Judges Lodging, 9 Lendal, York, North Yorkshire YO1 2AQ
Tel: 01904 638733 Fax: 01904 679947

Originally built as two privately owned houses in the middle of the 19th century, and backing onto one of the prettiest squares in York stands **Holmwood House**.

Holmwood House

The original listed buildings have been lovingly restored to retain the ambiance of a private home and provide peaceful, elegant rooms where the pressures of the day can be eased away. All of the 11 guest bedrooms have been individually decorated and furnished to a high standard, each offering full en-suite facilities and two rooms come complete with a romantic four poster bed. Guests will find many extra touches in addition to the usual colour TV, coffee and tea maker, radio-alarm clock, hairdryer and direct dial telephone and for those who find stairs difficult there are two rooms at ground level and one at garden level. There is a comfortable and attractive sitting room in which to relax and browse amongst books or local information and Holmwood House has also been awarded a *Roy Castle Gold* award for a nonsmoking environment. Breakfasts at Holmwood House are definitely worth getting up for, offering a choice of fruit juices, grapefruit segments, prunes and cereals; followed by a wide selection which includes full English breakfast, kippers, fruit platter, vegetarian, hot croissants and toast! For those special occasions Holmwood House offer special two night Gourmet Breaks in conjunction with one of York's top restaurants and for the more active, try their *Walking Breaks*.

Holmwood House, 114 Holgate Road, York, North Yorkshire YO2 4BB
Tel: 01904 626183 Fax: 01904 670899

Just to the south of York the green in **Naburn**, which looks more like a traffic island, has a maypole that doubles as a flagpole. There is a small marina and private yacht club at the end of this small village. At one time a ferry on the River Ouse operated between here and Bishopthorpe, a mile or so to the north.

The Blacksmith's Arms

A short distance from the riverbank is the well recommended pub and eating house, **The Blacksmith's Arms**. Parts of the inn date back 300 years and were formerly a small holding and blacksmith's shop. Throughout its long history it has been extended and remodelled many times but the present owners, Patricia and David Smith, have been successful in retaining the pub's traditional atmosphere. They offer an excellent selection of top quality pub meals at lunch times and every evening (7 pm–9 pm) except Sunday, throughout the summer months. The ales are well kept and include Ridings Bitter and Mansfield Bitter and Smooth. In fine weather, customers can sit outside in the pleasant walled garden. The adjacent former blacksmith's shop has been converted into a self-catering cottage called, appropriately, Blacksmith's Cottage. The cottage sleeps up to six people and is very characterful and cosy.

The Blacksmith's Arms, Naburn, North Yorkshire Tel: 01904 623464

Early on in its history, **Cawood** village, also south of York, belonged the Archbishops of York being the site of one of their palaces. The gatehouse of the Archbishop's palace remains standing, as does a 15th century building referred to locally as the banqueting hall. Cawood also contains some outstanding examples of buildings with Dutch gables dating back to the end of the 1600s and which are unique to this area. There was also once an important boat building industry here to compliment the village's position as a port but this is now confined to Selby. The ferry continued to play an important role though, until the bridge was built at the end of the 19th century.

The 16th century **Ferry Inn** is a pretty as a picture in its setting next to the River Ouse, so step back in time and enjoy this wonderful olde worlde inn. The interior is cosy and traditionally furnished with wooden bench style seating, exposed brickwork and roaring open fires. Keep an eye out for the plaque which tells the history of the village. This family run establishment is renowned for its real ales, of which there are at least eight or nine casks at any one time throughout the year.

The Ferry Inn

The bar menu is equally varied, with dishes to suit every palate and pocket! The vegetarian selection is perhaps the most impressive though, the best that anyone is likely to find in any pub. The owners, the Thorpe family, even offer bed and breakfast accommodation, and their three letting rooms are both comfortable and cosy with the added convenience of packed lunches supplied for those who wish to stroll and explore this beautiful part of North Yorkshire. Outside there is a most attractive beer garden and paved terraced area that overlooks the River Ouse and surrounding countryside, the perfect place to sit and enjoy a drink or a light lunch. All in all, the Ferry Inn is a truly wonderful pub that should not be missed.

The Ferry Inn, King Street, Cawood, near Selby, North Yorkshire YO8 0TL
Tel: 01757 268515

NORTH YORK MOORS NATIONAL PARK   *Map 14 ref M7*

The North York Moors is an area of approximately 650 square miles and holds expectations of a rather inhospitable, bleak terrain, which could not, as it happens, be further from the truth. The largest expanse of moorland in England, there is much to see here, with pretty cottaged hamlets, open heather moorland and miles of rugged coastline. This is also sheep country and the hardy Swaledale breed is by far the most common. In the 19th century a railway line was built to improve the links of the region and, though it fell into disuse, the **North Yorkshire Moors Railway** now offers visitors an ideal opportunity to discover the wonders of this countryside from the comfort of a steam train.

On the western side of the North York Moors National Park lies the village of **Hawnby**, where to the south, can be found the marvellous remains of **Rievaulx Abbey**. Said to be one of the most beautiful monasteries in the country and now in the care of English Heritage. The original abbey was founded in 1132 and was the first Cistercian abbey in the north of England. The most famous abbot of Rievaulx was Aelred, originally an Anglo-Saxon nobleman from Hexham in Northumberland, and a statue dedicated to him stands in the centre of Helmsley. The abbey was razed to the ground during the Reformation and the stones were take to construct a number of local buildings. Like many of the ancient ruins in the area, the abbey is occasionally used for musical and theatrical events.

Situated close to Rievaulx Abbey in a sheltered valley deep in the National Park, stands **Laskill Farm**. Built on an old medieval site dating back to the early 1400, Laskill Farm has been owned and run by Sue for over 27 years. This attractive old farmhouse offers its guests the chance to experience good old fashioned British hospitality amidst this peaceful and restorative haven. Sue offers bed and breakfast accommodation with the option of an evening meal and, as all of the freshly prepared food is cooked using only the finest home-grown and local

Laskill Farm

produce, the dinner is thoroughly recommended. The former outbuildings on the farm have been skillfully converted by local craftsmen using many original materials and features to provide guests with the very best in modern conveniences. The self-catering cottages are grouped around the courtyard of Sue's farmhouse home and offer panoramic views over surrounding woodland. The interiors of the cottages have been furnished and decorated to a very high standard and all feature an attractive inglenook fireplace, original beams and

patio and barbecue areas. *The Smithy Cottage* sleeps up to four in two bedrooms and *The Forge* sleeps up to six in three bedrooms, each having its own bathroom and lounge, dining and kitchen areas. Although all the cottages provide full self-catering facilities, Sue will be delighted to provide breakfast or dinner personally delivered to the door for those who wish to spoil themselves. In the extensive one acre of gardens there is a delightful summerhouse and fresh spring water; a lake, including ducks, completes this idyllic and tranquil picture. Also, in nearby Kirbymoorside, Sue has another three listed self-catering stone cottages, sleeping up to five guests, these charming terraced cottages have been tastefully renovated to a high standard and still retain all of their old world charm.
Laskill Farm, Hawnby, near Helmsley, North Yorkshire YO6 5NB
Tel: 01439 798268

Further east and on the southern outskirts of the National Park lies the village of **Hutton-le-Hole**. **Hammer and Hand House** is a charming listed, Georgian property built in 1784 in a mellow York stone as the village beer house. It features in the Royal Commission (Historical Monuments of England) publication *Houses of the North York Moors*. This attractive property has been owned and personally run by Ann and John Wilkins for the past decade and stands in a sheltered spot on the east side of this picturesque village, facing the green and beck and within the North York Moors National Park. The house contains many

Hammer and Hand House

original features including old stone fireplaces, cruck beams, panelled doors, whilst the antique furniture provides true character accommodation. The comfortable sitting room, with its beamed ceilings and impressive Georgian fireplace, is the perfect place to rest and relax after a busy day exploring the surrounding attractions. All of the individually styled and furnished bedrooms have en-suite facilities, colour TV and a complementary tea and coffee tray. In the Fitzherbert Room is an ornately carved and draped king size bed and luxury en-suite bathroom complete with gold 'Victorian' fittings and beautiful views—

perfect for that romantic break. Hammer and Hand House offers its guests the chance to experience warm and friendly service in charming surroundings that will provide both a carefree and memorable holiday.

Hammer and Hand House, Hutton-le-Hole, North Yorkshire YO6 6UA
Tel: 01751 417300 Fax: 01751 417711

Located high up on the moors, the picturesque village of **Goathland** has earned recent notoriety for being the setting of the TV series *Heartbeat*. Sheltered from cold winds by the surrounding moorlands, it has a surprisingly mild climate for a village so high above sea level, and the beautiful situation certainly makes it very special. As one might imagine with an isolated community such as this one, the traditions go back far, and none so far as the origins of the *Plough Stots Service*, a ritual sword dance performed in the town every January. The Nordic settlers brought this particular ceremony to these parts over a thousand years ago, the stot being derived from the Scandinavian word for a bullock. In the ancient procession, young men of the village drag a plough through the street, in place of the bullocks that would normally perform the task. The dancers follow, brandishing 30 inch swords, in a pagan ritual that the Norsemen were keen to retain after their invasion of the area.

One of the most outstanding attractions of this area is the privately operated, steam-hauled **North Yorkshire Moors Railway** which runs between Pickering and Grosmont, stopping in Goathland. This spectacular line passes through some of the most dramatic landscapes in the National Park including several Sites of Special Scientific Interest. The railway was designed before the age of steam by the great railway engineer, George Stephenson, in order to provide Whitby with a modern land link with the outside world.

When the line first opened the trains were made up of stage coaches on top of simple bogies, pulled along the rails by horses. One of the most interesting features was the 1 in 10 incline from Beck Hole to Goathland where wagons were hauled by rope. The incline caused many accidents until, in 1865, the Deviation Line was blasted through solid rock. Although the gradient is still one of the steepest rail sections in the country at 1 in 49, it opened up the line to steam trains.

In a splendid location overlooking the wide expanses of Goathland Moor, is the **Mallyan Spout Hotel**, named after the waterfall of the same name, which flows into a wooded valley a short distance away. This handsome ivy clad, stone built hotel provides a perfect base for those interested in outdoor pursuits or the peaceful pleasures of fine food, good wine and charming hospitality.

Inside the atmosphere is friendly and the surroundings are luxurious. There is a cocktail bar and three spacious guest lounges with views over attractive gardens to the moors and the beautiful Esk valley beyond. Each of the 24 individually decorated bedrooms has a private bathroom, colour television, telephone and radio. Most are decorated in cottage style and have breathtaking views over the surrounding countryside and moorland. Four rooms have recently been completely refurbished and are of a particularly high quality. They are located at the rear of the hotel and have outstanding panoramic views over the moors towards Egton. Their facilities include electric curtains and full hi-fi systems. In the *Coach House*, two double and two twin rooms are available at ground floor level for those who find stairs a problem. The hotel has been owned and personally run by Judith and Peter Heslop since the early 1970s. They ensure that their guests receive a professional standard of service which makes them feel instantly at home. The hotel restaurant is renowned for its cuisine and is open to residents and non-residents alike. The menu is long and adventurous and features freshly caught seafood from Whitby. The chef's specialities include such delights as fresh pear poached in rosemary and lime with fresh coriander and Stilton and creme fraiche mousse for starters and sautéed medallions of monkfish with a pink and green peppercorn sauce served on a bed of wild rice for a main course. All dishes are freshly cooked to order and they may require a short while to prepare. The results, however, are mouthwatering and well worth waiting for.

Mallyan Spout Hotel

The Mallyan Spout Hotel provides an ideal base for exploring the many nearby beauty spots and places of historical interest. The privately owned North Yorkshire Moors Railway stops at nearby Goathland station and offers a fascinating excursion through heather-clad hills, wooded valleys and charming moorland villages. The hotel also runs a programme of special weekends for the gourmet or those interested in activities such as hill walking and fishing.
Mallyan Spout Hotel, Goathland, North Yorkshire Tel: 01947 896486

WHITBY
Map 14 ref M7

This area is full of landmarks of the life of its greatest son, Captain James Cook, who learnt his skills in seamanship in this town. This historic fishing port serves as an excellent base for jaunts around the coast and is, in itself, worthy of several days exploration on its own. Visitors stopping here might be forgiven for imagining that the town would be shrouded in mist and have a distinctly gothic air to it. The novelist Bram Stoker can be blamed for this image of the town as he based part of his Gothic horror *Dracula* in Whitby. For fans there is a **Dracula Walk**, which takes place on a weekly basis (further information from the Tourist Information Centre).

Fiction aside there is a rich historical background to Whitby. Its traditions as a Christian settlement and whaling port are ancient and inspiring indeed. In AD 664, the synod of Whitby determined the date of Easter. A few years later St Hilda, a Northumbrian princess, founded a community for monks and nuns here. The imposing ruins of **Whitby Abbey** on the cliff top date mainly from the 13th century and dominate the town and harbour. From the old town, there is a famous climb of 199 steps to the **Church of St Mary**, next to the abbey remains, the place of worship for fishermen and seafarers for centuries. The interior has a distinctly nautical feel to it, due to alterations carried out by local shipwrights in the 17th century. Today, Whitby still retains its air of a seafarers' town, with the fishing boats and cobles anchored alongside more modern keel boats, and the yachts that one can see heading towards the marina situated up river.

The town is divided by the River Esk into two distinct areas. The old town is made up of narrow, cobbled streets and contains some small interesting shops. The newer part contains amusement arcades and souvenir shops but is worth investigating nevertheless. For those with tastes of a more nautical flavour, one can visit the cottage in Grape Lane where James Cook served his apprenticeship. In fact, reminders of the great man are never far away in one's ramblings through Whitby. A handsome monument to him stands on the West Cliff, looking down towards the abbey, not far from the whalebone arch which is another famous landmark.

Another thing that one can find when exploring Whitby, are the lovely sepia-tone photographs by Frank Meadow Sutcliffe which form a nostalgic record of the sailing ship traditions and lives of the local fisherfolk of days gone by. The **Sutcliffe Gallery**, on Flowergate, documents this remarkable man's life and works and also displays a great many of the pictures. A trip to the **Whitby Museum**, in Pannet Park, will provide more information as to the lives and industry of the people of Whitby, as well as more detailed documentation on Cook's endeavours.

Between 1753 and 1833, Whitby was the capital of the whaling industry, bringing home 2761 whales in 80 years. Much of that success was due to the skills of the great whaling captains William Scoresby and his son. William Scoresby Senior was renowned for his great daring and navigational skills, as well as for the invention of the crow's nest or mast-head lookout. His son, also called William, possessed leanings of a more scientific nature, and occupied himself with various experiments during his long days at sea in the icy Arctic waters. He is most noted for his discoveries of the forms of snow crystals, and the invention of the "Greenland Magnet", which made ships' compasses more reliable. The whaling industry is now, thankfully, long dead, but fortunately the fishing industry is not, as many of Whitby's restaurants will prove, being famous for their seafood menus.

Whitby Glass Ltd

In one of the ancient parts of Whitby called Sandgate, is the renowned studio of **Whitby Glass Ltd**, home of the world famous "Whitby Lucky Duck". The studio was founded in the early 1960s by Peter Rantell and today it is personally run by Dorothy Clegg, twice former Mayor of Whitby, and also former Deputy Mayor of Scarborough. Visitors are invited to call in at the 400 year old building to observe the skilled crafts people as they draw, bend and fashion coloured glass into the intricately shaped good luck talismans. These have been exported to places as far away as Mexico and Japan, with their alleged success including financial windfalls and the ending of a drought in Southern France.
Whitby Glass Ltd, 9 Sandgate, Whitby, North Yorkshire YO22 4DB
Tel: 01947 603553

"There is a right way, a wrong way, and a Whitby way of doing things", so for those who want to know Whitby better and reach the parts that other visitors miss, then join a guided tour with **Walk Whitby Way**. The Baron, dressed in character

Walk Whitby Way

costume, will tells stories and answers visitors questions, on a 90 minute Historic Town Tour, designed to inform and amuse, as the folklore of this ancient seaport is explored.

In the evening The Man in Black invites visitors to join him on a Ghost Walk, to discover the strange and supernatural tales of murder, mystery and suspense. 'In search of Dracula' is a late night walk and talk where Dracula stalked. It may be a holiday pastime but this is certainly an experience that no one forgets. Walk Whitby Way is a unique, leisurely learning experience for groups and individuals. Contact Harry Collett.

Walk Whitby Way, Ashford Guest House, 8 Royal Crescent, Whitby, North Yorkshire YO21 3EJ Tel: 01947 602138

In a splendid position on Whitby's bustling quayside, there stands a first rate eating house called **The Magpie Café**. This attractive building dates back from the 18th century and was once the home of the Scoresbys. It was then used as a shipping office for many years before being reopened as a café in the 1950s. The Magpie is more like a top class restaurant than a café, being Egon Ronay recommended and featuring in the *Good Food Guide*, *Wholefood Guide* and *British Relais Routier Guide*. It has also been featured as the Just a Bite Guide Restaurant of the Year. Owners Alison and Ian Robson have built their reputation on the quality of the food served and of the service provided. The house speciality is fresh, locally caught fish and seafood and it is said that they serve the best fish and chips in the area. The menus offer a very wide choice and there is much more to choose from than just fish. A variety of salads and vegetarian meals are on offer and the dessert selection is impressive to say the least! The chefs will also cater for those on special diets without a

The Magpie Café

fuss. The seating areas have an atmosphere which is both relaxed and welcoming, with flowers on each table and prints of old Whitby on the walls. The upper eating level also boasts magnificent views over the harbour and the café is open daily from March through to November from 11.30 am to 6.30 pm.

The Magpie Café, 14 Pier Road, Whitby, North Yorkshire YO21 3PU Tel: 01947 602058/821723

On the outskirts of Whitby, just off the Scarborough road is an elegant Georgian mansion, steeped in local history, called **Larpool Hall**. The present mansion was built by Lady Jonathan Lacey in 1796, but records show that there has been a building on the site since the 12th century. In recent years the hall has been an orphanage, service quarters during the Second World War and an outdoor pursuits centre until the present owners, Keith and Electra Robinson bought it in 1986. Today Larpool Hall Hotel offers luxurious accommodation with attentive personal service and peaceful surroundings. The hotel stands in 10 acres of delightful gardens and woodland which are perfect for a relaxing or leisurely stroll. From the beautiful entrance hall visitors are led to the large and elegant bedrooms. All have en-suite bathrooms and all the facilities expected from a top

Larpool Hall

class hotel. There are, in addition, ground floor bedrooms for those unable to climb the stairs. For very special occasions, the hotel boasts a romantic bridal suite on the top floor. The public rooms include the Cholmley Lounge which overlooks the forecourt of the hotel and the Esk Valley beyond. The Dales Restaurant is also a very beautiful room and is a lovely setting for a meal. The menu reflects Electra's wide interest and knowledge of cooking and ranges from traditional English and regional Yorkshire fare, to more exotic dishes for the adventurous. There is always a selection of vegetarian dishes and special diets are catered for with advance notice.

Larpool Hall ,Whitby, North Yorkshire YO22 4ND Tel: 01947 602737
Fax: 01947 820204

On the southern edge of the North Riding Forest Park, between Pickering and Scarborough, lies **Ebberston**. Standing in its own grounds, boasting panoramic views across the vale to the Yorkshire Wolds, **Foxholm** is a stone built farmhouse converted into a modern and comfortable country hotel. This splendid hotel has been owned and managed since 1978 by Kay Clyde and offers its guests the best in good old fashioned British hospitality. All of the comfortable bedrooms are situated on the ground floor and have full en-suite facilities, colour TV, clock-radio and complimentary tea and coffee tray. During 1992 the bar area was extended when the hotel became a fully licensed free house and it has retained much of its old charm, mainly in the wooden carved bar which is covered in old coins.

The games room offers a pool table and dart board and Sky television is available to keep abreast of the sports and news. The cosy residents' lounge has south facing French doors that lead into the extensive grounds, whilst the pleasant dining room can seat up to 20 guests in comfort. The comprehensive à la carte menu provides a good choice of home-cooked dishes which have been prepared using only the freshest locally grown seasonal ingredients. Situated in the tranquil village of Ebberston, Foxholm is the perfect place to escape the stresses of everyday life and just sit back and relax.

Foxholm

Foxholm, Ebberston, North Yorkshire YO13 9NJ Tel: 01723 859550

Further west, midway between Kirbymoorside and Pickering, the hamlet of **Sinnington** is where the River Leven leaves the moors and the valley of Rosedale for the more open country to the south. The main part of the village features houses overlooking a broad green with the river running alongside and the tiny packhorse bridge in the middle of the green presumably served a purpose at one time but it now spans a dry watercourse.

Set amidst beautiful scenery and ideal for those who enjoy walking and the peace of the countryside, the **Fox and Hounds** is a wonderful example of a true country retreat yet it is only 400 yards from the main road. Back in the 18th century, this was a thriving coaching inn on the main route from the East coast to Thirsk and all points west.

Fox and Hounds

A welcoming richness of antiques, ancient wood panelling and oak beams greet guests on arrival. The owners Andrew and Catherine Stephens and their courteous, well trained staff offer a friendly welcome and a relaxing atmosphere. A choice of ground floor or first floor accommodation is available from the 10 comfortable en-suite bedrooms. The restaurant has a full à la carte menu which offers a comprehensive selection of imaginative dishes all cooked to order. Meals are also available in the Bar and Brasserie. Special midweek and weekend breaks are available. ETB 4 Crowns Highly Commended.

Fox and Hounds, Main Street, Sinnington, North Yorkshire YO6 6SQ
Tel: 01751 431577

MALTON   *Map 14 ref M8*

This busy market town sits at the most eastern edge of the Howardian Hills, beside the River Derwent. Its Roman name was 'Derventio' a settlement of some note, and in the museum are many Roman relics that have been excavated from this area. Malton has been the historic centre of Ryedale since those times and, to the north of the Roman fort site, is the original town of Old Malton, with its ancient stone houses and quaint dwellings. At the centre stands the beautiful fragment of the only remaining Gilbertine Priory in use in England—**St Mary's Church**, founded by Eustance Fitzjohn in the 12th century. On a stout oak door of the church can be seen the famous mouse design of Robert Thompson of Kilburn and his distinctive work can also be seen on the pulpit and lectern.

The building of a Norman castle near to the river crossing encouraged the growth of a second town, the modern day Malton. Alongside farming, brewing is a traditional Malton industry and, at one time, nine breweries flourished here along the banks of the Derwent.

Three miles outside Malton, just off the new main road is **Scagglethorpe** village which has won awards in recent 'Britain in Bloom' competitions and also for its delightful village hall. Here can be found the **Wold Edge**, a charming and

Wold Edge

characterful country house built in 1675 and most attractively furnished to the period. The house is situated in a quiet cul-de-sac in the village nestling at the foot of the Wolds, and it is here that proprietor Mrs Roddie Brown provides a warm and friendly welcome for those seeking comfortable bed and breakfast accommodation. There is a large rear garden and ample private parking in this peaceful location.

Apart from the historic market town of nearby Malton many pretty villages surround the area. The Orangery at Settrington is a very popular venue for weddings and special occasions and draws from far distance places, whilst Flamingo Park Zoo, Scarborough, Whitby and other coastal areas remain favourite locations easily reached by car. Castle Howard, historic York and the nearby excellent golf course in Malton offers further hours of pleasure to guests of Wold Edge. Mrs Brown also has a joint referral facility with the owner of the local Manor House and can thus accommodate larger parties when required. The local inn is in walking distance and offers good quality meals.

Wold Edge, Scagglethorpe, near Malton, North Yorkshire YO17 8DU
Tel: 01944 758248

Scagglethorpe Manor

Scagglethorpe Manor is a 17th century Grade II listed farmhouse which has been enthusiastically restored and decorated during the past three years by Jim and Joyce Evans. The house now combines a blend of oak beams, log fires and warm colour tones in keeping with its period. The atmosphere is tranquil, friendly and comfortable and guests will enjoy the warm welcome and home comforts. A traditional and varied breakfast is Aga-cooked using local homegrown produce and preserves. The bedrooms have private facilities, there's a guest sitting room and extensive parking and gardens.

Scagglethorpe Manor, Scagglethorpe, near Malton, North Yorkshire
YO17 8DT   Tel & Fax: 01944 758909

Some eight miles west of Malton lies the charming and interesting little village of **Crayke**, situated on the crest of a hill with the houses clustered around the church and castle. A Saxon fortress was said to have marked this spot many years ago; there is also little left of the Norman castle once sited here, save the foundations. The battlemented house now seen amongst the trees behind the church is the tower house known as the Great Chamber built in the 15th century. It has a beautiful garden and a splendid view from its windows. By it are the remains of the New Tower, a majestic ruin cloaked in ivy.

The church is said to mark the place where St Cuthbert's body was finally laid to rest after its long wanderings and there are many fine features, including two stone figures, said to be Sir John Gibson and his wife who lived here in Elizabethan days. The fact that St Cuthbert's body was taken from here to Durham Cathedral is thought to give rise the name of the local inn.

In the centre of the village is the fine 18th century inn called **The Durham Ox**, which is ideal for those looking for good food and traditional Yorkshire hospitality. The old fashioned lounge bar of this stylish inn is furnished with period seats and settles on a stone flagged floor and is dominated by an imposing inglenook fireplace filled with gleaming old copper and brass. The log fires that blaze in winter are replaced by fresh flowers in the summer months and the pictures and old local photographs add to the general ambience. An archway divides off a bustling lower bar with a good lively atmosphere and, above the

The Durham Ox

cosy Victorian fire grate, is a written account of the local history dating back to the 12th century and, on the opposing wall, a large framed print of the original famous beast. The hosts, the Chadwick's, have built up an enviable reputation for good cooking combined with excellent value for money. The emphasis is on fresh produce and home-made food served in generous portions. The menu, chalked on a blackboard to ensure variety and change, includes traditional English favourites and popular international and vegetarian dishes cooked to order. Specialities include—Lamb with apricots, Aubergine and tomato bake, Port shank Italian style, beef Wellington, Local rabbit pie, Irish stew with crusted dumplings, interesting pasta dishes and home-made hot and cold puddings plus a good selection of wines. The Durham Ox also has three self-catering holiday cottages available which are grouped around an attractive courtyard at the rear of the Inn.

The Durham Ox, Crayke, North Yorkshire YO6 4TE Tel: 01347 821506

East Yorkshire

INTRODUCTION

The majority of the East Riding of Yorkshire lies on the Holderness peninsula, which lies to the east of Hull and between the River Humber and the North Sea. Flat and fertile, this is farming country and the peninsula terminates in a long spit of land which culminates in the sea-eroded headland of **Spurn Head**. Further up the coast there are a whole host of typical English seaside resorts that all benefit from bracing sea breezes coming off the North Sea.

Flamborough Head, the northern most tip of Bridlington Bay, was designated part of a Heritage Coast in 1979 and, as well as the numerous geological features found there, the Head is home to a splendid and important bird sanctuary.

HULL   *Map 14 ref N10*

The town lies on the southern margin of the plain of Holderness and takes its name from the River Hull on which the original port was founded (the Kingston of its original name of Kingston upon Hull was dropped to differentiate it from Kingston-on-Thames near London). The port has now moved to deeper water and the original docks have been refurbished as a marina.

The area was presided over in medieval days by the warlike Lords of Holderness, the land here much prized due to its accessibility for shipping and trade. The Romans had used it as a port to supply the fortresses and garrisons in the area, although it really only started to take on real significance in the 1200s. In Tudor days, it was a well known and prosperous town and there are many period houses and mansions in the area. The infamous Pilgrimage of Grace during Henry VIII's reign took place here, the closest to civil war England had come prior to the conflict between the Royalists and Parliamentarians two centuries later. It involved several notable families in the region, including the Lords of Holderness. Henry's reply to the insurrection was swift and terrible and ended the lines of many of these ancient houses. During the Civil War in Charles I's reign, Hull again became a focal point and the Royalists spent much time and effort, mostly wasted, on attempting to wrest the control of the Humber from the Parliamentarian forces.

Hull is perhaps known by many visitors as being the birthplace of the famous of reformer, William Wilberforce, noted for his campaign to abolish the slave trade. The impressive **Elizabethan House** in High Street where he was born, is now used as a museum to commemorate his life and works. The **Transport Museum**, just a few yards further down the same road is also worth a visit. Here one can see such curiosities as the Velocipede and "Automobile a Vapeur"—a steam driven car. Tourists visiting the museum invariably cluster around Lady Chesterfield's ornamental sleigh.

Many of the oldest parts of Hull were bombed out of existence in World War II, but fortunately the subsequent rebuilding has not resulted in so much of the urban, concrete replacements that other such towns and ports have suffered. There is still a wealth of beautiful, ancient and grand architecture including the Queen's Gardens, the **Maritime Museum** and the Holy Trinity Church. The old town, much of which dates back 800 years, is full of narrow cobbled streets, quays and old waterside inns which are popular with visitors to the city. The high rise tower blocks of so many cities are fortunately lacking here, offering clear views of the city's old architecture and the Humber estuary, spanned by the famous bridge.

The entertainments are many, but for those especially interested in the arts, theatre and music, as well as the pageantry associated with the area, the Spring might make a good time to visit, as this is when the Hull Festival takes place, which offers an excellent selection of events.

The River Humber, which drains one-fifth of all England's river water, is one of the country's largest estuaries and commercial waterways. The **Humber Bridge**, a well known landmark of this city, was the longest single span suspension bridge in the world at its opening in 1981. A toll is payable on the bridge, which has a total span of 2220 metres. The towers above the supporting piers are 510 feet high and, although both are vertical, because of the curvature of the earth they actually lean away from each other by several inches. At night the bridge is lit up with arc lights that are placed all over it.

At the north end of the bridge is the **Humber Bridge Country Park** which gives the visitor a true 'back to nature' tour only a short distance from one of man's greatest feats of engineering. Walks through woodlands, meadows and ponds are plentiful, with a nature trail. The Park itself has an interesting history too— it was used for chalk extraction as far back as 1317.

Situated in the picturesque East Yorkshire village of **Old Ellerby**, to the north of Hull, is the wonderful old English village pub, **The Blue Bell** which has been owned and run by Shirley and Dave Diamond for the past 5 years. Dating back

The Blue Bell

England

to 1675, this inn does have that olde world charm with red tiled floors, polished brass, low beamed ceilings and blazing fires. The beer lover will find a good selection of at least five real ales and, for those who wish for something a little more active, there is a newly created bowling green in the gardens. Despite its obvious popularity, The Blue Bell doesn't serve food as Shirley and Dave have decided to concentrate all their efforts on producing a warm and relaxing atmosphere with the welcoming aroma of burning apple wood rather than burnt chips! So for those who fancy experiencing the genuine ambience of a truly traditional inn then look no further than the Blue Bell for a memorable day out. *The Blue Bell, Crabtree Lane, Old Ellerby, near Hull, East Yorkshire HU11 5AJ Tel: 01964 562364*

BEVERLEY   *Map 14 ref N9*

This gracious and ancient market town is a place of curious and eccentric place-names steeped in history. It gained its power as the centre of trade and industry that served the port of Hull during medieval times but was tightly controlled by the 38 trade guilds that implemented a complex set of ordinances. One of the more curious rules was that bakers were not allowed to employ Scotsmen—whether or not this was due to the bad feelings generated by the many invasions by their more northerly neighbours, or whether it was simply because their culinary abilities were considered rather inadequate, nobody knows!

Around the town there were four (or maybe five!) gateways or bars. Unlike most other towns and cities in England at this time, Beverley was not encircled by a wall but by a ditch, the remains of which are still being researched. The only surviving gateway is the North Bar and it was at the adjoining Bar House that King Charles I and his sons stayed in the mid-17th century.

The cloth weaving, dyeing and tanning were all represented in the ancient guilds who staged mystery plays and attracted traders from as far afield as London to their Cross fair. In fact it was these guilds that paid for the building of **St Mary's Church** in the 13th century. Sadly, 400 years later the tower collapsed killing 400 worshippers but it was rebuilt and can be seen still standing below the North Bar. Many years before the building of this church, John, Bishop of York retreated to Beverley and subsequently the town became a place of pilgrimage for believers in his miracles. Following the Bishop's canonisation, King Athelstan granted the first Minster lands and privileges. The arrival of first the Vikings and then the Normans saw the buildings both changed and then destroyed and it was not until 1220 that the magnificent **Minster** was first begun. St John's tomb is marked by a giant slab in the centre of the building and the Minster's soaring twin towers are a well known landmark for miles around.

The market place, in the centre of Beverley, is separated into three sections. There is the Saturday Market Place on one side and the Wednesday Market Place to the other. The Butterdings Pavement, which as the name implies was once

426

reserved for the sales of butter and dairy produce, lies in the centre, separating the two. Dominating this central area is the 270 year old market cross bearing the arms of Queen Anne. Local legend says that it replaces an earlier cross which was large enough for stagecoaches to pass beneath.

Most of the town's ancient timber buildings are now hidden under Georgian façades, which were used to gentrify the town in the 1700s. It is the legacy of this time that visitors are still able to enjoy in the elegant terraces, promenades and overall planning of the town. This pleasing blend of different centuries' architecture has shaped the Beverley seen today.

A whole gallery of interesting historical, literary and artistic figures have connections with Beverley. One of the town's most famous sons was James Edward Elwell, the creator of the Gothic-style screen, as well as some of the house frontages in North Bar Without. The house once occupied by him has carvings of his, based on subject matter from Punch magazine. In conservative Beverley, these created a stir in their day, as one can see such national leaders as Disraeli and Gladstone graphically and irreverently depicted. His son Frederick W Elwell, RA was another famous and versatile artist and his works can be seen at **Beverley Heritage Centre**. Mary Woolstonecroft, pioneer feminist and mother of Mary Shelley, lived as a child in one of the Market Places, and Anthony Trollope stood as a Parliamentary candidate in the infamous corrupt election of 1868 and later satirised the town in a novel.

HORNSEA   *Map 14 ref O9*

Most famous for its pottery factory, which is the largest visitor attraction in the East Riding and provides all year activities for the family. In addition to a factory viewing area there is a car collection, factory shops and **Butterfly World** with over 200 butterflies in a tropical greenhouse.

Hornsea is a quieter resort than its neighbour up the coast, Bridlington, but still has plenty to offer the active tourist. There are excellent sands with gardens and amusements separated from the beach by the promenade. **Hornsea Mere** is a well known nature reserve, with facilities for boating, sailing and angling. It is Yorkshire's largest freshwater lake and is a refuge for over 170 species of birds. Also nearby at Hornsea Bridge is the **North Holderness Museum of Village Life**, with carefully recreated period rooms, and an exhibition of agricultural equipment and tools of local trades.

The quaint church of St Nicholas is a charming example of a fisherman's church, built mainly of sea-cobbles. One local character of note was the parish clerk in the 1700s, who apparently used the crypt to hide smuggled goods. The church was un-roofed one night during a terrifying storm and so troubled was the miscreant by the ominous nature of this sign from above that he suffered a fatal stroke as a result.

England

CHAPTER EIGHT
Northwest England

Albert Dock, Liverpool

8
Northwest England

Cheshire

INTRODUCTION

Cheshire is a county of contrasts: on the one hand there are many old rural communities surrounded and on the other there are the industrial towns on the banks of the River Mersey. To the east there are the deeply cut valleys of the edge of the Peak District and, in the south, the level plains of rich farming land.

The ancient county town of Chester, which was founded as a Roman fort on the banks of the River Dee, lies close to the western border with Wales. A bastion of defence against Welsh incursions it still remains a natural entry point into the country. Famous for its medieval Rows, the city is popular with tourists and an excellent shopping centre.

Further east, can be found many old textile villages which grew up along the banks of fast flowing streams and rivers at the time of the Industrial Revolution. Though the industry has almost ceased and the villages have become desirable homes for business people in Manchester, one such textile mill and associated buildings has been preserved. Quarry Bank Mill, at Styal, lies on the banks of the River Bollin, was a leading mill in the industry's heyday around the 1830s. The textile industry in Cheshire did not only concentrate on cotton and calico; Macclesfield is well known for its silk.

The historic salt industry in Cheshire dates beyond the time of the Roman occupation and it is no coincidence that the great chemical works on the banks of the Mersey in north Cheshire were founded close to the salt mines.

CHESTER   *Map 12 ref H12*

This ancient walled city lies on the border with North Wales and has been welcoming visitors since Roman times. The mighty Roman armies built the fortress Deva here and surrounded it with the famous city walls to defend it against attacks by ferocious Welsh tribes. Today, thousands of visitors to Chester walk the two mile circuit of the walls, taking in the splendid views of the city's illustrious past which is etched in the architecture of each building.

A tour of the walls will takes in the largest **Roman Amphitheatre** ever uncovered in Britain, the site of extravagant festivals watched by 7000 spectators and a training ground for Roman legionaries. Another beautiful sight is the city's **Cathedral** which celebrated 900 years of history in 1992 with various events including a production of the Chester Cycle of Mystery Plays.

Within the city walls there are plentiful treasures to discover. The unique world famous two tiered galleries of shops known as **The Rows**, line both sides of the main street and date from the Middle Ages. The beautifully ornate Eastgate Clock has been watching over this scene since 1897 and, apart from Big Ben in London, it is probably the most photographed timepiece in the world.

Among the many places worth visiting is **The Grosvenor Museum** which houses exhibitions chronicling the Roman occupation of Chester, as well as outstanding collections of paintings and silver. More about the city's fascinating past can be discover through exciting audiovisual shows at **Chester Heritage Centre**, while for a taste of nostalgia, the **Toy Museum** in Lower Bridge Street is a veritable treasure house of antique playthings from every age, including the largest collection of Dinky and Lesney vehicles in the world.

Chester is renowned for its shopping, with many shops retaining the magnificent architecture and elegance of a bygone era. However, there are more than just familiar High Street names here; Chester also has a great number of specialist and antique shops to appeal to the habitual browser looking for something a little different. As with its shops, Chester offers a cosmopolitan choice of food, ranging from traditional half-timbered English inns, to Cantonese, French and Cajun restaurants and chic wine bars, all of which offer cuisine of the highest standard. For a real taste of Chester, look out for Cheshire Cheese and fresh Dee salmon.

Of course, no visit to Chester would be complete without a trip to **Chester Zoo**. Lying outside the city and signposted off the A41 at Upton, this is Britain's largest garden zoo, set in 110 acres of landscaped grounds. Open all year round, except Christmas Day, this is definitely the place to come for a fun family day out. The monorail system gives visitors an exciting ride across the zoo and an alternative view of the residents and to make life even easier.

One has to admit that Italian restaurants do vary in their quality and presentation. These days the kitchen background noise, Italian language and carafe of vin very ordinaire is hardly acceptable. So, for those who have been searching for an authentic Italian restaurant, make for **Vito's Ristorante** in Lower Bridge Street. Here is traditional regional Italian cooking at its best, run by husband and wife team Vito and Lucia Monaco. Italian born Vito set up the restaurant six years ago after learning his craft from friends in his home town of Naples. In 1993 the restaurant was voted 'Pasta Restaurant of the Year' in the Pizza and Pasta Awards ceremony in London. Vito's Restaurant won high praise for its superbly presented meals and continues to win praise from the many regular customers who keep this restaurant packed and very successful. Everything at Vito's restaurant is made to order—pasta dishes, pizza and even the desserts. To taste the true flavour of Italian cooking, this is where it's at!

Vito's Ristorante

Vito's Ristorante, 25 Lower Bridge Street, Chester, Cheshire CH1 1RS
Tel: 01244 317330

Finding a quiet location in a city centre can prove very frustrating, however, for the businessman or visitor to Chester, the **Cavendish Hotel** could prove the ideal solution. Situated only one mile from the centre in a quiet and exclusive residential area, the hotel is convenient for all the amenities of the city. Jenny and Ian give a warm and personal welcome to all their guests as they enter this

Cavendish Hotel

distinctive and charming Georgian house. Here guests can relax in the comfort of gracious surroundings and period furnishings. The intimate dining room is warm and inviting and in the evening, food and wine are served by candlelight. Meals are of the highest quality, prepared with a French influence, and freshly cooked. The 19 en-suite bedrooms are individually designed to provide a relaxing haven, the rooms are equipped with many features for guests' personal comfort. A country house ambience with elegance and style.

Cavendish Hotel, 42-44 Hough Green, Chester, Cheshire CH4 8JQ
Tel: 01244 675100 Fax: 01244 681309

To the southwest of Chester, at **Rossett**, nestling in beautiful countryside just on the border of Wales, the chequered history of **The Golden Groves Inn** is felt in the very atmosphere as visitors enter its portals for the first time! The entrance and reception area of what is now the bar, (including a tiny snug bar) was the original 13th century Inn in its entirety. The low oak beams and ornate carved dark wood bar were additions during the 1600s. There are three dates carved into the intricate workings of the bar; they are well hidden.

The Golden Groves

Today, The Groves restaurant is situated exactly where the courtyard used to be. To this day, the headstone of James Clark stands in silent memorial to the lover of a long past landlady of the house. His presence is regularly felt, quite mischievously moving things (and smashing the odd plate or two). The emphasis is on food prepared with absolutely fresh ingredients, home-cooking values with a definitive rustic overtone. A great deal of effort is made in finding the correct source of raw materials locally, thus giving back to the community from which it chiefly earns its living. Presentation is all important, as it is the diners' first impression of the quality of what is to follow—and here, visitors are sure to be well satisfied.

The garden also provides an excellent opportunity for summer al fresco music, with a large (undercover) bar area and barbecue. There is a full assault course and adventure playground to amuse the children, while the adults are allowed to relax a while.

The Golden Groves, Llyndir Lane, Burton Green, Rossett, Clwyd
Tel: 01244 570445

FRODSHAM   *Map 12 ref I12*

This is an attractive town with a broad High Street lined with thatched cottages and spacious Georgian and Victorian houses. It was once an important coaching town during the 18th and 19th centuries and there are several fine coaching inns. Built in 1632, The Bear's Paw, with its three stone gables, recalls the bear-baiting that used to take place nearby. However, the town itself dates back to, at least, Norman times when the Earls of Chester built a castle here. The castle was later destroyed in the 17th century and only fragments remain on Overton Hill. Below the north face of the hill is the **Church of St Laurence**, with views spread out over the town, the Mersey Estuary and the Manchester Ship Canal. The church still has some fragments of Norman carving, but it is the exquisite north chapel with its 17th century panelling which is of particular note.

The outstanding **Squires Restaurant** stands on the main street in this beautiful Cheshire village. Housed on the first floor of this Grade II listed building the restaurant is beautifully decorated in rich, warm colours that create a relaxed and peaceful atmosphere. Michael Whalley, who has much experience of the catering business, opened Squires six years ago and has gained an excellent reputation for his glorious food. Open everyday except Sundays, the restaurant is well known throughout the area. During the day, between 10 am and 2 pm, there is a tasty menu of snacks and light lunches that make this a super meeting place.

Squires Restaurant

Come evening and the mood changes. The menu is extensive, with a host of special gourmet evenings throughout the year where diners can sample such culinary delights as Roasted quail filled with ostrich pate and Wild boar steaks complemented with an orange, nutmeg and yoghurt sauce. Thursday night is Fish Night, incorporated with the à la carte menu. There is a choice of at least eight different varieties of fish fresh from the market that morning, plus a choice of 10 sauces to accompany the fish. In intimate and cosy surroundings guests can

enjoy the very best of English, French and Italian cuisine, with all the dishes prepared to order. When a table is booked it is for the evening, a final touch that makes a meal here the perfect dining experience.
Squires Restaurant, 4A High Street, Frodsham, Cheshire WA6 7HE
Tel: 01985 735246

Just on the border of Frodsham is the **Aston Arms Hotel**, a pleasant mellow building set on the Isle of Aston where the River Weaver flows on one side of the hotel and the Weaver Navigational Canal on the other. Sailing and water skiing are a feature of this area as is clay pigeon shooting. This rather unusual hotel has its own bowling green and continues the sporting theme indoors with traditional pub games including pool, darts and dominoes. A great pint can be relished here where a top class selection of ales are always available. The Aston is featured in the CAMRA *Good Beer Guide* for 1997. The area is great for local exploration and the fine areas of Cheshire draw many visitors to the region. The hotel has five comfortable guest bedrooms with en-suite facilities and a good selection of food is served is served to order. Well worth a visit.

Aston Arms Hotel

Aston Arms Hotel, Isle of Aston, Frodsham, Cheshire WA6 7JA
Tel: 01928 732333

NORTHWICH   *Map 12 I12*

Lying on the confluence of the Rivers Weaver and Dane, the town's name derives from 'wych', meaning salt town; salt has been extracted from Cheshire since before Roman times. In 1670 rock salt was discovered in nearby Marston and Northwich developed as a major salt producer. In the 19th century, Brunner and Mond set up their salt works at nearby Winnington to manufacture alkali products based on brine. Extensive pumping of brine has, however, caused subsidence and large holes often used to appear, even swallowing up buildings. Salt extraction is now carefully controlled but the flooded areas, or flashes, around the town can still be seen and, on Witton Street, the White Lion Inn has sunk an entire storey! The subsidence led to the design of a new type of timber framed building in the area which can be jacked up as required.

Situated in the Northwich Workhouse building on London Road is Britain's only **Salt Museum**. With its unique collection of traditional working tools and lively displays which include working models and videos, the Salt Museum tells the fascinating story of Cheshire's oldest industry. Not only can ancient remains such as Roman evaporating pans and medieval salt rakes be seen, but there is much to remind visitors of the vital part that salt plays in the modern chemical industry.

Situated on the A559 just north of Northwich, in the village of **Wincham** lies the country residence, **Wincham Hall Hotel**. Standing within five acres of spectacular grounds featuring a walled garden and lily pond, this family run hotel has proved very popular as the ideal location for holding Wedding receptions and ceremonies. An historic establishment dating back to the beginning of the 12th century, the present hall has recently undergone an extensive refurbishment that ensures that the accommodation is second to none. The proprietors, Richard and Jane Clemetson can be justly proud of their establishment; they won the Cheshire

Wincham Hall Hotel

Life Hotel of the Year Award. The restaurant offers a comprehensive à la carte menu and an ever changing daily menu for both lunch and dinner with all dishes having been freshly prepared using only the best local produce. The selection is both varied and superb cooked, with dishes ranging from a Medley of seafood with chive cream sauce and puff pastry net to the sublime Tornados chasseur, served on a crouton bed with a rich meat glaze, chervil and mushrooms. Though in a rural setting, the hotel is conveniently placed for both the M6 and M56 motorways, making it an ideal venue for family celebrations as well as conferences and corporate events.

Wincham Hall Hotel, Hall Lane, Wincham, Cheshire CW9 6OG
Tel: 01606 43453 Fax: 01606 40128

Close by in the village of **Marston** is **The Salt Barge**. Built around 1890 and originally called the New Inn, it can be found 3/4 of a mile from the interesting town of Northwich and close to the Lion Salt Works Museum. This is a much larger pub than one first expects, with approximately eight areas in which to drink and dine. Carole and Keith are very friendly hosts and visitors will certainly enjoy their hospitality. The real fire is a welcoming sight on a cold day and the interior is on split levels where the furnishings are immaculate, and the old beams add a touch of character.

The Salt Barge

The Salt Barge has been the winner of a Gold Hygiene and Health Award for two consecutive years now; all food is freshly prepared by the chef who caters for an extensive range of tastes with English, Continental and vegetarian choices. On Sundays, a special two course traditional Sunday roast is available at a very reasonable price indeed. To supplement the menus, a selection of daily specials are listed on a blackboard. Children are catered for with their own menu and an outdoor play area. Less abled guests are given every assistance.
The Salt Barge, Ollershaw Lane, Marston, Northwich, Cheshire CW9 6ES Tel: 01606 43064

LYMM   *Map 12 ref I12*

This is another delightful village, with half-timbered houses, a market cross and village stocks, close to Warrington and also situated on the Bridgewater Canal. Lymm developed as an important centre for the fustian cloth trade in the 19th century. **Lymm Dam** is a large man-made lake in a lovely woodland centre which is linked to surrounding countryside and to the canal towpath by a network of footpaths and bridleways. The Dam is popular for angling and birdwatching.

For lovers of fine food, **The Lymm Bistro** in Bridgewater Street can be found in an attractive 200 year old building and has been run for the past nine years by Jo Shenton and Michael Venning. Since opening the bistro, Jo and Michael have earned themselves an excellent reputation for providing first class food and wines. Michael is the chef and he has obviously gone to great lengths to ensure that his diners receive only the very best and freshest of produce. Meals are cooked to order and served in the cosy, friendly atmosphere which the bistro exudes. Michael's speciality is fish and this can be anything from a simple, but exquisite, whole Dover Sole to really exotic and exciting dishes. For example, it is not unknown for Michael to offer amongst his daily specials such unusual dishes as giant Australian Snow Crab, Fresh Lobster, or Parrot Fish. As one can imagine, offering dishes such as these makes the Lymm Bistro very popular and it is not surprising that diners travel from far and wide to sample such excellent cuisine. Jo and Michael are on hand every evening to look after the personal requirement of their diners; the bistro also caters for special tastes including vegetarian meals and private parties. Blackboard specials are always popular and a selection of starters may consist of King prawns Thai style with coriander, ginger, lemon grass and kaffir lime or Monkfish wrapped in smoked bacon and grilled. The main courses are just as mouthwatering with such delights as fresh Marlin fish sautéed with various shellfish and served with a cream sauce and Wild boar—a roast saddle of wild boar served in a sauce made from its own juices, juniper berries and port. As might be imagined, the Lymm Bistro does become extremely busy (it is best to book a table) and with a table d'hôte menu available during the week as well, represents superb value for money.

The Lymm Bistro

The Lymm Bistro, 16 Bridgewater Street, Lymm, Cheshire WA13 0AB
Tel: 01925 754852

KNUTSFORD *Map 12 ref I12*

This attractive market town lies on the edge of gentle lowland countryside off the A556. Dating from medieval times it retains a certain quaintness and olde worlde charm; its narrow streets lined with a variety of fine shops, pubs, restaurants, and splendid Georgian houses.

During the 18th century Knutsford rapidly developed into a major coaching town on the main London–Liverpool route and, not surprisingly, still has many former coaching inns. However, it is as the setting for Elizabeth Gaskell's novel *Cranford* that the town is probably best known. The novel is a chronicle of the daily events and lives of the people of a small Victorian country town, written with a blend of sympathy, sharp observation and gentle humour which still delights readers today.

An interesting feature in the town is the **Heritage Centre** in Tatton Street which opened in 1989. This is a reconstruction of a 17th century timber-framed building which had been a Smithy in the 19th century. During the restoration, the old forge and bellows were found in a remarkable state of preservation. The wrought iron gate which leads up into the courtyard in front of the centre was designed as part of an environmental art project and depicts dancing girls taking part in the local May Day celebrations—another popular tradition that continues today. The festivities of Royal May Day, which are considered the most impressive of their kind in England, began in 1864 and earned their Royal prefix when the town was visited by the Prince of Wales in 1887. The celebrations consist of Maypole dancing and a large procession headed by Jack in Green and the May Queen in a horse-drawn landau. All vehicles are banned from the town centre and the streets are carpeted with coloured sand in which patterns are traced.

One of the best known landmarks of Knutsford is the **Belle Epoque** restaurant and hotel, Cheshire's Edwardian showpiece seen by many in various television plays and productions. The charming building has an Art Nouveau interior and is the work of Richard Harding Watt who admired the Mediterranean architecture which he saw on his travels. Lovingly restored and run by the Mooney family for 23 years, it is one of the most romantic restaurants in the North; the deeply fringed, jewel coloured drapes, intimate alcoves and Art Nouveau adornments recreates the Parisian Belle Epoque era. The delightful garden room overlooking the secluded roof garden is an ideal venue for wedding receptions; up to eight people can be seated. The garden providing the perfect backdrop for wedding photographs.

Belle Epoque

A lunch menu is available from Monday to Friday from 12–2 pm plus a full à la carte menu which is also available for evening dining. Every dish is individually cooked and, as this is a busy restaurant, a delay may sometimes occur. Whatever the choice, it is well worth any waiting and dishes such as Gressingham duck, Lamb shank or good old Sausage and mash will not disappoint. Belle Epoque has seven delightful bedrooms all en-suite and with colour television and tea and coffee making facilities. With the beautiful town of Knutsford literally on the doorstep and the delights of Cheshire all around, Belle Epoque is a perfect location. Less than two miles from junction 19 on the M6 Motorway.

Belle Epoque, 60 King Street, Knutsford, Cheshire WA16 6DT Tel: 01565 633060 Fax: 01565 634150

High Legh Garden Centre, which celebrated its tenth anniversary in 1997, is one of the country's premier centres and conveniently placed near the motorway network. With plenty on offer this garden centre of excellence makes a great day out for all the family, whether they are expert gardeners or enthusiastic beginners. The nursery, with its numerous outdoor beds and covered areas, contains a wide variety of trees, plants and shrubs and, as a member of the Hillier Premier Plant Scheme enjoys access to more unusual outdoor plants. All are grown with great care and attention and the friendly, knowledgeable staff are on hand to help with any queries visitors have on the growing of their purchases. Having the right tools for the job makes gardening much more of a pleasure and High Legh stocks all the leading brands of gardening equipment as well as a whole range of composts, chemicals and fertilisers to help create the perfect medium for the plants and shrubs. Situated to the rear of the nursery visitors will find a number of franchises which specialise in garden and home improvements, these include patios and driveways, conservatories, greenhouses and sheds and suppliers of turf and a specialist aquatic centre. To keep the children entertained there is also a safe and enjoyable outdoor play area.

High Legh Garden Centre

Gardening is not all hard work and High Legh stocks an impressive range of garden furniture and accessories so that, after the work is over, gardeners can sit back and enjoy their labours. From attractive sun loungers and parasols to barbecues and fireworks, there is everything here to ensure that the garden becomes a place for peaceful relaxation. Also undercover is the Planthouse which, throughout the year contains a magnificent display of colourful and fragrant indoor plants that not only make the perfect gift but also brighten up any home or conservatory.

The delightful gift shop offers a superb range of unusual pottery, glassware, fragrant and aromatherapy products, speciality foods, designer knitwear, leisure clothing, greeting cards and gift wrappings, complemented by a comprehensive book department offering titles to suit all ages. For the young gardener there is an excellent range of garden toys and accessories from which to choose.

The changing seasons are reflected in the impressive and unusual displays seen at High Legh and towards Christmas the centre is transformed into a Winter Wonderland with glittering decorations, garlands, wreaths, Christmas trees of all shapes and sizes and a spectacular grotto where children can visit Father Christmas.

Any visit to High Legh would not be complete without a stop at the Greenhouse Cafe. Visitors can sit and relax with family and friends over a drink or delicious home-cooked meals and consider their next purchase whilst children can enjoy their favourite foods from the special children's menu. High Legh's commitment to excellence extends further to include a wide variety of special events they hold throughout the year which include informative and interesting demonstrations, talks, preview evenings and garden events. With extensive car parking, level site access and disabled facilities, High Legh Garden Centre is well worth a visit at any time of the year.

High Legh Garden Centre, High Legh, Knutsford, Cheshire WA16 0QW
Tel: 01925 756991 Fax: 01925 757417

A visit to the renowned **Tatton Park**, which lies just outside the centre of Knutsford, heading towards Rostherne, has always been regarded as one of the best days out in the Northwest and is not surprisingly the National Trust's most visited property. It is the complete historic country estate. A magnificent Georgian mansion by Wyatt rises from the glorious gardens, widely regarded amongst England's Top Ten. The opulent staterooms contrast with the stark servants' rooms and cellars, working as they did for the Victorian household of the noble Egerton family.

Tatton has a history stretching back to 8000 BC, when man hunted deer for food and clothing. Eight hundred red and fallow deer still roam the 1000 acres of parkland and round the two lakes. Tatton's history and variety of historic buildings provide the means to interpret the visitors' day out as 'A story for Every Age' which, as visitors go from one attraction to another, explains by means of boards, leaflets and guides, the relationship of the farm to the mansion, the development of the landscape and so forth. Tatton can be regarded, historically speaking, as a typical country estate but the evidence of early occupation by man precedes the 18th century emparkment which makes Tatton all the more fascinating and exceptional.

The original breeds of animals still live down on the **Home Farm**, a short walk from the Mansion—working as it did in the 1930s, the farm is the heart of the estate, with its workshops and old estate office. A 'new' steam engine has recently been restored in the engine house.

Tatton Park

Old Hall nestles in a wood in the deer park. Visitors are given a guided tour through time from the late Middle Ages up to the 1950s. Flickering light from candles reveals the ancient timber roof of the Great Hall, supported by ornate quatrefoils. Underfoot, the floor is strewn with rushes, providing a warm place for the medieval Lord of the Manor and his servants to sleep. Built around 1520, Old Hall conjures up a hauntingly real image of a journey through history.

To complete the day's enjoyment, visitors can take lunch in the restaurant. Many public events are held indoors and outside in the Park, ranging from a giant classic car show to classical concerts. Also of interest is the annual concert performed by the Hallé Orchestra, fireworks are choreographed to the music. The children's adventure playground is specially tailored for preschool up to twelve year olds and children can happily amuse themselves while parents relax in the picnic area. Those interested can telephone Tatton Park for further information prior to their visit, the 24 hour information line number is 01565 750250.

Tatton Park, Knutsford, Cheshire WA6 6QN Tel: 01565 654822

Tabley House is a beautiful Georgian stately home designed by John Carr of York, for the Leicester Family who lived at Tabley for over 700 years. The first collection of English pictures ever made can be seen in the State Rooms for which they were created, together with furniture, by Chippendale and Bullock and Gillow of Lancaster. The house contains fascinating family memorabilia spanning three centuries, a 17th century Chapel and a hidden house which now belongs to the Victoria University of Manchester. JMW Turner, Henry Thompson and James Ward were among the many painters who stayed at Tabley.

Today, important works by them can be seen in the rooms for which they were created. St Peter's Chapel which is situated adjacent to the house was originally built on an island in Tabley Mere in 1678 and was subsequently moved to its present site in 1927. Tabley now has a licence for civil weddings and offers a superb opportunity for newlyweds to add their own small contribution to the history to this gracious mansion. Various events are held at Tabley during the season and all visitors are welcome including groups and those with special needs. The Tea Room is open from April until the end of October on Thursday, Friday, Saturday and Sunday and Bank Holidays between 2—5pm. Please ring the administrator for further information.

Tabley House

Tabley House, Knutsford, Cheshire WA16 0HB Tel: 01565 750151 Fax: 01565 653230

To the northwest of Knutsford at **Mere, The Kilton Inn** has a history dating from the early 18th century and it is said that Dick Turpin could return so quickly to this inn after holding up local travellers, that his alibi of being there all day could

Kilton Inn

not be disproved. Today, almost 300 years later, the Kilton Inn is still a safe haven for travellers, offering excellent value for money food in the Millers Kitchen, cask ales, good wine and comfortable accommodation. All bedrooms are en-suite and are equipped with satellite television, telephone, hospitality tray and other amenities. The Kilton Inn is one of the Premier Lodge chain and offers dedicated rooms for wheelchair users and people with disabilities. Located three miles from the M6, it is ideally placed for south Manchester and its International Airport. Terms are on a per room basis and will be particularly interesting to families.

Kilton Inn, Warrington Road, Hoo Green, Mere, near Knutsford, Cheshire WA16 0PZ Tel: 01565 830420 Fax: 01565 830411

North of Knutsford there is a scenic walk, from the centre of the village of Styal, through the Carrs, a pleasant park by the River Bollin to **Styal Country Park**. Owned by The National Trust, this comprises over 250 acres of woodland and riverside walks surrounding **Quarry Bank Mill**, built in 1784 and one of the first generation of cotton mills which powered by a huge iron waterwheel fed by the River Bollin. Also within the park is the delightful model village, which was established by the mill's original owner, Samuel Greg, a philanthropist and pioneer of the factory system. He took children from the slums of Manchester to work in his mill and, in return for their labour, provided them with food, clothing, housing, education and worship.

Visitors follow the history of the mill through various galleries and displays within the museum, including weaving and spinning demonstrations, and can experience for themselves what life was like for the hundred girls and boys who once lived in the Apprentice House, with guides dressed in period costume.

ALDERLEY EDGE   *Map 13 ref J12*

This small town takes its name from a long wooded escarpment, nearly two miles in length and rising 600 feet above sea level, culminating in sandy crags overlooking the Cheshire Plain. Alderley Edge itself is a popular area of countryside, rich in history and legend. Walkers will enjoy the network of footpaths through the woods which offer superb views of the surrounding scenery. It is only a short walk to the Wizard's Well, where the following verse can be found: "Drink of this and take thy fill, for the water falls at the Wizard's will."

Local legend tells of a farmer who was on his way to Macclesfield market to sell his white horse, when he was stopped by a wizard who wished to buy the horse. The farmer refused, but he failed to sell the horse at market and, on his return, was forced to sell it to the wizard. The wizard showed the farmer a cave, barred by iron gates, in which a sleeping army of knights and their steeds lay ready to ride out to save the country in its hour of need. The wizard, who in some versions of the story is portrayed as Merlin, explained to the farmer that he was a horse short and he rewarded the farmer handsomely. Readers of the highly popular novels by local author Alan Garner, will recognise that this story and the setting of Alderley Edge forms the core of his classic children's story *The Weirdstone of Brisingamen*.

More factually, Alderley Edge once contained a large neolithic settlement and many Bronze Age tools and implements have been found here. The area is also riddled with old copper mines, some of which are dangerous and should not be explored unguided. It is now a National Trust property and a car park on the main Macclesfield road gives access to the woodlands.

One of the finest Chinese restaurants in the area can be found in a quiet shopping parade on the outskirts of Alderley Edge. The **Mandarin Restaurant** occupies spacious modern premises with seating for around 60 diners which is set back from the main A34 Manchester to Congleton road. Inside, the tasteful combination of Oriental and European influences creates an atmosphere which is stylish and welcoming. The present proprietor, Colin Lee, was employed in the restaurant for 20 years before becoming the owner in 1992. Since taking over,

Mandarin Restaurant

he has established a reputation for providing the warmest of welcomes, excellent service and some of the most superb Cantonese cuisine in north Cheshire. The Mandarin specialises in four course set dinners and spectacular seven course banquets, and offers a choice of table d'hôte menus which vary according to season. There is also an extensive à la carte menu which features a full range of chicken, duck, meat, seafood and vegetarian dishes, along with a wide selection of starters, desserts and English dishes. The restaurant is open each evening from 6 pm to 11 pm and from 12 noon to 2 pm on Fridays, Saturdays and Sundays; closed Mondays.

Mandarin Restaurant, 2-3 The Parade, Alderley Edge, Cheshire SK9 7JX
Tel: 01625 584434/584704

Those looking for exceptional farmhouse accommodation which is situated within easy reach of Manchester Airport, the M6, M56 and M63 should make a point of finding the attractive Cheshire hamlet of **Over Alderley**, the location of **Lower Harebarrow Farm**. A handsome stone built farmhouse dating from around 1800, it lies on the B5087 midway between Alderley Edge and Macclesfield. Proprietor Mrs Beryl Leggott offers her guests the warmest of welcomes, comfortable accommodation and one of the finest farmhouse breakfasts in the district. ETB 1 Star Commended, the three guest bedrooms (one double, one twin and one single) are all beautifully appointed and equipped with washbasins and tea and coffee making facilities. There is also an attractive television lounge on the ground floor. Lower Harebarrow Farm lies within a few hundred yards of Hare Hill, the National Trust owned woodland estate which is renowned for its beautiful walled garden. Many of Cheshire's finest beauty spots, stately homes and the Peak District National Park also lie within easy driving distance.

Lower Harebarrow Farm

Lower Harebarrow Farm, Macclesfield Road, Over Alderley, near Macclesfield, Cheshire SK10 4SW Tel: 01625 829882

MACCLESFIELD   *Map 13 ref J12*

Nestling below the adjacent Peak District hills, this town was once an important silk manufacturing centre and a market town with its origins in medieval times. The town's link with silk developed in the 17th century from a cottage industry, expanding in 1743 when Charles Roe built the first silk mill. There then followed a rapid expansion, the industry reaching its peak of activity in the 19th century. Man-made fabrics are still manufactured in the town but textiles no longer dominate its economy. Appropriately enough, Macclesfield has the country's only **Silk Museum**, which covers all the aspects of the silk industry, from cocoon to loom. Nearby **Paradise Mill**, which was built in the 1820s, is now a working museum demonstrating silk weaving on 26 jacquard hand looms.

Modern Macclesfield is an interesting town well worth exploring, with small narrow cobbled streets and alleyways, many lined with black and white timbered houses and old weavers' cottages. There is a fine market square with a market cross and, set on a hill, a handsome church that was originally founded by King Edward and Queen Eleanor. It is probably best viewed from the railway station first, before climbing the 108 steps to view its interior. **St Michael and All Angels' Church** was extended at the end of the 19th century but it retains its 14th century core. Inside is the Legh Chapel, built in 1422 to receive the body of Piers Legh who fought at Agincourt and died at the Siege of Meaux.

Macclesfield Sunday School was built in 1813 for the education of local working children. It was finally closed in 1970 and as well as housing the Silk Museum, it forms the **Heritage Centre** with exhibitions on Macclesfield's rich and exciting past and on the story of the Sunday School itself. On the outskirts of the town is **West Park Museum**, a purpose-built museum founded in 1898 by the Brocklehurst family. The collection includes Egyptian artifacts, fine and decorative arts, and paintings by Charles Burnicliffe, the well known bird artist. The museum itself is set in one of the oldest public parks in England and has reputedly the largest bowling green in the country.

To the east of the town centre lies the **Macclesfield Canal**, one of the highest inland waterways in England, running for much of its length at over 500 feet above sea level. It was surveyed by Thomas Telford and opened in 1831, linking the Peak Forest Canal at Marple with the Trent and Mersey Canal near Kidsgrove, a distance of 26 miles. Between Macclesfield and Congleton, the canal descends over a hundred feet in a spectacular series of 12 locks at Bosley, before crossing the River Dane via Telford's handsome iron aqueduct. Another unusual feature of the canal is its roving bridges which carried the towpath across the canal, thus allowing horses to pass beneath the bridge before crossing it, and therefore making it unnecessary to unhitch the tow line.

The **Chatterbox Tea Rooms** are situated in Sunderland Street, in the older part of Macclesfield. This traditional Victorian building has been recently refurbished throughout by its new owner Marjorie Canning Smith and now offers its visitors a bright and airy eating area whilst retaining a warm and friendly atmosphere. Marjorie is an excellent cook and the first thing that visitors will notice when stepping inside is the delicious aroma of real home-cooking. The food is absolutely delicious and besides the comprehensive menu there are plenty of freshly prepared daily specials and a tempting and mouthwatering array of puddings and home-baked cakes. Open five days a week from Tuesday until Saturday, visitors will find an eating area both on the ground floor and upstairs whilst if the weather is fine, the colourful terrace area outside proves very

The Chatterbox Tea Rooms

popular. A must to seek out and find where no one will be disappointed.
The Chatterbox Tea Rooms, 33 Sunderland Street, Macclesfield, Cheshire Tel: 01625 618024

Macclesfield Garden Centre is clearly signposted from the Macclesfield–Leek road (A523) in the direction of Sutton and Langley. The centre was originally purchased in 1957 as derelict allotments and was subsequently cleared and developed for the growing and cultivation of high quality shrubs and trees. Famous in the surrounding area for their innovation and introduction of new and unusual varieties of outdoor plants, there is always something special to see. In addition to the wide range of garden accessories, there is a beautiful gift shop that offers a whole host of choice gifts and cards for all occasions. This is truly an outstanding garden centre that offers something for everyone yet still manages to retain that personal touch and as their slogan says, "Macclesfield Garden Centre—the natural choice, where traditional views still flourish."

Macclesfield Garden Centre

Macclesfield Garden Centre, Bullocks Lane, Off Byrons Lane, Macclesfield, Cheshire SK11 0HE Tel: 01625 618933 Fax: 01625 503485

The **Cat and Fiddle** is a renowned pub and eating place which has the distinction of being the second highest inn in England. Standing at 1690 feet above sea level, it can be found at the highest point on the A537 Buxton to Macclesfield road in what has become known as the Cat and Fiddle Pass. On a clear day the view is breathtaking, with the Jodrell Bank radio telescope and the Mersey estuary being clearly visible. The building was constructed in the early 19th century by a Macclesfield banker and now stands at one end of a 120 mile walk which links the two highest pubs in England, the highest being the Tan Hill Inn in North Yorkshire. On the entrance porch is a carving of a cat playing a fiddle, although the establishment's unusual name probably derives from two early pub entertain-

Cat and Fiddle

ments: the game of cat, a form of trap ball, and the fiddle, which was used to accompany dancing. Today, the inn is run by Sue and Ian Ryder along with their chef son Steve. Together, they provide a warm welcome, a wide range of traditional ales, and some of the finest food in the area. Indeed, such is the reputation for fine cooking that customers travel from miles around to sample the delicious morning coffees, lunches, dinners and bar snacks. The Cat and Fiddle is open all day throughout the summer and usual pub hours during the rest of the year, with food being available daily from 11 am to 2.30 pm and 7–9 pm.
Cat and Fiddle, Buxton Road, near Macclesfield, Cheshire SK11 0AR
Tel: 01298 23364

To the south of Macclesfield, at **Sutton**, lies **Sutton Hall**, once the baronial residence of the Sutton family and more recently a convent under the diocese of Shrewsbury. The Hall has now been converted, regardless of expense, to create a unique inn of distinction providing superb food and sumptuous accommodation. The fully licensed lounge bar, which is open to nonresidents and has a wealth of early 16th century oak and three open log fires, welcomes guests upon arrival. A fine range of cask conditioned ales as well as a complete selection of wines and spirits is available. The elegant dining room offers an intimate atmosphere in which to enjoy fresh seasonal dishes traditionally prepared from the finest ingredients. Following this delightful experience, guests may move through to the library and browse through the books.

Sutton Hall

Those wishing to spend the night or who have wisely elected to make Sutton Hall their holiday or business base, will ascend the wide oak staircase to one of the magnificent bedrooms each with its own character, beautifully maintained. Apart from the facilities usually associated with this type of establishment, guests will be enchanted with the sumptuous, lace draped four poster beds. Sutton Hall is perfectly situated for travellers north and south, being only a few miles from the motorway routes, and equally well placed for the beautiful areas of Cheshire and its many places of interest.
Sutton Hall, Bullocks Lane, Sutton, near Macclesfield, Cheshire SK11 0HE
Tel: 01260 253211 Fax: 01260 252538

Further west, at **Lower Withington** is **Welltrough Dried Flowers**, one of the North's largest silk and dried flower workshops. There is a vast selection of dried and silk flowers plus baskets, ceramic pots, ribbons, pot pourri and much more. Three showrooms are packed with arrangements and if these do not suit a particular requirement then specific designs can be made to order. A National Demonstrator gives demonstrations throughout the year as well as taking day workshops. The business, which was started in 1991, has continued to expand and now comprises of seven showrooms, demonstration room, permanent Christmas room and Dickensian Street so do allow plenty of time for a visit to Welltrough Dried Flowers.

Welltrough Dried Flowers, Welltrough Hall Farm, Lower Withington, near Macclesfield, Cheshire SK11 9EF Tel & Fax: 01477 571616

The redbrick and black and white cottages grouped round the village green of **Astbury**, to the southwest of Macclesfield, are quite a contrast from the grey-brown villages of the Peak. In spring the green sports a thick carpet of daffodils. The splendid recessed spire of **St Mary's Church**, that dominates the village, is considered one of the most striking in Cheshire.

Little Moreton Hall lies approximately three miles south of Astbury, just off the A34, and is undoubtedly one of the finest black and white timbered and moated manor houses in England. Ralph Moreton began its construction in about 1480 and the fabric of this magnificent house has changed little since the 16th century. Huge carved overhanging gables and distorted panels create a kaleidoscope of black and white patterns. A richly panelled Great Hall, parlour and chapel show off superb Elizabethan plaster and wood work. There is also a beautifully reconstructed Elizabethan knot garden with clipped box hedges and a period herb garden.

The Horseshoe Inn can be found approximately two miles from Mowcop Castle and one mile from Astbury village. Set within 11 acres of grounds, where different social events take place in the summer, The Horseshoe Inn was until recently a working farm run by Mervin and Siobhan. This delightful inn offers a warm hospitality and a great welcome. Open throughout the day, here guests

England

can enjoy good food and fine ale. Food is available every day at normal meal times and during the evening. The food itself sounds delicious with plenty of traditional fare to choose from. All meals are well priced and come in good-sized portions. The inn is listed in the CAMRA *Good Beer Guide* so visitors are sure of a good selection of quality ales. Outside is a spacious beer garden with enclosed children's play area.

The Horseshoe Inn

The Horseshoe Inn, Fence Lane, Newbold, Astbury, Congleton, Cheshire CW12 3NL Tel: 01260 272205

WINSFORD

Map 12 ref I12

Despite its growth in recent years with housing development, the town still retains several features of historic interest, including some timber framed pubs in the centre and an unusual timber framed church built for bargees travelling on the River Weaver. Winsford is actually formed from two older townships, Over and Wharton on either side of the River Weaver. Winsford Bottom Flash is a popular area for angling, canoeing and pleasure boating.

The **Vale Royal** is an area of some 150 square miles, incorporating some of the most beautiful Cheshire countryside. Within this vast area there is a wealth of historic sites revealing the rich heritage of this lovely rural country. The name originated when Prince Edward, 8th Earl of Chester declared it to be "The Vale Royal of England" because he felt it was so beautiful. Among the many places to visit there is the **Anderton Boat Lift**, an impressive structure recently restored to its former glory. The lift was conceived and designed by Edward Leader Williams, who later found fame for designing the Manchester Ship Canal, and it played a major part in the industrial development of the area. Using amazing hydraulics this cast iron construction was a marvel of the era, literally 'lifting' boats and transferring them from the river to the canal.

For the sporting enthusiast, The Vale Royal has a wide range of facilities, including Rudheath Leisure Centre, complete with sports hall, village room and fitness suite, Northwich Swimming Pool, Winsford Indoor Sports Complex with amenities for all kinds of sporting activities and Knights Grange Sports Complex which caters for a wide variety of sports ranging from golf to indoor bowls and crazy golf.

The abundance of countryside walks, meres, canals and rivers for the nature enthusiast, ensure that within this wonderful area there is something to appeal to everyone.

Anderton Boat Lift

Vale Royal Borough Council, Wyvern House, The Drumber, Winsford, Cheshire CW7 1AH Tel: 01606 862862

Bank Hall Hotel is situated approximately one mile from Winsford on the B5074. This lovely hotel represents a great deal of hard work by its owners Reenie and Graham George, who took a crumbling old property some 200 years old and rebuilt it to exacting standards, using original bricks and beams throughout. All the rooms are beamed and furnished in Georgian style. The bedrooms have full en-suite facilities with television and hospitality trays. Open log fires burn in the lounge and dining room which continue the Georgian theme.

Bank Hall Hotel

England

An evening menu is available and of course a hearty breakfast can be enjoyed as you start your day. To the rear of the hotel is a lake which guests may fish and where ducks and swans complete the tranquillity of this country setting. Disabled guests will be given assistance and children and well behaved pets are welcome—there's children's play area. Prices are very reasonable and special weekly rates apply.

Bank Hall Hotel, Swallow Lane, Winsford, Cheshire CW7 4BL
Tel: 01606 559163

The first impression of **The Fox and Hounds Inn** at **Sproston Green**, to the east of Winsford, is the lovely black and white timbered building: bright, clean and inviting, and doubtless with a good show of colour from the plants and shrubs in the summertime. Jane and Mike are the recent licensees though all the family contribute to producing the scrumptious home-cooked country food. There's lots to choose from and for those who can't find their ideal dish, then ask about the daily specials. There are log and open fires burning and the interior is spacious and very clean with characterful old oak beams. Outside there is a beer garden, bowling green and children's play area, all very pleasant in this quiet and peaceful area. Situated on the A535 Holmes Chapel Road, between junction 18 M6 and Middlewich. Definitely worth a visit.

The Fox and Hounds Inn

The Fox and Hounds Inn, Holmes Chapel Road, Sproston Green,
Middlewich, Cheshire SW4 7LW Tel: 01606 832303

KELSALL   *Map 12 ref I12*

Lying approximately six miles west of Northwich and signposted from the A556, **Delamere Forest** is a rambler's delight, its 4000 acres of woodland incorporating a wealth of lovely walks and various picnic sites for a peaceful family day out in the country.

In Norman times the word forest meant a protected hunting ground for royalty or nobility. Delamere was originally used by the Earls of Chester and it became a Royal Forest in the 14th century, with James I being the last king to hunt deer

454

here. Large areas of oak were cleared from the forest in Tudor times for ship building and boat construction, as well as for the familiar black and white half-timbered cottages of Cheshire. Since the early 20th century, Delamere Forest has been under the control of the Forestry Commission, who undertook an intensive programme of tree planting and woodland management. Now very much a working forest, 90% of the trees are eventually destined for the saw mills.

Close to the historic city of Chester and the delightful nearby Delamere Forest lies **Northwood Hall**. An elegant Victorian farmhouse set amongst mature oak and chestnut trees in the heart of the Cheshire countryside. It is the family home of Andrew, Caron and their young children, a warm and friendly welcome awaits all their guests in a relaxed family atmosphere. It is an ideal base for walking and picnics in and around the Delamere Forest or discovering the wealth of interesting attractions in the nearby city of Chester.

Bed and breakfast accommodation is available in the main hall, with all rooms traditionally appointed to either full or part en-suite, and with television and other homely comforts provided. Set around a romantic cobblestone courtyard adjacent to the hall are the old barns which now form a lovely conversion to a high standard of self catering accommodation. Many of the original features have been retained whilst providing all the modern comforts of home to make a stay as comfortable as possible.

Northwood Hall

In an idyllic setting hidden from the main hall amongst Chestnut trees there is also an attractive Caravan Park. All the facilities are on hand including modern toilets, laundry room, and a children's playground. The pitches have all weather access and are circled by a hard road. Well behaved dogs are welcome but must be kept on a lead. Whatever a guest's particular lifestyle Northwood Hall has many pleasing options and all can be sure that Andrew and Caron will make their stay as relaxed and as memorable as possible.

Northwood Hall, Frodsham Street, Kelsall, Tarporley, Cheshire CW6 0RP
Tel: 01829 752569

BEESTON and PECKFORTON   *Map 8 ref I13*

The western side of Cheshire approaching the Welsh border begins to have the feel of border country, where ancient tribal feuds and wars between Saxon and Celt have their memory in the great castles of the Warlords of the Marches, which were designed to defend disputed territory. Positioned on a craggy cliff towering over the Cheshire Plain, **Beeston Castle** is reputedly the site of some buried treasure left there by King Richard II, although no gold or jewels have ever been discovered. The castle's fascinating history spans 2500 years and the present fortress goes back to 1220, when it was built by Earl Randle, 7th Earl of Chester, as protection against the army of the Welsh Prince, Llewellyn the Great. Now in the care of English Heritage, it is open to the public and its hilltop location provides the most spectacular views of the surrounding countryside.

Peckforton Castle, visible from Beeston, has a very different history, its purposes being far from military. It is a grand Victorian mansion, occupying a three and a half acre hilltop site. It was built between 1844 and 1851 in exact Norman style to the designs of the architect Anthony Salvin, for Lord Tollemarch, Member of Parliament for Cheshire between 1841 and 1872. Described by the Victorian architect Sir George Gilbert Scott as "the largest and most carefully and learnedly executed Gothic mansion of the present", Peckforton Castle with its 60 foot high towers is a fantasy in stone. It has been superbly restored and is now open to the public with guided tours, refreshments and a speciality shop.

Merseyside

INTRODUCTION

The county of Merseyside was formed in 1974 and it combines parts of Lancashire and Cheshire around and including Liverpool and the River Mersey. Very much dominated by the city of Liverpool, Britain's leading trans-Atlantic port, there are some surprisingly rural areas which are given over to the market gardener.

One of the liveliest and most fascinating cities in the country, Liverpool has a lot to offer. The docks, on which its fortune was built, still handle over 25 million tons of cargo each year and then there are the two 20th century cathedrals, the two top class football teams, the Grand National, the impressive architecture and, of course, the Beatles. For a real Merseyside experience, however, a trip on the *Ferry 'Cross the Mersey* is a must. The services today continue in the tradition of Mersey river crossings that began in 1207. These powerful little vessels, strong enough to withstand the Mersey tides, have been refurbished in traditional style and provide a miniature cruise between Pier Head at Liverpool, Seacombe and Woodside in Birkenhead. The views from the ferry back down the estuary to the famous Liverpool waterfront, are truly memorable.

The Wirral describes itself, with good reason, as the Leisure Peninsula. Though the once great industry of shipbuilding at Birkenhead has declined, much of the area has undergone a change, not only with the restoration and smartening up of ferry terminii, but with the creation of attractive walkways along the seafront. If elegant Hamilton Square no longer contains the smart town houses of sea captains, Birkenhead Priory, the chapter house of a Benedictine monastery established in 1150, now a church, has changed little.

To the north of Liverpool, on route to Southport, lie the sand dune nature reserves that are the home of red squirrels and the endangered Natterjack toad. Retaining all its elegant Victorian beauty, the genteel seaside resort of Southport still attracts many visitors each year who come to stroll along the wide main street and window shop. All the usual resort facilities are here as well and, of course, this is the home of the second largest flower show in Britain.

LIVERPOOL   *Map 12 ref H12*

For many Liverpool is immediately associated with ferries across the Mersey, the Beatles, Red Rum, Shirley Valentine and two world famous football teams, but there is much more to this amazing city. In the 19th century, the Port of Liverpool was the gateway to a new world with thousands of British and European emigrants making their way across the Atlantic to start a new life in America. Today the historic waterfront with its 1000 listed buildings— including **Albert Dock**, Britain's biggest and most popular heritage attraction— is as busy as ever, for this is a city which is discovering itself as a major northern tourist centre.

The centre of Liverpool, rather than the water front area, also has some magnificent buildings and, tucked away off Church Street, on School Lane is the **Bluecoat Chambers**. This is a superb example of Queen Anne architecture and was built originally as the Bluecoat School. To the rear is the **Bluecoat Gallery** which displays the work of many local artists and craftspeople and is a great place to pick up a gift or souvenir. A short walk from here is Mathew Street, site of the **Cavern Club**, immortalised by the Beatles, and where there are some very good places to eat and drink including the very trendy Armadillo tea rooms.

A prince among pubs has to be the **Philharmonic Rooms**, virtually opposite the concert hall of the same name on Hope Street which is the road that runs between the city's two 20th century cathedrals. The splendid wrought iron gates are a clue to the opulence of the interior which is a riot of stained glass and wood panelling. Parties of tourists are frequently ushered in to see the brass and marble fittings in the gentleman's toilets.

The two great **Cathedral's**, one Roman Catholic and the other Anglican, were both built in the 20th century but they are of very different styles: the Anglican is traditional and took a whole lifetime to complete whilst the Metropolitan cathedral was quickly constructed in a very modern design. Both have their very loyal fans and, as they are also situated above the city, their distinctive profiles dominate the city skyline.

Many of the great merchant warehouses, banks and trading houses of this once mighty port survive along broad streets to give Liverpool a sense of grandeur which lives on. Behind the warehouses and newly pedestrianised areas run narrow streets and alleyways, some with old inns and restaurants which were once the haunt of mariners. Since the 1960s, these have been linked to the names of four young men who gave the city a new fame—the Beatles, whose music and Mersey Beat in the Cavern Club became known worldwide. There is a daily Beatles Magical History Tour which visits the places that influenced their music, such as Penny Lane and Strawberry Fields.

Liverpool is also a great cultural centre today. The Royal Liverpool Philhar-monic Orchestra has an international reputation and is based in the Philharmonic Hall in Hope Street. The Liverpool Playhouse, in Williamson Square, is Britain's oldest repertory theatre and the Everyman Theatre and Empire also have an outstanding reputation. The **Walker Art Gallery** has a splendid collection of Great Masters from early Flemish painters to the 20th century, including fine Rembrandts and Cézannes, while the **Northern Tate Gallery** at Albert Dock houses one of the most impressive collections of contemporary art outside London. Albert Dock is also home to the **Merseyside Maritime Museum** and the **Museum of Emigration** where, among other fascinating exhibits, there is the reconstructed interior of a 19th century emigrants' ship which gives an impression of what it was like for so many people seeking a new life across the Atlantic.

Sefton Park was, at one time, the place to live in Liverpool and all around the perimeter are houses which were once the homes of the rich merchants of the city. Most are, alas, now divided into flats and a couple now serve as hotels, such are their size. The park itself is still a wonderful facility for all to enjoy and is best explored on foot. Out of the park heading towards the airport there is a turning to the right down Jericho Lane where there is a marvellous waterside promenade and Otterspool Park, which adjoins the site of the Garden festival which Liverpool hosted some years ago.

Travelling along the A561 up Mersey estuary, leads to Speke airport and also **Speke Hall**, a beautiful half-timbered Elizabethan manor house whose grounds have a wealth of interesting features for the whole family to explore. Visitors to the hall can discover the secrets behind the eavesdrop chamber, or find out what life was like below stairs in the servants' hall and kitchen. They may even bump into the tapestry ghost on their travels. The oldest parts of Speke Hall were built nearly 500 years ago by the Norris family. Over succeeding generations, the building developed around a cobbled courtyard which is dominated by two yew trees, known locally as Adam and Eve. The Great Hall dates back to Tudor times, but has considerably altered over the years. The house as we see it today owes much to the refurbishments carried out in Victorian times, with many of the smaller panelled rooms containing fine furnishings from the arts and crafts movement, designed by William Morris. Outside, there are superb grounds and gardens. The moat which surrounded the house in the 17th century has now been drained and forms a feature of the grounds, which include a Victorian Rose Garden, a Croquet lawn, ancient woodland and the raised walk, which offers fine views across the Mersey.

The Yew Tree Hotel

Just across the Mersey at **Rock Ferry** can be found **The Yew Tree Hotel and Restaurant**, located only 10 minutes by car from Liverpool, with the Cheshire countryside and Welsh hills and coastline, near at hand. Set back from the road in grounds of half an acre, pleasantly bounded by a variety of mature trees, this family run Georgian hotel offers comfort and consideration to its business and tourist clients. The 12 generously proportioned en-suite bedrooms are individually furnished giving a home-from-home feeling of comfort and are equipped with television and hot drink making facilities. The Mariner's Cavern Restaurant is a unique feature of the hotel, with its warm relaxing charm, offering a special residents' menu, table d'hôte and à la carte, designed to suite all tastes. All food is freshly prepared allowing the chef imaginative scope from top quality ingredients. Basic French, German and Portuguese is spoken. ETB 3 Crown Classification.

The Yew Tree Hotel, 56-58 Rock Lane West, Rock Ferry, Merseyside
L42 4PA Tel & Fax: 0151 645 4112

FORMBY   *Map 12 ref H11*

To the north of Liverpool, along the coast lies Formby Point, a place of national importance for its nature conservation interest. Lying between the Mersey and Ribble estuaries, **Formby Point** is an area of constant change where man battles with the elements in an effort to prevent the merciless erosion of the coastline.

England

The dunes protect the hinterland from flooding like a natural sea wall, but they also bring their own problems. Sand blown by storms has in the past threatened inland villages with engulfment and since around 1700, leaseholders in the area were required by law to plant marram grass to help stabilise the dunes. The woods were first planted at the beginning of this century for the same reason, and the intention was that an esplanade would be constructed along the coast if the sand could be held at bay.

The fact that nature refuses to be so easily tamed has proved to be of great benefit to nature lovers who visit the area, as much of it is now a **Nature Reserve**. Almost 500 acres of Formby's dunes and woodlands were bought by the National Trust in 1967, and it now provides a natural habitat for a wide range of animals and plants. Two animals in particular make Formby Point well known. The red squirrel colony descends from the variety introduced here from the Continent many years ago and owes its success largely to being so well fed by visitors. The fact that so few trees grow on Formby's hinterland means that the colony is also well protected from its enemy, the grey squirrel, which is prevented access. The other animal which is eagerly looked for, but far more difficult to spot than the red squirrel due to its nocturnal habits, is the rare Natterjack Toad. Artificial freshwater pools have been dug to encourage this protected creature to breed.

SOUTHPORT   *Map 12 ref H10*

This attractive seaside town remains one of the northwest's most popular resorts. If it doesn't have quite the bravura of Blackpool, it does have style, with **Lord Street** and its arcades still being one of the region's most elegant shopping streets. Even though it is a seaside resort, visitors sometimes have to travel some distance across broad expanses of sand to reach the sea. There is all that one would expect to find at a seaside resort: lots of sand (especially dunes), refreshments, funfairs, rides, walks, boating pools, toy trains and fine gardens, including superb herbaceous borders and dahlia beds in late summer.

Situated on Lord Street is the delightful **Atkinson Art Gallery** with fine collections of British art, English glass and Chinese porcelain. On Derby Road is the **Southport Railway Centre** which has a large display of steam and diesel locomotives, housed in the old engine shed.

The Sunnyside Hotel occupies a position very close to the Promenade and Southport's Theatre and Floral Hall Complex. Run by Lisa Houghton, guests will be personally greeted with a warm smile upon their arrival. Most of the well appointed, centrally heated bedrooms have en-suite facilities and all have colour television and hospitality trays. A small number are set aside for nonsmokers, including a ground floor twin bedded room. Breakfast is served in the nonsmoking dining room where a delicious three course evening meal is available for residents. After dining, guests can relax in the very pleasant lounge and enjoy

Sunnyside Hotel

a drink from bar. The hotel is open throughout the year and has a spacious car park. Just two minutes walk from the ever popular Lord Street shopping boulevard and it's many arcades, the town's other attractions are easily reached, including the world famous Royal Birkdale Golf Club.

Sunnyside Hotel, 47 Bath Street, Southport, Merseyside PR9 0DP
Tel: 01704 536521

Southport's interesting and very colourful **Botanical Gardens** are located on the B5244 road in the picturesque old world village of **Churchtown** on the Preston side of Southport—two miles from the town centre. Entrance to the gardens is free as also are the coach and car parking facilities. The amenities of the Botanical Gardens are many and include an open air aviary and pets corner which are extremely popular with all age groups, a Museum, a unique fernery, boating lake, picturesque rose gardens, floral displays and two good bowling greens. A tour of the gardens may be taken by train. It is worth noting that the Museum attracts more than 75,000 visitors a year including many children, entrance is free

Botanical Gardens and Cafés

and should not be missed. In addition to a fully equipped children's playground, there's a extensive recreation field where youngsters can let off steam. Close by the main entrance and parking facilities are two attractive cafés where a wide variety of hot and cold meals, snacks and drinks are served throughout the day. The quality of the food is good and the staff helpful and considerate. Have an enjoyable day out and take the family. For those who prefer traditional entertainment, there is also the opportunity to relax and enjoy the Brass Bands performing on summer days. Open all year round.

Botanical Gardens and Cafés, Churchtown, Southport, Merseyside
Tel: 01704 28535

Lancashire

INTRODUCTION

Before the reorganisation of the county boundaries in 1974, Lancashire stretched from the industrial belt of Liverpool and Manchester to the scenic Furness region which is now part of Cumbria. Even with losing these two considerable and differing areas, Lancashire is a county which offers beautiful countryside, a varied coastline and a glimpse into the industrial heritage of the North.

The county town of Lancaster, a historic, university town, lies just a few miles from Morecombe Bay, the home of shrimps, treacherous sands and an abundance of sea birds. Further down the coast there is Blackpool, the North's answer to Brighton, and also the restrained resort of Lytham St Anne's. Inland is the picturesque Forest of Bowland and, though it is a forest no longer but an area of high, peaty moorland on the edge of the Pennines, there are some fine walks here.

Lancashire is also famous for its witches and, particularly in the area around Pendle Hill, the stories are legendary. These were, and to some extent still are, isolated communities whose economy was dependent on the textile industry. The larger towns such as Burnley and Blackburn, which served these villages, are, today, great reminders of the Industrial Revolution which turned Lancashire from a farming community into Britain's cotton belt.

LANCASTER   *Map 12 ref H8*

The capital of this beautiful county, Lancaster proudly boasts of its legacy, which extends back many centuries. Unlike York, which has long been internationally known as a tourist attraction, its Red Rose cousin has taken longer to be discovered. In fact, Lancaster has an equally important place in English history and there is much for the serious visitor to explore. It is also a surprisingly compact city, easily reached by either road, just off the M6, or by rail from a centrally positioned station where most Intercity trains call. Within yards of the railway station is **Lancaster Castle**, a great medieval fortress, founded by Normans to keep out Scottish invaders, and strengthened by John of Gaunt, Duke of Lancaster, in the 15th century. Standing proudly on a hill top, this great castle has an imposing presence and dominates the skyline above Lancaster. Its huge square keep dates back to 1200 and was raised in height and impregnability at the time of The Armada. Astonishingly perhaps, most of the building still functions as a prison but certain sections are open to the public, including the 18th century Shire Hall, the cells (where the witches of Pendle were imprisoned), the Crown Court, Hadrian's Tower and, a touch of the macabre, the Drop Room where prisoners were prepared for the gallows.

Close by, sharing the hill with the Castle, is a building with less grim associations—the lovely **Priory Church of St Mary**, which once served a Benedictine Priory established here in 1094. Most of the present church dates from the 14th and 15th centuries and particularly interesting things to see are fragments of Anglo-Saxon crosses, magnificent medieval choir stalls, and some very fine needlework. Nearby is a link with Roman Lancaster—the remains of a bath house which also served soldiers as an inn.

Judge's Lodging

A short walk from the castle leads into the largely pedestrianised city centre, for shops, the market and much besides. The **City Museum** in the Market Place occupies the Old Town Hall, built between 1781–3 by Major Jarrett and Thomas Harrison. As well as the city's art collection and an area of changing exhibitions, there are displays and collections of material illustrating aspects of the city's industrial and social history. Also here is the **Museum of the King's Own Royal Regiment**, a regiment which was based in Lancaster from 1880 onwards.

In Church Street is the **Judge's Lodging**, a beautifully proportioned building dating from the 1620s when it was built as a private house for Thomas Covell, but later used for judges during the Lancaster Assizes. It now houses two separate museums; the **Museum of Childhood** containing the Barry Elder doll collection, and a **Furniture Museum** containing many examples of the work-manship of Gillows, the famous Lancaster cabinet makers. In fact it was Richard

England

Gillow who designed the city's Maritime Museum. Around the corner in Sun Street is **The Music Room**, an exquisite early Georgian building originally designed as a pavilion in the long vanished garden of Oliver Marton.

Lancaster has grown up by the River Lune, navigable as far as Skerton Bridge, so there has always been a strong association between the town and its watery highway. It was in the late 17th and 18th centuries that Lancaster's character as a port fully emerged. The splendid buildings of the 18th century were born out of the port wealth and the layout and appearance of the town was much altered by this building bonanza. Lancaster as a port gradually declined throughout the 19th century so that many buildings put up for specific maritime purposes were taken over for other uses. Naturally the city has been affected by the arrival of the canal, the railways and 19th century industry; yet the hallmark of Lancaster, its Georgian centre, remains as the product of this maritime prosperity.

Lancaster's rich maritime history is celebrated at St George's Quay, which with its great stone warehouses and superb Custom House, is now an award winning **Maritime Museum**. In Georgian times this was a thriving port with the warehouses receiving shiploads of mahogany, tobacco, rum and sugar from the West Indies. Visitors today are given a vivid insight into the life of the mariners and quayside workers, with opportunities for knot tying and other maritime skills. Every year, over the four days of Easter weekend, St George's Quay is the site home to the Lancaster Maritime Festival with smugglers, sea songs and shanties.

Built between 1797 and 1819, the **Lancaster Canal** stretches 57 miles from Preston through the centre of Lancaster to Kendal. Today it is navigable between Preston and Tewitfield, north of Lancaster, the longest lock-free stretch of canal in the country. The canal offers a diversity of scenery and wildlife with opportunities for long distance trips and short circular walks with fine views through peaceful countryside. With 41 lock-free miles it offers relaxed boating with canalside pubs, restaurants and boat-hire facilities. It provides a good touring route for canoeists and is excellent for coarse fishing.

While exploring the city it is worth travelling via East Road and Wyresdale Road on the eastern edge, to Williamson Park. Here can be found the impressive **Ashton Memorial**—a great green copper domed building, a kind of miniature St Paul's—standing on a hilltop in the centre of a wonderful Edwardian park. It forms a landmark seen for miles around and gives a magnificent viewpoint across Morecambe Bay, the Lakeland Hills and the Forest of Bowland. It now houses exhibitions and multi-screen presentations about the Life and Times of Lancaster's Lord Ashton and the Edwardians. There is also a delightful **Tropical Butterfly House** in the former conservatory.

Owned and personally run by Don and Lynette Cullen for the past three years, **Elliots** is a restaurant for the discerning, serving a mix of French, English and

Swiss cuisine within superb surroundings. The building is traditional Edwardian style, but Don and Lynette have managed to capture the authentic Swiss Alpine style and produced a truly intimate atmosphere. Before they took over Elliots in 1994, the Cullens spent the last 25 years travelling round the world, working within the catering industry in such places as Victoria Jung Frau Interlaken in Switzerland and The King David Hotel in Jerusalem, Israel. The all female staff serve a wide selection of superbly presented dishes from a menu that includes such classic dishes as Frogs Legs à la Meuniere, Chateaubriand Bearnaise and good old Lancashire Hot Pot. Elliots Restaurant can be found in Market Street, which is situated just off the main road through Lancaster and only 50 yards from the historic castle, the city's main attraction.

Elliots

Elliots, 64 Market Street, Lancaster, Lancashire LA1 1HP
Tel: 01524 36092

CARNFORTH   *Map 12 ref H8*

Once a busy railway junction, the station has a claim to fame as the setting for the 1940s film classic *Brief Encounter*. Though the station has declined in importance, now being an unstaffed halt, the old engine sheds and sidings are now occupied by **Steamtown**, one of the largest steam railway centres in the north of England. Here, visitors are likely to see such giants of the Age of Steam as the Flying Scotsman or an A4 Pacific, together with a permanent collection of over 30 British and Continental steam locomotives. There are steam rides in the summer months on both standard gauge and miniature lines.

To the north of Carnforth the small village of **Silverdale** is worth visiting for the network of footpaths crossing the nearby escarpments whose limestone woodlands are a joy for the botanist, being rich in wild flowers in spring—primroses, violets, orchids, bird's eye primroses, rockroses and eglantines abound.

For keen gardeners, beginners or simply those who enjoy admiring beautiful gardens, then **Waterslack Farm Garden Centre** is well worth a visit. Hidden away in beautiful countryside and surrounded by National Trust woodland, this garden centre is acclaimed by many to be the prettiest on the Cumbria–Lancashire border—it's not difficult to see why, for its plant displays are always superbly presented. Run by Colin Simpson, the centre has been established since 1974 and not only stocks a wide and varied range of plants and shrubs, but also possesses a lovely tea room where visitors can enjoy a delicious, home-cooked light lunch or an afternoon tea. They may also be tempted to try one of the many mouthwatering Austrian gateaux or home-baked cakes which are also on offer. In the same building is a delightful gift shop which stocks all manner of country gifts. The Waterslack Garden Centre is situated near to the **Leighton Moss Bird Reserve** and **Leighton Hall**, on the road to Arnside. The garden centre is open every day from 10 am to 5.30 pm and is closed on Mondays and Tuesdays during the winter.

Waterslack Garden Centre

Waterslack Garden Centre, Tea Room and Gift Gallery, Silverdale, near Carnforth, Lancashire LA5 0UH Tel: 01524 701255

CLITHEROE   *Map 12 ref I9*

The old stone town of Clitheroe is the capital of the Forest of Bowland. Like Lancaster, it too is dominated by an 800 year old **Castle** on a hill, set on a limestone crag high above the little town. Little more than a ruin in a small park, when visitors stand in the keep, hidden voices relate aspects of the castle's history with suitable sound effects.

Extending across the northern half of Lancashire, the **Forest of Bowland** is a region of scenic splendour. Designated an Area of Outstanding Natural Beauty, this is a veritable paradise for walkers and country lovers, dotted with picturesque villages. Somewhat a misnomer, the area was once a hunting ground rather than a densely wooded area. Its present landscape provides numerous clues to its past history. The remains of a Roman road can be clearly seen from the viewpoint at Jeffrey Hill on Longridge Fell.

The village of **Downham**, to the northeast of Clitheroe, was purchased by the Assheton family in 1558, along with Whalley Abbey, and it is one of the loveliest villages in Lancashire as it has been maintained in virtually its original condition by the Assheton family. The present squire, Lord Clitheroe of Downham, still refuses to permit the skyline to be spoilt by TV aerials, satellite dishes or even dormer windows, which are all strictly prohibited. Because the village is so unspoilt it is often used in period films: *Whistle Down the Wind* was filmed here. Also don't miss the toilets in the car park, they have won several awards! The church tower is a splendid example of 15th century architecture.

Situated off the A59 in the middle of the village, opposite the church, is **The Assheton Arms**. There are records of licensed premises on this site going back as far as 1765. Look out for the initials carved over the stone fireplace, they are believed to be those of the original builder.

The Assheton Arms

The pub has a very olde worlde feel to it, with low ceilings, exposed beams and open fires. The Assheton Arms has an excellent reputation for food, the menu is extensive and impressive and usually includes a surprising variety of fresh seafood specialities. The ales are traditional and all hand-pulled. For those who happen to notice them, the wooden busts of guardsmen wearing 'busby' hats, they are in fact newel posts from the Busby family's department store, which later became Debenhams in Bradford.
The Assheton Arms, Downham, near Clitheroe, Lancashire
Tel: 01200 441227

The quaint country village of **Worston** is situated two miles from Clitheroe and is a ecclesiastical Parish of Chatburn, a place possessing almost universal interest from its association with witchcraft in the 17th century. Situated in this historic part of Lancashire is **The Calf's Head Inn**, a 200 year old pub that was previously a farmhouse and has now been recently refurbished by its new proprietors, Pat and Doug Ord, a couple who offer the weary traveller superb accommodation within a tranquil retreat. The Calf's Head offers its guests the choice of four superb en-suite bedrooms, all offering direct dial telephone, television, video, trouser press and complimentary tea and coffee making facilities. Weddings and special occasions can be professionally catered for by the Calf's Head team or trained staff, whilst the superb gardens prove to be the ideal setting for those memorable photographs. The 80 seater restaurant provides a varied and comprehensive à la carte menu, whilst the bar serves a wide range of bar meals and snacks, whatever their choice all will be very satisfied. In an age when the hustle and bustle of everyday activity takes its toll, its refreshing to find an inn where the friendliness and service hark back to a gentler period.

The Calf's Head Inn

The Calf's Head Inn, Worston, near Clitheroe, Lancashire BB7 1QA
Tel: 01200 441218 Fax: 01200 441510

To the south of Clitheroe, **Whalley** is a town that few visitors to Lancashire wish to miss, with its grey ruined Cistercian Abbey, founded in 1296 and rich in historic and architectural interest (the grounds are open to the public). The town of Whalley itself has great character and charm and lanes link it to the village of Sabden, from where a steep and scenic pass crosses Nick o'Pendle, a notable viewpoint and hair-raising descent towards Pendleton, Clitheroe and the Ribble Valley.

The **Whalley Viaduct** is a major landscape feature more than 600 metres long and up to 21 metres high. There are 48 arches in total, and the viaduct is built of 7 million bricks, all made locally. It was built to carry the Blackburn–Clitheroe railway line across the Calder Valley in 1850. Where it crosses the lane to Whalley Abbey, three of the arches have been given Gothic details to harmonise with the nearby 14th century gatehouse.

The Dog Inn on the main street in Whalley dates back, in parts, to the 17th century but there first appeared a licensed premises of that name on the Town

Census in 1830. A former farmhouse, the Dog Inn sits right in the heart of historic Whalley. Personally run for the past four years or more by Norman and Christine Atty, it is a real picture with an olde worlde appearance and memorabilia decorating the walls. At lunchtime, home-made traditional food is available with the menu displayed on three blackboards. Cooked to order and absolutely delicious the meals can be enjoyed whilst listening to the classical music playing in the background. In the evenings things change a little: there is no food, just a selection of excellent well kept ales, lagers and wines to enjoy.

The Dog Inn

The Dog Inn, King Street, Whalley, Lancashire BB7 9SP Tel: 01254 823009

HASLINGDEN   *Map 12 ref J10*

This area of **Rossendale** is one the most picturesque, varied and interesting areas of Lancashire's Hill Country. Nestling in the unspoilt beauty of the Irwell Valley, the market towns of Rawtenstall, Haslingden and Bacup are time capsules from Britain's industrial past.

Set amidst the beautiful countryside of rural Haslingden and housed in the former St Stephen's Church, **Holden Wood Antiques** offers a wealth of items of interest for the discerning collector. This listed building has been sympathetically

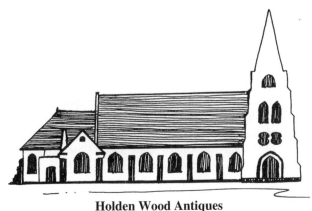

Holden Wood Antiques

England

restored and provides the perfect setting for the antiques on display. Browse amongst the 40 stalls that display a wide range of quality antique ceramics and books, unusual collectable items and contemporary works of merit. The two spindled staircases echo the original rafters of the church roof and provide access to the lofty gallery floor. The beautiful stained glass window forms the perfect backdrop to the wealth of quality objects on display here, including distinctive paintings, jewellery, clocks and fine antique furniture. The competitive pricing ensures that the items on display change regularly, so there is always something new to see and after the shopping there is the local heritage tea room to visit which will give an interesting insight into the church's own history and provide some welcome refreshment. Whether buying or selling, Holden Wood Antiques cannot fail to capture the imagination.

Holden Wood Antiques, Grane Road, Haslingden, Lancashire BB4 4AJ
Tel: 01706 830803

ROCHDALE   *Map 13 ref J11*

This town lies in a shallow valley formed by the little River Roch on the slopes of the Pennines, whose broad summits just above the outskirts of the town are often snow covered in winter. With its roots in medieval times, this is another once prosperous cotton town whose handsome Town Hall rivals Manchester in style if not in size.

Rochdale, to the east of Greater Manchester, was the birthplace of both the 19th century political thinker, John Bright, and the celebrated entertainer Gracie Fields, but perhaps its chief claim to fame is with the birth of the Co-operative movement. In carefully restored **Toad Lane** to the north of the town centre, is the world's first consumer co-operative store, the Rochdale Pioneers. The Co-op movement now represents a staggering 700 million members in 90 countries and the celebration of its 150th anniversary in 1994 has focused worldwide attention on the original Co-op shop on Toad Lane, now a museum.

Between Rochdale and Littleborough lies **Hollingworth Lake**, originally built as a supply reservoir for the Rochdale Canal, but for many years a popular area for recreation known colloquially as The Weavers' Seaport, for cotton workers unable to enjoy a trip to the seaside. It is now part of the Hollingworth Lake Country Park.

Jane Neave has been providing bed and breakfast accommodation at **Leaches Farm** since 1985 and has established a regular clientele who return on many occasions to her beautiful 17th century hill farm. Perched high, it has unrestricted views over Lancashire, Cheshire and Derbyshire and is ideal for those wishing to explore this wonderful countryside. With the motorway network close by, it is also perfect for a stopping place between other beauty spots such as Pendle, Bowland, the Yorkshire Dales, the Peak and Lake Districts and North Wales.

Jane has three guest bedrooms with hand-basins, television and tea and coffee facilities provided, which have separate bathroom, toilet and shower. A family room is available with an extra bed or cot. The comfortable residents' lounge has an open fire and television and video for guests' enjoyment. In addition, Leaches Farm has two static Holiday Homes in the farm yard. They are known as Brushwood and Swiss Chalet and each is suitable for families or several adults. All are well fitted, each having central heating, gas fire, colour television, shower and with bedding provided. Approved by North West Tourist Board and AA Listed.

Leaches Farm

Leaches Farm, Ashworth Road, Ashworth, Rochdale, Lancashire OL11 5UN
Tel: 01706 41116

To the north of Rochdale, in a cobbled street in the village of **Todmorden** stands **The Coffee Club**, a coffee shop that has been personally run by Barbara and Janet for the past five years. Open from Monday–Saturday 9.30 am until 4.00 pm, there is room to seat up to 32 people, The Coffee Club is enjoyed by both locals and tourists alike. The atmosphere is warm and cosy, with the definite country kitchen feel being created by the traditional pine tables and chairs and

The Coffee Club

England

attractive decor. All of the food on the extensive menu has been home-cooked
and include such delicious dishes as Cheese and Onion Pie and Shepherd's Pie
whilst the turkey sandwiches are served hot with apple and seasoning, delicious.
Barbara and Janet also provide an excellent take away service, where customers
can ring through their order and pick it up whenever they required. There is a
choice of hot and cold sandwiches, jacket potatoes, toasties and a range of hot and
cold drinks with hot meal specials changing on a daily basis.
The Coffee Club, 13 Water Street, Todmorden, Lancashire OL14 5AB
Tel: 01706 817231

OLDHAM   *Map 13 ref J11*

The great square red cotton mills still dominate the town, though many have now
been put to new uses. Now linked to central Manchester by the new Metrolink
Supertram, Oldham is notable for its lively Coliseum Theatre and for its position
close to superb scenery in the South Pennines and the Peak District.

"You've had your final briefing, you're in the base waiting for the battle to
commence. You know that on the far side of the huge city, the enemy is waiting,
will you be able to hold them back..." Face the enemy in the post-Apocalyptic
City of the future known as **The Arena**. Situated less than a mile outside of
Oldham, Junction 20 off the M62, The Arena is one of the largest indoor paintball
sites in Europe. With over 42,000 square feet on one floor, visitors are offered
the chance to play a wide variety of games in a unique, purpose built environment. Now recognised as the fastest growing sport in Europe, paintball is the
ultimate adrenaline rush. Included in the entrance fee is the use of a Radar 2000
pump action marker, a Vents Predator or Scotts goggle system and 50 Forest
Light paintballs.

For those who want a break from shooting up their friends then the Arena also
has a cafeteria that serves hot and cold drinks throughout the day, but to make the
day really special then a memorable buffet can be arranged. Open from 10 am
until 10 pm, seven days a week, The Arena also offers a selection of tailor made
packages including corporate bookings and birthdays complete with cake and
novelties. So for those looking for an experience to remember, look no further
than the Arena for three hours of exhilaration and unadulterated fun.

THE ARENA

The Arena, Unit G5, Granville Mill, Vulcan Street, Oldham, Lancashire
OL1 4LQ Tel & Fax: 0161 6280028

ASHTON-UNDER-LYNE

Map 13 ref J11

Situated in the centre of this town, in its Victorian Town Hall, is the **Museum of the Manchesters**. Opened by the Queen Mother in 1987 it tells the story of the Manchester Regiment in the context of the local community that its soldiers came from. The lives of the troops and civilians during the time of the Peterloo massacre, in the trenches of the First World War and during the Blitz can be discovered. The Town Hall stands on the Market Place and the museum is open Monday to Saturday 10 am to 4 pm.

The Tame and Etherow Valleys, both higher tributary valleys of the River Mersey, have been kept as attractive linear green spaces and walkways through otherwise busy urban districts, and contain some lovely areas of unspoiled countryside on the edge of both the Peak District and the South Pennines.

Country lovers will discover a beautiful oasis at **Etherow Country Park**, which is situated at Compstall on the B6104 between Romiley and Marple Bridge. Once part of the estate belonging to George Andrew who built Compstall Mill in the 1820s, the park covers an area of 240 acres. A haven for ramblers and birdwatchers, the park lies at the halfway point of the Etherow–Goyt Valley Way Footpath. The Goyt Way, a 10 mile trail to Whaley Bridge, also starts here. The park provides an ideal habitat for a rich variety of bird and wildlife as well as many different plant species. The nature reserve here, which is managed by Cheshire Conservation Trust, has been designated a Site of Special Scientific Interest.

Located above the William Monk Dealership in Ashton-under-Lyne just off Oldham Road, lies the **Top Wok**, a Chinese Restaurant that specialises in authentic Peking and Cantonese cuisine. This team of professionals is headed by Stephen Ip who has owned and run the restaurant and take away for the past year. The attractive bar is well stocked with a wide selection of beers, wines and spirits from around the world and whatever a guest chooses from the extensive menu, they will find a drink to compliment it. The restaurant is fully air-conditioned, will seat 130 diners with ease and has a menu that is both varied and

Top Wok

often unusual, though booking is advisable to avoid disappointment. Dishes range from delicious Cantonese Style Fillet Steak served on a Sizzling Hot Plate, to the spicy and full bodied Scallops in a Szechuan Sauce. The opening hours are Monday–Friday noon until 2.30 pm and 6 pm until 11 pm, Saturday 5.30 pm until 11 pm and Sunday 3 pm until 10 pm. Whatever the occasion, the Top Wok is the ideal setting, whether it is for a family celebration, business meeting or just a quick working lunch this superb Chinese restaurant offers an eating experience at very reasonable prices. The Top Wok also has a large customer car park complete with full security lighting and cameras so guests can enjoy their meal with complete peace of mind.

Top Wok, Boodle Street, Ashton-under-Lyne, Lancashire OL6 8NF
Tel: 0161 3398888

Situated at the very heart of Ashton old town, opposite the rear entrance to the indoor market is **The Fish Net**, a 70 seater restaurant that offers its visitors a chance to sample some of the freshest fish around. A member of the National Federation of Fish Fryers, this is a fish and chip shop with a difference. There is plenty of friendly waitress service in the restaurant, whilst the menu is a varied one with meals ranging from traditional fish and chips which are freshly produced using only the finest produce to a good selection of home-made pies and puddings always available. The kids will find their very own extensive children's menu which offers a good choice of delicious snacks and meals.

The Fish Net

Open Monday to Friday from 11 am until 3 pm and Saturdays from 11 am until 5 pm the Fish Net offers its customers good quality British fayre at excellent prices.

The Fish Net, 14 Market Street, Ashton-under-Lyne, Lancashire OL6 6BX
Tel: 0161 3396103

In the pretty village of **Mossley**, three miles from Ashton-under-Lyne town centre, can be found **The Billy Goat**. First licensed back in 1760, this village pub was originally named The Ball Inn, changed its name several more times until its new name Billy Goat in 1982 and is the only such named inn in the whole of England. Personally run by Michael and Sandra Dobson since 1993, the couple have just completed a complete refurbishment of the premises but seem not to have rid the inn of its unpaying guests, three ghosts that have been reputedly seen in the pub over the past years. Michael and Sandra also offer accommodation in the form of three guest bedrooms; one double, one family room and one with three single beds. All the rooms offer a colour TV and complimentary tea and coffee making facilities. Situated near to Saddleworth Moor, the inn has a good sized beer garden at the rear of the property with a public footpath that leads over

The Billy Goat

the surrounding hills to Lees. The Billy Goat received third prize in Mossley for the Britain in Bloom competition in 1995, for which Mossley itself won first prize as the best new entrant; so a glorious array of scent and colour can be expected by those who visit this picturesque village in the summer months. The evenings at this village pub are always busy with entertainment ranging from discos and Karaoke to live bands, attracting a large crowd from the surrounding neighbourhood, all wanting to relax and enjoy themselves in the Billy Goat's welcoming atmosphere.

The Billy Goat, 71-73 Stamford Street, Mossley, near Ashton-under-Lyne, Lancashire OL5 0JS Tel: 01457 838818

To the southwest of Stalybridge and situated in bustling Armentiers Square in the town of **Stalybridge**, **Le Café** is a pretty eating establishment that is set off the main road near to the recently renovated canal. Open six days a week from 9 am until 5 pm, Le Café has been operating for over 10 years but was recently bought by Linda and Jose who will greet all visitors with a cheerful smile and a warm welcome.

As well as the café, there is also a take-away facility available throughout the day and Linda and Jose also offer outside catering for weddings, birthdays, engage-

Le Café

ments or parties. The furnishings and decor are certainly reminiscent of a traditional country kitchen and a cosy atmosphere pervades throughout the eatery.

Le Café, 1 Princess Place, Armentiers Square, Stalybridge, Lancashire
Tel: 0161 304 9800

A little further south, the **Harbour Lights Restaurant** is situated in the heart of Werneth Low Country Park, at **Gee Cross**, overlooking spectacular views of six counties. Enjoy the friendly atmosphere while dining in the restaurant or sit back and listed to live entertainment in the main bar every Friday and Saturday evening. On Sunday visitors can work up an appetite with a leisurely stroll around the country park before dining in the attractive restaurant or having a snack in the bar. There is a full à la carte menu available every evening of the week and the extensive bar snack menu is served throughout the day with a special Jolly Roger menu provided for the kids.

The Harbour Lights

There are also facilities for parties and functions, with a capacity of up to 150 people, making this excellent establishment perfect for weddings, birthdays, retirements and anniversaries. The Harbour Lights is open Monday to Friday from 12 pm until 3 pm and Monday to Saturday evenings from 6 pm, whilst customers will find their favourite restaurant and bar is open all day on Sundays. *The Harbour Lights, Windy Harbour, Werneth Low Road, Werneth Low, Gee Cross, Hyde, Cheshire SK14 3AF Tel: 0161 3683640*

BURY   *Map 13 ref J11*

This town, famous for its black puddings, has a fine Pennine moorland back-cloth. One fascinating development has been the reopening of the old railway line between Bury, Ramsbottom and Rawtenstall as the East Lancashire Steam Railway. The former **Bolton Street Station** is now a small museum, with regular steam services through the Upper Irwell valley at weekends and during holiday times.

The **Normandie Hotel and Restaurant** has much to commend it, particularly its wonderful location. In the late 1950s, a very talented Frenchman from Normandy bought what was then the Crown Inn at **Birtle**, and set about realising his dream of bringing French cuisine to the Northwest of England. Yves Champeau developed a fine reputation for good food over many years, one which the present owners of the Normandie are perpetuating. Rooms were added to the restaurant in 1968 and the Normandie became an hotel. A more recent addition of 11 superb bedrooms has further enhanced the hotel.

Normandie Hotel

One of the Normandie's unique advantages is its location, right in the foothills of the Pennines and yet only minutes from the motorway system, thus allowing easy access to the Lake District, Yorkshire Dales, Chester, Liverpool and Blackpool, all within a hours drive. And yet, by contrast, a mere 200 yards from the hotel guests may look upon the beautiful Cheesden Gorge with no civilisation in sight.

The Normandie has an international reputation for superb food, setting the highest standards of modern French and English cuisine. Guests are treated to a gastronomic experience which is a combination of presentation, texture, taste and service. The restaurant is stylish and designed with plenty of space and comfort, whilst the friendly and knowledgeable staff are supportive and helpful in every way. The Normandie's cellars can reveal the finest vintages as well as excellent quality lesser known wines, in addition, a fine selection brandy and liqueurs are available. The luxurious en-suite guest bedrooms are very peaceful, each beautifully furnished and equipped with all modern luxuries. Further services are provided including laundry, shoe cleaning and typing services. Birtle is seven minutes from Bury just off the B6222 Bury to Rochdale Road. *Normandie Hotel, Elbut Lane, Birtle, near Bury, Greater Manchester BL9 6UT Tel: 0161 764 3869 Fax: 0161 764 4866.*

Heron Lodge Guest House

Heron Lodge Guest House, located at **Edgworth** a few miles northwest of Bury, is a substantial, recently built, detached residence of mature stone with mullioned windows built by Roland Milton and his family. The cobblestone approach to the double door entrance of this attractive house prepares guests for the quality within. The accommodation at Heron Lodge can only be described as sumptuous with comfort being the keynote. Three of the bedrooms have en-suite facilities whilst the forth has a private adjacent luxury bathroom. Rich floral curtains, deep pile carpets and traditional period furniture combined with every facility will make any stay here a wonderful experience. Light suppers and packed lunches may be ordered in advance but a wide variety of Continental and traditional meals are available close by at the local hostelry. Situated in the designated Lancashire Hill Country, host Roland will be delighted to suggest rambles or walks to suit every taste as well as inform visitors of the local history and other points of interest. Within five minutes walk are the Jumbles Country Park, Chapletown with its ancient stocks and Chetham Arms, medieval Turton Tower and a pack horse bridge at the bottom of Roland's garden. The Heron Lodge has a no smoking policy.
Heron Lodge Guest House, 8 Bolton Road, Edgworth, Turton Bottoms, Bolton, Lancashire BL7 0DS Tel: 01204 852262

BOLTON

Map 13 ref I11

This is another mill town that defies expectations, its very fine Victorian town hall being the central point in a recently extensively refurbished pedestrianised shopping and leisure area with shopping malls, a restored market hall, a superb leisure centre including a swimming pool, the celebrated Octagon Theatre, and an excellent local museum.

Bolton Festival, at the end of August, is a very popular event. It runs for a whole week and there is a vast range of attractions, which include Morris Dancing and brass bands. The Victorian market is a favourite event, with everyone dressing up in full period costume.

Bradford Park Guest House

For those needing economy priced accommodation, **Bradford Park Guest House** argues against the need to stay in Manchester for city visits, or pre-departure stop-overs from the Airport, from which it is only 20 minutes drive. Bradford Park has been established for 10 years in a large Victorian house which is easy to find and offers good accommodation in a choice of nine comfortable guest rooms. A good breakfast is served in the dining room and guests can book for an evening meal. Tea and coffee is on a help yourself basis. Satellite television is installed and Bradford Park offers a comfortable and economical stay. Leave M61 at Junction 2 and join A666 to Bolton. Turn off at Bolton South (A579) and turn right at the traffic lights. The Bradford is 400 yards on the right. *Bradford Park Guest House, 44 Bradford Street, Bolton, Lancashire BL2 1JJ Tel: 01204 525480*

WIGAN

Map 13 ref I11

This is the town that turned a music hall joke on its head. The old canal basin on the Leeds–Liverpool Canal had a coal wharf known as **Wigan Pier**, jokingly referred to by George Formby and by George Orwell in a documentary book about working-class life in the North in the 1930s. But Wigan has used the complex of old warehouses and mills around the canal basin to create a new Wigan Pier, a major leisure attraction with its own Piermaster. There are canal boat rides and remarkable exhibitions based on local social history of "The Way We Were", with costumed actors whose activities in the reconstructed schoolroom bring back vivid memories of childhood.

Wigan is not a town living in the past but has a modern town centre, with fine countryside on its own doorstep such as the Douglas Valley Trail. Even Wigan's coal mining past has interesting links with the natural world—**Pennington Flash**, a large lake caused by mining subsidence, is now a wildlife reserve and country park.

The **Bird i'th Hand** provides an ideal break for those journeying in the Wigan area. It is positioned midway between junctions 26 and 27 of the M6 motorway, near **Orrell**. Here a warm welcoming atmosphere combines with fine ale and excellent food to provide welcome refreshments and relaxation. Approximately 100 years old, it was at one time used for local inquests and more recently was run as a restaurant. Thankfully, it has been restored to a pub, though it does have a separate dining area with comfortable seating for 50 people. Delicious home-made food is available daytime and evening supported by top quality cask ales. The pub is due to be featured in The Good Beer Guide. Pleasantly decorated in country style everyone is sure to enjoy their visit to the Bird i'th Hand.

Bird i'th Hand

Bird i'th Hand, Gathurst Road, Orrell, near Wigan, Lancashire WN5 0LH
Tel: 01942 212006

CHAPTER NINE
North England

Devil's Bridge, Kirkby Lonsdale

9
North England

Cumbria

INTRODUCTION

Cumbria is the second largest English county and it combines the former counties of Cumberland and Westmorland with parts of Lancashire and Yorkshire. This is the land where the British Celts managed to preserve their independence from the Saxons, though there are later Norse influences. The place names are very different from those in the counties to the south and east and reflect the individual history of the area.

Carlisle, the county town, lies in the north, close to the Scottish border and near the western end of Hadrian's Wall. For centuries it was a base for English soldiers who planned their invasions of Scotland here as well as defending the town from the marauding Scots.

To the south lies the Lake District. A beautiful national park that is home to England's highest peak, Scafell Pike, and the countries largest lake, Windermere. The magnificent ancient crags, the isolated fells and the wide lakes inspired the poet Wordsworth and his works triggered an interest in the area which today makes it one of the most popular places in England.

Cumbria also has a long coastline and, though there are areas of industry, particularly at Sellafield, the Furness peninsula in the far southwest is attractive. The small town of Grange-over-Sands overlooks the sandflats of Morecambe Bay and is an excellent centre from which to explore the delights of the Furness area.

AMBLESIDE   *Map 15 ref H7*

This pretty town, situated on the banks of Lake Windermere, is a popular tourist centre during the summer and from here lake cruises can be made to Newby Bridge and Bowness. **Old Bridge House**, a tiny cottage perched on a little packhorse bridge in the centre of the town, is now a National Trust shop. In the 1850s this was the home of Mr and Mrs Rigg and their six children—the main room of this one-up, one-down house measures 13 feet by 6 feet!

A centre for extremely good walks, most notably into the high fells to the north of the town, a steep road climbs sharply out of the town centre that is known locally as The Struggle. It leads up to the dramatic **Kirkstone Pass** and over to Ullswater, making this a convenient position from which to explore the whole of the Lake District.

Visitors to Ambleside will receive a warm welcome at **The Royal Oak** situated on Main Street. Originally built in 1846, it was apparently Wordsworth's local and had a brewery at the back of the pub. It has been run by Bill and Pat Cook for the past 25 years and is a charming pub with rustic tables outside where visitors can enjoy a drink in fine weather, and clematis cascading over the entrance porch. Inside there is an attractive beamed ceilings and the walls are covered with photographs of ships, mementoes of Bill's year in the Merchant Navy. During the winter months visitors can make use of the pool table and bar snacks are available all year round.

The Royal Oak

The Royal Oak, Main Street, Ambleside, Cumbria LA22 9BU
Tel: 015394 33382

RAVENGLASS   *Map 15 ref G7*

The town lies on the estuary of three rivers—the Esk, the Mite and the Irt. Because of its sheltered position, Ravenglass became an important naval base for the Romans in the 2nd century: it was a supply point for the military zone around Hadrian's Wall. Except for a remarkable Bath House, little remains now of their large fort of **Glannaventra** on the cliffs above the village. The Bath House is an impressive building and one of the best surviving Roman structures in England, with walls over 12 feet high.

In the 18th century Ravenglass was a base for smugglers bringing contraband in from coastal ships—tobacco and French brandy. Today the estuary has silted up but there are still scores of small boats and the village is a charming resort, full of atmosphere. The layout has changed little since the 16th century and the main street is paved with sea pebbles and leads up from a shingle beach. Once, iron ore was brought to the estuary by narrow gauge railway from the mines near Boot, in Eskdale, about eight miles away.

The **Ravenglass and Eskdale Railway**, which runs for seven miles up the lovely Mite and Esk River valleys, was first opened to passengers in 1876 since when it has survived several threats of extinction. In 1915 it was converted from 3 feet gauge track to a new miniature 15 inch gauge and carried passengers and freight—which later included granite—between Ravenglass and Dalegarth. However, towards the end of the 1950s, the closure of the granite quarries seemed to spell disaster for T'laal Ratty (as the railway is affectionately known). At the auction of the railway in 1960 a band of enthusiasts outbid the scrap-dealers and a company was formed to keep the little railway running. Today there are 12 locomotives, both steam and diesel, and 300,000 people a year come from all over the world to ride on T'laal Ratty and enjoy the splendour of Eskdale. At Ravenglass there is a fascinating small **Museum of Iron Ore Mining** and the history of the line.

Muncaster Mill, a mile or so up the River Mite, is reached by Eskdale trains and has working machinery dating from the late 18th century. A mill has stood here since the 15th century, though the present building only dates from around 1700. Carefully restored by the Railway Company in 1976–8, it is powered by a great, overshot waterwheel and still produces a wide variety of stone-ground, whole-meal flours.

A mile or so east of Ravenglass stands **Muncaster Castle**, an impressive castellated mansion which has been owned by the Pennington family since 1208. It has grown from the original Pele tower built on Roman foundations to the impressive structure that can be seen today. Outstanding features are the Great Hall, Salvin's octagonal library and the drawing room with its barrel ceiling. Muncaster contains many treasures including beautiful furniture, tapestries, silver and porcelain. In 1464, King Henry VI sheltered here from his enemies after losing the Battle of Hexham and, in gratitude, he left his glass enamelled drinking bowl, now known as the Luck of Muncaster, saying that the Pennington family will live at the castle as long as the bowl remains unbroken.

The woodland gardens cover 77 acres and command spectacular views of the Lakeland Fells. The grounds also contain a fascinating **Owl Centre** where visitors can meet the birds daily at 2.30 pm (April to end October) and a talk is given on the work of the centre. The gardens and owl centre are open daily throughout the year; castle open afternoons from the end of March to the end of October (closed Mondays).

The famous **Ratty Arms** is housed within the old station buildings at Ravenglass Railway Station and is the Ravenglass and Eskdale Railway's own pub, in what used to be the old station. Malcolm and Joyce became managers in 1982 and then leaseholders in 1991 and have transformed the Ratty Arms into a haven for railway memorabilia. Well known for its excellent food, the restaurant can seat up to 100 diners and offers its guests a good selection of bar snacks and three course evening meal. All meals are freshly prepared using only the best local ingredients and offers dishes ranging from the simple but delicious Ploughman's Lunch to the enormous Mixed grill which includes steak, sausage, lamb chops, gammon, black pudding, egg and mushrooms—definitely not for the faint hearted! There is also a choice of well kept real ales and the warm and friendly atmosphere of a traditional local pub.

The Ratty Arms

The Ratty Arms, Ravenglass, Cumbria CA18 1SN Tel: 01229 717676

Up the valley and on the Ravenglass and Eskdale Railway lies **Eskdale Green** and the **King George IV Inn**, a centuries old traditional Lakeland inn with a checkered history. With the oldest parts possibly standing since Roman times, the inn retains the olde worlde character expected in a pub of its age; flagged floors, open fires, oak beams and low ceilings. The inn has been owned and

King George IV Inn

personally run by Harry and Jackie for the past eight years and is locally renowned for its excellent bar meals and full à la carte dinners. Dishes range from a simple Smoked salmon and cucumber sandwiches to the luxurious Entrecote steak with brandy and green peppercorn sauce. Daily changing specials boards complement a fine range of real ales, world wide wines and an extensive collection of over 200 malt whiskies. A recent extension and refurbishment of accommodation has provided three well appointed en-suite bedrooms offering all the usual amenities including Jackie's personal touches that will make everyone feel completely at home.

King George IV Inn, Eskdale Green, Cumbria Tel: 019467 23262
Fax: 01946 23334

To the north of Ravenglass, on the coast at **St Bees**, can be found **The Queens Hotel**. This handsome 17th century free house and hotel stands in the ancient main street of this small seaside town. Inside, there is a wonderful traditional atmosphere with oak beamed ceilings and the conspicuous absence of a juke box or fruit machines. Owned and personally run by Geoff and Kay for the past 11 years, this attractive hotel's bar offers three cask conditioned ales and a range of over 70 malt whiskies (those managing to sample 50 during their stay become members of the 50 Malt Club). Delicious, freshly prepared meals are served in the panelled dining area adjacent to the bar, but for those who prefer a totally nonsmoking dining area then the magnificent conservatory at the rear of the establishment is the perfect location for that memorable meal. Recently refurbished, the Queens offers 15 guest bedrooms, all with en-suite facilities, colour televisions and beverage making facilities. There is also an attractive secluded beer garden at the rear complete with a large barbecue area and in the winter months there is a regular monthly Folk Night on the 1st Sunday in each month.

The Queens Hotel
The Queens Hotel, St Bees, Cumbria CA27 0DE Tel: 01946 822287

COCKERMOUTH   *Map 15 ref G6*

This Cumbrian market town has managed to retain its unspoiled character and is less overrun by tourists than its neighbours to the west. There are pleasant shops and restaurants along a busy main street set against a majestic backdrop of fells. There has been a livestock auction in Cockermouth since 1873, a part of the rural scene in the Lakes which tourists do not often see.

Wordsworth was born here and his old home in Main Street, which has been at various times a shop, a cobbler's and a tearoom, was the National Trust's first Information Centre, a function which it still retains. Now known as the **Wordsworth House**, it was built in 1745 and the original staircase, fireplace and fine plaster ceilings can still be seen. There are some personal effects of the poet and visitors can also see his childhood garden. Another famous son of Cockermouth was Fletcher Christian, the man who led the mutiny on *The Bounty*. He was born in 1764, at Moorland Close, a farm about a mile south of the town, and attended the same school as Wordsworth.

Cockermouth Castle dates from the 13th and 14th centuries but is not open to the public. Part of it was built with material from the Roman fort Derventio, at Papcastle, immediately northwest of Cockermouth. It has had an eventful history; it was besieged by Robert the Bruce and saw action in both the Wars of the Roses and the Civil War.

The charming village of **Dean**, to the south of Cockermouth, is full of old houses and farms. The churchyard is entered through a lychgate and outside the church is an ancient preaching cross probably dating from the 12th century. Three original 15th century gargoyles, one face downwards, decorate the south wall.

Royal Yew Inn

Dean is signposted off the A5086 Cockermouth to Egremont road and is the picturesque location of **The Royal Yew**, a charming country pub run by Alastair and Ann Chalmers. Dating back to the last century, the inn takes its name from the ancient yew tree which stands outside. It has not been possible to date the tree but it is thought that it could be between 800 and 1000 years old. In addition to the main building, two adjoining barns have been converted to enlarge the establishment. These areas are particularly characterful and feature the original stone walls and steps which lead to the first floor—now demolished! Open seven days a week, this cosy, welcoming public house is renowned locally for its superb bar food and justly so. The menu is varied and imaginative, with best selling dishes such as Old Peculiar Pie, a home-made steak and mushroom pie, and Pavlova, the most popular dessert. There are a wide range of steak dishes as well as other main courses, and a children's menu. All are very reasonably priced and with the accompanying wine list, which includes wines from all over the world, The Royal Yew makes the perfect venue for lunch or dinner.

Royal Yew Inn, Dean, near Workington, Cumbria CA14 4TJ
Tel: 01946 861342

DALSTON   *Map 15 ref H5*

Lying on the banks of the River Caldew, Dalston became a thriving cotton town in the late 18th century thanks to George Hodgson of Manchester, who used the river as the source of power for the flax mill and four cotton mills that were established here. The local economy was sustained still further by the emergence of a forge and two corn mills.

In the main square of Dalston is **Country Kitchen**, a traditional tea shop run by Carolyn Orr where customers can enjoy home-cooking at its best, surrounded by a magnificent collection of over 112 teapots. Country Kitchen is a cosy, friendly establishment tempting locals and tourists alike to pop in and sample the freshly baked gingerbread or fruit pies and scones with a warming drink. There are always freshly prepared daily specials made by Carolyn using only the finest

Country Kitchen

local produce. Visitors can even take away with them some cakes, biscuits, sponges and much more as a tasty memento. Open Tuesday–Saturday 10 am–4.30 pm, with lots of parking spaces available in the village square.
Country Kitchen, 5 The Square, Dalston, near Carlisle, Cumbria CA5 7PJ Tel: 01228 711431

PENRITH   *Map 15 ref I6*

The town is dominated by **Beacon Hill Pike**, which stands amidst wooded slopes high above the town. The tower was built in 1719 and marks the place where, since 1296, beacons have been lit to warn of war and invasion. The beacon was last lit during the Napoleonic wars in 1804; it was seen by the author Sir Walter Scott who was visiting Cumberland and it prompted him to hasten home to rejoin his local volunteer regiment. It is well worth the climb from Beacon's Edge, along the footpath to the summit, to enjoy a magnificent view of the Lakeland fells.

Penrith itself is a lively market town with handsome old buildings. It is a charming mixture of narrow streets and wide open spaces, such as Great Dockray and Sandgate, into which cattle were once herded during the border raids. Later they became market places and markets are still held every Tuesday and Saturday.

Penrith has a splendid Georgian **Church** in a very attractive churchyard, surrounded by a number of interesting buildings. The oldest part of St Andrew's dates from Norman times but the most recent part, the nave, was rebuilt between 1719 and 1772. Of particular interest is the three-sided gallery. Look out too for the brass candelabra, suspended from the roof, which was a gift from the Duke of Cumberland in 1745—a reward for the town's loyalty during the Jacobite Rising.

In the 9th and 10th centuries Penrith was the capital of Cumbria, a semi-independent state which, until 1070, formed part of the Kingdom of Strathclyde and Scotland. It is said that the King of Cumbria, Owen Caesarius, is buried in the churchyard amidst the group of gravestones known as **Giant's Grave**. The group consists of two ancient crosses, each 11 feet high, and four 10th century hogback tombstones which have arched tops and sharply sloping sides.

The ruins of **Penrith Castle** bear witness to the town's important role in defending the surrounding country from marauding Scots. The castle was built around 1399 but was enlarged for the Duke of Gloucester (later Richard III) when he was Lord Warden of the Western Marches and responsible for keeping the peace along the border with Scotland. The castle has been in ruins since 1550 but remains an impressive monument.

MC Ferguson, ceramic importers, have their shop on the main road into Penrith from the M6 motorway. Previously the building housed The Gardeners,

Penrith's largest grocers shop and the premises still retains the license to sell tobacco. Spanning three generations the business has undergone many changes over the years. Today, as customers enter the shop, it is like entering Aladdin's cave: there are ceramic articles of every conceivable colour, style and use. Floor and wall tiles, baths, sanitary ware, fittings, garden furniture, statues, pots, fire surrounds and stoves, to mention a few. Owned and run by father and son, Mark and Adam Ferguson, this is the place to come to view the finest in European ceramics from something grand to the more cottage-style.

MC Ferguson

MC Ferguson, 24-25 Brunswick Road, Penrith, Cumbria CA11 7JU
Tel: 01768 862851

Malones, in Burrowgate Square, lies in the heart of this old market town. The traditional cottage building, dating from the 1680s, with its low beams, has

recently been restored and is a Grade II listed building. Many of the original features remain including the old walkway at the side of the cottage building which was used by the horses for the George Hotel stable. Patricia has been personally running these tea rooms for the past year and has created a delightful eating establishment on two floors, serving traditional Cumberland dishes that, along with the cakes and pastries, are all home-cooked. Patricia also offers an excellent take-away service as well as daily specials and breakfast from 8 am until 11 am for those early birds. Malones is certainly a retreat from the bustle of this busy town and with

Malones

its warm and friendly atmosphere customers return again and again.
Malones, 46 Burrowgate, Penrith, Cumbria CA11 7TA Tel: 01768 863110

KESWICK

Map 15 ref H6

This is the largest town within the Lake District Park and its stunning position, surrounded by the mountains of Skiddaw and Borrowdale and on the shores of Derwent Water, makes it one of Britain's most popular inland holiday resorts.

The volcanic rocks of Borrowdale, newer than the Skiddaw slate group, are rich in minerals, and the discovery of one of the strangest, graphite, led to the development of the pencil industry in Keswick. In the fascinating **Cumberland Pencil Museum** visitors can discover the history behind this everyday object, the pencil, through machinery displays and video shows. Children will like the drawing corner with a free drawing competition to enter, as well as the brass rubbing which always proves popular. This unique museum, which follows the story of Cumberland graphite and the development of the pencil manufacturing industry in Keswick, is of interest to all.

A short walk out of the town centre, along the Lake Road and past the bustling lakeside promenade, leads to the popular Century Theatre and **Friar's Crag**. This famous view of the Derwent Water and its islands, now National Trust property, formed one of John Ruskin's early childhood memories.

At the lower end of the market square stands **The Wild Strawberry**, a delightful tea room run by Margaret and James Wilkinson, with assistant baker, Janet Lysser. A nonsmoking establishment, the tea room is charming and traditional, with local green slate floors, beamed ceilings and boasts what is probably the best view of the Moot Hall Clock Tower. Here the emphasis is on tasty home-cooked snacks and cakes, accompanied by a choice of quality teas and coffees served in fine strawberry china specially made for the tea room. There is a great atmosphere with excellent food and friendly service and customers are sure to return time and time again. A founder member of the Tea Council's Guild of Tea Shops.

The Wild Strawberry, 54 Main Street, Keswick, Cumbria CA12 5JS Tel: 01768 774399

To the west of Keswick and not far from **Braithwaite** is **Lingholm**, the home of Lord and Lady Rochdale, and its very impressive gardens and woodlands are open to the public during the summer. Beatrix Potter's family used Lingholm for many years as a holiday home and it crops up in many of her stories.

Through the village and over a stone bridge is the **Coledale Inn**, a hidden place well worth seeking out. Set high above and overlooking Braithwaite, this is still the locals' pub and the busy Georgian and Victorian bars reflect its popularity. The Coledale is run by Peter and Susan Mawdsley and their two sons, Geoffrey and Michael who like to remember their guests by sending them Christmas cards. An idea of the esteem in which they are held is shown by the fact that previous landlords return here to spend their own leisure time.

The inn was built originally in 1824 as a woollen mill, changed its identity to a pencil mill and eventually became licensed premises during the mid-1900s. Set well away from passing traffic and with Grizedale Pike on the doorstep, it is situated on the Coledale Round and there are many other walks in the area. The garden in front of the house can be used for eating and drinks and is where Mr Mawdsley sometimes holds barbecues. The house has been sensitively adapted for modern day use yet is full of Victorian prints, furnishings and antiques; open fires bring extra cheer during the winter months. The 12 bedroom accommoda-

The Coledale Inn

tion is all en-suite and the rooms have colour TV and coffee making facilities. Many of the rooms enjoy magnificent views of the surrounding countryside. The basic tariff is for bed and breakfast only, but lunches and evening meals are served daily and packed lunches are available on request. Residents have their own dining room and reading lounge, and meals are served in either of the two bars or the dining room. This is a free house serving real ales (including a good local one) and an inexpensive range of wines is available by the carafe or bottle. Well known for the high standard of its food, the Coledale serves starters, light meals, main courses, salads, desserts, farmhouse cheeses and a children's menu as well as having a daily Chef's Special. Hot chocolate, tea and coffee (plain or liqueur) are also on the menu.

In addition to the Coledale, Peter and Susan also own **The Mary Mount** hotel situated on the shores of Derwentwater. Surrounded by over 4 acres of woodland gardens there are a number of walks from the hotel around the lake and nearby fells. This peaceful country house offers 14 en-suite bedrooms in the main hotel and nearby Four Oaks Garden Bungalow.

The Coledale Inn, Braithwaite, near Keswick, Cumbria CA12 5TN
Tel: 017687 78272

To the south of Keswick, at the foot of Helvellyn on the A591 Grasmere to Keswick road, can be found **Thirlspot** and **The Kings Head Hotel**, an impressive 17th century former coaching inn. Careful refurbishment has provided modern refinements whilst retaining the hotel's original charm and character. Here guests can enjoy a good selection of well kept traditional ales and the excellent menu offers a wide range of tasty offerings to appeal to every palate. This must be one of the most extensive bar menus in the country, featuring such unusual dishes as Blue fin tuna sandwiches, Moroccan chicken and Coquilles St Jacques. St John's Restaurant offers more formal dining for both residents and nonresidents and provides the finest of local produce in the form of traditional English dishes featuring local specialities. The restaurant enjoys such an excellent reputation that booking ahead is essential.

Kings Head Hotel

Accommodation is provided in 19 well equipped, en-suite bedrooms, all furnished in keeping with hotel's character. The welcoming hosts are the Sweeney family who own another popular inn, the **Traveller's Rest** in Grasmere and their experience in the hotel business is self-evident in the friendly atmosphere and excellent service.

Travellers Rest Inn

Kings Head Hotel, Thirlspot, near Keswick, Cumbria CA12 4TN
Tel: 017687 72393
Travellers Rest Inn, Grasmere, Cumbria LA23 9RR Tel: 015394 35604

WINDERMERE

Map 15 ref H7

Windermere is perhaps the Lake District's best known tourist centre. The confusion of names between the town and the lake goes back to the days when the Kendal and Windermere Railway Company was opened in 1847. Its terminal station was at the village of Birthwaite—hardly a name to bring the tourists flocking in—so the railway company called their station Windermere, even though it is over a mile away from the lake. In the early days, carriages and, in later years, buses linked the station with the landing stages in the village of Bowness on the shores of the lake.

Such was the popularity of the Lake District, even in Victorian times, that a town filled with hotels, boarding houses, comfortable villas and shops soon grew up around the railway station. It spread rapidly down the hill towards the lake until Bowness and Birthwaite were linked together under the name of Windermere Town, the lake being given the unnecessary prefix 'Lake'.

Windermere's railway line remains open as a single track branch—**The Lakes Line**—now the only surviving British Rail line to run into the heart of the Lake District. Modern diesel railcars provide a busy shuttle service to and from the express services at Oxenholme. The rail journey via Kendal, Burneside and Staveley is a delight and a very pleasant alternative to the crowded A591 road. Within a few yards of Windermere station, there is a footpath that leads through the woods to one of the finest viewpoints in Lakeland, **Orrest Head**. It takes about an hour from the station to climb and descend the little hillock but there is no better introduction to this part of Cumbria.

The lake itself is largest in England and is 1 mile wide at its broadest point. For many visitors to the Lake District time spent on the water is a must and it is a well known and well used watersports centre. There is also a car ferry across the lake from Bowness to Far Sawrey.

Merewood Country House Hotel, at **Eccle Rigg**, is an impressive establishment standing in 20 acres of landscaped woodland gardens, overlooking Lake Windermere. Here the warm welcome is matched by the comfort and luxury of the sumptuous surroundings. The Conservatory Bar is evocative of the Edwardian era, with its mahogany panelling, beautiful mosaic floor and red chesterfield sofas. In the restaurant, with its elegant yew tables, guests can enjoy a first class

Merewood Country House Hotel

England

menu of English and French cuisine, including a creative range of vegetarian dishes all accompanied by an extensive international wine list. Upstairs equal thought and care has gone into the individually decorated bedrooms. All are very spacious, beautifully furnished and with the top class facilities expected in a top quality hotel. It therefore comes as no surprise to learn that Merewood has received the five crown, highly commended award, one of the English Tourist Board's highest accolades. This is the ideal place to come to for a 'spoil yourself' weekend.

Merewood Country House Hotel and Restaurant, Eccle Rigg, Windermere, Cumbria LA23 1LH Tel: 015394 46484 Fax: 015394 42128

Across the lake lies the village of **Hawkshead** which has changed little since William Wordsworth, at the age of eight, attended the Grammar School here. The village is all the better preserved since visitors are obliged to leave their cars outside the centre and walk through it on foot. Next to the car park is the **National Park Information Centre**, a good starting point for exploring Hawkshead. A nice way to go into the village is past the Grammar School and through the churchyard. The 15th century church dominates Hawkshead from its high position, and is worth a look inside for its series of painted murals which date from 1680.

The National Trust now owns some of the buildings in Hawkshead, including Bend or Bump, which was formerly a house and shop and features in Beatrix Potter's *The Pie and the Patty Pan*; it was also a solicitor's office of William Heelis, who was Beatrix Potter's husband. This building is now the **Beatrix Potter Gallery**.

One of the most interesting places to visit from Hawkshead is **Grizedale Forest**, famous for its theatre and sculpture. In the forest more than 100 sculptures have been commissioned over the last 15 years, all made from natural materials found in the forest and by some of Britain's best known contemporary artists, including the sculptor Andy Goldsworthy, as well as artists from all over the world. The great beauty of these sculptures is their understated presence—visitors are left entirely to their own devices to explore the wonders of this forest, with the help of a printed guide, either on foot or on mountain bike, which can be hired at the Visitor Centre.

Grizedale Forest Sculpture

The **Theatre-in-the-Forest** has an excellent programme throughout the year of musical and theatrical events of the highest quality and the Visitor Centre now

406

includes an art gallery and workshop which is also open to the public, where the artists in residence will happily take a break from their work to describe their experiences of living and working in this unique environment.

Overlooking the square of this Elizabethan village stands **The Kings Arms Hotel**, an ancient Lakeland inn full of character, complete with log fires for those chilly evenings. Rosalie Johnson, the proprietor, offers a warm welcome to all her guests and looks after them very well. She will happily provide packed lunches for those day long excursions and, in the evening, guests can choose from an excellent range of home-cooked dishes. The imaginative traditional and Continental cuisine is served in the bar area and dining room and in warm weather customers can eat in the beer garden. With an extensive wine list to accompany the meal plus a choice of four real ales and wide selection of malt and Irish whiskeys at the bar, the evening is complete. Finally, guests can retire to one of the nine well-equipped guest rooms, or make use of the self-catering accommodation in one of three nearby cottages.

The Kings Arms Hotel

The Kings Arms Hotel, Hawkshead, Cumbria LA22 0NZ Tel: 015394 36372

BROUGHTON-IN-FURNESS   *Map 15 ref G7*

This charming little market town, built on the side of a hill above the Duddon Valley, is filled with handsome 18th century houses. The Market Hall still has its original 1766 clock and the Market Square, from where the Market Charter is still proclaimed annually, has its original stone-slabbed stalls. **Jack Hadwin's Motor Cycle Collection**, in the old Town Hall, boasts 50 machines dating from between 1899 to 1959 as well as items from the early days of motoring.

Broughton is an ideal base from which to explore the Duddon Valley and the relatively little known fell country all around, as well as the coast and northern Furness. About two miles west of Duddon Bridge, high up on Swinside Fell, and only reached by footpath, is **Swinside Stone Circle**, sometimes known as Sunkenkirk. This prehistoric monument could be 3500 years old, and was built for a purpose that can only be guessed.

The old bakery, which is very much part of the character of The Square in Broughton-in-Furness, is a favourite with visitors interested in the history of this picturesque old market village. Few are disappointed to find that it has now been tastefully converted into Christine and David Roe's **Beswicks Restaurant** with a reputation for excellent cuisine. Christine, with her flair for cooking, has created a collection of recipes which combine unusual ingredients with wonderful sauces, but she is pleased to prepare almost anything by special request. The house speciality is game—venison, quail and pheasant being very popular in season.

Beswicks Restaurant

The Roes also have an extensive wine list with over 80 different wines from nine countries and the character of each is helpfully described. Guests are first welcomed into the lounge to enjoy an aperitif, a leisurely look at the menu and a chance to absorb the unique atmosphere of Beswicks. After dinner, accompanied by soft classical music, coffee may be taken in the lounge. As the restaurant is popular and not open daily, booking ahead is advisable. Private dinners are catered for in special rooms by prior arrangement.

Beswicks Restaurant, Langholme House, The Square, Broughton-in-Furness, Cumbria LA20 6JF Tel: 01229 716285

MILLOM
Map 15 ref G8

The town stands at the mouth of the River Duddon on the banks of the estuary, with the 1970 foot Black Combe Fell behind it. Like neighbouring towns in this region, it grew with the development of the iron industry, and the town's **Folk Museum** tells its history. The museum also contains a permanent memorial to Norman Nicholson which tells of his books of verse and prose on local life and customs.

When the famous Millim Ironworks closed in the 1970s, Gerard and Pearl Milligan bought a piece of its land. Seventeen years passed before the magnificent **Duddon Pilot Hotel** opened its doors and the history of the period from ironworks to hotel can be seen displayed in photographic form within the hotel. Named after the River Duddon, this attractive family run establishment has a definite seafaring theme throughout with historic uniforms and model boats on full display. Gerard and Pearl's daughter Marjorie is the in-house chef and freshly prepares numerous delicious dishes using only the best local produce. The restaurant seats up to 40 diners and offers a full à la carte menu as well as a daily specials board, though it does prove very popular at weekends so ensure that you book to avoid disappointment.

The Duddon Pilot Hotel

The Duddon Pilot Hotel, Devonshire Road, Millom, Cumbria
Tel: 01229 774116

DALTON-IN-FURNESS   *Map 15 ref G8*

Lying in a narrow valley on the part of Furness which extends deep into Morecambe Bay, this ancient town was once the leading town of Furness and an important centre for administration and justice. The 14th century pele tower, **Dalton Castle**, stands almost hidden by surrounding buildings. It was built around 1330–36 to provide a place of refuge for the monks of Furness Abbey against Scottish raiders. Over the centuries, in its twin role as both prison and court, it has been substantially altered internally, although it still retains most of its original external features. It is now owned by the National Trust and there is a small museum with an interesting display of 16th and 17th century armour.

Dalton became established as a market town in the 13th century when the Cistercians began to hold fairs and markets in the town. Before the Dissolution of the Monasteries, it was the Abbot who held court and administered justice. Indeed, Dalton's decline coincided with the decline of the monks and the growing importance of Ulverston and Greenodd as ports.

To the south of Dalton is **Furness Abbey**, a magnificent ruin of eroded red sandstone set in fine parkland, the focal point of South Cumbria's monastic heritage. Visitors can still see the canopied seats in the presbytery and the graceful arches overlooking the cloister, testaments to the Abbey's former wealth and influence.

Furness Abbey stands in the **Vale of Deadly Nightshade**, a shallow valley of sandstone cliffs and rich pastureland. The Abbey itself was established in 1123 at Tulketh, near Preston, by Stephen, Count of Blois and King of England. Four years later it was moved to its present site and, after 20 years, became absorbed into the Cistercian Order. Despite its remoteness, the abbey flourished with the monks establishing themselves as guides across the treacherous sands of Morecambe Bay. Rich endowments of land, which included holdings in Yorkshire and Ireland, led to the development of trade in products such as wool, iron and charcoal. It became the second wealthiest monastery in Britain after Fountains Abbey in Yorkshire. After Dissolution in 1537 it became part of Thomas Cromwell's estate and was allowed to decay into a picturesque and romantic ruin. It is now owned by English Heritage who have a small Interpretative Centre nearby detailing its history.

The Golden Ball

The **Golden Ball Inn** is worth a visit particularly for those who like a friendly atmosphere and live entertainment. The exterior has an attractive Tudor style upper frontage while the interior has been completely refurbished retaining its old style character. This is a lively establishment run by Alex and Lynne Dacre where live entertainment is featured on Thursday, Saturday and Sunday evenings each week. Entry on these evenings is free of charge and visitors could enjoy the talents of a band or a comedy act. Bar snacks are served daily until 7 pm, there is a choice of good ales and the beer garden at the rear offers a breathe of air. Situated on the Old Town Road through Dalton.
The Golden Ball, Ulverston Road, Dalton-in-Furness, Cumbria LA15 8RJ
Tel: 01229 467757

ULVERSTON   *Map 15 ref H8*

This is a fine market town in the centre of Furness, with old buildings and a labyrinth of cobbled streets and alleyways to explore. The town dates from the 12th century when Stephen, Earl of Boulogne and King of England, owned the Manor. In 1280 the town was granted a charter to hold a market and every Thursday and Saturday it bustles with activity as livestock are brought for sale and street traders set up their stalls. Each September the charter is celebrated with events taking place daily for a two week festival, culminating in a lantern procession, when the children of Ulverston make their own lanterns and parade through the streets at dusk.

The railway station, on what is now the Furness Line, was once the junction for the branch to Lakeside, and is a fine example of early Victorian railway architecture. The oldest building in Ulverston is the Church of St Mary which, in part, dates from 1111. It was restored and rebuilt in the 1860s and a chancel added in 1903–4. The original steeple was destroyed in a storm in 1540 and the present tower dates from the reign of Elizabeth I.

Ulverston's most famous son is Stan Laurel, of Laurel and Hardy fame, who was born here in 1890. His real name was Arthur Stanley Jefferson and he spent his first 15 years in a small terraced house, 3 Argyll Street. It now has a plaque commemorating him and a local pub has been renamed The Stan Laurel. Nearby, at Upper Brook Street, is the **Laurel and Hardy Museum** crammed with photographs and relics of the comedian and his Hollywood partner, Oliver Hardy.

Once a staging post for coaches that crossed the sands of Morecambe Bay to Lancaster in the 18th century, the **Bay Horse Hotel and Restaurant** has, since 1988, been the home of Robert Lyons, the host. The house stands at the waters edge of the Leven estuary commanding views of both the Lancashire and Cumbrian fells. Originally a brewery, inn and fishermen's cottages, today the hotel remains very much a family home which offers comfort to all visitors. The atmosphere is friendly and informal a place where guests can relax and unwind from the stress and strain on every day life.

Bay Horse Hotel and Restaurant

The award winning conservatory restaurant overlooking the water is open for lunch from Tuesday to Saturday, and each evening for dinner. All the food, from the bread at the start of the meal to the chocolates with the coffee are made in the hotel kitchens. The cuisine is of such a high standard that, by popular demand, cookery demonstrations are held in the purpose-built kitchen. Ring for full details of dates and availability.

Seven en-suite bedrooms are available in the house and six of these have French windows opening onto a terrace giving panoramic views over the estuary. Each room is individually decorated and furnished and contains plenty of magazines, books and board games, along with all the facilities expected to provide a home-from-home.

Bay Horse Hotel and Restaurant, Canal Foot, Ulverston, Cumbria LA12 9EL Tel: 01229 583972 Fax: 01229 580502

CARTMEL   *Map 15 ref H8*

One of the prettiest villages in Furness, Cartmel is a delightful cluster of houses and cottages set around a square, from which lead winding streets and arches into charming back yards. The village is dominated by the famous **Cartmel Priory**, founded in 1188 by Augustine Canons. According to legend, it was originally intended to be sited on nearby Mount Barnard, but St Cuthbert appeared in a vision to the monastic architect and ordered him to build the priory between two springs of water.

Like all such monastic institutions, the priory was disbanded in 1537 and several of its members were executed for participating in the Pilgrimage of Grace. Today, only the 14th century gatehouse and the **Church of St Mary and St Michael** have survived. Indeed, after the dissolution, only the south aisle was used as a parish church, but in 1620 George Preston of Holker began to restore the entire building, re-roofing it and presenting the church with the richly carved black oak screens and stall canopies.

Apart from its glorious east window, one of its most noticeable features is the unique tower set diagonally on the tower stage. Inside, in the southwest corner of the church, is a door known as **Cromwell's Door**. The holes in it are said to have been made by indignant parishioners firing at Cromwellian soldiers who had stabled their horses in the nave. Parliamentary troops were in the area in 1643 and, indeed, fragments of lead were found in the wood during restoration work in 1955.

Occupying a fine position on the main square in the centre of historic Cartmel is the impressive **Kings Arms**. This picture postcard public house additionally offers a restaurant, tea rooms and gift shop—it certainly has something for everyone. The excellent service throughout the establishment is due to the care and attention to detail of the owners, Graham and Jacqui Hamlett. A traditional inn, The Kings Arms welcomes all ages and caters for every taste with all that is best is home-cooking. There are several menus which cater for the whole family including dishes for children and vegetarians. The dishes are a combination of New Zealand and Cumbrian cuisines, reflective of the years that Graham and Jacqui have spent there. In the summer, food can be enjoyed outdoors, either at tables facing the village square or on the patio overlooking the River Eea. Above the bar area are the newly opened tea rooms and gift shop. The tea room

The Kings Arms

serves cold drinks, real coffee and a choice of fine teas throughout the day with a selection of excellent home-made cakes. The Kings Arms is a characterful establishment where all can be assured of excellent and friendly service.
The Kings Arms and Hamletts Country Cottage Restaurant, The Square, Cartmel, Cumbria LA11 6QB Tel: 015395 36220

Situated in Cartmel's village square is **Country Classics**, a hidden place well worth seeking out. This fine clothing shop is housed in a Virginia creeper-clad Grade II listed building and is run by Ian and Karen Conroy, who pride themselves on the quality of the clothes that they stock and the high standard of friendly and informal service which they offer. The shop stocks classic style clothing ranges for all; ladies clothes by Janique, men's clothes by Pegasus, children's ranges and appliqué sweatshirts by Scallywag. A good range of men's, ladies' and children's shoes are also stocked. Why not call in for a rummage, everyone is sure to find something to suit them (and their purse). Open all day every day.

Country Classics
Country Classics, The Square, Cartmel, Cumbria LA11 6QB Tel: 015395 36165

Tucked away off the village square, in a small courtyard behind the medieval priory, is **Courtyard Cottage**. This delightful stone built cottage was once a stable block, but has recently been sensitively converted to provide a high standard of accommodation. It is available for self-catering breaks all year round and is ideally placed as a base for exploring all of the places described in this book.

Courtyard Cottage

The accommodation consists of a well equipped kitchen (including a gas hob and electric oven), dining hall and two single bedrooms (cots are available) with a bathroom on the ground floor and, on the first floor, a double bedroom with private washing facilities and a generously sized lounge which enjoys a superb view of the priory. A TV and video and a selection of games are also provided for guests to use.

The garden has a small patio area and there is a private parking space. Well behaved pets are welcome. ETB 4 keys commended.
Courtyard Cottage, The Square, Cartmel, Cumbria Tel: 015395 36165

The Cavendish at Cartmel is a picturesque establishment dating back to the 15th century and stands in the centre of the historic town of Cartmel. A plaque outside the front door records the part that the inn played in the local history of the area. It reads: "After the Cartmel Commons Enclosures Act of 1796, the Commissioners' first meeting took place at this hotel, then known as Mrs Hulland's Cavendish Arms Inn."

Today, The Cavendish is under the care of Tom Murray, with his sons, Howard and Nick, as it has been for over 20 years. The inn is charming and characterful retaining many original features including low beamed ceilings and creaky floorboards! It has an established reputation for its warmth of welcome, excellence of food and own traditional beers. The restaurant delights customers old and new with meals skilfully prepared to suit all tastes. On Sunday, the roast is prepared on an open spit and proves to be very popular. Staying at The

The Cavendish at Cartmel

Cavendish, there are a choice of 10 tastefully furnished bedrooms, some dating from the 16th century and other more recently completed. All have en-suite facilities, TV and drinks facilities. The inn was voted Brew Pub of the Year in 1996 by the *Good Beer Guide*.

The Cavendish at Cartmel, Cartmel, Cumbria LA11 6QA
Tel: 015395 36240 Fax: 015395 36620

A mile from the historic village of Cartmel and overlooking Morecambe Bay is the impressive **Uplands Hotel**. Uplands was opened in 1985 by Tom and Diana Peter, with John Tovey of the renowned Miller Howe Hotel in Windermere. Tom and Diana both worked with John at Miller Howe before opening Uplands. As might imagined, the food is terrific but also worth noting is the warm, friendly and informal atmosphere of the place. The dinner menus change daily and use only the freshest of ingredients. As well as the restaurant, the hotel has five en-suite bedrooms, all comfortably furnished and prettily decorated. Standing in over two acres of truly delightful gardens, with magnificent panoramic views over the Leven estuary, this is a particularly special place to enjoy a meal and be spoilt.

Uplands Country House Hotel

Uplands Country House Hotel, Haggs Lane, Cartmel, Cumbria LA11 6HD
Tel: 015395 36248 Fax: 015395 36848

To the southwest of Cartmel can be found the **Lakeland Riding School** near the village of **Flookburgh**. Just south of the Lake District, the school offers a wide variety of horse rides with something to suit beginners and the more experienced ride whatever their age. With over 30 horses, and with all training under the supervision of professional instructors, there is a horse for everyone.

The riding school itself has a large outdoor arena for jumping and dressage lessons, and with some wonderful countryside just minutes away, there are a range of rides available: one hour park or village rides, fell rides of varying lengths and beach rides by prior arrangement. Long distance trail rides of five hours take more experienced riders to Grizedale Forest and the Lakeland Fells. Beginners can improve their riding and the more experienced can take the opportunity to explore the region more fully with a three day break staying in the nearby caravan park. This is certainly an exhilarating way to discover the area.

Lakeland Riding School

Lakeland Riding School, Lakeland Leisure Park, Moor Lane, Flookburgh, near Grange-over-Sands, Cumbria LA11 7LT Tel: 015395 58131

Fifty years ago Dick Taylor opened a little nursery growing lettuces and tomatoes in the nearby village of **Cark**. Today, **Southern Lakeland Nurseries** has grown to a large and successful garden centre specialising in pot plants, bedding plants and hardy plants, under half an acre of glass housing. There are outdoor gardens as well as undercover areas, a shop supplying all types of garden sundries and a café. Dick and his wife Joan, ably assisted by their son Michael, look after the day to day running of the garden centre while daughter Alison and her helpers run the café and do all the cooking. It is open for delicious home cooked food, teas, coffees, salads, cakes and snacks seven days a week.

As visitors walk around the centre they will find a huge variety to choose from and a member of the family will usually be on hand to assist with help and

Southern Lakeland Nurseries

information. While here, visitors can also take the opportunity to send some flowers to a friend or relative through the Interflora service. Located opposite the railway station on the B5278, a quarter mile from Holker Hall.
Southern Lakeland Nurseries, Cark, near Grange-over-Sands, Cumbria LA11 7JZ Tel: 015395 58237

Rose and Crown Inn

Standing in the picturesque village of Cark-in-Cartmel, not far from Holker Hall, is the lovely **Rose and Crown Inn**. Recently taken over by Gary and Lynne Altham it is evident that the venture is going to be a success. Gary is a top class chef and this shows in the excellent bar menu supplemented by daily specials. Although 40 diners can be seated comfortably, is to recommended to book for Friday and Saturday evenings and Sunday lunch. Behind the bar is a good selection of refreshment including Hartleys XB and Robinsons ale. Also on offer is bed and breakfast accommodation in one of two en-suite letting rooms of which one has a four poster bed—ideal for that romantic weekend break!
Rose and Crown Inn, Cark, near Grange-over-Sands, Cumbria LA11 7NU Tel: 015395 58501

GRANGE-OVER-SANDS   *Map 15 ref H8*

Once a small coastal village, Grange-over-Sands was transformed into a fashionable resort by the coming of the Furness Railway linking it with Lancaster. Villas and hotels were built to take advantage of the exceptionally mild climate. Though the sands are not safe for bathing, this is more than compensated by the extensive promenade gardens along the sea front. Due to the mild climate these boast rock plants, alpines and even subtropical species. Away from the hotels, shops and cafés there are some lovely walks, none nicer than the path behind the town which climbs through the magnificent limestone woodlands, rich in wild flowers.

The path leads to **Hampsfell Summit** and **The Hospice**, a little stone tower from which there is an unforgettable view of Morecambe Bay and the craggy peaks of the Lake District. The Hospice was provided by a pastor of Cartmel in the last century for the 'shelter and entertainment of wanderers'. An external flight of stairs leads to a flat roof and the viewing-point. Grange is also the starting point of the **Cistercian Way**, an exceptionally interesting, 37 mile footpath route through Furness to Barrow, linking many sites of Cistercian interest.

Dating back to the 17th century, **The Commodore** on Main Street enjoys unbeatable views over Morecambe Bay towards Silverdale. The cross sands coach service from Lancaster to Ulverston began in 1785 and by 1820 travellers were able to stop at this coaching inn, then called The Bay Horse. Today, travellers to the area still take advantage of the warm and welcoming hospitality.

The Commodore

The Commodore is open from 11 am to 11.30 pm each day and offers excellent food, drink and accommodation. The upstairs dining area can seat up to 70, with the bar and outside terraced areas catering for another 80. The menu caters for all with a good selection for all appetites. Behind the bar are some well kept ales, including Directors, Theakston and John Smiths, with a regular guest ale as well. For a more lively atmosphere there is usually a band each Thursday and some Saturdays. The accommodation comprises five double rooms and two family rooms, with all enjoying views over the bay.
The Commodore, Main Street, Grange-over-Sands, Cumbria LA11 6DY
Tel: 015395 32381

Situated on a private estate in the beautiful Winster Valley overlooking Whitbarrow Scar and the Kent Estuary, within old Victorian outbuildings and a magnificent former 16th century manor house stands **Witherslack Hall Equestrian Centre**.

Witherslack Hall Equestrian Centre

The stables are arranged around a cobbled yard and offer riding for both experienced and novice riders with private and group lessons for adults and children. These attractive stables are personally run by Careth and Lynne and offer one and two hour rides, side saddle, evening lessons and weekend breaks in their well appointed bed and breakfast en-suite accommodation. The atmosphere is warm and welcoming, with Careth and Lynne ensuring that everyone feels relaxed and comfortable. They also welcome disabled riders and school parties and offer trekking, hacks and an outdoor menage.

Witherslack Hall Equestrian Centre, Witherslack Hall Farm, Witherslack, near Grange-over-Sands, Cumbria LA11 6SO Tel: 015395 52244

Standing in the picturesque village of **High Newton**, to the north of Grange-over-Sands and on the edge of Cartmel Fell, the **Duck and Crown Inn** offers its visitors the very best in food, drink and accommodation. This magnificent 17th century former coaching inn has been run by Leigh and Claire for over two years and it is Leigh's skills in the kitchen that has made the inn locally renowned for its excellent cuisine. The comprehensive menu includes an enormous house

Duck and Crown Inn

special that is designed to be shared and is called the Duck and Crown, this comprises half a Crispy duck and a Crown of lamb, definitely not for the faint hearted!

Leigh and Claire also offer a good range of real ales and have four en-suite guest bedrooms for those visitors who cannot tear themselves away from the delightful ambiance that pervades this traditional establishment. Also available are mid-week fishing breaks which are based on two nights dinner, bed and breakfast and fishing permits for five local lakes and reservoirs including the famous Newton Fisheries.

Duck and Crown Inn, Newton-In-Cartmel, near Grange-over-Sands, Cumbria LA11 6JH Tel: 015395 31793

Close by and near the crossroads at the village of **Lindale** is the John Wilkinson Memorial; a tall obelisk made from black iron. It commemorates the life of this local man, who invented the iron boat, and has been all but forgotten by historians and engineers alike.

The Lindale Inn is a charming, former coaching inn at the crossroads in the centre of this small village of Lindale. Renowned for serving the Best Steaks in the Lakes, the inn has a extensive menu of traditional pub food, mouthwatering grills and salads. All meals are freshly prepared to order using many local ingredients such as Morecambe Bay brown shrimps and an award winning Cumberland Sausage! As the food has such a good reputation the inn often gets busy, but don't worry there is plenty of room to seat diners. The hosts, Nick and Jane Kirkpatrick, also have an extensive range of malt whiskies behind the bar and serve a selection of fine real ales including Boddingtons, Flowers and Castle Eden. For those who enjoy live music, then make a point of visiting on a Monday when there is usually a band playing. There are four charming en-suite bedrooms, all decorated to a high standards, making this is an ideal place to stay.

The Lindale Inn

The Lindale Inn, Lindale, near Grange-over-Sands, Cumbria LA11 6LJ Tel: 015395 32416

Further east at **Beetham** and within earshot of a waterfall is the **Church of St Michael and All Angels**, approached through a pergola of rambling roses. The church dates from Saxon times and, during restoration work in 1834, a hoard of about a hundred old coins was discovered at the base of a pillar. The coins were from the reigns of Edward the Confessor, William the Conqueror and William Rufus. During the Civil War, the church was badly damaged, its windows smashed and effigies broken. However, a glass fragment of Henry IV in an ermine robe has survived.

Tucked away in the heart of the delightful village of Beetham is the charming **Wheatsheaf Hotel**. Overlooking Beetham's historic Norman church, the hotel has been run by Margaret Shaw, and her parents before her, for the past 30 years, and was originally built in 1609 as a coaching inn. It was ideally situated, lying only 100 yards off the A6, which was then the main road linking the south to Scotland, and it allowed travellers to rest and refresh themselves whilst the horses were changed.

The Wheatsheaf Hotel

The Wheatsheaf is a popular and busy hotel, full of character, and, although it has been obviously updated and refurbished, it has retained its original charm and exudes a warm, friendly atmosphere. The bar offers a wide choice of fine ales and a varied selection of bar meals are available daily. On the first floor there is a cosy, intimate restaurant which provides an excellent, reasonably priced menu, including a variety of home-made pies and hotpots, tasty roasts, fresh fish and freshly made fruit tarts and meringue dishes, as well as an extensive cold buffet. Its popularity makes prior bookings advisable for weekend evenings or Sunday lunchtime. In addition to the fine fare on offer, Margaret also provides top class accommodation. There are six letting bedrooms, all en-suite, spacious, and with that little extra personal touch which make The Wheatsheaf a lovely place to stay. Downstairs visitors should look out for the showcase which houses a vast selection of dolls that have been collected from all over the world.
The Wheatsheaf Hotel, Beetham, near Milnthorpe, Cumbria LA7 7LA
Tel: 015395 62123

KIRKBY LONSDALE   *Map 15 ref I8*

The old town on the banks of the River Lune (hence its name), is almost on the edge of the Yorkshire Dales National Park. Despite the conflict of allegiances, this town has maintained its character over the years and, as it is set well back from the main A65 road, it remains a very traditional, handsome market town, where life still revolves around the market place and its 600 year old cross.

Lovely Georgian buildings crowd along the winding main street and there are interesting alleyways and courtyards to explore with good shops to browse in, delicious bakeries and some wonderful tea shops. The view from the churchyard is delightful, extending over the valley of the Lune to the fells beyond. JMW Turner was inspired to paint this very scene and John Ruskin wrote enthusiastically about what he saw: "The Valley of the Lune at Kirkby Lonsdale is one of the loveliest scenes in England." Since then, the name Ruskin's View has stuck.

The arched bridge over the River Lune below the town, **Devil's Bridge**, is reputed to be at least 600 years old and got its name from the legend of an old woman who, unable to cross the deep river with her cattle, asked the devil to build her a bridge. He duly did this in return for the soul of the first creature to cross. But the clever woman threw a stick across the bridge which was collected by her dog, cheating the devil of a human soul, and he disappeared with a howl of rage, leaving behind his neck collar which some say can still be seen in the river below. Today on summer Sundays leather-clad bikers use the bridge as an informal gathering place and an impressive display of motorbikes from every era can be admired.

The drive from Kirkby Lonsdale to Sedbergh, on the A683 which follows the River Lune upstream, is quite beautiful. The river forms the geographic western boundary of the Yorkshire Dales National Park, a gentle valley on the edge of fertile farmland and rolling hills.

The **Snooty Fox Tavern** is a listed Jacobean inn in the centre of Kirkby Lonsdale and for a long time has had a reputation for good wholesome cooking, efficient friendly service and fine cask ales. Under the guiding hand of proprietor Jack Shone, his young and enthusiastic team set amazing standards; in this Westmorland Market Town they average over one hundred meals a day—all year round.

With a team of five professionals in the kitchen, the chefs, led by Darren Jones, are very serious about what they do for a living. Darren is responsible for the daily preparation of over 40 freshly cooked dishes including soufflés, lobster, home-made bread, home-crafted desserts, including ice-creams, and original chocolates. The chefs also produce delightful pastries which are served from a French patisserie within the establishment. The newly refurbished accommodation at the Snooty boasts nine en-suite rooms all with luxury facilities, attractive drapes and antique furnishings. A breakfast buffet is provided in the restaurant

Snooty Fox Tavern

where both Continental and full English breakfast is served. The two traditional bars serve hand-pumped real ales and the bar menu covers all levels of requirements while maintaining the quality.

Snooty Fox Tavern, Kirkby Lonsdale, Cumbria LA6 2AH Tel: 015242 71308 Fax: 015242 72642

KENDAL   *Map 15 ref I7*

This ancient town, in the valley of the River Kent, was once one of the most important woollen textile centres of Northern England. The Kendal woollen industry was founded in 1331 by John Kemp, a Flemish weaver. It flourished and sustained the town for almost 600 years until the development of competition from the huge West Riding mills in the Industrial Revolution of the 19th century. The town was also famous for its Kendal Bowmen, skilled archers clad in Kendal Green cloth, whose longbows were made from local yew trees on the nearby limestone crags. It was these men who fought so decisively against the Scots at the Battle of Flodden Field in 1513. Kendal has royal connections too. Katherine Parr, the last of Henry VIII's six wives, lived at **Kendal Castle** in the 16th century before she became Queen of England. Today its ruins, high on a hill overlooking the town, locate one of the original Roman camps that guarded the route to the Scottish Border.

Kendal, the largest town in the old county of Westmorland, has always been a bustling place, from the days when it was on the main route to Scotland. Nowadays the M6 and the Kendal by-pass divert much of the traffic away from the town centre, but its narrow main streets, Highgate, Stramongate and Stricklandgate, are still busy, and the fine stage coaching inns of the 17th and 18th century, to which Bonnie Prince Charlie is said to have retreated after his abortive 1745 rebellion, still line these streets.

Another distinctive feature of the historic centre is the series of named or numbered 'yards', tucked away down alleyways and through arches, once the

513

focus of local small industry. Walking down Highgate their intriguing, narrow entrances are irresistible to anyone with a sense of curiosity. Stricklandgate runs passed the Town Hall, which still houses Katherine Parr's Book of Devotions and, on Highgate, the Brewery Arts Centre combines a theatre, with an excellent programme of touring productions, an art gallery, cinema and a cafe.

At the bottom of Highgate is the **Abbot Hall Museum of Lakeland Life and Industry**, themed around traditional rural trades of the region, such as black-smiths' or wheelwrights' workshops, agricultural activity, weaving and print-ing. There are recreated cottage interiors and elegantly furnished period rooms. Abbot Hall Art Gallery forms part of a complex within **Abbot Hall Park** and includes work by John Ruskin and the celebrated Kendal painter, George Romney. Adjacent to Abbot Hall is the 13th century Parish Church, one of the largest in England with five aisles and a peel of ten bells.

The Sawyers Arms is a friendly, old fashioned pub, where locals and tourists happily swap tales over a pint of fine ale. Rebuilt in its present position in the early 1800s, the pub takes its name, Sawyer, from a person who saws timber professionally, and indeed, the area of Kendal was home to many industries around that time including carpentry. There have been many landlords over the years and today, the Sawyers Arms is very ably run by Geoff and Babs. As well as offering a range of excellent real ales the delicious home-cooked meals, the inn also has eight en-suite guest rooms. Completely refurbished in Spring 1997, the letting rooms provide wonderful accommodation and, in keeping with the high standard of hospitality found here, the breakfasts are certainly not to be missed.

The Sawyers Arms

The Sawyers Arms, 137 Stricklandgate, Kendal, Cumbria LA9 4RF
Tel: 01539 729737

On the main street of Highgate, can be found **The Kendal Bowman**. This former coaching inn dates back to the 18th century, but only changed its name to The

Kendal Bowman in 1957, paying tribute to the famous men who fought on the fields of Agincourt. Phil and Jo Metcalfe became the tenants here just two years ago and now offer the very best in food, drink and accommodation for visitors and locals alike. A Vaux Inn, there are a number of different real ales, including Vaux Bitter and Mild, Samson and Lambtons, all kept in fine fettle. Open all day every day with hot snacks served throughout the day and menu meals between 12 and 2.30 pm each lunchtime. For visitors to the area The Kendal Bowman has seven good letting rooms available all year round, all with showers and wash basins. This is a lively establishment with entertainment provided on Thursday nights and Sunday afternoons. A great atmosphere with excellent service.

The Kendal Bowman

The Kendal Bowman, 155 Highgate, Kendal, Cumbria LA9 4EN
Tel: 01539 724023

Not far from Levens Hall, just off the A590, is **Heaves Hotel**, owned and run by Miles and Catherine Whitelock whose family have been here for over 50 years. A magnificent example of Georgian architecture, this 15 bedroom hotel is set in 10 acres of gardens and woodland and offers peace and tranquillity plus superb

Heaves Hotel

England

views of the Pennines, Morecambe Bay and the Lakeland hills. Elegantly furnished in period style, the interior has many features of interest; marble floors, an Adam-style staircase, elaborate plasterwork and an imposing fireplace and overmantle reputed to be the work of Grinling Gibbons. Hotel facilities include a well stocked library, billiard room, residents' lounge and bar. Only a mile away is the village of Levens, Sizergh Castle and a salmon leap on the River Kent, while the market town of Kendal with its many attractions is three miles away. Heaves Hotel restaurant is open to nonresidents and has established a firm reputation locally.

Heaves Hotel, near Kendal, Cumbria LA8 8EF Tel: 015395 60396
Fax: 015395 60269

Just west of Kendal, the magnificent **Punch Bowl Inn** stands off the A5074 in the village of **Crosthwaite**. Privately owned, the inn enjoys a delightful setting surrounded by the outstanding scenery of the Lyth Valley and adjacent to an historic 16th century church. A former coaching inn dating back to the 16th century the facilities have been updated to a high standard yet retaining the original character, style and atmosphere. The bar serves John Smiths and Theakstons and there are always two guest ales. The restaurant is very cosy and the food is of a very high standard, having earned two AA rosettes. The reputation of the Punch Bowl for excellent food and drink extends far and wide so it is advisable to book ahead for those wishing to dine in the restaurant. Comfortable bed and breakfast accommodation is provided in three en-suite rooms.

The Punch Bowl Inn

The Punch Bowl Inn, Crosthwaite, near Kendal, Cumbria LA8 8HR
Tel: 015395 68237 Fax: 015395 68875

The village of **Underbarrow** lies in a beautiful area of rolling hills midway between Bowness and Kendal. This area to the east of Lake Windermere is relatively little known, but it is delightful to explore, dotted with little hamlets, good country pubs and beautiful views across the rolling, hilly landscape.

In this area steeped in history and, lying on the old woolpack route, is **The Underbarrow Punchbowl**, a traditional English pub dating back to the 1500s.

Run by former Merchant Navy officer David Howarth, with Allan King, the Punchbowl is noted for traditional draft ales of which the draft Bass was rated by the Daily Telegraph as the best pint in the Northwest. It is also renowned for its plentiful bar meals which are reasonably priced and available throughout the day. The quality of the food is excellent with selections made from the ever changing blackboard menu. To the east of the Lake, which is relatively little known, the pub itself is situated on the Westmorland Way walk, and has some of the best walking on its doorstep. It is a delight to explore, with little hamlets and other interesting landmarks dotted along the route.

The Underbarrow Punchbowl

The Underbarrow Punchbowl, Underbarrow, Kendal, Cumbria LA8 8HQ
Tel: 015395 68234

Staveley, further north, is a village of great charm through which runs a stream crossed by footbridges. It lies at the foot of the little Kentmere Valley, a quiet cul-de-sac leading to the hamlet of Kentmere itself. As its name implies, part of this valley was once a lake, drained to provide precious bottom pasture land. A large millpond remains to provide a head of water on the River Kent for use at a paper mill.

As many new by-pass roads are built for swifter progress, some established businesses unfortunately lose their prominence but benefit from the reduction of traffic noise. **The Eagle and Child** is just such a place. It is a 19th century inn situated in Staveley at the foot of Kentmere Valley on the A591 between Kendal and Windermere, and had a mention in Dorothy Wordsworth's Journal. It provides an excellent touring centre, for walkers and motorists, for the Lakes, Yorkshire Dales and Morecambe Bay areas; within a few yards walkers can join the Dalesway Walk. Lyn and Alan McCuaig, with their son Robert, are the well established owners coming from an impressive background in the catering trade—Alan was a chef and lecturer at Kendal Collage for 12 years and Lyn is the fifth generation of her family to be a hotelier. There are six letting bedrooms with satellite television, hand basins, and tea making facilities. Bar meals are available at lunchtime and in the evening. The Eagle and Child is open daily from Whit to the end of September. Families are welcome and will find it well situated for bus and train services. There is an attractive beer garden which is best enjoyed on warm sunny days.

The Eagle and Child Hotel

The Eagle and Child Hotel, Staveley, near Kendal, Cumbria LA8 9LP
Tel: 01539 821320

County Durham

INTRODUCTION

For hundreds of years County Durham was ruled by its viceregal Prince Bishops who made a major contribution to the area's rich and unique heritage. The county town, Durham, is dominated by its cathedral which stands on a hill in a horseshoe bend of the River Wear. The County has also played an important part on the Industrial Revolution, Darlington, in the south of the county, is a historic railway town, the home of George Stephenson's Stockton to Darlington Railway which opened in 1825.

Today, the fascinating blend of heritage, combined with some of England's most beautiful and unspoilt countryside, is guaranteed to surprise and delight most visitors. Lying between the Yorkshire Dales and Northumberland National Parks, the Durham Dales form part of the North Pennines, one of the largest areas of Outstanding Natural Beauty in England.

DURHAM   *Map 16 ref K5*

This city is dominated by its mighty cathedral and no visit to Durham is complete without time spent at this magnificent shrine of Christianity. Though in ecclesiastical significance **Durham Cathedral** lags behind Canterbury and York it does perhaps excel them in architectural splendour. It is widely acknowledge to be the finest and grandest example of early Norman architecture in the country. This was the cathedral of the powerful and wealthy Prince Bishops of Durham who once held almost regal power in their territories. They could administer civil and criminal law; they had the power of pardon and the right to mint their own money, create baronetcies, and give market charters— they could even raise an army!

More significantly, inside the building are the tombs of two of the greatest figures of the early Christian church in England: the remarkable St Cuthbert, shepherd saint of Northumbria, and the Venerable Bede, saint, scholar and Britain's first historian. The cathedral owes its origin to a Saxon Benedictine community who, in 995, fled to this rocky peninsula which is surrounded by the serpentine River Wear, to hide the body of St Cuthbert in a little church made from the boughs of trees. The real founder of the cathedral, however, was a Norman, William de St Carileph, the Bishop of Durham from 1081 to 1096. He brought to the small Saxon church not only holy relics but also a group of scholars from Monkwearmouth and Jarrow.

The foundation stone was laid in 1093, witnessed by King Malcolm III of Scotland and the main part of the building was erected in a mere 40 years. Over the years, much has been added, however, amid all the splendour are the simple fragments of carved wood which survive from St Cuthbert's coffin, made for the saint's body in 698 and carried round the North of England for almost 300 years.

Sharing the same rocky peninsula as the cathedral is **Durham Castle**, founded in 1072 and once belonging to the Prince Bishops. Such was the impregnability of this site that Durham was one of the few major towns in Northumbria that was never captured by the Scots. Among its most impressive features are the chapel, dating from 1080, and the great hall, which was built in the middle of the 13th century. The castle is used as a hall of residence for students of Durham University and so is only open to the public at limited times.

The rest of the city reflects the long history of the castle and cathedral it served, including generations of pilgrims who had to be fed and watered. There are winding streets, such as Fishergate and Silver Street, whose names and appearance reveal their medieval origins, an ancient Market Place, elegant Georgian houses, and quiet courts and alleyways. Yet, for all its industrial development in the 19th and 20th centuries, there is a sense of open space which is never more evident than in the view across the town from the university or in the fine park behind the railway station.

On the outside of the long river loop around the castle and cathedral is the **Old Fulling Mill**, which now houses an archaeological museum containing material from excavations in and around the city. A very different museum but equally outstanding is the **Durham University Oriental Museum**, which houses a collection of oriental art of international importance.

The fascinating **Durham Light Infantry Museum** is situated just off Framwellgate, in the centre of the city. The history of this famous regiment is presented through an imaginatively laid out display of photographs, medal, uniforms and weapons. Also in the same building, the **Durham Art Gallery** hosts a constantly changing programme of exhibitions, workshops and demonstrations. The surrounding landscaped gardens are a venue for summer brass band concerts and an annual military vehicle rally. The museum and art gallery are open daily except Mondays, with only a minimal admission fee.

Durham Light Infantry Museum and Durham Art Gallery

Durham Light Infantry Museum and Durham Art Gallery, Aykley Heads, Durham DH1 5TU Tel: 0191 384 2214

The impressive **Mount Oswald Manor and Golf Course** lies to the south of Durham city centre, off the A177 Sedgefield road. A renowned eating place, this imposing Georgian mansion is open every day from 9.30 am to 9.30 pm. The extensive and reasonably priced menu offers a range of dishes, including vegetarian options and children's portions. A number of function suites are also available for hire which are ideal for business meetings, conferences and wedding receptions. The manor grounds are the setting for a beautiful 18-hole golf course. The green fees are very reasonable and golf clubs and trolleys are available for hire. Open to the public, visiting groups are especially welcome.

Mount Oswald Manor and Golf Course

Mount Oswald Manor and Golf Course, South Road, Durham DH1 3TQ Tel: 0191 386 7527

CHESTER-LE-STREET
Map 16 ref K5

This is a busy market town built around the confluence of Cow Burn and the River Wear. The street on which the town once stood was a Roman road, later replaced by the Great North Road, and the settlement developed in the protective care of a Roman fort. The medieval **Church of St Mary and St Cuthbert** is built on the site of a cathedral that was established in 883 by the monks of Lindisfarne as they carried St Cuthbert's body around the north of England. His coffin rested here for 113 years until the monks were forced to move on to Ripon before finding a final resting place for the saint at Durham.

Next to the church is the **Ankers House Museum**, the anchorite where the Ankers order of monks lived their solitary lives of prayer in the 14th and 15th centuries. It houses a Roman stone with inscription, the shaft of a Saxon cross and the stone head of a Roman emperor.

To the east of the town lies **Lumley Castle**, built in 1390 by Sir Ralph Lumley. The building once stood with its rear view towards the town, this was changed in the 18th century by Vanburgh. Before this major alteration, the castle was embellished by the 6th Lord Lumley who added a tablet to proclaim his ancestry and busts of Plato and Aristotle to advertise his knowledge. The castle was occupied by the Lumley family until 1953 when it became the property of Durham University. It is now a luxury hotel.

To the west of Chester-le-Street, the small village of **Beamish** is the home of the **Beamish Open Air Museum**, an award winning attraction situated in 200 acres of landscaped parkland. Here, life in County Durham about 100 years ago has been vividly recreated: there is a tramway serving old mining communities, a drift mine, streets with cottages, shops and a pub.

DARLINGTON
Map 13 ref K6

Lying just off the Great North Road, Darlington has every right to be considered Durham's second town, both in terms of its importance as a regional centre and for its heritage. It has a bustling town centre, with a large market place and a grand Victorian market hall that brings people in from the surrounding dales of both Durham and Yorkshire. High Row, with its elevated street of shops, makes an impressive sight and it forms part of a compact but characterful shopping centre.

Perhaps Darlington's greatest claim to fame lies in the role the town played, along with its neighbour Stockton, in the creation of the world's first commercially successful public railway which opened in 1825. It was the Darlington Quaker and banker, Edward Pease, who became the main driving force behind the railway scheme to link the Durham coalfield with the port of Stockton. The present Darlington Station at Bank Top came from a much later period in the railway age, as lines were being constructed to link England and Scotland. The original Darlington Station, built in 1842, was at what is now North Road. Today it is the **Darlington Railway Centre and Museum**, a museum of national importance, housing relics of the pioneering Stockton and Darlington Railway, including Stephenson's Locomotion No 1, an early S&D carriage and Hackworth's mighty engine, the Derwent. Timothy Hackworth, who came from Shildon as Stephenson's Locomotive Superintendent, was the man with the practical skills to make the engines actually work. He designed his own breed of rugged, tough colliery engines, which really demonstrated the superiority of steam power over the horse in terms of strength and reliability. Hackworth also built the first locomotives to be used in Russia and Canada.

Le Tiffin Coffee Shop

Renowned as one of the friendliest and cosiest eating places in Darlington, **Le Tiffin Coffee Shop** is a great place to enjoy a coffee, pastry, snack or full lunch. Fifteen years ago, proprietors Barbara and Paul Dobinson left their jobs and took over what was then a semi-derelict property in Skinnergate and, through sheer hard work and dedication, they have turned it into one of the premier daytime eating establishments in the area. Situated in one of the oldest parts of the town, the building lies near a pretty Quaker meeting house. The interior is beautifully furnished and decorated with a fine collection of teapots and prints by local artists, many of which are for sale. Le Tiffin can seat up to 45 people, so there is plenty of room to enjoy a hearty lunch. Paul prepares the lunches and Barbara makes all the pies and desserts (her home-baked scones have quite a reputation). The food is varied, reasonably priced and of a very high standard. The menu features an impressive selection of coffees and teas from all over the world. Loose tea, coffee beans and ground coffee can also be purchased to enjoy at home or as a charming gift.

Le Tiffin Coffee Shop, 11 Skinnergate, Darlington, County Durham DL3 7NJ Tel: 01325 485431

Northumberland

INTRODUCTION

Northumberland is England's most northerly county and it is also one of the most remote and unspoilt. Following the county reorganisation of 1974, when the new county of Tyne and Wear was created, Northumberland lost the industrial areas around Newcastle, Gateshead and Sunderland. Though these towns are not, strictly speaking, within the county, they share many of the same ancient features as the rest of Northumberland. Only their recent, industrial history is different.

From ancient times, the county of Northumberland has been subjected to raids and rustling from beyond the Scottish border. This bleak and lonely borderland is littered with ruined castles, pele towers and bastles which bear witness to the turbulent past. Once a powerful Anglo-Saxon kingdom, called Northumbria, the rulers presided over the introduction of Christianity in the north of England and the golden age of monastic art that is exemplified by the Lindisfarne Gospels.

Straddling the border with Scotland the Cheviot Hills provide excellent and challenging walking country, the highest peak is The Cheviot at 2684 feet. Northumberland National Park includes sections of these rounded grass covered hills and, in the south, remains of Hadrian's Wall, built in AD 122 to repeal the Picts, can still be seen. To the west of the Park lies Kielder Forest, a popular recreational area which also includes Kielder Water, the largest man-made reservoir in Europe. The Forest's information centre can be found at Kielder Castle which was once the Duke of Northumberland's shooting lodge. Belonging to the Forestry Commission, Kielder has many leisure facilities on offer including watersports, forest trails and fishing.

HEXHAM   *Map 16 ref J4*

The great **Abbey**, in this busy little market town, dates back to AD 674, at which times it was reputed to be the "largest and most magnificent church this side of the Alps." Though it may now have a few rivals for such a title, the present building is still on a magnificent scale, with many Saxon remains from the original church. These include the crypt, said to be the finest of its period in existence, and the 1300 year old St Wilfrid's Chair or Frith Stool. There is also some wonderful late medieval architecture, mainly from the 12th and 13th centuries. Not only is there a rich heritage of carved stonework here, but Hexham is also famous for its woodcarving. The early 16th century rood screen has been described as the best in any monastic church in Britain.

Found in the 14th century Manor House is **The Middle March Centre for Border History**. This museum vividly tells the story of the border struggles between the two nation states of England and Scotland. The territory was hotly disputed and, for many centuries, was virtually without rule of law and subject to the activities of the notorious Reivers —cattle rustlers and thieves who took advantage of the disputed lands. The powerful Wardens, or Lords of the Marches, themselves warlords of pitiless ferocity, were given almost complete authority by the King to control the Reiver and anyone else who crossed their path. This was a desperate time and it gave rise to many of the great medieval Border Ballads, violent and colourful tales of love, death, heroism and betrayal.

The former mining village of **Bardon Mill**, on the north bank of the South Tyne, is found to the west of Hexham. It was here that an important drovers road crossed the river and cattle were fitted with iron shoes to help them on their way to the southern markets. The village is convenient starting point for walks along Hadrian's Wall and the Roman fort of **Vindolanda** is nearby. Here, at this lonely fort, is the **Roman Museum** where the remains of no less than eight successive forts built to house troops can be seen. There is also a full scale replica of a section of the wall and actual Roman writing implements, textiles, leather and wooden objects.

AMBLE   *Map 16 ref K3*

This is a small port on the mouth of the River Coquet, which prospered on the export of coal but is now a busy marina and sea fishing centre with a carefully restored harbour.

Just a mile offshore lies **Coquet Island** which, in Anglo-Saxon times, had a monastic foundation known as Cocwadae, and a Benedictine settlement of which only fragments of the foundations remain. The island had a bad reputation in former times for causing shipwrecks but it is now a celebrated bird sanctuary, noted for its colonies of terns, puffins and eider ducks. Managed by the RSPB, the island can be visited by boat from Amble on prearranged trips.

ALNWICK   *Map 16 ref K2*

One of the most impressive towns in Northumbria, Alnwick (pronounced Annick) is dominated by a magnificent castle that was the stronghold of the great Percy dynasty from 1309 to the middle of the 18th century. It still has the feel and appearance of a great medieval miliary and commercial centre, being an important market town since the granting of its charter in 1291.

Alnwick Castle began, like most in the area, as a Norman motte and bailey structure which was replaced in the 12th century by a circular stone keep, to which much has been added over the centuries. It was extensively rebuilt and restored in the 1850–60s by the Victorian architect, Anthony Salvin, for a later duke who sought to recapture the medieval feel whilst transforming it into a great country house with all the modern comforts of the time. A number of rooms are open to the public and amongst its treasures are paintings by Titian, Tintoretto, Canaletto and Van Dyck, collections of Meissen china and superb furniture.

There is also an important **Archaeological Museum** and extensive archive collections, as well as the **Royal Northumberland Fusiliers Regimental Museum**.

The town itself is worthy of exploration, with narrow streets with such evocative names as Hotspur Gate (a surviving part of the town's 15th century fortifications and built by the 2nd Earl of Northumberland), Fenkle Street, Green Batt, Bondgate Within and Bondgate Without. The popular and colourful Alnwick Fair, dating from the 13th century, takes place each June and July.

LINDISFARNE   *Map 16 ref K1*

This most evocative of English islands was known as Lindisfarne until the 11th century when a group of Benedictine monk settled here, giving it the name Holy Island, although both names are now used. The ruins of their great sandstone priory, in massive Romanesque style, can still be explored.

The links with early Christianity are even more significant than that of the Benedictines, for it was here, in AD 635, that St Aidan and his small community of Irish monks came from Iona to found a base from which to help convert northern England to Christianity. The monks are also remembered for having produced some of the finest surviving examples of Celtic art, the richly decorated Lindisfarne gospels, which were begun in the 7th century. When the island was invaded by Vikings in the 9th century, the monks fled, taking their precious gospels with them. These have, miraculously, survived and are now in the safe hands of the British Museum.

St Cuthbert also came here, living on a tiny islet as a hermit before seeking even further seclusion on the Farne Islands. A cross marks the site of his tiny chapel, which can be reached over the sand and rocks at low tide.

Lindisfarne Castle was established in Tudor times as yet another fortification to protect the exposed flanks of Northumbria from invasion by the Scots. It was extensively rebuilt and restored in 1903 as a private house by the great Edwardian architect, Edward Lutyens, and is now in the hands of the National Trust.

BERWICK-UPON-TWEED   *Map 16 ref J1*

This town, lying close to the border with Scotland, has been fought and quarrelled over for a thousand years and more. It has changed hands no less then 14 times, so even now, the inhabitants are not certain where their allegiance lies. It was started by William the Lion of Scotland who gave the town to the English Crown in 1147 as part of his ransom after he had been captured at Alnwick. Richard the Lionheart then had to surrender it to Scotland to raise money to pay for his crusades and the town continued to change hands until 1482 when it was finally confirmed as being part of England.

Even then, for a time, Berwick became almost a country in itself, an independent 'free town' which had to be specifically mentioned in Acts of Parliament until 1746. To confuse the issue more, having lost its status as a Scottish burgh in 1368, it was restored by Lord Lyon in 1958. This makes it now a town which technically belongs to both nations.

Berwick's original medieval walls, built in the 13th century and modified by Henry VIII, can still be walked, and the old town within them is a colourful blend of warm sandstone and red pantiles. The many fine buildings are mostly Georgian and include the **Ravensdowne Barracks**, designed by Vanburgh and built between 1717 and 1721. They were reputed to be the first barracks ever built, as a result of complaints by local people about constantly having to billet soldiers.

The later fortifications, ordered by Elizabeth I to replace part of the earlier town wall are regarded as the finest preserved example of walled defences in the whole of Europe. They were built in 1558 by Italian engineers, who were experts at creating defences to exploit the full use of artillery to defend the town and the huge grassy ramparts still have an uncannily modern appearance.

The Tweed estuary is spanned by three distinctive bridges linking the town centre with the communities of Tweedmouth and Spittal. The oldest of these bridges is the 17th century Berwick Bridge, a handsome stone bridge with 15 arches dating from 1624. The Royal Tweed Bridge is the most modern, having been built in 1928 whilst the enormous 126 foot high, 28 arch Royal Border Bridge carrying the East Coast main line railway was built in 1847 by Robert Stephenson and opened by Queen Victoria in 1850.

The old town goal, inside the mid 18th century town hall, now houses the **Cell Block Museum**. The adjacent bell chamber has a charming history and visitors are sometimes allowed to ring the eight named bells. Each bell has its own function: Cuthbert, for instance, was rung only on Shrove Tuesday.

The town's parish church was one of only two churches built during the reign of Oliver Cromwell and, though it has no spire, two octagonal turrets were added during the 19th century. Facing the church is the main entrance to the Barracks which now houses three museums. In the Clock Block is the **Berwick Borough Museum and Art Gallery**, which invites the visitor to peer through a 'Window on Berwick' and there is also the **Kings Own Scottish Borderers' Regimental Museum**, with displays of medals, uniforms, military regalia and silverware.

Tourist Information Centres

British Tourist Authority
Thames Tower, Black's Road, Hammersmith, London, W6 9EL

Cumbria Tourist Board
Holly Road, Windermere, Cumbria, LA23 2AQ
Tel: 015394 44444

East Anglia Tourist Board
Topsfield Hall, Hadleigh, Suffolk, IP7 5DN
Tel: 01473 822922

East Midlands Tourist Board
Exchequergate, Lincoln, LN2 1PZ
Tel: 01522 531521

Heart of England Tourist Board
Woodside, Larkhill Road, Worcester, WR5 2EF
Tel: 01905 763436

London Tourist Board
26 Grosvenor Gardens, London, SW1W 0DU
Tel: 0171 7303450

North West Tourist Board
Swan House, Swan Meadow Road, Wigan Pier
Wigan, WN3 5BB
Tel: 01942 821222

Northumbria Tourist Board
Aykley Heads, Durham, DH1 5UX
Tel: 0191 3846905

South East England Tourist Board
The Old Brew House, Warick Park, Tunbridge Wells
Kent, TN2 5TU
Tel: 01892 540766

Southern Tourist Board
40 Chamberlayne Road, Eastleigh, Hampshire, S05 5JH
Tel 01703 620006

West Country Tourist Board
60 St Davids Hill, Exeter, EX4 4SY
Tel: 01392 76351

Yorkshire & Humberside Tourist Board
321 Tadcaster Road, York, YO2 2HF
Tel: 01904 707961

Town & Village Index

A

Abbotsbury   105
Abingdon   129
Albury   56
Alderley Edge   445
Aldermaston   66
Aldershot   79
All Stretton   301
Alnwick   524
Amble   524
Ambleside   483
Amesbury   127
Andover   83
Appledore   194
Arkle Town   403
Arundel   40
Ascot   66
Ash   62
Ashbourne   314
Ashton-under-Lyne   473
Ashwater   193
Astbury   451
Avebury   126
Axminster   156

B

Bakewell   315
Balls Cross   47
Bampton   188
Banbury   133
Barbrook   187
Bardon Mill   524
Barney   351

Barnsley   372
Barton Bendish   357
Bath   108
Battle   37
Beaminster   94
Beamish   521
Beaulieu   88
Bedford   332
Beechamwell   356
Beeston   456
Beetham   511
Ben Rydding   379
Berkeley   253
Berkhamstead   331
Berwick-upon-Tweed   525
Beverley   426
Biddenden   16
Birtle   477
Bishop Monkton   398
Bishop's Stortford   331
Blandford Forum   93
Bodmin   212
Bodmin Moor   199
Bolton   479
Boscastle   206
Boston Spa   376
Boughton-in-Furness   497
Bournemouth   93
Bovey Tracey   175
Bowd   148
Bradford   382
Bradford-on-Avon   122
Braithwaite   492
Breadstone   255

Bridgerule   194
Bridgnorth   296
Bridport   103
Brighton   24
Bristol   106
Broadstairs   10
Broadwindsor   96
Broomfield   24
Buckfastleigh   179
Buckingham   70
Bucklers Hard   89
Buckover   257
Bude   201
Budleigh Salterton   143
Bugle   232
Burbage   293
Burghclere   82
Burnham   69
Burnham Market   346
Burnham Overy Staithe   347
Burton upon Trent   309
Bury   477
Bury St Edmunds   334
Buscot   131
Bush   204
Buxton   316

C

Cam   264
Camborne   236
Cambridge   359
Cannock Chase   307
Canterbury   3
Cark   506
Carnforth   465
Cartmel   502
Castle Acre   354
Castle Drogo   191
Cawood   410
Chalfont   269
Chalfont St Giles   69
Chapeltown   371
Charfield   262
Charmouth   99
Cheddar   119
Chelmsford   328
Cheltenham   247
Cheriton Fitzpaine   190

Chesham   70
Chester   431
Chester-le-Street   521
Chichester   42
Chiddingfold   58
Chideock   101
Chipping Sodbury   259
Chudleigh   178
Church Lawford   287
Church Stretton   300
Churchtown   461
Cirencester   270
Clayton   39
Cleethorpes   365
Climping   42
Clitheroe   466
Clyst Hydon   163
Coalbrookdale   303
Coalpit Heath   260
Coalville   293
Cockermouth   488
Colchester   325
Colkirk   353
Compton   62
Cookham   64
Corfe Castle   92
Coventry   288
Crayke   422
Crosthwaite   516
Crow Edge   372

D

Dalston   489
Dalton-in-Furness   499
Darlington   521
Dartmouth   172
Deal   11
Dean   488
Denby Dale   389
Denholme   383
Derby   311
Dersingham   341
Desborough   292
Devoran   225
Dewsbury   393
Doncaster   373
Dorchester   90

Dorking   54
Dover   12
Downham   467
Drewsteignton   191
Dunkeswell   160
Dunster   116
Durham   518
Dursley   261
Dymchurch   15

E

East Bergholt   338
East Dereham   349
East Looe   214
East Retford   322
Eastbourne   29
Ebberston   419
Eccle Rigg   495
Edgworth   478
Edwinstowe   321
Elvaston   313
Ely   361
Epsom   52
Esher   51
Eskdale Green   486
Eton   64
Exeter   137
Exmouth   142
Exton   141

F

Falfield   258
Falmouth   242
Faringdon   130
Farnborough   80
Farnham   61
Fenny Bridges   162
Flookburgh   506
Folkestone   14
Forde Abbey   96
Forest of Dean   251
Formby   459
Foulsham   350
Fowey   228
France Lynch   270
Frant   37
Frensham   60
Frodsham   435

G

Gainsborough   364
Gee Cross   476
Gittisham   161
Glastonbury   113
Glossop   318
Glynde   28
Goathland   414
Godalming   57
Goudhurst   17
Grange-over-Sands   507
Grantham   365
Great Bircham   342
Great Bookham   55
Guestling   34
Guildford   49

H

Hadstock   330
Halifax   384
Harrogate   395
Hartland   194
Harwich   327
Haslemere   59
Haslingden   469
Hastings   33
Hatfield   332
Havant   78
Hawkridge   117
Hawkshead   496
Hawnby   412
Helston   241
Henley-on-Thames   131
Henwood   222
Hereford   272
Herne Bay   8
Herstmonceux   32
Hever   22
Hexham   523
High Newton   509
Highclere   83
Highcross   294
Hindhead   59
Hinton   260
Hitchin   331
Holmfirth   388
Honiton   157

Horbury   392
Horley   53
Hornsea   427
Hove   25
Huddersfield   386
Hull   424
Hunstanton   343
Huntingdon   360
Hutton-le-Hole   413
Hythe   14

I

Ilfracombe   182
Ilkley   378
Ironbridge   303
Ivybridge   170

K

Keighley   380
Kelsall   454
Kendal   513
Kenilworth   284
Keswick   491
Kettlesing   398
King's Lynn   340
Kingsclere   82
Kirkby Lonsdale   512
Knutsford   439

L

Lacock   123
Lamberhurst   18
Lambourn   67
Lamorna   240
Lancaster   462
Lansallos   217
Launceston   200
Lavenham   337
Leeds, Kent   24
Leeds, West Yorkshire   374
Lewes   27
Lichfield   308
Lincoln   363
Lindale   510
Lindisfarne   525
Liskeard   221
Little Bookham   55

Little Malvern   274
Littledean   252
Littleham   143
Liverpool   457
Long Melford   338
Looe   214
Lostwithiel   230
Lower Breinton   273
Lower Withington   451
Luddenden   385
Ludlow   297
Lurgashall   48
Lutterworth   294
Lyme Regis   96
Lymm   438
Lympstone   141
Lyndhurst   88
Lynmouth   185
Lynton   185

M

Macclesfield   447
Maidencombe   174
Malmesbury   124
Malton   421
Margate   9
Market Bosworth   293
Marlow   68
Marston   437
Masham   399
Melton Mowbray   292
Mere   444
Meriden   290
Meshaw   188
Mevagissey   225
Middleham   400
Midhurst   46
Millom   498
Milton Keynes   71
Minions   200
Morwenstow   204
Mossley   474
Mullion   241

N

Naburn   410
Nailsworth   268

New Mills   317
Newbury   67
Newmarket   336
Newport Pagnell   71
Newquay   233
North Nibley   263
Northwich   436
Northwick   258
Norton   303
Norwich   340
Nottingham   319

O

Oakengates   302
Odiham   81
Okehampton   192
Old Ellerby   425
Oldham   472
Orrell   480
Ottery   180
Ottery St Mary   151
Over Alderley   446
Oxford   128

P

Payhembury   163
Peckforton   456
Pelynt   219
Penrith   490
Penzance   238
Petersfield   79
Petworth   47
Piltdown   39
Plymouth   164
Polperro   218
Pool   236
Poole   92
Port Isaac   209
Porthcothan   233
Portreath   237
Portsmouth   76
Poughill   202
Princethorpe   287

R

Ravenglass   484
Reading   63

Redruth   236
Reigate   53
Richmond   401
Ripley   50
Rochdale   470
Rochester   23
Rock   213
Rock Ferry   459
Romsey   87
Rossett   434
Rousdon   155
Royal Tunbridge Wells   19
Rugby   286
Rushall   21
Rye   35

S

Saffron Walden   329
Salcombe   170
Salcombe Regis   150
Salisbury   119
Sandplace   221
Sandwich   11
Scagglethorpe   421
Seaton   153
Shallowford   306
Sheffield   369
Shepton Mallet   112
Sheringham   348
Shipton Gorge   104
Shrewley   276
Shrewsbury   302
Sidford   149
Sidmouth   145
Silchester   82
Silsden   381
Silverdale   465
Sinnington   420
Sissinghurst   17
Sittingbourne   23
Sonning   132
South Creake   347
South Elmsall   391
Southerton   152
Southport   460
Southwell   321
Spalding   365
Sproston Green   454

St Agnes   234
St Albans   330
St Austell   228
St Bees   487
St Ives   237
Stafford   304
Stalybridge   475
Stanley   392
Staveley   517
Stoke Abbott   95
Stoke Heath   289
Stratford-upon-Avon   277
Stratton   203
Styal   445
Sutton   450
Sutton Cheney   293
Swaffham   355
Swinford   295
Symondsbury   104

T

Taunton   116
Tavistock   180
Telford   302
Tenterden   15
Tetbury   265
Tewkesbury   250
Thirlspot   494
Thornbury   256
Thursford   352
Tintagel   207
Tiverton   189
Toad Rock   20
Todmorden   471
Tonbridge   22
Topsham   140
Torquay   173
Trelights   212
Truro   224
Tunbridge Wells   19

U

Ulverston   500
Underbarrow   516
Uplyme   98
Upper Quinton   283
Utley   382

W

Wakefield   391
Walkhampton   181
Walton on the Naze   328
Wanswell   254
Warwick   275
Watchet   118
Wellingborough   291
Wells   112
Wells-next-the-Sea   345
Wembury   169
West Looe   214
Westerham   22
Weston   160
Weston-Super-Mare   118
Wetherby   377
Weybridge   51
Weymouth   90
Whalley   468
Whitby   415
Whitstable   7
Wigan   479
Willen   71
Wilton   121
Wincham   437
Winchester   84
Windermere   495
Windsor   64
Winsford   452
Wisbech   361
Withycombe   142
Woburn   333
Woodstock   132
Wookey Hole   113
Woolsthorpe   366
Wootton Fitzpaine   101
Worcester   273
Worston   467
Worthing   40

Y

York   404
1066 Story, Hastings   33

Places of Interest Index

A

Abbey Church of St Mary & Ethelflaeda, Winchester 87
Abbey Gardens, Bury St Edmunds 334
Abbey Grounds, Cirencester 271
Abbeydale Industrial Hamlet, Sheffield 370
Abbot Hall Museum of Lakeland Life & Industry, Kendal 514
Abbot Hall Park, Kendal 514
Abingdon Abbey 129
Airborne Forces Museum, Aldershot 79
Albert Dock, Liverpool 457
Albury Park 56
Alderman's Barrow, Exmoor 117
Aldermaston Lock 67
Alexander Keiller Museum, Avebury 126
All Hollows School, Rousdon 155
All Saints' Church, Dewsbury 393
All Saints' Church, Huntingdon 360
All Saints's Church, Okehampton 192
Almonry, The, Battle 37
Alnwick Castle 524
Ancient High House, Stafford 306
Anderton Boat Life, Winsford 452
Andover Museum 83
Angel Hill, Bury St Edmunds 335
Angel Hotel, Helston 241
Anglican Cathedral, Bristol 106
Anglican Cathedral, Liverpool 457
Anglican Cathedral, Sheffield 370

Ankers House Museum, Chester-le-Street 521
Anne of Cleeves House, Melton Mowbray 292
Anne of Cleves House, Lewes 27
ARC, The, York 406
Archaeological Museum, Alnwick 525
Armley Mill, Leeds 375
Arundel Castle 41
Arundel Museum & Heritage Centre 42
Arundel Toy & Military Museum 41
Arwenack House, Falmouth 243
Ashmolean Museum, Oxford 128
Ashton Memorial, Lancaster 464
Assembly Rooms, Bath 110
Atkinson Art Gallery, Southport 460
Audley End House, near Saffron Walden 329
Automata Museum, York 406
Avebury Stone Circle 126
Axe Edge 317

B

Backs, The, Cambridge 360
Balkerne Gate, Colchester 326
Banbury Cross 133
Banbury Museum 133
Bankfield Museum, Halifax 384
Banks Common 55
Barbara Hepworth Museum, St Ives 238

Barbara Hepworth Sculpture Garden, St Ives 238
Barbican Gate, Sandwich 11
Barbican, The, Plymouth 165
Bass Museum of Brewing, Burton upon Trent 309
Bath Abbey 109
Bath House, Bakewell 316
Bath Industrial Heritage Centre 111
Bath Postal Museum 111
Battle Museum of Local History 37
Beachy Head 30
Beacon Hill Pike, near Penrith 490
Beamish Open Air Museum 521
Beaney Institute, Canterbury 4
Beatrix Potter Gallery, Hawkshead 496
Beaulieu 88
Beaulieu Abbey 88
Becka Falls, Bovey Tracey 175
Beckford's Tower, Bath 111
Beeston Castle 456
Benedictine Abbey of St Michael, Farnborough 80
Berkeley Castle 253
Berkhamstead Castle 331
Berwick Borough Museum & Art Gallery, Berwick-upon-Tweed 526
Betty's Coffee House, Ilkley 379
Beverley Heritage Centre 427
Beverley Minster 426
Biggin, The, Hitchin 331
Bishop Bonner's Cottages, East Dereham 350
Bishop's House Museum, Sheffield 371
Bishop's Palace, Chichester 43
Bishop's Palace, Salisbury 121
Bishop's Palace, Wells 112
Black Down, near Abbotsbury 105
Blake's Lock Museum, Reading 64
Bleak House, Broadstairs 10
Blenheim Palace, Woodstock 133
Blue Anchor Inn, Helston 241
Bluecoat Chambers, Liverpool 457
Bluecoat Gallery, Liverpool 457
Blundell's Old School, Tiverton 190
Bodmin Moor 199
Bolton Street Station Museum, Bury 477
Bond's Hospital, Coventry 289
Bookham Common 55
Botanical Gardens, Southport 461
Box Hill, Dorking 55
Bradford Cathedral 383
Branksea Castle, near Poole 92
Brass Rubbing Centre, Ely 362
Breakwater, Plymouth 165
Bridge, Bradford-on-Avon 122
Bridge of Sighs, Cambridge 360
Bridgnorth Castle 296
Bridport Museum 103
Britannia Royal Naval College, Dartmouth 173
British Engineerium, Hove 25
British Folk Art Collection, Bath 110
British Typewriter Museum, Bournemouth 93
Broadlands, Romsey 87
Broads 340
Brook Experience, The, Winchester 84
Brooklands Museum, near Weybridge 51
Brooklands, near Weybridge 51
Brown Willy, Bodmin Moor 199
Brownsea Island 92
Bryanston Park, Blandford Forum 94
Bucklers Hard 89
Bude Canal 201
Bude Museum 201
Buffs Regimental Museum, Canterbury 4
Building of Bath Museum, Bath 110
Bull Ring, Cirencester 271
Bunyan Meeting House, Bedford 333
Bunyan Museum, Bedford 333
Burnham Beeches 69
Burrator Reservoir, near Walkhampton 181
Butter Cross, Swaffham 355
Butterfly World, Hornsea 427
Butterwalk, Dartmouth 173
Buxton Museum 316

C

Cadhay, Ottery St Mary 151
Calderdale Industrial Museum, Hali-

fax 384
Calleva Atrebatum, Silchester 82
Cam Long Down 264
Camber Castle, near Rye 36
Cambridge Folk Museum 360
Canal Basin, Leeds 375
Canal Museum, The, Nottingham 320
Cannon Hall, Barnsley 372
Cannop Valley Nature Reserve, Forest of Dean 252
Canterbury Castle 5
Canterbury Cathedral 3
Canterbury Heritage Museum 5
Canterbury Tales, The 5
Carn Brea, near Redruth 237
Carpet Gardens, Eastbourne 30
Cartmel Priory 502
Casa Magni Shelley Museum, Bournemouth 93
Castle Acre Castle 354
Castle Acre Priory 354
Castle Canyke, Bodmin 212
Castle Drogo 191
Castle Hill, near Huddersfield 386
Castle House, Buckingham 71
Castle Museum, Colchester 326
Castle Park, Bristol 106
Cat & Fiddle Inn 317
Cathedral of Our Lady & St Philip Howard, Arundel 41
Cathedral, Portsmouth 78
Cavern Club, Liverpool 457
Cell Block Museum, Berwick-upon-Tweed 526
Chained Library, Hereford 272
Chalice Hill, near Glastonbury 114
Chantry Chapel, Wakefield 391
Charles' Church, Plymouth 166
Charles Dickens Birthplace Museum, Portsmouth 77
Charterhouse School, Godalming 57
Chartwell, Westerham 23
Chatsworth House, near Bakewell 315
Cheddar Gorge 119
Cheesewring, The, Bodmin Moor 200
Chelmsford & Essex Museum, Chelmsford 329
Chelmsford Cathedral 329

Cheltenham Art Gallery & Museum 248
Cheltenham Racecourse 248
Chesil Beach, Abbotsbury 105
Chester Cathedral 432
Chester Heritage Centre 432
Chester Zoo 432
Cheylesmore Manor House, Coventry 289
Chicheley Hall, Newport Pagnell 72
Chichester Cathedral 43
Chichester District Museum 44
Chiltern Open Air Museum, The, Chalfont St Giles 69
Church, Faringdon 130
Church, Newport Pagnell 72
Cider Museum & Distillery, Hereford 273
Cirencester Park 271
Cistercian Way, Grange-over-Sands 508
Citadel, The, Plymouth 165
City Museum & Art Gallery, Derby 312
City Museum & Art Gallery, Leeds 375
City Museum, Lancaster 463
City Museum, Sheffield 370
City Museum, Winchester 86
Clandon Park, Guildford 50
Clara's Cottage, Weston-Super-Mare 118
Claremont House, Esher 52
Claremont Landscape Garden, Esher 52
Clayton Tunnel 39
Cliffe Castle, Keighley 380
Clitheroe Castle 466
Clive House, Shrewsbury 302
Clock Tower, Herne Bay 8
Clock Tower, Newbury 67
Coastal Defence Museum, Eastbourne 29
Cobb, Lyme Regis 96
Cockermouth Castle 488
Cockington, Torquay 174
Colchester Castle 326
Colchester Zoo 327

Collegiate Church, Ottery St Mary 151
Colour Museum, Bradford 383
Commandery Civil War Centre,
    Worcester 274
Compton Acres, Poole 93
Conqueror's Stone, Hastings 34
Cooper Gallery, Barnsley 372
Copper Castle, Honiton 158
Coquet Island 524
Corfe Castle 92
Corinium Museum, Cirencester 270
Cornish Folk Museum, East Looe 215
Costume & Accessories Museum,
    Deal 12
County Hall, Abingdon 129
County Museum, Dorchester 90
Coventry Cathedral 288
Cow Castle, Exmoor 117
Cowdray House, Midhurst 46
Cowdray Park, Midhurst 47
Cox's Cave, Cheddar 118
Crampton Tower, Broadstairs 11
Cranmere Pool, Dartmoor 176
Crescent, The, Buxton 316
Cromwell Museum, The,
    Huntingdon 360
Cromwell's Door, Cartmel 502
Cross Street, Redruth 237
Crown Inn, Chiddingfold 59
Cumberland Pencil Museum,
    Keswick 492
Curioxity, Oxford 129
Custom House, Dartmouth 172
Custom House, Exeter 139
Cutlers Hall, Sheffield 370

D

Dalton Castle 499
Dalton Mill, Keighley 380
Darlington Railway Centre & Mu-
    seum 522
Dartmoor National Park 175
Dartmouth Castle 172
Deal Castle 12
Deep Sea Adventure, Weymouth 91
Delamere Forest, near Kelsall 454
Derby Cathedral 311

Devil's Bridge, Kirkby Lonsdale 512
Devil's Dyke, Beechamwell 357
Devil's Punch Bowl, near Hindhead 59
Devonport Dockyard, Plymouth 166
Dewsbury Museum of Childhood 393
Dinosaur Museum, Dorchester 90
Dinosaurland, Lyme Regis 97
Dirty Duck, The, Stratford-upon-
    Avon 278
Doctor's Gate, Glossop 318
Doll Museum, The, Warwick 276
Doll's House, Windsor Castle 65
Dolphin Yard, Sittingbourne 23
Dome, The, Brighton 25
Dome, The, Plymouth 166
Doncaster Museum & Art Gallery 373
Dormy House Club, Rye 36
Dorney Court, near Burnham 69
Dorset Military Museum,
    Dorchester 90
Dover Castle 13
Dracula Walk, Whitby 416
Drake's Island, Plymouth 165
Duke of Cornwall Light Infantry
    Museum, Bodmin 213
Dunster Castle 117
Dunster Working Water Mill 116
Durham Art Gallery 520
Durham Castle 519
Durham Cathedral 518
Durham Light Infantry Museum 520
Durham University Oriental Mu-
    seum 519
Dyson Perrins Museum, Worces-
    ter 274

E

Easby Abbey, near Richmond 402
East Looe Museum 215
East Riddlesden Hall, near
    Keighley 381
Eastbridge Hospital, Canterbury 4
Eddystone Lighthouse, near Ply-
    mouth 165
Educational Museum, Haslemere 59
Egyptian House, Penzance 239
Electric Palace Cinema, Harwich 328
Elizabethan House, Hull 424

Elizabethan House, Plymouth   166
Elvaston Castle   313
Ely Cathedral   362
Epsom Racecourse   52
Etherow Country Park, near Ashton-
       under-Lyne   473
Eton College   64
Eureka!, Halifax   384
Eurotunnel Exhibition Centre, Folke-
       stone   14
Exchange, The, Bristol   107
Exmoor   106
Exmoor National Park   117
Eye Water Well, Bodmin   213

F

Falmouth Arts Centre   243
Faringdon Hall   130
Farnborough Hill   80
Farnham Castle   61
Farnham Museum   62
Fernacre Stone Circle, Bodmin
       Moor   199
Festival Theatre, Chichester   43
Finchcocks, Goudhurst   17
Fishermen's Museum, Hastings   33
Fistral Beach, Newquay   233
Fitzwilliam Museum, Cambridge   360
Flamborough Head   424
Flatford Mill, near East Bergholt   339
Folk Museum, Helston   241
Folk Museum, Millom   498
Forbury Gardens, Reading   63
Forde Abbey   96
Ford's Hospital, Coventry   289
Foredown Tower Countryside Centre,
       near Brighton   26
Forest of Bowland, near Clitheroe   466
Forest of Dean   251
Formby Point   459
Fossils & Country Life Museum,
       Charmouth   99
Friar's Crag, Keswick   492
Furness Abbey, near Dalton-in-
       Furness   499
Furniture Museum, Lancaster   463

G

Gallants Bower, Dartmouth   172
Geological Museum, Camborne   237
Geological Museum, Penzance   239
Giant's Grave, Penrith   490
Gibbet Hill, near Hindhead   60
Gilbertine Priory, Lincoln   363
Glannaventra, Ravenglass   484
Glastonbury Abbey   115
Glastonbury Tor   113
Globe Works, Sheffield   370
Glynde Place   28
Glyndebourne Opera House,
       Glynde   29
Goodwin Sands, Deal   12
Gordale Scar   394
Gough's Cave, Cheddar   118
Grammar School, Ashbourne   314
Grammar School, Midhurst   46
Grand Union Canal   276
Grantham Museum   366
Great & Little Ponds, Frensham   60
Great Barn Museum, Avebury   126
Great Mew Stone, Wembury · 169
Great Western Canal   190
Green Man & Black's Head Royal
       Hotel, Ashbourne   313
Grimspound, near Widecombe-in-the-
       Moor   176
Grizedale Forest, near Hawkshead   496
Grosvenor Museum, The, Chester   432
Guildford Castle   49
Guildford Cathedral   49
Guildford Museum   50
Guildhall, Exeter   138
Guildhall, Guildford   50
Guildhall, Lavenham   337
Guildhall, Sandwich   11
Guildhall, The, Windsor   65
Guildhall, Worcester   274
Gulbenkian Theatre, Canterbury   5
Gustav Holst Birthplace Museum,
       Cheltenham   248

H

Haddon Hall, near Bakewell   315
Hampsfell Summit, Grange-over-

Sands 508
Hardy's Wessex, Dorchester 90
Harlow Car Botanical Gardens, Harro-
gate 395
Hartland Point 194
Hastings Castle 33
Hastings Embroidery 34
Hatfield House 332
Hawk & Owl Trust Centre, Chalfont St
Giles 70
Henry Moore Sculpture Gallery,
Leeds 375
Herbert Art Gallery & Museum,
Coventry 289
Hereford Castle 272
Hereford Cathedral 272
Heritage Centre, Knutsford 440
Heritage Centre, Macclesfield 448
Heroes Shrine, The, Aldershot 80
Herstmonceux Castle 32
Hever Castle 22
Hexham Abbey 523
High Lighthouse, Harwich 327
High Street, Guildford 50
High Street, Portsmouth 76
Highclere Castle 83
Hind Hotel, Wellingborough 291
History of Waxworks, Wookey
Hole 113
HMS Victory, Portsmouth 77
HMS Warrior, Portsmouth 78
Hollingworth Lake, near Rochdale 470
Hollytrees Museum, Colchester 326
Holmfirth Postcard Museum 388
Holy Cross Abbey, Shrewsbury 302
Holy Trinity Church,
Buckfastleigh 179
Holy Trinity Church, Shrewsbury 302
Hornsea Mere 427
Horses at Work Museum, Halifax 384
Hospice, The, Grange-over-Sands 508
Hospital of St Cross, Winchester 86
Household Cavalry Museum, Wind-
sor 66
Humber Bridge Country Park,
Hull 425
Humber Bridge, Hull 425
Hurlers Stone Circle, Bodmin

Moor 200

I

Ilkley Moor 378
Industrial Museum, Bradford 383
Industrial Museum, Derby 312
Ironbrige Gorge Museum,
Ironbridge 303
Izaak Walton's Cottage,
Shallowford 306

J

Jack & Jill Windmills, Clayton 40
Jack Hadwin's Motor Cycle Collection,
Broughton-in-Furness 497
James Gilbert Rugby Museum,
Rugby 287
Jenner Museum, Berkeley 254
Jews House, Lincoln 363
Jockey Club, Newmarket 336
John Moore Countryside Museum,
Tewkesbury 251
Jorvik Centre, York 404
Judge's Lodging, Lancaster 463

K

Kelham Island Museum, Sheffield 370
Kendal Castle 513
Kenilworth Castle 284
Kent's Cavern, Torquay 174
King Arthur's Halls, Tintagel 207
King John's Hunting Lodge,
Romsey 88
King's College Chapel, Cam-
bridge 359
King's Heath, Malmesbury 125
Kings Own Scottish Borderers's
Regimental Museum, 526
King's Pipe, Falmouth 243
Kingston Russell, near
Abbotsbury 105
Kirkstall Abbey, near Leeds 375
Kirkstone Pass, near Ambleside 484
Knockhundred Row, Midhurst 46

L

Lace Centre, The, Nottingham 320

Lace Hall, The, Nottingham   320
Lakes Line, The, Windermere   495
Lamb House, Rye   35
Lambourn Trainers Association   67
Lancaster Canal   464
Lancaster Castle   462
Land Gate, Rye   35
Lanes, The, Brighton   25
Lanhydrock House, near Bodmin   213
Lantern Hill, Ilfracombe   182
Lanterns, The, Folkestone   14
Launceston Castle   200
Laurel & Hardy Museum,
      Ulverston   501
Lawrence House, Launceston   200
Leeds Castle, Kent   24
Leeds Industrial Museum   375
Leighton Hall, near Silverdale   466
Leighton Moss Bird Reserve, near
      Silverdale   466
Lewes Castle   27
Lichfield Cathedral   308
Lincoln Castle   364
Lincoln Cathedral   364
Lindisfarne Castle   525
Lingholm, near Braithwaite   492
Lister's Mill, Bradford   383
Little Germany, Bradford   383
Little Hall, Lavenham   337
Little Moreton Hall   451
Little Museum, Tewkesbury   251
Living History Model, Lewes   27
Llandoger Trow, Bristol   107
Lord Street, Southport   460
Loseley House, Compton   63
Loseley Park   63
Lostwithiel Museum   230
Low Lighthouse, Harwich   327
Low Mill, Keighley   380
Ludlow Castle   297
Lumley Castle, near Chester-le-
      Street   521
Lumsford Mill, near Bakewell   316
Lymm Dam   438

M

Macclesfield Canal   448
Magna Via, Halifax   384

Maison Dieu, Arundel   41
Maison Dieu, Dover   13
Major Oak, The, near Edwinstowe   322
Malham Cove   394
Malmesbury Abbey   124
Malmesbury House, Salisbury   121
Malting, The, Ely   362
Manor House Museum, Bury St
      Edmunds   335
Mansion House, Doncaster   373
Mappa Mundi, Hereford   272
Margate Caves   9
Maritime & Local History Museum,
      Deal   12
Maritime Museum, Beaulieu   88
Maritime Museum, Exeter   139
Maritime Museum, Falmouth   243
Maritime Museum, Harwich   327
Maritime Museum, Hull   425
Maritime Museum, Lancaster   464
Maritime Museum, Penzance   239
Maritime Museum, Poole   92
Market Cross, Chichester   42
Market Cross, Shepton Mallet   112
Market House, Penzance   239
Market Jew Street, Penzance   239
Marlow Place, Marlow   68
Marlowe Theatre, Canterbury   5
Martello Tower, Dymchurch   15
Marwood House, Honiton   157
Mary Rose, Portsmouth   77
Mathematical Bridge, Cambridge   360
Maumbury Rings, Dorchester   90
Mayflower Steps, Plymouth   166
Melandra Castle, Glossop   318
Melford Hall, Long Melford   338
Merchant Adventurers's Hall,
      York   405
Merchant's House, Plymouth   166
Merry Maidens, near Lamorna   240
Merseyside Maritime Museum   458
Metropolitan Cathedral, Liverpool   457
Mevagissey Museum   226
Micrarium, Buxton   316
Middle March Centre for Border
      History, The, Hexham   523
Middleham Castle   400
Military Museum, Aldershot   79

Millbay Docks, Plymouth   165
Milton's Cottage, Chalfont St Giles   70
Mompesson House, Salisbury   121
Monk Bretton Priory, near
     Barnsley   373
Montpelier Parade, Harrogate   395
Morrab Gardens, Penzance   239
Mount Caburn, Glynde   28
Moyses Hall Museum, Bury St
     Edmunds   335
Muncaster Castle, near Ravenglass   485
Muncaster Mill, near Ravenglass   485
Museum Art Gallery, Brighton   25
Museum of British Road Transport,
     Coventry   289
Museum of Cannock Chase   308
Museum of Childhood, Lancaster   463
Museum of Costume and Textile,
     Nottingham   320
Museum of Costume, Bath   110
Museum of Dartmoor Life,
     Okehampton   192
Museum of Emigration, Liverpool   458
Museum of Fairground Equipment,
     Wookey Hole   113
Museum of Industry & Rural Life,
     Milton Keynes   71
Museum of Iron, Coalbrookdale   303
Museum of Iron Ore Mining,
     Ravenglass   485
Museum of Lincolnshire Life, Lin-
     coln   364
Museum of Local History,
     Godalming   57
Museum of Local History, Stratford-
     upon-Avon   277
Museum of Maritime & Local History,
     Salcombe   171
Museum of Oxford   128
Museum of Social History, Colches-
     ter   326
Museum of South Yorkshire Life,
     Doncaster   374
Museum of St Albans   331
Museum of Sussex Archeology,
     Lewes   27
Museum of the History of Science,
     Oxford   129
Museum of the Iron Age, Andover   83
Museum of the King's Own Royal
     Regiment, Lancaster   463
Museum of the Manchesters, Ashton-
     under-Lyne   473
Museum of the River,
     Coalbrookdale   303
Museum of the Royal Warwickshire
     Regiment, Warwick   276
Museum of the Staffordshire Yeomanry,
     Stafford   306
Music Room, The, Lancaster   464

N

Nash's House, Stratford-upon-
     Avon   277
National Cycle Museum, Lincoln   364
National Horse Racing Museum,
     Newmarket   336
National Motor Museum, Beaulieu   88
National Museum of Film, Photography
     & Television, Bradford   383
National Park Information Centre,
     Hawkshead   496
National Railway Museum, York   406
Natural History Museum, Colches-
     ter   326
Nature Reserve, Formby   460
New Forest Museum & Visitors Centre,
     Lyndhurst   88
Newbury Lock   67
Newbury Museum   67
Noah's Ark Museum, Fowey   228
North Brink, Wisbech   361
North Devon Maritime Museum,
     Appledore   195
North Holderness Museum of Village
     Life, near Hornsea   427
North Norfolk Railway,
     Sheringham   349
North York Moors National Park   411
North Yorkshire Moors Railway   412
North Yorkshire Moors Railway,
     Goathland   414
Norwich Castle   340
Norwich Cathedral   340
Nothe Fort, Weymouth   91

Nottingham Castle   319

O

Observatory, Herstmonceux   32
Octagon, The, Budleigh Salterton   144
Okehampton Castle   192
Oken's House, Warwick   276
Old Bell Hotel, Malmesbury   125
Old Bridge House, Ambleside   483
Old Cloth Hall, Biddenden   16
Old Fulling Mill, Durham   519
Old House Museum, Bakewell   315
Old House Museum, Hereford   273
Old Parsonage, Marlow   68
Old Post Office, Tintagel   207
Old Town Gaol, Dover   13
Opera House, Buxton   316
Orrest Head, Windermere   495
Overbecks, Salcombe   171
Owl Centre, near Ravenglass   485
Oxford Story Museum   128
Oxford University Museum   129

P

Pallants, The, Chichester   43
Pantiles, The, Royal Tunbridge
     Wells   19
Paradise Mill, Macclesfield   447
Parish Church, Dorking   55
Parish Church, Halifax   384
Parish Church, St Ives   237
Parish Church, Tintagel   207
Parish Church, Windsor   65
Parke, Bovey Tracey   175
Peace Pagoda & Buddhist Temple,
     Willen   71
Peak District National Park   309, 369
Peckforton Castle, near Beeston   456
Peckover House, near Wisbech   361
Pendennis Castle, Falmouth   242
Pendennis Point, Falmouth   242
Peninsula Barracks, Winchester   86
Pennine Way   369
Pennington Flash, Wigan   480
Penponds, Camborne   237
Penrith Castle   490
Pepperpot, The, Godalming   57

Petworth House   47
Petworth Park   47
Philharmonic Rooms, Liverpool   457
Philpot Museum, Lyme Regis   97
Pickford House, Derby   311
Piece Hall, Halifax   384
Piece Hall Museum, Halifax   384
Pier, Hastings   34
Pipe Well, Liskeard   222
Pipers, near Lamorna   240
Pittville Pump Room Museum, Chelten-
     ham   248
Plymouth Hoe   165
Polesden Lacey, near Great
     Bookham   56
Police Bygones Museum, Tetbury   265
Porlock Hill, Exmoor   117
Porth Island, Newquay   233
Portsdown Hill, Portsmouth   78
Portsea Island, Portsmouth   76
Prebendal School, Chichester   43
Preston Manor, Brighton   26
Priory, Hitchin   331
Priory, The, Lavenham   337
Prysten House, Plymouth   166
Pulteney Bridge, Bath   110
Pump Room, Buxton   316

Q

Quaker Meeting House, near
     Doncaster   373
Quarry Bank Mill, Styal   445
Quebec House, Portsmouth   77
Quebec House, Westerham   23

R

Ravenglass & Eskdale Railway   485
Ravensdowne Barracks, Berwick-upon-
     Tweed   526
Reading Abbey   63
Reading Museum   64
Red Cross Museum, Winchester   86
Red Lodge, The, Bristol   107
Redoubt, The, Harwich   328
Redoubt Tower, Eastbourne   29
Regimental Museum, Barnsley   372
Regimental Museum of the Green

Howards, Richmond   402
Regimental Museum, Salisbury   121
Remnantz, Marlow   68
Restormel Castle, Lostwithiel   230
Rhenish Tower, Lynmouth   185
Rhodes Memorial Museum, Bishop
   Stortford   332
Richmond Castle   401
Rickham Coastguard Station,
   Salcombe   171
Rievaulx Abbey, near Hawnby   412
Rochester Cathedral   23
Rocky Valley, near Boscastle   206
Roman Amphitheatre, Chester   432
Roman Baths, Bath   108
Roman Museum, near Bardon
   Mill   524
Roman Painted House, Dover   13
Rose Hill, Dorking   55
Rossendale   469
Rothesay Museum, Bournemouth   93
Rotunda Museum of Antique Dolls's
   Houses, Oxford   129
Rougemont Castle, Exeter   138
Rough Tor, Bodmin Moor   199
Round & Square Towers, Port-
   smouth   76
Round Hill, Aldershot   80
Rows, The, Chester   432
Royal Aircraft Establishment, Farnbor-
   ough   80
Royal Cresecent, Bath   110
Royal Crown Derby, Derby   311
Royal Garrison Church, Portsmouth   78
Royal Military Police Museum, Chiches-
   ter   43
Royal Museum & Art Gallery, Canter-
   bury   4
Royal National Lifeboat Museum,
   Eastbourne   30
Royal Naval Museum, Portsmouth   77
Royal Northumberland Fusiliers
   Regimental Museum,
   Alnwick   525
Royal Pavilion, Brighton   25
Royal Pump Room Museum, Harro-
   gate   395
Royal William Victualling Yard,

Plymouth   166
Royal Worcester Porcelain, Worces-
   ter   274
Royalty & Empire Exhibition, Wind-
   sor   66
RSC Collection, Stratford-upon-
   Avon   279
Rudding Park, Harrogate   395
Rugby School   286
Rusell-Cotes Art Gallery & Museum,
   Bournemouth   93
Ruskin Mill, Nailsworth   268
Rye Museum   36

S

Saints' Way, The, Bodmin   213
Salcombe Castle   171
Salisbury & South Wiltshire Mu-
   seum   121
Salisbury Cathderal   119
Salmeston Grange, Margate   9
Salt Museum, Northwich   437
Saltwood Castle, Hythe   15
Salutation Inn, Nottingham   320
Samuel Johnson Birthplace Museum,
   Lichfield   309
Sandham Memorial Chapel,
   Burghclere   82
Sandown Castle, Deal   12
Saracen's Head, Southwell   321
Scotney Castle, Lamberhurst   18
Scott Polar Research Institute, Cam-
   bridge   360
Sea Life Centre, Hunstanton   344
Seal Island   344
Seaton Tramway   153
Sefton Park, Liverpool   458
Serle's House, Winchester   86
Sett Valley Trail, near New Mills   317
Shakespeare Memorial, Stratford-upon-
   Avon   279
Shambles, The, York   405
Sheeps Tor, near Walkhampton   181
Sheffield Town Hall   370
Shell Grotto, Margate   9
Sherwood Forest Visitor Centre, near
   Edwinstowe   322
Shibden Hall & Park, near Halifax   384

Shillinglee Park, Chiddingfold   59
Shrewsbury Castle   302
Silk Mill, Derby   312
Silk Museum, Macclesfield   447
Sissinghurst Castle Gardens   17
Smugglers Adventure, Hastings   33
Smugglers' Museum, Polperro   218
Snake Inn, The, near Glossop   318
Snake Pass, near Glossop   318
Somerset County Museum, Taunton   116
Somerset Rural Life Museum, Glastonbury   116
South Devon Railway, Buckfastleigh   179
South Gate, Launceston   200
Southover Grange, Lewes   27
Southport Railway Centre   460
Southsea Common, near Portsmouth   78
Southwell Cathedral   321
Speke Hall, Liverpool   458
Spurn Head   424
Squerryes Court, Westerham   23
St Agnes Museum   234
St Albans Cathedral   330
St Albans Organ Museum   331
St Andrew's Church, Penrith   490
St Anne's Well Gardens, Hove, Brighton   25
St Augustine's Abbey, Canterbury   5
St Botolph's Priory, Colchester   327
St Catherine's Hall, Lincoln   363
St Clement's Church, Hastings   33
St Edmund Hall, Oxford   128
St George's Chapel, Windsor Castle   65
St George's Church, Esher   52
St George's Church, Tiverton   190
St George's Guildhall, King's Lynn   341
St George's Island, Looe   215
St Guron's Well, Bodmin   213
St Ives Museum   238
St John's Church, Cirencester   271
St John's Hospital, Lichfield   307
St John's House, Warwick   276
St Laurence's Church, Church
Stretton   300
St Laurence's Church, Frodsham   435
St Lawrence's Church, Bradford-on-Avon   122
St Margaret's Hospital, Honiton   157
St Martin's Abbey, Battle   37
St Mary & St Cuthbert's Church, Chester-le-Street   521
St Mary & St Michael's Church, Cartmel   502
St Mary's Church, Aldermaston   66
St Mary's Church, Andover   83
St Mary's Church, Astbury   451
St Mary's Church, Beechamwell   356
St Mary's Church, Berkeley   254
St Mary's Church, Beverley   426
St Mary's Church, Chiddingfold   58
St Mary's Church, East Bergholt   338
St Mary's Church, Frensham   60
St Mary's Church, Launceston   200
St Mary's Church, Malton   421
St Mary's Church, Rye   36
St Mary's Church, Silchester   82
St Mary's Church, Stafford   305
St Mary's Church, Whitby   416
St Mary's Collegiate Church, Warwick   276
St Mary's Priory Church, Lancaster   463
St Michael & All Angels' Church, Beetham   511
St Michael & All Angels' Church, Macclesfield   447
St Michael's Church, Helston   241
St Nectan's Kieve, near Boscastle   206
St Nicholas's Church, Arundel   41
St Nicholas's Church, Compton   62
St Nicholas's Church, Dunkeswell   160
St Nicholas's Church, East Dereham   349
St Nicholas's Church, Great Bookham   55
St Nicholas's Priory, Exeter   138
St Peter & St Paul's Church, Swaffham   356
St Peter's Cathedral, Exeter   138
St Peter's Church, Ashwater   193
St Petroc's Church, Bodmin   213

St Saviour's Parish Church,
Dartmouth   172
St Thomas's Church, Bovey
Tracey   175
Stafford Castle   307
Stag Inn, Hastings   33
Stained Glass Museum, Ely   362
Stamford Hill, near Stratton   203
Stanford Hall, near Swinford   295
Stanley Spencer Gallery, Cookham   64
State Apartments, Windsor Castle   65
Statue of Alfred, Winchester   84
Statue of William III, Petersfield   79
Steamtown, Carnforth   465
Stephen G Beaumont Museum,
Wakefield   391
Stonehenge, near Amesbury   127
Stray, The, Harrogate   395
Stripple Stones, Bodmin Moor   200
Styal Country Park   445
Subtropical Gardens, Abbotsbury   105
Suspension Bridge, Marlow   68
Sussex Combined Services Museum,
Eastbourne   30
Sussex Toy & Model Museum,
Brighton   25
Sutcliffe Gallery, Whitby   416
Sutton Harbour, Plymouth   166
Swaffham Museum   356
Swannery, Abbotsbury   105
Swinside Stone Circle, near Broughton-
in-Furness   497

T

Tabley House, near Knutsford   443
Tales of Robin Hood, Nottingham   320
Tarka Trail, Barnstaple   182
Tarr Steps, Hawkridge   117
Tate Gallery Annexe, St Ives   238
Tate Gallery, Liverpool   458
Tatton Park, near Knutsford   442
Taunton Castle   115
Tavistock Abbey   180
Telford Park   302
Temple Newsam House, near
Leeds   375
Tewkesbury Abbey   250
Tewkesbury Town Museum   251

Theakston's Brewery, Masham   399
Theatre Royal, Bristol   107
Theatre Royal, Bury St Edmunds   336
Theatre-in-the-Forest, near
Hawkshead   496
Thornbury Castle   256
Three Tuns Hotel, Windsor   65
Timeball Tower, Deal   12
Tintagel Castle   208
Tithe Barn, Abbotsbury   105
Tithe Barn, Bradford-on-Avon   123
Tithe Barn, Glastonbury   116
Tithe Barn, Wellingborough   291
Tiverton Castle   190
Toad Lane, Rochdale   470
Tolgus Tin Mill, near Redruth   237
Tonbridge Castle   22
Torre Abbey, Torquay   173
Town Gaol, Reading   64
Town Hall, Buckingham   71
Town Hall, Huntingdon   360
Town Museum, Bodmin   213
Town Museum, Saffron Walden   329
Towner Art Gallery, Eastbourne   30
Toy Museum, Chester   432
Transport Museum, Hull   424
Treadwheel Crane, Harwich   328
Tree Inn, Stratton   203
Trenance Garden, Newquay   233
Trevaunance Cove, near St Agnes   235
Trinity House Tower, Walton on the
Naze   328
Trip to Jerusalem, Nottingham   320
Tropical Butterfly House, Lancas-
ter   464
Truro Cathedral   225
Tucker's Hall, Exeter   138
Tudor House, Margate   9
Tumble Down Dick, Farnborough   81
Tunnel Baths, Ilfracombe   183
Tunnel House, Clayton   40
Turkish Baths, Harrogate   395
Tutankhamun, The Exhibition,
Dorchester   90
Tyndale Monument, near North
Nibley   263

U

Uffington Castle, near Faringdon 131
Uffington White Horse, near
 Faringdon 130
Undercliffe Cemetery, Bradford 383
Underground Passages, Exeter 138
University Botanic Garden, Cam-
 bridge 360
University of Surrey, Guildford 49

V

Vale of Berkeley 253
Vale of Deadly Nightshade, near
 Dalton 499
Vale Royal, near Winsford 452
Valley of the Rocks, near Lynton 186
Venta Belgarum, Winchester 84
Verulamium Museum, St Albans 330
Verulamium Park, St Albans 331
Vicar's Cross, Wells 112
Victorian Art Gallery, Bath 110
Victoriana Museum, Deal 12
Vindolanda 524
Virginia Water, near Windsor 66

W

Wakefield Cathedral 391
Wakefield Museum 391
Walker Art Gallery, Liverpool 458
Walmer Castle 12
Warwick Castle 275
Water House, Rye 36
Water Tower, Colchester 326
Waterfront & Scalpen's Court Museum,
 Poole 92
Watersmeet, Lynton 186
Watts' Memorial Gallery, Compton 63
Waverley Abbey, near Farnham 62
Wells & Walsingham Steam Railway,
 Wells-next-the-Sea 345
Wells Cathedral 112
Wells Museum 113
West Park Museum, Macclesfield 448
Westgate Museum, Winchester 86
Wetherby Bridge 377
Wey Navigation, Weybridge 51

Weymouth Museum 91
Whalley Viaduct 468
Whitby Abbey 416
Whitby Museum 416
White Cliffs Experience, The, Do-
 ver 13
White Horse, Dorking 55
Whitefriars, Coventry 289
Whitstable Castle 8
Wigan Pier 479
Wild Animal Kingdom & Leisure Park,
 Woburn 333
Wildfowl & Wetlands Trust,
 Arundel 42
William Salt Library, Stafford 307
William Shakespeare Museum, Strat-
 ford-upon-Avon 277
Willy Lot's Cottage, near East
 Bergholt 339
Wilton Carpet Factory 121
Wilton House, Wilton 122
Winchester Castle 84
Winchester Cathedral 85
Winchester City Mill 86
Winchester College 86
Winchester Heritage Centre 84
Windmill Church, Reigate 53
Windsor Castle 64
Windsor Great Park 66
Wink, The, Lamorna 240
Winkworth Arboretum, Godalming 58
Wisbech Museum 361
Wish Tower, Eastbourne 29
Woburn Abbey 333
Wolvesey Castle, Winchester 85
Woodspring Museum, Weston-Super-
 Mare 118
Woodspring Priory, Weston-Super-
 Mare 119
Wookey Hole 113
Wool Hall, Lavenham 338
Worcester Cathedral 274
Wordsworth House, Cockermouth 488
Worlebury Camp, Weston-Super-
 Mare 118
Worsbrough Country Park,
 Barnsley 373
Worsbrough Mill, Barnsley 373

Worthing Museum & Art Gallery   40

Y

Yarner Wood Nature Reserve, near
      Bovey Tracey   175
York Castle Museum   406
York Minster   405
Yorkshire Dales National Park   394
Yorkshire Mining Museum,
      Wakefield   391
Ypres Tower, Rye   36

The Hidden Places Series

ORDER FORM

To order more copies of this title or any of the others in this series
please complete the order form below and send to:

**Travel Publishing Ltd,7a Apollo House, Calleva Park
Aldermaston, Berks, RG7 8TN**

Title	Price	Quantity	Value
Channel Islands	£6.99	....	....
Devon & Cornwall	£4.95	....	....
Dorset, Hants & Isle of Wight	£4.95	....	....
East Anglia	£4.95	....	....
Gloucestershire	£6.99	....	....
Heart of England	£4.95	....	....
Lancashire & Cheshire	£4.95	....	....
Lake District & Cumbria	£4.95	....	....
North Wales	£4.95	....	....
Northumberland & Durham	£4.95	....	....
Peak District	£6.99	....	....
Potteries	£6.99	....	....
Somerset	£6.99	....	....
South East	£4.95	....	....
South Wales	£4.95	....	....
Thames & Chilterns	£5.99	....	....
Welsh Borders	£5.99	....	....
Wiltshire	£6.99	....	....
Yorkshire & Humberside	£4.95	....	....
England	£9.99	....	....
Ireland	£8.99	....	....
Scotland	£8.99	....	....
Wales	£8.99	....	....
TOTAL		_____	_____

**For orders of less than 10 copies please add £1 per book for
postage & packing. Orders over 10 copies P & P free.**

I enclose a cheque for £ .... made payable to Travel
Publishing Ltd

NAME ....

ADDRESS ....

....

POSTCODE ....

TEL NO ....

The Hidden Places Series
READER REACTION FORM

The Hidden Places research team would like to receive reader's comments on any visitor attractions or places reviewed in the book and also recommendations for suitable entries to be included in the next edition. This will help ensure that the **Hidden Places** series continues to provide its readers with useful information on the more interesting, unusual or unique features of each attraction or place ensuring that their stay in the local area is an enjoyable and stimulating experience.

To provide your comments or recommendations would you please complete the forms below as indicated and send to: **The Research Department, Travel Publishing Ltd., 7a Apollo House, Calleva Park, Aldermaston, Reading, RG7 8TN.**

Please tick as appropriate: Comments ☐   Recommendation ☐

Name of *"Hidden Place"*:

Address:

Telephone Number:

Name of Contact:

Comments/Reason for recommendation:

Name of Reader:

Address:

Telephone Number:

Map Section

The following pages of maps encompass the main cities, towns and geographical features of England, as well as all the many interesting places featured in the guide. Distances are indicated by the use of scale bars located below each of the maps

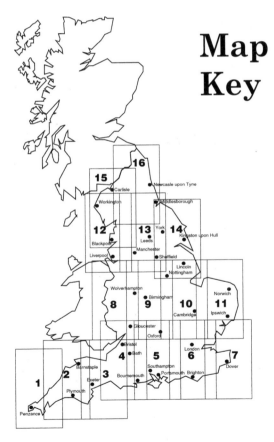

Map Key

These maps are small scale extracts from the *England and Wales Leisure Map*, reproduced with kind permission of *Estates Publications*.

England

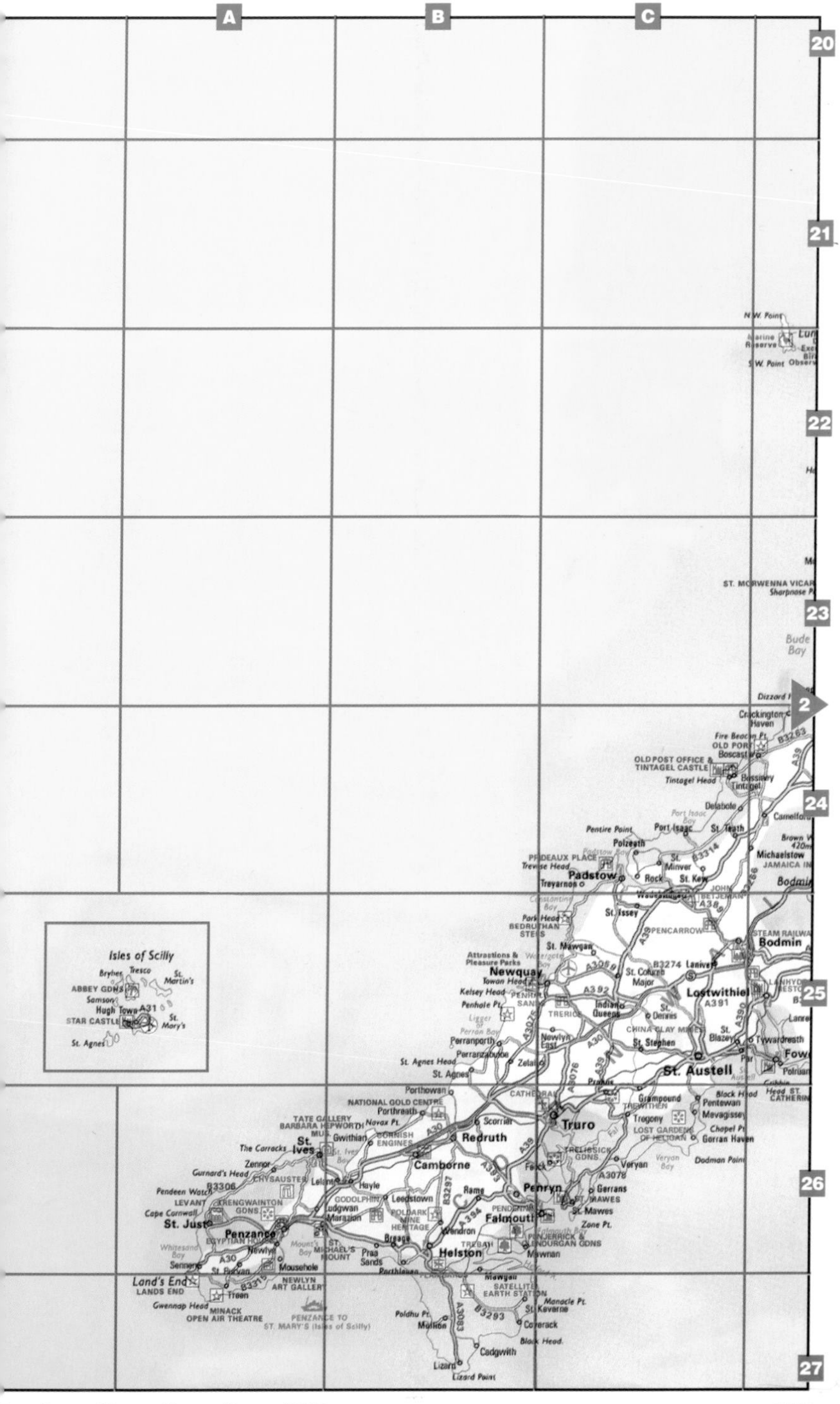

MAP 1

20

21

22

23

24

25

26

27

A

B

C

N.W. Point
Marine
Reserve
N.W. Point Observ.
East
Bird

Lun

Bude
Bay

Dizzard
Crackington
Haven
Fire Beacon Pt.
OLD PORT &
Boscastle
OLD POST OFFICE &
TINTAGEL CASTLE
Tintagel Head
Tintagel

Port Isaac
Pentire Point
Port Isaac
St. Teath
Delabole

Polzeath
Rock
St. Kew

Camelford

Brown W.
420m
Michaelstow
JAMAICA INN

St. Endellion

B3263

A39

Trevose Head
Treyarnon

PRIDEAUX PLACE
Padstow
St. Issey

OPENCARROW

A39

Bodmin

Minver

Park Head
BEDRUTHAN
STEPS
St. Mawgan
St. Columb
Major

Newquay
Attractions &
Pleasure Parks
Watergate
Bay

STEAM RAILWAY

Bodmin

Lostwithiel

Kelsey Head
Penhale Pt.
Holywell

B3274
Lanivet

Indian
Queens

A392

A391

Ligger
Perran Bay
Perranporth
Perranzabuloe
Zelah

Newlyn
East
TREVIO

CHINA CLAY MINES

Bugle

St. Dennis
St. Blazey
Tywardreath
Par

St. Agnes Head
St. Agnes
St. Stephen

Fow

St. Austell

Delabole

St. Ives Bay
Porthtowan
NATIONAL GOLD CENTRE

Grampound
St. Ewe
Pentewan

Black Head
HEAD ST.
CATHERINE

Redruth

Scorrier

TRURO
Truro
CATHEDRAL

Tregony
LOST GARDEN
OF HELIGAN

Mevagissey
Chapel Pt.

TATE GALLERY
BARBARA HEPWORTH
MUSEUM
St.
Ives
Navax Pt.
Godrevy Pt.
CORNISH
ENGINES

Camborne
Hayle
Leedstown

A3078

A30

Ponsanooth
Feock

Garran Haven
Dodman Point

Gwithian

A3047

Gerrans
St. Mawes
Veryan
Bay

Veryan

Zone Pt.

Gurnard's Head
The Carracks
Zennor
Lelant

B3297

Penryn

Falmouth

Pendeen Watch
LEVANT
Cape Cornwall
B3306
CHYSAUSTER
TREGWAINTON GDNS

Ludgvan
Marazion

POLDARK
MINE
HERITAGE

PENDENNIS

St. Just
Penzance
Newlyn

ST.
MICHAEL'S
MOUNT

Wendron

TRELISSICK GDNS

GLENDURGAN &
TREBAH GDNS

Whitesand
Bay
Sennen

A30

Heamoor
Gulval

Helston

Mawnan

SATELLITE
EARTH STATION

Land's End
LANDS END
Gwennap Head

Mousehole

Praa
Sands

Porthleven

Mawgan

Manacle Pt.
St. Keverne

MINACK
OPEN AIR THEATRE

Treen
NEWLYN
ART GALLERY

PENZANCE TO
ST. MARY'S (Isles of Scilly)

Poldhu Pt.
Mullion

B3293

Coverack

Black Head

Cadgwith
Lizard
Lizard Point

MAP 2

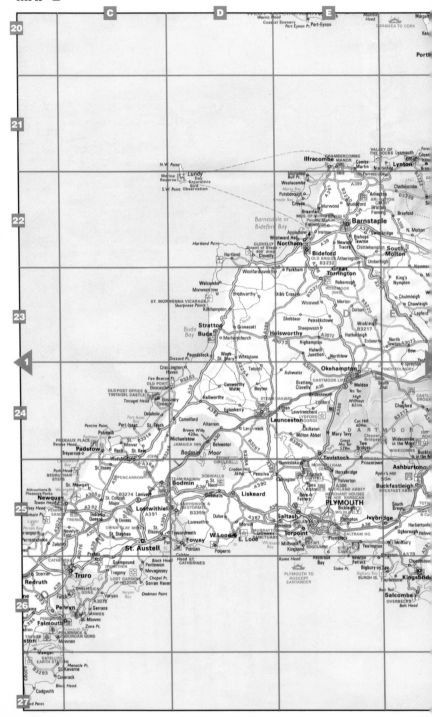

MAP 3

MAP 4

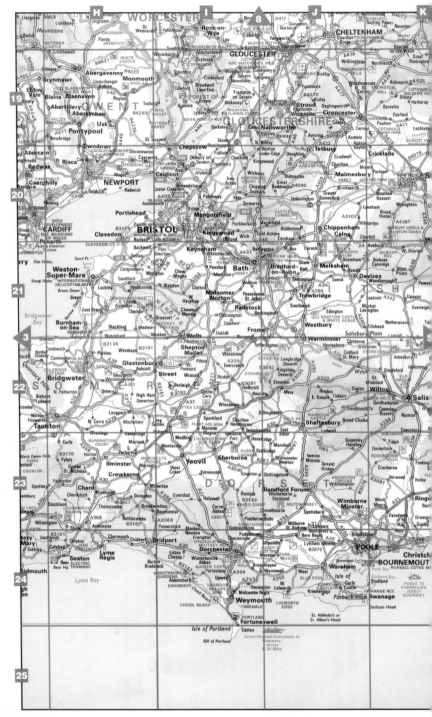

MAP 5

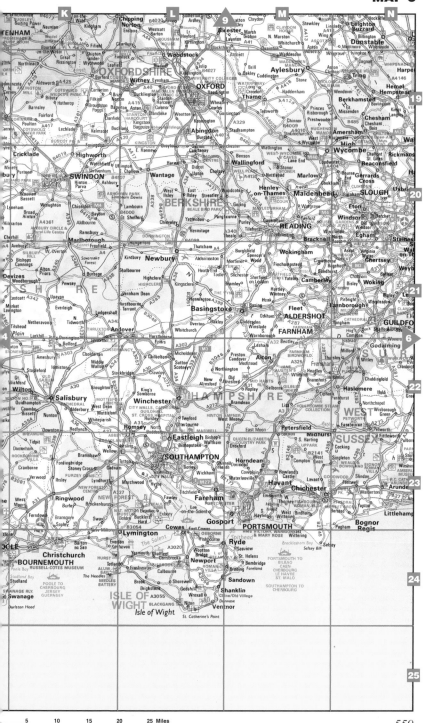

MAP 6

©Estate Publications   Crown Copyright Reserved

MAP 7

MAP 8

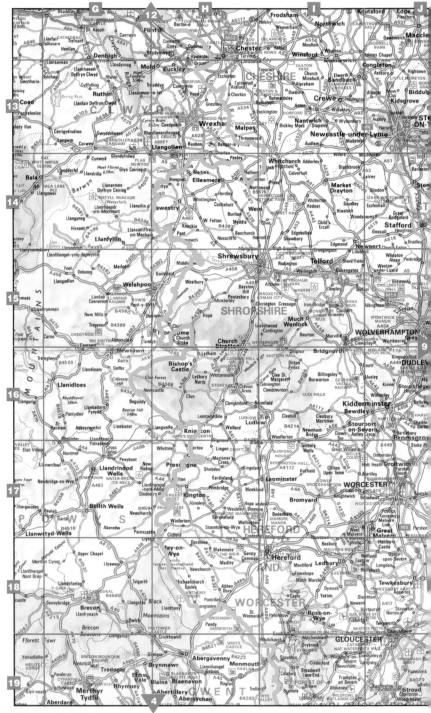

©Estate Publications   Crown Copyright Reserved

MAP 9

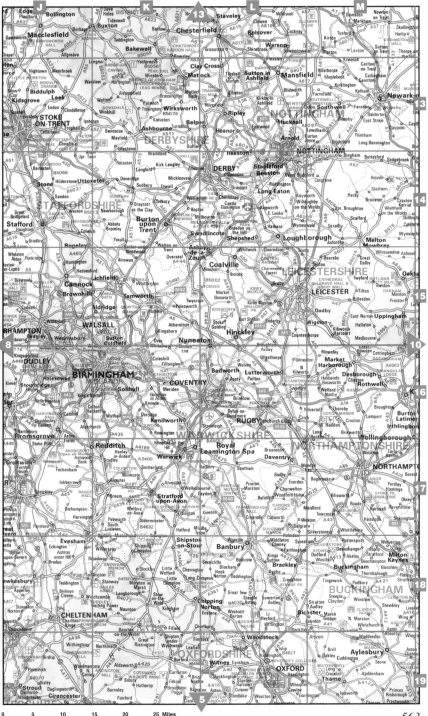

MAP 10

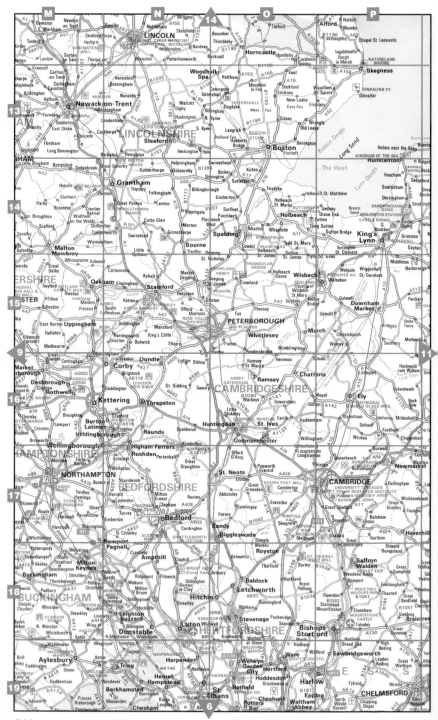

MAP 11

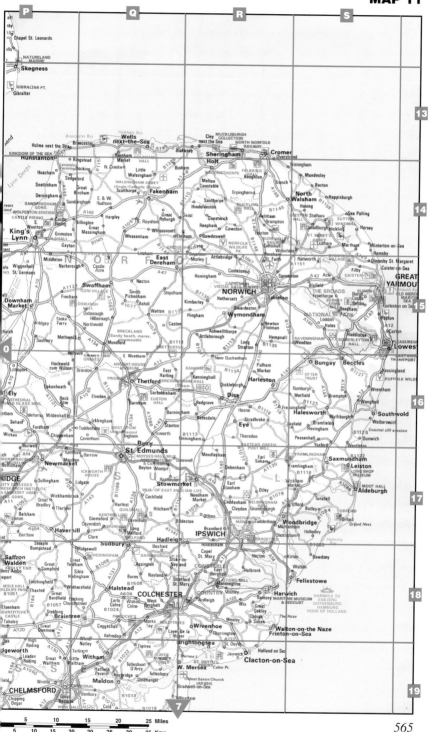

MAP 12

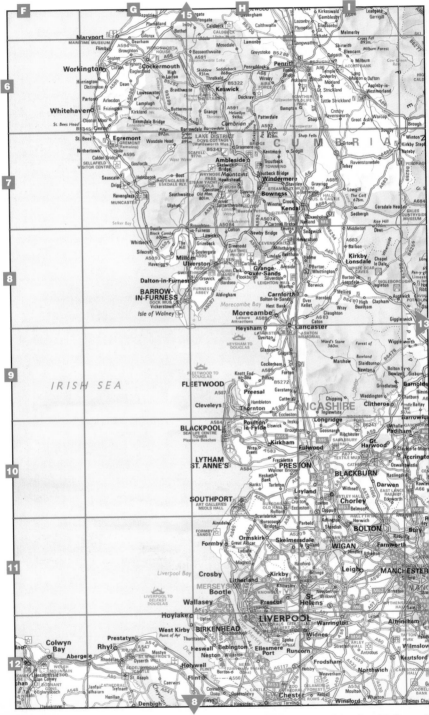

©Estate Publications   Crown Copyright Reserved

MAP 13

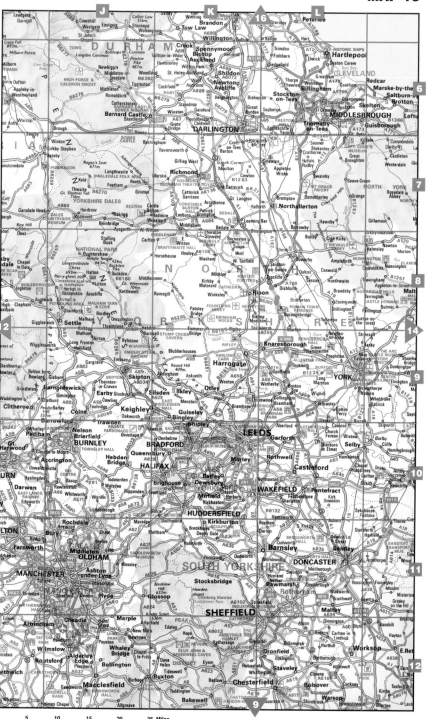

MAP 14

MAP 15

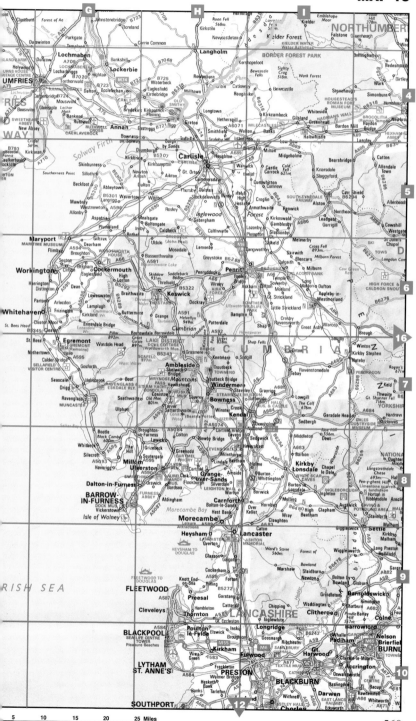

MAP 16

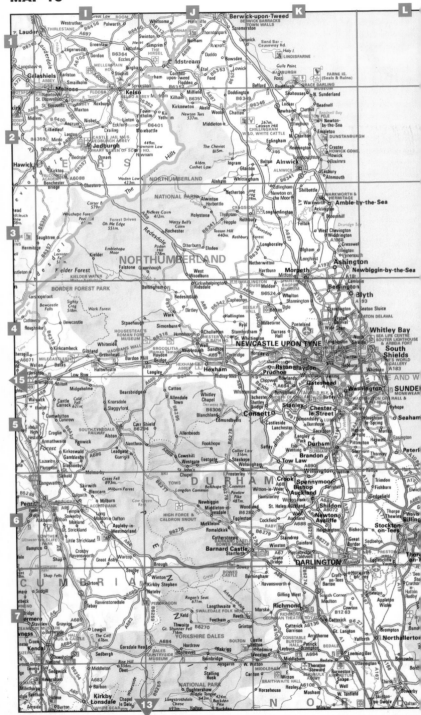

570

©Estate Publications   Crown Copyright Reser